procedure definition

```
procedure One(Y : real; var C : arraytype; var F : text);
{ Sample procedure definition. Y is a value parameter;
  C and F are variable parameters. }
var  i : integer;               { local variable }
begin                           { procedure body }
    <statement₁>;
    .
    .
    .
    <statementₙ>
end;  { One }
```

function definition

```
function Max(A, B : integer) : integer;
{ Sample function definition. }
begin                           { function body }
   Max := A;
   if A < B
   then Max := B
end;  { Max }
```

program body

```
begin  { Main Program }
    <statement₁>;
    .
    .
    .
    <statementₙ>;
    One(X + 5.1, A, DataFile);  { procedure call }
    N := Max(5, N);             { function call }
    .
    .
    .
end.  { Program }
```

Intermediate Problem Solving and Data Structures

WALLS AND MIRRORS

SECOND EDITION

The Benjamin/Cummings Series in Computer Science

G. Booch
Object-Oriented Design with Applications (1991)

G. Brookshear
Computer Science: An Overview, Third Edition (1991)

F. M. Carrano
Assembler Language Programming for the IBM 370 (1988)

D.M. Etter
Structured FORTRAN 77 for Engineers and Scientists, Third Edition (1990)

P. Helman, R. Veroff, and F. Carrano
**Intermediate Problem Solving and Data Structures: Walls and Mirrors
Second Edition (1991)**

P. Helman and R. Veroff
Walls and Mirrors: Intermediate Problem Solving and Data Structures—Modula II (1988)

N. Miller and C.G. Peterson
File Structures with Ada (1990)

A. Kelley and I. Pohl
A Book on C, Programming in C, Second Edition (1990)

A. Kelley and I. Pohl
C by Dissection: Essentials of Programming in C (1988)

I. Pohl
C++ for C Programmers (1990)

I. Pohl
C++ for Pascal Programmers (1991)

I. Pohl
Turbo C++ (1991)

W. J. Savitch
Pascal: An Introduction to the Art and Science of Programming, Third Edition (1991)

W. J. Savitch
Turbo Pascal 4.0/5.0 with 5.5 Supplement (1990)

R. Sebesta
VAX: Assembly Language Programming, Second Edition (1991)

Titles of Related Interest

M. Sobell
A Practical Guide to the UNIX System, Second Edition (1989)

M. Sobell
A Practical Guide to the UNIX System V, Second Edition (1991)

Intermediate Problem Solving and Data Structures

WALLS AND MIRRORS

SECOND EDITION

Paul Helman
Robert Veroff
University of New Mexico

Frank M. Carrano
University of Rhode Island

The Benjamin/Cummings Publishing Company, Inc.
Redwood City, California ■ Fort Collins, Colorado
Menlo Park, California ■ Reading, Massachusetts
New York ■ Don Mills, Ontario ■ Wokingham, U.K.
Amsterdam ■ Bonn ■ Sydney ■ Tokyo ■ Madrid ■ San Juan

Sponsoring Editor: Alan R. Apt
Production Editor: Mary Shields
Production Service: The Book Company
Design: The Book Company
Copy Editor: Rebecca Pepper
Cover Design: Joe DiChiarro
Composition: Graphic Typesetting Service

TURBO Pascal is a trademark of Borland International, Inc.
Cover Photo: SuperStock/Four by Five

Library of Congress Cataloging-in-Publication Data

Helman, Paul.
    Intermediate problem solving and data structures : walls and
mirrors / Paul Helman, Robert Veroff, Frank M. Carrano.
        p.   cm.
    Includes bibliographical references and index.
    ISBN 0-8053-0321-9
    1.   Electronic digital computers—Programming.   2.   Data structures
(Computer science)   I.   Veroff, Robert.   II.   Carrano, Frank M.
III.   Title.
    QA76.6.H453   1991
005.1—dc20   90-47001
                                                                              CIP

ISBN 0-8053-0321-9

3 4 5 6 7 8 9 10 -RN- 95 94 93 92 91

The Benjamin/Cummings Publishing Company, Inc.
390 Bridge Parkway
Redwood City, California 94065

This book is intended primarily for ACM's recommended core curriculum course CS2. However, in a field as dynamic as computer science, it is common to see great diversity in undergraduate computer science curricula. This book includes comprehensive coverage of enough topics to make it appropriate for other courses in areas such as lower-division data structures, advanced programming and problem solving, and elementary software engineering.

As I set out to revise this book, my goal was to update and, if possible, strengthen an already excellent presentation, while retaining the outstanding problem-solving approach of the first edition. This second edition represents a thorough rewrite of the original innovative work. Every page has been changed—and I hope improved—and material and figures have been added or rearranged to make the book more accessible and readable.

APPROACH

This book contains classic computer science topics and problem areas that are consistent with the ACM CS2 course. In addition, the latter sections of Part III together with Part IV contain the material necessary to satisfy the needs of a traditional lower-division data structures course.

Problem Solving

One of the most important roles of the second course is to help the student learn to integrate problem solving and programming abilities. This book emphasizes both the thought processes and the methods used by the computer scientist. Learning how a computer scientist develops, analyzes, and implements a method is just as important to the student as learning the mechanics of the method. A computer science major cannot learn the subject from a cookbook approach to the material.

This book presents analytical tools for the development of solutions within the context of example problems. Top-down design and the successive refinement of algorithms and data structures (through data abstraction) are applied to problems throughout the book, including two large case studies. Similarly, the use of good documentation, debugging aids, and loop invariants to develop and verify solutions is part of our problem-solving methodology.

Flexibility

The extensive coverage in this book should provide you with the material that you want for your course. You can select the topics you desire and present them in a flexible order. In Part I, you can choose or ignore Pascal review topics according to your students' background. In Part II, you can cover recursion before data abstraction. In Parts III and IV, you can, for example, introduce tables before queues or cover hashing, 2-3 trees, graphs, or priority queues any time after tables and in any order. You can also cover topics from the last chapter earlier. For example, you can cover external sorting after you cover mergesort. The *Instructor's Guide* suggests other ways to order the topics in this book.

Data Abstraction and Recursion

Three early chapters provide an extensive introduction to data abstraction and recursion. Both topics are important, and people have various opinions about which should be taught first. Although in this book the chapter on data abstraction precedes the chapters on recursion, you can simply modify this order, as you will see later.

In addition to being covered in these introductory chapters, data abstraction and recursion are woven throughout this book. The design and use of abstract data types permeate our problem-solving approach. Likewise, we continually emphasize the value of recursive thinking.

Choosing a Solution

We introduce Pascal pointers and linked list processing early and use the techniques in building data structures. This approach allows the consideration—first at an informal level and then more quantitatively—of the advantages and disadvantages of array-based and pointer-based data structures. We also introduce at an elementary level the analysis of algorithms. Thus, we continually emphasize the trade-offs between potential solutions, and this emphasis becomes a central problem-solving theme.

Applications

Classic application areas arise in the context of the major topics of this book. For example, searching and sorting are discussed in the context of both recursion and the abstract data type (ADT) table. Binary search, quicksort, and mergesort, being naturally recursive algorithms, appear early and are used to introduce order-of-magnitude analysis. In the context of the ADT table, later parts of the book introduce such topics as binary search trees, 2-3 trees, hashing, and file indexing. Searching and sorting is again considered in the context of external files.

Algorithms for recognizing and evaluating algebraic expressions are first introduced in the context of recursion, and are considered again later as an application of stacks. Other applications include, for example, the Eight Queens problem as an example of backtracking, event-driven simulation as an application of queues, and graph searching and traversals as other important applications of stacks and queues.

CHANGES IN THIS EDITION

This second edition contains much new material as follows:

- **Additional review of Pascal.** Coverage of arrays, records, and sets, as well as appendixes that summarize Pascal, all facilitate the transition from the introductory course to this one.

- **Expanded and earlier coverage of data abstraction.** Data abstraction is introduced in Chapter 1 and covered in depth in Chapter 4. Several new examples elaborate the purpose and use of an abstract data type, while clarifying the distinction between an ADT and its implementation as a data structure.

- **Expanded coverage of software engineering.** Additional material includes the software life cycle, loop invariants, pre- and postconditions, and the use of abstraction.

- **Expanded and earlier coverage of order-of-magnitude (Big O) analysis.** An introductory approach to the analysis of algorithms has been augmented and moved from the last chapter to Chapter 7.

- **New topics for CS2.** Material particularly useful in CS2 has been added or improved as follows:

- Enhanced coverage of processing linked lists recursively
- A new discussion of backtracking
- Additional sorting algorithms
- More accessible presentation of the conditional *and* and *or* operators and their implementations

- **Expanded coverage of data structures.** Material particularly useful in data structures courses has been added or improved as follows:

  - A new chapter on graphs
  - Expanded coverage of hashing
  - Expanded coverage of AVL trees

- **Significant pedagogical enhancements.** Additions that make learning easier include

  - Self-test exercises with answers
  - Margin notes
  - A glossary of terms

- **An appendix on mathematical induction.** This appendix, which includes examples and exercises, provides a convenient introduction to inductive proofs.

SPECIAL FEATURES

- **Pedagogical features.** This book contains the following features that help students not only during their first reading of the material, but also during subsequent review:

  - Chapter previews
  - Key Concepts boxes
  - Margin notes
  - Chapter summaries
  - Common Pitfalls/Debugging sections

  Each chapter begins with a table of contents and a preview that orient students toward the material in the chapter. Major ideas are denoted as Key Concepts. Margin notes identify important points and facilitate a review of the material. Each chapter summary highlights the principal themes in the chapter and places the content in proper perspective. The Common Pitfalls/Debugging section at the end of every chapter alerts the reader to common misconceptions about the concepts and techniques just presented.

- **Self-test exercises with answers, exercises, and projects.** A collection of self-test exercises, with answers at the end of the book, are included in each chapter to reinforce points from the text. Additional exercises and projects, suitable for homework, provide additional practice, provoke further thought, and supply appropriate programming assignments. The most challenging exercises are labeled with asterisks. Answers to these additional exercises appear in the *Instructor's Guide*.

- **Case studies.** In an attempt to illustrate "real-world programming," case studies develop and later modify a large interactive inventory program. The goal is to demonstrate that top-down design and modularity are invaluable aids in the development and modification of a large program. We attempt to make this and other problems more realistic by requiring the solutions to use external files. Many of our programs interact with Pascal files, and in Chapter 14 we also consider direct access files.

- **Appendixes.** The appendixes are new to this edition. If you plan to include in your course the inductive proofs that appear in this book, students will find the appendix on mathematical induction helpful. In addition, other appendixes and the inside covers summarize Pascal in a form that students will find useful while writing programs.

- **Glossary of terms.** Not surprisingly, this book contains terminology that will be unfamiliar to your students. A glossary has been added to this edition to help them cope with the many new terms.

- **Supplementary materials.** The following items are available to help you with your course:

  - *Instructor's Guide*
  - Software diskette

  The *Instructor's Guide* for this book contains teaching notes and suggestions, solutions to exercises and programming projects, additional material that you may want to include in your course, and transparency masters. Also available is a diskette containing all the programs that appear in the book and the programs for the case studies.

- **Class-tested material.** Acknowledged later in this preface are the numerous people who used the original manuscript in class while this book was under development. In addition, this second edition reflects the experience of the instructors who used the first edition in their courses. The first edition was one of the most widely adopted CS2 books, and an extensive poll of its users provided many useful suggestions that have been incorporated into the present work.

OVERVIEW

The chapters in this book are organized into four parts. This organization allows the instructor to easily tailor the book to a particular course. In most cases, Parts II and III will form the core of a one-semester course. The coverage given to Parts I and IV will depend on what role the course plays in your curriculum. More detailed suggestions for use in different courses appear in the next section of this preface.

Part I: Programming and Software Engineering

Much of Part I resembles an extension of an introductory course in that its emphasis is more on programming than on the earlier stages of the problem-solving process. The topics in this part include structured programming with Pascal; major issues in software engineering; Pascal arrays, records, files, sets, and pointer variables; and linked lists. The presentation of pointer variables and linked lists does not assume any previous knowledge of this material. Part I concludes with a case study in which we design and implement an interactive inventory system. You can cover or omit topics in Part I according to the background of your students.

Part II: Problem-Solving Tools

Part II introduces the student to data abstraction, recursion, and order-of-magnitude analysis as problem-solving tools. We focus on the role of data abstraction in the problem-solving process along with the successive refinement of algorithms. Several examples demonstrate how to design an abstract data type as part of the overall design of a solution. The distinction between an ADT and the data structure that is used to implement it remains in the forefront throughout the discussion. We emphasize the importance of weighing trade-offs when selecting a data structure for a particular application.

The ability to think recursively is one of the most useful skills that a computer scientist can possess. The insights into a concept, problem, or algorithm gained through a recursive approach are often of great value in gaining a better understanding of its nature. Our treatment of recursion emphasizes intuition over mechanics. We believe that a true understanding of recursion comes from repeated encounters with recursive definitions of both concepts and problems. We include examples ranging from simple recursive definitions to recursive algorithms for searching and sorting. We hope that when students complete this part of the book, recursion will be an integral part of their problem-solving repertoire.

The final chapter in Part II introduces the student to order-of-magnitude analysis and Big O notation by examining the efficiency of several searching and sorting algorithms. In doing so, the chapter introduces several classic sorting algorithms, including the recursive mergesort and quicksort.

We have chosen to discuss data abstraction (Chapter 4) before recursion (Chapters 5 and 6). If you prefer to present recursion first, you can cover Chapter 5 or both Chapters 5 and 6 before you cover Chapter 4.

Part III: Problem Solving with Abstract Data Types

Part III continues the use of data abstraction as a problem-solving tool. We present such basic abstract data types as the stack, queue, table, and priority queue, along with the data structures used to implement them. We note that these abstract data types fall into two categories: those that organize their data by position (stacks and queues) and those that organize their data by value (tables and priority queues). Also included in Part III is extensive coverage of binary trees, graphs, and heaps.

The discussions of the abstract data type table constitute a key element of this book. For example, a table must efficiently support the classic information storage and retrieval operations of inserting data by value, removing data by value, and searching for data by value. Our exploration of the various implementations of a table leads us to consider issues of efficiency. This continues, at an informal level, the order-of-magnitude analysis begun in Part II. The application of this analysis to the linear (array-based and pointer-based) implementations of tables motivates the need for the binary search tree implementation.

Notice that if you want to develop the ADT table even further before you cover other topics, you can skip or postpone Chapters 11 and 12, and move directly to the advanced techniques in Part IV.

Part IV: Advanced Techniques for the Management of Data

Part IV presents more complex data structures and advanced algorithms for searching and sorting. We develop 2-3 trees and hashed table implementations and analyze which operations each supports best. We then consider the problem of sorting and indexing data stored in direct access external files. We apply mergesort to external direct access files and show how external hashing and B-tree indexes are generalizations of the internal hashing schemes and 2-3 trees already developed.

TO THE INSTRUCTOR: USING THIS BOOK IN YOUR COURSE

As instructors ourselves, we had you in mind while organizing this book. By appropriately choosing which parts of the book to emphasize, you can easily tailor the material to fit your particular curriculum. Here are a few suggestions.

Courses closely following ACM's CS2.   If your introductory Pascal course emphasizes structured programming and covers the advanced Pascal topics presented in Chapter 2, students can review most of the first two chapters on their own. On the other hand, if the introductory course manages to cover only the basics of the Pascal language, then you should devote a fair amount of class time to Chapters 1 and 2. In either case, the development of linked lists in Chapter 3 should be covered well in class. You can optionally use the case study in Chapter 3 to reinforce the concepts discussed in Chapters 1 and 2, even if the students have already studied this material in the introductory course. Although you can choose to have your students write the entire program for the case study, you can also have them write portions of the program or modify it, since the program is available to you on diskette.

The course should cover the material through Chapter 10, at least. You can select topics from Chapters 11 through 14 as time permits. You can cover many topics within these chapters in any order.

> *CS2:*
>
> Part I: moderate to complete coverage
>
> Part II: complete coverage
>
> Part III: complete coverage of first half; light to moderate coverage of second half
>
> Part IV: light to moderate coverage

Lower-division data structures courses.   At many schools, the primary undergraduate data structures course comes early in the curriculum. You can use this book in such a course by giving high priority to the material in Chapter 4 and Chapters 7 through 14. This means that you should spend as little time as possible on Chapters 1 and 2, and you may even find it necessary to omit some of the material on recursion. You should assign projects, such as the one suggested in Chapter 13, in which the students develop programs for 2-3 trees or hashing.

> *Lower-Division Data Structures:*
>
> Part I: light coverage
>
> Part II: moderate coverage
>
> Part III: complete coverage
>
> Part IV: complete coverage

Second- and third-quarter courses.   This book should work very well for schools on the quarter system. If the first quarter is an introductory Pascal course, then Parts I and II and the beginning of Part III would constitute a reasonable second quarter. This would leave the remainder of Part III and all of Part IV for the third quarter.

Second Quarter:

Part I: complete coverage

Part II: complete coverage

Part III: complete coverage of first half

Third Quarter:

Part III: complete coverage of second half

Part IV: complete coverage

TO THE STUDENT

As former college students and educators who are constantly learning, we wrote this book with you in mind also. You will find such learning aids as margin notes, chapter summaries, self-test exercises with answers, and Pascal reference material in the appendixes and inside the covers. If you have not already done so, you should review the list of this book's features given earlier in this preface in the section "Special Features."

Our presentation makes some basic assumptions about your knowledge of Pascal. Some of you may need to review this material or learn it for the first time by consulting, for example, the book you used in your Pascal course and Chapter 2 of this book. You will need to know about arrays, records, files, and—to a lesser extent—sets. Although Chapter 2 presents these topics, your instructor might not cover them in class.

Realize that this book will expand your knowledge of Pascal. Although you should be able to use the four simple data types, integer, real, character, and boolean; subrange types; and one-dimensional arrays of each of these types, we recognize that many of you will need to develop a sense of which types are appropriate in a particular situation. This book will help you by answering the following kinds of questions: When does the use of a subrange add to the readability of a program, and when does it detract from it? How does the use of a subrange interact with program debugging and the handling of "bad" input data? When is an array the most efficient data structure as opposed to, say, a linked list—a structure you soon will encounter?

We also assume that you are familiar with the way Pascal evaluates expressions and executes statements. Moreover, you should have good judgment in choosing between control structures: *while* versus *for* versus *repeat*; *if-then* versus *if-then-else* versus *case*. You should appreciate the evils of the *goto*. There are, however, some subtleties in these matters that we shall explore. Similarly, we assume that you can write procedures and functions and are well versed in such matters as parameter passing and scope rules for variables. However, we shall continually demonstrate the role of modularity as perhaps the single most important factor that contributes to good program development, readability, and modifiability. We assume no experience with recursive subprograms, which are included in Part II of this book.

ACKNOWLEDGMENTS

It is a pleasure to acknowledge the outstanding work of Paul Helman and Robert Veroff, the authors of the first edition of *Walls and Mirrors*. As one who has taught from this innovative work, I am grateful for the opportunity to contribute to its evolution by preparing this revision.

Many wonderful people have helped create this book. Alan Apt, editor of both editions, initiated this project, and always provided invaluable guidance and assistance. Others at Benjamin/Cummings were always there for help and support, in particular, Mark McCormick, Jean Foltz, Mary Ann Telatnik, Shirley McGuire, John Thompson, Laura Kenney, Mary Shields, and Guy Mills. Special thanks to George and Wendy Calmenson of The Book Company for their production talents (it was great working with you again) and to Rebecca Pepper, an outstanding copy editor.

My sincere appreciation goes to many others. Among them are Doug McCreadie, Ted Emmott, Ed Lamagna, Mike Hayden, Janet Prichard, Lorraine Berube, Marge White, John Turner, Jim LaBonte, John Cardin, David Tetreault, Irene Azzinaro, and David Clayton.

Many educators provided input for the second edition at various stages of its development. All of their comments contributed greatly to this edition's present form. In alphabetical order they are:

Wolfin Brumley—*Colorado State University*

Michael Cleron—*Stanford University*

Charles Denault—*Stanford University*

Jane Wallace Mayo—*University of Tennessee*

Rayno Niemi—*Rochester Institute of Technology*

Roy Pargas—*Clemson University*

Keith Pierce—*University of Minnesota*

Stuart Regis—*Stanford University*

Sharon Salveter—*Boston University*

Linda Shapiro—*University of Washington*

Neil Snyder—*Wright State University*

Mark Stehlick—*Carnegie-Mellon University*

Harriet Taylor—*Louisiana State University*

Susan Wallace—*University of North Florida*

Carol Wolfe—*Pace University, Manhattan*

Henderson Yeung—*California State University, Fresno*

I want particularly to thank Keith Pierce and Mark Stehlick, not only for their reviews of the first edition, but also for their extensive critiques of the manuscript for the second edition.

Our collective thanks to the many people who helped develop the first edition of this book. Larry Olsen contributed greatly to its production. The following people used the original manuscript and made several useful suggestions. Thanks to Sto Bell, Kris Jensen, Sue Medeiros, Cleve Moler, John Rowe, and all of the students at the University of New Mexico who had to suffer through the early drafts. Our appreciation also goes to Philip Carrigan and the students at Northeastern University for class-testing the manuscript. We would also like to thank Stephanie Horoschak, who drew the diagrams for these early drafts.

Again we acknowledge the reviewers for the first edition:

Richard Botting—*California State University, San Bernardino*

Philip Carrigan—*Northeastern University*

Michael Clancy—*University of California, Berkeley*

Shaun Cooper—*University of New Mexico*

Ken Lord—*Queens College, New York*

Andrew Oldroyd—*Washington University, St. Louis*

David Radford—*University of Illinois, Chicago*

Richard Snodgrass—*University of North Carolina*

Paul Spirakis—*New York University*

Clinton Staley—*University of California, Santa Barbara*

Brad Wilson—*Western Kentucky University*

Finally, your comments, suggestions, and corrections will be greatly appreciated. Please send them to

Computer Science Editorial Office

The Benjamin/Cummings Publishing Co., Inc.

390 Bridge Parkway

Redwood City, CA 94065

Thank you all.

F. M. C.

BRIEF CONTENTS

CONTENTS

APPLICATIONS

Programming and Software Engineering

CHAPTER *1*

Principles of Programming and Software Engineering

Problem Solving and Software Engineering
> What Is Problem Solving?
> Problem-Solving Tools: Top-Down Design, Procedural and Data
>   Abstraction, Information Hiding, and Recursion
> The Life Cycle of Software
> Loop Invariants
> What Is a Good Solution?

A Summary of Key Issues in Programming
> Modularity Through Top-Down Design
> Modifiability
> User Interface
> Fail-Safe Programming
> Style
> Debugging

Summary
Common Pitfalls/Debugging
Self-Test Exercises
Exercises
Projects

PREVIEW   This chapter summarizes several fundamental principles that serve as the basis for dealing with the complexities of large programs. The discussion both reinforces the basic principles of structured programming, which are further illustrated by the case study in Chapter 3, and demonstrates that writing well-structured and well-documented programs is cost-effective. The chapter also presents a brief discussion of algorithms and data abstraction, and indicates how these topics relate to the book's main theme of developing problem-solving and programming skills. Later, in Parts II, III, and IV of the book, the focus will shift from discussions of programming principles to the development and use of new problem-solving tools. Even when the focus of discussion is on these new tools, you should note how all solutions adhere to the basic principles discussed in this chapter.

PROBLEM SOLVING AND SOFTWARE ENGINEERING

Where did you begin when you wrote your last Pascal program? After reading the problem specifications and after the requisite amount of procrastination, most novice programmers simply begin to write Pascal statements. Obviously, their goal is to get their programs to execute, preferably with correct results. Therefore, they run their programs, examine error messages, insert semicolons, change the logic, delete semicolons, pray, and otherwise torture their programs until they work. Most of their time is probably spent debugging both syntax and program logic. Certainly, your programming skills are better now than when you wrote your first program, but will you be able to write a really large program by using the approach just described? Maybe, but there are better ways.

Coding without a solution design increases debugging time

Realize that an extremely large software development project generally requires a team of programmers rather than a single individual. Teamwork requires an overall plan, organization, and communication. A haphazard approach to programming will not serve a team programmer well and will not be cost-effective. Fortunately, there is a branch of computer science—**software engineering**—that provides techniques to facilitate the development of computer programs.

Software engineering facilitates development of programs

Whereas a first course in computer science typically emphasizes programming issues, the focus in this book will be on the broader issues of problem solving. This chapter begins with an overview of the problem-solving and programming processes and their close relationship.

What Is Problem Solving?

Here the term **problem solving** refers to the entire process of taking the statement of a problem and developing a computer program that solves that problem. This process requires you to pass through many phases, from gaining an understanding of the problem to be solved, through designing a conceptual solution, to implementing the solution with a computer program.

A solution specifies algorithms and ways to store data

Exactly what is a solution? Typically, a **solution** consists of two components: algorithms and ways to store data. An **algorithm** is a concise specification of a method to solve a problem. One action that an algorithm often performs is to operate on a collection of data. For example, an algorithm may have to put new data into a collection, remove data from a collection, or ask questions about a collection of data. When constructing a solution, you must organize your data collection so that you can operate on the data easily in the manner that the algorithm requires.

Perhaps this description of a solution leaves the false impression that all the cleverness in problem solving goes into developing the algorithm and that how you store your data plays only a supporting role. This is far from the truth. You need to do much more than store your data; you also need to operate on the data. In Chapter 4, you will learn that an **abstract data type**, or ADT, is a collection of data *and* a set of operations on that data. For example, suppose that you need to store a collection of names in a manner that allows you to search rapidly for a given name. One solution to this problem is to store the names sorted in an array and to use a binary search algorithm to search the array for a specified name. You can view the *sorted array together with the binary search algorithm* as an ADT that solves this problem.

An ADT is a collection of data and a set of operations on that data

Problem-Solving Tools: Top-Down Design, Procedural and Data Abstraction, Information Hiding, and Recursion

Several tools will help you to design a solution to a given problem. Five of these tools are top-down design, procedural abstraction, data abstraction, information hiding, and recursion.

Top-down design.   When you begin to write programs of moderate size and complexity, you will find it difficult to cope with the entire program at once. Most people who write programs and most people who read programs are similarly limited. Modularity through top-down design is a solution to this and other problems associated with large programs. What is meant by top-down design and modularity? The philosophy of top-down design is that you should address a task at successively lower levels of detail. You should partition a program into independent **modules**—procedures, functions, and other blocks of code—as Figure 1-1 depicts.

To illustrate the concept of a modular solution, consider a simple example. Suppose that you wanted to find the median among a collection of test scores. Figure 1-2 uses a **structure chart** to illustrate the hierarchy of modules that solve this problem. At first, each module is little more than a statement of *what* it needs to solve and is devoid of detail. You refine each module, in turn, by partitioning it into additional smaller modules. The result is a hierarchy of modules; each module is refined by its successors, which solve smaller problems and contain more detail about *how* to solve

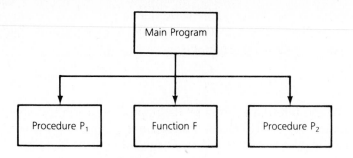

Figure 1-1

A program partitioned into independent modules

the problem than their predecessors. The refinement process continues until the modules at the bottom of the hierarchy are simple enough for you to translate directly into Pascal procedures, functions, and isolated blocks of code that solve very small, independent problems. Such a program is said to be **modular.** This strategy of dividing a program into isolated components should be fairly familiar to you.

Notice from Figure 1-2 that you can break the solution into three independent tasks:

```
Read the test scores into an array
Sort the array
Get the "middle" element of the array
```

A solution consisting of independent tasks

You can develop the module that solves each of these tasks in virtual isolation from the other modules. In fact, you want to design modules that are as independent as possible, except of course for their **interfaces,** which are the communication mechanisms between modules. If the three modules perform their tasks, then by calling them in order you will correctly find the median, regardless of *how* each module performs its task.

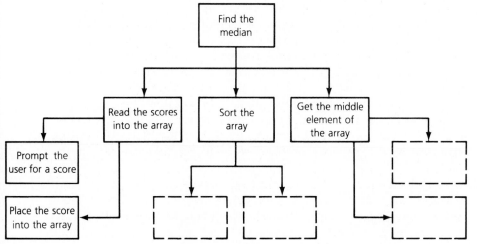

Figure 1-2

A structure chart showing the hierarchy of modules

You begin to develop each module by dividing it into subtasks. For example, you can refine the task of reading the test scores into an array by dividing it into the following two modules:

Subtasks

```
Prompt the user for a score
Place the score into the array
```

You continue the solution process by developing, in a similar manner, modules for each of these two tasks. A modular program has many advantages, several of which are discussed in the following sections. In general, modularity and top-down design help to simplify the problem-solving process. Thus, you should practice modularity at all points of the problem-solving process.

Specify what to do, not how to do it

Procedural abstraction.   When you use top-down design and modularity to solve a problem, each algorithm begins as a "black box." As the problem-solving process proceeds, you gradually refine the black boxes until eventually you implement their actions by writing Pascal code. Each black box specifies *what* it does, but not *how* it does it. No one black box may "know" how any other black box performs its task—it may know only what that task is. For example, if one part of a solution is to sort some data, one of the black boxes will be a sorting algorithm. The other black boxes will know that the sorting black box sorts, but they will not know how it sorts. In this way the various components of a solution are kept isolated from one another.

Typically, these black boxes are implemented as subprograms. **Procedural abstraction** separates the purpose of a subprogram from its implementation. Once a subprogram is written, you can use it without knowing the particulars of its algorithm as long as you have a statement of its purpose and a description of its parameters. Assuming that the subprogram is documented properly, you will be able to use it knowing only its header statement and its initial descriptive comments; you will not need to look at its code.

Modularity and procedural abstraction complement each other. Modularity involves breaking a solution into modules; procedural abstraction involves specifying each module clearly *before* you implement it in Pascal. For example, what does the module assume and what action does it take? Such specifications will clarify the design of your solution because you will be able to focus on the high-level functionality of your solution without being distracted by implementation details. In addition, these principles allow you to modify one part of a solution without significantly affecting the other parts. For example, you should be able to change the sorting algorithm in the previous problem without affecting the rest of the solution.

Procedural abstraction is essential to team projects. After all, in a team situation, you will have to use subprograms written by others without detailed knowledge of their algorithms. Will you actually be able to use such a subprogram without studying its code? In fact, you do each time you use a Pascal built-in function such as `sqrt`.

Data abstraction.   Most introductory courses stress the modular development of algorithms, and you will see many more examples that illustrate this technique further. For most of you, however, the application of modular development to data is a new concept. Procedural abstraction means focusing on what a module does instead of the details of its algorithm. Similarly, with **data abstraction** you focus on the operations that you will perform on the data instead of on how you will implement the operations. Clearly, you will eventually be concerned about programming detail. However, the principle of abstraction asks that you suppress your implementation concerns—for both algorithms and data structures—while you design the high-level functional aspects of the solution.

Specify what you will do to data, not how to do it

As was mentioned previously, an **abstract data type**, or ADT, is a collection of data and a set of operations on that data. Such operations might add new data to the collection, remove data from the collection, or search for some data. The other modules of the solution will "know" *what* operations the ADT can perform. However, they will not know *how* the data is stored or *how* the operations are performed.

For example, you have used a Pascal array, but have you ever stopped to think about what an array actually is? You will see many pictures of arrays throughout this book. The artist's conception of an array may resemble the way a Pascal array is implemented on a computer, and then again it may not. The point is that you are able to use an array without knowing what it "looks like"—that is, how it is implemented. Although different systems may implement Pascal arrays in different ways, the differences are transparent to the programmer. For instance, regardless of how the array A is implemented, you can always store the value x in location i of A by using the statement

    A[i] := x

and later write out that value by using the statement

    write(A[i])

Thus, you can use an array without knowing the details of its implementation, just as you can use the function *sqrt* without knowing the details of its implementation.

Likewise, you can perform operations on the data in an ADT without knowing the details of the ADT's implementation. Ultimately, you will implement each ADT by using **data structures.** A data structure is a construct that you can define within a programming language to store a collection of data. For instance, you might store some data in a Pascal array of integers, or in an array of records, or in a record of arrays. You will learn much more about abstract data types and data structures in Chapter 4.

An ADT is not a fancy name for a data structure

Within problem solving, abstract data types support algorithms, and algorithms are part of what constitutes an abstract data type. As you design a solution, you should develop algorithms and ADT's in tandem. The global algorithm that solves a problem suggests operations that you need to perform on the data, which in turn suggest ADT's and algorithms for performing the operations on the data. However, the development of the solution may proceed in the opposite direction as well. The kinds of ADT's that you are able to design can influence the strategy of your global algorithm for solving a problem. That is, your knowledge of which data operations are easy to perform and which are difficult can have a large effect on how you approach a problem.

As you probably have surmised from this discussion, there frequently is not a sharp distinction between an "algorithms problem" and a "data structures problem." It is often possible to look at a program from one perspective and feel that the data structures support a clever algorithm and then to look at the same program from another perspective and feel that the algorithms support a clever data structure.

Information hiding. As you have seen, abstraction identifies the essential aspects of both modules and data structures, which you can treat as black boxes. Abstraction tells you to write functional specifications for each black box; it is responsible for their outside, or **public**, views. However, abstraction also helps you to identify details that you should *hide* from public view—details that should not be in the specifications but should be **private.** The principle of **information hiding** not only hides such details within the black box, it also ensures that no other black box can access these hidden details. Thus, you should hide certain details within your modules and ADT's and make them inaccessible to all other modules and ADT's.

All modules and ADT's should hide something

Information hiding limits the ways that you need to deal with modules and ADT's. As a user of a module or ADT, you do not worry about implementation details. As an implementer of a module or ADT, you do not worry about their uses.

Recursion. Recursion is another extremely powerful problem-solving tool. Problems that at first appear to be quite difficult often have simple recursive solutions. Like top-down design, recursion breaks a problem into several smaller problems. What is striking about recursion is that these smaller problems are of *exactly the same type* as the original problem. That is, a recursive solution solves a problem by solving a smaller instance of the same problem! It solves this new problem by solving an even smaller instance of the same problem. Eventually, the new problem will be so small that its solution will be either obvious or known. This solution will lead to the solution of the original problem.

For example, suppose that you could solve problem P_1 if you had the solution to problem P_2, which is a smaller instance of P_1. Suppose further that you could solve problem P_2 if you had the solution to problem P_3, which is a smaller instance of P_2. If you knew the solution to P_3 because it was small enough to be trivial, you would be able to solve P_2. You could then use the solution to P_2 to solve the original problem P_1.

Recursion can provide simple solutions to difficult problems

Recursion can seem like magic, especially at first, but as you will see in Chapters 5 and 6, recursion is a very real and important problem-solving tool that is an alternative to **iteration.** An iterative solution involves loops, a concept with which you are undoubtedly quite familiar. Although not all recursive solutions are better than iterative solutions, recursion can provide straightforward solutions to problems that have complex iterative solutions.

The Life Cycle of Software

The development of good software involves a lengthy and continuing process known as the software's **life cycle.** This process begins with an initial idea, includes the writing and debugging of programs, and continues for years to involve corrections and enhancements to the original software. Here, then, is a list of the phases in the life cycle of typical software:

Phase 1: Specification. Given an initial statement of the software's purpose, you must specify clearly all aspects of the problem. Note that often the people who describe the problem are not programmers and that the initial problem statement might be imprecise. The specification phase, then, requires that you bring precision and detail to the original problem statement and that you communicate with both programmers and nonprogrammers.

Here are some questions that you must answer as you write the specifications for the software. What is the input data? What data is valid and what data is invalid? Who will use the software, and what user interface should be used? What error detection and error messages are desirable? What assumptions are possible? Are there special cases? What is the form of the output? What documentation is necessary? What enhancements to the program are likely in the future?

Make the problem statement precise and detailed

One way to improve communication between people and to clarify the software specifications is to write a prototype program that simulates the behavior of portions of the desired software product. For example, a simple—even inefficient—program could demonstrate the proposed user interface for analysis. It is better to discover any difficulties or to change your mind now than after programming is underway or even complete.

Prototype programs can clarify the problem

Realize that your previous programming assignments included program specifications. Perhaps aspects of these specifications were unclear and you had to seek clarification, but most likely you have had little practice in writing your own program specifications.

Phase 2: Design. Once you have completed the specification phase, you must design the algorithms that will accomplish the required tasks. Determine whether you can use programs or subprograms that already exist to perform some of the work. By using top-down design principles, divide the project into modules. Next, indicate the interaction between modules; a structure chart provides a clear picture of these relationships.

A structure chart shows the relationship between modules

At this point, it is important that you clearly specify not only the purpose of each module but also the **data flow** between modules. For example, you should provide answers to these questions for each module: What data is available to the module before its execution? What does the module assume? What does the data look like after the module executes? Thus, you should specify in detail the assumptions, input, and output for each module. One way to make these specifications is by writing both a **precondition**, which is a statement of the conditions that must exist at the beginning of a module, and a **postcondition**, which is a statement of the conditions at the end of a module. For example, you might describe a procedure that sorts an array as follows:

Subprogram specifications include preconditions and postconditions

```
procedure Sort(A, N)
{ Sorts an array into ascending order.
   Precondition: A is an array of N integers, 1 <= N <= Max.
   Postcondition: A[1] <= A[2] <= ... <= A[N], N is
   unchanged. }
```

Finally, you can use pseudocode to specify the details of the algorithms.

It is likely that you have spent little or no time in the design phase for your programs. It is imperative that you change this habit! The end result of top-down design is a solution that is easy to translate into the control structures and data structures of a particular programming language. By spending adequate time in the design phase, you will spend less time when you write and debug your program.

Phase 3: Verification.   There are formal, theoretical methods for proving properties about an algorithm that you could use to establish that an algorithm is correct. Although research in this area is incomplete, it is useful to mention some aspects of the verification process.

An **assertion** is a statement about a particular condition at a certain point in an algorithm. Preconditions and postconditions are simply assertions about conditions at the beginning and end of modules. An **invariant** is a condition that is always true at a particular point in an algorithm. A **loop invariant** is a condition that is true before and after each execution of an algorithm's loop. Later in this chapter, you will see how to use loop invariants to write correct loops.

There are theoretical ways to prove that some algorithms are correct

Proving that an algorithm is correct is like proving a theorem in geometry. For example, to prove that a module is correct, you would start with the preconditions (the axioms and assumptions in geometry) and demonstrate that the steps of the algorithm lead to the postconditions. To do so, you would consider each step in the algorithm and show that an assertion before the step leads to a particular assertion after the step. There are formal ways to make these demonstrations for various constructs such as *if* statements, *while* loops, and assignment statements.

As you prove that individual statements are correct, you need to collect them together to prove that sequences of statements, and then modules, and finally the program is correct. For example, suppose that you show that if assertion A_1 is true and statement S_1 executes, then assertion A_2 is true. Also, suppose that you have shown that assertion A_2 and statement S_2 lead to assertion A_3. You can then conclude that if assertion A_1 is true, executing the sequence of statements S_1 and S_2 will lead to assertion A_3. By continuing in this manner, you eventually will be able to show that the module is correct.

Clearly, if you discovered an error during the verification process, you would correct your algorithm and possibly modify the problem specifications. Thus, by using invariants, it is likely that your algorithm will contain fewer errors *before* you begin coding. As a result, you will spend less time debugging your program.

Phase 4: Coding.   Next, you must translate the algorithms into a particular programming language and remove the syntax errors. Although this phase is probably your concept of programming, realize that the coding phase is not the major part of the life cycle for most software—actually, it is a relatively minor part.

Coding is a relatively minor phase in the software life cycle

The solution that a top-down design produces is a hierarchy of subproblems, which will correspond to modules in a program. In Figure 1-3, the solution to problem A is defined in terms of subproblems S_1, S_2, and S_3. Before you begin to code the module that solves problem A, it seems reasonable that you should first implement the solutions to subproblems S_1, S_2, and S_3. This is a **bottom-up implementation**. Once you are confident that the modules for S_1, S_2, and S_3 are working, you can use them to continue to implement the solution to problem A.

In some situations it might be reasonable to implement a module before implementing some of its submodules—that is, to work in a top-down fashion. For example, in Figure 1-3, you might choose to implement module A before module S_3. In this case you would write a dummy procedure for S_3 that does nothing but report that it has been called. These dummy procedures, which are often called **stubs**, allow you to focus your attention on the central parts of the solution.

You also can implement a certain module at various levels of refinement. For example, suppose that you want to implement S_3 before you implement S_1, but S_3 needs the data that S_1 reads. You could use assignment statements in S_1 that define some typical values for S_3 to use. In this way you can concentrate on S_3 without the distraction of entering input. Alternatively, you could implement S_3 by itself in its own special main program that thoroughly tests S_3. Your approach will depend in part on the complexity of the module in question.

Phase 5: Testing.   During the testing phase, you need to remove as many logical errors as you can. At first, test the program with valid input data

Design a set of test data to test your program

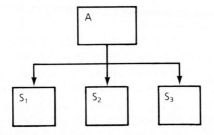

Figure 1-3

Top-down design, bottom-up implementation

that leads to a known solution. If certain data must lie within a range, include values at the endpoints of the range. For example, if the input value for N can range from 1 to 10, be sure to include test cases in which N is 1 and 10. Also, include invalid data to test the error-detection capability of the program. Try some random data, and finally try some actual data.

Develop a working program under simplifying assumptions, then add refining sophistication

Phase 6: Refining the solution.   The result of the previous steps of the solution process is a correct program, which you have tested extensively and debugged as necessary. If you have a program that solves your original problem, you might wonder about the significance of this step of the solution process.

Often the best approach to solving a problem is first to make some simplifying assumptions during the top-down design of the solution—for example, you could assume that the input will be in a certain format and will be correct—and next to develop a complete working program under these assumptions. You can then add more sophisticated input and output routines, additional features, and more error checks to the working program. Of course, you must take care to ensure that the final refinements do not require a complete redesign of the solution. You can usually make these additions cleanly, however, particularly when you have used a modular design. In fact, the ability to proceed in this manner is one of the key advantages of having a modular design! Thus, the approach of simplifying the problem initially makes a refinement step necessary in the solution process.

Here is a good example of the fact that the phases within this life cycle—or alternatively, the steps within a solution process—are not completely isolated from one another. To make realistic simplifying assumptions early in the design process, it is necessary to have some idea of how you will account for those assumptions later on.

Phase 7: Production.   When the software product is complete, it is distributed to its intended users, installed on their computers, and used.

Phase 8: Maintenance.   Maintaining a program is not like maintaining a car. Software does not wear out if you neglect it. However, users of your software invariably will detect errors that you did not discover during the testing phase. Correcting these errors is part of maintaining the software. Another aspect of the maintenance phase is the enhancement of the software by adding more features or by modifying existing portions to better suit the users.

Figure 1-4 pictures the eight phases of the software life cycle, which were just discussed. The circular arrangement suggests that the phases are part of a cycle and are not simply a linear list. It is likely, for example, that during the maintenance phase you will have to return to the problem specifications to verify or modify them. Also notice that the eight phases surround a documentation core in the figure. Documentation is not a sep-

Figure 1-4

The life cycle of software

arate phase, as you might expect. Rather, it is integrated into all phases of the software life cycle.

Is a program's life cycle relevant to *your* life? It definitely should be! You should view Phases 1 through 6 as the steps in a problem-solving process. Using this strategy, you first design and implement a solution (Phases 1 through 5) based on some initial simplifying assumptions. The outcome is a well-structured program that solves a somewhat simplified problem. The last step of the solution process (Phase 6) refines your work into a sophisticated program that meets the original problem specifications.

Loop Invariants

As was mentioned earlier, a loop invariant is a condition that is true both before and after the execution of a loop. This section discusses loop invariants further and shows you how to use them to demonstrate the correctness of iterative algorithms. By using invariants, you can detect errors before you begin coding and thereby reduce your debugging and testing time. Overall, invariants can save you time.

Consider this simple example of a loop that computes the sum of the first *N* elements in the array A:

```
{ Compute the sum of A[1], A[2], . . ., A[N] }
Sum := 0;
j := 1;
while j <= N do
begin
   Sum := Sum + A[j];
   j := j + 1
end
```

Before this loop begins execution, *Sum* is 0 and *j* is 1. After the loop executes once, *Sum* is A[1] and *j* is 2. In general,

Sum is the sum of the elements A[1] through A[j − 1]   *Loop invariant*

This statement is the invariant for this loop.

You can use invariants to establish the correctness of an iterative algorithm by showing that each of the following four points is true:

Steps to establish the correctness
of an algorithm

- **The invariant must be true initially**, before the loop begins execution for the first time. In the previous example, *Sum* is 0 and *j* is 1 initially. In this case, the invariant states that *Sum* contains the sum of the elements *A[1]* through *A[0]*, which is true because there are no elements in this range.

- **An execution of the loop must preserve the invariant.** That is, if the invariant is true before any given iteration of the loop, then you must show that it is true after the iteration. In the example, the loop adds *A[j]* to *Sum* and then increments *j* by 1. Thus, after an execution of the loop, the most recent element added to *Sum* is *A[j - 1]*; that is, the invariant is true after the iteration.

- **The invariant must capture the correctness of the algorithm.** That is, you must show that if the invariant is true when the loop terminates, the algorithm is correct. When the loop of the example terminates, *j* contains *N* + 1 and the invariant is true: *Sum* contains the sum of the elements *A[1]* through *A[(N + 1) - 1]*, which is the sum that you intended to compute.

- **The loop must terminate.** That is, you must show that the loop will terminate after a finite number of iterations. In the example, *j* begins at 1 and then increases by 1 at each execution of the loop. Thus, *j* eventually will exceed *N* regardless of *N*'s value. This fact and the nature of the `while` statement guarantees that the loop will terminate.

Notice the clear connection between the previous demonstration and **mathematical induction.**[1] Showing the invariant to be true initially, which establishes the **base case**, is analogous to establishing that a property of the natural numbers is true for 0. Showing that each iteration of the loop preserves the invariant, which is the **inductive step**, is analogous to showing that if a property is true for an arbitrary natural number *k*, then the property is true for the natural number *k* + 1. After performing the previous four steps, you can conclude that the invariant is true after every iteration of the loop—just as mathematical induction allows you to conclude that a property is true for every natural number.

Identifying loop invariants will help you to write correct loops. You should state the invariant as a comment that precedes each loop. For example, in the previous example, you might write the following:

State loop invariants in your
programs

```
{ Invariant: 1 <= j <= N + 1 and Sum = A[1] + . . . + A[j-1] }
while j <= N do
    . . .
```

---

[1]A review of mathematical induction appears in Appendix A.

What Is a Good Solution?

Before you devote your time and energy to the study of problem-solving tools, it seems only fair that you see at the outset why mastery of these tools will help to make you a good problem solver. An obvious statement is that the use of these tools will produce good solutions. This statement, however, leads to the more fundamental question, what *is* a good solution? A brief attempt at answering this question concludes this section.

Because a computer program is the final form your solutions will take, consider what constitutes a good computer program. Presumably, you write a program to perform some task. In the course of performing that task, there is a real and tangible **cost**. This cost includes such factors as the computer resources (computing time and memory) the program consumes, the difficulties encountered by those who use the program, and the consequences of a program that does not behave correctly.

However, the costs just mentioned do not give the whole picture. They pertain to only one phase of the life cycle of a solution—the phase in which it is an operational program. In assessing whether or not a solution is good, you also must consider the phases during which you developed the solution and the phases after you wrote the initial program that implemented the solution. Each of these phases incurs costs, too. The total cost of a solution must take into account the value of the time of the people who developed, refined, coded, debugged, and tested it. A solution's cost must also include the cost of maintaining, modifying, and expanding it.

Thus, when calculating the overall cost of a solution, you must include a diverse set of factors. If you adopt such a multidimensional view of cost, it is reasonable to evaluate a solution against the following criterion:

> *A solution is good if the total cost it incurs over all phases of its life cycle is small.*

A multidimensional view of a solution's cost

It is interesting to consider how the relative importance of the various components of this cost has changed since the early days of computing. In the beginning, the cost of computer time relative to human time was extremely high. In addition, people tended to write programs to perform very specific, narrowly defined tasks. If the task changed somewhat, a new program was written. Program maintenance was probably not much of an issue, and there was thus little concern if a program was hard to read. It was common for a program to have only one user, its author. As a consequence, programmers tended not to worry about misuse or ease of use of their programs; a program's interface generally was not considered important.

In this type of environment, one cost clearly overshadowed all others: computer resources. If two programs performed the same task, the one that required less time and memory was better. How things have changed! Since the early days of computers, computing costs have dropped dramatically, thus making the value of the problem solver's and programmer's time a much more significant factor in the cost of a solution. Another consequence of the drop in computing costs is that computers now are used to perform tasks in a wide variety of areas, many of them nonscientific. People who interact with computers often have no technical expertise and no knowledge of the workings of programs. People want their software to be easy to use.

Programs must be well structured and documented

Today, programs are larger and more complex than ever before. They are often so large that many people are involved in their design, use, and maintenance. Good structure and documentation are thus of the utmost importance. As programs perform more highly critical tasks, the prices for malfunctions will soar. Thus, society needs both well-structured programs and techniques for formally verifying their correctness. People will not and should not entrust their livelihoods—or their lives—to a program that only its authors can understand and maintain.

These developments have made obsolete the notion that the most efficient solution is always the best. If two programs perform the same task, it is no longer true that the faster one is necessarily better. Programmers who use every trick in the book to save a few microseconds of computing time at the expense of clarity are not in tune with the cost structure of today's world. You must write programs with people as well as computers in mind.

Efficiency is only one aspect of a solution's cost

At the same time, do not get the false impression that the efficiency of a solution is no longer important. To the contrary, there are many situations in which efficiency is the prime determinant of whether or not a solution is even usable. The point is that a solution's efficiency is only one of many factors that you must consider. If two solutions have approximately the same efficiency, then other factors should dominate the comparison. However, when the efficiencies of solutions differ *significantly,* this difference can be the overriding concern. The stages of the problem-solving process at which you should be most concerned about efficiency are those during which you develop the underlying methods of solution— the algorithms and the data structures. It is the choice of the algorithms and data structures, far more than the manner in which you code them, that leads to significant differences in efficiency.

The problem-solving philosophy that we advocate in this book reflects our view of the multidimensional cost of a solution. We believe that this philosophy is reasonable in today's world and that it will be reasonable in the years to come.

A SUMMARY OF KEY ISSUES IN PROGRAMMING

Given that a good solution is one that, in the course of its life cycle, incurs a small cost, the next questions to ask are, what are the characteristics of good solutions, and how can you construct good solutions? This section summarizes the answers to these very difficult questions. You will find more complete answers by observing the principles of problem solving that are practiced throughout the book. For example, Chapter 3 presents a large case study. A major goal of this case study is to demonstrate how you can solve a formidable problem by carefully following a few key programming principles. Throughout the remainder of the book, even as the emphasis shifts from programming to the earlier stages of the design of a solution, you should note how the programs attempt to adhere to these principles.

The programming issues that this section discusses should be familiar to you. However, it is usually the case that the beginning student does not truly appreciate their importance. After the first course in programming, many students still simply want to "get the thing to run." We hope that the discussion to follow and the case study in Chapter 3 will help to emphasize just how important these issues really are.

One of the most widespread misconceptions held by beginning students is that a computer program is "read" only by a computer. As a consequence, the beginning student tends to consider only whether or not the *computer* will be able to "understand" the program—that is, will the program compile, execute, and produce the correct output? The truth is, of course, that other people often must read and modify programs. In a typical programming environment, many individuals share a program. One person may write a program, which other people use in conjunction with other programs written by other people, and a year later, a different person may modify the program. It is therefore essential that you take great care to design a program that is easy to read and understand.

People read programs, too

You should always keep in mind the following six issues of program structure and design:

Six Key Programming Issues

1. Modularity through top-down design
2. Modifiability
3. User interface
4. Fail-safe programming
5. Style
6. Debugging

Modularity Through Top-Down Design

As will be continually emphasized, you should practice modularity through top-down design at all phases of the problem-solving process, beginning with the initial design of a solution. A modular implementation generally follows naturally from a solution that you developed through top-down design. As was noted earlier, a modular program has several advantages.

As the size of a program grows, many programming tasks become more difficult. Modularity is a means of slowing down the rate at which the level of difficulty grows. The primary difference between a small modular program and a large modular program is simply the number of modules each contains. Because the modules are independent, working on one large modular program is not very different from working on many small, independent programs. On the other hand, working on a large nonmodular program is more like working on many interrelated programs simultaneously.

More specifically, modularity has a favorable impact on the following aspects of programming:

Modularity facilitates programming

- **Constructing the program.** Keeping track of what is going on in a large, complex program can quickly become very difficult. By restricting attention to small, independent modules, *the task of writing a large program is reduced to one of writing many small programs.* This approach also permits team programming, where several programmers work independently on their own modules.

- **Debugging the program.** Debugging a large program can be a monstrous task. Imagine that you type a 10,000-line program and eventually get it to compile. Neither of these tasks would be very much fun. Now imagine that you execute your program and, after a few hundred lines of output, you get the message

```
subscript value of 34 is out of range at line 5679
```

You quickly turn to line 5679 and, sure enough, there is the assignment statement

```
A[place] := A[place + 1]
```

How did that subscript get out of range? You should anticipate spending the next day or so tracing through the intricacies of your program before discovering what has gone wrong.

A great advantage of writing modular code is that the task of debugging a large program is reduced to one of debugging many small programs. When you begin to code a module, you should be almost certain that all other modules coded so far are correct. That is, before you consider a module finished, you should test it extensively, both separately and in context of the other modules, by calling it with actual parameters carefully chosen to induce all possible behaviors of the modules. If this testing is done thoroughly, you can have a high degree of certainty that any problem is a result of an error in the last module added. *Modularity isolates errors.*

Modularity isolates errors

More theoretically, as was mentioned before, there are formal methods for proving properties of programs that you can use to establish the correctness of a program. Modular programs are amenable to this verification process.

Modular programs are easy to read

- **Reading the program.** A person reading a large program may have trouble seeing the forest for the trees. Just as a top-down design helps the programmer cope with the complexities of solving a problem, so too will it help the reader of a program to understand how a program works. A modular program is easy to follow because the reader can get a good idea of what is going on without reading any of the code. A well-written module can be understood fairly well from only its name, header comment, and the names of the other modules that it calls. The reader of a program needs to study actual code only if he or she requires a detailed understanding of how the program operates. This is discussed further in the section on style later in this chapter.

- **Modifying the program.** Modifiability is the topic of the next section, but as the modularity of a program has a direct bearing on its modifiability, it is briefly mentioned here. A small change in the requirements of a program should require only a small change in the code. If this is not the case, it is likely that the program is poorly written and, in particular, that it is not modular. To accommodate a small change in the requirements, a modular program usually requires a change in only a few of its modules. *Modularity isolates modifications.* A simple example is presented in the discussion of modifiability in the next section.

  Modularity isolates modifications

- **Eliminating redundant code.** Another advantage of modular design is that you can identify operations that occur in many different parts of the program and implement them as subprograms. This means that the code for an operation will appear only once, resulting in an increase in both readability and modifiability. The example in the next section demonstrates this point.

  Modularity eliminates redundancies

Modifiability

Imagine that the specification for a program changes after some period of time. Frequently, people require that a program do something differently than they specified originally, or they ask that it do more than they requested originally. This section examines two techniques that make a program easy to modify: the use of subprograms and the use of user-defined constants.

Subprograms.   Suppose, for instance, that a library has a large program to catalog its books. The program represents a book with a record[2], which the following statements define:

```
const stringsize = 20;

type  string = packed array [1..stringsize] of char;
```

---

[2]Do not worry if you have not studied records or if you do not remember them. You still should be able to understand the point of this example. Note that Chapter 2 reviews records.

```
book = record
    callno : real;
    author : string;
    title  : string
end;

var    Request : book;
```

Suppose that at several points the program needs to print out the information about a requested book. At each of these points, the program could include this sequence of statements:

```
with Request do
begin
    writeln('Call number : ', callno:6:2);
    writeln('Author : ', author);
    writeln('Title : ', title)
end { with }
```

Alternatively, you could replace this sequence with a call to the following procedure, *PrintInfo*:

```
procedure PrintInfo(Request : book);
begin
    with Request do
    begin
        writeln('Call number : ', callno:6:2);
        writeln('Author : ', author);
        writeln('Title : ', title)
    end { with }
end   { PrintInfo }
```

Subprograms make a program easier to modify

Not only does the use of the procedure have the obvious advantage of eliminating redundant code, it also makes the resulting program more modifiable. Suppose that, after the library's program has been running for a year, the library's staff notices that their patrons often wish to know the length of a given book. This addition requires changing only the type definition of *book* to

```
book = record
    callno : real;
    author : string;
    title  : string;
    length : posint    { new field; posint = 1..maxint }
end
```

and adding the statement

```
writeln('Length : ', length:5) { print out the new field }
```

to the *writeln* statements in the definition of the procedure *PrintInfo*. If you had not used a procedure, the modification would have required you to insert the *writeln* statement at each point where the program prints the information. Merely finding each of these points could be difficult, and you probably would overlook a few. In this simple example, the advantages of using subprograms should be clear.

For a slightly more subtle illustration, recall an earlier example of a solution that, as one of its tasks, sorted some data. Developing the sorting algorithm as an independent module and eventually implementing it as a procedure would make the program easier to modify. For instance, if you found that the sorting algorithm was too slow, you could replace the sort procedure without even looking at the rest of the program. You simply could "cut out" the old procedure and "paste in" the new one. If instead the sort was integrated into the program, the required surgery might be quite intricate.

In general, it is a very bad sign if you need to rewrite a program to accommodate small modifications. Usually, it is easy to modify a well-structured program slightly: Because each module solves only a small part of the overall problem, a small change in problem specifications usually affects only a few of the modules.

User-defined constants. The use of user-defined, or named, constants is another way to enhance the modifiability of a program. For example, Pascal's restriction that an array must be of a predefined, fixed size causes a bit of a difficulty. Suppose that a program used an array to process the SAT scores of the computer science majors at your university. When the program was written, there were 202 computer science majors, so the array was defined by

User-defined constants make a program easier to modify

```
type scores = array[1..202] of integer
```

The program processes the array in several ways: For example, it reads the scores, prints the scores, and averages the scores by using a construct such as

```
for i := 1 to 202 do
    Process the score
```

If the number of majors should change, not only do you need to redefine the type *scores*, but you must also change each loop that processes the array to reflect the new array size. In addition, there may be other references in the code that depend on the size of the array. A 202 here, a 201 there—which to change?

On the other hand, if you use a constant such as

```
const size = 202
```

you can define the array by using

```
type scores = array[1..size ] of integer
```

and write the processing loops in this form:

```
for i := 1 to size do
    Process the score
```

If you write references that depend on the size of the array in terms of the constant *size* (such as *size*, *size* - *1*, and so on), you can change the array size simply by changing the definition of the constant *size*.

User Interface

Another area in which you need to keep people in mind is the design of the user interface. Humans often process a program's input and output. Here are a few obvious points:

Prompt the user for input

- In an interactive environment, the program should always prompt the user for input in a manner that makes it quite clear what it expects. For example, the prompt "?" is not nearly as enlightening as the prompt "Enter account number for deposit." You should never assume that the users of your program will know what response the program requires.

Echo the input

- A program should always echo its input. Whenever a program reads data, either from a user at a terminal or from a file, the program should include the values it reads in its output. This inclusion serves two purposes: First, it gives the user a check on the data entered—a guard against typos and errors in data transmission. This check is particularly useful in the case of interactive input. Second, the output is more meaningful and self-explanatory when there is a record of what input generated the output.

Label the output

- The output should be well labeled and easy to read. An output of

```
1800   6   1
Jones, Q.   223 2234.00 1088.19   X, Y   Smith, T. 111
110.23 L,   Harris, V.   44   44000.00 22222.22
```

is more prone to misinterpretation than is

```
CUSTOMER ACCOUNTS AS OF 1800 HOURS ON JUNE 1

Status codes:
X = new account, Y = joint account, L = inactive account
```

NAME	ACC#	CHECKING	SAVINGS	STATUS
Jones, Q.	223	$ 2234.00	$ 1088.19	X, Y
Smith, T.	111	$ 110.23	---------	L
Harris, V.	44	$44000.00	$22222.22	------

These characteristics of a good user interface are only the basics. Several more subtle points separate a program that is merely usable from one that is user friendly. Students tend to ignore a good user interface, but by investing a little extra time here, you can make a big difference: the difference between a good program and one that only solves the problem. For example, consider a program that requires a user to enter a line of data in some fixed format, with exactly one blank between the fields. A free-form input that allows any number of blanks between the fields would be much more convenient for the user. It takes so little time to add a loop that skips blanks, so why require the user to follow an exact format? Once you make this small additional effort, it is a permanent part of both your program and your library of techniques. The user of your program never has to think about input format. Contrast this with having all users worry about input format every time they use your program.

Fail-Safe Programming

A fail-safe program is one that will perform reasonably no matter how anyone uses it. Unfortunately, this goal is usually unattainable. A more realistic goal is to anticipate the ways that people might misuse the program and to guard carefully against these abuses.

This discussion considers two types of errors. The first type is an *error in input data*. For example, suppose that a program expects a nonnegative integer but reads –12. When a program encounters this type of problem, it should not abort without displaying some sort of useful message. The message

Check for errors in input

```
subscript out of range ... program terminated
```

is not as useful as the message

```
-12 is not a valid number of children.
Please reenter this number.
```

The second type of error is an *error in the program logic*. Although a discussion of this type of error belongs in the debugging section at the end of this chapter, detecting errors in program logic is also an issue of fail-safe programming. A program that appears to have been running correctly may at some point behave unexpectedly, even if the data that it reads is valid. For example, the program may not have accounted for the particular data that elicited the surprise behavior, even though you tried your best to test the program's logic. Or perhaps you modified the program and that modification invalidated an assumption that you made in some other part of the program. Whatever the difficulty, a program should have built-in safeguards against these kinds of errors. It should monitor itself and be able to indicate that *there is something wrong with me and you should not trust my results*.

Check for errors in logic

Guarding against errors in input data. Suppose that you are computing statistics about the people in income brackets between $10,000 and

$100,000. The brackets are rounded to the nearest thousand dollars: $10,000, $11,000, and so on to $100,000. The raw data is a file of zero or more lines of the form

```
<G> <N>
```

where N is the number of people with an income that falls into the G-thousand-dollar group. Several people have compiled the data, so there may be several entries for the same value of G. As the user enters data, the program must add up and record the number of people for each value of G. From the problem's context, it is clear that G is an integer in the range 10 to 100 inclusive, and N is a nonnegative integer.

As an example of how to guard against errors in input, we will consider the input procedure for this problem. The first attempt at writing this procedure will illustrate several common ways in which a program can fall short of the fail-safe ideal. Consideration of several possible modifications to the procedure will lead to some dos and don'ts about fail-safe programming in general and for the use of subrange types in particular. Eventually you will see an input procedure that is much closer to the fail-safe ideal than the original solution.

Many of the points here specifically concern Pascal, so actual code rather than pseudocode will be used. A first attempt at the procedure might be

```
const low = 10;              { low end of incomes considered }
      high = 100;            { high end of incomes considered }

type  thousands   = low..high;
      IncomeTable = array[thousands] of integer;
```

This procedure is not fail-safe
```
procedure ReadData(var IncomeData : IncomeTable);
{ ------------------------------------------------------------
  Reads and organizes income statistics.
  Precondition: Input data is error-free and each input line
  is in the form <G> <N> where N is the number of people
  with an income in the G-thousand-dollar group.
  Postcondition: IncomeData[G] = total number of people with
  an income in the G-thousand-dollar group.
  ------------------------------------------------------------ }
var   Group, Number : integer;        { input values }
      i : thousands;                  { loop control }

begin
    for i := low to high do            { zero out the array }
        IncomeData[i] := 0;

    while not eof do
    begin
        readln(Group, Number);                    {read data}
        writeln('Income group = ', Group:3,
                ' and Number = ', Number:7);      {echo print}
```

```
        IncomeData[Group] := IncomeData[Group] + Number
    end   { while }
end   {ReadData}
```

This procedure has some problems. If an input line contains unexpected data, the program will not behave reasonably. Consider two specific possibilities:

- The program accepts a negative value for *Number*. Although a negative value for *Number* is invalid because you cannot have a negative number of people in an income group, the program will add *Number* to the group's array entry. Thus, the statistics that other parts of the program produce will not be valid.

- The first integer on the line is not in the range *low..high*. The reference *IncomeData[Group]* will then cause execution to terminate with a message such as

```
subscript value of 9 is out of range at line ...
```

A first attempt at addressing these two problems uses Pascal's facility for subrange types. As you will see, however, *it is not appropriate to use subrange types as a mechanism for catching errors in input.* For example, because the number of people in any income group should never be negative, you might change the global type definitions to

Do not use subrange types to detect invalid input data

```
type   nonneg     = 0..maxint;      { new type }
       thousands  = low..high;      { remains the same }
       IncomeTable = array[thousands] of nonneg { an array
           of this type can contain only nonnegative
           integers}
```

Does this change really address the concern about a negative input value for *Number*? First, notice that it is possible to add a negative value to an entry of *IncomeData* without that entry becoming negative. For example, if *Number* is –4,000 and *IncomeData* is 10,000, then *IncomeData* + *Number* is 6,000. Thus, a negative value for *Number* could remain undetected and invalidate the results of the rest of the program.

Not only would the subrange fail to catch many input errors, but also when it did catch errors, it might generate a very confusing message. For example, suppose that *Number* is –4,000 and *IncomeData* is 2,143. When the program computed *IncomeData* + *Number*, it would terminate with a message such as

```
value of −1857 is not in range
```

This message is not particularly useful! It does not specifically tell you that *Number* was negative. This ungraceful termination caused by an error in input is not consistent with the desire for a fail-safe program.

Thus, making *IncomeData* an array over the subrange *nonneg* does not adequately address the problem of invalid input values for *Number*. However, there is another reason for wanting *IncomeData* to be an array of this type, as you will see in the next section, "Guarding Against Errors in Program Logic."

The next attempt at solving the problem of invalid input might be to declare the variable *Number* to be type *nonneg*. However, this idea is not good either. If the data contains a negative value for *Number*, the program will abort with a message such as

```
value of -4000 is not in range
```

A fail-safe program should detect the invalid data but not abort. A better solution is to leave *Number* as an integer, but always to check its value before storing it in the array, as this pseudocode indicates:

Test for invalid input data

```
readln(Group, Number)
. . .
if Number ≥ 0
    then add Number to IncomeData
    else handle the error
```

Notice that Pascal allows you to assign a variable of type *T* (in this case, *integer*) to a variable whose type is a subrange of *T* (in this case, *nonneg*), as long as the value of the first variable is within the specified range.

Now that you have seen a satisfactory solution to the problem of an invalid input value for *Number*, it is clear how you can solve the problem of an invalid input value for *Group*. After the program reads a value for *Group*, it must check to see if it is in the range *low..high*. If the value is in range, you may use *Group* to subscript the array *IncomeData*. However, if it is not in range, you must handle the input error.

There are several reasonable courses of action for the program to take after it has encountered an error in the input. One possibility is for the program to print out an informative message, such as

```
The value 9 supplied for the income group
is not in the required range of 10..100
```

and terminate. Another possibility is to print out a similar message, ignore the bad input line, and continue. Which action is correct really depends on how the program uses the data once it is read.

These points are illustrated with a solution that attempts both to make the input procedure as universally applicable as possible and to make the program that uses it as modifiable as possible. In the following solution, when the input procedure encounters an error in input, it will print out a message, set a flag, ignore the data line, and continue. By setting a flag, the procedure leaves it to the calling routine to determine the appropriate action—such as abort or continue—when there is an input error. Thus, you can use the same input procedure in many contexts and can easily modify the action taken upon encountering an error. Error handling is discussed further in the section on style later in this chapter.

```
const low = 10;          { low end of incomes considered }
      high = 100;        { high end of incomes considered }

type  nonneg      = 0..maxint;
      thousands   = low..high;
      IncomeTable = array[thousands] of nonneg;

procedure ReadData(var IncomeData : IncomeTable;
                   var DataError : boolean);
{ ------------------------------------------------------------
  Reads and organizes income statistics.
  Precondition: Each input line contains exactly 2 integers
  in the form <G> <N> where N is the number of people with
  an income in the G-thousand-dollar group.
  Postcondition: IncomeData[G] = total number of people with
  an income in the G-thousand-dollar group. If either G or N
  is erroneous (G not in the range [low..high] or N
  negative), the program ignores the data line, prints a
  message, sets the flag DataError to true, and continues.
  In this case, the calling routine should take action.
  DataError is false if there are no data errors.
  ------------------------------------------------------- }
var  Group, Number : integer;      { input values }
     i : thousands;                { loop control }

begin
   DataError := false;             { no data error found yet }

   for i := low to high do         { zero out the array }
      IncomeData[i] := 0;

   while not eof do
   begin
      readln(Group, Number);
      writeln('Input line contains income group   ',
              Group:3, '  and  Number  ', Number:7);
      if ( (Group >= low) and (Group <= high) )
                               and (Number >= 0)
         then    { the input is valid - add it to the tally }
            IncomeData[Group] := IncomeData[Group] + Number
         else    { error in input data }
         begin
            writeln('Error in input:');
            if ( Group < low ) or ( Group > high )
               then writeln('Income group not',
                            ' in range 10..100.');

            if ( Number < 0 )
               then writeln('Number is negative.');
```

A procedure that includes fail-safe programming

```
                    writeln('This input line will be ignored.');
                    writeln;
                    DataError := true { set error flag }
                end  { else }
        end  { while }
    end  { ReadData }
```

This input procedure will behave gracefully in the face of most common input errors. However, it is not completely fail-safe. What happens if an input line contains only one integer? What happens if an input line contains a noninteger? The procedure would be more fail-safe if it read its input character by character, converted the characters to integer, and checked for end of line. In most contexts, this processing would be a bit extreme. However, if the people who enter the data frequently err by typing nonintegers, you could alter the input procedure easily because the procedure is an isolated module. In any case, the procedure's header comment should include any assumptions it makes about the data and an indication of what might make the program abort abnormally.

Guarding against errors in program logic.   Now consider the second type of error that a program should guard against: errors in its own logic. These are errors that you may not have caught when you debugged the program, or you may have introduced them through program modification.

Unfortunately, there is no reliable way for a program to let you know when something is wrong with it. (Could you rely on a program to tell you that something was wrong with its mechanism for telling you that there is something wrong?) However, you can build checks into a program that ensure that certain conditions always hold when the program is correctly implementing its algorithm. As was mentioned earlier, such conditions are called invariants.

As a simple example of an invariant, consider again the array *IncomeData* from the previous example. *All integers in this array must be greater than or equal to zero.* Recall that *IncomeData* was left as an array of *nonneg* values. Although this choice does not help to guard against input errors, to some extent it does guard against errors in the program's logic. For example, if at any time the program attempts to store a negative value in the array, the program terminates. The termination is not very graceful, but it is far better for a program to terminate ungracefully than it is for it to continue to produce output that—unbeknownst to the users—is incorrect.

Pascal's type checking should really be your last line of defense against errors in a program's logic. If, for example, the program computes a value to add to an entry of the array *IncomeData*, it might be reasonable for the program to check first that this computed value is within some range of believability. If the value is outside such a range, the program can terminate with a message that alerts its users to a potential problem and requests that debuggers be called in.

Another general way in which you should make a program fail-safe is to make each subprogram check the values of its parameters. For example, consider the following function, *SumBetween*, which returns the sum of all the integers between integers *x* and *y*.

Subprograms should check the values of their parameters

```
function SumBetween(x, y : integer) : integer;
{ -----------------------------------------------------------
  Returns the sum of all the integers between x and y.
  Precondition: x and y are integers such that x <= y.
  Postcondition: Returns SumBetween = x + (x + 1) + ... + y.
  x and y are unchanged.
  ----------------------------------------------------------- }
var Sum, i : integer;
begin
    Sum := 0;
    for i := x to y do
        Sum := Sum + i;
    SumBetween := Sum
end   { SumBetween }
```

The header comment of this function contains a precondition—information about what assumptions are made—*as should always be the case*. The value that this function returns is valid only if the precondition is met. If *x* is greater than *y*, then the function will return the incorrect value of zero.

In the context of the program for which this function was written, it may be reasonable to make the assumption that *x* will be less than or equal to *y*. That is, if the rest of the program is working correctly, then it will call *SumBetween* only with correct values of *x* and *y*. Ironically, this last observation gives you a good reason for *SumBetween* to check the relationship between the values of *x* and *y*: If it turns out that *x* is greater than *y*, then the warning that results from the check indicates that something may be wrong elsewhere in the program.

Another reason the function *SumBetween* should check whether *x* is less than or equal to *y* is that the function should be correct outside the context of its program. That is, if you borrow the function for use in another program, the function should warn you if you use it incorrectly by passing it an *x* that is greater than *y*. A stronger check than simply the statement of the assumptions in the header comment is desirable. Thus, *a subprogram should state its assumptions and, when possible, check that its parameters conform to these assumptions.*

Style

The following eight issues of personal style in programming are considered here:

Eight Issues of Style

1. Extensive use of subprograms
2. Avoidance of global variables in subprograms
3. Use of variable parameters
4. Use of functions
5. Avoidance of `goto`
6. Error handling
7. Readability
8. Documentation

Admittedly, much of the following discussion reflects the personal taste of the authors; there certainly are other good programming styles.

It is difficult to overuse subprograms

Extensive use of subprograms.   You should use subprograms extensively; it is very difficult to overuse subprograms. If a set of statements performs an identifiable, recurring task, it should be a subprogram. However, a task need not be recurrent to justify the use of a subprogram.

There are two arguments against the extensive use of subprograms. First, subprograms may incur a large overhead. A program with all its code in line runs faster than one that calls subprograms to execute the same statements. However, it is false to infer from this fact that it is cheaper to use programs that do not contain subprograms. The use of subprograms is cost-effective if you consider human time as a significant component of the program's cost. In addition to the consideration of the cost of human time, current research trends support extensive use of subprograms. Compilers can reduce the penalties for subprogram calls. Transformation tools take a program with subprograms and transform it for execution into an equivalent program with the subprograms represented in line.

A second objection to the extensive use of subprograms is that they can be difficult to read. *Perhaps* you have overused subprograms if they cause a reader to flip back and forth constantly through the program. However, if the subprograms implement recurring tasks, the distraction they may cause is made up for by the increase in the program's modifiability. In short, it is possible to overuse subprograms, but it is far easier to underuse them.

Avoidance of global variables in subprograms.   One of the main advantages of subprograms is that they can implement the concept of an isolated module. This isolation is sacrificed when a subprogram accesses a global variable, because the effects of a subprogram's action are no longer self-contained or limited to variable parameters. Hence, the isolation of both errors and modifications is greatly compromised when global variables appear in subprograms.

Should a subprogram ever access global variables? Sometimes, but only if the sacrifice of isolation is justifiable. Several programs in this book access global variables in subprograms for the sake of readability. *If some piece of data is so inherently important to a program that almost every subprogram must access it, then the data is global in nature.* Allowing the subprograms global access to the variables that contain this data best reflects the relationship between the data and the program as a whole. You will see several examples of this situation as they arise.

Use global variables sparingly

Use of variable parameters. A subprogram does interact, in a controlled fashion, with the rest of the program via the use of parameters. **Value parameters**, which are the default when you do not specify the keyword *var*, pass values into the subprogram, but any change that the subprogram makes to these parameters is not reflected in the actual parameters back in the calling routine. The communication between the calling routine and the subprogram is one-way. Because the restriction to one-way communication supports the notion of an isolated module, *you should use value parameters when possible.*

Value parameters

When is it appropriate to use **variable parameters?** The obvious situation is when a procedure needs to return values to the calling routine. However, if the procedure needs to return only a single value, it may be more appropriate to use a function. If a function is not appropriate, then variable parameters are probably in order.

Variable parameters

There is another situation in which variable parameters might be desirable, but the issues are very subtle. Suppose that a subprogram has a parameter X whose value it does not alter. The natural choice is for X to be a value parameter. However, the invocation of a subprogram with a value parameter X causes the subprogram to copy the value of the actual parameter that corresponds to X into temporary storage that is local to the subprogram. This copying incurs very little overhead if X is a simple variable, but the computing time and storage required to copy a large array might be significant. However, if X were a variable parameter, no copy of it would be made, which could lead to significant savings in computer resources.

The problem with making X a variable parameter is that it conveys misinformation about the subprogram's relation to the rest of the program. By convention, you use a variable parameter to communicate a value from the subprogram back to the calling routine. However, variable parameters whose values remain unchanged make the program more difficult to read and more prone to errors if modifications are required. The situation is analogous to using a constant instead of a variable whose value never changes. Thus, there is a trade-off between readability and modifiability on the one hand and efficiency on the other. Unless there is a significant difference in efficiency, we generally take the side of readability and modifiability. Later, this book explores such trade-offs more fully.

Use of functions. Because Pascal could not possibly include all potentially useful statements in its set of primitive statements, it provides the programmer with procedures, a mechanism for writing new statements out of the built-in primitives. You can call a procedure from any point in a program at which you need the user-defined statement. Similarly, a function is a mechanism by which the programmer can write new *expressions*. Any time you need to calculate a value, you can call a user-defined function as if it were part of the language.

Functions should not have side effects

Because you use a function as an expression, you should use it, as you would any other expression, only to compute a simple value. This use corresponds to the mathematical notion of a function. Therefore, it would be strange indeed if a function did *anything* other than return the required value. Imagine evaluating the expression $2 * x$ and having the values of five other variables change! *A function should never do anything but return the required value.* That is, a function should never have a **side effect**.

What functions have potential for side effects?

Functions with the potential for side effects

- **Functions with global variables.** If a function references a global variable, it has the potential for a side effect. *In general, functions should not assign values to global variables.*

- **Functions with variable parameters.** A variable parameter indicates that its values will change within the function. (However, recall the previous discussion on the use of variable parameters.) This is a side effect. *In general, functions should not use variable parameters.*

- **Functions that perform I/O.** Input and output (I/O) are side effects. *In general, functions should not perform I/O.*

- **Avoidance of `goto`.** One of the most important factors contributing to well-structured programs is an orderly flow of control. An orderly flow of control implies the following:

KEY CONCEPTS **Orderly Flow of Control**

1. The general flow of a program is forward.
2. A module is entered only at its beginning and exited only at its end.
3. The conditions for terminating loops are clear and uniform.
4. The alternative cases of conditional statements are clear and uniform.

The use of a `goto` almost always violates at least one of these conditions. In addition, it is very difficult to verify the correctness of a program that contains a `goto`. Therefore, in general, you should avoid the `goto`. There are, however, *rare* situations where you will need an exceptional flow of control and the use of a `goto` is appropriate. Such a case is considered next.

Error handling.   A fail-safe program checks for errors in both its input and its logic, and attempts to behave gracefully when it encounters them. Error handling often necessitates exceptional actions that would constitute bad style in normal program execution. For example, error handling may involve the use of functions with side effects and the use of *goto*'s. You often must choose between several courses of action, no single one of which is completely satisfactory.

A subprogram should check for certain types of errors, such as invalid input or parameter values. What action should a subprogram take when it encounters an error? The procedure *ReadData* in the income statistics program earlier in this chapter printed an error message and returned a boolean flag to the calling routine to indicate that it had encountered an invalid line of data. Thus, the procedure left it to the calling routine to decide on the appropriate action. In some situations, however, it is more appropriate for the subprogram itself to take the action—for example, when the required action does not depend on the point from which the subprogram is called.

If a *function* handles errors by printing an error message or returning a flag, it violates the rule against functions with side effects. Despite this fact, these actions seem reasonable for functions as well as procedures.

Depending on context, the appropriate action in the face of an error can range from ignoring erroneous data and continuing execution to terminating the program. In the case of a fatal error that calls for termination, a *goto* might be the cleanest way to abort. Suppose that you are nested deep within procedure calls, *while* loops, and *if-then-else* statements when you encounter a fatal error. The first course of action could be to call a diagnostics procedure, which would print out as much information as possible to help the user determine why the program had to abort—including, for example, current values of variables and an echo of erroneous data. After the procedure has reported all this information, the program should terminate. However, if the diagnostic procedure returns control to the point from which it was called, you still must exit from many layers of nested control structures. A cleaner solution is for the last statement of the diagnostic procedure to be *goto 999*, where *999* labels the end of the program. This situation is one of the rare instances where the use of a *goto* can actually enhance program readability.

Readability.   For a program to be easy to follow, it should have a good structure and design, a good choice of variable names, good indentation and use of blank lines, and good documentation. You should avoid clever programming tricks that save a little computer time at the expense of much human time. You will see examples of these points in the programs throughout the book.

Use a good indentation style to enhance the readability of a program. The layout of a program should make it easy for a reader to identify the program's modules. Use blank lines to offset each subprogram. Also, within both subprograms and the main program, you should offset with blank lines and indent individual blocks of code visibly. These blocks are generally—but are not limited to—the actions performed within a control structure, such as a *while* loop or an *if-then-else* statement.

There are several good indentation styles to choose from. The four most important general requirements of an indentation style are that

Guidelines for indentation style

- Blocks should be indented sufficiently so that they stand out clearly.
- In a compound statement, the *begin* and the *end* should line up:

```
begin
   <statement₁>
   <statement₂>
         .
         .
         .
   <statementₙ>
end
```

- Indentation should be consistent: Always indent the same type of construct in the same manner.
- The indentation style should provide a reasonable way to handle the problem of **rightward drift**, the problem of nested blocks bumping against the right-hand margin of the page.

Within these guidelines there is room for personal taste. Here is a summary of the style you will see in this book.

Indentation style in this book

- A *while* or *for* loop is indented for a simple action as

```
while <cond> do
   <statement>
```

and for a compound action as

```
while <cond> do
begin
   <statements>
end
```

- An *if-then-else* statement is indented for simple actions as

```
if <cond>
   then <statement₁>
   else <statement₂>
```

and for compound actions as

```
if <cond>
   then
   begin
```

```
        <statements>
    end

    else
    begin
        <statements>
    end
```

There is one special use of the *if-then-else* statement for which another style is used: when cascading *if-then-else-if*'s choose among three or more different courses of action. Instead of writing

```
if <cond₁>
   then <action₁>
   else if <cond₂>
      then <action₂>
         else if <cond₃>
            then <action₃>
```

we write

```
if <cond₁> then
   <action₁>
else if <cond₂> then
   <action₂>
else if <cond₃> then
   <action₃>
```

This indentation style better reflects the nature of the construct, which is like a generalized *case* statement:

```
<cond₁> : <action₁>
<cond₂> : <action₂>
<cond₃> : <action₃>
```

- We often use *begin/end*'s to increase readability, even when they are not a syntactic necessity. For example, in the construct

```
while <cond₁> do
begin
   if <cond₂>
       then <action₁>
       else <action₂>
end
```

the *begin/end* is syntactically unnecessary because an *if-then-else* is a single statement. However, the *begin/end* highlights the scope of the *while* loop.

Documentation. A program should be well documented so that others can read, use, and modify it easily. There are many acceptable styles for documentation, and exactly what you should include often depends on the particular program. The following are the essential features of any program's documentation:

KEY CONCEPTS   **Documentation**

1. A header comment for the program that includes
   a. Statement of purpose
   b. Author and date
   c. Description of the program's input and output
   d. Description of how to use the program
   e. Assumptions such as the type of data expected and what could go wrong. *This is very important!*
   f. Brief description of the global algorithms and data structures
   g. Description of the key variables

2. A "miniheader" comment in each module, similar to the program's header, that contains information pertinent to that module, including its preconditions and postconditions

3. Comments in the body of each module to explain important and confusing parts of the program

---

Beginning programmers tend to downplay the importance of documentation because the computer does not read comments. By now, you should realize that people do read programs. There is also a tendency for beginners to document programs as a last step. However, you should write documentation as you develop the program. The task of writing a large program might extend over a period of several weeks. You may find that the procedure that seemed so obvious when you wrote and debugged it last week will seem confusing when you try to debug it again next week.

Debugging

No matter how much care you take in writing a program, there inevitably will be bugs that you need to track down. Fortunately, programs developed under the guidelines presented in the previous sections are generally amenable to debugging. Programs that are modular, clear, and well documented are certainly easier to debug than those that are not. Fail-safe techniques, which guard against certain errors and report them when they are encountered, are also a great aid in debugging.

Many students seem to be totally baffled by bugs in their programs and have no idea how to proceed. These students simply have not learned to track down a bug systematically. Without a systematic approach, finding a small bug in a large program can indeed be a difficult task.

The difficulty that many people have in debugging a program is perhaps due in part to a desire to believe that their program is really doing what it is supposed to do. For example, on receiving the error message

```
subscript value of 11 out of range on line 1098
```

a student might say, "That's impossible. The statement at line 1098 was not even executed, because it is in the `else` clause, and I am positive that the `then` clause was executed." This student must do more than simply protest. The proper approach is to add `write` statements that show which clause was executed and to verify the value of the boolean condition. If the condition is false when you expect it to be true—as the error message indicates—then the next step is to determine how it became false.

How, then, can you find the point in a program at which something becomes other than what it should be? The trick to debugging is simply to use a program's output to tell you what is going on. This technique may sound pretty mundane, but the real trick is to use the program's output in an effective manner. After all, you do not simply put `write` statements at random points of the program and have them report random information. The *effective use of output* is one of the keys to debugging.

What is meant by the effective use of output? The main idea is to systematically use the output to locate the points of the program that cause the problem. A program's logic implies that certain conditions should be true at various points in the program. (Recall that these conditions are called invariants.) A bug means that a condition that you think ought to be true is not. To correct the bug, you must find the first point in the program at which one of these conditions differs from expectation. By inserting `write` statements at strategic locations of a program—such as at the entry and departure points of loops and subprograms—you can systematically isolate the bug.

Use temporary `write` statements to find bugs

Each `write` statement, through both its placement and content, should inform you of whether things start going wrong before or after a given point in the program. Thus, after you run the program with an initial set of diagnostic `write` statements, you should be able to trap the bug between two points. For example, suppose that things are fine before you call procedure `P1`, but something is wrong by the time you call `P2`. This kind of information allows you to concentrate the next batch of diagnostics between these two points. You continue the process until eventually the search is limited to only a few statements. There is really no place in a program for a bug to hide.

The ability to place `write` statements in appropriate locations and to have them report appropriate information comes in part from thinking logically about the problem and in part from experience. Here are a few general guidelines:

What a `write` statement should report. You should use `write` statements such as the following ones to report both the values of key variables and the location in the program at which the variables have those values:

```
writeln('At point A in procedure Compute:');
writeln('x=', x, ' y=', y, ' z=', z)
```

write statements in subprograms.   Two key locations to place *write* statements are at the beginning and end of a subprogram, as has been done in this example:

```
procedure P(. . .);
begin
   writeln('Parameter values on entering procedure P:',
                                        ...); .
                                                   .
                                                   .
                                                   .
   writeln('Parameter values on leaving procedure P:', ...)
end
```

write statements in loops.   You should place *write* statements at the beginnings and ends of loops to report the values of the control variables, as this example indicates:

```
writeln('Before entering the for loop A, ',
        'the variables have the following values: ',
        ' start=', start, ' stop=', stop, ... );

{ this is for loop A }
for i := start to stop do
begin
   writeln('At the beginning of iteration when i = ', i,
           ', the variables have the following values', ... );
      .
      .
      .
   writeln('At the end of iteration when i = ', i,
           ', the variables have the following values', ... )
end;

writeln('After exiting the for loop A, ',
        'the variables have the following values:  ',
        ' start=', start, ' stop=', stop, ... )
```

write statements in *if-then-else* statements.   You should place a *write* statement before the test in an *if-then-else* statement. You should also use *write* statements to report both the branch taken as a result of the test and the values of the variables involved in the test, as this example indicates:

```
writeln('Before if-then-else A, variables have values ' ... )

{ if-then-else A }
```

```
{ if-then-else A }
if <cond>
        then
        begin
           writeln('Condition is true, so follow the then branch');
             .
             .
             .

        end
        else
        begin
           writeln('Condition is false, so follow the else
                                           branch');
             .
             .
             .

        end
```

Special dump routines. Often the variables whose values you wish to print are arrays or other, more complex data structures. If so, you should write dump routines to accomplish the task. You can easily move the single statement that calls each dump routine from one point in the program to another as you track down a bug. The routines should display the data structures in a highly readable manner. The time that you spend on these routines often proves to be worthwhile, as you can call them repeatedly while debugging different parts of the program.

Hopefully, this discussion has conveyed the importance of the *effective use of output in debugging.* Even the best programmers have to spend some time debugging. Thus, to be a truly good programmer, you must be a good debugger.

SUMMARY

1. Software engineering is a branch of computer science that studies ways to facilitate the development of computer programs.

2. The life cycle of software consists of eight phases: specifying the problem, designing the algorithm, verifying the algorithm, coding the programs, testing them, refining the solution, using the software, and maintaining the software.

3. A loop invariant is a property of an algorithm that is true before and after each iteration of a loop. Loop invariants are useful in developing iterative algorithms and establishing their correctness.

4. When evaluating the quality of a solution, you must consider a diverse set of factors: the solution's correctness, its efficiency, the

time that went into its development, its ease of use, and the cost of modifying and expanding it.

5. When designing a solution, you should proceed in a top-down fashion and break the tasks into independent modules, which you gradually refine. Some of these modules perform algorithmic-type tasks, such as sorting an array, and others perform data-management-type tasks, such as retrieving a data item. In either case, each module should be a "black box" from the perspective of the rest of the program.

6. Take great care to ensure that the final solution is as easy to modify as possible. Generally, a modular program is easy to modify because changes in the problem's requirements frequently affect only a handful of the modules. The use of user-defined (named) constants—for example, in the declarations of array bounds—is another factor that can greatly enhance a program's modifiability.

7. A program should be as fail-safe as possible. For example, a program should guard against errors in input and errors in its own logic. By checking invariants—which are conditions that are true at certain points in a program—you can monitor correct program execution. You should use Pascal's facility for subrange types as a last line of defense against errors in program logic and not in general to guard against errors in input.

8. A subprogram should correspond as much as possible to the notion of an isolated module. To this end, do not overuse global variables, and avoid functions with side effects whenever possible.

9. A subprogram should always include a header comment that states its purpose, its precondition—that is, the conditions that must exist at the beginning of a module—and its postcondition—the conditions at the end of a module.

COMMON PITFALLS/DEBUGGING

1. The effective use of output is one of the keys to debugging. You should use *write* statements to report the values of key variables at key locations. These locations include the beginnings and ends of procedures and loops and the branches of conditional statements.

2. To facilitate the use of output in debugging, you should write dump routines that display the contents of the data structures. You can easily move calls to such routines as you track down a bug.

3. Your programs should guard against errors. A fail-safe program checks that an input value is within some acceptable range and

reports if it is not. An error in input should not cause a program to terminate before it clearly reports what the error was. A fail-safe program also attempts to detect errors in its own logic. For example, in many situations subprograms should check that the parameters have valid values.

4. You should use subrange types only as a last line of defense against errors. A variable into which data is read should not be of a subrange type, because an out-of-range value causes an ungraceful termination. A proper use of subrange types is to help enforce a condition in the program's logic.

SELF-TEST EXERCISES

The answers to all Self-Test Exercises are at the back of this book.

1. What is the loop invariant for the following?

```
j := 1;
Sum := A[1];
while j < N do
begin
    j := j + 1;
    Sum := Sum + A[j]
end
```

2. Write specifications for a procedure that computes the sum of the first five positive integers in an array of *N* arbitrary integers.

EXERCISES

1. Consider the following program, which interactively reads and writes the identification number, name, age, and salary (in thousands of dollars) of a group of employees. How can you improve the program? Some of the issues are obvious, while others are more subtle. Try to keep in mind all the topics discussed in this chapter.

```
program stats(input, output);

var x1, x2, x3, i : integer;
    name : array[1..8] of char;

begin
    while not eof do
    begin
        read(x1);
        for i := 1 to 8 do
            read(name[i]);
```

```
            readln(x2, x3);
            writeln(x1, name, x2, x3)
        end
    end.
```

2. This chapter stressed the importance of adding fail-safe checks to a program wherever possible. What can go wrong with the following function? How can you protect yourself?

```
function tan(x : real) : real;
begin
    tan := sin(x)/cos(x)
end
```

3. Modify the function *SumBetween*, which appears in the section "Fail-Safe Programming," to ensure that $x <= y$.

4. Consider a program that will read employee information into an array of records, sort the array by employee identification number, write out the sorted array, and compute various statistics on the data, such as the average age of an employee. Write complete specifications for this problem and design a modular solution. What subprograms did you identify during the design of your solution? Write specifications, including preconditions and postconditions, for each subprogram. Implement your solution by using stubs.

5. Write the procedure that Self-Test Exercise 2 describes, and state the loop invariants.

6. Write the loop invariants for the function *SumBetween* that appears in this chapter.

7. Demonstrate that the algorithm in Self-Test Exercise 1 correctly computes $A[1] + A[2] + \cdots + A[N]$ by using loop invariants.

8. The following program is supposed to compute the **floor** of the square root of its input value x. (The floor of a number n is the largest integer less than or equal to n.)

```
program sqrt(input, output);
{ Computes and prints floor(sqrt(x)) for an input value
  x >= 0}

var x, ans, temp1, temp2 : integer;

begin
    { initialize }
    readln(x);
    ans := 0;
    temp1 := 1;
    temp2 := 1;
    { compute floor }
    while temp1 < x do
```

```
begin
    ans := ans + 1;
    temp2 := temp2 + 2;
    temp1 := temp1 + temp2
end;

writeln('The floor of the square root of ',
        x:1, ' is ', ans:1)
end.
```

There is a bug in this program.

a. What output does the program produce when $x = 64$?

b. Debug the program on the computer. How did you choose the placement of extra *write* statements?

c. How can you make the program more user friendly and fail-safe?

9. On rare occasions a *goto* can actually enhance the readability of a program. One of these occasions is when, due to some severe error, you must abort a program from a location deep inside nested procedure calls, *while* loops, and *if-then-else* statements. Write a diagnostic procedure that you can call from anywhere in a program. This procedure should take an error code as an argument (some mnemonic enumerated type), print an appropriate error message, and *goto* the end of the program.

PROJECTS

10. Write a program that sorts and evaluates bridge hands.

INPUT

The input is a stream of character pairs, which represent playing cards. For example,

```
2C QD TC AD 6C 3D TD 3H 5H 7H AS JH KH
```

represents the 2 of clubs, queen of diamonds, 10 of clubs, ace of diamonds, and so on. Each pair consists of a rank followed by a suit, where rank is A, 2, ..., 9, T, J, Q, or K, and suit is C, D, H, or S. You can assume that there will be no errors in the input and that exactly 13 cards will be represented on each input line. Input is terminated by an end of file. For this problem you are to form a hand of 13 cards from each input line.

OUTPUT

Print each hand of 13 cards in a readable form arranged both by suits and by rank within suit (aces are high). Then evaluate the hand by using the following standard bridge values:

Aces count 4

Kings count 3

Queens count 2

Jacks count 1

Voids (no cards in a suit) count 3

Singletons (one card in a suit) count 2

Doubletons (two cards in a suit) count 1

Long suits with more than 5 cards in the suit count 1 for each card over 5 in number

For example, for the previous sample input line, the program should produce the output

```
CLUBS          10   6    2
DIAMONDS       A    Q    10   3
HEARTS         K    J    7    5    3
SPADES         A
Points = 16
```

because there are 2 aces, 1 king, 1 queen, 1 jack, 1 singleton, no doubletons, and no long suits. (The singleton ace of spades counts as both an ace and a singleton.)

Optional: See how much more flexible and fail-safe you can make your program. That is, try to remove as many of the previous assumptions in input as you can.

11. Write a program that will act as an interactive calculator capable of handling very large (larger than $maxint$) nonnegative integers. This calculator need perform only the operations of addition and multiplication.

In this program each input line is of the form

```
<num1> <op> <num2>
```

and should produce output such as

```
    num1
op  num2
---------
    num3
```

where *num1* and *num2* are (possibly very large) nonnegative integers, *op* is the single character + or *, and *num3* is the integer that results from the desired calculation.

Design your program carefully. You will need the following:

a. A data structure to represent large numbers; for example,

array[1..maxsize] **of** 0..9

b. A procedure to read in numbers. Skip leading zeros. Do not forget that zero is a valid number.

c. A procedure to write numbers. Do not print leading zeros, but if the number consists of all zeros, print a single zero.

    d. A procedure to add two numbers.

    e. A procedure to multiply two numbers.

In addition, you should

    f. Check for overflow (numbers with more than *maxsize* digits) when reading, adding, and multiplying numbers.

    g. Have a good user interface.

Optional: Allow signed integers (negative as well as positive integers) and write a procedure for subtraction.

CHAPTER *2*

Review of Advanced Pascal

PREVIEW Most of this chapter reviews the Pascal structured data types: arrays, records, files, and sets. Even if you choose not to read this review material, you should not skip the last section. It shows how to compensate for the deficiency of Pascal's *and* and *or* operators and discusses separately compiled units.

Every high-level programming language provides a collection of built-in data types, which are called the language's **primitive data types**. Integers, reals, characters, and arrays are primitive data types that almost all high-level languages support. Pascal is unusually rich in the data types it allows. The **simple data types** are integer, real, character, boolean, enumerated types, and subrange types. This chapter reviews **structured data types**: arrays, records, files, and sets. The next chapter introduces a third data type, the pointer.

A note about Standard Pascal.   This presentation attempts to conform to the current ISO definition of Standard Pascal.[1] However, experience has shown that very few implementations completely conform to the standard, particularly with regard to files. Our best advice is to program defensively. If your program fails and you have considered all likely possibilities, begin to suspect that your compiler is stricter than the specifications in the standard. You should design tests to verify this hypothesis. On the other hand, if your compiler includes extensions to the standard, avoid them in general. (A common extension to the standard is to allow functions to return arrays and records.) This approach will increase the chances that your program will run on another system and that it will continue to run if a new version of the compiler is installed on your own system.

ARRAYS

Recall that an array is a collection of **elements**, or **components**, that have the same data type. An array contains a finite, fixed number of elements, which have an order. Thus, there is a first element, a second element, and so on, as well as a last element. You must know the maximum number of elements possible in a particular array when you write your program, *before* you execute it. Because you can access the array elements directly and in any order, an array is a **direct access**, or a **random access**, data structure.

An array has a fixed size: do not exceed it

Although you are probably comfortable with **one-dimensional arrays**, a brief review will set the stage for multidimensional arrays and arrays of arrays.

---

[1]Second DP 7185. *Specification for the Computer Programming Language Pascal*, December 1980.

One-Dimensional Arrays

When you decide to use an array in your program, you must declare it and, in doing so, indicate its maximum size. The following statements declare a one-dimensional array, *MaxTemps*, which contains the daily maximum temperatures for a given week:

An array with integer subscripts

```
type    arraytype = array[1..7] of real;
var     MaxTemps : arraytype;
```

You can refer to any of the seven real elements in this array directly by using an expression, which is called the **index**, or **subscript**, enclosed in square brackets. For example, *MaxTemps[5]* is the fifth element in the array. Also, if *K* is an integer variable whose value is 5, then *MaxTemps[K]* is the fifth element in the array, and *MaxTemps[K + 1]* is the sixth element. Figure 2-1 illustrates the array *MaxTemps*, which at present contains only five temperatures. *MaxTemps[5]* is the last value in the array and *MaxTemps[6]*, for example, is undefined.

Clearly, before you can retrieve an element of an array, you must assign it a value. You can assign or retrieve element values either one element at a time by using the previously described notation or all at once. That is, if *X* and *Y* are arrays of the same type, the statement

```
X := Y
```

assigns to each element of *X* the value in the corresponding element of *Y*.

Although the indexes for *MaxTemps* must be integer valued, indexes in general can be of other ordinal data types as well. For example, consider the following type definitions and variable declarations:

Arrays with enumerated subscripts

```
type    days = (Sun, Mon, Tues, Wed, Thurs, Fri, Sat);
        arraytype1 = array[days] of real;
        arraytype2 = array['A'..'Z'] of integer;

var     Temps : arraytype1;
        Codes : arraytype2;
```

Temps is another array of seven real elements, but it does not have integer indexes. Instead, *Temps[Thurs]* is the fifth element in the array. Similarly, the 5th integer of the 26 integers in the array *Codes* is *Codes['E']*.

You can use one-dimensional arrays for simple lists: for example, a list of at most 7 temperatures or a list of at most 50 exam scores. Note that you refer to the elements in a one-dimensional array by using one index. How-

Figure 2-1

A one-dimensional array of at most seven elements

ever, you can also declare **multidimensional arrays**, which have more than one index.

Multidimensional Arrays

Suppose that you wanted to represent the minimum temperature for each day during 52 weeks. The following statements declare a **two-dimensional array**, *MinTemps*:

```
type   arraytype = array[1..7, 1..52] of real;            A 7 × 52 array
var    MinTemps : arraytype;
```

These statements specify the ranges for two indexes: The first index can range from 1 to 7, while the second index can range from 1 to 52. Most people picture a two-dimensional array as a rectangular arrangement, or **matrix**, of elements that form rows and columns, as Figure 2-2 indicates. Each column in this matrix represents the seven daily minimum temperatures for a particular week.

To reference an element in a two-dimensional array, you must indicate both the row and the column that contain the element. You make these indications of row and column by writing two indexes. For example, *MinTemps[5, 12]* is the element in the 5th row and the 12th column. In the context of the temperature example, this element is the minimum temperature recorded for the 5th day of the 12th week. Note that what was said about the indexes of one-dimensional arrays applies also to multidimensional arrays.

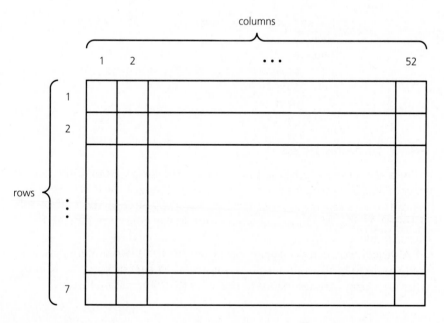

Figure 2-2

A two-dimensional array

As an example of how to use a two-dimensional array in a program, consider the following procedure, which determines the smallest value in the previously described array *MinTemps*:

```pascal
procedure LowestDailyTemp(MinTemps : arraytype;
                var LowestTemp : real; var day, week : integer);

{ -------------------------------------------------------
  Determines the lowest daily temperature during a 52-week
  period.
  Precondition: MinTemps is a 2-dimensional array of daily
  minimum temperatures for 52 weeks, where MinTemps[d, w] is
  the minimum temperature for day d of week w.
  Postcondition: LowestTemp is the smallest value in
  MinTemps, day and week are indexes such that LowestTemp =
  MinTemps[day, week], MinTemps is unchanged.
  ------------------------------------------------------- }

var d, w : integer;           { array indexes }
begin
   {initialize: assume lowest temperature is first in the
    array}
   LowestTemp := MinTemps[1,1];
   day := 1;
   week := 1;

   { search array for lowest temperature }
   for w := 1 to 52 do          { for all weeks }
      for d := 1 to 7 do        { for all days in a week }
      begin
         if LowestTemp > MinTemps[d,w]
            then
            begin
               LowestTemp := MinTemps[d,w];
               day := d;
               week := w
            end   { if }
      end   { for }
end   { LowestDailyTemp }
```

It is also entirely possible to declare *MinTemps* as a one-dimensional array of 364 (7 * 52) elements, in which case you might use *MinTemps[82]* instead of *MinTemps[5, 12]*. (Why? See Exercise 1 at the end of this chapter.) However, doing so would not make your program easier to understand!

More than three dimensions is unusual
Although you can declare arrays with more than two dimensions, generally more than three dimensions is unusual. The techniques for working with such arrays are analogous to those for two-dimensional arrays.

Arrays of Arrays

Consider again the daily minimum temperatures for 52 weeks. Instead of declaring a two-dimensional array to represent these temperatures, as was done previously, you could declare a one-dimensional array of 52 one-dimensional, 7-element arrays, as follows:

```
type    weektype = array[1..7] of real;
        yeartype = array[1..52] of weektype;

var     Temps : yeartype;
```

An array of 52 arrays

Here, *Temps* is an array of arrays where *Temps[12]*, for example, is an array of 7 temperatures for the 12th week. If it is useful to think about individual weeks, then this organization is preferable to the previous two-dimensional array. For example, you could pass *Temps[12]*, which is the data for week 12, to a function that calculates an average of the 7 temperatures in a one-dimensional array. (See Self-Test Exercise 2.)

However, you reference the temperature recorded for the 5th day of the 12th week by writing *Temps[12][5]*. You might find this notation more awkward than the notation for a two-dimensional array. Thus, if you will consider individual days rather than individual weeks, you may find that a two-dimensional array is preferable to an array of arrays.

This section concludes by considering an array of character strings. For example, the following one-dimensional array of names might represent the people on your gift list. (Assume that *NameLength* and *Number* are appropriate integer constants.)

```
type    name = packed array[1..NameLength] of char;
        namelist = array[1..Number] of name;

var     GiftList : namelist;
```

Here, the packed array of characters makes it possible to reference an entire name conveniently by writing, for example, *GiftList[5]*, which is the fifth name on the list.

RECORDS

While an array is a collection of elements that are all of the same data type, a **record** is a group of related items that are not necessarily of the same data type. Each item in a record is called a **field**. For example, a record that describes you might contain three fields: your name, your identification number, and your grade point average. The following statements define a data type for such a record:

```
const   NameLength = 15;      { Length of name }
type    StudentRecord = record
```

```
                            Name : packed array[1..NameLength] of char;
                            Id : integer;
                            GPA : real
                        end;   { record }
```

The identifiers *Name*, *Id*, and *GPA* are called **field identifiers**.

Now you can use the data type *StudentRecord* when declaring variables. To declare the record variable *Student1*, you would write

```
    var     Student1 : StudentRecord;
```

Figure 2-3 depicts the record *Student1*. To reference the fields within a particular record, you write the record variable, a period, and the field identifier. For example, the second field in the record *Student1* is *Student1.Id*, as in the statement

```
    Student1.Id := 123456789;
```

The third letter in the first field of *Student1* is

```
    Student1.Name[3]
```

Notice that it is convenient to make a copy of an entire record. The following statement copies the record *Student1* into the record *Student2*:

Copying a record

```
    Student2 : = Student1
```

where *Student2* has a data type of *StudentRecord*.

The with Statement

When you make several references to fields that are in a particular record, writing the record variable for each reference can get tedious. By using the *with* statement, you can reference the fields simply by writing the field identifiers. For example, to assign values to the three fields in the record *Student1*, which was defined previously, you could write

```
    with Student1 do
    begin
        Name := 'Jamie Perfect  ';
        Id := 123456789;
        GPA := 4.0
    end;   { with }
```

Field identifiers that are within the *with* statement reference the fields that are within the record *Student1*. However, outside of the *with* statement, the record variable *Student1* is necessary, as in the following statement:

```
    writeln(Student1.Name:15, ' has a GPA of ',
            Student1.GPA:4:2);
```

Student1.Name	Student1.Id	Student1.GPA
Jamie Perfect	123456789	4.0

Figure 2-3
The record *Student1*

Although the *with* statement can save you a good deal of tedious typing, if overused it can detract from the readability of a program. The potential problem has to do with what some have called the **principle of locality**. This principle states that the effects of any statement should, as much as possible, be limited to other statements in its immediate locality. Adherence to this principle enhances readability, as it reduces the number of things that a reader must remember to understand the meaning of a statement.

A statement should affect only statements in its immediate locality

A *with* statement that has a scope of more than a few lines is likely to violate the principle of locality. You must remember that you are within the scope of a *with* statement to know that identifiers are field names of the same record rather than disjoint variables. You use a record to convey the message that its fields all contain information about the same entity; the use of a *with* statement tends to obscure this message.

Restrict the scope of a with statement to a few lines

There are a few situations in which a *with* statement is useful. Although no steadfast rules exist for when you should use *with*, here are three situations that come to mind.

Using the *with* Statement

KEY CONCEPTS

1. When reading values into the fields of a record, you can nest the *read* statement within a *with* statement.

2. When writing values out from the fields of a record, you can nest the *write* statement within a *with* statement.

3. When assigning values to the fields of a record, you can nest the block of assignment statements within a *with* statement.

Records Within Records

Sometimes it is desirable for a field within a record to be itself a record. For example, suppose that you need to add an address field to the student's record that was defined earlier. It is convenient for the address to be a record with fields such as street, city, state, and zip code. The following definitions and declarations include these changes to the data type *StudentRecord*:

Fields can be records

```
const  StringLength = 15;  { Length of character string }

type   CharString = packed array[1..StringLength] of char;
```

```
AddressRecord = record
    Street    : CharString;
    City      : CharString;
    State     : packed array[1..2] of char;
    Zip       : packed array[1..10] of char
end;  { record }

StudentRecord = record
    Name      : CharString;
    Id        : integer;
    Address   : AddressRecord;
    GPA       : real
end; { record }

var    Student1 : StudentRecord;
```

Note the order of the type definitions: The definition of *AddressRecord* must precede its use in *StudentRecord*. Now *Student1.Address.Zip* references the zip code field in the record *Student1*.

Arrays of Records

Now suppose that an instructor wants a record for each student in a class. You can add the data type

```
Class = array[1..50] of StudentRecord;
```

to the previous type definitions and then declare, for example, the variable *CSC212* to be of the data type *Class*. The following are examples of references to this array:

> *CSC212[9].Name* is the *Name* field in the ninth record.
>
> *CSC212[9].Name[1]* is the first letter of the *Name* field in the ninth record.
>
> *CSC212[9].Address.State* is the *State* field in the ninth record.

Variant Records

A variant record has a fixed part, which includes the tag field, and a variant part

Sometimes, within a group of records there are fields that you use only for certain records. Rather than defining a record variable that contains all possible fields for all situations, you can use a **variant record** to save memory space. A variant record has a fixed part, which contains the fields that are common to all records, and a variant part, which contains fields that differ for certain records.

For example, consider the following statements, which include a record definition for a student:

```
const  NameLength = 15;
```

```
type    MajorType = (CompSci, CompEgr, OtherEgr, Other);
        StudentRecord = record
            Name : packed array[1..NameLength] of char;
            Id   : integer;
            GPA  : real;
            case Major : MajorType of
                CompSci, CompEgr : ( CscGPA : real;
                                      CscCredits : integer );
                OtherEgr         : ( MajorGPA : real );
                Other            : ( )
        end;  { record }

var     Student2 : StudentRecord;
```

The fixed fields *Name*, *Id*, and *GPA* must appear first in the record definition. You define the variant part by using a construct, which is similar to a *case* statement. The field *Major* is called the **tag field** and is analogous to the selector in a *case* statement. Notice, however, that you must declare the tag field's data type. For the possible values of the tag field, you describe the fields in the variant part of the record and enclose each description in parentheses. For example, when the value of the tag field *Major* is either *CompSci* or *CompEgr*, the variant part of the record contains two fields: *CscGPA* and *CscCredits*. Notice that the field identifiers must all be unique. Also notice that you can leave the variant part empty by writing ( ) and that there is no matching *end* for the reserved word *case*. Figure 2-4 depicts some of the records that *Student2* can contain.

You must be careful to reference only those fields that exist for a particular value of the tag field. For example, within the record *Student2*, if the value of *Student2.Major* is *CompSci*, you can reference the field *Student2.CscGPA*, but not *Student2.MajorGPA*. You can reference the fixed fields within *Student2* for any value of *Student2.Major*.

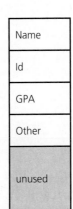

Figure 2-4

Instances of the variant record *Student2*

FILES

The components of a file must all be of the same data type

A **file** is a *sequence* of components of the same data type. The file is a structured data type; we will present and use it here in the same spirit as other data types. However, a file differs from the other data types in that a file can be permanent; it can live on after program execution terminates.

Variables that have data types other than a file data type represent memory that is accessible only within the program that creates them. When program execution terminates, the operating system reuses this memory and loses its contents. Files, on the other hand, reside in auxiliary storage, such as on a disk, and can exist and be accessible independently of any particular program. Files are thus more system dependent than the other data types because the mechanisms for creating and accessing them from outside a program depend on the particulars of a system. However, from within a Pascal program, files behave in a standard, system-independent manner.

It is useful to contrast files with their closest Pascal relatives, arrays. Files and arrays are similar in that they are both collections of components of the same type. For example, just as you can have an array of type `char`, so also can you have a file of type `char`. In both cases, the components are characters. However, in addition to the previous distinction between files and all other data types—including arrays—there are two other differences:

Differences between files and arrays

- **File size is dynamic; array size is static.** When you declare an array, you must specify its size. Thus, the Pascal compiler reserves a fixed amount of memory for the array. A well-written program always checks that an array can accommodate a new piece of data before attempting to insert it. If the array cannot accommodate the data, the program might have to terminate with a message of explanation. The only recourse is to increase the array size—hopefully by changing the value of a constant—and to run the program again. On the other hand, if you declare the array's size to be larger than you need, you would waste memory. In contrast, the size of a file is not fixed. When the system first creates a file, the file requires almost no storage space. As a program adds data to the file, the file's size increases dynamically. Thus, at any given time, the file occupies only as much space as it actually requires. This dynamic nature is a great advantage.

- **Pascal files provide sequential access; arrays provide direct access.** Before you get the impression that files are superior to arrays in all respects, consider that with arrays you can go directly to the element you want. If you want the 100th element in the array `A`, you can get at it by writing `A[100]`; you do not need to look at the elements `A[1]` through `A[99]` first. However, you can get to elements in a Pascal file only sequentially. If you want the 100th element in a file, you must read past the 99 elements that precede it. File processing is therefore considerably slower and less flexible than array processing. The **direct access** nature of arrays is a great advantage. Some programming languages do support direct access files; such files are discussed in Chapter 14. However, Standard Pascal supports only **sequential access** files.

You have used files ever since you wrote your first program. Your typical program header,

```
program typical(input, output);
```

specifies that the program *typical* uses two files: one is called *input*, which is the **standard input file**, and the other is *output*, which is the **standard output file**. These particular file definitions are system dependent, but often they both are your terminal. That is, a Pascal program treats your terminal as a file—even though there are many differences between a terminal and more conventional files. A program can take its input directly from the terminal and display its output on the terminal. Note that many systems allow you to specify that the standard input and output files be something other than your terminal.

There are both external and internal files. An **external file** exists after program execution. External files not only provide a permanent record for human users, they also allow communication between programs. Program *A* can write its output into a file that program *B* can later use for input. An **internal file** is temporary and exists only during program execution. Although an internal file resides in auxiliary storage, the system does not retain it after program execution ends. You use an internal file as a scratch pad when there is too much data to retain conveniently in memory.

You name a file by using any valid Pascal identifier called a **file variable**, and you write the names of the *external* files in the program header. Thus, you could have

```
program LotsOfFiles(NailFile, WoodFile, FileCabinet, output);
```

List only the external files in the program header

This declaration tells the operating system that the program *LotsOfFiles* will use the external files *NailFile*, *WoodFile*, and *FileCabinet*. By convention, *output* must always appear in the header, even if you do not use the standard output file. Some of these files may exist already; others may not exist yet but will be created when the program *LotsOfFiles* executes. In either case, these files will exist after program execution terminates. Although the program might also use internal files, you do not list them in the program header.

Within the program, you treat a file name much as you treat any other type of variable. You must declare both external and internal files in the variable declaration section of your program; that is, file variables must be global. However, you do not declare the standard files *input* and *output*.

Declare all files except `input` and `output` in the variable declaration section

Pascal classifies files further. A **textfile** is a file of characters that are organized into lines. The standard files *input* and *output* are textfiles, as are the files that you create—by using an editor—to contain your Pascal programs. A file that is not a textfile is called a **general file** or sometimes a **binary file** or a **nontext file**. The following statements, which could appear in the program *LotsOfFiles*, declare textfiles, general files, external files, and internal files:

```
type    intfile    = file of integer;
        namefile   = file of packed array[1..15] of char;
        woods      = (oak, pine, mahogany);

var     NailFile    : intfile;         { external general file}
        WoodFile    : file of woods;   { external general file}
        FileCabinet : text;            { external textfile}
        TempFile    : namefile;        { internal general file}
```

The type definition for a general file is of the form

```
    file of <T>
```

where *T* is any predefined or user-defined data type other than *file*; you cannot have a file of files. You declare a textfile by using the predefined data type *text*. A textfile is similar to a *file of char*; however, a textfile is divided into lines, but a *file of char* is not. Also, notice that even though *TempFile* contains characters, it is a general file—not a textfile—because each of its elements is an array, not a single character. *TempFile* is also an internal file because it does not appear in the program header for *LotsOfFiles*.

There is one last point to be made before we consider the details of textfiles and general files. Conceptually, you can speak of a special **end-of-file (eof) symbol** that follows the last component in a file. There actually may be no such symbol in the file; however, allowing this slight abstraction permits a clear and concise explanation of the behavior of Pascal programs.

Textfiles

Textfiles are designed for easy communication with people. As such, textfiles are flexible and easy to use, but they are relatively inefficient with respect to computer time and storage. As you will see, some aspects of textfiles are true of all files, while other aspects are peculiar to textfiles.

Textfiles appear to contain lines

One special aspect of textfiles is that they *appear* to be divided into lines. This illusion is often the source of much confusion. In reality, a textfile—like any other file—is a sequence of components of the same type. That is, a textfile is a sequence of characters. A special **end-of-line (eoln) character** causes the illusion that a textfile contains lines by making the file *behave* as if it were divided into lines. When an output device encounters an end-of-line character, the device generates a carriage return and line feed, which cause the output device to move to the beginning of the next line. When you create a textfile by entering data at a terminal, each carriage return inserts one end-of-line character into the file. In addition,

Figure 2-5

A textfile with end-of-line
characters

Standard Pascal treats all textfiles—including the empty file—as if they end
with both an end-of-line character and an end-of-file symbol. Figure 2-5
depicts a textfile with these special characters. Note that there is no end-
of-line character at the beginning of a file. Note also that the existence of
end-of-line characters in a textfile is what distinguishes a textfile from a
general *file of char*.

Associated with each file in a program is a special variable called the
file buffer. The file buffer has the same data type as the individual components of the file. In the case of a textfile, each component is a character,
so the file buffer's data type is *char*. You form the file buffer's identifier by
appending a caret (∧) to the file's identifier. Thus, associated with the
textfile *F* is the file buffer *F∧*, which is a variable of type *char*. Note that
you do not explicitly declare *F∧* in the variable declaration section of your
program. In addition to the file buffer, there is a **file window**, which marks
the current position in the file. The following sections describe the behavior of both the file window and the file buffer during input and output.

Input.   When you use a file *F* for input, the file window is over the component that you will read next. The file buffer *F∧* has this component as
its value, as Figure 2-6 illustrates.

Before you can read anything from a file, you must prepare, or **open**, it
for input by using the *reset* procedure. For the programmer, the important step in opening a file is the initialization of the file window's position.
For example, for the file *F*,

*You must use **reset** before
reading from a file for the first
time*

    reset(F)

moves the file window over the first component in the file and sets *F∧* to
the value of this component. You can call the *reset* procedure at any time

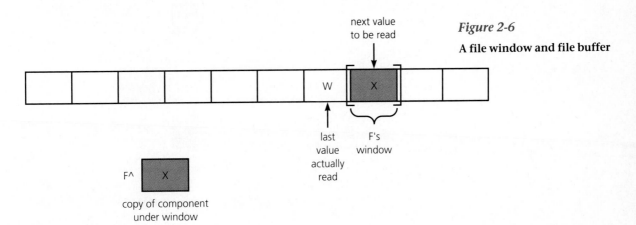

Figure 2-6

A file window and file buffer

Never use `reset(input)`

in your program, and you can reset the same file more than once. Note that you never use *reset* with the standard input file.

Although there is no way to move the file window to any particular component other than the first one, you can advance the window sequentially from one component to the next by using the *get* procedure. For example,

get advances the file window to the next component

```
get(F)
```

advances *F*'s window to the next component and thus changes the value of *F*^. Realize that by using an assignment statement, you can store the value of *F*^ into another variable for processing.

Figure 2-7 illustrates both the *reset* and *get* procedures with a simple textfile. Note how *reset* and *get* affect the file window in the figure.

Figure 2-7

The effect of *reset* **and** *get* **on a textfile**

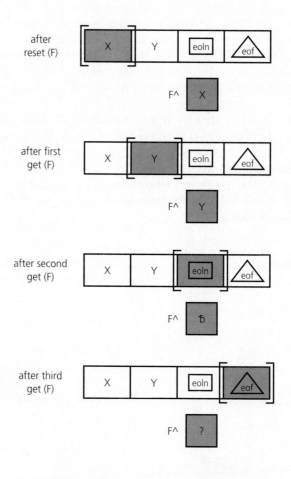

future get (F)
results in   ERROR: ATTEMPT TO READ PAST END OF FILE

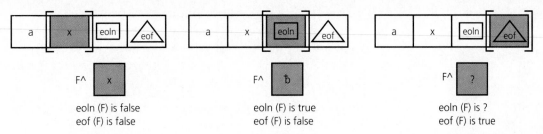

eoln (F) is false   eoln (F) is true   eoln (F) is ?
eof (F) is false   eof (F) is false   eof (F) is true

Figure 2-8

The end-of-line (eoln) and end-of-file (eof) functions

When the file window is over the last component (the Y) in the file, a call to *get* advances the file window to the end-of-line character. Another call to *get* advances the window to the end-of-file symbol. A subsequent call to *get* would result in an error and a message like the following:

    ERROR: ATTEMPT TO READ PAST END OF FILE

When the file window is over the end-of-line character, the value of the file buffer *F*^ is a blank. Thus, an end-of-line character behaves like a blank when you read it. When the file window is over the end-of-file symbol, the value of *F*^ is undefined, and an attempt to reference it is an error.

You can detect when the file window is over either an end-of-line character or the end-of-file symbol by using, respectively, the predefined boolean functions *eoln* and *eof*. The function *eoln(F)*, which is defined only when *F* is a textfile, is true if *F*'s window is over an end-of-line character, and false otherwise. However, if the window is over the end-of-file symbol, *eoln(F)* is undefined. The function *eof(F)* returns the value true if and only if *F*'s window is over the end-of-file symbol. Figure 2-8 illustrates the meaning of these functions. Notice that when *eoln(F)* is true, *eof(F)* is false, because the end-of-line character is a character that is actually in the file.

*When **eof(F)** is true, both **F**^ and **eoln(F)** are undefined; do not reference them*

The Pascal procedure *read*, which you already know, also applies to files. *Read* takes two arguments: The first is the file name and the second is a variable. When this variable is a character variable, the statement

    read(F, x)

read accesses the file buffer and advances the file window

is exactly equivalent to the sequence

    x := F^; { Assign the value of the file buffer to x }
    get(F)   { Advance the file window to the next component }

Figure 2-9 illustrates the effect of this *read* statement.

You can use the Pascal procedure *readln* only with textfiles. It reads a value from a file and then moves the window just past the next end-of-line character. Thus, as Figure 2–10 illustrates, the effect of

    readln(F, x)

*Use **readln** only with textfiles.*

Figure 2-9

The effect of `read(F, x)` **on a textfile**

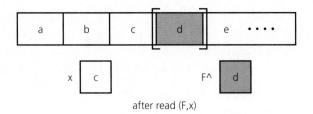

is equivalent to

```
x := F^;                    { Assign the value of the
                              buffer to x }
while not (eoln(F)) do  { Skip to the next end-of-line }
    get(F);                 { character }
get(F)                      { Advance window just beyond
                              end-of-line character }
```

readln(F) advances the file window just beyond the end-of-line character

By omitting the assignment statement $x := F^$ from these statements, you get the effect of `readln(F)` without the argument x. Thus, `readln(F)` advances the window just beyond the end-of-line character to what is usually the beginning of the next line.

To summarize, consider the textfile F that appears in Figure 2-10. If `Ch` is a character variable, the statements in the following sequence assign values to `Ch` as indicated:

```
reset(F);
read(F, Ch);    { Ch = 'a' }
readln(F, Ch);  { Ch = 'b' }
read(F, Ch);    { Ch = 'e' }
readln(F, Ch);  { Ch = 'f' }
reset(F);
read(F, Ch);    { Ch = 'a' }
readln(F, Ch);  { Ch = 'b' }
readln(F, Ch);  { Ch = 'e' }
read(F, Ch);     { Error: attempted read past end of file }
```

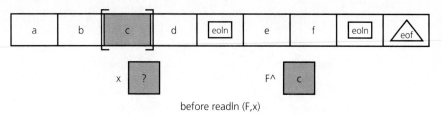

Figure 2-10

The effect of `readln(F, x)` on a textfile

before readln (F,x)

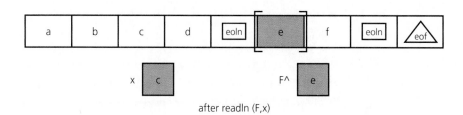

after readln (F,x)

Output. Before you can write anything to a file F, you must open it for output by calling the *rewrite* procedure as follows:

```
rewrite(F)
```

If you are creating a new file, *rewrite* creates the file and positions the file window at the beginning (or the end) of the new file, which is empty. If the file F already exists, then *rewrite(F)* erases the data in the file and positions the window at the beginning (or the end) of the now empty file. You can call the *rewrite* procedure any time in your program and you can rewrite the same file more than once, although each time you do, you erase the file. Note that you never use *rewrite* with the standard output file.

You must use **rewrite** *before writing to a file for the first time*

rewrite creates a new file or erases the data in an existing file

Never use **rewrite(output)**

After you have opened a file F for output, you use the file buffer $F^\wedge$ to assign values to the file. A call to the Pascal *put* procedure, such as

```
put(F)
```

appends to the file F the component whose value is in $F^\wedge$ and advances the file window. This call to *put* also causes the value of $F^\wedge$ to become undefined, as Figure 2-11 illustrates. Notice that the file window for an output file is positioned just past the last component in the file.

put appends $F^\wedge$ to the file and advances the file window

The Pascal procedure *write*, which you already know, also applies to files. *Write* takes two arguments: The first is the file name and the second is an expression whose value has the same data type as the components in the file. The statement

```
write(F, <expression>)
```

is exactly equivalent to the sequence

```
F^   := <expression>;   { Assign value to the file
                            buffer }
```

write appends a value to the file and advances the file window

Figure 2-11

The effect of *put (F)* **on a textfile**

```
put(F)                      { Append value in F^ to file;
                              advance window }
```

You can use the Pascal procedure *writeln* only with textfiles. It appends a value to a file, writes an end-of-line character, and then moves the window just past the end-of-line character. Thus, the effect of

Use *writeln* only with textfiles

```
writeln(F, <expression>)
```

is equivalent to

```
write(F, <expression>);
write(F, <the end-of-line character>)
```

Figure 2-12 illustrates the effect of such a *writeln* statement. Note that by calling *writeln* without the expression argument, as in

```
writeln(F)
```

you can append just the end-of-line character to the file *F*.

Copying a textfile.   Suppose that you have a textfile *OriginalFile* and that you want to make a copy of it. Unfortunately, the following assignment statement is illegal:

```
CopyFile := OriginalFile { THIS STATEMENT IS ILLEGAL }
```

Copying a textfile requires some work and provides a good example of the statements that you have just studied. It is necessary to copy the file one character at a time, taking into account both the end-of-line characters and the end-of-file symbol. The following program assumes that the textfile *OriginalFile* exists and creates a duplicate textfile *CopyFile*:

```
program CopyTextfile(OriginalFile, CopyFile, output);
{ Copies the textfile OriginalFile to the textfile CopyFile.}

var OriginalFile, CopyFile : text;
    Ch : char;
begin
    writeln('Beginning file copy...');
    reset(OriginalFile);           { open given file for input }
    rewrite(CopyFile);             { open new file for output }

    while not eof(OriginalFile) do     { read to end of file }
```

```
begin
   while not eoln(OriginalFile) do  { read to end of line }
   begin
       read(OriginalFile, Ch); { copy line from old file }
       write(CopyFile, Ch)     { to new file a char.
                                 at a time }
   end;  { inner while }
   writeln(CopyFile);          {write end-of-line character}
   readln(OriginalFile)        { advance window beyond
                                 end-of-line character }
end;  { outer while }

writeln('File copy completed.')
end.  { CopyTextfile }
```

Self-Test Exercise 5 at the end of this chapter asks you to trace this program for a particular file, paying close attention to the values of the *eoln* and *eof* functions.

In the previous program, notice the first and the last *writeln* statements that write messages to the standard output file. If they did not exist, you would receive no visible output when you ran the program. A program that produces no visible output is called a **silent program**. A silent program will probably bewilder its user, and for this reason, you should not write a program that produces no output to the standard output file.

Programs should not be silent

Adding to a textfile.   You can use the same file for both input and output within a program. For example, consider the following sequence of *reset* and *rewrite* statements with the file *F*:

```
reset(F);        { You can now read the file F. }
   .
   .
   .
rewrite(F);      { You can now write to the file F,
                   but previous contents are lost. }
   .
   .
   .
reset(F);        { You can now read the file F. }
```

Observe that a file cannot be available simultaneously for both input and output. This rule makes it difficult to perform a task such as appending a

F before writeln

F after writeln (F, 'mom')

Figure 2-12

The effect of `writeln` **on a textfile**

new component to a file. For example, suppose that you first reset the file and then read to its end. Before you can write an additional component to the file, you must first call *rewrite*—but *rewrite* will destroy the file contents!

Adding a component to a file requires that you first copy the file

Thus, to append a component to a file, you must first make a copy of the file. Then, while the duplicate file is still open for output, you can write the new component to the file. You then have two files: the original file and an augmented copy. If desired, you can replace the original file with a copy of the augmented file. In this case, you could make the augmented file a temporary internal file, because once you have copied it into the original external file you have no need for it after program execution ends. Exercises 10 and 11 at the end of this chapter ask you to write such a program.

Numeric data within textfiles.   As you know, you can read integer and real values from the standard input file into variables whose data types are integer or real, as appropriate. You also know that the standard input file is a textfile, and that a textfile is a sequence of characters. Although these facts may seem contradictory to you, integer and real values can be read from and written to a textfile. (You also can write, but not read, boolean values.) Although this presentation uses integers to illustrate the concepts, the other data types follow by analogy.

The representation of a numeric value in a textfile differs from its representation in an integer or real variable

When your program reads from a textfile into an integer variable, the system expects a sequence of characters that it can convert into an integer. For example, if the textfile contains the character sequence '2', '3', '4' and if you read from the textfile into the integer variable x, the system will convert these three characters into the computer's internal representation for the integer 234 and assign this value to x. More precisely, the textfile contains the ASCII codes for the characters '2', '3', and '4'—which are, respectively, the decimal values 50, 51, and 52. However, these codes appear in the file in binary, as Figure 2-13a indicates. If you read those characters into the integer variable x, then x will contain the computer's internal representation for the integer 234, which appears in binary as shown in Figure 2-13b. The important point here is that there is a difference between the ASCII representation of digits in a textfile and the representation in memory of the number that those digits symbolize.

To summarize, for the textfile F and the integer variable x, the statement

```
read(F, x)
```

has the following effect:

while $F^\wedge$ *= ' ' do* { *Skip to the first nonblank character* }
    get(F)

Convert into an integer the sequence of characters that begins at the current position of F's window and ends just before the next character c that is not in the range '0'..'9'

(a) textfile

Figure 2-13

(a) The ASCII characters 2, 3, and 4 represented in binary in a textfile; (b) the internal binary representation of the integer 234

(b)

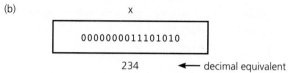

Assign this integer value to x
Advance the file window so that it is over the character c

Observe that if the sequence begins with a character other than +, −, or 0 through 9, an error will occur. For example, the system cannot convert the sequence *w123* into an integer, but it will convert the sequence *123wrt45* into the integer 123. As you can see in Figure 2-14, the file window will then be positioned over the *w* when the read concludes.

Similarly, when your program writes an integer value such as 234 to a textfile, the system first converts the integer from the computer's internal binary representation (0000000011101010) to the character sequence '2', '3', '4' and then writes these characters to the file. For the textfile *F* and the integer variable *x*, the statement

```
write(F,x)
```

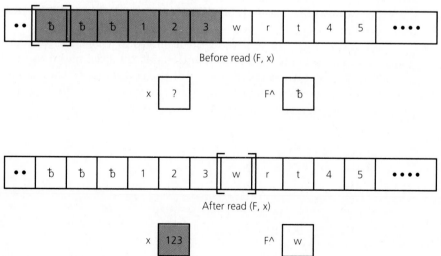

Figure 2-14

Reading an integer from a textfile

has the following effect:

> *Convert the value of x into a sequence of characters*
> *Append this sequence of characters to the file F*
> *Position F's window just past the last character*
>   *written*

Now consider a pitfall that awaits you when you try to read an entire textfile of numeric data. The following program is supposed to read and echo a series of integers from the textfile *F*. However, it contains a serious bug.

```pascal
program EchoFile(F, output);
{ THIS PROGRAM CONTAINS A BUG }
var F : text;
    x : integer;
begin
    reset(F);
    while not eof(F) do
    begin
        read(F, x);
        writeln('Integer read is ', x)
    end { while }
end.   { program }
```

This program will read past the end-of-file symbol, producing an error. Why? After the system reads the last integer in the file, *F*'s window will be over either the end-of-line character or, if there are blanks at the end of the last line, a blank that is before the end-of-line character. (See Figure 2-15.) In either case, *eof(F)* is false, so the *while* loop will continue. The *read(F, x)* statement will advance *F*'s window to the next nonblank character, but there is none. (Recall that *read* treats the end-of-line character as if it were a blank.) Hence, while searching for a nonblank character, the *read* statement will attempt to advance the window beyond the end-of-file symbol, causing the error.

A solution to this problem is to write a procedure called *SkipBlanks* that will skip both blanks and end-of-line characters, leaving the window over either the next nonblank character or the end-of-file symbol in case there are no more nonblank characters. Once you have written such a procedure, you can read the integers by using these statements:

An example of using Skip-
Blanks *when reading integers*
from a file

```pascal
reset(F);
SkipBlanks(F);
while not eof(F) do
begin
    read(F, x);
    writeln('Integer read is ', x);
    SkipBlanks(F)
end
```

Figure 2-16 shows the effect of *SkipBlanks(F)*.

Figure 2-15

Reading the last integer in a textfile

Before reading 4 into x

After reading 4 into x, subsequent
read (F, x) will cause error

eof (F) is false

eof (F) is false

The pseudocode for *SkipBlanks* is

while (**not** *eof(F)*) **and** *(the file window is over a blank)* **do**
   Advance the file window

This pseudocode seems simple enough, but your instinct is probably to implement the test at the top of the *while* loop as

    *(**not** eof(F)) **and** (F^ = blank)*

However, when *eof(F)* becomes true, it is an error to inspect *F^*, because its value is undefined. Because Pascal evaluates both operands of the *and* operator even when the first operand is false, the test can lead to an error. The solution is to inspect *F* only after you have ascertained that *eof(F)* is false.

   This observation leads to the procedure *SkipBlanks*:

```
procedure SkipBlanks(var F: text);
{ --------------------------------------------------------
  Skips blanks before numbers in a textfile.
  Precondition: F is a textfile of either integers or reals.
  Postcondition: Advances F's file window to either the next
  nonblank character or the end-of-file symbol.
  -------------------------------------------------------- }
const blank = ' ';
var Done : boolean;         { Done is true when F^ <> blank }

begin
    Done := false;

    { advance the window until either eof
      or a nonblank character is found }
    while (not eof(F)) and (not Done) do
    begin
       if F^ = blank
           then get(F)      { advance window }
           else Done := true
```

Figure 2-16

The effect of *SkipBlanks*

Before SkipBlanks (F)

eof (F) is false

After SkipBlanks (F)

eof (F) is true

```
    end  { while }
end  { SkipBlanks }
```

You also should use the *SkipBlanks* procedure when reading real numbers from a textfile.

Notice that the file *F* is a parameter of *SkipBlanks*. When a parameter is a file, you must declare it as a variable parameter. This restriction is a logical consequence of the more general restriction on files that was already mentioned: You cannot use an assignment statement to copy one file to another file, even if the files are of the same type. Because a value parameter "copies" its value from the actual parameter, *you therefore must pass a file as a variable parameter.*

Pass files to subprograms as variable parameters

The last section of this chapter discusses the Pascal *and* operator in more detail and provides guidance for writing procedures such as *SkipBlanks*.

Multiargument *read* and *write*.   Standard Pascal allows a single *read* or *readln* statement to read any number of values from a file, and a single *write* or *writeln* statement to write any number of values to a file. The call

```
    read(F, x1, x2, x3)
```

is exactly equivalent to

```
    read(F, x1);
    read(F, x2);
    read(F, x3)
```

and the call

```
    readln(F, x1, x2, x3)
```

is exactly equivalent to

```
    read(F, x1, x2, x3);
    readln(F)
```

Similarly, the call

```
    write(F, <expression₁>, <expression₂>, <expression₃>)
```

is exactly equivalent to

```
write(F, <expression₁>);
write(F, <expression₂>);
write(F, <expression₃>)
```

and the call

```
writeln(F, <expression₁>, <expression₂>, <expression₃>)
```

is exactly equivalent to

```
write(F, <expression₁>, <expression₂>, <expression₃>)
writeln(F)
```

Default files.   Several of the predefined functions and procedures that this section introduces use the standard input or standard output as the default when you omit the file parameter. In particular,

- *eof*, *eoln*, *read*, and *readln* all default to the standard input file *input* when you omit the file parameter.

- *write* and *writeln* default to the standard output file *output* when you omit the file parameter.

General Files

Files that are not textfiles are called **general** (or **binary** or **nontext**) **files.** Like a textfile, a general file is a sequence of components of the same data type, which is any type other than a file. Consider the following statements, which declare some general files:

```
type    intfile     = file of integer;
        realfile    = file of real;
        string      = packed array[1..10] of char;
        stringfile  = file of string;

var     I : intfile;    { a general file of integers }
        R : realfile;   { a general file of reals }
        S : stringfile; { a general file of arrays }
```

It is important to emphasize that each file component is an indivisible entity. For example, each component of the general file *I* is an integer in the computer's internal representation. If you write the integer value 234 to the integer file *I*, the system would write the computer's internal representation of 234, which is 0000000011101010 in binary, to the file, rather than the three ASCII characters '2', '3', '4', which are, respectively, 00110010, 00110011, and 00110100 in binary. If your system allowed you to print out *I* (some systems allow you to print out only textfiles), you would get gibberish. You create *I* not by using an editor—as you could for a textfile—but rather by running a program. Similar comments are true for the file *R* of real numbers. Figure 2-17 illustrates the file *I*.

Similarly, consider the file S, where each component is a string of 10 characters, as Figure 2-18 illustrates in human-readable form. Input and output with the file S are at the string level, not the character level. Thus, if the variable A has data type *string*, you could read an entire component, which is a string, at once from S into A; but if the variable Ch has data type *char*, you could not read a single character from S into either Ch or $A[i]$. However, once you have read a string into the array A, you can access the individual characters as usual: $A[i]$ is the ith character in the string.

General files do not contain end-of-line characters

A general file has an end-of-file symbol at its end, just as a textfile does. However, the notion of lines does not exist for a general file: There are no end-of-line characters in a general file. The Pascal procedures *reset*, *rewrite*, *get*, *put*, *read*, and *write* as well as the function *eof* all apply to general files and are defined as they are for textfiles. For example, Figure 2-19 illustrates *reset*, *get*, and *eof* with a file of integers, which are indicated here in decimal rather than binary. Note that *readln*, *writeln*, and *eoln* do not apply to general files.

Do not use readln, writeln, and eoln with general files

Now consider an example that will demonstrate how to use general files. Suppose that you have two integer files, $F1$ and $F2$. Each file component is an integer in the computer's internal representation. Suppose further that each file is sorted into ascending order: In each file, every integer component is less than or equal to the integer component that follows it. Suppose that you want to write a program that will merge $F1$ and $F2$ to produce a third file $F3$ of type *integer* that is the sorted combination of $F1$ and $F2$. In addition, you want to write the final contents of $F3$ to the standard output file, which, remember, is a textfile.

The problem breaks down naturally into two tasks:

Tasks for merging two files

```
Merge F1 and F2 into F3
Write F3 to the standard output file
```

You can refine the first of these tasks as

The first task

```
Open F1 and F2 for input
Open F3 for output
while both input files have more components do
begin
    Consider the values in the two file buffers F1^
        and F2^
    Write the smaller of these values to F3
    Advance the appropriate file window
end
```

Figure 2-17

A general file of integers

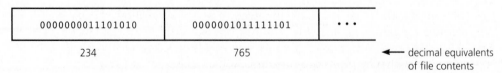

234   765   ← decimal equivalents
                                                                of file contents

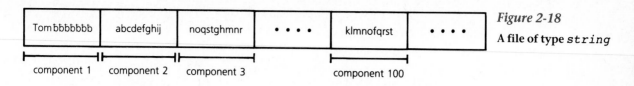

Figure 2-18

A file of type `string`

Tom bbbbbbb	abcdefghij	noqstghmnr	. . . .	klmnofqrst	. . . .

component 1   component 2   component 3   component 100

```
{ At this point, exactly one of the input files will
   have more components to write to F3 }

     Write the remaining components of the
        unfinished file to F3
```

Figure 2–20 illustrates these steps in the merge task.

To enhance modularity, you can implement this pseudocode as a procedure with three formal parameters, which correspond to the three files. This implementation allows the procedure to merge any pair of sorted integer files into a third. Assuming the type definition

```
     type intfile = file of integer
```

the following is the *MergeFiles* procedure:

```
procedure MergeFiles(var F1, F2, F3 : intfile);
{ ----------------------------------------------------------
  Merges two sorted general files of integers into a third
  sorted file.
  Precondition: F1 and F2 are each sorted general integer
  files.
  Postcondition: F3 is a sorted integer file that is the
  merger of F1 and F2. F1 and F2 remain unchanged.
  ---------------------------------------------------------- }
begin
   { ready the files }
   reset(F1);
   reset(F2);
   rewrite(F3);

   { merge while both input files are not empty }
   while (not eof(F1)) and (not eof(F2)) do
   begin
      if F1^ < F2^
         then
         begin
            write(F3, F1^);
            get(F1)
         end

         else
         begin
            write(F3, F2^);
```

```
                        get(F2)
                      end
              end; { while }

      { finish off the files (one will already be finished) }

          { finish off F1 if necessary }
          while not eof(F1) do
          begin
              write(F3, F1^);
              get(F1)
          end; { while }
          { finish off F2 if necessary }
          while not eof(F2) do
          begin
              write(F3, F2^);
              get(F2)
          end { while }
      end   { MergeFiles }
```

It would have been more difficult to implement *MergeFiles* by using *read*'s instead of both *get*'s and file buffers. In particular, the comparison between the "current" integers of the two files is stated elegantly in the procedure as

```
      if F1^ < F2^
```

The alternative of

```
      read(F1, x);
      read(F2, y);
      if x < y
            then...
```

is clumsy because the two *read*'s advance both file windows. It is simpler to advance only the window of the smaller integer's file.

The refinement of the second task,

> *Write F3 to the standard output file*

is straightforward:

The second task
> *Open F3 for input*
> *{ The standard output file is always open for output }*
>
> **while** *there are more components in F3* **do**
> **begin**
>   *Write the value of the component that is under*
>   *F3's window to the standard output file*
>   *Advance F3's window*
> **end**

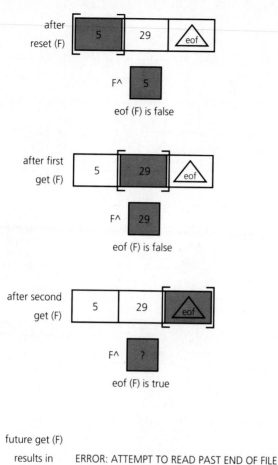

after
reset (F)

F^ 5

eof (F) is false

after first
get (F)

F^ 29

eof (F) is false

after second
get (F)

F^ ?

eof (F) is true

future get (F)

results in   ERROR: ATTEMPT TO READ PAST END OF FILE

The Pascal implementation of this pseudocode results in the following procedure, *WriteFile*:

```
procedure WriteFile(var F : intfile);
{ ------------------------------------------------------------
  Writes the general integer file F to standard output.
  Precondition: F is a general file of integers.
  Postcondition: Copies F to the standard output file, F is
  unchanged.

  ------------------------------------------------------------ }
begin
    reset(F);              { ready the file F for reading }
    while(not eof(F)) do
    begin
        write(F^);         { write the component under the
                             window to standard output }
```

Figure 2-20

Merge steps

F1 ready for input   F2 ready for input   F3 ready for output

(Integer files shown with components as "human readable integers")

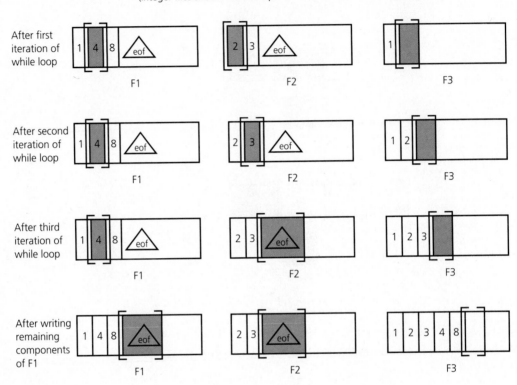

```
        get(F)              { advance the window }
    end; { while }

    writeln                 { advance to the next line }
end { WriteFile }
```

The following complete program incorporates the previous procedures and declares the files *F1*, *F2*, and *F3*.

```
program merge(output, F1, F2, F3);
{ *********************************************************
  Merges two sorted general files of integers into a third
  file, which is then printed.
  Input: F1 and F2 are general files of integers that are in
  ascending order.
```

```
    Output: F3 contains all integers in F1 and F2 in ascending
    order; copies F3 to the standard output file; F1 and F2
    are unchanged.

    Remember that F1 and F2 are NOT textfiles and thus you
    cannot create or inspect them by using a text editor.
    ****************************************************** }

type   intfile = file of integer;

var    F1, F2, F3 : intfile;
procedure MergeFiles(var F1, F2, F3 : intfile);
    { body of procedure presented earlier }

end;   { MergeFiles }

procedure WriteFile(var F : intfile);

    { body of procedure presented earlier }

end;   { WriteFile }

begin   { Main Program }
    MergeFiles(F1, F2, F3);   { merge F1 and F2 into F3 }
    WriteFile(F3)                { write out F3 }
end.   { Program }
```

Note that this program must use the particular files *F1*, *F2*, and *F3*. That is, in Standard Pascal you cannot read a file name into a variable and then use the variable name instead of the file name in Pascal statements such as *read* and *write*. Some versions of Pascal have corrected this deficiency of Standard Pascal.

The case study in Chapter 3 further illustrates the use of files in the solution to a large, real-world problem.

SETS

In mathematics and in Pascal, a **set** is a collection of distinct elements. If you want your program to check a value against several possible values, you can use a set to make this determination. For example, suppose that the program reads a one-letter response to a yes-or-no question into the character variable *Response*. Acceptable values for *Response* would be *Y* or *y* for "yes" and *N* or *n* for "no." The boolean expression

```
    Response in ['Y', 'y', 'N', 'n']
```

is true if the value of *Response* is valid—that is, if it is in the set *['Y', 'y', 'N', 'n']*. This section will review set declarations and set operations.

Declaring Sets and Assigning Them Values

You can declare a set data type by writing a statement of the following form within the type declaration section of your program:

  set of <*base_type*>

Here, <*base_type*> represents any ordinal data type. For example, consider the following type and variable declarations:

```
type   AgeSetType    = set of 1..100;

       UpperCase     = 'A'..'Z';
       LetterSetType = set of UpperCase;

var    AgesPresent : AgeSetType;
       LettersRead : LetterSetType;
```

Set variable declarations do not assign values to sets

The variable *AgesPresent* is a set whose elements can be integers in the range 1 through 100. The variable *LettersRead* is a set whose elements can be uppercase letters. Note that the previous variable declarations *do not assign values to the variables*. A common mistake is to think that the value of *AgesPresent* is a set of 100 integers. However, the **base type** *1..100* simply specifies the permissible elements that the set *AgesPresent* can contain. Note that many Pascal implementations restrict the size of a set's base type.

Set constants.   To assign values to a set, you use a set constant, which is a list of elements separated by commas and enclosed in square brackets. For example, you denote the set of the responses *Y* and *N* by using the set constant *['Y', 'N']*. Similarly, *[1, 4, 5]* is a set of the three integers 1, 4, and 5. In addition, *[18.. 21, 25]* has the same meaning as *[18, 19, 20, 21, 25]*. Note that *[]* is the empty set, which you can use to initialize a set variable. Thus, the following assignment statements are possible:

```
       LettersRead := ['Y', 'N'];
       AgesPresent := [18..21, 25];
       AgesPresent := [];
```

Elements in a set are not ordered

You should also note that the elements within a set do not have an order, even though programmers often write the elements in order. Thus, the sets *['Y', 'N']* and *['N', 'Y']* are identical.

Illegal assignments

The following assignment statements are *illegal* for the reasons given:

```
AgesPresent := [5, 101]; { 101 is not in the set's base type }
LettersRead := 'A';      { 'A' is not a set; use ['A'] instead }
```

Now consider an enumerated data type as the base type for a set, as in the following statements:

```
type   Errors = (NegInput, ZeroInput, NonInteger, NoInput);
       ErrorSetType = set of Errors;

var    ErrorsOccurred : ErrorSetType;
```

A common mistake is to treat the data type *Errors* as a set. Here, the variable *ErrorsOccurred* is the set, and you could assign it a value such as *[ZeroInput, NoInput]*.

Note that you cannot use set constants in the *const* statement. Thus, the following statement is illegal:

```
const YesNo = ['Y', 'y', 'N', 'n']    { ILLEGAL }
```

Set-valued expressions.   Set constants and set variables are two examples of set-valued expressions. A more general set-valued expression allows arbitrary expressions of the appropriate type to appear between the square brackets. For example, if *J* and *K* are integer variables, then *[J..K, J + K]* is a set-valued expression. You can form more complex set-valued expressions by combining set-valued expressions, parentheses, and set operators; set operators are considered next.

Set Operators

Eight set operators are available in Pascal: membership, equality, inequality, subset, superset, union, intersection, and difference. Each operator has two operands. The first five operators in this list are boolean valued: They return a value of *true* or *false*. The remaining three operators produce a set.

Membership in a set.   Perhaps the most useful feature of sets is the test for membership in a set. Suppose that you want to determine whether or not the value of the integer variable *N* is in one of these ranges: *0..10*, *25..30*, or *50..maxint*. You could use either a lengthy boolean expression such as

```
((0 <= N) and (N <= 10)) or ((25 <= N) and (N <= 30))
or (N >= 50)
```

or the simpler expression

```
N in [0..10, 25..30, 50..maxint]
```

Set membership simplifies range tests

Both expressions are true if *N* is within the desired range. The Pascal membership operator *in* has two operands. The first (*N*) is an expression of the same type as an individual element in the set that the second operand specifies; the second operand can be any set-valued expression.

The expression *not (N in [0..10])* is true when *N*'s value is not in the range 0 through 10. Notice that *N not in [0..10]* is syntactically incorrect.

Other set operators.   The remaining seven set operators have set-valued expressions as operands. The first four operators return a boolean value, and the rest return a set. Here is a list of the operators and their definitions:

- **Equality (=).** If the sets *S* and *T* are identical, then they are **equal**. If *S* and *T* are equal, then the Pascal expression *S = T* is true; otherwise it is false.

- **Inequality** (<>). If the sets S and T are not identical, then they are **not equal**. If S and T are not equal, then the Pascal expression S <> T is true; otherwise it is false.
- **Subset** (<=). S is a **subset** of T if every element of S is also an element of T. If S is a subset of T, then S <= T is true.
- **Superset** (>=). S is a **superset** of T if T is a subset of S. If S is a superset of T, then S >= T is true.
- **Union** (+). The **union** of sets S and T (denoted in Pascal as S + T) is the set of all elements that are in either S or T (or both).
- **Intersection** (*). The **intersection** of sets S and T (S * T) is the set of all elements that are in both S and T.
- **Difference** (–). The **difference** of sets S and T (S − T) is the set of all elements that are in S but not in T.

Note that the following expressions are all true:

Examples of true expressions

```
['Y', 'N'] = ['N', 'Y']
[2] <> [2, 3]
[2] <= [2, 3]
[2, 3] >= [2]
[2, 4, 6] + [8] = [2, 4, 6, 8]
[10..40] + [30..60] = [10..60]
[10..60] * [50..70] = [50..60]
([10..40] + [30..60]) * [50..70] = [50..60]
[2, 4, 6, 8] − [4, 6, 9] = [2, 8]
```

Operator precedence

For expressions that involve the intersection (*), union (+), and difference (–) operators, intersection has a higher precedence than the union and difference operators. Thus, * has a higher precedence than + and –; this is the same precedence that the arithmetic operators *, +, and – have. In addition, if an expression involves both set-valued operators (*, +, –) and boolean-valued operators (=, <>, <=, >=, in), then the set-valued operators are always performed first. For example, the union operation is performed first in both the expression S + T in R and the expression S + T >= R.

The operands of the set operators must be **type compatible**. Recall that the value of a set-valued expression is always a set, which contains a subrange or subranges of a single ordinal data type. This ordinal data type (*integer*, *char*, *boolean*, or user-defined enumerated) is called the **host type**. The operand sets must have the same host type to be type compatible. For example, the following sets are type compatible because their host types are the same—*integer*:

```
var S1 : set of 1..50;
    S2 : set of 1..100;
```

You cannot use sets directly in I/O statements

Finally, note that you cannot use sets directly in *read* and *write* statements. For example, the following statements write the elements in the set *S1*, which was just declared:

```
writeln('The elements in the set S1 are: ');
```

```
for J := 1 to 50 do          { J is an integer variable }
    if J in S1
        then write(J:3);
```

Exercises 15 and 16 at the end of this chapter consider I/O with other sets, including those whose host type is an enumerated data type.

FINAL COMMENTS ON PASCAL

This final section on Pascal discusses two miscellaneous issues of programming with this language. The remainder of the book discusses problem solving in general.

Pascal's *and* and *or* Operators

Pascal is a very well-designed language, but it is not perfect. Perhaps its worst flaw is the behavior of its *and* and *or* operators. In particular, you know that when the boolean expression <*expression₁*> is false, then the expression

$$\text{<}expression_1\text{>} \text{ and } \text{<}expression_2\text{>}$$

is false regardless of the value of <*expression₂*>. However, Pascal evaluates <*expression₂*> anyway. Similarly, you know that when <*expression₁*> is true, then the expression

Pascal always evaluates both operands of the operators and *and* or

$$\text{<}expression_1\text{>} \text{ or } \text{<}expression_2\text{>}$$

is true regardless of the value of <*expression₂*>. Again, Pascal evaluates <*expression₂*>. The problem in both of these examples is that if <*expression₂*> is ever undefined, then evaluating it will cause an error. This behavior makes many conceptually simple programming tasks very clumsy.

For example, suppose that the array A is of the following data type:

```
type  arraytype = array[1..MaxSize] of integer;
```

Consider the following statements to determine whether or not the value of *Target*, which is an integer variable, occurs in the first N elements of A:

```
i := 1;
while (i <= N) and (A[i] <> Target) do
    i := i + 1;
if i <= N
    then writeln(Target, ' occurs at position ', i,
                     ' of the array.')
    else writeln(Target, ' does not occur in the array.')
```

A problem occurs when N = *MaxSize* and *Target* does not occur in A. Because Pascal evaluates the expression A[i] <> *Target* even though i

<= *N* is false—that is, when *i* = *N* + *1*—the reference to A[N + 1], which does not exist, causes an error.

If Pascal's *and* operator had been defined so that it did not evaluate its second operand when the first operand was false, the previous *while* loop would work without change. Some programming languages do support such an operator, which is called **conditional and**. Similarly, many programming languages also support a **conditional or** operator that does not evaluate its second operand if the first operand is true. Pascal's failure to support these conditional operators complicates many common programming tasks.

You can use Cand and Cor in pseudocode solutions

Although you cannot change Pascal, you certainly can define your own pseudocode. Therefore, the remainder of this book will use the notation **Cand** to mean *conditional and* and **Cor** to mean *conditional or* in pseudocode solutions. Thus, for example, you would write the pseudocode for the previous *while* loop as

```
i := 1;
while (i <= N) Cand (A[i] <> Target) do
    i := i + 1;
```

Even though this notation simplifies algorithms greatly, it does not solve Pascal's problem. How, then, do you implement the previous loop in Pascal? When your pseudocode contains a loop such as

```
while <x> Cand <y> do
    <S> { body of the loop }
```

replace it with the following statements, where *Done* is a boolean variable, *x* and *y* represent boolean expressions, and *S* is the body of the loop:

```
Done := false;
while <x> and (not Done) do
begin
    if <y>
        then <S> { body of loop }
        else Done := true
end
```

Thus, the *while* loop in the previous array example becomes

```
i := 1;
Done := false;
while (i <= N) and (not Done) do
begin
    if A[i] <> Target
        then i := i + 1
        else Done := true
end
```

Notice that the *SkipBlanks* procedure presented earlier contains a similar loop. Recall that the procedure advances the file window to the next nonblank character in the file; if there are no more nonblank characters, it advances the window to the end-of-file symbol. Conceptually, the procedure is simply

```
while (not eof(F)) Cand (F^ = blank) do
    get(F)
```

The *Cand* avoids the evaluation of the expression $F^\wedge = blank$ when *not* *eof(F)* is false (that is, when *eof(F)* is true) and thus avoids the error that can result from an attempt to examine $F^\wedge$ when its value is undefined. *SkipBlanks* implements this pseudocode by using the technique just demonstrated.

Now consider some other instances of *Cand* and *Cor*, which occur later in this book. When *Cand* occurs in an *if* statement in your pseudocode, such as

```
if <x> Cand <y>
    then <S₁>
    else <S₂>
```

you implement it in Pascal by using statements of the following form:

```
if not <x> then
    <S₂>
else if not <y> then
    <S₂>
else <S₁>
```

When *Cor* occurs in an *if* statement in your pseudocode, such as

```
if <x> Cor <y>
    then <S₁>
    else <S₂>
```

you write the following Pascal code instead:

```
if <x> then
    <S₁>
else if <y> then
    <S₁>
else <S₂>
```

Self-Test Exercise 7 at the end of this chapter considers the case in which *Cor* occurs in a *while* statement. Other exercises at the end of this chapter will give you practice in implementing the *Cand* and *Cor* operators in Pascal.

Building a Large Pascal Program in Pieces

Chapter 1 spoke of the virtues of modular programming. One advantage is that you can implement subprograms independently of other subprograms. You also may find it possible for several different programs to use a particular subprogram. As a result, you can build a library of subprograms that you can include in future programs.

How can you use previously written subprograms in a current program? Many modern operating systems support a **source-inclusion facility**, which allows the system to *include* the contents of a file automatically at a specified point in a program before the program is compiled. Thus, for example, you can store one or more subprograms in a file and have the system include it in any program that uses the subprograms. The assumption, of course, is that the subprograms are in **source** form—that is, they need to be compiled. This book assumes that a source-inclusion facility is available and adopts the convention that the system should replace the statement

```
#include <filename>
```

with the contents of the file `<filename>`.

It certainly would be more efficient to compile the subprograms once, independently of any particular program, and then later merge the results of the compilation with any program that you desire. Many programming languages allow you to do just that. Unfortunately, Standard Pascal does not provide for this type of separate compilation. However, there are Pascal compilers, such as TURBO Pascal,[2] that allow separate compilation. For example, you can compile a **unit**, which is a collection of subprograms, constant definitions, type definitions, and variable declarations, for later use in a program. If `unit1` is the name of a unit, you can use it in your program by including a statement such as

Units are compiled separately from the program that uses them

```
uses     unit1
```

A unit has both public and private portions. An **interface** provides the **public** portion; it is what you see when you want to use the unit. Through the interface, you pass the unit input parameters and it passes back output parameters. The unit's implementation is its **private** portion. That is, you cannot see how the unit performs its task. Specifically, the unit is the result of previously compiled Pascal statements, which are no longer available to you. Perhaps you did not even write the unit, just as you did not write the standard Pascal functions such as *sqrt*. Thus, you can use a unit in the same spirit that you use standard functions. Although standard functions are available to you automatically, you need to tell the compiler that you want to use a particular unit by writing a *uses* statement.

Units enforce procedural abstraction. You must think of units in terms of what they can do for you and not how they are implemented. You should think of all your subprograms this way, even if you eventually implement them yourself.

---

[2]TURBO Pascal is a trademark of Borland International, Inc.

SUMMARY

1. An array is a collection of elements that have the same data type. You can refer to the elements of an array by using an index.

2. A record is a group of related items—called fields—which may be of different data types. You can use the *with* statement to simplify references to the fields within records.

3. Fields in a record can themselves be records.

4. A group of records is variant if the records contain both fixed fields, which are common to all records, and variant fields, which differ for certain records. A tag field references the fields in the variant part of the records.

5. A file is a sequence of components of the same data type. A file is the only Pascal data type that allows data to exist independently of a program. A program can write data to an external file, and this data will not disappear when the program terminates. An external file provides a way to keep a permanent record of a program's output as well as a way for one program to use another program's output as its input. An internal file exists only during program execution.

6. A textfile is a file of characters that contains end-of-line characters. Although end-of-line characters make the file appear as if it were divided into lines, these characters are in most respects like any other component in the textfile.

7. In a textfile, the value of the file buffer *F^* is blank when the file window is over an end-of-line character. In such cases, the function *eoln(F)* is true and the function *eof(F)* is false. In addition, when the file window is over the end-of-file symbol, *eof(F)* is true and *eoln(F)* is undefined.

8. The standard input file *input* and the standard output file *output* are textfiles:
   a. Do not declare *input* or *output* in a variable declaration.
   b. Do not use the *reset* or *rewrite* procedures with these files; *input* is always open for reading and *output* is always open for writing.
   c. When you omit the file parameter from either a *read* or a *write* statement, the default files are *input* and *output*, respectively.
   d. The program header must always specify *output*.

9. Although textfiles are files of characters, you can write integer, real, or boolean values to them. For example, if *x* contains the integer value 234, writing *x* to a textfile places the character

sequence '2', '3', '4' in the file. The *write* procedure performs the conversion from the internal representation of the integer to the representation of the corresponding character sequence. Similarly, you can read characters, which represent either integer or real values, from a textfile into an appropriate integer or real variable.

10. A set is a collection of distinct elements. Of the eight set operators, membership, equality, inequality, subset, and superset are boolean-valued operators, while union, intersection, and difference are set-valued operators.

11. Here are some situations where sets may be appropriate:

   a. There is no implied order for the objects.
   b. You need to keep track of which objects are present, but you do not need a count of how many of each object is present.
   c. You need to perform the standard set operations.

COMMON PITFALLS / DEBUGGING

1. An array has a fixed size, which you choose before program execution. You must be careful that an index does not exceed this size.

2. Be careful when you reference the fields within a record. You must write both the record variable and the field identifier when you are outside the scope of a *with* statement. Be particularly careful when several record definitions have some of the same field identifiers.

3. The components in a file must all be of the same data type.

4. You must read a file's components into a variable of the corresponding type. For example, if the file is of type *string* (which, for instance, is an array of *char*), you can read a component only into a variable of type *string* and not into a variable of type *char*.

5. Do not forget to use *reset(F)* before you read from the file *F* and to use *rewrite(F)* before you write to *F*. The standard input and output files are exceptions; do not use *reset* and *rewrite* with *input* and *output*.

6. Remember that *rewrite* erases the data in an existing file.

7. When the file window is over the end-of-file symbol, *eof(F)* is true, the value of the file buffer $F^\wedge$ is undefined, and the value of the function *eoln(F)* is undefined. It is an error to attempt to reference either $F^\wedge$ or *eoln(F)* in such a case.

8. Use *readln*, *writeln*, and *eoln* only with textfiles.

9. You must pass a file to a subprogram as a variable parameter.

10. Be careful when reading integers (or reals) from a textfile. A common programming error leads to an attempt to read past the end of the file while searching for the "last" integer. For example, the loop

```
{ F is a textfile, x is an integer variable )
while not eof(F) do
    read(F, x)
```

results in such an error. To avoid this error, you should use the procedure *SkipBlanks*.

11. Generally, Pascal implementations impose a limit on the size of a set's base type.

12. Pascal does not support a "conditional and" operator or a "conditional or" operator. As a result, Pascal evaluates both operands of both the *and* and *or* operators. For example, evaluating an expression such as

```
not eof(F)) and (F^ <> x)
```

results in an error if *eof(F)* is true, because Pascal still evaluates the operand *(F^ <> x)*. (Recall that it is an error to reference *F^* when *eof(F)* is true, because *F^* is undefined in this case.)

SELF-TEST EXERCISES

1. Consider the array that the following statements define:

```
type    arraytype = array[1..7, 1..52] of real;
var     MinTemps : arraytype;
```

Suppose, as you saw earlier in this chapter, that each column of the array represents the minimum temperatures for the seven days in a particular week. Write the Pascal statements that perform the following:

a. Write the minimum temperature for each day of the first week.
b. Write the minimum temperature for the first day of each of the first five weeks.
c. Write all of the minimum temperatures so that the temperatures for each week appear on a separate line.

2. Consider the array *Temps* that the following statements define:

```
type    weektype = array[1..7] of real;
        yeartype = array[1..52] of weektype;
var     Temps : yeartype;
```

Temps[12] is a one-dimensional array of seven real numbers. Suppose that you want to compute the average of these seven numbers by calling a function *Average*. Write the header statement for the function *Average* so that *Average(Temps[12])* returns the desired average.

3. Consider the definition of the record *Student1* within the section of this chapter entitled "Records Within Records." Write the Pascal references for the following items in this record:

    a. The state
    b. The first digit in the zip code
    c. The GPA
    d. The first letter in the name

4. Let *A*, *B*, and *C* be sets of integers. Assume that

    A := [1..5, 9]; B := [2, 4, 6, 8]; and C := [9..15, 20, 22]

    What is the value of each of the following expressions?

    a. **not** *(8 **in** A)*   e. *A * C*
    b. *A − B*   f. *B <= A*
    c. *B − A*   g. *A + B*
    d. *A + [9]*   h. *A + C*

5. Consider the program *CopyTextfile*, which makes a copy of a textfile and was discussed in this chapter in the section "Textfiles." Trace the execution of this program when *OriginalFile* looks like

    a b <eoln> c d <eoln> <eof>

    where *<eoln>* represents the end-of-line character and *<eof>* represents the end-of-file symbol. Indicate the contents of *Ch* and *Copy-File*, the position of the file windows, and the values of the *eoln* and *eof* functions as you trace through the program.

6. Implement the following pseudocode in Pascal by removing the *Cand* operator:

```
{ locate the first (if any) nonzero element in the array
  A of N integers }
i := 1
while (i ≤ N) Cand (A[i] = 0) do
    i := i + 1
if i > N
    then all elements are zero
    else the first nonzero element is A[i]
```

7. What does the Pascal implementation of the following pseudocode

```
while <x> Cor <y> do
    <S>   { body of the loop }
```

    look like when you remove the *Cor* operator? *Hint*: Use a boolean variable.

EXERCISES

1. Assume the array *MinTemps* that Self-Test Exercise 1 describes. Consider the one-dimensional array *MT* of 364 (7 * 52) real numbers.

   a. Suppose that the first seven elements of *MT* represent the days in the first week, the second seven elements of *MT* represent the days in the second week, and so on. Which element of *MT* represents the 5th day in the 12th week? (That is, which element of *MT* corresponds to *MinTemps[5, 12]*?)

   b. Suppose that the first 52 elements of *MT* correspond to the first row of *MinTemps*, the second 52 elements of *MT* correspond to the second row of *MinTemps*, and so on. Which element of *MinTemps* corresponds to *MinTemps[5, 12]*?

2. Write the function *Average* that Self-Test Exercise 2 describes.

3. Consider the variable *CSC212* as defined in the section of this chapter entitled "Arrays of Records."

   a. Repeat Self-Test Exercise 3, but use the record *CSC212[3]* instead of *Student1*.

   b. Write statements that read names into the *Name* fields of *CSC212*. Do this both by using and by not using a *with* statement.

4. Change the definition of the *Name* field within the record type *StudentRecord*, which appears in the section "Records Within Records," so that *Name* is a record with three fields: *First*, *Middle*, *Last*.

5. Consider the variant record *Student2* that this chapter defines in the section "Variant Records." Write statements that display (print) the fields in this record by using a *case* statement. Do this both by using and by not using a *with* statement.

6. Consider the following definitions:

```
const   maxsize = 8;
type    string = packed array[1..maxsize] of char;
        person = record
            name : string;
            age  : 0..maxint
        end; { record }

var     ch : char;
        i : integer;
        aname : string;
        aperson : person;
        F1 : file of string;
        F2 : file of person;
```

What is wrong with the following statements?

```
read(aname);
for i := 1 to maxsize do { this is syntactically correct }
    readln(aname[i]);
for i := 1 to maxsize do
    read(F1, aname[i]);
if not eoln(F1)
    then read(F1, aname);
read(F2, aperson.name)
```

On the other hand, make sure that you understand that the following is legal and makes sense.

```
while not eof(F2) do

begin
    read(F2, aperson);
    writeln(aperson.name, aperson.age)
end
```

7. The procedure *SkipBlanks* advances the window of a textfile either to the next nonblank character or—if there is none—to the end-of-file symbol. Write a procedure that will skip to the next nonblank character on a line. If there is no nonblank character on the rest of the current line, your procedure should stop on the end-of-line character. In this problem there is no need to use the *Cand* operator. Why?

8. Write two procedures that each print the contents of a textfile. One procedure should use *get* and the other should use *read*.

9. Write a procedure

    ```
    AdvanceTo(var F : text; Target : char)
    ```

    that will position the file window directly over the first occurrence in the file *F* of the character that *Target* specifies. If *Target* is a blank, the procedure should position the window over the first blank in the file and *not* over an end-of-line character. If *Target* does not appear in the file, the procedure should print a message to this effect.

10. a. Consider a textfile *F* of nonnumeric data. Write a program that appends to *F* the 20 characters that it reads from the standard input file. Your program should use an internal textfile.
    b. Repeat Part *a* of this exercise, but this time assume that the textfile *F* contains integer data and that you want to append to *F* the 20 integers that you read from the standard input file.

11. Write a procedure that will append the contents of the textfile *F2* to the end of the general file *F1*. Assume that both files contain integer data. Recall that the call *rewrite(F1)* will destroy the contents of file *F1*. (*Hint:* Use a temporary internal file.)

12. Repeat Exercise 11, but this time assume that *F2* is a general file instead of a textfile.

13. Let *f* be declared by

    ```
    f : file of integer
    ```

    Write a procedure that will write to the standard output file the *last five* integers in *f*. Your procedure may call *reset* only once. You must write the integers in the same order in which they appear in the file. If there are fewer than five integers in *f*, your program should print a message to that effect, and it should print as many integers as there are.

14. Let *A*, *B*, and *C* be sets of integers. Assume that

    ```
    A := [1..5, 9]; B := [2, 4, 6, 8]; and C := [9..15, 20, 22]
    ```

    What is the value of each of the following expressions?

    a. *(4 in A) and (4 in B)*
    b. *(A * B) + [3]*
    c. *A − C*
    d. *C − [20]*
    e. *A + [10]*
    f. *B * C*
    g. *A <= B*
    h. *A >= (B − [6, 8])*
    i. *C >= C*
    j. *A + C*

15. Write some Pascal statements to read an integer into the set *S1* of *1..50*.

16. Assume the following declarations:

    ```
    type   ColorType = (red, blue, green, yellow);
    var    ColorSet : set of ColorType;
    ```

    a. Write some Pascal statements to read color names into *ColorSet* by reading one-letter codes that correspond to the colors, and by adding the appropriate color name to the set by using a *case* statement.
    b. Write some Pascal statements, including a *case* statement, to write the color names in the set *ColorSet*.

17. Write a Pascal procedure to determine which characters in a computer's character set appear at least once in a given textfile. Use a set of *char*. (Note that a reasonable alternative is to use a boolean array indexed by *char*.)

18. Write statements that keep track of which of several possible non-fatal errors occur in the course of a program's execution. Use a set of *errors*, where *errors* is an enumerated data type.

PROJECTS

19. Write a program that will read English prose and list in alphabetical order all the words that occur in the prose, along with a count of the number of times each word occurs.

The heart of this program will be a procedure that reads in a word. If you agree to treat any character other than the letters A through Z as a delimiter, then you can define a word to be any string of up to eight characters that is surrounded by delimiters. If a string between delimiters is more than eight characters, read the entire string, but truncate it to eight characters when you record it.

You can assume that there will be at most 100 distinct words in the text.

20. Write a program that simulates binary operations with n-bit quantities. Use a set of $1 . . n$ to represent an n-bit quantity: The value i is in the set if and only if the ith bit of the n-bit quantity is 1. You can state the binary operations in terms of union, intersection, and difference.

CHAPTER 3

Linked Lists

Preliminaries
> Maintaining Sorted Data in an Array
> Pointers and Linked Lists

Programming with Linked Lists
> Displaying the Contents of a Linked List
> Deleting a Specified Node from a Linked List
> Inserting a Node into a Specified Position
> Insert and Delete Procedures for a Sorted Linked List
> Saving and Restoring a Linked List by Using a File
> Using Structured Types in Data Fields

Variations of the Linked List
> Circular Linked Lists
> Dummy Head Nodes
> Doubly Linked Lists

A Case Study: Maintaining an Inventory
> Statement of the Inventory Problem
> Top-Down Design of a Solution
> Bottom-Up Implementation of the Solution
> Final Set of Refinements to the Program

Summary
Common Pitfalls/Debugging
Self-Test Exercises
Exercises
Projects

PREVIEW   This chapter introduces one more Pascal data type, the pointer, and discusses the linked list as a data structure. You can use pointers to implement a linked list in Pascal. We will develop algorithms for inserting items into and deleting items from a sorted linked list that is implemented with pointers. The techniques for performing these fundamental linked list operations are the basis of many of the data structures that appear throughout the remainder of this book. The material in this chapter is thus essential to much of the presentation in the following chapters.

The chapter concludes with a large case study of the development of a computerized system for managing the inventory of a videocassette store. The design and implementation of the solution will show you the principles and concepts of the previous two chapters in action. The size and complexity of this problem make it essential that the solution be developed in a top-down fashion and that the program be highly modular. The problem also provides a natural application for files and linked lists.

PRELIMINARIES

Why would you need another data structure, such as the linked list? We will answer this question by illustrating the deficiencies of an array. We then define Pascal pointers and use them to establish the structure of a linked list.

Maintaining Sorted Data in an Array

One of the most frequently performed computing tasks is the maintenance, in some specified order, of a collection of data. Many examples immediately come to mind: students placed in order by their names, baseball players listed in order by their batting averages, and corporations listed in order by their assets.

The problem of *maintaining* ordered data requires more than simply sorting the data. Often you need to insert some new data item into its proper, ordered place. Similarly, you often need to delete some data item. For example, suppose your university maintains an alphabetical list of the students who are currently enrolled. The registrar must insert names into and delete names from this list because students constantly enroll in and leave school.

Suppose that the array *Students* contains the list of students, as shown in Figure 3–1a. In Pascal, you could implement the array of students with the following definition:

```
const   maxstudents = 1000;
        strlen = 10;
```

```
type    string    = packed array[1..strlen] of char;
        namelist  = record
            lastpos : 0..maxstudents; { number of students }
            names   : array[1..maxstudents] of string
        end;  { record }

var     Students : namelist
```

To insert a new student name, you must find the position in the array
where the name belongs, shift to the right the names from this position
on, and insert the new name in the newly created opening. Figure 3–1b
depicts this insertion, and the following Pascal procedures perform it.

Insertion into an array requires shifting elements to make room for the new item

(a)

Figure 3-1

(a) An array of names;
(b) shifting for insertion

(b)

```
function Find(Target : string; List: namelist) : integer;
{ ---------------------------------------------------------
  Determines the insertion point for the procedure Insert.
  Precondition: The array List.names contains List.lastpos
  names in alphabetical order; List.lastpos >= 0.
  Postcondition: Returns the position (in the range
  1..List.lastpos) of the first element in the array
  List.names that is greater than or equal to Target. If
  there is no such element, returns List.lastpos + 1. If
  List.lastpos = 0 (that is, List.names is empty), returns
  1. Target and List are unchanged.
  --------------------------------------------------------- }
var Place : integer;

begin
  Place := 1;

  { find the proper position in the array }
  {loop invariant:
   all elements in List.names[1..Place-1] are < Target }
  while (Place < List.lastpos)
                  and (List.names[Place] < Target) do
    Place := Place + 1;
```

```
                { check for insertion after the last name }
            if (List.lastpos > 0) and (List.names[Place] < Target)
                then Place := Place + 1;

            Find := Place
        end;  { Find }

    procedure Insert(Newname : string; var List : namelist;
                        var Success : boolean);
    { ------------------------------------------------------
      Inserts a name into a sorted array of names.
      Precondition: The array List.names contains List.lastpos
      names in alphabetical order; List.lastpos >= 0.
      Postcondition: Inserts Newname into its proper place in
      the array List.names and sets Success to true. If the
      array is full, sets Success to false, but does not insert.
      If one or more elements already in the array are identical
      to Newname, inserts Newname in front of these elements. If
      insertion occurs, List.lastpos is increased by 1. Newname
      is unchanged.
      Calls: Find.
      ------------------------------------------------------ }
    var i, Place : 1..maxstudents;

    begin
        if List.lastpos >= maxstudents
            then Success := false

            else
            begin
                Place := Find(Newname, List); {find insertion point}

                { make room for insertion by shifting elements }
                { Note: if Place = List.lastpos + 1, the loop is
                  skipped; simply insert at end }
                for i:= List.lastpos downto Place do
                    List.names[i+1] := List.names[i];

                { insert element and count it }
                List.names[Place] := Newname;
                List.lastpos := List.lastpos + 1;
                Success := true
            end { if }
    end { Insert }
```

Now consider how to delete a student's name from the list. You could blank it out after finding the name in the list. However, this strategy can lead to gaps in the array, as Figure 3-2a illustrates. An array that is full of gaps has two significant problems:

Problems with gaps in an array

- Variable *List.lastpos* could have the value *maxstudents* even though there are empty cells in the array. As a conse-

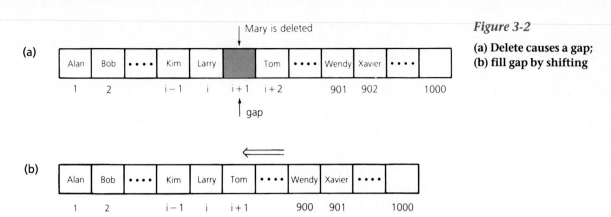

Figure 3-2

(a) Delete causes a gap;
(b) fill gap by shifting

quence, it could become impossible to insert new names into the array even when fewer than *maxstudents* names are present.

- Because the names are spread out, the *Find* procedure might have to look at every cell of the array even when only a handful of names are present.

Thus, what you really need to do is shift the elements of the array to fill the gap left by the deleted name, as shown in Figure 3-2b.

The following Pascal procedure performs the deletion by shifting. Both the type definitions and the function *Find* are the same as before.

```
procedure Delete(Name : string; var List : namelist;
                 var Success : boolean);
{ -------------------------------------------------------
  Deletes an element from a sorted array of names.
  Precondition: The array List.names contains List.lastpos
  names in alphabetical order; List.lastpos >= 0.
  Postcondition: Deletes Name from the array List.names by
  shifting array elements and sets Success to true. If Name
  is not in the array, sets Success to false and does not
  change List. If deletion occurs, List.lastpos is decreased
  by 1. Name is unchanged.
  Calls: Find.

  ------------------------------------------------------- }

var i, Place : integer;

begin
    Place := Find(Name, List); { find position of Name in array }

    { if position is after array end }
    if (Place > List.lastpos) then
       Success := false
```

```
                  { else if Name is not where expected }
                else if (Name <> List.names[Place]) then
                   Success := false

                else                                      { Name is present }
                begin                                     { shift to delete }
                   for i := Place to (List.lastpos—1) do
                        List.names[i] := List.names[i+1];

                   List.lastpos := List.lastpos — 1; { decrement count }
                   Success := true
                end
          end { Delete }
```

Pointers and Linked Lists

As you have just seen, when you use an array to maintain the sorted list of student names, you must shift data both when you insert a new data item between a specified pair of data items and when you remove an item from a specified position. It would be preferable to use other methods that did *not* require you to shift data for both insertions and deletions. How can you avoid shifting data? To get a conceptual notion of such a scheme, consider Figure 3-3.

In these diagrams, each member of the list *points to* the next member. Thus, the members of the list are *linked* to one another. Such a list is called a **linked list**. If you need to insert a new member, you simply find its place in the list and set two **pointers**. Similarly, to delete an item, you find the item and set a pointer so that the item is bypassed.

Figure 3-3 should help free you from the notion that the only way to maintain a given order of data is to store the data in that order. Although the most intuitive means of imposing an order on data is to order it physically, it is possible to use other means. In a physical ordering, the next data item in sequence after some item x is the data item that is "to the right" of x. However, in a linked list, x actually *points to* the next data item. That is, if you know where x is, you can determine x's **successor**. Thus, x's successor can be anywhere physically. This flexibility not only allows you to insert and delete data items without shifting data, it also allows you to increase the size of a linked list easily. That is, *a linked list is able to grow as needed, whereas an array can hold only a fixed number of data items.* In many applications, this flexibility gives a linked list a significant advantage.

An item in a linked list points to its successor

You can think of the linked list as an abstract data type (ADT). That is, you can describe operations on a linked list and design applications for a linked list without knowing—or caring—how to get one data item to point to another. Thus, if someone gave you Pascal subprograms that performed certain operations on a linked list, you could use them in a program to maintain a linked list without knowing the details of the subprograms' implementations. Chapter 4 will discuss abstract data types—including the linked list—in detail and demonstrate the importance of this concept. However, this chapter will focus on Pascal pointers and present the linked

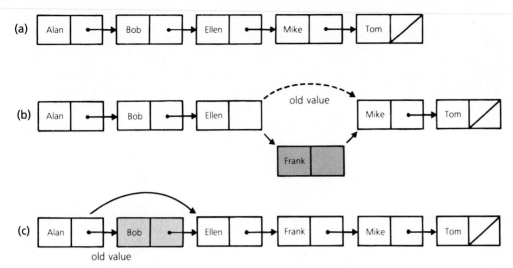

Figure 3-3
(a) A linked list of names;
(b) insertion; (c) deletion

list as a data structure. That is, you will learn how to use pointers to implement a linked list. You should note, however, that you do not need pointers to implement linked lists; other implementations are possible.

Consider the following statements, which declare the variable *p* to be an integer **pointer variable**, or simply a **pointer**:

```
type    ptr = ^integer;
var     p : ptr
```

The variable *p* is said to be an *integer pointer variable* because it can *reference a memory cell* that contains an integer. (Similarly, you can declare pointers to any other type except files.) What does it mean to *reference a memory cell?* When you declare an ordinary variable *x* to be *integer*, the Pascal compiler allocates a memory cell that can hold an integer. You use the identifier *x* to refer to this cell. To put the value 5 in the cell, you would write

```
x := 5
```

To print out the value that is in the cell, you would write

```
write('The value of x is ', x)
```

However, the declaration

```
var p : ptr
```

allocates a memory cell that can hold a reference to another memory cell that holds an integer. This reference to another memory cell is the computer's representation of the location, or **address** in memory, of the cell. Figure 3-4 illustrates a pointer that points to an integer.

The notion of one memory cell that references another memory cell is a bit tricky. In the previous example, it is important to keep in mind that the content of *p* is not an integer in the usual sense. The content of *p* is of

Figure 3-4

A pointer to an integer

interest only because it tells you where in memory to look for the integer value (5 in Figure 3-4). That is, you can get to the integer value *indirectly* by following the reference that *p* contains.

Now consider how you can actually use *p* to get to the integer to which *p* points. In Pascal you are not allowed to look at the address that *p* contains. For example, you cannot say

```
write(p)
```

p^ is the memory cell pointed to by p

So how can you get to the integer in the memory cell that *p* references? Suppose that *p* points to a memory cell that contains the value 5. More precisely, *p* contains the address of a memory cell that contains the value 5. In Pascal, *p^* refers to *the memory cell to which p points,* as shown in Figure 3-5. Thus, in this example, the value of *p^* is 5 and *write(p^)* writes 5.

You also use the *p^* notation to store a value in the memory cell to which *p* points. For example, you can put the value 7 into the memory cell that *p* points to by using the assignment statement

```
p^ := 7
```

After this assignment, the expression *p^* has the value 7, because 7 is now the value in the memory cell to which *p* points. Notice that the assignment statement

```
p := 7        { THIS STATEMENT IS ILLEGAL }
```

is illegal because there is a type clash: 7 is an integer, while *p* is a pointer, which can contain only a *reference* to (that is, an *address* of) a memory cell that contains an integer.

If you also had the declaration

```
var q : ptr
```

you could assign to *q* the value in *p* by using the assignment statement

```
q := p
```

Figure 3-5

p versus p^

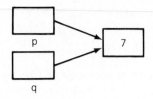

Figure 3-6

Two pointers that reference the same memory cell

Pointer *q* now points to the same memory cell that *p* points to, as Figure 3-6 illustrates.

Now for the big question: How do you get a pointer variable to point to a memory cell in the first place? To begin, there is an important restriction on what a pointer variable can point to. If you had the declarations

```
var    p : ^integer;
       x : integer
```

you could *not* get *p* to point to the memory cell associated with *x*. (Remember that *p* := *x* is illegal.) The compiler allocates **static** memory to all variables that you declare by using standard variable declarations—static because the memory is allocated before the program (or subprogram) executes. This execution does not affect the memory requirements of these variables.

In contrast, pointer variables do not point to these statically allocated memory cells, but rather to memory cells that the system allocates **dynamically**. Until there is a memory cell for *p* to reference, *p* does not point to anything, its value is undefined, and it is in effect useless, as Figure 3-7a illustrates. Pascal allocates dynamic memory by means of the predefined procedure *new*, which takes a pointer variable for its argument, as in

```
new(p)
```

new allocates memory dynamically

This procedure call allocates a new memory cell and initializes *p* so that *p* points to this new cell, as Figure 3-7b illustrates. Because *p* is an integer

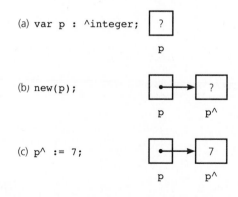

Figure 3-7

(a) Declaring a pointer variable; (b) allocating memory dynamically; (c) assigning a value

pointer, the new cell can contain only an integer. However, if you declare *p* as

> **var** p : ^char   { pointer to a character }

then *new(p)* would create a memory cell in which you could place a character.

Observe that this newly created memory cell has no name in the usual sense. The only way to get at its contents or to put contents in it is indirectly via the pointer *p*. That is, *p*^ references the newly created cell. As Figure 3-7c shows, the statement *p*^ *:= 7* assigns 7 to the newly created memory cell. The simple program in Figure 3-8 should serve to illustrate these concepts further.

The last assignment statement in Figure 3–8 indicates a problem: What should you do with a memory cell that you no longer need? Simply removing all references to the cell is wasteful, as the cell is no longer accessible, even though it remains allocated to the program. Pascal provides the pre-

dispose returns memory to the   defined procedure *dispose* as a counterpart to *new*. Conceptually, the call
system for reuse   *dispose(p)* returns to the system the memory cell pointed to by *p* and sets *p* to an undefined value. That is, *dispose* in effect deallocates memory from a program, thus freeing the memory for future use by this or other programs.

Although most of the mechanics of pointers have been illustrated, it is

Figure 3-8

Programming with pointer variables

not yet completely clear how you can use them to implement a linked list (like the one pictured in Figure 3-3). After all, each item on a linked list

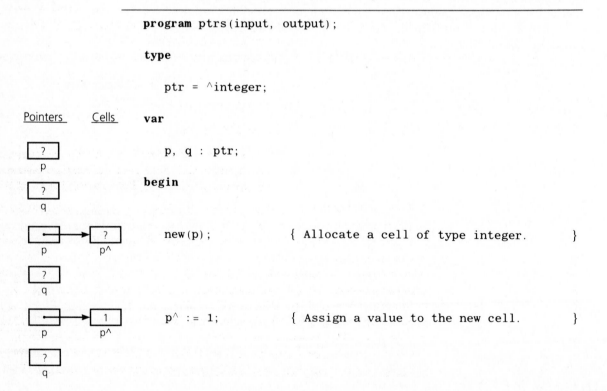

```
program ptrs(input, output);

type

    ptr = ^integer;

var

    p, q : ptr;

begin

    new(p);              { Allocate a cell of type integer.      }

    p^ := 1;             { Assign a value to the new cell.       }
```

Pointers   Cells

Pointers   Cells

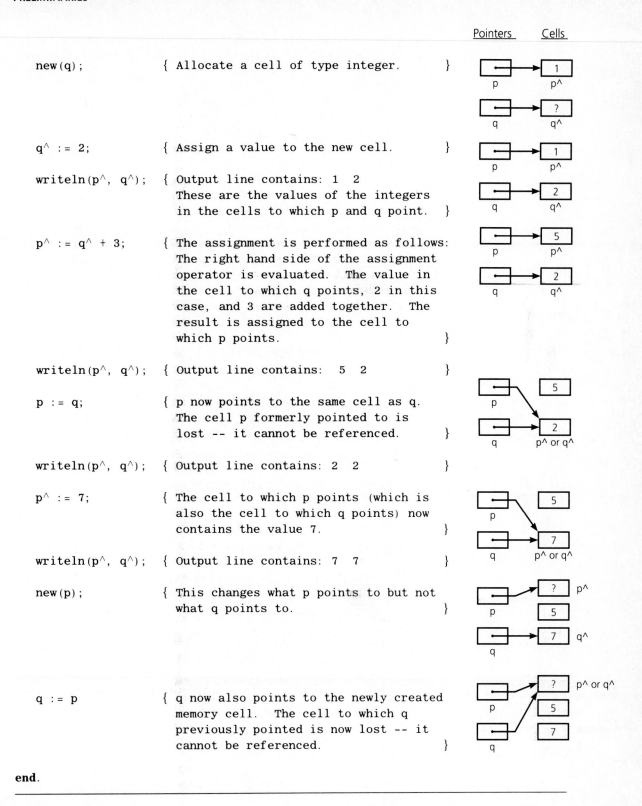

new(q);   { Allocate a cell of type integer.   }

q^ := 2;   { Assign a value to the new cell.   }

writeln(p^, q^);   { Output line contains: 1   2
                          These are the values of the integers
                          in the cells to which p and q point.   }

p^ := q^ + 3;   { The assignment is performed as follows:
                          The right hand side of the assignment
                          operator is evaluated. The value in
                          the cell to which q points, 2 in this
                          case, and 3 are added together. The
                          result is assigned to the cell to
                          which p points.   }

writeln(p^, q^);   { Output line contains: 5   2   }

p := q;   { p now points to the same cell as q.
                          The cell p formerly pointed to is
                          lost -- it cannot be referenced.   }

writeln(p^, q^);   { Output line contains: 2   2   }

p^ := 7;   { The cell to which p points (which is
                          also the cell to which q points) now
                          contains the value 7.   }

writeln(p^, q^);   { Output line contains: 7   7   }

new(p);   { This changes what p points to but not
                          what q points to.   }

q := p   { q now also points to the newly created
                          memory cell. The cell to which q
                          previously pointed is now lost -- it
                          cannot be referenced.   }

end.

contains both a data value—an integer, for example—and a pointer to the next item. Consider now how you can set up such a list, how you can print out the information on a linked list, and how you can insert into and delete from a linked list.

Since each item on the list must contain two pieces of information—the data value and a reference to the next item on the list—it is natural to conclude that each item on the list should be a record. One field of the record is the data and the other is a pointer. A record of this form is usually called a **node**.

Suppose that the data portion of each node contained an integer. What type of pointer should you use within a node, and to what will it point? You might guess that the pointer should point to an integer, but actually it must point to a record, because the nodes of the list are indeed records and not integers. Thus, a record of type *node* will have as one of its fields a pointer to type *node*. This idea is perhaps difficult to comprehend: Each record of type *node* contains a pointer to another record of type *node*.

The type definitions are thus

A node in a linked list is usually a record

```
type  ptr = ^node;   { note that node is not yet defined }
      node = record
          data : integer;
          next : ptr
      end
```

Note that these statements define *ptr* to be ^*node* before they define *node*. In all other contexts, Pascal does not allow you to use a type in a *type* definition before you define it. However, for pointers, this syntax is legal. The compiler flags *node* as an unknown type and comes back to that type when it eventually encounters its definition. Figure 3-9 illustrates a node described by the previous record definitions.

Now the declaration

```
var p : ptr
```

declares a pointer variable *p* to be of type *ptr*; that is, *p* can point to a node of type ^*node*.

There are two minor issues to consider. First, what is the value of the *next* field in the last node on the list? Pascal provides the constant *nil*, which you can assign to a pointer of any type. By convention, a *nil* pointer value means that the pointer does not point to anything. By setting the *next* field of the last record of the list equal to *nil*, you can easily detect when you are at the end of the list. It is common to confuse a pointer variable whose value is *nil* with one whose value is not initialized. Until you explicitly assign a value to a pointer variable, its value—like that of

A pointer whose value is nil does not point to anything

Figure 3-9

A list node

data   next

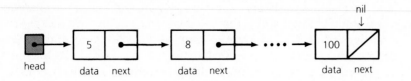

Figure 3-10

A head pointer to a list

any other variable—is undefined. You should not assume that its value is *nil*.

Second, nothing points to the beginning of the list, and if you cannot get to the beginning of the list, you cannot get to the second node on the list, and if you cannot get to the second node on the list, you cannot get to the third node on the list, and so on. The solution is to have an additional pointer whose purpose is to point to the first node on the list. Such a node is called the **head pointer** or simply the **head** of the list. Figure 3-10 pictures a linked list with a head pointer.

The head pointer points to the first node in a linked list

Observe in Figure 3-10 that the pointer variable *head* is different from the other pointers in the diagram in that it is not part of a record. Rather, it is a simple pointer variable that is external to the list, and it serves as a way of getting to the list's beginning. Also, note that the variable *head* always exists, even at times when there are no nodes on the list. The declaration

```
var head : ptr
```

creates the variable *head* whose value, like that of other uninitialized variables, is undefined. To what value should you initialize *head* and to what value should you change it if a list ever becomes empty? In both cases, assigning *head* the value *nil* is a logical choice, as this indicates that *head* does not point to anything.

If head is nil, the list is empty

It is a common mistake to think that before you can assign *head* a value, you must make the call *new(head)*. This misconception is rooted in the belief that the variable *head* does not exist before the call. This is not at all true; *head* is a declared pointer variable waiting to be assigned a value. Thus, for example, you can assign *nil* to *head* without first calling *new(head)*. In fact, the effect of the sequence

```
new(head);        { An incorrect use of new }
head := nil
```

is to cause the only reference—*head*—to the newly created node to be lost, as Figure 3-11 illustrates.

So far, you have seen that you can use pointer variables to implement a linked list. However, you have not seen how to perform operations that

 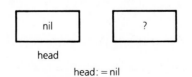

Figure 3-11

A lost cell

alter the structure of the list. The next section develops these operations. As you study the operations that alter the structure of a list, the potential advantages of a linked list over an array will become more apparent. One of these advantages was indicated already: You do not need to shift the data when you insert items into or delete items from a linked list. A second advantage of perhaps more importance is a result of the use of pointers to implement the linked list. It concerns the ability to use the Pascal procedure *new* to dynamically allocate memory cells for a program. Because you can use *new* to allocate memory cells as needed, you do not require an estimate of the amount of data that the program will have to handle. Contrast this with a static array. If you use an array to store a list of student names, you need an upper bound on the number of students that you must handle. *The ability of a linked list to grow as needed is a major advantage.*

Linked lists do not have a fixed size

However, linked lists can have disadvantages. For example, suppose that you wanted to access the nth node in the linked list in Figure 3-10. You would have to access the first node and get the pointer to the second node, access the second node and get the pointer to the third node, and so on until you finally accessed the nth node. Clearly, the time it takes you to access the first node is less than the time it takes to access the tenth node. That is, the **access time** depends on n. In contrast, you can access the nth item in the array A by using $A[n]$. Accessing either $A[1]$ or $A[10]$ takes the same amount of time. That is, the access time is constant for an array.

The time to access the nth node in a linked list depends on n

Beginning in the next sections and continuing through most of the book, we shall emphasize the importance of choosing between a **pointer-based solution** and an **array-based solution**. Although you have just seen the advantage of using a pointer-based linked list, it is not always the best choice. For many applications, an array-based solution is more appropriate. You will learn how to choose an appropriate structure to solve a particular problem as you progress through this book. For now, you should become comfortable with the mechanics of what was done in this section.

PROGRAMMING WITH LINKED LISTS

The previous section illustrated how you can use pointer variables to implement a linked list. This section develops algorithms for displaying the data portions of such a linked list and for inserting items into and deleting items from a sorted linked list. These linked list operations play a central role in the case study that appears later in this chapter, and they are the basis of many of the data structures that appear throughout the remainder of the book. Thus, the material in this section is essential to much of the discussion in the following chapters.

Displaying the Contents of a Linked List

Suppose now that you have a linked list, as was pictured in Figure 3-10, and that you want to write out the contents of its data fields. A high-level pseudocode solution is

```
Set the current position to the first record on the list
while not at the end of the list do
begin
    Print out the data field of the record at the current
      position
    Advance the current position to the next record on the
      list
end
```

This solution makes it clear that you need to keep track of the current position on the list. That is, you need a pointer variable to point to the record that you are working with. Thus, you must have the following additional declaration:

```
var cur : ptr
```

To initialize *cur* to point to the first record, simply let *cur* point to the same record that *head* points to by writing

```
cur := head
```

To write out the data field of the current record, you use the statement

```
writeln(cur^.data)
```

This statement makes sense because *cur^* refers to a record, which you must qualify by supplying a field name. Finally, to advance the current position to the next record, you write

```
cur := cur^.next
```

Figure 3-12 illustrates this action. If the previous assignment statement is not clear, consider

```
temp := cur^.next;
cur := temp
```

and then convince yourself that the intermediate variable *temp* is not necessary.

Figure 3-12

The effect of the assignment
cur := cur^.next

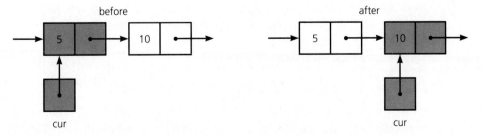

These ideas lead to the *PrintList* procedure.

```
procedure PrintList(head : ptr);
{ -----------------------------------------------------------
  Prints the data in a linked list.
  Precondition: head is a pointer variable that points to
  the linked list.
  Postcondition: Writes the data in the linked list to the
  standard output file. Both head and the list are unchanged.
  ----------------------------------------------------------- }
var cur : ptr;
begin
    cur := head;

    { Loop invariant: cur points to the next node to be
      printed }
    while cur <> nil do
    begin
       writeln(cur^.data);
       cur := cur^.next
    end { while }
end { PrintList }
```

Notice the condition in the *while* statement. As written, *cur* points to each node in a nonempty list during the course of the *while* loop's execution, and so the data portion of each node is printed. After the last node is printed, *cur* becomes *nil* and the *while* loop terminates. When the list is empty—that is, when *head* is *nil*—the *while* loop is correctly skipped.

A common error is to use *cur^.next* instead of *cur* in the *while* statement. When *cur* points to the last node of a nonempty list, *cur^.next* is *nil*, and so the *while* loop would terminate before printing the data in the last node. In addition, when the list is empty—that is, when *cur* is *nil*—*cur^.next* is undefined and causes an error.

A traverse operation visits each node in the list

The procedure *PrintList* uses **list traversal**, which is a common operation. A traversal sequentially **visits** each node on the list until it reaches the end of the list. *PrintList* prints the data field of each node when it visits the node. Later in this book, you will see that there are other useful things that you can do to a node during a visit.

To write the contents of a linked list, you had to assume that somehow the linked list was set up in advance. We will now show you operations that actually alter the structure of a linked list. These operations allow you to delete nodes from and insert nodes into an existing linked list. Ultimately, you will see how to build a linked list from scratch.

Deleting a Specified Node from a Linked List

So that you can address the problem of deleting a specified node from a linked list, assume that the list shown in Figure 3-13 already exists. Notice that, in addition to *head*, the diagram includes two external pointer variables, *cur* and *prev*, which the following statements declare:

```
var    cur  : ptr;   { pointer to current node }
       prev : ptr    { pointer to previous node }
```

The task is to delete the node to which *cur* points. The role of the pointer variable *prev* will become apparent in a moment.

As Figure 3-13 indicates, you can delete node *N*, which *cur* points to, by altering the value of the pointer field *next* in the node that precedes *N*. You need to set this pointer so that it points to the node that follows *N*, thus bypassing *N* on the chain. Notice that this pointer change does not directly affect the node *N*. Node *N* remains in existence, and it points to the same node that it pointed to before the deletion. However, the node has effectively been deleted from the list. For example, notice that the procedure *PrintList* from the previous section would not print the contents of the node *N*.

To accomplish this pointer change in Pascal, notice first that if you had only the pointer *cur* that points to *N*, there would be no direct way of getting to the node that precedes *N*. After all, you cannot follow the links on the list backward. However, notice the pointer variable *prev* in Figure 3-13. *If you are to delete the node N from a linked list, you need a pointer to the node that precedes N.*

If you do have a pointer variable *prev* that points to the node preceding *N*, the pointer change suggested by Figure 3-13 is easy to implement in Pascal. The following assignment statement is all that you require to delete the node that *cur* points to:

```
prev^.next := cur^.next
```

Deleting an interior node

There are two questions to answer about the deletion of a node from a linked list.

- How did the variables *cur* and *prev* come to point to the appropriate nodes?
- Does the previous method work for any node *N*, regardless of where in the linked list it appears?

To answer the first question, consider the context in which you might expect to delete a node. In one common situation, you need to delete a

Figure 3-13

Deleting a node from a linked list

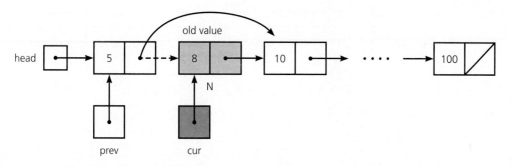

node that contains a particular data value. In other words, you do not pass the values of *cur* and *prev* to the `Delete` procedure, but instead `Delete` establishes these values as its first step by searching the list for the node *N* that contains the data value to be deleted. Once `Delete` finds the node *N*—and the node that precedes *N*—the deletion of *N* proceeds as described previously. The details of such a `Delete` procedure appear later in this section.

In answer to the second question, the method described does not work if the node to be deleted is the *first* node on the list. If the node to be deleted is the first node on the list, it certainly does not make sense to assert that *prev* points to the node that precedes this node! Thus, *deletion of the first node on a linked list is a special case,* as Figure 3-14 depicts.

When you delete the first node of the list, you must change the value of *head* to reflect the fact that, after the deletion, there is a new first node on the list. That is, the node that was second prior to the deletion is now first. You make this change to *head* by using the assignment statement

Deleting the first node

```
head := cur^.next
```

As was the case for the deletion of an interior node, the pointers bypass the old first node, although it still exists. Notice also that if the node to be deleted is the *only* node on the list—and thus it is also the first node—the previous assignment statement assigns the value *nil* to the variable *head*. Recall that the value *nil* in *head* indicates an empty list, and so this assignment statement handles the deletion of the only node on a list correctly.

It is really a bit wasteful that node *N* still exists after its deletion from the list. Once you change the value of *cur* so that it no longer points to *N*, *N* will be in a state of limbo—it still requires storage space, even though the program can no longer access it. If a program were to accumulate many nodes in this limbo state, its storage requirements might become unreasonably high. Therefore, before you change the value of *cur*, you should use the statement

Return deleted nodes to the system by using `dispose`

```
dispose(cur)
```

to return node *N* to the system.

Figure 3-14

Deleting the first node

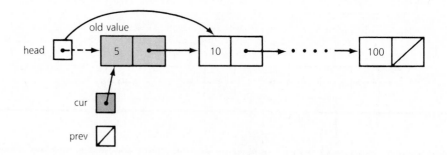

You have seen the mechanics of deleting a specified node from a linked list. Shortly, we shall incorporate these techniques into a Pascal procedure for deleting a node that contains a specified data value.

Inserting a Node into a Specified Position

Figure 3-15 illustrates the technique of inserting a new node into a specified position of a linked list. You insert the new node, to which the pointer variable *newitem* points, between the two nodes that *prev* and *cur* point to. As the diagram suggests, you can accomplish the insertion by using the pair of assignment statements

```
newitem^.next := cur;
prev^.next := newitem
```

Inserting a node between nodes

The following two questions are analogous to those previously asked about the deletion of a node:

- How did the variables *newitem*, *cur*, and *prev* come to point to the appropriate nodes?
- Does the method work for inserting a node into any position of a list?

The answer to the first question, like the answer to the corresponding question for the *Delete* operation, is found by considering the context in which you will use the *Insert* operation. The case study given later in this chapter, for example, maintains a sorted linked list of cassette titles. That problem requires a procedure to insert a new title into its proper sorted position in the list. The first step of such an *Insert* procedure is to establish the values of *cur* and *prev* by traversing the list until you find the proper sorted position for the new title. You then create a new node, to which *newitem* points, by calling Pascal's *new* procedure:

```
new(newitem)
```

After you establish the data portion of this new node, you insert it into the list, as was just described. The details of the *Insert* procedure appear in the next section.

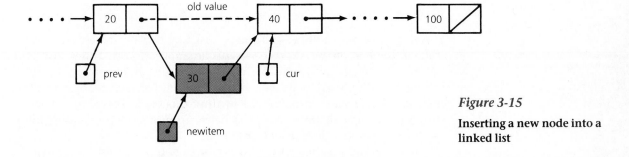

Figure 3-15

Inserting a new node into a linked list

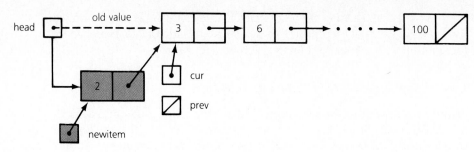

Figure 3-16

Inserting at the beginning of a linked list

The answer to the second question is that *insertion, like deletion, must account for special cases*. First, consider the insertion of a node at the beginning of the list, as shown in Figure 3-16. You must make *head* point to the new node and the new node point to the node that had been at the beginning of the list. You accomplish this by using these statements:

Inserting a node at the beginning of a list

```
newitem^.next := head;
head := newitem
```

Observe that if the list is empty before the insertion, *head* is *nil*, so the *next* field of the new item is set to *nil*. This step is correct because the new item is the last item—as well as the first item—on the list.

Inserting a new node at the end of a list, as shown in Figure 3-17, is also a special case, because the intention of the pair of assignment statements

If cur is nil, inserting at the end of a list is not a special case

```
newitem^.next := cur;
prev^.next := newitem
```

is to insert the new node *between* the node that *cur* points to and the node that *prev* points to. If you are to insert the new node at the end of the list, to what node should *cur* point? In this situation it makes sense to view the value of *cur* as *nil* because as you traverse the list, *cur* becomes *nil* as it moves past the end of the list. Observe that if *cur* has the value *nil* and *prev* points to the last node on the list, then the previous pair of assignment statements will indeed insert the new node at the end of the list.

Insert and Delete Procedures for a Sorted Linked List

You will often have a linked list that is sorted by its data values. The case study at the end of this chapter presents an application that uses such a linked list. There are also many problems that require you to order a linked list in ways other than by its data values. Examples of such problems and their solutions appear throughout Part III of this book. This section constructs procedures to insert into and delete from a sorted linked list by using the previously developed techniques.

To be more precise, this section implements the following two procedures:

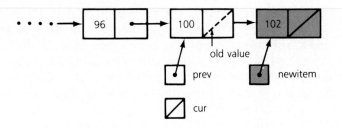

Figure 3-17

Inserting at the end of a linked list

```
Insert(head, X, Success)
```

{ Inserts a new node into a sorted linked list.
  Precondition: head points to a sorted linked list; X is
  the value to be inserted.
  Postcondition: Inserts X into its proper sorted position
  in the sorted linked list unless the list already contains
  an item with value X, in which case no insertion occurs. X
  is unchanged; the list and possibly head are changed if X
  is inserted. The boolean flag Success is true if the
  insertion is successful, otherwise it is false. }

```
Delete(head, X, Success)
```

{ Deletes a specified node from a sorted linked list.
  Precondition: head points to a sorted linked list; X is
  the value to be deleted.
  Postcondition: Deletes the data item equal to X, if it is
  present, from the sorted linked list. X is unchanged; the
  list and possibly head are changed if X is deleted. The
  boolean flag Success is true if the deletion is
  successful, otherwise it is false. }

Implementation of *Insert*.   The specification of the *Insert* procedure
does not allow the list to contain two items with the same value. This
restriction is arbitrary, and, in fact, you might very well wish to allow
duplicate values in some applications, in which case you would modify the
Insert procedure accordingly. In the case study to follow, duplicates are
not allowed, so this implementation of *Insert* does not allow duplicates.
However, the treatment of duplicates is a final refinement to the solution.
Initially, the assumption is that the list does not already contain the new
data that you want to insert.

There are three high-level steps in the insertion process:

1. Determine the point of insertion.   *Three steps to insert a new node*
2. Create a new node and store the new data in it.
3. Connect the new node to the list by changing pointers.

As was observed previously, to determine the point at which the value
X should be inserted into a sorted list, you must traverse the list from its
beginning until you find the appropriate place for X. This appropriate place
is just before the node that contains the first data item greater than X. You

know that you will need a pointer *cur* to the node that is to follow the new node; that is, *cur* points to the node that contains the first data item greater than *X*. You also need a pointer *prev* to the node that is to precede the new node; that is, *prev* points to the node that contains the last data item smaller than *X*. Thus, as you traverse the list, you keep a *trailing* pointer. When you reach the node that contains the first value larger than *X*, the trailing pointer points to the previous node. At this time, you can insert the new node between the two nodes that *prev* and *cur* point to, as was described earlier.

A first attempt at some pseudocode that refines the three steps in the algorithm follows:

A first attempt at a solution

```
{ STEP 1: Determine the point of insertion }
{ initialize prev and cur to start the traversal from the
  beginning of the list }
prev := nil
cur := head

{ advance prev and cur as long as X > the current data item }
{ Loop invariant: X > all data portions in node 1 through
  node that prev points to }
while X > cur^.data do
begin
    prev := cur
    cur := cur^.next
end

{ STEP 2: Create a new node—with newitem pointing to it—and
          store the new data in it }
new(newitem)
newitem^.data := X

{ STEP 3 : Connect the new node, which newitem points to, to
           the list by changing pointers so that insertion
           is between the two nodes that prev and cur point to }
newitem^.next := cur
prev^.next := newitem
```

The earlier discussion should have alerted you to the fact that there are two special cases to watch for:

Special cases

- The insertion of a node at the beginning of the list
- The insertion of a node at the end of the list

You have already seen how to handle these special cases, but in the context of this *Insert* procedure, the detection of the special cases is somewhat tricky.

First consider the insertion of a node at the beginning of the list. This situation arises when the value *X* to be inserted is *smaller* than all the values currently on the list. In this case, the *while* loop in Step 1 of the previous pseudocode is never entered, so *prev* and *cur* maintain their original values. In particular, *prev* maintains its original value of *nil*. Since this is the only situation in which the value of *prev* is equal to *nil* after the *while* loop, you can detect an insertion at the beginning of the list by comparing *prev* to *nil*. Thus, you can refine the insertion pseudocode by replacing Step 3 with the following:

When `prev = nil`*, insertion is at the beginning of the list*

```
{ STEP 3 : Connect the new node }
{ test for insertion at the beginning of the list }
if (prev = nil)
    then           { insert new node at beginning of the list }
    begin
       newitem^.next := head
       head := newitem
    end

    else           { insert new node between the two nodes that }
    begin          { prev and cur point to }
       newitem^.next := cur
       prev^.next := newitem
    end
```

Correct version of Step 3

The second special case, insertion at the end of the list, arises when the value *X* to be inserted is *greater* than all the values currently on the list. As was noted earlier, you can handle insertion at the end of the list by using the standard pair of assignment statements:

```
newitem^.next := cur
prev^.next := newitem
```

provided that *prev* points to the last node on the list and that the value of *cur* is *nil*. However, the *while* loop

```
while X > cur^.data do   { this loop causes an error }
begin
   prev := cur
   cur := cur^.next
end
```

The loop in Step 1 causes a problem

in Step 1 of the pseudocode causes a difficulty because *X* is greater than all the values on the list. Eventually, the *while* statement compares *X* to the value in the last node. During that execution of the loop, *cur* is assigned the value *nil*. After this iteration, *X* is again compared to *cur^.data*. This reference to the pointer *cur*, when its value is *nil*, results in a program error.

To solve this problem, you need another test in the termination condition of the *while* loop so that the loop exits when *cur* becomes *nil*. Thus, in Step 1 of the pseudocode, you replace the *while* statement with

```
while (cur <> nil) Cand (X > cur^.data) do
```

The correct `while` *statement for Step 1*

Recall that the *Cand* (conditional and) operator does not evaluate its second operand if its first operand is false. (Also recall that you implement

Cand in Pascal by using a boolean flag.) Notice how this `while` statement solves the problem of inserting a node at the end of the list. In the case where *X* is greater than all the values on the list, *prev* points to the last node on the list and *cur* becomes *nil*, thus terminating the `while` loop. Therefore, you can insert the new node at the end of the list by using the standard pair of assignment statements

```
newitem^.next := cur
prev^.next := newitem
```

Observe that the solution correctly handles insertion into an empty list as a special case of insertion at the beginning of the list. When the list is empty, the statement `cur := head` assigns *cur* an initial value of *nil*, and thus the `while` loop is never entered. Therefore, *prev* maintains its original value of *nil*, indicating an insertion at the beginning of the list. In the revised Step 3, the statement `newitem^.next := head` executes next and assigns *nil* to the new node's *next* field. Thus, the new node is set up correctly as both the first and the last node on the list.

You now have a satisfactory solution at the pseudocode level for inserting *X* into a linked list that does not already contain *X*. Notice that the major difficulty in developing a Pascal *Insert* procedure from this solution is the fact that Pascal does not support the *Cand* operator. This limitation forces you to simulate its action by using a boolean flag. Thus, the pseudocode for Step 1, which is

```
prev := nil
cur := head

{ advance prev and cur as long as X > the current data
  item }
{ Loop invariant: X > all data portions in node 1
  through node that prev points to }
while (cur <> nil) Cand (X > cur^.data) do
begin
    prev := cur
    cur := cur^.next
end
```

is implemented in Pascal as follows:

```
{ STEP 1: Determine the point of insertion }
    prev := nil;
    cur := head;

    Done := false;
    { boolean Done becomes true when cur points to a
      value <= X }

    { advance prev and cur as long as X > the current data
      item }
```

```
while (cur <> nil) and (not Done) do
{ Loop invariant: X > all data portions in node 1
  through node that prev points to }
begin
   if (X > cur^.data)
       then
       begin
          prev := cur;
          cur := cur^.next
       end

       else Done := true
end   { while }
```

Notice that if *X* did exist in the list and if you allowed duplicates, then the solution would insert *X* before the first node that contained *X*.

Finally, suppose that you want to prevent the insertion of a value that is already present in the list. You can accomplish this task by checking, upon termination of the *while* loop in Step 1, whether *X* is equal to the value in the node that *cur* points to. If it is, then a duplicate of *X* is in the list, so the insertion is disallowed. Notice that you must be careful to avoid this check when the value of *cur* is *nil*. You can write this check most naturally in pseudocode by using the *Cor* (conditional or) operator as follows:

```
{ STEP 1a: Check for duplicates }
if (cur = nil) Cor (X <> cur^.data)
    then X is not a duplicate value
    else X is a duplicate value
```

Disallow duplicates

As Pascal does not support the *Cor* operator, you need to eliminate it, as you saw in Chapter 2. Notice how we implemented *Cor* in the Pascal procedure that follows shortly.

There is only one small Pascal issue that is left to discuss: how to pass the list's head pointer variable to the procedure. Should the head pointer be a value parameter or a variable (*var*) parameter? It must be a variable parameter, but the reasoning is complex. If your first instinct is that *head* must be a variable parameter because the procedure will alter the nodes on the list to which *head* points, you have reached the right conclusion, but for the wrong reason.

Consider what would happen if you passed the head pointer as a value parameter. Figure 3-18 illustrates that although the procedure copies the actual parameter *p* into the formal parameter *head*, the list nodes themselves are *not* copied. Thus, if the procedure makes any changes to the nodes on the list, the changes are made to the actual nodes, not to local copies of the nodes; that is, *any changes the procedure makes to the list are not localized to the procedure.*

Thus, passing the head of a list to a procedure as a value parameter allows the procedure to modify the nodes on the list and even to insert and delete nodes. Therefore, it now would seem that *head* could be a value parameter in the *Insert* procedure. This assumption would be correct if not for the possibility that the procedure will change the value of *head* itself. If the procedure inserts the new node at the beginning of the list, it changes the value of *head*, and this change must be reflected in the actual parameter (*p* in Figure 3-18) that corresponds to *head*. This required change in *p* is the only reason that *head* needs to be a variable parameter!

The Pascal version of the *Insert* procedure is as follows:

*The final code for **Insert***

```
procedure Insert(var head : ptr; X : integer;
                     var Success : boolean);
{ ---------------------------------------------------------
  Inserts a node into a sorted linked list; disallows
  duplicates.
  Precondition: head points to a sorted linked list; X is
  the value to be inserted.
  Postcondition: Inserts X into its proper sorted position
  in the sorted linked list unless the list already contains
  an item with value X, in which case no insertion occurs. X
  is unchanged; the list and possibly head are changed if X
  is inserted. The boolean flag Success is true if the
  insertion is successful, otherwise it is false.
  --------------------------------------------------------- }
var cur, prev, newitem : ptr;
    Done, Duplicate : boolean;

begin
    { STEP 1: Determine the point of insertion }
    { initialize prev and cur to start the traversal from }
    { the beginning of the list }
    prev := nil;
    cur := head;

    Done := false;
    { boolean Done becomes true when cur points to a
      value >= X }

    { advance prev and cur as long as X > the current data
      item }
    while (cur <> nil) and (not Done) do
```

Figure 3-18

A head pointer as a value parameter

```
    { Loop invariant: X > all data portions in node 1
      through node that prev points to }
begin
    if (X > cur^.data)
        then
        begin
            prev := cur;
            cur := cur^.next
        end

        else Done := true
end   { while }

{ STEP 1a: Check for duplicates: is X in list already?
  Boolean Duplicate is true if X is already in list,
  otherwise it is false.}
if (cur = nil) then                { if list is empty }
    Duplicate := false             { then X is not in list }
else if (X <> cur^.data ) then { if X <> value in node }
    Duplicate := false             { then X is not in list }
else Duplicate := true;            { else X is in list }

if not Duplicate                   { if X is not in list, }
    then                           { insert it by connecting }
    begin                          { new node to the list }
        { STEP 2: create a new node, which newitem points
          to, and store the new data in it }
        new(newitem);
        newitem^.data := X;

        { STEP 3: Connect the new node to the list }
        if (prev = nil) {is insertion at beginning of list?}
            then   { insert new node at beginning of list }
            begin
                newitem^.next := head;
                head := newitem
            end

            else  { insert new node between the two nodes }
            begin {    that prev and cur point to }
                newitem^.next := cur;
                prev^.next := newitem
            end;

            Success := true { insertion is successful }
    end   { not a duplicate }

    else Success := false    {disallow insertion — X in list
                              already }
end   { Insert }
```

Implementation of `Delete`.   Now turn your attention to implementing the `Delete` procedure for a sorted linked list. Much of the reasoning for `Delete` is analogous to that for `Insert`, so we present only one level of pseudocode and leave the Pascal procedure as an exercise. You may wish to review the earlier discussion of the mechanics of deleting a specified node.

There are three high-level steps in the deletion process.

Three steps to delete a node

1. *Locate the node in the list that you want to delete.*
2. *Disconnect this node from the list by changing*
   pointers.
3. *Return the node to the system.*

These steps refine into the following pseudocode for the `Delete` procedure:

```
Delete(head, X, Success)

{ Deletes a specified node from a sorted linked list.
  Precondition: head points to a sorted linked list; X is
  the value to be deleted.
  Postcondition: Deletes the data item equal to X, if it is
  present, from the sorted linked list. X is unchanged; the
  list and possibly head are changed if X is deleted. The
  boolean flag Success is true if the deletion is
  successful, otherwise it is false. }
begin
{ STEP 1: Locate node in the list that you want to delete }
    { initialize for traversal from the beginning of the list }
    prev := nil
    cur := head

    { traverse until you find X or pass the point where
      it would be——notice the conditional and }
    while (cur <> nil) Cand (X > cur^.data) do
    begin
       prev := cur
       cur := cur^.next
    end   { while }

{ STEP 2: If X is present, disconnect its node from the list by
  changing pointers. Note the conditional and }
    if (cur <> nil) Cand (X = cur^.data)
       then
       begin     {check for deletion from beginning of the list }
          if (prev = nil)
             then head := cur^.next
             else prev^.next := cur^.next
          Success := true
       end
```

```
    else Success := false
{ STEP 3: Return the node to the system }
   dispose(cur)
end  {Delete}
```

The major stumbling block to a Pascal implementation is again the *Cand* operator. However, you saw how to remove *Cand* in Chapter 2 and again in the implementation of the *Insert* procedure. The implementation of *Delete* is left as an exercise.

There is one more issue to raise: What is the fate of any pointer variable that points to a disposed node? The procedure call *dispose(p)* returns an undefined value for *p*. Thus, it is impossible for a program to follow *p* to a node that is no longer active. However, consider the situation

```
   q := p;
   dispose(p)
```

The pointer q points to a disposed node

as illustrated in Figure 3-19. Even though *dispose* returns *p* as undefined, *q* still points to the disposed node. Later the system might reallocate this node—via the *new* procedure—and *q* may still point to it. You can imagine some of the errors that might ensue if a program mistakenly followed the pointer *q* and reached a node within an entirely unexpected data structure! It would be useful if the *dispose* procedure could eliminate the potential for this type of program error by setting to *nil* all pointers to a disposed node. Unfortunately, this task is very difficult. Because the procedure *dispose* cannot determine which variables—in addition to *p*—point to the node to be freed, it will have to remain the programmer's responsibility not to follow a pointer to a freed node.

Saving and Restoring a Linked List by Using a File

As a final problem, we discuss how you can save and restore a linked list by using an external file, so that you can preserve the list between runs of a program. The case study in this chapter utilizes this technique in a business application. The program maintains a linked list of information about a retail store's inventory. Since the program is not running continually, you

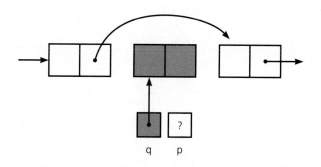

Figure 3-19

An incorrect reference to a deleted and disposed node

need a way to save the list so that the program can restore it each time you run the program.

The technique is demonstrated here by saving and restoring a linked list of integers like the lists that were used earlier in this chapter. Recall the following definitions and declaration:

```
type    ptr = ^node;
        node = record
            data : integer;
            next : ptr
        end;

var     head : ptr
```

To begin, suppose that your program needs to write a linked list of integers to a file in a way that will allow you to restore the list later. What should you write to the file? You might be tempted to write each node in its entirety—that is, to write each entire record, which contains an integer field and a pointer field, to a file of type *node*. However, writing the pointer fields serves no useful purpose, because once the program has terminated, the saved pointer values from the records are meaningless. Although the address in a pointer field, which referenced a memory location, was valid before you wrote the list out to the file, the interpretation of the address is not well defined after program execution terminates. For example, when you execute the program again, the saved address may reference a memory location of some completely different structure within the program or even within another program altogether. Thus, the solution of writing out the entire node to a file is not a good one.

Do not write the pointer fields to the file

It turns out that all you need to do is to write the data portion—in this case an integer—of each node to the file, because it is easy to restore the list structure from only this information. The following procedure, *SaveList*, performs this task by writing the integers to a general file of integers, although you just as easily could write them to a textfile. Figure 3-20 illustrates the action of *SaveList*.

Save a linked list by writing only its data to a file

```
procedure SaveList(head : ptr; var F : intfile);
{ --------------------------------------------------------
  Saves a linked list's data in a general file.
  Precondition: head points to the linked list; F is a
  general file of type intfile; intfile must be previously
  defined.
  Postcondition: F is created; head and the linked list are
  unchanged.
  -------------------------------------------------------- }
var cur : ptr;

begin
{ initialize }
    rewrite(F);
    cur := head;
```

head   linked list   Save   file

Figure 3-20

Saving a linked list in a file

```
{ traverse the list to the end, writing out each item }
    while (cur <> nil) do
    begin
        write(F, cur^.data);
        cur := cur^.next
    end  { while }
end  { SaveList }
```

Once you have saved the linked list's data in the file, you can recreate the list anytime you wish. After the program that originally created the list has terminated, the data endures in the file. Thus, when the program (or another program) is active again, it can restore the list by reading the data from the file.

To develop a procedure to restore a linked list, you should first notice that the procedure *SaveList* writes the integers to the file in the order that they appear on the list. The *RestoreList* procedure thus must build the list by reading the file and placing each newly read integer at the end of the list, as Figure 3-21 illustrates.

A pseudocode solution for *RestoreList* is

```
while not end of file do
begin
    Read in the next integer
    Place the integer at the end of the list
end
```

To add a new integer to the end of the list, you must perform these four steps:

1. Use *new* to allocate a new node for the list.
2. Set the pointer field in the last node on the list to point to the new node.
3. Put the new integer in the new node.
4. Set the pointer field in the new node to *nil*.

Four steps to add a node to the end of a linked list

Figure 3-21

Restoring a linked list from a file

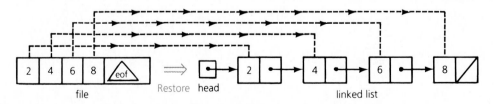

file   Restore head   linked list

Figure 3-22

A linked list with head and tail pointers

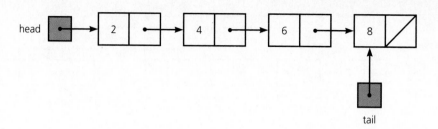

Each time you read a new integer, you must get to the last node on the list. One way to accomplish this is to traverse the list each time you read a new integer. A much more efficient method uses a pointer variable *tail* to remember where the end of the list is—just as *head* remembers where the beginning of the list is. Like *head*, *tail* is external to the list. Figure 3-22 illustrates a linked list that has both head and tail pointers.

Use a tail pointer to facilitate adding nodes to the end of a linked list

With *tail* pointing to the end of the list, you can perform both Step 1 and Step 2 by using the single statement

```
new(tail^.next)
```

This call to *new* allocates a new node and sets the *next* field of the last node on the list to point to this new node. Notice that you could have accomplished the same task by using a temporary pointer variable as follows:

```
new(temp);
tail^.next := temp
```

You thus have an easy method for adding a new integer to the end of the list. Initially, however, when you insert the first integer into an empty list, *tail* does not point to anything. One way to handle this fact is to treat the first insertion as a special case before the *while* loop. This approach leads to the Pascal procedure *RestoreList*:

Treat the first insertion as a special case

Creating a linked list from data in a file

```
procedure RestoreList(var head : ptr; var F : intfile);
{ ------------------------------------------------------------
  Creates a linked list from the data in a general file.
  Precondition: F is a general file of type intfile; intfile
  must be previously defined.
  Postcondition: head points to the linked list; F is
  unchanged. If F is empty, head is nil.
  ------------------------------------------------------------ }
var tail : ptr;

begin
   reset(F);              { open F for input }

   if not eof(F)          { test for an empty file }
      then
      begin
```

```
              { add the first integer to the list }
              new(head);
              read(F, head^.data);
              head^.next := nil;
              tail := head;

              { add the remaining integers to the list }
              while not eof(F) do
              begin
                  new(tail^.next);
                  tail := tail^.next;
                  read(F, tail^.data);
                  tail^.next := nil
              end { while }
          end

          else head := nil   { the file is empty — return the
                                empty list }
end   { RestoreList }
```

Now suppose that a file contains integers that are not in the order you want. For example, suppose that you want the integers to appear in ascending order on your linked list, but in the file they are in no particular order at all. You can solve this problem easily by using the previous *Insert* procedure. Because *Insert* inserts new items into their proper sorted order, the following Pascal procedure will create an ordered linked list from an unordered file:

```
procedure BuildSortedList(var head : ptr; var F : intfile);
{ --------------------------------------------------------
  Constructs a linked list that contains in sorted order the
  integers from a general unordered file.
  Precondition: F is a general file of type intfile; intfile
  must be previously defined. For simplicity, assume that F
  contains no duplicates.
  Postcondition: head points to the created linked list, as
  previously described; F is unchanged.
  Calls: Insert.
  -------------------------------------------------------- }
var   X : integer;
      Success : boolean;     { Success is provided for
                  Insert, but ignored here; Insert will always
                  return Success = true because F contains no
                  duplicates }

begin
    head := nil;
    reset(F);
    while (not eof(F)) do
```

*Creating a sorted linked list
from arbitrary data in a file*

```
    begin
       read(F, X);
       Insert(head, X, Success)
    end   { while }
end   {BuildSortedList}
```

This type of sorting algorithm is known as an **insertion sort** and is among the sorting algorithms that Chapter 7 will consider.

Using Structured Types in Data Fields

Although for simplicity the previous linked lists used integer data fields, you need not restrict yourself to simple data types. In fact, the advantages of a linked list are more dramatic when you use data fields of a structured data type such as an array or a record. For example, suppose that you want a linked list of customer names, where each name is a packed array of characters. The following statements describe such a list:

```
const   maxstring = 20;
type    datatype = packed array[1..maxstring] of char;
        ptr = ^node;
        node = record
                  data : datatype;
                  next : ptr
               end;   { record }
var     head : ptr
```

In fact, you could redefine *datatype* so that it is a record with several fields that include additional details about each customer. (Notice how easy such a change would be. The use of *datatype* is one way to make a program simple to modify.)

VARIATIONS OF THE LINKED LIST

This section briefly introduces several variations of the linked list that you have just seen. These variations often are useful, and you will encounter them later in this text. Many of the implementation details are left as exercises. Note that in addition to the data structures discussed in this section, it is possible to have structures such as arrays of pointers to linked lists and linked lists of linked lists. These structures are also left as exercises.

Circular Linked Lists

When you access a computer by using a remote terminal, you are sharing the computer with many other users. The **time-sharing system** must organize the users so that only one user at a time has access to CPU time. By ordering the users, the system can give each user a turn. Because users regularly enter and exit the system (by logging on or logging off), a linked list of user names allows the system to maintain order without shifting names when it makes insertions to and deletions from the list. Thus, the system can traverse the linked list from the beginning and give each user on the list a turn at CPU time. What must the system do when it reaches the end of the list? It must return to the beginning of the list. However, the fact that the last node of a linked list does not point to another node can be an inconvenience.

If you want to access the first node of a linked list after accessing the last node, you must resort to the head pointer. Suppose that you change the *next* field of the list's last node so that, instead of containing *nil*, it points to the first node. The result is a **circular linked list**, as illustrated in Figure 3-23. In contrast, the linked list you saw earlier is said to be **linear**.

Every node in a circular linked list points to a successor, so you can start at any node and traverse the entire list. Although you could think of a circular list as not having either a beginning or an end, you still would have an external pointer to one of the nodes in the list. Thus, it remains natural to think of both a first and a last node in a circular list. If the external pointer points to the "first" node, you still would have to traverse the list to get to the last node. However, if the external pointer—call it *List*—points to the "last" node, as it does in Figure 3-24, you can access both the first and last nodes without a traversal, because *List^.next* points to the first node. In fact, the somewhat strange notation *List^.next^.data* is the data field of the first node.

A *nil* value in the external pointer indicates an empty list, as it did for a linear list. However, no node in a circular list contains *nil* in its *next* field. Thus, you must alter the algorithm for detecting when you have traversed an entire list. By simply comparing the current pointer *cur* to the external pointer *List*, you can determine when you have traversed

Every node in a circular linked list has a successor

No node in a circular linked list contains nil

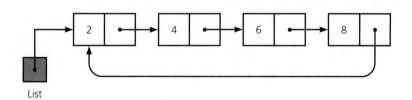

Figure 3-23

A circular linked list

List

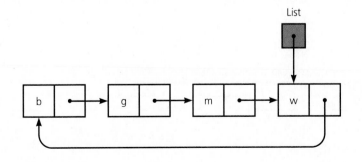

Figure 3-24

A circular linked list with an external pointer to the last node

List

the entire circular list. For example, the following Pascal statements write the data fields of every node in a circular list, assuming that *List* points to the "last" node and *Print* is a procedure to write a data field in an appropriate format:

Write the data that is in a circular linked list

```
if List <> nil
    then                            { if list is not empty }
    begin
        cur := List;               { initialize cur }
        repeat
            cur := cur^.next;      { point to next node }
            Print(cur^.data)       { write data portion }
        until cur = List           { quit at end of list }
    end
```

Operations such as insertion into and deletion from a circular linked list are left as exercises.

Dummy Head Nodes

Both the *Insert* and *Delete* procedures presented earlier for linear lists require a special case to handle action at the first position of a list. Although these procedures correctly handle this case, many people prefer a method that eliminates the need for the special case. One such method is to add a **dummy head node**—as Figure 3-25 depicts—that is always present, even when the list is empty. In this way, the item at the first position of the list is actually in the second node.

When you use a dummy head node, there is no special case in the *Insert* and *Delete* procedures, because these procedures will initialize *prev* to point to the dummy head node rather than to *nil*. Thus, for example, in the *Delete* procedure the statement

```
prev^.next := cur^.next
```

deletes from the list the node to which *cur* points, regardless of whether or not this node is the first element in the list.

Despite the fact that a dummy head node eliminates the need for a special case, we do not, in general, advocate its use in a linked list. We feel that handling the first list position separately is less distracting than is altering the list's structure by adding a dummy head node. However, dummy head nodes are useful in doubly linked lists, as you will see in the next section.

Figure 3-25

A dummy head node

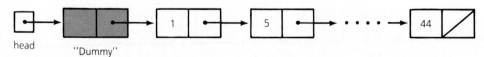

head   "Dummy"

(a) Dummy Head Node

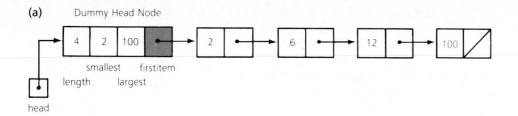

smallest firstitem

length largest

head

(b) Head Record (head)

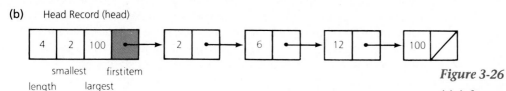

smallest firstitem

length largest

Figure 3-26

(a) A dummy head node with global information; (b) a head record with global information

Some people like to put global information about the list—such as its length and the smallest and largest value in the list—in a dummy head node, as Figure 3-26a shows. Unless the dummy head node is exactly the same type of record as the other nodes on the list, the list operations will still require a special case for the first position. This situation occurs because one Pascal pointer variable can point to only one type of record. Thus, if the data type of the dummy head node differs from the other nodes, you cannot use the same pointer variable to point both to the dummy head node and to another list node. For example, you cannot initialize *prev* to point to the dummy head node and then advance it to traverse down the list. One way to program around this problem is to use a variant record.

Our own preference for handling global information is to put the information in a **head record** that contains the external pointer to the first node on the list, as shown in Figure 3-26b. The following Pascal statements establish the head record *head*:

```
type    headrecord = record
            length, smallest, largest : integer;
            firstitem : ptr   { ptr is of type ^node as
                                before }
        end;

var     head : headrecord
```

You can use a head record for global information instead of a dummy head node

Whether or not you use a dummy head node or a head record is, however, a matter of personal taste.

Doubly Linked Lists

Suppose that you have a method for directly accessing the node that you wish to delete from a linked list. If you have been able to locate the node

Each node in a doubly linked list points to both its predecessor and its successor

without a traversal, you will not have established a trailing pointer to the node that precedes it on the list. Without a trailing pointer, you will be unable to delete the node. You could overcome this problem if you had a way to back up from the node that you wish to delete to the node that precedes it. A **doubly linked list** will solve this problem because each of its nodes has pointers to both the next node and the previous node.

Consider a sorted list of customer names such that each node contains, in addition to its data fields, two pointer fields, `precede` and `next`. As usual, the `next` field of node N points to the node that follows N on the list. The `precede` field points to the node that precedes N on the list. Thus, the form of the sorted linked list of customers is as shown in Figure 3-27.

Notice that if `cur` points to a node N, you can get a pointer to the node that precedes N on the list by using the assignment statement

```
prev := cur^.precede
```

A doubly linked list thus allows you to delete a node without traversing the list to establish a trailing pointer.

Because there are more pointers to set, the mechanics of inserting into and deleting from a doubly linked list are a bit more involved than for a singly linked list. In addition, the special cases at the beginning or the end of the list are more complicated. It is common to eliminate the special cases by structuring a doubly linked list to contain a dummy head node. Although dummy head nodes may not be worthwhile for singly linked lists, the more complicated special cases for doubly linked lists make them very attractive.

Dummy head nodes are useful in doubly linked lists

As is shown in Figure 3-28a, the external pointer `ListHead` always points to the dummy head node. Notice that the head node is of the same type as the other nodes on the list; thus it also contains `precede` and `next` pointer fields. You can link the list so that it becomes a **circular doubly linked list**. The `next` field of the head node then points to the first "real node"—for example, the first customer name—on the list, and the `precede` field of the first real node points back to the head node. Similarly, the `precede` field of the head node then points to the last node on the list, and the `next` field of the last node points to the head node. Note that the dummy head node is present even when the list is empty. In this case, both pointer fields of the dummy head node point to the head node itself, as Figure 3-28b illustrates.

By using a circular doubly linked list, you can perform insertions and deletions without special cases: Inserting into and deleting from the first

Figure 3-27

A doubly linked list

head

ListHead

Dummy Head Node

(a)

(b)   ListHead

Figure 3-28

(a) A circular doubly linked list with a dummy head node; (b) an empty list with a head node

or last position is the same as for any other position. First consider how to delete the node *N* that *p* points to. As Figure 3-29 illustrates, you need to

A circular doubly linked list eliminates special cases for insertion and deletion

1. Change the *next* field of the node that precedes *N* so that it points to the node that follows *N*.
2. Change the *precede* field of the node that follows *N* so that it points to the node that precedes *N*.

The following assignment statements accomplish these two steps:

Deleting a node

```
{ delete the node that p points to }
p^.precede^.next := p^.next;
p^.next^.precede := p^.precede
```

You should convince yourself that these statements work even when the node to be deleted is the first, last, or only data (nonhead) node on the list.

Now consider how to insert a node into a circular doubly linked list. In general, the fact that the list is doubly linked does not save you from having to traverse the list to find the proper place for the new item. For example, if you insert a new customer name, you must find the proper place in the sorted linked list for the new record. The following traversal sets *cur* to point to the node that should follow the new node on the list:

```
cur := ListHead^.next
while (cur <> ListHead) Cand (Newname > cur^.name) do
    cur := cur^.next
```

Traverse the list to locate the insertion point

Figure 3-29

Pointer changes for deletion

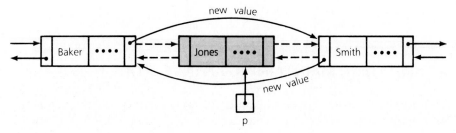

new value

new value

p

Figure 3-30

Pointer changes for insertion

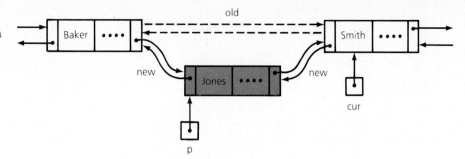

Notice that if you want to insert the new record either at the end of the list or into an empty list, the loop will set *cur* to point to the dummy head node.

As Figure 3-30 illustrates, once *cur* points to the node that is to follow the new node, you need to

1. Set the *next* field of the new node to point to the node that is to follow it.
2. Set the *precede* field of the new node to point to the node that is to precede it.
3. Set the *precede* field of the node that is to follow the new node so that it points to the new node.
4. Set the *next* field of the node that is to precede the new node so that it points to the new node.

The following assignment statements accomplish these four steps, assuming that *p* points to the new node:

Inserting a node

```
{ insert the new node pointed to by p before the node
  pointed to by cur }
p^.next := cur;
p^.precede := cur^.precede;
p^.next^.precede := p;
p^.precede^.next := p
```

You should convince yourself that these statements work even when you insert the node into the beginning of a list, at the end of a list—in which case *cur* points to the head node—or into an empty list, in which case *cur* also points to the head node.

A CASE STUDY: MAINTAINING AN INVENTORY

The case study in this section illustrates the issues of program design and development that the previous chapters discuss. The solution to this particular problem, maintaining an inventory, demonstrates how you can solve a complex problem effectively by using the principles of top-down design and modularity. The solution also illustrates Pascal list processing and file handling.

Statement of the Inventory Problem

The object is to write an interactive program that will maintain an inventory for a videocassette dealer. The inventory consists of a list of movie titles and the following inventory information associated with each title:

- **Have value:** number of cassettes currently in stock.
- **Want value:** number of cassettes that should be in stock. (When the have value is less than the want value, more cassettes are ordered.)
- **Wait list:** list of names of people waiting for the title if it is sold out.

Because the inventory program will not be running at all times, there should be a mechanism for saving the inventory in a file and for restoring the inventory when the program is run again.

Input and output are as follows:

INPUT

- A file that contains a previously saved inventory.
- A file that contains information on an incoming shipment of cassettes. (See command D under "Action Commands.")
- Single-letter commands—with arguments where necessary— that inquire about or modify the inventory and that the user will enter interactively.

OUTPUT

- A file that contains the updated inventory. (Note that any inventory items with have value = 0, want value = 0, and an empty wait list are removed from the inventory and do not appear in the file.)
- Output as specified by the individual commands.

The program should be able to execute the following commands:

Information Commands

H	(help)	Print a summary of the available commands.
I *<title>*	(inquire)	Print the inventory information for a specified title.
L	(list)	List the entire inventory (in alphabetical order by title).

Action Commands

A *<title>*	(add)	Add a new title to the inventory. Prompt for initial want value.

Action Commands

M <*title*>	(modify)	Modify the want value for a specified title.
D	(delivery)	Take delivery of a shipment of cassettes, assuming that the clerk has entered the shipment information (titles and counts) into a file. Read in the file, mail out cassettes to the people on the wait list, and update the have values in the inventory accordingly. Note that the program must add an item to the inventory if a delivered title is not present in the current inventory.
O	(order)	Write a purchase order for additional cassettes based on a comparison of the have and want values in the inventory, so that the have value is brought up to the want value.
R	(return)	Write a return order based on a comparison of the have and want values in the inventory and decrease the have values accordingly (make the return). The object is to reduce the have value to the want value.
S <*title*>	(sell)	Decrease the count for the specified title by 1. If the title is sold out, put a name on the wait list for the title.
Q	(quit)	

You can use this problem statement as a high-level specification for a computer program. The sections that follow describe the process of going from a statement of the problem to a program that effectively solves the problem—that is, meets its specification. You can view this problem-solving process as having three main stages:

1. The top-down design of a solution
2. The bottom-up implementation of the solution
3. The final set of refinements to the program

Although these stages appear as isolated topics in the following discussion, you must always keep a global perspective. You cannot complete a stage in total isolation from the others.

Top-Down Design of a Solution

This section describes the highlights of a methodical, top-down approach to the inventory problem. At many steps in the development of the solution, you must make choices. Although the following discussion may give the illusion that the choices are clear-cut, such is not always the case. In reality there are more trade-offs between the choices and more false starts (wrong choices considered) than we possibly can describe in a reasonable amount of space. However, the presentation tries to convey, as much as possible, the spirit of the problem-solving process.

The discussion may also give the illusion that we solved all subproblems in complete isolation from other subproblems. In reality, as we have said, many are best solved in tandem with other subproblems and with a perspective of the overall picture in mind. The methodology that we describe gives a framework for the systematic solution of large problems. We deal with some of the more subtle aspects of weighing trade-offs and keeping the big picture in proper perspective in Parts III and IV of this book.

Consider now the top-down design of a solution to the inventory problem. From the statement of the inventory problem, it is clear that at the highest level you can break the inventory problem into the following subtasks, as Figure 3-31 illustrates:

I. Restore the current inventory from an external file.

II. Execute user commands to ask about or modify the inventory.

III. Save the current inventory in an external file.

Before proceeding with the refinement of the three subproblems, consider the choice of a data structure. Both Chapter 4 and Part III of this book demonstrate that you should base the choice of an abstract data type on the operations that you expect to perform on the data. Because the ADT is an integral part of all phases of the solution process, you should refine it in a top-down fashion along with the algorithm. At this time, however, the emphasis is on using data structures rather than on developing and choosing among ADT's.

The problem description suggests some common operations that you will perform on the inventory:

- List the inventory in alphabetical order by title (L command).

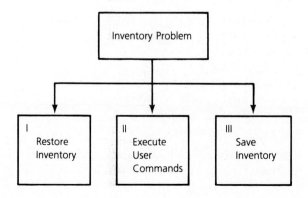

Figure 3-31

Division of the problem into subproblems

- Find the inventory item associated with a title (I, M, D, and S commands).

- Insert new inventory items (A and D commands).

Recall that associated with each title there might be a list of people who are waiting for that title. You must be able to add new people to the end of this list when they want a cassette that is sold out and to delete people from the beginning of the list when new cassettes are delivered.

Part III of this book discusses various ADT's that support these kinds of operations in an efficient way. For now, we settle for a data structure that is both reasonable with respect to more advanced analysis and is consistent with the level of material presented so far. Chapter 12 revises this solution so that it utilizes ADT's and more sophisticated data structures.

You can represent the inventory as follows:

- The inventory will be a linked list of data items, sorted by the title that each item represents.

- Each item will contain a title, the number in stock (a have value), the number desired (a want value), and a pointer to the beginning of a linked list of people's names (the wait list).

- Because you must be able to add new names to the end of an item's wait list, each item will also contain a pointer to the last name on its list. (Recall the insert and delete operations for a linked list that were illustrated earlier in the chapter.)

Figure 3-32 and the following Pascal type definitions summarize these choices:

```
const   maxstring = 15;
type    string = packed array[1..maxstring] of char;

        { wait list — people waiting for certain
          cassettes }
        waitptr = ^waitnode;
        waitnode = record
            who : string;
            next : waitptr
        end;   { record }

        { inventory list — list of stock items }
        stockptr = ^stocknode;
        stocknode = record
            title : string;
            have, want : integer;
            wait, last : waitptr;
            next : stockptr
        end   { record }
```

Now consider how the data structures will interact with the rest of the program. In Chapter 1 you saw reasons for avoiding global structures in general, but it might be appropriate to make a structure global if it is an integral part of all (or almost all) aspects of the program. If you design the inventory program to operate on a single, fixed inventory, then it is reasonable to treat the inventory structure globally. However, if you design— or might later modify—the program to manipulate more than one inventory (for example, if you want to look at saved histories of the inventory), then you want to have general subprograms, to which you can pass different inventory structures as arguments. We chose the second approach here, in anticipation of future modifications to the program.

With the data structure chosen, you can continue with the design of solutions to Subproblems I, II, and III. Consider Subproblems I and III first. You can consider these subproblems together because they are so closely associated: They both deal with communication between the internal data structure for processing the inventory and an external file for saving the inventory.

Figure 3-32

(a) Orthogonal structure for the inventory; (b) inventory list node; (c) wait list node

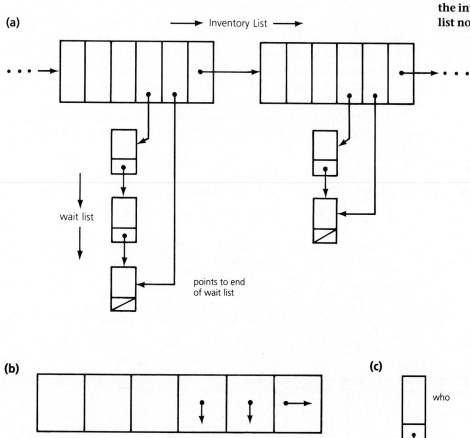

(a)

Inventory List

wait list

points to end
of wait list

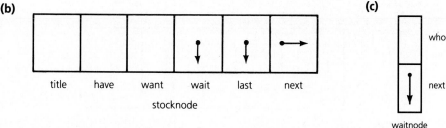

(b)

title   have   want   wait   last   next

stocknode

(c)

who

next

waitnode

At the highest level, Subproblem I requires you to read the inventory from a file into the data structure. Thus, for each inventory item you must be able to read the title, the have and want values, and the wait list. Similarly, Subproblem III requires you to write the inventory to a file.

Before you can proceed, you must consider how you will save the inventory in a file. Recall that you save a linked list in a file by saving only the data portion of the list items. However, there is one slight complication here: Each inventory item has an associated sublist—the wait list. Thus,

- You need a second file for the names on the wait lists because the items in a file must all be of the same type.
- To restore the wait lists, you must know their lengths. In particular, if you store the names on all the wait lists together in a single file, you must be able to determine where one list ends and the next begins.

The need for a second file is not a difficulty, but you must modify the original statement of the inventory problem to accommodate this change because it specifies "a file." This change is not at all unreasonable given the spirit of the problem.

To address the second observation, recall that the have value of a stock item is the number of items currently in stock. It is reasonable to adopt the convention that a negative have value is the number of cassettes that you are short—the size of the wait list!

The following statements summarize this discussion. They contain a slight modification to the previous type definitions and new definitions for the two files.

```
const   maxstring = 15;
type    string = packed array[1..maxstring] of char;

        { wait list--people waiting for certain cassettes }
        waitptr = ^waitnode;
        waitnode = record
            who : string;
            next : waitptr
        end;  { record }

        { data fields for a single stock item }
```

Figure 3-33

Modified node structure

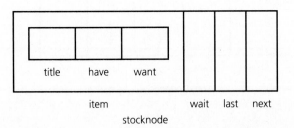

```
stockinfo = record
      title : string;
      have, want : integer
end;  { record }

{ node on inventory list }
stockptr = ^stocknode;
stocknode = record
      item : stockinfo;
      wait, last : waitptr;
      next : stockptr
end;  { record }

{ file of stock items for the inventory list }
stockfile : file of stockinfo;

{ file of names for the wait lists }
namefile : file of string;
```

If you redefine the inventory record, as Figure 3-33 shows, so that it contains a subrecord that consists of the title, its have value, and its want value, you can keep these items together in the file. Thus, the previous concern of saving and restoring a linked list is addressed.

With this data structure, you can attempt the first version of a solution to Subproblem I.

Subproblem I: Restore the current inventory from external files. At a very high level, the following procedure, *Getinv*, solves this subproblem:

Figure 3-34

```
Getinv(invlist, invfile, waitfile)

    while not eof(invfile) do
    begin
        Read a stock item from the inventory file
        Add the item to the end of the inventory list
        Read in the wait list associated with the stock item
    end
```

As was described earlier, the addition of the first node to a linked list is a special case. Therefore, you can refine the first attempt as follows:

```
Getinv(invlist, invfile, waitfile)

    if not eof(invfile)
        then
        begin
            { get the first item for the inventory list }
            Read the first item from the inventory file
            Add it as the first item on the inventory list
            Getwait(stockitem, waitfile) { Subproblem I.1 }
```

```
                              { get the rest of the list }
                              while not eof(invfile) do
                              begin
                                  Read the next item from the inventory file
                                  Add it to the end of the inventory list
                                  Getwait(stockitem, waitfile)
                              end
                          end
```

Figure 3-35

Subproblem I.1: Read in the wait list for a stock item.   This procedure uses the fact that you can determine the size of the wait list from the have value of the stock item.

```
Getwait(stockitem, waitfile)

    if have value < 0
        then
        begin
            size := negative of the have value
            for i := 1 to size do
            begin
                Read a name from the wait file
                Add the name to the end of the wait list
            end
        end
```

Figure 3-36

Subproblem III: Save the current inventory in external files.

FIRST PASS

```
Putinv(invlist, invfile, waitfile)

    for each item in the inventory do
    begin
        if the item is still part of the inventory
            then save the item (and its wait list)
    end
```

SECOND PASS

Recall that you remove an item from the inventory—by not saving it in the file—if both its want value and have value are zero and its wait list is empty. The following refinement implements this convention:

```
Putinv(invlist, invfile, waitfile)

    for each item in the inventory do
    begin
        if (the have value is not zero) or
                (the want value is not zero) or
                (the wait list is not empty)
```

```
        then
        begin
            { write the wait list to waitfile }
            Putwait(stockitem, waitfile) { Subproblem III.1 }

            Write out the stock item to the inventory file
        end
    end
end
```

Subproblem III.1: Save the wait list for a stock item in an external file.

```
Putwait(stockitem, waitfile)

    trav = stockitem.wait
    while trav <> nil do
    begin
        Write out the wait name to waitfile
        trav := trav^.next
    end
```

Figure 3-37

Note that the preceding assumes, for both saving and restoring the inventory, that the have value is a true indicator of the size of the wait list, which will be the case if the entire program is working correctly. But what if something goes wrong? For example, if a later modification to the program causes a violation of this indicator, the inventory structure could become invalid or the program could abort in a very inelegant way—a way that would be very unsatisfactory to a user. For example, when restoring the inventory, the program could attempt to read past the end of the file if it expected some wait list to be longer than it was.

As a fail-safe measure, you should check that the have counts truly reflect the sizes of the wait lists whenever you save or restore the inventory. However, you can postpone this important detail now and view it as one refinement to the program that you will make during the third and final stage of the problem-solving process.

With this portion of the problem out of the way, we can turn to the core of the inventory problem, Subproblem II. Many of the subproblems that we solve are very simple and have high-level solutions that are self-explanatory. We explain the solution only where it is necessary to support or clarify the refinements.

Subproblem II: Execute user commands to ask about or modify the inventory. You process user commands until the quit command occurs. At a very high level, you can state Subproblem II as follows:

FIRST PASS

```
main program

    Read the first command
    while command is not Q (quit) do
```

Figure 3-38

```
    begin
        Execute the appropriate command
        Read the next command
    end
```

SECOND PASS

```
main program

    Getcmnd(command)                      { Subproblem II.1 }
    while command <> 'Q' do
    begin
        case command of
            'H' : procH                   { Subproblem II.2 }
            'I' : procI(inventory)        { Subproblem II.3 }
            'L' : procL(inventory)        { Subproblem II.4 }
            'A' : procA(inventory)        { Subproblem II.5 }
            'M' : procM(inventory)        { Subproblem II.6 }
            'D' : procD(inventory)        { Subproblem II.7 }
            'O' : procO(inventory)        { Subproblem II.8 }
            'R' : procR(inventory)        { Subproblem II.9 }
            'S' : procS(inventory)        { Subproblem II.10 }
        end
        Getcmnd(command)
    end
```

As part of the final refinement of the user interface, you should test for undefined commands.

Figure 3-39

Subproblem II.1: Read the next command.   You should provide a flexible input format. At first, however, you can assume that *the command will be a single uppercase letter* and leave the addition of flexibility for the final refinement of the program. Because as a procedure *Getcmnd* is an isolated module, the later refinements should cause no difficulties. Of course, the choice is really arbitrary as to how simple the original input procedure should be and how much refinement you should postpone for later.

FIRST PASS

```
Getcmnd(command)

    Skip blanks in the input file
    Read the command
```

As a safeguard against an unexpected end of file, *Getcmnd* equates end of file with the quit command, as follows:

SECOND PASS

```
Getcmnd(command)

    { skip blanks in the input file }
```

```
    SkipBlanks(input)                { Subproblem II.1.1 }

    { read the command — test for end of file }
    if eof(input)
       then command := 'Q'
       else read(command)
```

Subproblem II.1.1: Skip blanks in a file.

```
SkipBlanks(infile)

    while (not eof(infile)) Cand (infile^ = ' ') do
        get(infile)
```

Note the use of the `Cand` (conditional and) operator.

Figure 3-40

Subproblem II.2: Process command H (summarize the available commands).

```
procH

    Write out a summary of each command
```

Figure 3-41

Subproblem II.3: Process command I (print information for a specified title).

FIRST PASS

```
procI(invlist)

    Read in a title argument
    Find the title in the inventory
    Write out the title, have value, and want value
    Write out the associated wait list
```

Figure 3-42

SECOND PASS

```
procI(invlist)

    { get the title argument }
    Gettitle(title)                  { Subproblem II.3.1 }

    { find the title in the inventory }
    loc := Find(invlist, title)      { Subproblem II.3.2 }

    { write out the information }
    if loc <> nil
       then
       begin
           with loc^.item do
               writeln(title, have, want)
           Waitnames(loc^.wait)      { Subproblem II.3.3 }
       end
```

Figure 3-43

Subproblem II.3.1: Read in a title.

FIRST PASS

```
Gettitle(title)

    Initialize the title to all blanks
    Skip blanks in the input file
    Read characters until the title is full or
     end of line is reached
```

SECOND PASS

```
Gettitle(title)

    { initialize }
    for i := 1 to maxsize do
        title[i] := ' '

    { read in the string }
    SkipBlanks(input)
    if not eof(input)
        then
        begin
            i := 1
            while (i ≤ maxsize) and (not eoln) do
            begin
                read(title[i])
                i := i + 1
            end
        end
```

Figure 3-44

Subproblem II.3.2: Find a title in the inventory.   Return *nil* if the title is not found. Observe that this task is very similar to the search portions of the *Insert* and *Delete* procedures discussed earlier in this chapter.

```
function Find(invlist, title) : returns pointer to a stock item

    { locate the title }
    cur := invlist
    while (cur <> nil) Cand (cur^.item.title < title) do
        cur := cur^.next

    { set the function value }
    if (cur <> nil) Cand (cur^.item.title = title)
        then Find := cur
        else Find := nil
```

Again, note the use of the *Cand* operator.

Subproblem II.3.3: Write out the names on the specified wait list.

```
Waitnames(ptr)

    while ptr <> nil do
    begin
        Write out the name that ptr points to
        ptr := ptr^.next
    end
```

Figure 3-45

Subproblem II.4: Process command L (list the current inventory).

FIRST PASS

```
procL(invlist)

    for each item in the inventory do
    begin
        Write out the title, have value, and want value
        Write out the associated wait list
    end
```

Figure 3-46

SECOND PASS

```
procL(invlist)

    trav := invlist
    while trav <> nil do
    begin
        with trav^.item do
            writeln(title, have, want)
        Waitnames(trav^.wait)
        trav := trav^.next
    end
```

Subproblem II.5: Process command A (add a new title to the inventory).
You can define the A command to mean that it will add a new title if the title does not already exist. If the title does exist, you can prompt the user to modify the existing want value.

Figure 3-47

FIRST PASS

```
procA(invlist)

    Read in a title argument
    Insert the new title in the inventory (if it is
        not there already)
    Read the want value
```

SECOND PASS

```
procA(invlist)

    { get the title argument }
    Gettitle(title)

    { insert a new stock item if necessary
      -- return loc pointing to the item }
    Insert(invlist, title, loc)   { Subproblem II.5.1 }

    { update the want value for the stock item }
    read the want value
```

Subproblem II.5.1: Insert a new item in the inventory, if it is not present already. Return a pointer to the item.

FIRST PASS

```
Insert(invlist, title, loc)

    Locate where the title should go
    Insert it if it is not there already
    Return a pointer to the item
```

Figure 3-48

SECOND PASS

```
Insert(invlist, title, loc)

    { locate where the title should go }
    prev := nil
    cur := inventory
    while (cur <> nil) Cand (cur^.item.title < title) do
    begin
       prev := cur
       cur := cur^.next
    end

    { insert title if necessary }
    if (cur = nil) Cor (cur^.item.title <> title)
       then insert new node between prev and cur

    loc is a pointer to the item
```

Figure 3-49   Note the use of the *Cand* and *Cor* operators.

Subproblem II.6: Process command M (modify the want value for a specified title). The M command is supposed to modify the want value of an existing title. You can define it to include the addition of a new title, if it does not exist already. Note that *procA* and *procM* are identical, so you can combine them into one routine, *procAM*.

Subproblem II.7: Process command D (take delivery of a shipment). The D command specifies that the shipment information for a delivery will be in an external file, so add the following variable declaration to the existing declarations:

> **var** shipfile : text

In the following, the shipment file name is passed to the procedure *procD* as a parameter.

Figure 3-50

FIRST PASS

```
procD(invlist, shipfile)

    while not eof(shipfile) do
    begin
        Read the delivery information (titles and counts)
        Locate the title (insert it if it is not there already)
        Update the have value for the title
        Hold cassettes for people on the wait lists
    end
```

SECOND PASS

```
procD(invlist, shipfile)

    while not eof(shipfile) do
    begin
        { read the count and title }
        read(shipfile, count)
        Gettitle(title)

        { update the have value in the inventory
          -- create a new item if necessary }
        Insert(invlist, title, loc)
        Update the have value

        { process back orders if necessary }
        while (wait list is not empty) and (count > 0) do
        begin
            Hold one cassette for the first person on the
                wait list
            Delete the first person from the wait list
            count := count - 1
        end
    end
```

Note that procedure *Gettitle* reads title arguments from the input file (for commands I, A, M, and S) and reads titles from the delivery file (for command D). You can accommodate these tasks by having procedure *Gettitle* take a file name as an argument *(procedure Gettitle(title, infile))*.

Subproblem II.8: Process command O (write a purchase order).

```
procO(invlist)

    for each item in the inventory do
    begin
        if have value < want value
            then write a purchase order
    end
```

Figure 3-51

Subproblem II.9: Process command R (write a return order).

```
procR(invlist)

    for each item in the inventory do
    begin
        if have value < want value
            then
            begin
                Write a return order
                Decrease the have value accordingly
            end
    end
```

Figure 3-52

Subproblem II.10: Process command S (sell a cassette).

FIRST PASS

```
procS(invlist)

    Read in a title argument
    Find the title in the inventory
    if the title is not in the inventory then
        Print a message
    else if the have value = 0 then
        Decrease the have value by 1
    else read in a name for the wait list
```

Figure 3-53

SECOND PASS

```
procS(invlist)

    { get the title argument }
    Gettitle(title, infile)

    { find the title in the inventory }
    loc := Find(invlist, title)

    { decrease the have value by 1 if possible }
    if loc = nil then
        Print message
```

```
   else if have value > 0 then
      have value := have value — 1
   else
   begin    { get a name for the wait list }
      Getname(name, infile)
      Add the name to the end of the wait list
   end
```

Observe that procedure *Getname* is really identical to procedure *Gettitle*, which was defined earlier. Therefore, rename *Gettitle* and *Getname* with the more general name *Getstring*. (*Getstring(string, infile)*).

A top-down design of a solution to the inventory problem is now complete. Figure 3–54 summarizes this design. The place at which the design of a solution ends and its implementation with a program begins is not at all clear. You easily could justify refining the solution further before turning to the coding. However, the intention of this discussion is not to walk you through every detail of this particular problem, but rather to give you a good feel for the spirit of the solution process. With this in mind, we now turn to the second stage of the problem-solving process: the implementation of the solution with a program.

Bottom-Up Implementation of the Solution

This stage of the process takes the solution and produces a working Pascal program. Although there is much coding detail at this stage, we emphasize the organization of the implementation and the order of doing things rather than programming details. That is, we demonstrate how to build a program systematically from the bottom up, adding a few new routines at a time until the program is complete. We shall summarize here the major steps that we took to get from the pseudocode solution to a complete working program.

The development of this program occurred in two main phases. In the first phase, we essentially chose to ignore the wait lists by treating calls to the wait list operations (procedures *Getwait*, *Putwait*, and *Waitnames*) as stubs. Recall that stubs are placeholder procedures, which simply report that they have been called. We chose this approach because the wait list operations are peripheral to the main focus of the problem. The second phase of the implementation consisted of replacing the stubs with the implementations of the corresponding modules. Within each phase, we added a few routines at a time, got them to work, and then added more routines.

Phase 1: Omit the wait list operations.   This discussion is broken into the following five steps:

1.   One of the most useful and important procedures that you can write is often not part of the solution at all. During the development of a large

Figure 3-54   **Complete design hierarchy**

program, it is useful to have a special debugging procedure that writes out the status of the primary data structures and program variables. Having this as a separate procedure allows you easily to either add diagnostics to or remove them from any place in the code during the remainder of the program development.

In this particular program, the debugging routine also happens to be one of the routines for the program: Procedure *procL* lists the current inventory. Therefore, procedure *procL* should be one of the first routines written. Note, however, that you cannot test *procL* unless there is some data in the data structure. Thus, the first coding task is to define and implement some minimal subset of the solution that would put something into the data structure and allow you to test *procL*. The following procedures accomplish this task:

Getcmnd	{ Subproblem II.1 }	Read in a command.
SkipBlanks	{ II.1.1 }	Skip blanks in an input file (needed for *Getcmnd*).
procAM	{ II.5 and II.6 }	Insert new items into the inventory.
Insert	{ II.5.1 }	Insert a new node into the data structure (needed for *procAM*).

We then implemented

procL	{ II.4 }	List the current inventory.

2. After the procedures in the previous step were working satisfactorily, we turned our attention to adding a new set of routines to expand the scope of the program. We chose from among many possibilities and decided to write the routines for saving and restoring the inventory:

Getinv	{ I }	Restore the inventory from a file.
Putinv	{ III }	Save the inventory in a file.

One reason for this decision was that it allowed us to continue the development of the program over a series of runs without having to create a new inventory from scratch each time. We did not code the procedures *Putwait* and *Getwait* (for saving and restoring the wait lists) until Phase 2 of the program development.

Notice that the program never actually deletes nodes from the linked list of inventory items. It removes items from the inventory simply by not writing them out to the file when it executes the Q command (that is, when it executes *Putinv*). Because this removal occurs just before the program terminates—and all memory is returned to the system—nothing is gained by explicitly disposing of these particular nodes.

3. At this point, the program was starting to look like a solution to the original problem. We chose to add the following routines next, primarily because they were easy to write:

procH	{ II.2 }	Write out a summary of the commands.
procO	{ II.8 }	Write a purchase order.
procR	{ II.9 }	Write a return order.

4. The choices here were fairly arbitrary. We focused on the addition of procedure *procI*.

procI	{ II.3 }	Write information about a specified title.
Getstring	{ II.3.1 }	Read a title argument (needed for *procI*).
Find	{ II.3.2 }	Locate a title in the inventory (needed for *procI*).

5. Finally, we added the last two procedures:

procD	{ II.7 }	Process a delivery.
procS	{ II.10 }	Sell a cassette.

Phase 2: Implement the wait list operations. At this point we had a working program that supported all the inventory commands but did not account for the wait lists. It was fairly easy to add the remaining subprograms:

Getwait	{ I.1 }	Read in (from a file) the wait list for a stock item.
Putwait	{ III.1 }	Write out (to a file) the wait list for a stock item.
Waitnames	{ II.3.3 }	Write out the wait list for a stock item.

Final Set of Refinements to the Program

After completing the bottom-up implementation of the solution, we had a complete working program for the original problem. During this last stage of the problem-solving process, we refined the program to make it more sophisticated. This stage included the following kinds of refinements:

1. During the top-down design of the solution, we made temporary simplifying assumptions about the input data. In this final stage we removed these assumptions.

   For example, in the pseudocode given earlier for Subproblem II.1 (the procedure *Getcmnd*) we made the assumption that commands would consist of single uppercase letters. In the final set of refine-ments, we removed this assumption by allowing both lowercase com-mands and uppercase commands and by adding code to recognize commands that appear as the first character of a word. The advantage of this second feature is that it allows a user to type, for example, the word "order" instead of the single character "O". The first version of the program would not have recognized "order" and would have ignored it.

2. A second type of refinement was to make the user interface more "intelligent." For example, you might want a program that is easy to use for both sophisticated and unsophisticated users. An example of a modification that can enhance the appeal of the program is as follows: If a command requires an argument such as the title of a cassette, then the user should be able to type either the full command with argu-ments (if the user is familiar with the command) or only the command name and get prompted for the arguments (if the user is not familiar with the command). That is, the program prompts for arguments only if the user omits them. We added this feature by modifying the *Getstring* procedure and by adding a procedure *Prompt* to prompt the user to give the appropriate input.

3. A third kind of refinement concerned adding internal checks to the program to test for program errors. Given the nature of the program, it is reasonable to assume that other people might modify it in the future. These modifications might violate some of the assumptions about the data and data structures, and the program should help you to avoid any serious consequences as a result of modification. This is in keeping with the discussion of fail-safe programming in Chapter 1.

   For example, consider the operations that restore and save the inventory. The correctness of the inventory program depends heavily on the integrity of these operations, and these operations in turn depend on the validity of the have value of each inventory item as a true indicator of the size of the associated wait list. If a modification to a program caused a violation of the relationship between the have value and the size of the wait list, the results could be severe: The entire inventory structure could lose its validity. One type of enhancement to this program was to include checks of this relationship in the places where the inventory structure was vulnerable to ruin. We chose to build this extra testing into the procedures *Getwait* and *Putwait*. Note that *Getinv* and *Putinv*—the procedures that restore and save the inventory structure—call *Getwait* and *Putwait*.

One of the reasons that we like this inventory problem is because there is so much room for growth. The exercises at the end of this chapter sug-gest modifications and enhancements. We hope that the ease of changing and adding to the program will help to convince you of the value and effectiveness of top-down design and modularity.

SUMMARY

1. Pointer variables are an extremely useful data type. You can use them to implement the data structure known as a linked list by using statements such as the following:

```
type    ptr = ^node;
        node = record
            data : <any data type except file>;
            next : ptr
        end;
var     head : ptr
```

If *p* is a variable of type *ptr* that points to a node in this linked list, then

- *p*^ is the node.
- *p*^.*data* is the data portion of the node.
- *p*^.*next* points to the next node.

2. The linked list is highly versatile and you will encounter it throughout the book. Algorithms for inserting data into and deleting data from a sorted linked list consist of two steps: Traverse the list from the beginning until you reach the appropriate position; perform pointer changes to alter the structure of the list.

3. An important advantage of a pointer-based linked list over an array is that you can increase the size of a linked list simply by using the *new* command to dynamically allocate additional nodes when needed. You can also insert items into and delete items from a linked list without shifting data.

4. While you can access any element of an array directly, you must traverse a linked list to access a particular node. Therefore, the access time for an array is constant, whereas the access time for a linked list depends upon the location of the node within the list.

5. Pascal's *dispose* procedure allows a program to recycle its nodes by returning them to the system for reallocation by the *new* procedure.

6. You can store a linked list in a file by writing the data portion of the nodes in the order in which they appear on the list. As a result, it is easy to restore the linked list directly from the file at a later time.

7. In a circular linked list, the last node points to the first node, so that every node has a successor. If the list's external pointer points to the last node instead of the first node, you can access both the last node and the first node without traversing the list.

8. Dummy head nodes provide a method for eliminating the special

cases for insertion into and deletion from the beginning of a linked list. The use of dummy head nodes is a matter of personal taste for singly linked lists, but it is helpful for a doubly linked list.

9. A head record contains global information about a linked list—such as its length—in addition to a pointer to the first node on the list.

10. A doubly linked list allows you to traverse the list in either direction. Each node points to its successor as well as its predecessor. Because insertions and deletions with a doubly linked list are more involved than with a singly linked list, it is convenient to use both a dummy head node and a circular structure to eliminate complicated special cases for the beginning and end of the list.

11. The case study demonstrated how you can use a methodical top-down approach to solve a large problem. The case study illustrated several problem-solving principles, including the following:

    a. You should split the problem into modules that you successively refine. For the most part, you should perform the refinements in isolation, although you should keep the overall picture in mind.

    b. After you have completed the design of the initial solution, you have a hierarchy of modules. As you begin implementing the modules with Pascal subprograms, you must decide which modules to code first. If the development of a module *M* depends on the actions of its submodules, then a reasonable approach is to start at the bottom of the hierarchy and work up. On the other hand, if the modules that *M* uses are peripheral, you can implement them initially by using dummy procedures—called stubs—that simply report that they have been called. By using stubs you can focus on the more central aspects of the problem.

    c. Before you consider the programming task complete, you should carefully perform a final set of refinements that include making the input modules as flexible as possible, adding fail-safe features, and polishing the documentation.

COMMON PITFALLS/DEBUGGING

1. You cannot look at the value of a pointer variable *p*. For example, *write(p)* is illegal.

2. An uninitialized pointer variable has an undefined value, not the value *nil*.

3. An attempt to reference a pointer variable that has the value *nil* is
    an error. For example, each of the following results in an error if
    p has the value *nil*: *write(p); write(p^.data); p :=*
    p^.next

4. Insertions into and deletions from the beginning of a linked list
    are special cases unless you use dummy head nodes. Failure to rec-
    ognize this fact can result in a reference to a pointer whose value is
    nil; such a reference is an error.

5. When traversing a linked list by using the pointer variable *cur*,
    you must be careful not to reference *cur* after it has "passed" the
    last node on the list, because it will have the value *nil* at that
    point. For example, the loop

    ```
    while (X > cur^.data) do
        cur := cur^.next
    ```

    causes an error if *X* is greater than all the data values in the linked
    list, because *cur* becomes *nil*. At the pseudocode level, the *Cand*
    operator solves this problem:

    ```
    while (cur <> nil) Cand (X > cur^.data) do
        cur := cur^.next
    ```

6. After you have returned a node to the system by using *dispose*,
    you should not reference any pointer variable that still points to
    the node. The procedure *dispose(p)* helps you to avoid this type
    of error by assigning *p* an undefined value. However, if variables
    other than *p* point to the freed node, there is still the potential that
    the program will reference it.

7. A doubly linked list is a construct that programmers tend to over-
    use. However, a doubly linked list is appropriate when you can
    access a node directly, without performing a traversal from the
    beginning of the list. Because doubly linking the list provides an
    easy way to get to the node's predecessor as well as its successor,
    you can, for example, delete the node readily.

SELF-TEST EXERCISES

1. Eliminate the statements that are syntactically incorrect in this pro-
    gram, and then trace the execution by hand.

    ```
    program testptr(output);

    type    intptr = ^integer;
            intptrptr = ^intptr;

    var     p, q : intptr;
            pp : intptrptr;
    ```

```
begin
    new(p);
    new(q);
    writeln(p, q);

    p^ := 7;
    q^ := 11;
    writeln(p^, q^);

    new(pp);
    pp^   := 20;
    pp^ := p;
    writeln(p^, pp^);

    pp^^ := pp^^ + q^;
    writeln(p^, pp^^);

    new(pp^);
    pp^^ := -3;
    pp^^ := q^ + p^ + pp^^;
    writeln(p^, q^,pp^^)
end.
```

2. Consider a sorted linked list of nodes that each contain a single character in its data portion. Initially, the list contains three nodes, as Figure 3-55 depicts. In addition, *prev* points to the first node in this list and *cur* points to the second node. Do not use any of the subprograms that were presented in this chapter when writing the solutions to this exercise.

  a. Write Pascal statements that delete the second node and return it to the system. (*Hint:* First modify Figure 3-55.)
  b. Now assume that *cur* points to the first node of the remaining two nodes of the original list. Write Pascal statements that delete the first node and return it to the system.
  c. Now *head* points to the only node that is left on the list. Write Pascal statements that insert a new node that contains "A" into the list so that the list remains sorted.
  d. Revise Figure 3-55 so that your new diagram reflects the results of the previous deletions and insertion.

3. Write a procedure that will print only the Nth node in a linked list of integers. You can assume that the linked list contains at least N nodes.

4. How many assignment operations does the procedure that you wrote for Self-Test Exercise 3 require?

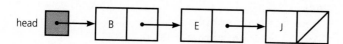

Figure 3-55

Linked list for Self-Test Exercise 2

5. Consider the array *Lists* of pointers that the following statements define:

```
type  ptr = ^node;
      node = record
          data : integer;
          next : ptr
      end;
      ptrarray = array[1..10] of ptr;
var   Lists : ptrarray
```

You can think of *Lists* as an array of linked lists. Suppose that each linked list is ordered. How can you use the *Insert* and *Delete* procedures, as developed in this chapter, on the ith linked list in *Lists*?

EXERCISES

1. Trace the execution of the following program by hand, and show its output.

```
program testptr(output);
const  maxname = 8;
       maxfamily = 100;

type   string = packed array[1..maxname] of char;

       person = record
           name : string;
           age  : 0..maxint
       end;

       family = array[1..maxfamily] of person;

       personptr = ^person;
       familyptr = ^family;

var    pptr : personptr;
       fptr : familyptr;
       i : integer;
begin
    new(pptr);
    pptr^.age := 25;
    pptr^.name := 'Fred    ';
    for i := 1 to maxname do
       write(pptr^.name[i]);
    writeln(' is ', pptr^.age:1,' years old.');

    new(fptr);
    fptr^[10] := pptr^;
    for i := 1 to maxname do
       write(fptr^[10].name[i]);
```

```
      writeln(' is ', fptr^[10].age:1,' years old.')
  end.
```

2. This exercise assumes that you have completed Self-Test Exercise 2 and know the final status of the linked list. For each of the following, write the Pascal statements that perform the requested operation on the list. Also draw a picture of the status of the list after each operation is complete. When you delete a node from the list, return it to the system. All insertions into the list should maintain the list's sorted order. Do not use any of the subprograms that were presented in this chapter.

   a. Assume that *prev* points to the first node and *cur* points to the second node. Insert "F" into the list.

   b. Assume that *prev* points to the second node and that *cur* points to the third node of the list after you revised it in Part *a*. Delete the last node on the list.

   c. Assume that *prev* points to the last node of the list after you revised it in Part *b*, and assume that *cur* is *nil*. Insert "G" into the list.

3. Complete the Pascal implementation of the procedure `Delete` described in the section "Insert and Delete Procedures for a Sorted Linked List."

4. a. Write a procedure `Traverse` that traverses an ordered linked list and determines either where *X* belongs on the list or where *X* occurs on the list. The procedure should return two pointers as follows: *cur* points to the node on the list whose data portion is greater than or equal to *X*, and *prev* points to the preceding node.

   b. Modify the `Insert` and `Delete` procedures that were presented in this chapter so that they use your `Traverse` procedure.

5. Compare the number of operations that the `PrintList` procedure— described in the section "Displaying the Contents of a Linked List"— requires to print each node in a linked list of integers with the number of operations that a procedure requires to print each item in an array of integers.

Exercises 6 through 27 all refer to the following definitions:

```
type  nodeptr = ^node;
      node = record
            data : integer;
            next : nodeptr
         end
```

6. Write a function

```
function count(head : nodeptr) : integer;
```

to count the number of records on the linked list pointed to by *head*.

7. Write a procedure that will return to the system all the nodes on a linked list. Use the procedure *dispose*.

8. Write a procedure that will copy a linked list to a new linked list.

9. Given a linked list, write a procedure that creates a second linked list whose nodes are the nodes of the first list in reversed order. That is, the first node on the first list is the last node of the second list.

10. Given a linked list, write a procedure that reverses its links. Thus, the last node becomes first and the first node becomes last. This exercise differs from Exercise 9 in that there is only one list.

11. Consider an unordered linked list of integers. Write a procedure that creates two additional unordered linked lists: One list contains the even integers that are in the original list, and the other contains the odd integers. Do not destroy the original list.

12. Repeat Exercise 11, but this time do not use the *new* procedure. Instead, move each node from the original list into one of the new lists as appropriate. When you are done, the original list will be empty.

13. Repeat Exercise 12, but this time move only the odd integers from the original list into a new list. When you are done, the original list will contain the even integers and the new list will contain the odd integers.

14. Repeat Exercises 11, 12, and 13, but this time assume that all of the lists are sorted.

15. Write a procedure that will delete the ith node from a linked list.

16. Write a function

```
function Find(head : nodeptr; target : integer) : nodeptr;
```

to return a pointer to the first record on an unordered linked list that contains the value in *target*. If there is no such record on the list, *Find* should return *nil*. Assume that *head* points to the linked list.

17. Write a procedure that will delete from a linked list the node that contains the largest data value. Can you do this with a single traversal of the list?

18. Write a procedure that will merge two linked lists that are sorted by data value. The result should be a linked list that is the sorted combination of the original lists.

19. Repeat Exercises 7, 8, and 15 through 18 for a circular linked list.

20. Assume that the pointer *List* points to the first node of a circular linked list. Write a loop that will print the data portion of every node on the list.

21. Write a procedure that will determine whether two circular lists are identical. Do this in two different ways as follows:

    a. In the first version, you may assume that a data item will occur at most once on any list.

    b. In the second version, you must account for possible duplicates on a list.

22. Write a procedure *Linear(var p : nodeptr)* that converts a circular list to a linear list that starts at the node that contains the smallest integer on the list. The parameter *p* points to some arbitrary node on the circular linked list. Upon return from the procedure, *p* points to the head of the new linear list.

23. Write a procedure that will reverse the links of a circular linked list, as Figure 3-56 depicts.

24. Write a program that will read a file of integers, insert each into a linked list so that the list is sorted by data value, and write out the final list.

25. Write the type definitions for the dummy head node that Figure 3-26a pictures. Also declare the pointer variable *head*.

26. Write procedures for insertion into and deletion from a sorted linked list that has a dummy head node.

27. Write a type definition for a variant record that will allow you to keep global information about a list in a dummy head node.

28. You can implement a character string as a linked list of characters. Write subprograms for some typical string operations such as concat-

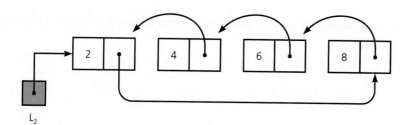

Figure 3-56

Two circular lists, one the reverse of the other

enation (append one string to another) and length computation. How can you implement the string so that you can obtain its length without traversing the linked list and counting?

29. Consider the ordered doubly linked list shown in Figure 3-28. This list is circular and has a dummy head node. Suppose that *Newname* contains a name that you want to add to the list in its proper order. Write a loop that traverses the list backward from the last node and sets *cur* to point to the node that should precede the new node in the list.

30. Write procedures *Insert* and *Delete* for the ordered doubly linked list shown in Figure 3-28. The list is circular and has a dummy head node. Each procedure has a pointer parameter *p*. *Insert* should insert the new node pointed to by *p* in its proper order in the list. *Delete* should delete the node to which *p* points.

31. Repeat Exercise 30 for the ordered doubly linked list shown in Figure 3-27. This list is not circular and does not have a dummy head node. Watch out for the special cases at the beginning and end of the list.

32. You can have a linked list of linked lists, as Figure 3-32 indicates. Assume the constant and type definitions on page 136. Suppose that *cur* points to the desired stock item (node) in the inventory list. Write a Pascal procedure that adds a name to the end of the wait list associated with the node to which *cur* points.

PROJECTS

33. Write a complete string manipulation package (see Exercise 28), including more sophisticated string operations such as finding the index of the leftmost occurrence of a character in a string and determining whether one string is a substring of another.

34. Write the inventory program that the case study describes.

35. Modify and expand the inventory program in the case study. Here are a few suggestions:
   a. Add the ability to manipulate more than one inventory with the single program.
   b. Add the ability to keep various statistics about each of the inventory items (such as the average number sold per week for the last 10 weeks).
   c. Add the ability to modify the have value for an inventory item (for example, when a cassette is damaged or returned from a customer). Consider the implications for maintaining the relationship between a have value and the size of the corresponding wait list.

    d. Make the wait lists more sophisticated. For example, keep names and addresses and mail letters automatically when a cassette comes in.

    e. Make the ordering mechanism more sophisticated. For instance, do not order cassettes that have been ordered already but have not been delivered.

Problem-Solving Tools

CHAPTER *4*

Data Abstraction: The Walls

PREVIEW   The first three chapters of this book reinforced principles of program design and implementation. Our primary concern now is to develop a repertoire of problem-solving tools. This chapter elaborates on data abstraction, which was introduced in Chapter 1, as a tool for increasing the modularity of a program—for building "walls" between a program and its data structures. During the design of a solution, you will discover that you need to support several operations on the data and therefore need to define abstract data types. Only after you have clearly defined the operations of an abstract data type should you consider data structures for implementing it. This chapter will introduce some simple abstract data types and use them to demonstrate the advantages of abstract data types in general. In Part III of this book, which involves the management of data, you will see several other important ADT's.

ABSTRACTION

By now the advantages of top-down design should be quite clear. Throughout the previous chapters of this book, we have espoused its virtues via argument and illustration. You can develop programs by piecing together functions and procedures that have yet to be written. The trick is to decide what *you would like* the subprograms to do and to proceed under the assumption that they exist and work. In this way you can write the subprograms in relative isolation from one another, knowing *what* each one will do but not necessarily *how* each will eventually do it. The underlying principle, which is called **procedural abstraction**, yields **modular** programs, whose advantages you saw in Chapter 1. To summarize those advantages, modularity is a method that keeps the complexity of a large program manageable by systematically controlling the interaction of its components. Thus, a modular program is easier to write because you can focus on one task at a time without other distractions.

Recall from Chapter 1 that procedural abstraction involves writing module specifications and in addition identifying details that you can hide within the module from other modules. The principle of **information hiding** involves not only hiding these details, but also making them *inaccessible* from outside a module. A graphic way to understand procedural abstraction and information hiding is to imagine **walls** around the various tasks a program performs. These walls prevent the tasks from becoming entangled. The wall around each task T prevents the other tasks from "seeing" how T is performed. As Figure 4-1 illustrates, one benefit of this isolation is that if the method for performing task T should change, task Q will not be affected, because the wall prevents task Q's method of solution from depending on task T's method of solution.

The isolation of the modules cannot be total, however. Although task Q is oblivious to *how* task T is performed, it may well have to know *what*

Isolate the implementation details of a module from other modules

Figure 4-1

**Isolated tasks: the imple-
mentation of task *T* does not
affect task *Q***

task *T* is and how to initiate it. For example, suppose that a program needs
to operate on a sorted array of names. The program may, for instance, need
to search the array for a given name or print out the names in alphabetical
order. The program thus needs a module *S* that sorts an array of names.
Although the rest of the program knows that module *S* will sort an array, it
should not care how *S* accomplishes its task.

   When you as program designer realize that there is a need to sort the
names, you write the specifications for the sort routine. For example,

*Write specifications for each
module before implementing it*

The routine will receive an array of no more than *maxname* names.
The length of each name is no more then *maxlen* characters. The
routine will return the array with the names in ascending
alphabetical order.

You can view these specifications as the terms of a **contract** that states that
the program can rely on *S* to sort the array. If you alone write the entire
program, this contract helps systematically decompose the problem into
smaller tasks. If the program is a team project, the contract helps to delin-
eate responsibilities. Whoever writes the sort routine has this contract to
live up to. After the sort routine has been written and tested, the rest of the

program will rely on it. The contract tells the other modules how to use the routine and the result of doing so. For example, the contract will specify how to call the sort routine properly and will state that upon return, the array is sorted in ascending order.

Thus, imagine a tiny slit in each wall, as Figure 4–2 illustrates. Things can pass through the slit into and out of the module. For example, you can pass the array into the sort routine, and the routine can pass the sorted array out to you. What goes in and comes out is governed by the terms of the module's contract: *If you use me in this way, this is exactly what I'll do for you.* It is very important to notice, however, that a module's contract does not commit the module to a particular method of performing its task. If another part of the program assumes anything about the method, it does so at its own risk. Thus, for example, if at some later date you use a different sort routine, you should not need to change the rest of the program at all. The slit in the wall is not large enough to allow the outside world to see the inner workings of the module. As long as the new module honors the terms of the original contract, the rest of the program should be oblivious to the change.

Specifications do not indicate how to implement a module

This discussion should not be news to you. Although we have not explicitly used the terms "wall" and "contract" before, the concepts certainly permeate the previous chapters of this book. For example, we have used the standard function *sqrt* as an example of a module that you know how to use. You know that if you pass *sqrt* either a real or an integer expression, it will return the real square root of the value of that expres-

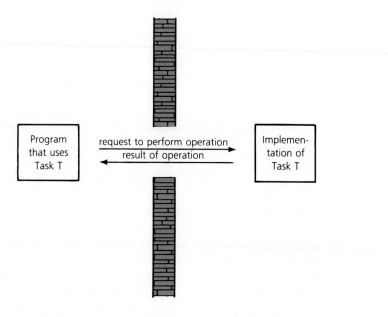

Figure 4-2

A slit in the wall

sion. You can use *sqrt* even though you do not know its implementation. In fact, the *sqrt* function is precompiled and is an example of a **unit**, which was introduced in Chapter 2. You do not have access to *sqrt*'s code. Furthermore, it may be that *sqrt* was written in a language other than Pascal! There is so much about *sqrt* that you do not know, yet you can use it in your program without concern.

Both procedural and data abstraction ask you to think what, not how

We have given you this synopsis of procedural abstraction now because we are about to expand on the other half of modular program development: **data abstraction.** Procedural abstraction advocates partitioning a program into independent algorithms, which perform small, isolated tasks, and asks you to think in terms of *what* an algorithm does independently of *how* it does it. Data abstraction asks that you think in terms of *what* you can do to a collection of data independently of *how* you do it. Data abstraction is a tool that allows you to develop each data structure in relative isolation from the rest of the solution. The other modules of the solution will "know" what operations they can perform on the data, but they should not depend on how the data is stored or how the operations are performed. Again, the terms of the contract are *what* and not *how*. Thus, data abstraction is a natural extension of procedural abstraction to data structures.

Often the solution to a problem requires the performance of operations that are broadly described in one of three ways:

- **Add** data to a data collection.
- **Remove** data from a data collection.
- **Ask questions** about the data in a data collection.

The details of the operations, of course, vary from application to application, but the overall theme is the management of data. Realize, however, that not all problems, and certainly not all ADT's, use or require these operations.

ABSTRACT DATA TYPES

A collection of data values together with a set of operations on that data are called an **abstract data type**, or ADT. The definition of the operations must be rigorous enough to specify completely the effect that they have on the data, yet the definition must not specify how to store the data nor how to carry out the operations. For example, the ADT operations cannot specify whether to store the data in consecutive memory locations or in disjoint memory locations that are linked with pointers. You choose a particular **data structure** when you implement an ADT. Recall that a data structure is a construct that you can define within a programming lan-

The specifications of ADT operations indicate what they do, but not how to implement them

Data structures implement ADT's

guage to store a collection of data. For example, a Pascal array is a data structure.

Data structures and structured data types are related. All structured data types—arrays, records, files, and sets—are data structures. There are, however, other data structures, which could be either user-defined data types in Pascal or data types in another language, that you could invent. For example, suppose that you wanted a data structure to store both the names and salaries of a group of employees. You could use the following definitions:

```
const   NumberEmployees = 500;
        Length = 20;
type    string    = packed array[1..Length] of char;
        nametype   = array[1..NumberEmployees] of string;
        salarytype = array[1..NumberEmployees] of real;
var     Names : nametype;
        Salaries : salarytype;
```

Here the employee *Names[i]* has a salary of *Salaries[i]*. The two arrays *Names* and *Salaries* together form a data structure, yet there is no single Pascal data type that describes it.

An abstract data type is not another name for a data structure. To give you a better idea of the conceptual difference between an ADT and a data structure, consider the machine in Figure 4-3. This machine accepts ice cubes as input and produces as output either crushed ice or cold water according to which one of two buttons you push. The machine is analogous to an abstract data type. The ice cubes are analogous to a data collection; the operations are *Crush* and *Liquefy*. At this level of design, the machine is a black box. You are not concerned with how it will perform its operations, only that it performs them. If you want crushed ice, do you really care how the machine accomplishes its task as long as it does so correctly? Thus, after you have specified the machine's functions, you can design many uses for crushed ice and cold water without knowing how the machine accomplishes its tasks and without the distraction of engineering details.

ADT's and data structures are not the same

Eventually someone must build the machine. Exactly how will this machine produce crushed ice, for example, from ice cubes? It might crush the cubes between two steel rollers, or it might use hammers to smash the cubes into small pieces. The internal structure of the machine corresponds to the implementation of the ADT in Pascal, that is, to a data structure. Although the user of the machine does not care about its inner workings, certainly the machine's manufacturer cares. Which design is easiest and cheapest to build? Which design is the most efficient in its operation? These are the same concerns that you should have when you choose a data structure to implement an ADT in Pascal.

Notice that the interior mechanisms for each operation are surrounded by steel walls. The only breaks in the walls accommodate the input (ice

Figure 4-3

A machine that transforms ice cubes into either crushed ice or water

ice cubes

cubes) to the machine and its output (crushed ice or cold water). Thus, the machine's mechanisms are not only hidden from the user but also are inaccessible. In addition, the mechanism of one operation is hidden from and inaccessible to the other operation. There are other benefits of the machine's design as a result of its modularity. You can improve the operation *Crush* by modifying its module without affecting the *Liquefy* module. You could also add an operation by adding another module to the machine without affecting the original two operations. Thus, both abstraction and information hiding are at work here.

When a program must perform on its data operations that are not directly supported by the language, you must construct the data structures.

Carefully specify an ADT's operations before you implement them

You should first design an abstract data type and then carefully specify what the ADT operations are to do (the contract). Then—*and only then*—should you implement the operations with a data structure. If you implement the operations properly, the rest of the program will be able to assume that the operations perform as specified—that is, that the terms of the contract are honored. However, the program must not depend on a particular method for supporting the operations.

To summarize, data abstraction results in walls between a program and its data structures. A slit in each wall allows you to pass requests to perform operations through to the data structure and allows the data structure to pass back the results of these operations, as Figure 4-4 illustrates. The data structure's specifications govern what those operations are and what they do: *This is the exact result of each of my operations.* This approach allows the program to be oblivious to any change in the implementations of its data structures. Much of the remainder of the book uses this data-abstraction approach.

A program should not depend on the details of an ADT's implementation

Providing for the requirements of an ADT sounds like a formidable task, and indeed it is. An ADT is both a mathematical concept and a problem-solving tool. The formal mathematical study of ADT's uses systems of **axioms** to specify the behavior of the operations. Our goal is to give you a sense of the value of ADT's as a problem-solving tool rather than to develop mathematically rigorous definitions. Therefore, we will rely primarily on informal, intuitive definitions. From time to time, however, we shall present a few axiomatic definitions for illustrative purposes.

The following pages describe how to use an abstract data type to realize data abstraction's goal of separating the operations on data from the implementation of these operations. In doing so, several examples of ADT's will be presented.

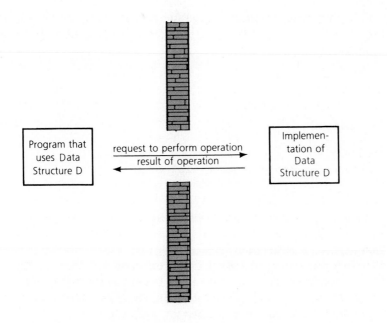

Figure 4-4

A wall that isolates data structures

Figure 4-5

A grocery list

The ADT Ordered List

To elaborate on the notion of an abstract data type, consider the familiar grocery list pictured in Figure 4-5. Although the six items on the list are in sequential order, they are not necessarily sorted by name. Perhaps the list items appear in the order in which they occur on the grocer's shelves, but more likely they appear in the order in which they occurred to you.

What can you do to such a list? You might count the items to determine the length of the list, insert an item at position *i* on the list, delete the item at position *i*, or look at the item at position *i*. Thus, you could define the ADT "grocery list" as a collection of grocery items together with the previous operations. In fact, this ADT is more formally known as an **ordered list**. However, do not bring to the following discussion any preconceived notion of a data structure that the term "ordered list" might suggest.

The following specifications define the operations for the ADT ordered list. Note that it is customary to include an initialization operation that creates an empty list.

KEY CONCEPTS   **ADT *Ordered List Operations***

```
Create(L)
{ Creates an empty ordered list L. }

Length(L)
{ Returns the number of items that are in the ordered list L. }

Insert(L, i, newitem)
{ Inserts newitem at position i of ordered list L. The value
  of i must be within the range 1 to Length(L)+1. If i ≤
  Length(L), items are shifted as follows: The item at
  position i becomes the item at position i+1, the item at
```

```
position i+1 becomes the item at position i+2, . . . , the
item at position Length(L) becomes the item at position
Length(L)+1. }
```

Delete(L, i)
```
{ Deletes the item at position i of the ordered list L. The
  value of i must be within the range 1 to Length(L). If i <
  Length(L), items are shifted as follows: The item at
  position i+1 becomes the item at position i, the item at
  position i+2 becomes the item at position i+1, . . . , the
  item at position Length(L) becomes the item at position
  Length(L)−1. }
```

Retrieve(L, i)
```
{ Returns the item at position i of the ordered list L. The
  value of i must be within the range 1 to Length(L). The
  list is left unchanged by this operation. }
```

The specifications of these five operations are the terms of the contract for the ADT ordered list. Notice that the specifications of the operations contain no mention of how to store the ordered list or how to perform the operations. The ADT definition tells you only what you can do to an ordered list. It is of fundamental importance that the definition of an ADT *not* include implementation issues. This restriction on the definition of an ordered list is what allows you to build a wall between an implementation of an ordered list and the program that uses it. The ADT operations are the sole terms of the contract between an implementation and a program: *If you request that these operations be performed, this is what will happen.* The behavior of the operations is the only thing on which a program should depend.

An ADT definition should not include implementation issues

A program should depend only on the behavior of the ADT

What does the definition of the ADT ordered list tell you about its behavior? It is apparent that the ordered list operations fall into the three broad categories presented earlier in this chapter.

- The operation *Insert* **adds** data to a data collection.
- The operation *Delete* **removes** data from a data collection.
- The operations *Retrieve* and *Length* **ask questions** about the data in a data collection.

These descriptions of the operations are only general, but the definition of an ordered list does specify exactly what the operations do. To get a more precise idea of how the operations work, apply them to this grocery list:

L = <milk, eggs, butter, apples, bread, chicken>

The notation implies that milk is the first item on the list and chicken is the last item.

To begin, consider how you can construct this list by using the ordered list operations. One way is first to create an empty list and then to use a series of *Insert* operations to successively append the items to the list as follows:

```
Create(L)
Insert(L, 1, milk)
Insert(L, 2, eggs)
Insert(L, 3, butter)
Insert(L, 4, apples)
Insert(L, 5, bread)
Insert(L, 6, chicken)
```

Notice that the ordered list's *Insert* operation can insert new items into any position of the list, not just its end. The definition of *Insert* specifies that if a new item is inserted into position i, then the position of each item that was at a position of i or greater is increased by 1. Thus, for example, if you start with the previous grocery list and you perform the operation

```
Insert(L, 4, nuts)
```

then the list becomes

L = <milk, eggs, butter, nuts, apples, bread, chicken>

All items that were at position numbers greater than or equal to 4 before the insertion are moved and are now each at the next higher position number after the insertion.

Similarly, the *Delete* operation specifies that if an item is deleted from position i, then the position of each item that was at a position greater than i is decremented by 1. Thus, for example, if L is the list

L = <milk, eggs, butter, nuts, apples, bread, chicken>

and you perform the operation

```
Delete(L, 5)
```

then the list becomes

L = <milk, eggs, butter, nuts, bread, chicken>

All items that were at position numbers greater than 5 before the deletion are moved and are now each at the next lower position number after the deletion.

These examples illustrate that the definition of an ADT can specify the effects of its operations without having to indicate how to store the data. However, we have stated the terms of an ordered list's contract—that is, the specifications of its operations—rather informally. For instance, we are relying on your intuition to know what we mean when we say that an item is "at position *i*" in the ordered list. This notion is simple, and most people will understand its intentions. However, some abstract data types are much more complex and less intuitive than an ordered list. For such ADT's it is necessary to use a more rigorous method of defining the behavior of their operations: You must supply a set of **axioms**. For example, the axiom

```
Retrieve(Insert(L, i, X), i) = X
```

specifies that `Retrieve` retrieves from position *i* the item that `Insert` has put there.[1]

Once you have satisfactorily specified the behavior of an ADT, you can design applications that access and manipulate the ADT's data solely in terms of its operations and without regard for its implementation. As a very simple example, suppose that you want to design a procedure that prints out the items in an ordered list. Even though the wall between the implementation of the ADT ordered list and the rest of the program prevents you from knowing how the ordered list is stored, you can write a procedure `PrintList` in terms of the operations that define the ADT ordered list. The pseudocode for such a procedure follows:

```
PrintList(L)
{ Prints the items on the ordered list L (in order) }

    for position := 1 to Length(L) do
    begin
       item := Retrieve(L, position)
       Print item
    end
```

An implementation-independent application of the ADT ordered list

Notice that as long as the ADT ordered list is implemented correctly, the `PrintList` procedure will perform its task; the procedure does not depend on *how* you implement the ordered list. Figure 4-6 illustrates the wall between `PrintList` and the implementation of the ADT ordered list.

As another application of the ADT operations, suppose that you want a procedure `Swap` that interchanges the items currently in positions *i* and *j*

---

[1]You may have noticed that there is a bit of an inconsistency in the way we have used the operations. In order for the above axiom to be syntactically correct, `Insert(L, i, X)` must be an ordered list. It will be an ordered list if `Insert` is a (Pascal-like) function that returns as its value the ordered list that results after the insertion. On the other hand, our earlier definition implies that `Insert` changes the value of its argument `L` and does not return a value. The inconsistency results from our desire to define the operations on an intuitive level. As long as you are aware of the issue, it should not cause any difficulties.

Figure 4-6

The wall between `Print-List` and the implementation of the ADT **ordered list**

of the ordered list. The following pseudocode for such a procedure assumes that there actually are items in positions *i* and *j* of the ordered list:

```
Swap(L, i, j)
{ Swaps the iᵗʰ and jᵗʰ items in the ordered list L. }

    first := Retrieve(L, i)   { copy iᵗʰ item }
    second := Retrieve(L, j) { copy jᵗʰ item }

    Delete(L, i)                  { replace iᵗʰ item with jᵗʰ }
    Insert(L, i, second)

    Delete(L, j)                  { replace jᵗʰ item with iᵗʰ }
    Insert(L, j, first)
```

Notice that the order of operations is important because when you delete an item, *Delete* renumbers the remaining items. Like *PrintList*, the *Swap* procedure does not depend on how you implement the ordered list.

You can use ADT *operations in an application without the distraction of implementation details*

In both of the preceding examples, notice how you can focus on the task at hand without the distraction of implementation details such as arrays or pointers. With less to worry about, you are less likely to make an error in your logic when you use the ADT operations in applications such as *PrintList* and *Swap*. Likewise, when you finally implement the ADT operations in Pascal, you will not be distracted by these applications. In addition, you will not have to change *PrintList* and *Swap*, because they do not depend on any implementation decisions that you make. These assertions assume that you do not change the specifications of the ADT operations during their implementation. However, as Chapter 1 pointed out, developing software is not a linear process. You may realize during implementation that you need to refine your specifications. Clearly, changes to the specification of any module affect any already-designed uses of that module.

To summarize, you can specify the behavior of an ADT independently of its implementation, either with informal definitions or with more formal axioms. Given such a specification, and without any knowledge of how the ADT will be implemented, you can design applications that utilize the ADT's operations to access its data.

Designing an ADT

You will see two implementations of the ADT ordered list later in this chapter. However, you probably have some ideas for implementations because the ADT ordered list shares some behaviors with both arrays and linked lists. Consider now some ADT's whose implementations will be less obvious to you. In doing so, you will learn more about the nature of an ADT and see that you should design ADT's as part of your solution to a problem.

The design of an abstract data type should evolve naturally during the problem-solving process. As an example of how this process might occur, suppose that you want to determine the dates of all the holidays in a given year. One way to do this is to examine a calendar. That is, you could consider each day in the year and ascertain whether that day is a holiday. The following pseudocode is thus a possible solution to this problem:

```
ListHolidays(Year)
{ Prints the dates of all holidays in the given year. }

    Date := date of first day of Year
    while Date is not the last day of Year do
    begin
      if Date is a holiday
          then write(Date, ' is a holiday')
      Date := Date + 1 { Date := date of next day }
    end   { while }
```

What data is involved here? Clearly, this problem operates on dates, where a date consists of a month, day, and year. Pascal does not have a standard data type *date*, so you will have to define your own. However, a Pascal user-defined (enumerated) data type does not suffice here. Even if you could specify all the dates that you require by using a user-defined data type, the data type would not specify and restrict the legal operations on the dates. For example, the standard data type *integer* implies arithmetic operations such as addition and multiplication as well as boolean operations such as comparison. An abstract data type differs from a user-defined data type in that an ADT specifies certain operations on the data values.

An ADT differs from a Pascal user-defined data type

What operations will you need to solve the holiday problem? You can see from the previous pseudocode that you must

- Determine the date of the first day of a given year.

- Determine whether a date is the last day of a year.
- Determine whether a date is a holiday.
- Determine the date of the day that follows a given date.

Thus, you could define the following operations for your ADT date:

```
FirstDay(Year)
{ Returns the date of the first day of the year specified. }
IsLastDay(Date)
{ Returns true if Date is the last day of the year,
  otherwise returns false. }

IsHoliday(Date)
{ Returns true if Date is a holiday, otherwise returns
  false. }

Next(Date)
{ Returns the date of the day after the specified date. }
```

All of these operations happen to be specified as functions.

The *ListHolidays* pseudocode now appears as follows:

```
ListHolidays(Year)
{ Prints the dates of all holidays in the year Year. }

    Date := FirstDay(Year)
    while not IsLastDay(Date) do
    begin
      if IsHoliday(Date)
          then write(Date, ' is a holiday ')
      Date := Next(Date)
    end   { while }
```

Thus, you can design an ADT by choosing operations that are suitable to your problem. After specifying the operations, you use them to solve your problem independently of the implementation details of the ADT.

An appointment book.   As another example of an ADT design, imagine that you want to create a computerized appointment book that spans a one-year period. Suppose that you make appointments only on the hour and half hour between 8 a.m. and 5 p.m. You want your system to store a brief notation about the nature of each appointment along with the date and time.

Thus, you can define an ADT appointment book. The data items in this ADT are the appointments, where an appointment consists of a date, time, and purpose. What are the operations? Two obvious operations are

- Make an appointment for a certain date, time, and purpose.
- Erase the appointment for a certain date and time.

You will want to be careful that you do not make an appointment at an already occupied time. In addition to these operations, it is likely that you will want to

- Ask whether you have an appointment at a given time.
- Determine the nature of your appointment at a given time.

These two operations are related and can be combined. After all, you cannot determine the nature of an appointment unless you have one, and if you have an appointment, you probably will want to know its purpose. Finally, ADT's typically have an initialization operation.

Thus, the ADT appointment book can have the following operations:

```
Create(AppointmentBook)
{ Creates an empty appointment book. }

Insert(AppointmentBook, Date, Time, Purpose)
{ Makes an appointment for the Date, Time, and Purpose
  specified. Assumes that there is not already an
  appointment at that time. }

Delete(AppointmentBook, Date, Time)
{ Deletes the appointment for the Date and Time specified. }

Query(AppointmentBook, Date, Time, IsAppointment, Purpose)
{ Determines whether there is an appointment for the Date
  and Time specified. If there is, sets IsAppointment to
  true and returns the purpose of the appointment in
  Purpose; otherwise sets IsAppointment to false. }
```

You can use these ADT operations to design other operations on the appointments. For example, suppose that you want to change the day or time of a particular appointment. The following pseudocode indicates how to accomplish this task by using the previous ADT operations:

```
{ change the date or time of an appointment }
read (OldDate, OldTime, NewDate, NewTime)
Query(AppointmentBook, OldDate, OldTime, IsAppointment, Purpose)
if IsAppointment { if old date/time is booked already }
    then
    begin            { then see if new date/time is available }
        Query(AppointmentBook, NewDate, NewTime, IsAppointment,
                                                  Purpose)

        if IsAppointment
            then write('You already have an appointment at ',
                            NewTime, ' on ', NewDate)
            else    { new date/time is available }
```

```
        begin
            Insert(AppointmentBook, NewDate, NewTime, Purpose)
            Delete(AppointmentBook, OldDate, OldTime)
        end
    end

    else write('You do not have an appointment at ', OldTime,
               ' on ', OldDate)
```

Again notice that you can design applications for ADT operations without knowing how the ADT is implemented. The exercises at the end of this chapter provide examples of others tasks you can perform with this ADT.

ADT's that suggest other ADT's.   This final example shows that the design of one ADT can suggest other ADT's. In fact, you can use one ADT to implement another ADT.

Suppose that you want to design a data base of recipes. You could think of this data base as an ADT: The recipes are the data items, and some typical operations on the recipes could include the following:

```
Create(RecipeBook)
{ Creates an empty data base. }

Insert(RecipeBook, Recipe)
{ Inserts a recipe into the data base RecipeBook. }

Delete(RecipeBook, Recipe)
{ Deletes a recipe from the data base RecipeBook. }

Retrieve(RecipeBook, Name, Recipe)
{ Retrieves the named recipe from the data base RecipeBook. }
```

This level of the design does not indicate such details as where `Insert` will place a recipe into the data base.

Now imagine that you want to write a procedure that scales a recipe retrieved from the data base. If the recipe is for n people, you want to revise it so that it will serve m people. Suppose that the recipe contains measurements such as 2½ cups, 1 tablespoon, and ¼ teaspoon. That is, the quantities are given as mixed numbers—integers and fractions—in units of cups, tablespoons, and teaspoons.

This problem suggests another ADT—measurements—with the following operations:

```
Read(Measure)
{ Reads a Measure. }

Write(Measure)
{ Writes a Measure. }

Scale(Measure, NewMeasure, ScaleFactor)
{ Multiplies a Measure by a fractional ScaleFactor, which
  has no units, to obtain NewMeasure. }
```

```
Convert(Measure, NewUnit, NewMeasure)
{ Converts Measure from its old units to a NewMeasure in new
  units. }
```

The ADT measurements require that you perform fractional arithmetic. As there is no Pascal data type *fraction*, another ADT called fraction is in order. Its operations could include addition, subtraction, multiplication, and division of fractions. For example, you could specify addition as

```
AddFractions(First, Second, Sum)
{ Adds two fractions and reduces the sum to lowest terms }
```

Moreover, you could include operations to convert a mixed number to a fraction and to convert a fraction to a mixed number when feasible.

When you finally implement the ADT measurements, you can use the ADT fraction. That is, you can use one ADT to implement another ADT. The exercises at the end of this chapter ask you to implement these ADT's.

The Linked List As an ADT

Although Chapter 3 presented the linked list as a data structure that involved pointers, you could design an ADT linked list, which you could implement in ways other than by using Pascal pointers. For example, you could define the ADT linked list of sorted integers that has the following operations:

```
Create(LL)
{ Creates an empty linked list LL. }

Insert(LL, X)
{ Inserts X into its proper sorted position in a sorted
  linked list LL unless the list already contains an item
  with value X, in which case no insertion occurs. }

Delete(LL, X)
{ Deletes the data item equal to X, if it is present, from
  the sorted linked list LL. }

Retrieve(LL, i, DataItem)
{ Retrieves the data item in node i of the linked list LL. }

Position(LL, X)
{ Returns the position number in the linked list LL of the
  node that contains X. }
```

As you did in Chapter 3, you can implement this ADT by using pointers. However, you also can implement it by using arrays, as Exercise 10c at the end of this chapter considers. Similarly, you can define other Pascal data structures such as files and sets as ADT's, but we leave these to you as exercises.

IMPLEMENTING ADT'S

Data structures implement ADT's   The question of how to **implement** an ADT—that is, how to store the data and carry out the operations—is in the realm of **data structures**. In other words, data structures implement ADT's. What does it mean to implement an ADT once its operations are clearly defined? Your first reaction to this question might be that an implementation is a set of Pascal type definitions, functions, and procedures. Although this point of view is not incorrect, hopefully you have learned not to jump right into code. Just as you use successive refinement in the top-down design of algorithms, so should you refine an ADT through successive levels of abstraction. You can view each of the successively more concrete descriptions of the ADT as implementing its more abstract predecessors. As you will see, there are decisions that you should make carefully at each level of the implementation. In a formal course on data structures, you will learn how to weigh quantitatively the trade-offs involved. For now, however, our analyses are at the intuitive level.

The refinement process stops when you reach an implementation at a level of abstraction that the programming language supports—that is, when the ADT is transformed gradually from a set of operations into a form that can be realized in a programming language. If the implementation uses constructs such as records and pointers, you can stop if your language is Pascal, because Pascal supports records and pointers. On the other hand, if your language is FORTRAN, you must devise a way to implement records and pointers by using the constructs that FORTRAN supplies. The more primitive your language, the more levels of implementation you will require.

Implementations of the ADT Ordered List

The implementation of the ADT ordered list will illustrate ADT implementation in general. Recall that the ADT ordered list operations are

```
Create(L)
Length(L)
Insert(L, i, newitem)
Delete(L, i)
Retrieve(L, i)
```

An array-based implementation.   Your first thought about implementing an ordered list is probably to store the list's items in an array. In fact, you might believe that the ordered list is simply a fancy name for an array. If you do, we hope that by the time you finish reading this chapter, you will see the error in this point of view.

In any case, the array-based implementation appears to be a natural choice because both an array *Items* and an ordered list reference their

Figure 4-7

**An array-based implementa-
tion of an ordered list**

items by position number. Thus, you can store the ordered list's i^{th} item in
`Items[i]`. How much of the array will the ordered list occupy? Possibly
all of the array, but probably not. That is, you need to keep track of the
array elements that you have assigned to the ordered list and those that
are available for use in the future. The length of the array is a known, fixed
value such as `maxlen`. Thus, a simple solution is to keep track of the number of items on the list, that is, the list's length. An obvious benefit is that
it will be simple for you to implement the operation `Length(L)`.

You should implement each ADT operation as either a procedure or a
function. Each operation will require both the array `Items` and the length
`Len` of the ordered list. One way to facilitate the passing of both `Items` and
`Len` to each subprogram is to define the ordered list `L` as a record with two
fields:

> `Len`: an integer that is the length of the list

> `Items`: an array that contains the items on the list

*An ordered list as a record with
two fields*

as Figure 4-7 illustrates. Thus, the following statements declare `L` to be an
ordered list:

```
const  maxlen = <maximum length of list>;
type   itemtype = <desired type of list item>;
       orderedlist= record
            Len : integer;
            Items : array[1..maxlen] of itemtype
       end;
var    L : orderedlist;
```

The pseudocode for the five ordered list operations follows:

```
Create(L)

    L.Len := 0

Length(L)

    Length := L.Len

Insert(L, i, newitem)

    if (i < 1) or (i > Length(L) + 1) or (Length(L) = maxlen)
        then indicate an error
        else
```

```
                    begin
                        { shift all items at positions i or greater
                          ( no shift if i = Length(L)+1 ) }
                        for j := Length(L) downto i do
                            L.Items[j + 1] := L.Items[j]
                        { insert new item }
                        L.Items[i] := newitem
                        L.Len := L.Len + 1
                    end

        Delete(L, i)

            if (i < 1) or (i > Length(L))
                then indicate an error
                else
                begin
                    { shift all items at positions greater than i
                      ( no shift if i = Length(L) ) }
                    for j := i + 1 to Length(L) do
                        L.Items[j — 1] := L.Items[j]
                    L.Len := L.Len — 1
                end

        Retrieve(L, i)

            if (i < 1) or (i > Length(L))
                then indicate an error
                else return the item L.Items[i]
```

This pseudocode is very close to a Pascal implementation of the ADT ordered list. However, there are a few details to work out, such as how *Retrieve* can return an item and what to do in the event of an error. The completion of this implementation is left as an exercise.

A pointer-based implementation.   A close examination of the array-based implementation uncovers a difficulty. An array has a fixed size—at least in most commonly used programming languages—but the ADT ordered list can have an arbitrary length. Thus, in the strict sense, you cannot use an array to implement an ordered list, because it is certainly possible for the number of items on the list to exceed the fixed size of the array. When developing implementations for ADT's, you are often confronted with this **fixed-size** problem. In many contexts, you must reject an implementation that has a fixed size in favor of an implementation that can grow dynamically.

Thus, this section considers how you can develop a dynamic implementation. Pascal supports the dynamic allocation of storage through its predefined procedure *new*. Recall that the procedure call *new(p)* returns *p* pointing to a newly allocated node of storage. You can use the techniques developed in Chapter 3 to link these nodes together, thereby creating a linked list that represents the ADT ordered list. As the length of the ordered list increases, you need only use the procedure *new* to allocate nodes for the additional items. Unlike the array-based implementation, a pointer-based implementation does not impose a fixed maximum length on the list—except, of course, as imposed by the storage limits of the system.

Figure 4-8 indicates one possible way to design a linked list to implement an ordered list. You can use a head record *L* that has two fields as follows:

> *Len*: an integer that is the length of the list

> *Head*: a pointer to the item in the first position of the list

A head record that points to an ordered list

Thus, the following statements declare *L* to be an ordered list:

```
type    itemtype = <desired type of list item>;
        ptr = ^node;
        node = record
             item : itemtype;
             next : ptr
        end;
        orderedlist = record
             Len : integer;
             Head : ptr
        end;
var     L : orderedlist;
```

Of the five ordered list operations, `Create` and `Length` are straightforward:

```
Create(L)

    L.Len := 0
    L.Head := nil

Length(L)

    Length := L.Len
```

For the implementation of the operations `Retrieve`, `Insert`, and `Delete`, it is convenient to define a function `Setptr`, which returns a pointer to the node at a specified position on the list. Because a linked list does not provide direct access to a specified position, `Setptr` must traverse the list from its beginning until the specified point is reached. As you will

Figure 4-8

A pointer-based implementation of an ordered list

see, this task is common to the implementation of the operations *Retrieve*, *Insert*, and *Delete*. The pseudocode for *Setptr* is as follows:

```
Setptr(L, pos)
{ Returns a pointer to the node at position pos in ordered
  list L. If pos < 1 or pos > Length(L), Setptr returns the
  value nil. }

    if (pos < 1) or (pos > Length(L))
        then Setptr := nil
        else { count from the beginning of the list }
        begin
            trav := L.Head
            for i := 1 to pos−1 do
                trav := trav^.next
            Setptr := trav
        end
```

Now the *Retrieve* operation appears in pseudocode as follows:

```
Retrieve(L, i)

    if (i < 1) or (i > Length(L))
        then indicate an error
        else
        begin
            p := Setptr(L, i)
            Return the item p^.item
        end
```

Notice that this implementation of *Retrieve* is substantially less efficient than the array-based implementation. The array-based implementation accesses the ith item directly because it is stored in *Items[i]*. The pointer-based implementation, on the other hand, traverses the linked list until the ith item is encountered.

The pointer-based implementations of *Insert* and *Delete* use the general linked list processing techniques developed in Chapter 3. To insert an item at position i of a list when $i > 1$, you must obtain a pointer to the node at position $i - 1$. Insertion into the first position of a list is a special case.

```
Insert(L, i, newitem)

    if (i < 1) or (i > Length(L) + 1) then
        Indicate an error
    else if (i = 1) then
        Insert newitem at the beginning of the list
    else
    begin
        p := Setptr(L, i−1)
        Insert newitem after the node pointed to by p
    end
```

The *Delete* operation is analogous to *Insert*. To delete an item from position i of a list when $i > 1$, you must obtain a pointer to the node at position $i - 1$. Deletion from the first position of a list is a special case.

```
Delete(L, i)

    if (i < 1 ) or (i > Length(L)) then
        Indicate an error
    else if (i = 1) then
        Delete the first node from the list
    else
    begin
        p := Setptr(L, i—1)
        Delete the node following the node pointed to by p
    end
```

The completion of this pointer-based implementation is left as an exercise.

Because *Setptr* returns a pointer, you would not want any module outside of the ADT to call it. To do so would violate the walls of the ADT. That is, the walls should hide the pointer-based implementation of the ADT from the modules outside of the ADT. Such modules should be able to use the ADT without knowledge of the pointers that the implementation uses. Thus, only *Retrieve*, *Insert*, and *Delete* should call *Setptr*. It is perfectly reasonable for the implementation of an ADT to define private variables, procedures, and functions that are not accessible by the rest of the program.

Setptr is hidden from the user within the walls of the ADT

Violating the walls. Consider the consequences of violating the walls of an ADT and the advantages of not doing so. Recall the *PrintList* procedure that printed the items on an ordered list L.

```
PrintList(L)
{ Prints the items on the ordered list L (in order) }

    for position := 1 to Length(L) do
    begin
        item := Retrieve(L, position)
        Print item
    end
```

Again note that this procedure invokes the ADT operations *Length* and *Retrieve*, and therefore is independent of the particular implementation of the ADT ordered list that you happen to choose. That is, *PrintList* will work regardless of whether you use an array-based implementation, a pointer-based implementation, or some other implementation. This feature is a definite advantage of abstract data types. In addition, by thinking in terms of the available ADT operations, you will not be distracted by implementation details such as pointers. For example, the following is an implementation of *PrintList* that assumes the pointer-based implementation that was just described:

```
PrintList2(L)
{ Prints the items on the ordered list L (in order).
  Assumes a pointer-based implementation. }

    cur := head
    while cur <> nil do
    begin
        Print cur^.data
        cur := cur^.next
    end
```

PrintList2 certainly takes more effort to write than *PrintList*. (Note that *PrintList2* is the same as the *PrintList* procedure in Chapter 3.)

Suppose that after writing *PrintList2*, you decide to change from the pointer-based implementation that *PrintList2* assumes to an array-based implementation of the ADT ordered list. You would need a completely new implementation of *PrintList2* because it depends on the data structure—the linked list—that you chose for the implementation of the ordered list. Violating the walls of the ADT is a definite disadvantage here.

Sometimes people use the ADT operations but violate the walls of the ADT inadvertently. For example, under the array-based ordered list implementation that we described earlier in this chapter, you might accidentally reference the first item in the ordered list by writing *L.Items[1]* instead of *Retrieve(L, 1)*. If you changed to another implementation, your program would be incorrect. To correct your program, you must locate and change all references to *L.Items[1]*—but first you must realize that *L.Item[1]* is in error!

Comparing Array-Based and Pointer-Based Implementations

Typically, the various implementations that a programmer contemplates for a particular ADT have advantages and disadvantages. When you must select an implementation, you should weigh these advantages and disadvantages before you make your choice. As you will see, the decision between possible implementations of an ADT is one that you must make time and time again. This section compares the two implementations of the ADT ordered list that you just saw as an example of how you should proceed in general.

Arrays are easy to use, but they have a fixed size

The array-based implementation appears to be a reasonable approach. An array behaves like an ordered list, and arrays are easy to use. However, as was already mentioned, an array has a fixed size; it is possible for the number of items in the ordered list to exceed this fixed size. In practice, when choosing among implementations of an ADT, you must ask the question, does the fixed-size restriction of an array-based implementation present a problem in the context of a particular application? The answer to this question depends on two factors. The obvious factor is whether or not, for a given application, you can predict in advance the maximum number of items in the ADT at any one time. If you cannot, then the array-based solution is not adequate; it is quite possible that an operation—and hence the entire program—will fail because the ADT in the context of a particular application requires more storage than the array can provide.

Can you predict the maximum number of items in the ADT?

On the other hand, if you can predict in advance the maximum number of items in the ADT at any one time for a given application, you must explore a more subtle factor: Would you waste storage by declaring an array to be large enough to accommodate this maximum number of items? Consider a case in which the maximum number of items is large, but you suspect that this number will rarely be achieved. For example, suppose that there could be as many as 10,000 items in an ordered list, but the actual number of items in the ordered list rarely exceeds 10. Although you must declare at least 10,000 array locations, at least 9,990 array locations will be wasted for the majority of the program's execution.

Will an array waste storage?

In both of the previous cases, the pointer-based implementation of an ordered list is preferable to the array-based implementation. Because a pointer-based implementation uses the *new* procedure to provide dynamic storage allocation, it will provide as much storage as the ordered list needs (within the bounds of the particular computer, of course). Thus, you need not be able to predict the maximum size of the ordered list. Also, the ordered list will be allocated only as much storage as it needs, so you will not waste storage. In addition, the pointer-based implementation recycles storage for use elsewhere by using the *dispose* procedure.

Thus, there are many types of applications for which the fixed-size restriction of an array-based implementation of an ADT is unacceptable. The need for dynamic storage is one factor that would lead you to choose a pointer-based implementation. There are also other, more subtle factors that would push you in this direction. Some of these factors will come to light in Chapter 10, which compares implementations of the ADT **table**.

It is important to point out, however, that there are many contexts in which the fixed-size limitation of an array-based implementation is not a problem. For example, it would not be a problem if, from the context of the application, you knew that the length of an ordered list would never be greater than 25. You could allocate enough storage in the array for the ordered list and know that you would waste little storage when the ordered list contained only a few items.

There are other contrasts in the natures of the array-based and pointer-based implementations. Any time you store a collection of data in a structure such as an array or a linked list, the data items become ordered; that is, there is a first item, a second item, and so on. This order implies that given any item in the structure there is a notion of the next item after it. In an array A, the location of the next item after the item in $A[i]$ is *implicit*—it is in $A[i + 1]$. In a linked list, however, the location of the next item after the item in node N must be determined *explicitly* by using the pointer in the node N. This notion of an implicit versus explicit *next* is one of the primary differences between an array and a linked list.

The item after the ith item in an array is implied; in a linked list, it is pointed to explicitly

Thus, the most obvious advantage of an array-based implementation is that it saves space because it does not have to store explicit information about where to find the next data item. Another, more subtle advantage is that it can provide **direct access** to a specified item. For example, if you use the array *Items* to implement an ordered list, you know that the item associated with list position *i* is stored in *Items[i]*. On the other hand, if you use a linked list to implement the ordered list, you have no way of knowing the location of the node that contains this item. To get to the appropriate node, you would have to use the *next* pointers to traverse the linked list from its beginning until you reached the *i*th node. The advantages provided by direct access will be considered often as we select implementations for many of the ADT's in the remainder of this book.

Changing from One Implementation to Another

Suppose that your program originally employs the array-based ordered list implementation, but you soon realize that the limitations of a fixed-sized ordered list are not acceptable for your particular application. Because the wall created by the data-abstraction approach isolates a program from changes in the implementations of its ADT's, changing from one implementation to another requires only a minimal amount of surgery.

In theory, you must replace only the body of each of the five ordered list operations. In practice, however, you must make a few other small changes. As an example, the following summarizes the necessary program modifications for changing from an array-based to a pointer-based implementation:

1. **Change the subprograms.** As you would expect, you must remove the five subprograms that the array-based implementation uses to perform the ordered list operations and replace them with the subprograms for the pointer-based implementation.

2. **Change global type definitions.** The need for this modification is really a result of Pascal's requirement that the type definitions for the ordered list be global: Because variables that are not local to the routines—for example, actual parameters in the procedure calls—must use the type definitions, the definitions must be global. If the type definitions could be local to the subprograms that implement the ordered list operations, then the definitions would be replaced as a result of replacing the subprograms. As this is not the case, you have to replace the type definitions that you saw earlier in this chapter as well as the subprograms.

3. **Change the calling sequence.** Although this change does not apply to our implementations of the ADT ordered list, we note it here anyway. Sometimes there will be slight differences between the parameters of a subprogram in one implementation and those of the corresponding subprogram in another implementation. If this is the case, you could change the calling sequences when you change implementations. However, this change does violate the spirit of the ADT contract.

Instead you could revise the specifications of the ADT operations to remove any implementation dependencies; that is, you could change the definitions of the subprograms so that their parameter lists correspond to an implementation-independent calling sequence.

These modifications are like the ones that you generally must make when you change from one implementation of an ADT to another. Notice that none of the modifications require any sort of substantial revisions to the program. For all practical purposes, the wall allows the rest of the program to be oblivious to a change in the implementation of an ADT.

SUMMARY

1. Data abstraction is a technique for controlling the interaction between a program and its data structures. It builds walls around a program's data structures, just as other aspects of modularity build walls around a program's algorithms. Such walls make programs easier to design, implement, read, and modify.

2. The specification of a set of data-management operations together with the data values upon which they operate define an abstract data type (ADT).

3. Only after you have fully defined an ADT should you think about how to implement it with a data structure. Even after you have selected an implementation, the remainder of the program should not depend on your particular choice.

4. The proper choice of a data structure to implement an ADT depends both on the details of the ADT operations and on the context in which you will use the operations.

5. An array-based implementation uses an implicit ordering scheme—for example, the item that follows `A[i]` is stored in `A[i + 1]`. A pointer-based implementation uses an explicit ordering scheme—for example, the item that follows the one in node N is found by following node N's pointer.

6. You often must choose between an array-based and a pointer-based implementation. One important criterion on which to base this choice is whether or not, in the context of a particular problem, the fixed-size limitations of an array are acceptable. If not, the dynamic storage allocation provided by a pointer-based implementation is required. On the other hand, an array provides direct access to its ith element, whereas a linked list does not. In the chapters that follow, you will encounter applications with a wide range of data-management requirements. The process of selecting data structures for these applications will illustrate some of the other important criteria on which to base the choice of a data structure.

COMMON PITFALLS / DEBUGGING

1. A program should not depend upon the particular implementations of its ADT's.

2. If you choose an array-based implementation for an ADT, there will be a maximum number of items that you can store. Thus, the implementation will have to check whether there is room in the data structure before inserting a new item, and the calling program will have to take appropriate action if there is no room.

3. Standard Pascal does not allow functions to return complex structures such as arrays and records. Therefore, you generally should write an ADT's retrieval operations as procedures that use a variable parameter to return the item. This approach allows you to define the ADT's items to be of any type.

4. The syntax of Pascal requires you to place the type definitions of ADT's globally, outside of the ADT subprograms. As a consequence, when switching from one implementation to another, you must replace the type definitions as well as the subprograms.

SELF-TEST EXERCISES

1. What is the significance of "wall" and "contract"? Why do these notions help you to become a better problem solver?

2. Write a procedure that replaces the ith item in an ordered list L. Define the procedure in terms of the ADT ordered list operations. Thus, your procedure should be independent of any particular implementation of the ordered list.

3. You can think of a Pascal textfile abstractly. Define a set of operations that are a part of the ADT textfile.

4. Write preconditions and postconditions for each of the ADT ordered list operations.

EXERCISES

1. Develop an array-based implementation of the ADT ordered list. Be sure to consider the issue of error checking and handling.

2. Develop a pointer-based implementation of the ADT ordered list.

3. Compare the array-based and pointer-based implementations of the

Delete(L, i) operation for an ordered list. Describe the work required for various values of *i* under each implementation. What are the implications for efficiency if the cost of shifting data is large compared to the cost of following a pointer? When would this situation occur? What if the costs are approximately the same?

4. Implement the procedure *Swap(L, i, j)* that interchanges the *i*th and *j*th items of the ordered list *L*, as described in the section "The ADT Ordered List." Add a parameter *Success* that indicates whether the swap was successful.

5. Use the procedure *Swap* that you wrote in Exercise 4 to write the following procedures:

    a. Write a procedure that reverses the order of the items in an ordered list *L*.

    b. Write a procedure that sorts the items in an ordered list *L* into ascending order.

6. If Pascal did not contain sets, you could define your own abstract data type set. Define operations that are a part of the ADT set. (Exercise 10b asks you to implement this ADT.)

7. Define operations that are a part of the ADT character string.

8. Write a pseudocode procedure in terms of the ADT appointment book, described in the section "Designing an ADT," for each of the following tasks:

    a. Change the purpose of the appointment at a given date and time.

    b. Print all the appointments for a given date.

    Do you need to add operations to the ADT to perform these tasks?

9. Consider the ADT polynomial—polynomials in a single variable *x*— that the following operations define:

    Create(P)
    { Initializes P to be the zero polynomial. }

    Degree(P)
    { Returns the degree of the polynomial P. The degree is
    * the highest power of a term with a nonzero*
    * coefficient. }*

    Set(P, i, value)
    { Sets the coefficient of the degree i (x^i) term to
    * value. }*

    Retrieve(P, i)
    { Returns the coefficient of the degree i (x^i) term. }

    For this problem, consider only polynomials—such as the following polynomial—whose exponents are nonnegative integers:

$P = 4x^5 + 7x^3 - x^2 + 9$

The following examples demonstrate the ADT operations on this polynomial:

`Degree(P)` = 5 (the highest power of a term with a nonzero coefficient)

`Retrieve(P, 3)` = 7 (the coefficient of the degree 3 (x^3) term)

`Retrieve(P, 2)` = –1 (the coefficient of the degree 2 (x^2) term)

`Retrieve(P, 4)` = 0 (the coefficient of a missing term is implicitly 0)

`Retrieve(P, 6)` = 0 (the coefficient of a missing term is implicitly 0)

`Set(P, 7, −3)` produces the polynomial:

$P = -3x^7 + 4x^5 + 7x^3 - x^2 + 9$

By using these ADT operations, write statements to perform the following tasks:

a. Print the coefficient of the term that has the highest degree.
b. Increase the coefficient of the x^3 term by 8.

10. Some programming languages—for example, FORTRAN—do not directly support the data types *record*, *set*, and *pointer*. In these languages, you have to implement structures such as records, sets, and linked lists by using the structures that are available.

a. Define an ADT record and implement it by using only arrays and simple variables. How can you implement an array of records?
b. Define an ADT set and implement it by using only arrays and simple variables. (See Exercise 6.)
c. Implement the ADT linked list of sorted integers as described in the section "The Linked List As an ADT" by using two integer arrays—*Data* and *Next*—and a single integer-valued variable *Head*. When appropriate, use a boolean parameter, *Success*, to indicate whether an operation is successful.

On the surface, it may seem to you that this implementation sacrifices the primary motivation for having linked structures: dynamic allocation. In Chapter 10, however, you will see that dynamic allocation is not the only motivation for having linked structures; a fixed-sized array-based implementation of a linked structure can in fact be useful. Furthermore, in a more advanced course on data structures, you will be exposed to techniques for using large arrays that will be "shared" by several data structures. In this context you will see that a linked list that has been implemented with arrays can indeed be viewed as a dynamic structure.

PROJECTS

11. Consider the ADT character string that you defined in Exercise 7. Develop an implementation for your operations. (Note that Exercises 28 and 33 of Chapter 3 asked you to write a pointer-based implementation of character strings.)

12. Consider the ADT polynomial that Exercise 9 defined.

    a. Define the ADT polynomial operations in terms of the ADT ordered list operations.

    b. Write a procedure *Add* that will add two polynomials. Write *Add* in terms of the ADT polynomial operations.

    c. Consider a sparse implementation of the ADT polynomial. That is, suppose you would like to implement the ADT in such a way that only the terms with nonzero coefficients are explicitly stored. For example, you can represent the polynomial *P* in Exercise 9 with the linked list in Figure 4-9. Complete the sparse implementation.

    d. Define a traverse operation for the ADT polynomial that will allow you to add two sparse polynomials without having to consider terms with zero coefficients explicitly.

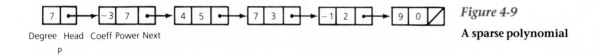

Degree Head Coeff Power Next
    P

Figure 4-9

A sparse polynomial

13. Implement the ADT appointment book, described in the section "Designing an ADT." Add operations as necessary. For example, you should add operations to read and write appointments.

14. Implement the ADT recipe book as described in the section "Designing an ADT" and, in doing so, implement the ADT's measurements and fraction. Add operations as necessary. For example, you should add operations to recipe book to read, write, and scale recipes.

CHAPTER 5

Recursion:
The Mirrors

PREVIEW   The goal of this chapter is to help you to develop a basic understanding of recursion, which is one of the most powerful methods of solution
available to the computer scientist. Several relatively simple problems demonstrate the thought processes that lead to recursive solutions. These problems
are diverse and include examples of computing, counting, and searching. In
addition to presenting recursion from a conceptual viewpoint, this chapter
discusses methods that will help you to understand the mechanics of recursion.
These methods are particularly useful for tracing and debugging recursive subprograms.

RECURSIVE SOLUTIONS

Typically, solutions to problems use either **iteration**—that is, they involve
loops—or **recursion**. You should know at the outset that not all recursive
solutions are better than iterative solutions. In fact, some recursive solutions are impractical. However, recursive algorithms often provide elegantly simple solutions to problems of great complexity. Such solutions
are, in general, very well structured and modular. In fact, the manner in
which the modules of a recursive solution interact is precisely what makes
recursion such a powerful and unique problem-solving tool.

Recursion will play a major role in many of the solutions that appear
throughout the remainder of this book. This chapter and the next present
several important applications of recursion, including recursive search
algorithms and recursive grammars for defining the syntax of languages.
Chapter 7 examines recursive sorting algorithms as part of its discussion of
algorithm efficiency. Recursion will also be an integral part of many of the
data structures studied in Parts III and IV.

What exactly is recursion? It is a technique for performing a task T by
performing another task T'. So far, this sounds like top-down design, in
which you solve a large problem by breaking it up into smaller problems.
The difference is that, with recursion, the task T' has *exactly the same nature*
as the original task T. Thus, a recursive solution of task T might be
described as follows:

```
Solution to T:
     Solve task T', which is identical in nature to
        task T
```

It may seem strange to solve a task by solving another task just like it. What
have you gained? The crucial point is that, although T' is identical in
nature to T, it is in some sense *smaller* than T.

As an illustration of the elements in a recursive solution, consider the
problem of looking up a word in a dictionary. Suppose you wanted to look

up the word "vademecum." Imagine starting at the beginning of the dictionary and looking at every word in order until you found "vademecum." That is precisely what a **sequential search** does, and, for obvious reasons, you want a faster way to perform the search. One such method is the **binary search**, which in spirit is similar to the way in which you use a dictionary. Although you can write an iterative binary search algorithm, consider the following recursive binary search of the dictionary:

```
{ Search the dictionary for a word }

    if the dictionary contains only one page
      then scan the page for the word

      else
      begin
          Open the dictionary to a point near the middle
          Determine which half of the dictionary contains the
            word

          if the word is in the first half of the dictionary
            then search the first half of the dictionary for
                    the word
            else search the second half of the dictionary for
                    the word
      end
```

Parts of this solution are intentionally vague: How do you scan a single page? How do you find the middle of the dictionary? Once the middle is found, how do you determine which half contains the word? The answers to these questions are not difficult, but we will not obscure the solution strategy with these details at present.

The previous search strategy reduces the problem of searching the dictionary for a word to a problem of searching half of the dictionary for the word, as Figure 5-1 illustrates. Notice two important points. First, once you have divided the dictionary in half, you already know how to search the appropriate half: You can use exactly the same strategy that you employed to search the original dictionary. Second, note that there is a special case that is different from all the other cases: After you have divided the dictionary so many times that you are left with only a single page, the halving

Figure 5-1

A recursive solution

ceases. At this point, the problem is sufficiently small that you can solve it directly by scanning the single page that remains for the word. This special case is called the **degenerate case**, or the **base case**.

A degenerate case is a special case whose solution you know

This strategy is one of **divide and conquer.** You solve the dictionary search problem by first *dividing* the dictionary into two halves and then *conquering* the appropriate half. You solve the smaller problem by using the same divide-and-conquer strategy. The dividing continues until you reach the degenerate case. As you will see, this strategy is inherent in many recursive solutions.

A binary search uses a divide-and-conquer strategy

To further explore the nature of the solution to the dictionary problem, consider a slightly more rigorous formulation.

```
Search(dictionary, word)

    if dictionary is one page in size
       then scan the page for word

       else
       begin
           Open dictionary to a point near the middle
           Determine which half of dictionary contains word

           if word is in the first half of dictionary
               then Search(first half of dictionary, word)
               else Search(second half of dictionary, word)
       end
```

Writing the solution as a procedure allows several important observations:

Four observations about a recursive solution

1. One of the actions of the procedure is to call itself; that is, the procedure `Search` calls the procedure `Search`. This action is what makes the solution recursive. The solution strategy is to split `dictionary` in half, determine which half contains `word`, and apply the same strategy to the appropriate half.

2. Each call to the procedure `Search` made from within the procedure `Search` passes a dictionary that is one-half the size of the previous dictionary. That is, at each successive call to `Search(dictionary, word)`, the size of `dictionary` is cut in half. The procedure solves the search problem by solving another search problem that is identical in nature *but smaller in size.*

3. There is one search problem that you handle differently from all of the others. When `dictionary` contains only a single page, you use another method: You scan the page directly. Searching a one-page dictionary is the degenerate case of the search problem. When you reach the degenerate case, the recursive calls stop and you solve the problem directly.

4. The manner in which the size of the problem diminishes ensures that you will eventually reach the degenerate case.

These facts describe the general form of a recursive solution. Though not all recursive solutions fit these criteria as nicely as this solution does, the similarities are far greater than the differences. As you attempt to construct a new recursive solution, you should keep in mind the following four questions:

KEY CONCEPTS   *Four Questions for Constructing Recursive Solutions*

1. How can you define the problem in terms of a smaller problem of the same type?
2. How does each recursive call diminish the size of the problem?
3. What instance of the problem can serve as the degenerate case?
4. As the problem size diminishes, will you reach this degenerate case?

Now consider two relatively simple problems: computing the factorial of a number and writing a string backward. Their recursive solutions further illustrate the points raised by the solution to the dictionary search problem. These examples also illustrate the difference between a recursive function and a recursive procedure.

A Recursive Function: The Factorial of n

Consider a recursive solution to the problem of computing the factorial of an integer *n*. We chose to start with this problem because its recursive solution is easy to understand and neatly fits the mold we described earlier. However, because there is a simple and efficient nonrecursive solution to the problem, you probably would not use the recursive solution in practice.

To begin, consider the familiar iterative definition of *Factorial(n)* (more commonly written *n!*):

An iterative definition of Factorial

$$Factorial(n) = n * (n-1) * (n-2) * \cdots * 1 \text{ for any integer } n > 0$$
$$Factorial(0) = 1$$

The factorial of a negative integer is undefined. You should have no trouble writing an iterative factorial function based on this definition.

To define *Factorial(n)* recursively, you first need to define *Factorial(n)* in terms of the factorial of a smaller number. To do so, simply observe that the factorial of *n* is equal to the factorial of (*n* – 1) multiplied by *n*; that is,

A recurrence relation

$$Factorial(n) \cdot n * Factorial(n-1)$$

The definition of *Factorial(n)* in terms of *Factorial(n* – 1), which is an example of a **recurrence relation**, implies that you can also define *Factorial(n* – 1) in terms of *Factorial(n* – 2), and so on. This process is analogous to the dictionary search solution, in which you search a dictionary by searching a smaller dictionary in exactly the same way.

The definition of *Factorial(n)* lacks one key element: the degenerate case. As was done in the dictionary search solution, here you must define one case differently from all the others, or else the recursion will never stop. The degenerate case for the factorial function is *Factorial(0)*, which you know is 1. Because *n* originally is greater than or equal to zero and each call to *Factorial* decrements *n* by 1, you will always reach the degenerate case. With the addition of the degenerate case, the complete recursive definition of the factorial function is

$$Factorial(n) = \begin{cases} 1 & \text{if } n = 0 \\ n * Factorial(n-1) & \text{if } n > 0 \end{cases}$$

A recursive definition of **Factorial**

To be sure that you understand this recursive definition, apply it to the computation of *Factorial(4)*. Since $4 > 0$, the recursive definition states that

$Factorial(4) = 4 * Factorial(3)$

Similarly,

$Factorial(3) = 3 * Factorial(2)$
$Factorial(2) = 2 * Factorial(1)$
$Factorial(1) = 1 * Factorial(0)$

You have reached the degenerate case, and the definition directly states that

$Factorial(0) = 1$

At this point, the application of the recursive definition stops and you still do not know the answer to the original question: What is *Factorial(4)*? However, the information to answer this question is now available:

Since $Factorial(0) = 1$, then $Factorial(1) = 1 * 1 = 1$
Since $Factorial(1) = 1$, then $Factorial(2) = 2 * 1 = 2$
Since $Factorial(2) = 2$, then $Factorial(3) = 3 * 2 = 6$
Since $Factorial(3) = 6$, then $Factorial(4) = 4 * 6 = 24$

Notice that the recursive definition of *Factorial(4)* yields the same result as the iterative definition, which gives $4 * 3 * 2 * 1 = 24$. To prove that the two definitions of *Factorial* are equivalent for all nonnegative integers, you would use **mathematical induction**. (See Appendix A.) Chapter 6 discusses the close tie between recursion and mathematical induction.

The recursive definition of the factorial function has illustrated two points: (1) *Intuitively*, you can define *Factorial(n)* in terms of *Factorial(n − 1)*, and (2) *mechanically*, you can apply the definition to determine the value of a given factorial. Even in this simple example, applying the recursive definition required quite a bit of work. That, of course, is where the computer comes in.

Once you have a recursive definition of *Factorial(n)*, it is easy to construct a Pascal function that implements the definition:

```
type nonneg = 0..maxint;

function Fact(n : nonneg) : nonneg;
{ -------------------------------------------------------
  Computes the factorial of the nonnegative integer n.
  Precondition: n must be greater than or equal to 0.
  Postcondition: Returns the factorial of n; n is
  unchanged.
  ------------------------------------------------------- }
begin
    if n = 0
        then Fact := 1
        else Fact := n * Fact(n - 1)
end   { Fact }
```

Suppose that the statement *writeln(Fact(3))* calls the function from the main program. Figure 5-2 depicts the sequence of computations that this call would require.

This function fits the model of a recursive solution given earlier in this chapter as follows:

Fact satisfies the four criteria of a recursive solution

1. One action of *Fact* is to *call itself*.

2. At each recursive call to *Fact*, the integer whose factorial you need to compute is *diminished by 1*.

3. The function handles the factorial of 0 differently from all the other factorials: It does not generate a recursive call. Rather, you know that *Fact(0)* is 1. Thus, *n* = 0 is the *degenerate case*.

4. Given that *n* is nonnegative, point 2 of this list assures you that you will always reach the degenerate case.

Figure 5-2

Fact(3)

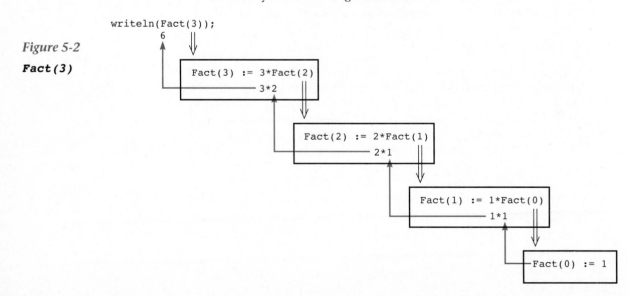

At an intuitive level, it should be clear that the function *Fact* implements the recursive definition of *Factorial*. Now consider the mechanics of executing this recursive function. *Fact* is straightforward except perhaps for the assignment statement in the *else* clause (*Fact := n * Fact(n — 1)*). This assignment statement has the following effect:

1. To evaluate the expression to the right of the assignment operator, each operand of the product is evaluated.

2. The second operand—*Fact(n — 1)*—is a call to the function *Fact*. Although this is a recursive call (the function *Fact* calls the function *Fact*), there really is nothing special about it. Imagine substituting a call to another function—Pascal's function *abs*, for example—for the recursive call to *Fact*. The principle is the same: Simply evaluate the function.

In principle, evaluating a recursive function is no more difficult than evaluating a nonrecursive function. In practice, however, the bookkeeping can quickly get out of hand.

Thus, we shall introduce the **box method**, which is a systematic way to trace the actions of a recursive function or procedure. You can use the box method both to help you to understand recursion and to debug recursive subprograms. However, such a mechanical device is no substitute for an intuitive understanding of recursion. The box method is illustrative of how compilers frequently implement recursion. As you read the following description of the method, realize that each box roughly corresponds to an **activation record**, which a compiler typically uses in its implementation of a subprogram call. Chapter 8 will discuss this implementation further.

An activation record is created for each subprogram call

The box method. The box method is illustrated here for the recursive function *Fact*. As you will see in the next section, this method is somewhat simpler for a recursive procedure, as no value needs to be returned.

1. Label each recursive call in the body of the recursive subprogram. There may be several recursive calls, and it will be important to distinguish among them. These labels help you to keep track of the correct place to which you must return after a function call completes. For example, mark the expression *Fact(n — 1)* within the body of the function with the letter A:

```
function Fact(n : nonneg) : nonneg;
begin
    if n = 0
        then Fact := 1
        else Fact := n * Fact(n — 1)
    end  { Fact }                    (A)
```

Label each recursive call in the subprogram

You return to point A after each recursive call, substitute the computed value for *Fact(n — 1)*, and continue execution by evaluating the expression *n * Fact(n — 1)*.

Each time a subprogram is called, a new box represents its local environment

2. Represent each call to the subprogram during the course of execution by a new box in which you note the subprogram's **local environment**. More specifically, each box will contain

    a. The value parameters of the formal parameter list.

    b. The subprogram's local variables.

    c. A placeholder for the value returned by each recursive call from the current box. Label this placeholder to correspond to the labeling in Step 1.

    d. The value of the function itself.

When you first create a box, you will know only the values of the parameters. You fill in the values of the other items as you determine them from the subprogram's execution. For example, you would create the box in Figure 5-3 for the call `Fact(3)`. (You will see in later examples that you must handle both variable parameters and global variables somewhat differently from value parameters and local variables.)

3. Draw an arrow from the statement that initiates the recursive process to the first box. Then, when you create a new box after a recursive call, as described in Step 2, you draw an arrow from the box that makes the call to the newly created box. Label each arrow to correspond to the label (from Step 1) of the recursive call; this label indicates exactly where to return after the call completes. For example, Figure 5-4 shows the first two boxes generated by the statement `writeln(Fact(3))` in the main program.

4. After you create the new box and arrow as described in Steps 2 and 3, start executing the body of the subprogram. Each reference to an item in the subprogram's local environment references the corresponding value in the current box, regardless of how you generated the current box.

5. On exiting the subprogram, cross off the current box and follow its arrow back to the box that called the subprogram. This box now becomes the current box, and the label on the arrow specifies the exact location at which execution of the subprogram should continue. Substitute the value returned by the just-terminated function call into the appropriate item in the current box.

Figure 5-5 is a complete box trace for the call `Fact(3)`, which is in the main program. In the sequence of diagrams in this figure, it is always clear which box is the current box: It is the deepest along the path of arrows and appears in color.

Figure 5-3

A box

```
n = 3
A:  Fact (n-1) = ?
Fact = ?
```

```
writeln(Fact(3))
```

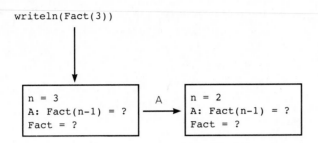

Figure 5-4

The beginning of the box method

The box method should give you a good indication of the special techniques you need to employ to debug a recursive subprogram. You should include `write` statements to report the values of all parameters and local variables at both entry to and exit from the subprogram. `Write` statements also should report the point in the program where each recursive call occurred. You will see this technique used in the next example.

Well-placed `write` *statements can help you to debug a recursive subprogram*

We end this section with a brief discussion of error checking within *Fact*. By declaring the function's parameter *n* to be of type *nonneg* rather than simply *integer*, you can guard against errors in the logic of the calling program. If the calling program ever passed a negative value to the function *Fact*, the program would abort immediately because of a type clash. On the other hand, if you had declared *n* as an integer, passing a negative value to *Fact* would result in an infinite sequence of recursive calls, terminated only by a system-defined limit, because the function would never reach the degenerate case. For example, *Fact (−4)* would call *Fact (−5)*, which would call *Fact (−6)*, and so on.

We admit that using Pascal's type checking to guard against logic errors does not result in a user-friendly function. However, Chapter 1 indicated that such error checking should be your last line of defense. In addition to declaring *n* to be of type *nonneg*, the function should test *n* and, if *n* < 0, the function should either issue an error message or set a flag. Chapter 1 discussed these ideas in the two sections "Fail-Safe Programming" and "Style"; you might want to review that discussion at this time.

A Recursive Procedure: Writing a String Backward

Now consider a problem slightly more difficult than computing the factorial of a number: Given a string of characters, print it out in reverse order. For example, write the string 'cat' as 'tac'. To construct a recursive solution, you should ask the four questions in the "Key Concepts" box on page 202.

You can construct a solution to the problem of writing a string of length *n* backward in terms of the problem of writing a string of length *n* − 1 backward. That is, each recursive step of the solution diminishes by 1 the length of the string to be written backward. The fact that the strings get shorter and shorter suggests that the problem of writing some "very short"

Figure 5-5

Box trace of
Fact(3)

The initial call is made and function Fact begins execution:

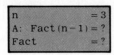

```
n            = 3
A: Fact(n-1) = ?
Fact         = ?
```

At point A, a recursive call is made and the new invocation of the function Fact begins execution:

```
n            = 3      n            = 2
A: Fact(n-1) = ?   A  A: Fact(n-1) = ?
Fact         = ?   →  Fact         = ?
```

At point A, a recursive call is made and the new invocation of the function Fact begins execution:

```
n            = 3      n            = 2      n            = 1
A: Fact(n-1) = ?   A  A: Fact(n-1) = ?   A  A: Fact(n-1) = ?
Fact         = ?   →  Fact         = ?   →  Fact         = ?
```

At point A, a recursive call is made and the new invocation of the function Fact begins execution:

```
n            = 3      n            = 2      n            = 1      n            = 0
A: Fact(n-1) = ?   A  A: Fact(n-1) = ?   A  A: Fact(n-1) = ?   A  A: Fact(n-1) = ?
Fact         = ?   →  Fact         = ?   →  Fact         = ?   →  Fact         = ?
```

This is the degenerate case, so this invocation of Fact completes.

```
n            = 3      n            = 2      n            = 1      n            = 0
A: Fact(n-1) = ?   A  A: Fact(n-1) = ?   A  A: Fact(n-1) = ?   A  A: Fact(n-1) = ?
Fact         = ?   →  Fact         = ?   →  Fact         = ?   →  Fact         = 1
```

The function value is returned to the calling box which continues execution.

```
n            = 3      n            = 2      n            = 1      n            = 0
A: Fact(n-1) = ?   A  A: Fact(n-1) = ?   A  A: Fact(n-1) = 1      A: Fact(n-1) = ?
Fact         = ?   →  Fact         = ?   →  Fact         = ?      Fact         = 1
```

The current invocation of Fact completes.

```
n            = 3      n            = 2      n            = 1      n            = 0
A: Fact(n-1) = ?   A  A: Fact(n-1) = ?   A  A: Fact(n-1) = 1      A: Fact(n-1) = ?
Fact         = ?   →  Fact         = ?   →  Fact         = 1      Fact         = 1
```

The function value is returned to the calling box which continues execution.

```
 n          = 3  A   n          = 2      n          = 1       n          = 0
 A: Fact(n−1)= ?  →  A: Fact(n−1)= 1     A: Fact(n−1)= 1      A: Fact(n−1)= ?
 Fact       = ?      Fact       = ?      Fact       = 1       Fact       = 1
```

The current invocation of Fact completes.

```
 n          = 3  A   n          = 2      n          = 1       n          = 0
 A: Fact(n−1)= ?  →  A: Fact(n−1)= 1     A: Fact(n−1)= 1      A: Fact(n−1)= ?
 Fact       = ?      Fact       = 2      Fact       = 1       Fact       = 1
```

The function value is returned to the calling box which continues
execution.

```
 n          = 3      n          = 2      n          = 1       n          = 0
 A: Fact(n−1)= 2     A: Fact(n−1)= 1     A: Fact(n−1)= 1      A: Fact(n−1)= ?
 Fact       = ?      Fact       = 2      Fact       = 1       Fact       = 1
```

The current invocation of Fact completes.

```
 n          = 3      n          = 2      n          = 1       n          = 0
 A: Fact(n−1)= 2     A: Fact(n−1)= 1     A: Fact(n−1)= 1      A: Fact(n−1)= ?
 Fact       = 6      Fact       = 2      Fact       = 1       Fact       = 1
```

The value 6 is returned to main call.

string backward can serve as the degenerate case. One very short string is
the empty string, the string of length zero. Thus, you can choose for the
degenerate case the problem

```
Write the empty string backward
```

The degenerate case

The solution to this problem is to do nothing at all—a very straightforward
solution indeed! (Alternatively, you could use the string of length 1 as the
degenerate case.)

Exactly how can you use the solution to the problem of writing a string
of length $n - 1$ backward to solve the problem of writing a string of length
n backward? This approach is analogous to the construction of the solution
to the factorial problem, where you specified how to use *Factorial*($n - 1$) in
the computation of *Factorial*(n). Unlike the factorial problem, however,
with the string problem it is not immediately clear how to proceed. Obviously, not any string of length $n - 1$ will do. For example, there is no
relation between writing 'apple' (a string of length 5) backward and writing
'pear' (a string of length 4) backward. You must choose the smaller problem carefully so that you can use its solution in the solution to the original
problem.

The string of length $n - 1$ that you choose must be a substring (part) of
the original string. Suppose that you strip away one character from the

*How can you write an n-charac-
ter string backward, if you can
write an (n − 1)-character string
backward?*

original string, leaving a substring of length $n - 1$. For the recursive solution to be valid, the ability to write the substring backward, combined with the ability to perform some minor task, must result in the ability to write the original string backward. Compare this approach with the way you computed *Factorial* recursively: The ability to compute *Factorial*($n - 1$), combined with the ability to multiply this value by n, resulted in the ability to compute *Factorial*(n).

You need to decide which character to strip away and which minor task to perform. Consider the minor task first. Since you are printing characters, a likely candidate for the minor task is printing a single character. As for the character that you should strip away from the string, there are several possible alternatives. Two of the more intuitive alternatives are

> `Strip away the last character`

or

> `Strip away the first character`

Consider the first of these alternatives, stripping away the last character, as Figure 5-6 illustrates.

For the solution to be valid, you must print the last character in the string first. Therefore, you must print the last character before you write the remainder of the string backward. A high-level recursive solution, given the string S, is

WriteBackward writes a
string backward

```
WriteBackward(S)

    if the string is empty
        then do not do anything--this is the degenerate case

        else
        begin
            Print the last character of S
            WriteBackward(S minus its last character)
        end
```

This solution to the problem is conceptual. To obtain a Pascal procedure, you must resolve a few implementation issues. Suppose that the procedure will receive two parameters: an array S that contains the string to

Figure 5-6

A recursive solution

be written backward and an integer *size* that specifies the size of the string. To simplify matters, you can assume that the string begins at position 1 and ends at position *size* of the array. That is, all characters, including blanks, in that range of the array are part of the string. Finally, define the constant *maxlen* to be equal to the length of the longest string that you will encounter. The Pascal procedure *WriteBackward* appears as follows:

```
type string = packed array[1..maxlen] of char;
procedure WriteBackward(S : string; size : integer);
{ --------------------------------------------------------
  Writes a character string backward.
  Precondition: The string is S[1..size], where size >= 0.
  Postcondition: Writes the string backward; does not change
  either parameter.
  ------------------------------------------------------- }
begin
   if size > 0
      then
      begin
         { write the last character }
         write(S[size]);

         { write the rest of the string backward }
         WriteBackward(S, size — 1)                {A}
      end

      { size = 0 is the degenerate case — do nothing }
end   { WriteBackward }
```

Notice that the recursive calls to *WriteBackward* use successively smaller values of *size*. This decrease in *size* has the effect of stripping away the last character of the string and ensures that the degenerate case will be reached.

You can trace the execution of *WriteBackward* by using the box method. As was true for the function *Fact*, each box contains the local environment of the recursive call—in this case, the value parameters *S* and *size*. Because *WriteBackward* is a procedure rather than a function, it returns no computed value. Figure 5-7 illustrates the box method for the procedure *WriteBackward* with the string 'cat'.

The procedure Write-Backward does not return a computed value

Now consider a slightly different approach to the problem. Recall that we mentioned two alternatives for the character that you could strip away from the string: the last character or the first character. The solution just given strips away the last character of the string. It will now be interesting to construct a solution based on the second alternative:

Strip away the first character

To begin, consider a simple modification of the previous pseudocode solution that replaces each occurrence of *last* with *first*. Thus, the pro-

Figure 5-7

Box trace of *Write-Backward('cat', 3)*

The initial call is made, and the procedure begins execution.

Point A (WriteBackward (S,size-1)) is reached, and the recursive call is made.

Output line just before call: **t**

The new invocation begins execution.

Point A is reached, and the recursive call is made.

Output line just before call: **ta**

The new invocation begins execution.

Point A is reached, and the recursive call is made.

Output line just before call: **tac**

The new invocation begins execution.

This is the degenerate case, so this invocation completes.
Control returns to the calling box, which continues execution.

| S = 'cat' | A | S = 'cat' | A | S = 'cat' | | S = 'cat' |
| size = 3 | | size = 2 | | size = 1 | | size = O |

Output line just after return from last call: **tac**

This invocation completes. Control returns to the calling box, which continues execution.

| S = 'cat' | A | S = 'cat' | | S = 'cat' | | S = 'cat' |
| size = 3 | | size = 2 | | size = 1 | | size = 0 |

Output line just after return from last call: **tac**

This invocation completes. Control returns to the calling box, which continues execution.

| S = 'cat' | | S = 'cat' | | S = 'cat' | | S = 'cat' |
| size = 3 | | size = 2 | | size = 1 | | size = 0 |

Output line just after return from last call: **tac**

This invocation completes. Control returns to the statement following the main call.

cedure prints the first character rather than the last and then recursively writes the remainder of the string backward.

```
WriteBackward1(S)

    if the string is empty
        then do not do anything--this is the degenerate case

        else
        begin
            Print the first character of S
            WriteBackward1(S minus its first character)
        end
```

WriteBackward1 does not write a string backward

Does this solution do what you want it to? If you think about this procedure, you will realize that it prints the string in its normal left-to-right direction instead of backward. After all, the steps in the pseudocode are

```
Print the first character of S
Write the rest of S
```

These steps simply print the string S. Naming the procedure *Write-Backward* does not guarantee that it will actually write the string backward—recursion really is not magic!

You can write S backward correctly by using the following recursive formulation:

```
Write S minus its first character backward
Print the first character of S
```

In other words, you write the first character of S only *after* you write the rest of S backward. This approach leads to the following pseudocode procedure:

```
WriteBackward2(S)

    if the string is empty
        then do not do anything--this is the degenerate case

        else
        begin
            WriteBackward2(S minus its first character)
            Print the first character of S
        end
```

WriteBackward2 writes a string backward

The translation of *WriteBackward2* into Pascal is similar to that of the original *WriteBackward* procedure and is left as an exercise.

It is instructive to carefully trace the actions of the two pseudocode procedures *WriteBackward* and *WriteBackward2*. First, add *writeln* statements to each procedure, to provide output that is useful to the trace, as follows:

```
WriteBackward(S)

    writeln('Enter WriteBackward with string: ', S)
    if the string is empty
      then do not do anything--this is the degenerate case

      else
      begin
        writeln('About to print last character of string: ',S)

        Print the last character of S
        WriteBackward(S minus its last character)        {A}
      end
    writeln('Leave WriteBackward with string: ', S)

WriteBackward2(S)

    writeln('Enter WriteBackward2 with string: ', S)
    if the string is empty
      then do not do anything--this is the degenerate case

      else
      begin
        WriteBackward2(S minus its first character)      {A}
        writeln('About to print first character of string: ',S)
        Print the first character of S
      end
    writeln('Leave WriteBackward2 with string: ', S)
```

Figures 5-8 and 5-9 show the output of the revised procedures Write-
Backward and WriteBackward2, when initially given the string 'cat'.

You need to be comfortable with the differences between these two
procedures. The recursive calls that the two procedures make generate a
different sequence of values for the parameter S. Despite this fact, both
procedures correctly write the string argument backward. They compensate for the difference in the sequence of values for S by printing different
characters in the string at different times relative to the recursive calls. In
terms of the box traces in Figures 5-8 and 5-9, procedure WriteBackward
prints a character just before generating a new box (just before a new recursive call), whereas procedure WriteBackward2 prints a character just after
crossing off a box (just after returning from a recursive call). When these
differences are put together, the result is two procedures that employ different strategies to accomplish the same task.

This example also illustrates the value of the box method, combined
with well-placed write statements, in debugging recursive subprograms.
The write statements at the beginning, interior, and end of the recursive
procedures report the value of the parameter S. In general, when debugging a recursive subprogram, you should also report both the values of
local variables and the point in the subprogram where each call occurs, as
in the example that follows on page 219.

The output file is initially empty.

The initial call is made and the procedure begins execution.

Point A is reached, and the recursive call is made.

Output file just before call:

```
Enter WriteBackward with string: cat
About to print last character of string:
t
```

The new invocation begins execution.

Point A is reached, and the recursive call is made.

Output file just before call:

```
Enter WriteBackward with string: cat
About to print last character of string: cat
t
Enter WriteBackward with string: ca
About to print last character of string: ca
a
```

The new invocation begins execution.

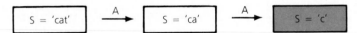

Point A is reached, and the recursive call is made.

Output file just before call:

```
Enter WriteBackward with string: cat
About to print last character of string: cat
t
Enter WriteBackward with string: ca
About to print last character of string: ca
a
Enter WriteBackward with string: c
About to print last character of string: c
c
```

The new invocation begins execution.

This invocation completes execution and a return is made.

(continues)

Figure 5-8

Box trace of *Write-Backward('cat')* in pseudocode

Figure 5-8
continued

Output file just after return:

```
Enter WriteBackward with string: cat
About to print last character of string: cat
t
Enter WriteBackward with string: ca
About to print last character of string: ca
a
Enter WriteBackward with string: c
About to print last character of string: c
c
Enter WriteBackward with string:
Leave WriteBackward with string:
```

This invocation completes execution and a return is made.

Output file just after return:

```
Enter WriteBackward with string: cat
About to print last character of string: cat
t
Enter WriteBackward with string: ca
About to print last character of string: ca
a
Enter WriteBackward with string: c
About to print last character of string: c
c
Enter WriteBackward with string:
Leave WriteBackward with string:
Leave WriteBackward with string: c
```

S = 'cat'   --A-->   S = 'ca'   S = 'c'   S = "

This invocation completes execution and a return is made.

Output file just after return:

```
Enter WriteBackward with string: cat
About to print last character of string: cat
t
Enter WriteBackward with string: ca
About to print last character of string: ca
a
Enter WriteBackward with string: c
About to print last character of string: c
c
Enter WriteBackward with string:
Leave WriteBackward with string:
Leave WriteBackward with string: c
Leave WriteBackward with string: ca
```

This invocation completes execution and a return is made.

Output file just after return:

```
Enter WriteBackward with string: cat
About to print last character of string: cat
t
Enter WriteBackward with string: ca
About to print last character of string: ca
a
Enter WriteBackward with string: c
About to print last character of string: c
c
Enter WriteBackward with string:
Leave WriteBackward with string:
Leave WriteBackward with string: c
Leave WriteBackward with string: ca
Leave WriteBackward with string: cat
```

Figure 5-9

Box trace of *Write-Backward2('cat')* in pseudocode

The output file is initially empty.

The initial call is made and the procedure begins execution.

```
┌──────────┐
│ S = 'cat'│
└──────────┘
```

Point A is reached, and the recursive call is made.

Output file just before call:

```
Enter WriteBackward2 with string: cat
```

The new invocation begins execution.

Point A is reached, and the recursive call is made.

Output file just before call:

```
Enter WriteBackward2 with string: cat
Enter WriteBackward2 with string: at
```

The new invocation begins execution.

Point A is reached, and the recursive call is made.

Output file just before call:

```
Enter WriteBackward2 with string: cat
Enter WriteBackward2 with string: at
Enter WriteBackward2 with string: t
```

(continues)

Figure 5-9
continued

The new invocation begins execution.

This invocation completes execution and a return is made.

Output file just after return:

```
Enter WriteBackward2 with string: cat
Enter WriteBackward2 with string: at
Enter WriteBackward2 with string: t
Enter WriteBackward2 with string:
Leave WriteBackward2 with string:
```

This invocation completes execution and a return is made.

Output file just after return:

```
Enter WriteBackward with string: cat
Enter WriteBackward with string: at
Enter WriteBackward with string: t
Enter WriteBackward with string:
Leave WriteBackward with string:
About to print first character of string: t
t
Leave WriteBackward2 with string: t
```

This invocation completes execution and a return is made.

Output file just after return:

```
Enter WriteBackward2 with string: cat
Enter WriteBackward2 with string: at
Enter WriteBackward2 with string: t
Enter WriteBackward2 with string:
Leave WriteBackward2 with string:
About to print first character of string: t
t
Leave WriteBackward2 with string: t
About to print first character of string: at
a
Leave WriteBackward2 with string: at
```

| S = 'cat' | S = 'at' | S = 't' | S = '' |

This invocation completes execution and a return is made.

Output file just after return:

```
Enter WriteBackward2 with string: cat
Enter WriteBackward2 with string: at
Enter WriteBackward2 with string: t
Enter WriteBackward2 with string:
Leave WriteBackward2 with string:
About to print first character of string: t
t
Leave WriteBackward2 with string: t
About to print first character of string: at
a
Leave WriteBackward2 with string: at
About to print first character of string: cat
c
Leave WriteBackward2 with string: cat
```

Example: Using `write` **statements to debug a recursive subprogram.** The following pseudocode indicates where to place `write` statements within a recursive subprogram during debugging:

```
Procedure R(... )

    { this is point A }
    writeln('Calling Procedure R from point A.',...)
    R(... )
        .
        .
        .
    { this is point B }
    writeln('Calling Procedure R from point B.',...)
    R(... )
        .
        .
        .
```

Sample **write** *statements that help to debug a recursive subprogram*

In addition to reporting each recursive call, the `write` statements should display the values of all parameters and local variables.

Before leaving the `WriteBackward` problem, suppose that the string S is in a linked list rather than an array. Given the nature of linked lists, the strategy of `WriteBackward` is very difficult to implement; however, the strategy of `WriteBackward2` is simple to implement. You will see why in the next chapter when you learn to process linked lists recursively.

COMPUTING THINGS

You should now be ready to use recursion to tackle some more challenging problems. The next two problems require you to compute some specified value.

Raising an Integer to a Power

Pascal has no exponentiation operator. That is, if you want to know the value of x^n, you have to write a function to compute it. This section presents three functions for performing exponentiation. To simplify matters, consider only integers raised to nonnegative integer powers.

Assuming the type definition

```
type nonneg = 0..maxint
```

the following *iterative* Pascal function performs the exponentiation:

Pow1 computes x^n iteratively

```
function Pow1(x : integer; n : nonneg) : integer;
{ -------------------------------------------------------------
  Exponentiation function--ITERATIVE SOLUTION.
  Precondition: x is an integer; n is a nonnegative integer.
  Postcondition: Returns x raised to the nth power.
  ------------------------------------------------------------- }
var   temp : nonneg;
      i : integer;

begin
   temp := 1;
      for i := 1 to n do
      temp := x * temp;
   Pow1 := temp
end  { Pow1 }
```

Now consider a recursive solution. How can you define raising x to the nth power in terms of raising x to a smaller power? The answer is found in the "rule of exponents":

$$x^n = x * x^{n-1}$$

That is, you can compute x^n by computing x^{n-1} and multiplying the result by x. This recursive solution lacks only a degenerate case. Recall that, by definition,

$$x^0 = 1$$

You thus have the following recursive formulation:

Computing x^n recursively

$$x^0 = 1$$
$$x^n = x * x^{n-1} \quad \text{if } n > 0$$

Since n is nonnegative, you will always reach the degenerate case, $n = 0$.

The following Pascal function implements this solution directly:

```pascal
function Pow2(x : integer; n : nonneg) : integer;
{ ----------------------------------------------------------
  Exponentiation function--RECURSIVE SOLUTION.
  Precondition: x is an integer; n is a nonnegative integer.
  Postcondition: Returns x raised to the nth power.
  ---------------------------------------------------- }
begin
    if n = 0
       then Pow2 := 1
       else Pow2 := x * Pow2(x, n-1)
end   { Pow2 }
```

Pow2 computes x^n recursively

To compute x^n, the function *Pow2* is called $n + 1$ times: once from the main program and n times recursively. You can reduce this number of calls greatly by exploiting another rule of exponents:

$$x^n = (x^{n/m})^m$$

In particular, for $m = 2$

$$x^n = (x^{n/2})^2$$

You can use this rule to construct a more efficient recursive power function. The strategy of the following function is to halve the value of n at each recursive call rather than simply to decrement it by 1. The result is that the function reaches the degenerate case with far fewer recursive calls than *Pow2*.

```pascal
function Pow3(x : integer; n : nonneg) : integer;
{ ----------------------------------------------------------
  Exponentiation function--MORE EFFICIENT RECURSIVE SOLUTION.
  Precondition: x is an integer; n is a nonnegative integer.
  Postcondition: Returns x raised to the nth power.
  ---------------------------------------------------- }
begin
    if n = 0 then
       Pow3 := 1
    else if odd(n) then
       Pow3 := x * sqr(Pow3(x, n div 2))
    else Pow3 := sqr(Pow3(x, n div 2))
end   { Pow3 }
```

Pow3 computes x^n recursively and more efficiently than Pow2

Observe that the function *Pow3* has a case for even n (when *odd(n)* is false) and a different case for odd n (when *odd(n)* is true). Consider first the case for even n. Here the function computes the value x^n as

```pascal
sqr(Pow3(x, n div 2))
```

(*sqr* is a predefined Pascal function for raising integers to the power of 2). This computation is valid because, when n is even,

$$(x^{n\ div\ 2})^2 = (x^{n/2})^2 = x^n$$

Now consider the case when n is odd. Notice that the value of n div 2 is not the same as $n/2$ when n is odd. For example, the value of 13 div 2 is 6 rather than 6.5, and consequently $(x^{13\ div\ 2})^2$ is equal to x^{12} rather than x^{13}. In general, when n is odd,

$$(x^{n\ div\ 2})^2 = x^{n-1}$$

To compensate for this fact, when n is odd the function *Pow3* computes

```
x * sqr(Pow3(x, n div 2))
```

Figure 5-10 illustrates the dramatic reduction in the number of required calls to the power function that you can achieve by halving n rather than decrementing n by 1. Exercise 15 further discusses the efficiency of the power functions.

Figure 5-10

Pow2(x, 11) versus
Pow3(x, 11)

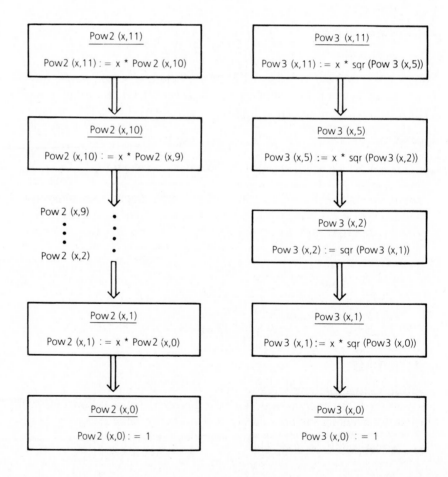

Multiplying Rabbits (The Fibonacci Sequence)

Rabbits are very prolific breeders. If rabbits did not die, their population would quickly get out of hand. Suppose we assume the following "facts," which we obtained in a recent survey of randomly selected rabbits:

- Rabbits never die.
- A rabbit reaches sexual maturity exactly two months after birth, that is, at the beginning of its third month of life.
- Rabbits are always born in male-female pairs. At the beginning of every month, each sexually mature male-female pair gives birth to exactly one male-female pair.

Suppose you started with a single newborn male-female pair. How many pairs would there be in month 6, counting the births that took place at the beginning of month 6? Since 6 is a relatively small number, you can figure out the solution easily:

Month 1:	1 pair, the original.
Month 2:	1 pair still, since it is not yet sexually mature.
Month 3:	2 pairs; the original pair has reached sexual maturity and has given birth to a second pair.
Month 4:	3 pairs; the original pair has given birth again, but the pair born at the beginning of month 3 is not yet sexually mature.
Month 5:	5 pairs; all rabbits alive in month 3 (2 pairs) are now sexually mature. Add their offspring to those pairs alive in month 4 (3 pairs) to yield 5 pairs.
Month 6:	8 pairs; 3 sexually mature pairs plus 5 pairs alive in the previous month.

You can now construct a recursive solution for computing *Rabbit(n)*, the number of pairs alive in month *n*. You must determine how you can use *Rabbit(n – 1)* to compute *Rabbit(n)*. Observe that *Rabbit(n)* is the sum of the number of pairs alive just prior to the start of month *n* and the number of pairs born at the start of month *n*. Just prior to the start of month *n*, there are *Rabbit(n – 1)* pairs of rabbits. Not all of these rabbits are sexually mature at the start of month *n*. Only those who were alive in month *n – 2* are ready to reproduce at the start of month *n*. That is, the number of pairs born at the start of month *n* is *Rabbit(n – 2)*. Therefore, you have the relationship

Rabbit(n) = Rabbit(n – 1) + Rabbit(n – 2)   *The number of pairs in month* n

Figure 5-11 illustrates this relationship.

This recursive relationship introduces a new point. In some cases, you solve a problem by solving more than one smaller problem of the same type. This change does not add much conceptual difficulty, but you must

Figure 5-11

Recursive solution to the rabbit problem

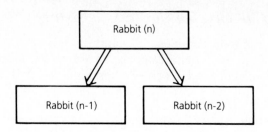

be very careful when selecting the degenerate case. The temptation is simply to say that *Rabbit*(1) should be the degenerate case because its value is 1 according to the problem's statement. But what about *Rabbit*(2)? Applying the recursive definition to *Rabbit*(2) would yield

$$Rabbit(2) = Rabbit(1) + Rabbit(0)$$

Thus, the recursive definition would need to specify the number of pairs alive in month 0—an undefined quantity.

One possible solution is to define *Rabbit*(0) to be 0, but this approach seems artificial. A slightly more attractive alternative is to treat *Rabbit*(2) itself as a special case with the value of 1. Thus, the recursive definition has two degenerate cases, *Rabbit*(2) and *Rabbit*(1). The recursive definition becomes

Two degenerate cases are necessary because there are two smaller problems

$$Rabbit(n) = \begin{cases} 1 & \text{if } n \leq 2 \\ Rabbit(n-1) + Rabbit(n-2) & \text{if } n > 2 \end{cases}$$

Incidentally, the series of numbers *Rabbit*(1), *Rabbit*(2), *Rabbit*(3), and so on is known as the **Fibonacci sequence**, which models many naturally occurring phenomena.

A pseudocode function to compute *Rabbit*(n) is easy to write from the previous definition:

Rabbit computes the Fibonacci sequence, but does so inefficiently

```
function Rabbit(n) : returns a positive integer
{ Assumption: n is a positive integer. }

    if n ≤ 2
        then Rabbit := 1
        else Rabbit := Rabbit(n — 1) + Rabbit(n — 2)
```

Should you implement this function in Pascal and run it? Figure 5-12 illustrates the recursive calls that `Rabbit(7)` generates. (To save space, the figure uses `Rab` instead of `Rabbit`.) Think about the number of recursive calls that `Rabbit(10)` generates. At best, the function `Rabbit` is inefficient; for large values of *n*, it is infeasible to use. We shall discuss this problem in more detail at the end of this chapter, at which time we shall give some techniques for generating a more efficient solution from this same recursive relationship.

COUNTING THINGS

The next two problems require you to count certain combinations of events or things.

Mr. Spock's Dilemma (Choosing k out of n Things)

The five-year mission of the *U.S.S. Enterprise* is to explore new worlds. The five years are almost up, but the *Enterprise* has just entered an unexplored solar system that contains n planets. Unfortunately, time will allow for only k explorations. Mr. Spock begins to ponder how many different ways he can choose k planets for exploration out of the n planets in the solar system.

Mr. Spock is especially fascinated by one particular planet, Planet X. He begins to think—in terms of Planet X—about how many ways there are to pick k planets out of the n. "There are two possibilities: Either we visit Planet X, or we do not visit Planet X. If we do visit Planet X, then I will have to choose $k - 1$ other planets to visit from the $n - 1$ remaining planets. On the other hand, if we do not visit Planet X, I will have to choose k planets to visit from the remaining $n - 1$ planets."

Mr. Spock is on his way to a recursive method of counting how many ways he can choose k planets from n. Let $C(n, k)$ be the number of ways of choosing k planets from n. Then, in terms of Planet X, Mr. Spock deduces that

$$C(n,k) = \text{(the number of ways of choosing a group of } k \text{ planets that includes Planet } X\text{)}$$

$$+$$

$$\text{(the number of ways of choosing a group of } k \text{ planets that does not include Planet } X\text{)}$$

But Mr. Spock has already reasoned that the number of ways to select a group that includes Planet X is $C(n - 1, k - 1)$, and the number of ways to select a group that does not include Planet X is $C(n - 1, k)$. Mr. Spock has figured out a way to solve his counting problem in terms of two smaller counting problems of the same type:

$$C(n, k) = C(n - 1, k - 1) + C(n - 1, k)$$

Mr. Spock now has to worry about the degenerate case(s). He also needs to demonstrate that each of the two smaller problems eventually reaches a degenerate case. First, what selection problem does he immediately know the answer to? If the *Enterprise* had time to visit all the planets (that is, if $k = n$), there would be no need for a decision; there is only one way to select all the planets. Thus, the first degenerate case is

$$C(k, k) = 1$$

The number of ways to choose k out of n things is the sum of the number of ways to choose k – 1 out of n – 1 things and the number of ways to choose k out of n – 1 things

Degenerate case: There is one way to choose everything

Figure 5-12

The recursive calls that
Rabbit(7) **generates**

If $k < n$, it is easy to see that the second term in the recursive definition $C(n-1, k)$ is "closer" to the degenerate case $C(k, k)$ than is $C(n, k)$. However, the first term, $C(n-1, k-1)$, is not closer to $C(k, k)$ than is $C(n, k)$—they are the same "distance" apart. *When you solve a problem by solving two (or more) smaller problems, each of the smaller problems must be closer to a degenerate case than the original problem.*

Mr. Spock realizes that there is another trivial selection problem that the first term does, in fact, approach. This problem is the counterpart of his first degenerate case, $C(k, k)$. Just as there is only one way to select all the planets to visit ($k = n$), there is also only one way to select zero planets to visit ($k = 0$). When there is no time to visit any of the planets, the

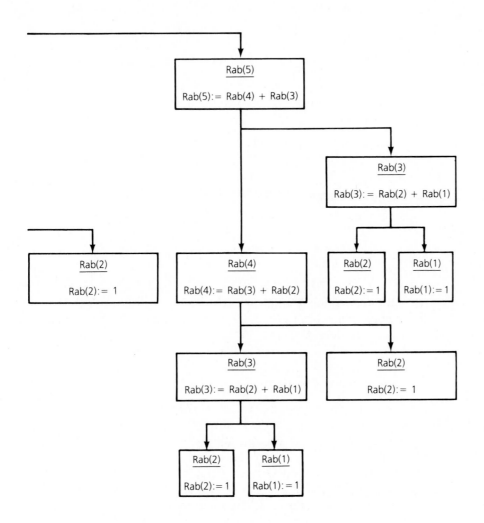

Enterprise must head home without any exploration. Thus the second degenerate case is

$$C(n, 0) = 1$$

Degenerate case: There is one way to choose everything

This degenerate case does indeed have the property that $C(n - 1, k - 1)$ is closer to it than is $C(n, k)$. (Alternatively, you could define the second degenerate case to be $C(n, 1) = n$.)

Mr. Spock adds one final part to his solution:

$$C(n, k) = 0 \qquad \text{if } k > n$$

Although k could not be greater than n in the context of this problem, the addition of this case makes the recursive solution more generally applicable.

To summarize, the following recursive solution solves the problem of choosing k out of n things:

$$C(n, k) = \begin{cases} 1 & \text{if } k = 0 \\ 1 & \text{if } k = n \\ C(n-1, k-1) + C(n-1, k) & \text{if } 0 < k < n \\ 0 & \text{if } k > n \end{cases}$$

You can easily derive the following pseudocode function from this recursive definition:

```
function C(n, k) : returns a nonnegative integer
{ Assumption: n and k are nonnegative integers. }

    if k > n then
        C := 0
    else if k = n then
        C := 1
    else if k = 0 then
        C := 1
    else C := C(n-1, k-1) + C(n-1, k)
```

The comments about efficiency that we made following the rabbit problem apply here also. Figure 5-13 shows the number of recursive calls that the computation of $C(4, 2)$ requires.

The Mad Scientist Problem

The mad scientist wishes to make a chain out of plutonium and lead pieces. There is a problem, however. If the scientist places two pieces of plutonium next to each other, BOOM! The question is, in how many ways can the scientist safely construct a chain of length n?

Assume that pieces of the same element are indistinguishable and that the scientist has at least n pieces of plutonium and n pieces of lead. Also note that the question asks for the number of ways to construct a chain. The chains *lead-plutonium* and *plutonium-lead*, for example, are different chains and count as two ways.

The scientist realizes that there are two classes of safe chains: safe chains that end with a lead piece and safe chains that end with a plutonium piece. The answer to the question is simply the sum of the number of chains of each type. That is, let

$C(n)$ be the number of safe chains of length n

$L(n)$ be the number of safe chains of length n that end with a piece of lead

$P(n)$ be the number of safe chains of length n that end with a piece of plutonium

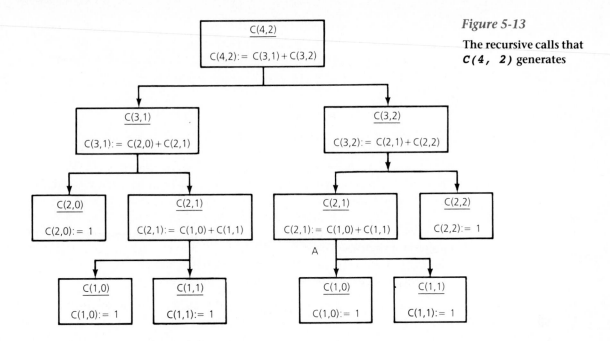

Figure 5-13

The recursive calls that
C(4, 2) generates

Then

$$C(n) = L(n) + P(n)$$

First, consider $L(n)$. The scientist can create a safe chain of length n that ends with a lead piece simply by tacking a lead piece onto the end of *any* safe chain of length $n - 1$. Hence, the number of safe chains of length n that end with a lead piece is precisely equal to the total number of safe chains of length $n - 1$; that is,

$$L(n) = C(n - 1)$$

The number of safe chains of length n that end in lead

Next, consider $P(n)$. The only way a safe chain can end with a plutonium piece is if the piece just before the end is lead. (If it is plutonium, the scientist cannot add another plutonium piece.) Thus, the only way to make a safe chain of length n that ends in plutonium is first to make a safe chain of length $n - 1$ that ends in lead and then add a piece of plutonium to the end. Therefore, the number of safe chains of length n that end with a plutonium piece is precisely equal to the number of safe chains of length $n - 1$ that end with a lead piece:

$$P(n) = L(n - 1)$$

The scientist then uses the earlier fact that $L(n) = C(n - 1)$ to obtain

$$P(n) = C(n - 2)$$

The number of safe chains of length n that end in plutonium

Thus, the scientist has solved $L(n)$ and $P(n)$ in terms of the smaller problems $C(n - 1)$ and $C(n - 2)$, respectively. The scientist then uses

$$C(n) = L(n) + P(n)$$

to obtain

The number of safe chains of length n

$$C(n) = C(n - 1) + C(n - 2)$$

The form of this recurrence relation is identical to the solution for the multiplying rabbits problem.

As you saw in the rabbit problem, two degenerate cases are necessary because the recurrence relation defines a problem in terms of two smaller problems. As you did for the rabbit problem, you can choose $n = 1$ and $n = 2$ for the degenerate cases. Although both problems use the same n's for their degenerate cases, there is no reason to expect that they use the same values for these degenerate cases. That is, there is no reason to expect that *Rabbit*(1) is equal to $C(1)$ and that *Rabbit*(2) is equal to $C(2)$.

A little thought reveals that for the chain problem,

Two degenerate cases are necessary because there are two smaller problems

$C(1) = 2$ (Chains that consist of either a single piece of pluto-nium or a single piece of lead.)

$C(2) = 3$ (The safe chains of length 2 are *lead-lead, plutonium-lead*, and *lead-plutonium*.)

In summary, the solution to this problem is

A recursive solution

$C(1) = 2$

$C(2) = 3$

$C(n) = C(n - 1) + C(n - 2)$ for $n > 2$

Moral of the story: Sometimes you can solve a problem by breaking it up into cases—for example, chains that end in plutonium and chains that end in lead.

Another moral of the story: The values that you use for the degenerate cases are extremely important. Although the recurrence relations for C and *Rabbit* are the same, the different values for their degenerate cases ($n = 1$ or 2) cause different values for larger n. For example, *Rabbit*(20) = 6,765, while $C(20) = 17,711$. The larger the value of n, the larger the discrepancy. You should think about why this is so.

SEARCHING FOR THINGS

Searching is an important task that occurs frequently. This chapter began with an intuitive approach to a binary search algorithm. In this section we will develop the binary search and examine other searching problems that have recursive solutions. Our goal is to develop further your notion of recursion.

Finding the Largest Element of an Array

This section begins by outlining a solution to a simple problem. You should complete the solution before continuing.

Suppose you have an array A of integers and you want to find its maximum element. You could construct an iterative solution without too much difficulty, but instead consider a recursive formulation:

```
if A has only one element then
    MaxArray(A) is the element in A

else if A has more than one element then
        MaxArray(A) is the maximum of
        (MaxArray(left half of A), MaxArray(right half of A))
```

Notice that this strategy fits the divide-and-conquer model we discussed at the beginning of this chapter when we introduced the binary search algorithm. That is, the algorithm proceeds by dividing the problem and conquering the subproblems, as Figure 5-14 illustrates. However, there is a difference between this algorithm and the binary search algorithm. While the binary search algorithm conquers only one of its subproblems at each step, *MaxArray* conquers both. In addition, after *MaxArray* conquers the subproblems, it must reconcile the two solutions—that is, it must find the maximum of the two maximums. Figure 5-15 illustrates the computations that are necessary to find the largest element in the array that contains 1, 6, 8, and 3 (denoted here by <1, 6, 8, 3>).

MaxArray conquers both of its subproblems at each step

We leave it to you to develop a recursive solution based on this strategy. In so doing, you may stumble on several subtle programming issues. We discuss virtually all of these issues in the binary search problem that follows, but this is a good opportunity for you to get some practice implementing a recursive solution.

Binary Search

At the beginning of this chapter, we presented—at a high level—a recursive binary search algorithm for finding a word in a dictionary. We will now fully develop this algorithm, illustrating some important programming issues.

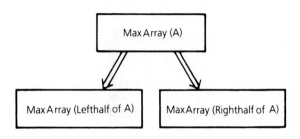

Figure 5-14

Recursive solution to the largest-element problem

Recall the earlier solution to the dictionary problem:

A binary search conquers one of its subproblems at each step

```
Search(dictionary, word)

    if dictionary is one page in size
        then scan the page for word

        else
        begin
            Open dictionary to a point near the middle
            Determine which half of dictionary contains word

            if word is in the first half of dictionary
                    then Search(first half of dictionary, word)
                    else Search(second half of dictionary, word)
        end
```

Now alter the problem slightly by searching an array `A` of integers for a given value `V`. The array, like the dictionary, must be sorted, or else a binary search is not applicable. Hence, assume that

An array must be sorted before you can apply a binary search to it

$$A[1] \le A[2] \le A[3] \le \cdots \le A[n]$$

where n is the size of the array. A high-level binary search for the array problem is

```
BinSearch(A, V)

    if A is of size 1
        then determine if its element is equal to V
```

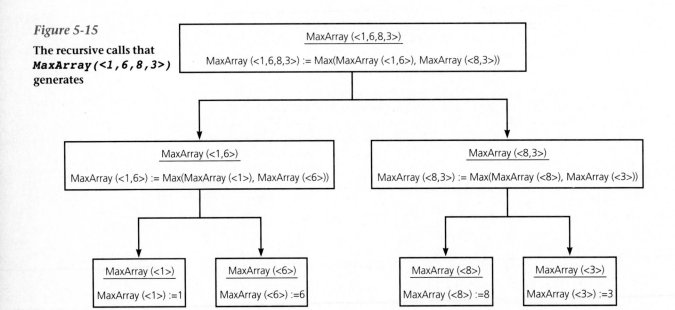

Figure 5-15

The recursive calls that `MaxArray(<1,6,8,3>)` generates

```
    else
    begin
        Find the midpoint of A
        Determine which half of A contains V
        if V is in the first half of A
            then BinSearch(first half of A, V)
            else BinSearch(second half of A, V)
    end
```

Although the solution is conceptually sound, various considerations demand changes in its organization. Three of these considerations are the following:

1. **How will you pass "half of *A*" to the recursive calls to *BinSearch*?** You can pass the entire array at each call, but have *BinSearch* search only the portion *A[first..last]*. Thus, you would also pass the integers *first* and *last* to *BinSearch*:

```
        BinSearch(A, V, first, last)
```

With this convention, the new midpoint is given by

```
        mid := (first + last ) div 2
```

Then *BinSearch(first half of A, V)* becomes

```
        BinSearch(A, V, first, mid — 1)
```

and *BinSearch(second half of A, V)* becomes

```
        BinSearch(A, V, mid + 1, last)
```

The array halves are A[first..mid-1] and A[mid+1..last]; neither "half" contains A[mid]

2. **How do you determine which half of the array contains *V*?** One possible implementation of

```
        if V is in the first half of A
```

is

```
        if V < A[mid]
```

However, there is no test for equality between *V* and *A[mid]*. This omission can cause the algorithm to miss *V*: After the previous halving algorithm splits *A* into halves, *A[mid]* is not in either half of the array. (In this case, two halves do not make a whole!) Therefore, you must determine whether *A[mid]* is the value you seek *now* because later it will not be in the remaining half of the array. The interaction between the halving criterion and the termination condition (the degenerate case) is subtle and is often a source of error. We need to rethink the degenerate case.

Determine whether A[mid] is V, the value you seek

3. **What should the degenerate case(s) be?** As written, *BinSearch* terminates only when an array of size 1 occurs; this is the only degenerate case. By changing the halving procedure so that *A[mid] remains in one of the halves,* it is possible to implement the binary search correctly so

Two degenerate cases

that it has only this single degenerate case. However, we believe that it is clearer to have two distinct degenerate cases as follows:

a. *first > last*. You will reach this degenerate case when the value *V* is not in the original array.

b. *V = A[mid]*. You will reach this degenerate case when the value *V* is in the original array.

These degenerate cases are a bit different from any you have encountered previously. In a sense, the algorithm determines the answer to the problem from the degenerate case it reaches. Many search problems have this flavor.

The Pascal function *BinSearch*, which follows, returns the index of the array element that is equal to *V*. Because we plan to show you a box trace of this function, we have labeled—as *X* and *Y*—the two recursive calls to *BinSearch*.

```
{ n is a constant equal to the size of the array }
type   list = array[1..n] of integer;

function BinSearch(A: list; V, first, last : integer): integer;
{ -----------------------------------------------------------
  Searches the array A[first..last] for the value V by using
  a binary search.
  Precondition: 1 <= first, last <= n, and A[first] <=
  A[first+1] <= ... <= A[last].
  Postcondition: If V is in the array, returns BinSearch > 0
  such that A[BinSearch] = V; otherwise returns BinSearch = 0.
  ----------------------------------------------------------- }
var mid : integer;

begin
    if first > last
        then BinSearch := 0 { V is not in the original array }

        else
        { Invariant: If V is in A, then A[first] <= V <= A[last] }
        begin
            mid := (first + last) div 2;
            if V = A[mid] then
                BinSearch := mid   { V found at A[mid] }
            else if V < A[mid] then
                BinSearch := BinSearch(A, V, first, mid-1) { X }
            else BinSearch := BinSearch(A, V, mid+1, last) { Y }
        end
end   { BinSearch }
```

Notice that *BinSearch* has the following invariant: If *V* occurs in the array, then $A[first] \le V \le A[last]$.

Figure 5-16 shows a box trace of *BinSearch* when it searches the array containing 1, 5, 9, 12, 15, 21, 29, and 31 for the integer 6. Notice how the labels *X* and *Y* of the two recursive calls to *BinSearch* appear in the dia-

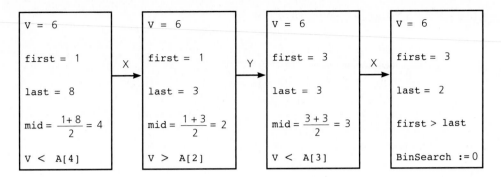

Figure 5-16

Box trace of **BinSearch** with **A** =< 1, 5, 9, 12, 15, 21, 29, 31>

gram. Exercise 6 at the end of this chapter asks you to perform other box traces with this function.

There is another implementation issue, which deals specifically with Pascal, to consider. In the function *BinSearch*, A is a value parameter. This fact implies that at each call to *BinSearch*, the function makes a copy of A and places it in its local environment. If A is large, many calls to *BinSearch* may be necessary, with each call requiring a copy of a large array.

There are two obvious ways to avoid this problem, but neither is satisfactory. Either you could declare the array A as a global variable or you could pass A to *BinSearch* as a variable parameter. Both of these solutions undermine modularity, however. First, you usually should avoid global variables, as they destroy the clean interface between a subprogram and the remainder of the program. Global variables also make the subprogram less general. In the case of *BinSearch*, a global declaration of the array A would allow the function to search only this specific array. Second, passing A as a variable parameter suggests that the function *BinSearch* makes a change to A. However, *BinSearch* does not change A, so passing A as a variable parameter conveys misinformation about *BinSearch*'s interface with the rest of the program.

Passing A either globally or as a variable parameter is not satisfactory

A third possibility is to embed the recursive search function within a nonrecursive function, which is called a **nonrecursive shell**. In the following, the function *dosearch* performs the recursive binary search—as *BinSearch* did earlier—and *BinSearch* is the nonrecursive shell:

```
{ n is a constant equal to the size of the array }
type list = array[1..n] of integer;

function BinSearch(A : list; V: integer) : integer;
{ -----------------------------------------------------
   Searches the array A for the value V by using a binary
   search.
   Precondition: A is sorted in ascending order.
   Postcondition: If V is in the array, returns BinSearch > 0
   such that A[BinSearch] = V; otherwise returns BinSearch = 0.
   ----------------------------------------------------- }
```

BinSearch is a nonrecursive shell

A is global to dosearch

```
function dosearch(V, first, last : integer) : integer;
{ ---------------------------------------------------------
   Precondition: A is global to dosearch.
   Postcondition: If V is in A[first..last], then returns
   dosearch > 0 such that A[dosearch] = V; otherwise
   returns dosearch = 0.
   --------------------------------------------------------- }
var mid : integer;
begin
   if first > last
      then dosearch := 0

      else
{ Invariant: If V is in A, then A[first] <= V <= A[last] }
         begin
            mid := (first + last) div 2;
            if V = A[mid] then
               dosearch := mid
            else if V < A[mid] then
               dosearch := dosearch(V, first, mid-1)
            else dosearch := dosearch(V, mid+1, last)
         end
   end;   { dosearch }

begin   { body of BinSearch }
   BinSearch := dosearch(V, 1, n)
end   { BinSearch}
```

The only action of the function *BinSearch* is to call the function *dosearch*. The function *dosearch* is local to *BinSearch* and performs the actual binary search. You pass the array *A* to *BinSearch* as a value parameter, and *dosearch* accesses it as a nonlocal variable; that is, *A* is global to *dosearch*. Because you call *BinSearch* only once (for each search problem), only one copy of *A* is made. The fact that *dosearch* is local to *BinSearch* minimizes the objection that *dosearch* accesses a nonlocal variable *A*: Only *BinSearch* invokes *dosearch*. The function *dosearch* can make no changes to *A* that will propagate outside *Bin-Search*. *BinSearch* is general because you can pass it any array of the appropriate type. The solution is a good compromise between the concerns of programming style and efficiency.

A nonrecursive shell allows a compromise between efficiency and style

However, there are some situations where even one copy of *A* is too many, and in these situations it is necessary to pass the array *A* as a variable parameter. You will need some mathematical techniques for analyzing algorithms to identify such a situation. Chapter 7 introduces some of these techniques briefly, but not until you take a formal course on the analysis of algorithms will you be exposed to them in earnest. Until then, we recommend that you use the nonrecursive shell approach as a reasonable compromise between efficiency and style.

A box trace of the recursive function *dosearch* reveals a new consideration. Because the array *A* is neither a value parameter nor a local variable, it is not a part of *dosearch*'s local environment, and so *A* should not appear within each box. Therefore, as Figure 5-17 shows, you represent the array *A* outside the boxes, and all references to *A* affect this single representation. Note that you represent a variable parameter in the box method in the same way as you represent a global variable.

Represent global variables and variable parameters outside of the boxes in a box trace

As a final comment, notice that the binary search algorithm is inappropriate for a linked list: How would you locate its midpoint? Chapter 10 examines a linked structure that permits a binary search.

***BinSearch** is inappropriate for a linked list*

Finding the kth Smallest Element of an Array

The previous two examples presented recursive methods for finding the largest element in an arbitrary array and for finding an arbitrary element in a sorted array. We conclude this discussion of searching with a high-level description of a recursive solution for finding the kth smallest element in an arbitrary array *A*. Would you ever be interested in such an element? Statisticians often want the median value in a collection of data. The median value in an ordered collection of data occurs in the middle of the collection. In an unordered collection of data, there are about the same number of values smaller than the median value as there are larger values. Thus, if you have 49 elements, the 25th smallest element is the median value.

Obviously, you could solve this problem by sorting the array. Then the kth smallest element would be *A[k]*. Although this approach is a legitimate solution, it does more than the problem requires; a more efficient solution

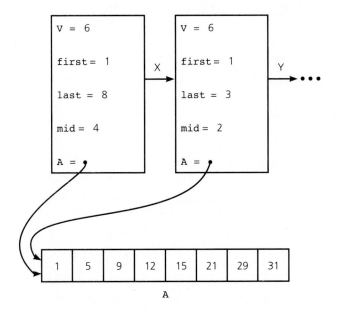

Figure 5-17

Box method with either a global variable or a variable parameter

is possible. The solution that we outline here finds the kth smallest element without completely sorting the array.

By now, you know that you solve a problem recursively by writing its solution in terms of one or more smaller problems of the same type in such a way that this notion of *smaller* ensures that you will always reach a degenerate instance of the problem. For all of the earlier recursive solutions, the amount of the reduction in problem size between recursive calls is *predictable*. For example, in the factorial problem, you always decrease the problem size by 1; in the exponentiation problem, you always halve the problem size. In addition, the degenerate cases for all the previous problems except the binary search have a static, predefined size. Thus, by knowing only the size of the original problem, you can determine the number of recursive calls that are necessary before you reach the degenerate case.

For all previous examples, you know the amount of reduction made in the problem size by each recursive call

The solution that we are about to present for finding the kth smallest element departs from these traditions. Although you solve the problem in terms of a smaller problem, just how much smaller this problem is depends on the elements in the array and cannot be predicted in advance. Also, the size of the degenerate case depends on the elements in the array, as it did for the binary search. (Recall that you reach a degenerate case for a binary search when the middle element is the one sought.)

You cannot predict in advance the size of either the smaller problems or the degenerate case in the recursive solution to the kth-smallest-element problem

This "unpredictable" type of solution is caused by the nature of the problem: The relationship between the rankings of the elements in any predetermined parts of the array and the ranking of the elements in the entire array is not strong enough to determine the kth smallest element. For example, suppose that A contains the elements shown in Figure 5-18. Notice that $A[4] = 6$ is the third-smallest element in the first half of A and that $A[5] = 8$ is the third-smallest element in the second half of A. Can you conclude from this anything about the location of the third-smallest element in all of A? The answer is no; this relationship is not strong enough to allow you to draw any useful conclusions. You should experiment with other fixed splitting schemes as well.

The recursive solution proceeds by

1.   Selecting a **pivot element** in the array
2.   Cleverly arranging, or **partitioning**, the elements in the array about this pivot element
3.   Recursively applying the strategy to *one* of the partitions

Now consider the details of the recursive solution. Suppose that you want to find the kth smallest element in the array segment $A[F..L]$. Let

Figure 5-18

A sample array

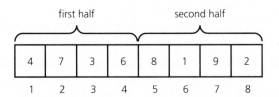

the pivot p be any element of the array segment. (For now, ignore how to choose p.) You can partition the elements of $A[F..L]$ into three regions: S_1, which contains the elements less than p; the pivot p itself; and S_2, which contains the elements greater than or equal to p. Notice that this partition implies that all the elements in S_1 are smaller than all the elements in S_2. Figure 5-19 illustrates this partition.

Partition A into three parts: elements $< p$, p, and elements $\geqslant p$

In terms of array subscripts, all elements in $A[F..pivotindex–1]$ are less than p and all elements in $A[pivotindex+1..L]$ are greater than or equal to p. Notice that the sizes of the regions S_1 and S_2 depend on both p and the other elements of $A[F..L]$.

This partition induces three "smaller problems," such that the solution to one of the problems will solve the original problem:

1. If there are k or more elements in $S_1 = A[F..pivotindex–1]$ (that is, if $k < pivotindex – F + 1$), then S_1 contains the k smallest elements of the array segment $A[F..L]$. In this case, the kth smallest element must be in S_1.

2. If there are $k – 1$ elements in S_1 (that is, if $k = pivotindex – F + 1$), then the kth smallest element must be the pivot p; this is the degenerate case.

3. If there are fewer than $k – 1$ elements in S_1 (that is, if $k > pivotindex – F + 1$), then the kth smallest element in $A[F..L]$ must be in $S_2 = A[pivotindex+1..L]$. Because there are $pivotindex – F$ elements in S_1, the kth smallest element in $A[F..L]$ is the $(k – (pivotindex – F + 1))^{st}$ smallest element in S_2.

A recursive definition can summarize this discussion. Let

$$Select(k, A, F, L) = k^{th} \text{ smallest element in } A[F..L]$$

The kth smallest element in $A[F..L]$

After you select the pivot element p and partition $A[F..L]$ into S_1 and S_2, you have that

$Select(k, A, F, L)$

$$= \begin{cases} Select(k, A, F, pivotindex–1) & \text{if } k < pivotindex–F+1 \\ p & \text{if } k = pivotindex–F+1 \\ Select(k – (pivotindex–F+1), A, pivotindex+1, L) & \\ & \text{if } k > pivotindex–F+1 \end{cases}$$

The kth smallest element in $A[F..L]$

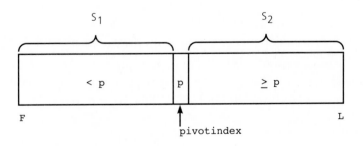

Figure 5-19

A partition about a pivot

There is always a pivot, and since it is not part of either S_1 or S_2, the size of the array segment to be searched decreases by at least 1 at each step. Thus, you will eventually reach the degenerate case: The desired element is a pivot. A high-level pseudocode solution is as follows:

```
function Select(k, A, F, L) : returns a value from the array

Choose a pivot element p from A[F..L]
Partition the elements of A[F..L] about p

if k < pivotindex — F + 1 then
    Select := Select(k, A, F, pivotindex—1)
else if k = pivotindex — F + 1 then
    Select := p
else Select := Select(k-(pivotindex-F+1), A, pivotindex+1, L)
```

This pseudocode is not far from a Pascal function. The only questions that remain are how to choose the pivot element p and how to partition the array about the chosen p. The choice of p is arbitrary. Any p in the array will work, although the sequence of choices will affect how soon you reach the degenerate case. Chapter 7 gives a procedure for partitioning the elements about p. There you will see how to turn the function $Select$ into a sorting algorithm.

RECURSION AND EFFICIENCY

Recursion is a powerful problem-solving tool that often produces very clean solutions to even the most complex problems. Recursive solutions can be easier to understand and to describe than iterative solutions. By using recursion, you can often write simple, short implementations of your solution.

The overriding concern in this chapter has been to give you a solid understanding of recursion so that you will be able to construct recursive solutions on your own. However, there are some drawbacks to recursion, which we briefly point out in this section.

These drawbacks have to do with the issue of efficiency. It is often the case that a nonrecursive, iterative subprogram is more efficient than a recursive one. Two factors contribute to the inefficiency of some recursive solutions:

Factors that contribute to the inefficiency of some recursive solutions

- The overhead associated with subprogram calls
- The inherent inefficiency of some recursive algorithms

The first of these factors does not pertain specifically to recursive subprograms but is true of subprograms in general. In most implementations of Pascal and other high-level programming languages, a subprogram call incurs a bookkeeping overhead. As Chapter 8 will indicate, this bookkeeping is not unlike the box method. Recursive subprograms magnify this overhead because a single initial call to the subprogram can generate a large number of recursive calls. For example, the call *Factorial(n)* generates *n* recursive calls. On the other hand, the use of recursion, as is true with modularity in general, can greatly clarify complex programs. This clarification frequently more than compensates for the additional overhead. Thus, the use of recursion is often consistent with the view of the cost of a computer program.

Recursion can clarify complex solutions

However, you should not use recursion just for the sake of using recursion. For example, you probably should not use the recursive *Factorial* function in practice. You can easily write an iterative *Factorial* function that is almost as clear as the recursive one and is more efficient. There is no reason to incur the overhead of recursion when its use does not gain anything. *The true value of recursion is as a tool for solving problems for which there is no simple nonrecursive solution.*

Recursion is not always appropriate, particularly when a clear, efficient iterative solution exists

The second point about recursion and efficiency is that some recursive algorithms are inherently inefficient. This inefficiency is a very different issue than that of overhead. It has nothing to do with how a compiler happens to implement a recursive subprogram but rather is related to the method of solution that the algorithm employs.

As an example, recall the recursive solution for the multiplying rabbits problem that you saw earlier in this chapter:

$$Rabbit(n) = \begin{cases} 1 & \text{if } n \leq 2 \\ Rabbit(n-1) + Rabbit(n-2) & \text{if } n > 2 \end{cases}$$

*The recursive version of **Rabbit** is inherently inefficient*

The diagram in Figure 5-12 illustrated the computation of *Rabbit(7)*; we asked you to think about what the diagram would look like for *Rabbit(10)*. If you thought about this question, you may have come to the conclusion that such a diagram would fill up most of this chapter. The diagram for *Rabbit(100)* would fill up most of this universe!

The fundamental problem with *Rabbit* is that it computes the same values over and over again. For example, in the diagram for *Rabbit(7)*, you can see that *Rabbit(3)* is computed five times. When *n* is moderately large, many of the values are recomputed literally trillions of times. Even if the computation of each of these values required only a trivial amount of work (for example, if you could perform a million of these computations per second), the enormous number of times that the values are recomputed still would make the solution infeasible.

However, do not conclude that the recurrence relation is of no use. One way to solve the rabbit problem is to construct an iterative solution based on this same recurrence relation. The iterative solution goes forward instead of backward and computes each value only once. You can use the following iterative function to compute *Rabbit(n)* even for very large values of *n*.

*You can use **Rabbit**'s recurrence relation to construct an efficient iterative solution*

```
function ItRabb(n : integer): integer;
{ ------------------------------------------------------------
  Iterative solution to the rabbit problem.
  ---------------------------------------------------------- }
var R, R1, R2, i : integer;

{ Just before the (i+1)st iteration of the loop, R and R1
  contain Rabbit(i), and R2 contains Rabbit(i—1). Thus, at
  the (i+1)st iteration, Rabbit(i+1) is simply R1 + R2. }
begin
    { initialize degenerate cases: R and R1 contain the value
      of Rabbit(2), R2 contains the value of Rabbit(1) }
    R1 := 1;
    R2 := 1;
    R  := 1;

    for i := 3 to n do
    begin
       R := R1 + R2;    { compute the value of Rabbit(i) }

       R2 := R1;        { get the values ready for }
       R1 := R          { the next iteration       }
    end;

    ItRabb := R         { return Rabbit(n) }
end   { ItRabb }
```

Convert from recursion to iteration if it is easier to discover a recursive solution but more efficient to use an iterative solution

There are thus times when an iterative solution is more efficient than a recursive solution. In certain cases, however, it may be easier to discover a recursive solution than an iterative solution. Therefore, you may need to convert a recursive solution to an iterative solution. This conversion process is easier if your recursive subprogram calls itself once, instead of several times. Be careful when deciding whether your subprogram calls itself more than once. Although the function *Rabbit* calls itself twice, the function *BinSearch* calls itself once, even though you see two calls in the Pascal code. Those two calls appear within an *if* statement; only one of them will be executed.

Conversion from a recursive solution to an iterative solution is even easier when the solitary recursive call is the last *action* that the subprogram takes. This situation is called **tail recursion**. For example, the procedure *WriteBackward* exhibits tail recursion because its recursive call is the last action that the procedure takes. Before you conclude that this observation is obvious, consider the function *Fact*. Although its recursive call appears last in the function definition, *Fact*'s last action is the multiplication. Thus, *Fact* is not tail recursive.

Although the original recursive formulation of the *Rabbit* algorithm was inherently inefficient, there are recursive algorithms that are extremely efficient. For example, the recursive binary search algorithm is quite efficient. You will develop the ability to determine whether a recursive algorithm is adequately efficient in more advanced courses concerned with the analysis of algorithms. For now, we shall continue to present recursive algorithms without worrying too much about this issue.

SUMMARY

1. Recursion is a technique that solves a problem by solving a smaller problem of the same type.

2. When constructing a recursive solution, keep the following four questions in mind:
    a. How can you define the problem in terms of a smaller problem of the same type?
    b. How does each recursive call diminish the size of the problem?
    c. What instance of the problem can serve as the degenerate case?
    d. As the problem size diminishes, will you reach this degenerate case?

3. You can use the box method to trace the actions of a recursive subprogram. These boxes resemble activation records, which many compilers use to implement recursion. (Chapter 8 discusses implementing recursion further.) Although the box method is useful, it cannot replace an intuitive understanding of recursion.

4. Recursion often produces straightforward solutions to even the most complex problems. Recursive solutions can be easier to understand, describe, and implement than iterative solutions. However, some recursive solutions can be less efficient than a corresponding iterative solution due to their inherently inefficient algorithms and the overhead of subprogram calls.

COMMON PITFALLS / DEBUGGING

1. A recursive algorithm must have a degenerate case, whose solution you know directly without making any recursive calls. Without a degenerate case, a recursive subprogram will generate an infinite sequence of calls.

2. A recursive solution must be stated in terms of one or more problems that are each closer to a degenerate case than is the original problem. When a recursive subprogram contains more than one recursive call, there often must be more than one degenerate case.

3. The box method, in conjunction with well-placed *write* statements, can be a good aid in debugging recursive subprograms. *Write* statements should report the values of parameters and local variables at both entry to and exit from the subprogram. *Write*

statements should also report the point in the program from which each recursive call occurs.

4. A recursive solution that recomputes certain values frequently can be inefficient. In such cases, iteration may be preferable to recursion.

SELF-TEST EXERCISES

1. The following function computes the product of the $n \geqslant 1$ real numbers in an array. Show how this function satisfies the properties of a recursive function.

```pascal
type  arraytype = array[1..50] of real;
function Product(A : arraytype; n : integer) : real;
{ Precondition: n >= 1.
  Postcondition: Returns the product of n elements in A,
  A is unchanged. }
begin
   if n = 1
      then Product := A[1]
      else Product := A[n] * Product(A, n-1)
end
```

2. Rewrite the function in Self-Test Exercise 1 as a procedure.

3. Write a recursive function that computes the product of the elements in the array A[first..last].

4. Given an integer $N > 0$, write a recursive procedure PrintIntegers that prints the integers $N, N-1, \cdots, 1$.

5. What is the purpose of a nonrecursive shell?

6. Of the following recursive procedures and functions that you saw in this chapter, identify those that exhibit tail recursion: Fact, WriteBackward, WriteBackward2, Pow2, Rabbit, C in the Spock problem, C in the mad scientist problem, MaxArray, BinSearch, and Select.

EXERCISES

1. Given an integer $N > 0$, write a recursive Pascal procedure that prints the integers $1, 2, \cdots, N$.

2. Write a recursive Pascal procedure that prints the digits of a positive decimal integer in reverse order.

3. The following recursive function Count counts the number of integers in the array A[1..n] that are equal to the integer x. For example,

if A contains the 10 integers 1, 2, 4, 4, 5, 6, 7, 8, 9, and 12, then
Count(A, 10, 4) returns the value 2 because 4 occurs twice in A.

```
type intarray = array[1..10] of integer;
function Count(A : intarray; n, x : integer) : integer;
var c : integer;
begin
    if n <= 0
        then Count := 0

        else
        begin
            if A[n] = x
                then c := 1
                else c := 0
            Count := Count(A, n-1, x) + c
        end
end   { Count }
```

Demonstrate that *Count* is recursive by listing the criteria of a recursive solution and stating how *Count* meets each criterion.

4. Embed the function *Count* that Exercise 3 defines in a nonrecursive shell. Write this shell as a function *CountIntegers*.

5. Perform a box trace of the following calls to recursive subprograms that appear in this chapter. Clearly indicate each subsequent recursive call.

a. *Rabbit(5)*
b. *Pow3(2, 5)*
c. *PrintIntegers(5)* (You wrote *PrintIntegers* in Self-Test Exercise 4.)

6. Perform a box trace of the recursive function *BinSearch*, which appears in the section "Binary Search," with the array 1, 5, 9, 12, 15, 21, 29, 31 for each of the following search values V: **a.** 5; **b.** 13; **c.** 16.

7. What output does the following program produce?

```
program main(output);

function test(a, b, n : integer) : integer;
var c : integer;
begin
    writeln('Enter: a = ', a:2, ' b = ', b:2);

    c := (a + b) div 2;
    if (sqr(c) <= n)
        then test := c
        else test := test(a, c-1, n);

    writeln('Leave: a = ', a:2, ' b = ', b:2);
end; { test }
```

```
begin { Main Program }
   writeln(test(1, 7, 7))
end.  { Program }
```

8. What output does the following program produce?

```
program testfsqrt(output);

function fsqrt(n : integer) : integer;

    function dosearch(first, last : integer) : integer;
    var mid : integer;
    begin
       writeln('Enter: first = ', first:2,' last = ',
                                              last:2);

       mid := (first + last) div 2;
       if (sqr(mid) <= n) and (n < sqr(mid+1)) then
           dosearch := mid
       else if sqr(mid) > n then
           dosearch := dosearch(first, mid-1)
       else dosearch := dosearch(mid + 1, last);

       writeln('Leave: first = ',first:2,' last = ',
                                              last:2)

    end;  { dosearch }

begin
    fsqrt := dosearch(1, n)
end;  { fsqrt }

begin { Main Program }
   writeln(fsqrt(30))
end.  { Program }
```

9. Consider the following function, which writes out a positive decimal number in base 8:

```
type posint = 1..maxint;

procedure PrintOctal(n : posint);
begin
    if n > 0
    then
    begin
       if n div 8 > 0
           then PrintOctal(n div 8);
       write(n mod 8 : 1)
    end
end
```

Describe how the algorithm works. Hand-execute the function with $n = 100$.

10. Consider the following program:

```
program demo(output);

var temp : integer;

function f(n : integer) : integer;
begin
    writeln('function entered with n = ', n:2);

    if n = 0 then
        f := 1
    else if n = 1 then
        f := 2
    else if n = 2 then
        f := 3
    else f := f(n - 2) * f(n - 4)
end; { f }

begin { Main Program }
    temp := f(8);
    writeln('The value of f(8) is ', temp:4)
end.  { Program }
```

Show the exact output of the program. Are there any parameter values that you could pass to the function f that would cause the program to run forever? If so, describe all such values.

11. Consider the following procedure:

```
procedure R(x, y : integer);
begin
    if y > 0
    then
    begin
        x := x + 1;
        y := y - 1;
        writeln(x, y);
        R(x, y);
        writeln(x, y)
    end
end
```

Execute the procedure with $x = 5$ and $y = 3$. How is the output affected if x is a variable (var) parameter instead of a value parameter?

12. Implement *WriteBackward2*, discussed in the section "A Recursive Procedure: Writing a String Backward," as a Pascal procedure.

13. Implement *MaxArray*, discussed in the section "Finding the Largest Element of an Array," as a Pascal function. What other recursive definitions of *MaxArray* can you describe?

14. Write a recursive function that will sum the elements in an array.

15. Consider the functions *Pow1*, *Pow2*, and *Pow3* discussed in the section "Raising an Integer to a Power." How many multiplications will each function perform (counting calls to function *sqr* as one multiplication) to compute 3^{32}? 3^{19}? How many recursive calls will *Pow2* and *Pow3* make to compute 3^{32}? 3^{19}?

16. Modify the recursive *Rabbit* function so that it is visually easy to follow the flow of execution. Instead of just adding "Enter" and "Leave" messages, indent the trace messages according to how "deep" the current recursive call is. For example, the call *Rabbit(4)* should produce the output

```
Enter Rabbit:    n = 4
    Enter Rabbit:    n = 3
        Enter Rabbit:    n = 2
        Leave Rabbit:    n = 2    value = 1
        Enter Rabbit:    n = 1
        Leave Rabbit:    n = 1    value = 1
    Leave Rabbit:    n = 3    value = 2
    Enter Rabbit:    n = 2
    Leave Rabbit:    n = 2    value = 1
Leave Rabbit:    n = 4    value = 3
```

Note how this output corresponds to figures such as Figure 5-12.

17. Consider the following recurrence relation:

$f(1) = 1; f(2) = 1; f(3) = 1; f(4) = 3; f(5) = 5;$
$f(n) = f(n - 1) + 3 * f(n - 5)$ for all $n > 5$.

a. Compute $f(n)$ for the following values of n: 6, 7, 12, 15.

b. If you were careful, rather than computing $f(15)$ from scratch (the way a recursive Pascal subprogram would compute it), you would have computed $f(6)$, then $f(7)$, then $f(8)$, and so on up to $f(15)$, recording the values as you computed them. This ordering would have saved you the effort of ever computing the same value more than once. (Recall the nonrecursive version of the *Rabbit* program discussed at the end of this chapter.)

Note that during the computation, you never need to remember all the previously computed values—only the last five. By taking advantage of these observations, write a Pascal function that uses a variation of the ADT ordered list to compute $f(n)$ for arbitrary values of n.

18. Write iterative versions of the following recursive subprograms: *Fact, WriteBackward, Rabbit, BinSearch, Select*.

*19. Consider the problem of finding the **greatest common divisor** (GCD) of two positive integers *a* and *b*. The algorithm we present is a variation of Euclid's algorithm, which is based on the following theorem:

THEOREM. If *a* and *b* are positive integers with $a > b$ such that *b* is not a divisor of *a*, then GCD(a, b) = GCD$(b, a \bmod b)$.

This relationship between GCD(a, b) and GCD$(b, a \bmod b)$ is the heart of the recursive solution. It specifies how you can solve the problem of computing GCD(a, b) in terms of another problem of the same type. Also, if *b* does divide *a*, then $b =$ GCD(a, b), so an appropriate choice for the degenerate case is $(a \bmod b) = 0$.

This theorem leads to the following recursive definition:

$$\text{GCD}(a, b) = \begin{cases} b & \text{if } (a \bmod b) = 0 \\ \text{GCD}(b, a \bmod b) & \text{otherwise} \end{cases}$$

The following Pascal function implements this recursive algorithm:

```
type posint = 1..maxint;

function GCD(a, b : posint) : integer;
{ Returns the greatest common divisor of a and b. }
begin
    if (a mod b) = 0         { degenerate case }
        then GCD := b
        else GCD := GCD(b, a mod b)
end    { GCD }
```

a. Prove the theorem.
b. What happens if $b > a$?
c. What is the notion of smaller? (That is, do you always approach a degenerate case?) Why is the degenerate case appropriate?

*20. Let $C(n)$ be the number of different ways to select integers from the integers 1 through $n - 1$ so that they add up to *n* (for example, $4 = 1 + 1 + 1 + 1 = 1 + 1 + 2 = 2 + 2 \cdots$). Write recursive definitions for $C(n)$ under the following variations:

a. Permutations are distinct versus permutations are not distinct (for example, $4 = 1 + 2 + 1$ and $4 = 1 + 1 + 2$).
b. You count *n* itself in the sum versus you do not count *n* (for example, $C(1) = 0$ versus $C(1) = 1$).

21. Consider the following recursive definition:

$$Acker(m, n) = \begin{cases} n + 1 & \text{if } m = 0 \\ Acker(m - 1, 1) & \text{if } n = 0 \\ Acker(m - 1, Acker(m, n - 1)) & \text{otherwise} \end{cases}$$

This function, called **Ackermann's function**, is of interest because it grows rapidly with respect to the sizes of m and n. What is *Acker(1, 2)*? Implement the function in Pascal and do a box trace of *Acker(1, 2)*. (*Caution:* Even for modest values of m and n, Ackermann's function requires many recursive calls.)

CHAPTER *6*

Recursion as a Problem-Solving Tool

PREVIEW   Most of the problems in this chapter are both difficult and important. For many of these problems, the recursive solutions are far more elegant and concise than the best of their nonrecursive counterparts. For example, the classic Towers of Hanoi problem appears to be quite difficult, yet it has an extremely simple recursive solution.

Although this chapter considers linked lists again—recursion simplifies the operations that you saw in Chapter 3—for the most part, it introduces new concepts such as backtracking and formal grammars. Backtracking is a technique that involves guesses at a solution. Formal grammars enable you to define, for example, syntactically correct algebraic expressions. The chapter concludes with a discussion of the close relationship between recursion and mathematical induction; you will learn how to use mathematical induction to study properties of algorithms.

More applications of recursion appear in the next chapter, where you will study some recursive sorting algorithms.

Now that we have presented the basic concepts of recursion, we are ready to move on to some extremely useful and somewhat complex applications. The examples in this chapter include two puzzles, recursive processing of linked lists, and grammars for defining languages.

DOING THINGS

This section uses recursion to "do things." Specifically, given some data organized in one way, the problem is to recursively organize the data in another way. Because you actually must effect some change and not, for example, simply search the data, you must use procedures rather than functions to accomplish such a task. The first problem of this section is called the Towers of Hanoi. Although this problem probably has no direct real-world application, we nevertheless begin with it because its solution so well illustrates the use of recursion.

The Towers of Hanoi

Many, many years ago, in a distant part of the Orient—in the Vietnamese city of Hanoi—the Emperor's wiseperson passed on to meet his ancestors. The Emperor needed a replacement wiseperson. Being a rather wise person himself, the Emperor devised a puzzle, declaring that its solver could have the job of wiseperson.

The Emperor's puzzle consisted of N disks (he didn't say exactly how many) and three poles: A (the source), B (the destination), and C (the spare). The disks were of different sizes and had holes in the middle so that they could fit on the poles. Because of their great weight, the disks could be placed only on top of disks larger than themselves. Initially, all the disks were on pole A, as shown in Figure 6-1a. The puzzle was to move the disks, one by one, from pole A to pole B. A person could also use pole C in the course of the transfer, but again a disk could be placed only on top of a disk larger than itself.

As the position of wiseperson was generally known to be a soft job, there were many applicants. Scholars and peasants alike brought the Emperor their solutions. Many solutions were thousands of steps long, and many contained *goto*'s. "I can't understand these solutions," bellowed the Emperor. "There must be an easy way to solve this puzzle."

And indeed there was. A great Buddhist monk came out of the mountains to see the Emperor. "My son," he said, "the puzzle is so easy, it almost solves itself." The Emperor's security chief wanted to throw this strange person out, but the Emperor let him continue.

"If there is only one disk (that is, $N = 1$), move it from pole A to pole B." So far, so good, but even the village idiot got that part right. "If there is more than one disk (that is, $N > 1$), simply

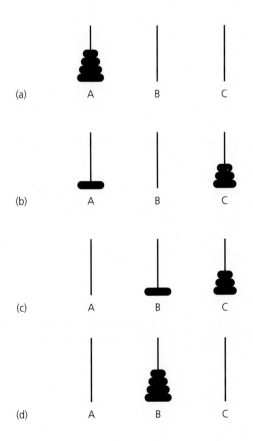

(a)

(b)

(c)

(d)

Figure 6-1

(a) The initial state; (b) move $N - 1$ disks from A to C; (c) move one disk from A to B; (d) move $N - 1$ disks from C to B

1. Ignore the bottom disk and solve the problem for $N - 1$ disks, with the small modification that pole C is the destination and pole B is the spare. (See Figure 6-1b.)

2. After you have done this, $N - 1$ disks will be on pole C, and the largest disk will remain on pole A. So solve the problem for $N = 1$ (recall that even the village idiot could do this) by moving the large disk from A to B. (See Figure 6-1c.)

3. Now all you have to do is move the $N - 1$ disks from pole C to pole B; that is, solve the problem with pole C as the source, pole B as the destination, and pole A as the spare." (See Figure 6-1d.)

There was silence for a few moments, and finally the Emperor said impatiently, "Well, are you going to tell us your solution or not?" The monk simply gave an all-knowing smile and vanished.

The Emperor obviously was not a recursive thinker, but you should realize that the monk's solution is perfectly correct. The key to the solution is the observation that you can solve the Towers problem of N disks by solving three smaller—in the sense of number of disks—Towers problems. Let `Towers(count, source, dest, spare)` denote the problem of moving `count` disks from pole `source` to pole `dest`, using pole `spare` as a spare. Notice that this definition makes sense even if there are more than `count` disks on pole `source`; in this case, you concern yourself with only the top `count` disks and ignore the others. Similarly, the poles `dest` and `spare` might have disks on them before you begin; you ignore these, too, except that you may place only smaller disks on top of them.

The problem statement   You can restate the Emperor's problem as follows: Beginning with N disks on pole A and 0 disks on poles B and C, solve `Towers(N, A, B, C)`. You can state the monk's solution as follows:

The solution   Step 1.   Starting in the initial state—with all the disks on pole A—solve

         `Towers(N−1, A, C, B)`

         That is, ignore the bottom (largest) disk and move the top $N - 1$ disks from pole A to pole C, using pole B as a spare. When you are finished, the largest disk will remain on pole A, and all the other disks will be on pole C.

    Step 2.   Now, with the largest disk on pole A and all others on pole C, solve

         `Towers(1, A, B, C)`

         That is, move the largest disk from pole A to pole B. Because this disk is larger than the disks already on the spare pole C, you really could not use the spare. However, fortunately—and obviously— you do not need to use the spare in this degenerate case. When you are done, the largest disk will be on pole B and all other disks will remain on pole C.

Step 3.   Finally, with the largest disk on pole *B* and all the other disks on pole *C*, solve

```
Towers(N-1, C, B, A)
```

That is, move the *N* – 1 disks from pole *C* to pole *B*, using *A* as a spare. Notice that the destination pole *B* already has the largest disk, which you ignore. When you are done, you will have solved the original problem: All the disks will be on pole *B*.

A pseudocode description of the solution is

```
Towers(count, source, dest, spare)

    if count = 1
        then move the disk directly from source to dest

        else
        begin
            Solve Towers(count-1, source, spare, dest)
            Solve Towers(1, source, dest, spare)
            Solve Towers(count-1, spare, dest, source)
        end
```

This recursive solution follows the same basic pattern as the recursive solutions you saw in the previous chapter:

1.   You solve a Towers problem by solving other Towers problems.

2.   These other Towers problems are smaller than the original problem; there are fewer disks to move. In particular, the number of disks decreases by 1 at each recursive call.

3.   When there is only one disk—the degenerate case—the solution is easy to solve directly.

4.   The way that the problems become smaller ensures that you will reach a degenerate case.

The solution to the Towers problem satisfies the four criteria of a recursive solution

Notice that this recursive solution will call itself many, many times. Figure 6-2 illustrates the calls for three disks.

Now consider a Pascal version of the Towers solution. Notice that since most computers do not have arms (at the time of this writing), the procedure moves a disk by printing directions to a human. Thus, the formal parameters that represent the poles are of type *char*, and the corresponding actual parameters are *'A'*, *'B'*, and *'C'*. The call *Towers(3, 'A', 'B', 'C')* produces this output:

The solution for three disks

```
Move disk from pole A to pole B
Move disk from pole A to pole C
Move disk from pole B to pole C
Move disk from pole A to pole B
```

Figure 6-2

The recursive calls for *Tow-ers(3, A, B, C)*

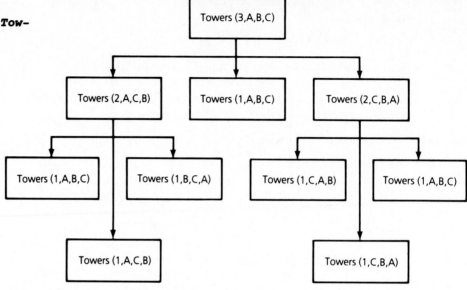

```
Move disk from pole C to pole A
Move disk from pole C to pole B
Move disk from pole A to pole B
```

The Pascal procedure follows:

```
procedure Towers(count : integer; source, dest, spare : char);
begin
    if count = 1
        then writeln('Move disk from pole ', source:1,
                            ' to pole ', dest:1)
        else
        begin
            Towers(count-1, source, spare, dest);   { X }
            Towers(1, source, dest, spare);         { Y }
            Towers(count-1, spare, dest, source)    { Z }
        end
end   { Towers }
```

The three recursive calls in the procedure are labeled X, Y, and Z. These labels appear in the box trace of *Towers(3, 'A', 'B', 'C')*. (See Figure 6-3.)

Processing Linked Lists Recursively

It is possible, and sometimes desirable, to process linked lists recursively. This section examines the examples of recursive traversal and insertion operations on a linked list.

The initial call is made, and procedure Towers begins execution:

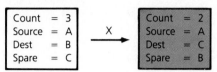

Figure 6-3

Box trace of *Towers(3, 'A', 'B', 'C')*

At point X, a recursive call is made, and the new invocation of the procedure begins execution:

At point X, a recursive call is made, and the new invocation of the procedure begins execution:

This is the degenerate case, so a disk is moved, the return is made, and the procedure continues execution.

At point Y, a recursive call is made, and the new invocation of the procedure begins execution:

This is the degenerate case, so a disk is moved, the return is made, and the procedure continues execution.

At point Z, a recursive call is made, and the new invocation of the procedure begins execution:

(continues)

Figure 6-3
continued

This is the degenerate case, so a disk is moved, the return is made, and the procedure continues execution.

This invocation completes, the return is made, and the procedure continues execution.

At point Y, a recursive call is made, and the new invocation of the procedure begins execution:

```
Count   = 3        Count   = 1
Source  = A    Y   Source  = A
Dest    = B  ----> Dest    = B
Spare   = C        Spare   = C
```

This is the degenerate case, so a disk is moved, the return is made, and the procedure continues execution.

```
Count   = 3        Count   = 1
Source  = A        Source  = A
Dest    = B        Dest    = B
Spare   = C        Spare   = C
```

At point Z, a recursive call is made, and the new invocation of the procedure begins execution:

```
Count   = 3        Count   = 2
Source  = A    Z   Source  = C
Dest    = B  ----> Dest    = B
Spare   = C        Spare   = A
```

At point X, a recursive call is made, and the new invocation of the procedure begins execution:

```
Count   = 3        Count   = 2        Count   = 1
Source  = A    Z   Source  = C    X   Source  = C
Dest    = B  ----> Dest    = B  ----> Dest    = A
Spare   = C        Spare   = A        Spare   = B
```

This is the degenerate case, so a disk is moved, the return is made, and the procedure continues execution.

```
Count   = 3        Count   = 2        Count   = 1
Source  = A    Z   Source  = C        Source  = C
Dest    = B  ----> Dest    = B        Dest    = A
Spare   = C        Spare   = A        Spare   = B
```

At point Y, a recursive call is made, and the new invocation of the procedure begins execution:

This is the degenerate case, so a disk is moved, the return is made, and the procedure continues execution.

At point Z, a recursive call is made, and the new invocation of the procedure begins execution:

This is the degenerate case, so a disk is moved, the return is made, and the procedure continues execution.

This invocation completes, the return is made, and the procedure continues execution.

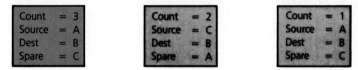

This invocation completes, and a return is made to the main program.

Traversal. As a first example, consider a character string *S* that is in a linked list. That is, assume you have the following:

```
type    ptr = ^node;
        node = record
             letter : char;
             next   : ptr
        end;
var     Str : ptr
```

Definitions for a linked list that contains a character string

The pointer variable *Str* points to the head of the list that contains the string.

Suppose that you want to print the string *S*. That is, you want to print the characters in the string in the order in which they appear in the linked list. The recursive strategy is simply

```
Print the first character of S
Write S minus its first character
```

The following Pascal procedure implements this strategy:

```
procedure WriteForward(Str : ptr);
{ ------------------------------------------------------------
  Writes the string S.
  Precondition: S is in a linked list that the pointer
  Str points to.
  Postcondition: S is printed, S and Str are unchanged.
  ------------------------------------------------------------ }
begin
    if Str <> nil
       then
       begin
          write(Str^.letter);     { print first character }
          WriteForward(Str^.next) { write S minus its
                                    first character }
       end
end   { WriteForward }
```

This procedure is uncomplicated. It requires that you have direct access only to the first character of the string. The linked list provides direct access to this character, as the list's head *Str* points to it. Furthermore, you easily can pass *S* minus its first character to `WriteForward`: If *Str* points to the beginning of the string *S*, then `Str^.next` points to *S* minus its first character. You should compare `WriteForward` to the iterative procedure `PrintList` that appears in Chapter 3.

Compare the recursive
WriteForward to Chapter
3's PrintList, which is
iterative

Now suppose that you want to print the string backward. The previous chapter already developed two recursive strategies for writing a string *S* backward. Recall that the strategy of the procedure `WriteBackward` is

> Print the last character of S
> Write S minus its last character backward

The strategy of the procedure `WriteBackward2` is

> Write S minus its first character backward
> Print the first character of S

You saw that these two strategies work equally well when *S* is in an array. However, when *S* is in a linked list, the first strategy is very difficult to implement: If `Str` points to the node that contains the first character of the string, how do you get to the last character? Even if you had some way to get to the last node on the list quickly—such as by having a tail pointer, as described in Chapter 3—it would be very difficult for you to move toward the front of the string at each recursive call. That is, it would be difficult for you to access the ends of the successively shorter strings that the recursive calls generate. (However, a doubly linked list would solve this problem. Why?)

This discussion illustrates one of the primary disadvantages of linked lists: While an array provides direct access to any character in the string, a linked list does not. Fortunately, however, the strategy of procedure `WriteBackward2` requires that you have direct access only to the first character of the string. This access is the same that `WriteForward` requires: The list's head `Str` points to the first character of the string *S*, and `Str^.next` points to *S* minus its first character.

When the string is in a linked list, `WriteBackward2` is much easier to implement recursively than `WriteBackward`

The following is a Pascal procedure for implementing `Write-Backward2` when *S* is stored in a linked list:

```
procedure WriteBackward2(Str : ptr);
{ ------------------------------------------------------------
  Writes the string S backward.
  Precondition: S is in a linked list that the pointer
  Str points to.
  Postcondition: S is printed backward, S and Str are
  unchanged.
  ------------------------------------------------------------ }
begin
    if Str <> nil
      then
      begin
         WriteBackward2(Str^.next); { write S minus its first
                                      character backward }
         write(Str^.letter)        { print first character }
      end
end { WriteBackward2 }
```

Insertion.   Now view the insertion of a node into a sorted linked list from a new perspective, that is, recursively. Later in this book you will need a recursive algorithm to perform this insertion. Interestingly, the recursive `Insert` eliminates the need for both a trailing pointer and a special case for inserting into the beginning of the list.

Consider the following recursive view of a sorted linked list: A linked list is sorted if its first data item is less than its second data item and the list that begins with the second data item is sorted. More formally, you can state this definition as follows:

The linked list that *L* points to is a sorted list if

L is *nil* (the empty list is a sorted linked list)

A recursive definition of a sorted linked list

or

L^.next is *nil* (a list with a single node is a sorted linked list)

or

L^.data < L^.next^.data, and *L^.next* points to a sorted linked list

You can base a recursive `Insert` procedure on this definition. Notice that the following algorithm inserts the node at one of the degenerate cases— either when the list is empty or when the new data item *X* is smaller than all the data items on the list. In both cases, you need to insert *X* at the beginning of the list.

```
Insert(L, X)
{ Inserts X into its proper sorted position in a sorted
  linked list. L points to the list. X does not exist
  already in the list. }

    if (L = nil) Cor (X < L^.data) { Cor was described in
                                          Chapter 2 }

            then { degenerate case }
            begin
                { Insert the new node at the beginning of the list
                  that L points to }
                new(p)
                p^.data := X
                p^.next := L
                L := p
            end

            else Insert(L^.next, X)
```

Insertion occurs at the de-generate case

Although `Insert` does not maintain a trailing pointer, the insertion of the new node is accomplished easily when the degenerate case is reached. The conceptually difficult part of this algorithm is the statement

```
    L := p
```

This assignment is all that is necessary to make the pointer field of the appropriate node point to the new node. Note that `L` points to the beginning of a sorted list. Recall that to insert the node to which `p` points at the beginning of this list, you need to make `L` point to that node. But does this action really change the appropriate pointer field in the actual argument list (the original list that the external pointer `Listhead` points to)? Yes it does, assuming that `L` is passed as a *variable parameter*.

L must be a variable parameter

To understand the previous remarks, first consider the case in which the new item is to be inserted at the beginning of the original list to which the external pointer `Listhead` points. In this case, no recursive calls are made, and thus when the degenerate case is reached ($X < L^{\wedge}.data$), `Listhead` is the actual parameter that corresponds to `L`, as Figure 6-4a illustrates. Hence, assuming that `L` is a variable parameter, the assignment `L := p` sets the value of `Listhead` to `p`—that is, `Listhead` now points to the new node, as Figure 6-4b shows.

The general case in which the new item is inserted into the interior of the list to which `Listhead` points is very similar. When the degenerate case is reached, what is the actual parameter that corresponds to `L`? It is the *next* field of the node that should precede the new node; that is, it is the *next* field of the last node whose data item is less than `X`. Therefore, since `L` is a variable parameter, the assignment `L := p` sets the *next* field of the appropriate node to point to the new node.

Though we could argue that you should perform the operations on a sorted linked list recursively (after all, recursion does eliminate special

Figure 6-4

**(a) The degenerate case—
first node of list; (b) the
assignment made for insertion at the beginning of the
list; (c) the search stops in
the middle of the list**

(a)

(b)

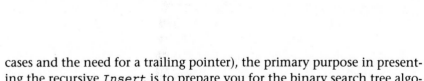

(c)

cases and the need for a trailing pointer), the primary purpose in presenting the recursive *Insert* is to prepare you for the binary search tree algorithms that we will present in Chapter 10.

BACKTRACKING

This section considers an organized way to make successive guesses at a
solution. If a particular guess leads to a dead end, you back up to that guess
and replace it with a different guess. This strategy of backing up when you
reach an impasse is known as **backtracking**. You can combine recursion
and backtracking to solve the following problem.

*Backtracking is a strategy for
guessing at a solution and backing up when an impasse is
reached*

The Eight Queens Problem

A chessboard contains 64 squares that form 8 rows and 8 columns. One of the most powerful pieces in the game of chess is the queen because it can attack any other piece within its row, within its column, or along its diagonal. The Eight Queens problem asks you to place eight queens on the chessboard so that no queen can attack any other queen.

Place eight queens on the chessboard so that no queen can attack any other queen

One strategy is to guess at a solution. However, there are 4,426,165,368 ways to arrange 8 queens on a chessboard of 64 squares—so many ways that it would be exhausting to check all of them for a solution to this problem. (Remember Mr. Spock's problem in Chapter 5!) Nevertheless, a simple observation eliminates many arrangements from consideration: No queen can reside in a row or a column that contains another queen. Alternatively, each row and column can contain exactly one queen. Thus, attacks along rows or columns are eliminated, leaving only 8! = 40,320 arrangements of queens to check for attacks along diagonals. A solution appears more feasible.

Place queens one column at a time

Suppose that you provide some organization for the guessing strategy by placing one queen per column, beginning with the first square of column 1. When you consider column 2, you eliminate its first square because row 1 contains a queen, you eliminate its second square because of a diagonal attack, and you finally place a queen in the third square of column 2. Figure 6-5 shows the placement of five queens as a result of this procedure. The dots in the figure indicate squares that are rejected because a queen in that square is subject to attack by another queen in an earlier column.

If you reach an impasse, backtrack to the previous column

Notice that the five queens in Figure 6-5 can attack any square in column 6. Therefore, you cannot place a queen in column 6, so you must back up to column 5 and move its queen. As Figure 6-6 indicates, the next possible square in column 5 is in the last row. When you consider column 6 once again, there are still no choices for a queen in that column. As you have exhausted the possibilities in column 5, you must back up to column

Figure 6-5

Five queens that cannot attack each other, but that can attack all of column 6

4. The next possible square in column 4 is in row 7, as Figure 6-7 indicates. You then consider column 5 again and place a queen in row 2.

How can you use recursion in the solution that was just described? Consider a procedure that places a queen in a column, given that you have placed queens correctly in the preceding columns. First, if there are no more columns to consider, you are finished; this is the degenerate case. Otherwise, after you successfully place a queen in the current column, you need to consider the next column. That is, you need to solve the same problem with one fewer column; this is the recursive step. Thus, you begin with eight columns, consider smaller problems that decrease in size by one column at each recursive step, and reach the degenerate case when you have a problem with no columns.

This solution appears to satisfy the criteria for a recursive solution. However, you do not know that you can *successfully place a queen in the*

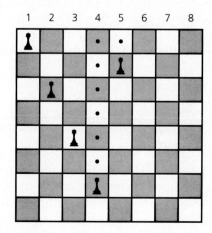

current column. If you can, then the procedure calls itself recursively for the next column. If you cannot place a queen in the current column, then you need to backtrack, as has already been described. The following pseudocode describes the algorithm for placing queens in columns, given that the previous columns contain queens that cannot attack each other:

The solution combines recursion with backtracking

```
PlaceNextQueen(Column)
{ Places queens in columns Column through 8. }

    if Column > 8
        then the problem is solved

        else
        begin
            while there are unconsidered squares in the column
                            and the problem is unsolved do
            begin
                Determine the next square in the column that is
                    not under attack by a queen in an earlier column
                if there is such a square
                    then
                    begin
                        Place a queen in the square
                        { try next column}
                        PlaceNextQueen(Column+1)
                        if no queen possible in column Column+1
                            then remove queen from column Column
                                    and consider next square in
                                    the column
                    end { if }
            end{ while }
        end{ if }
```

Before you implement *PlaceNextQueen* in Pascal, you need to consider a few details. For simplicity, you can use a two-dimensional array to represent the board. (The exercises at the end of this chapter consider other possibilities.) You can use an enumerated data type to represent the two states of each square on the board: A square either contains a queen or is empty. Thus,

The chessboard can be a two-dimensional array

```
const BoardSize = 8;
type  Square = (Queen, Empty);
      boardtype = array[1..BoardSize, 1..BoardSize] of Square;
var   Board : boardtype
```

The procedure *PlaceNextQueen* needs to determine whether the squares in the given column can be attacked by the queens in previous columns. Here the function *Attack*, which returns *true* if a given square can be attacked by queens that are in previous columns, makes this determination.

Finally, the procedure *PlaceNextQueen* is used in the following context:

```
ClearBoard              { set all squares to Empty }     Using PlaceNextQueen
PlaceNextQueen(1)       { begin with the first column }
if there is a solution
    then PrintBoard     { print solution }
    else print message  { no solution found }
```

The following is the Pascal implementation of *PlaceNextQueen*:

```
procedure PlaceNextQueen(Column : integer;
                         var Board : boardtype;
                         var Done : boolean);
{ ----------------------------------------------------------
    Places queens in columns Column through BoardSize of Board.
    Precondition: There are queens in columns 1 through
    Column-1. BoardSize is a global constant.
    Postcondition: If a solution is found, queens are in all
    columns of Board and Done = true; otherwise, there is no
    solution for a queen anywhere in column Column and Done =
    false.
    Calls: Attack.
    ---------------------------------------------------------- }
var Row : integer;            { square number in column }
begin
    if Column > BoardSize
        then Done := true    { degenerate case }

        else
        begin
            Done := false;
            Row := 1;
            while (Row <= BoardSize) and (not Done) do
            begin
                { if square can be attacked, }
                if Attack(Board, Row, Column)
                    then Row := Row + 1 { then consider next
                                          square in column }

                    else                { otherwise }
                    begin
                        { place queen and consider next column }
                        Board[Row, Column] := Queen;
                        PlaceNextQueen(Column+1, Board, Done);

                        { if no queen possible in next column, }
                        if not Done
                            then                { then backtrack }
                            begin
                                { remove queen placed earlier and
```

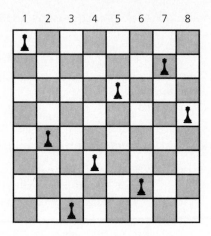

```
                                     try next square in column }
                                Board[Row, Column] := Empty;
                                Row := Row + 1
                          end   { then }
                    end   { else }
              end   { while }
        end   { if }
  end   { PlaceNextQueen }
```

Figure 6-8 indicates the solution that the previous algorithm finds.

By modifying the use of *PlaceNextQueen*, you can discover other solutions to the Eight Queens problem. You can also improve this algorithm. Although we used an 8 by 8 array to represent the board because it simplified the implementation, such an array is inefficient; after all, only 8 squares out of 64 are used. The exercises at the end of this chapter consider modifications and improvements to this algorithm.

DEFINING THINGS

*A language is a set of strings of
symbols*

This section demonstrates how to define languages by using recursion. A **language** is nothing more than a set of strings of symbols. For example, consider the language that comprises all syntactically correct Pascal programs. If you view a program as one long string of characters, you can define the set

Pascal-Programs = {strings *w* : *w* is a syntactically correct Pascal
program}

Notice that whereas all programs are strings, not all strings are programs. A Pascal compiler is a program that, among other things, determines whether a given string is a member of the set *Pascal-Programs;* that is, the compiler determines whether the string is a syntactically correct Pascal program. Of course, this definition of *Pascal-Programs* is not descriptive enough to allow the construction of a compiler. The definition specifies a characteristic of the strings in the set *Pascal-Programs*: The strings are syntactically correct Pascal programs. However, the definition does not give the rules for determining whether a string is in the set or not; that is, the definition does not specify what is meant by a syntactically correct Pascal program.

When we say "language," we do not necessarily mean a programming language or a communication language. For example, consider the following language:

Algebraic-Expressions = {*w* : *w* is an algebraic expression}

The language *Algebraic-Expressions* is the set of strings that meets certain rules of syntax. Once again, notice that the set's definition does not give these rules.

A **grammar** states the rules of a language. As it is a complex task to present a grammar for the set *Pascal-Programs*, we instead present grammars for some simpler languages, including several different common languages of algebraic expressions.

A grammar states the rules for forming the strings in a language

The Basics of Grammars

A grammar is a device for defining a language. One of the great benefits of using a grammar to define a language is that you can often write a straightforward recursive algorithm, based on the grammar, that determines whether a given string is a member of the language. Such an algorithm is called a **recognition algorithm** for the language.

A grammar uses several special symbols:

- $x \mid y$ means *x* or *y*.
- $x\, y$ means *x* followed by *y*. (When the context requires clarification, we will write $x \cdot y$.)
- *<word>* means any instance of *word* that the definition defines.

Symbols that grammars use

As an example of a grammar, consider the language

Pascal-Ids = {*w* : *w* is a legal Pascal identifier}

As you know, a legal Pascal identifier must begin with a letter and be followed by zero or more letters and digits. For simplicity, assume that there is no restriction on the maximum length of an identifier. One way to represent this definition of an identifier is with a syntax diagram, as shown in Figure 6-9.

A syntax diagram is convenient for people to use, but a grammar is a better starting point if you want to write a program that will recognize an

Figure 6-9

A syntax diagram for Pascal identifiers

identifier. A grammar for the language *Pascal-Ids* is

A grammar for the language of Pascal identifiers

$$\langle identifier \rangle = \langle letter \rangle \mid \langle identifier \rangle \langle letter \rangle \mid \langle identifier \rangle \langle digit \rangle$$
$$\langle letter \rangle = A \mid B \mid \cdots \mid Z$$
$$\langle digit \rangle = 0 \mid 1 \mid \cdots \mid 9$$

The definition reads as follows:

> *An identifier is a letter, or an identifier followed by a letter, or an identifier followed by a digit.*

The most striking aspect of this definition is that *identifier* appears in its own definition: This grammar is recursive, as are many grammars.

Given a string *w*, you can determine whether the string is in the language *Pascal-Ids* by using the grammar to construct the following recognition algorithm: If *w* is of length 1, then it is in the language if the character is a letter. (This statement is the degenerate case, so to speak.) If *w* is of length greater than 1, then it is in the language if

- The last character of *w* is a letter, and *w* minus its last character is an identifier

or

- The last character of *w* is a digit, and *w* minus its last character is an identifier

The pseudocode for a recursive function that determines whether a string is in *Pascal-Ids* follows:

A recognition algorithm for Pascal identifiers

```
function Id(w) : returns a boolean value
{ Determines if w is a legal Pascal identifier. }

    if w is of length 1 then     { degenerate case }
        if w is a letter
            then Id := true
            else Id := false

    else if the last character of w is a letter then
        Id := Id(w minus its last character)
    else if the last character of w is a digit then
        Id := Id(w minus its last character)
    else Id := false
```

Two Simple Languages

Now consider two more simple examples of languages, their grammars, and resulting recognition algorithms.

Palindromes. A palindrome is a string that reads the same from left to right as it does from right to left. For example, "radar" and "deed" are both palindromes. You can define the language of palindromes as follows:

> *Palindromes* = {*w* : *w* reads the same left to right as right to left}

How can you use a grammar to define the language *Palindromes*? You need to devise a rule that allows you to determine whether or not a given string *w* is a palindrome. In the spirit of recursive definitions, you should state this rule in terms of determining whether a *smaller string* is a palindrome. Your first instinct might be to choose *w* minus its last (or first) character for the smaller string. However, this does not work because there is no relationship between the statements

> *w is a palindrome*

and

> *w minus its last character is a palindrome*

That is, *w* might be a palindrome, although *w* minus its last character is not, as is the case for "deed." Similarly, *w* minus its last character might be a palindrome, although *w* is not, as is the case for "deeds."

A little thought reveals that you must consider characters in pairs: There *is* a relationship between the statements

> *w is a palindrome*

and

> *w minus its first* and *last characters is a palindrome*

Specifically, *w* is a palindrome if and only if

- The first and last characters of *w* are the same

and

- *w* minus its first and last characters is a palindrome

A recursive description of a palindrome

You need a degenerate case that you will reach after stripping away enough pairs of characters. If *w* is of even length, you will eventually be left with two characters, and then, after you strip away another pair, you will be left with zero characters. A string of length zero is called the **empty string** and is a palindrome. If *w* is of odd length, you will eventually be left with one character, after which you cannot strip away another pair. Hence, you must have a second degenerate case: A string of length 1 is a palindrome.

Strings of length 0 or 1 are the degenerate case

This discussion leads to the following grammar for the language *Palindromes*:

A grammar for the language of palindromes

$$<pal> = \text{empty string} \mid <ch> \mid \text{a} <pal> \text{a} \mid \text{b} <pal> \text{b} \mid \cdots \mid \text{Z} <pal> \text{Z}$$
$$<ch> = \text{a} \mid \text{b} \mid \cdots \mid \text{z} \mid \text{A} \mid \text{B} \mid \cdots \mid \text{Z}$$

Based on this grammar, you can construct a recursive function for recognizing palindromes. The pseudocode for such a function follows:

A recognition algorithm for palindromes

```
function Pal(w) : returns a boolean value
{ Determines if w is a palindrome. }

  if (w is the empty string) or (w is of length 1) then
     Pal := true

  else if the first and last characters of w are
               the same letter then
     Pal := Pal(w minus its first and last characters)

  else Pal := false
```

Strings of the form A^nB^n.   The symbol A^nB^n is standard notation for the string that consists of n consecutive A's followed by n consecutive B's. Another simple language consists of such strings:

$$L = \{w : w \text{ is of the form } A^nB^n \text{ for some } n \geq 0\}$$

The grammar for this language is actually very similar to the grammar for palindromes. You must strip away both the first and last characters and check to see that the first character is an "A" and the last character is a "B". Thus, the grammar is

A grammar for the language of strings A^nB^n

$$<legalword> = \text{empty string} \mid \text{A} <legalword> \text{B}$$

The pseudocode for a recognition function for this language follows:

A recognition algorithm for strings A^nB^n

```
function Recognize(w) : returns a boolean value
{ Determines if w is of the form A^nB^n. }

  if the length of w is zero then
    Recognize := true

  else if (the first character of w is A) and
              (the last character of w is B) then
    Recognize := Recognize(w minus its first and last characters)

  else Recognize := false
```

Algebraic Expressions

One of the tasks a compiler must perform is to recognize and evaluate algebraic expressions. For example, consider the Pascal assignment statement

```
y := x + z * (w/k + z * (7 * 6))
```

A Pascal compiler must determine whether the right side is a syntactically legal algebraic expression; if so, the compiler then must indicate how to compute the expression's value.

There are several common definitions for a "syntactically legal" algebraic expression. Some definitions force an expression to be fully parenthesized, whereas others are more lenient. In general, the stricter a definition, the easier it is to recognize a syntactically legal expression. On the other hand, it is an inconvenience for the programmer to have to conform to overly strict rules of syntax. For example, if the syntax rule requires full parenthesization, you would have to write $((x * y) * z)$ rather than $x * y * z$.

This section presents three different languages for algebraic expressions. The expressions in these languages are easy to recognize and evaluate but are generally inconvenient to use. However, these languages provide us with good, nontrivial applications of grammars. We will mention other languages of algebraic expressions whose members are difficult to recognize and evaluate but are convenient to use. To avoid unnecessary complications, assume you have only the binary operators +, −, *, and / (no unary operators or exponentiation). Also assume that all operands in the expression are single-letter identifiers.

Infix, prefix, and postfix expressions. The type of algebraic expressions you learned about in grade school are called **infix expressions.** The term "infix" indicates that every binary operator appears between its operands. For example, in the expression

$a + b$

the operand + is between its operands a and b. This convention necessitates associativity rules, precedence rules, and the use of parentheses to avoid ambiguity. For example, the expression

$a + b * c$

is ambiguous. What is the second operand of the +? Is it b or is it $(b * c)$? Similarly, the first operand of the * could be either b or $(a + b)$. The rule that * has higher precedence than + removes the ambiguity by specifying that b is the first operand of the * and that $(b * c)$ is the second operand of the +. If you want another interpretation, you must use parentheses:

$(a + b) * c$

Even with precedence rules, there is ambiguity in an expression like

$a / b * c$

Typically, / and * have equal precedence, so you could interpret the expression either as $(a / b) * c$ or as $a / (b * c)$. The common practice is to *associate from left to right*, thus yielding the first interpretation.

Two alternatives to the traditional infix convention are **prefix** and **postfix**. Under these conventions, an operator appears before its operands and after its operands, respectively. Thus, the infix expression

$$a + b$$

is written in prefix form as

In a prefix expression, an opera-
tor precedes its operands

$$+ a\ b$$

and in postfix form as

$$a\ b +$$

In a postfix expression, an oper-
ator follows its operands

To further illustrate the conventions, consider the two interpretations of the infix expression $a + b * c$ just considered. You write the expression

$$a + (b * c)$$

in prefix form as

$$+ a * b\ c$$

The + appears before its operands a and $(* b\ c)$, and the $*$ appears before its operands b and c. The same expression is written in postfix form as

$$a\ b\ c * +$$

The $*$ appears after its operands b and c, and the + appears after its operands a and $(b\ c *)$.

Similarly, you write the expression

$$(a + b) * c$$

in prefix form as

$$* + a\ b\ c$$

The $*$ appears before its operands $(+ a\ b)$ and c, and the + appears before its operands a and b. The same expression is written in postfix form as

$$a\ b + c *$$

The + appears after its operands a and b, and the $*$ appears after its operands $(a\ b +)$ and c.

Prefix and postfix expressions
never need precedence rules,
association rules, and
parentheses

The advantage of prefix and postfix expressions is that they never need precedence rules, association rules, and parentheses. Therefore, the grammars for prefix and postfix expressions are quite simple. In addition, the algorithms that recognize and evaluate these expressions are relatively straightforward.

Prefix expressions.   A grammar that defines the language of all prefix expressions is

$\langle pre\text{-}exp \rangle = \langle letter \rangle \mid \langle operator \rangle\ \langle pre\text{-}exp \rangle\ \langle pre\text{-}exp \rangle$
$\langle operator \rangle = + \mid - \mid * \mid /$
$\langle letter \rangle = A \mid B \mid \cdots \mid Z$

From this grammar you can construct a recursive algorithm that recognizes prefix expressions. Suppose that you treat the expression in question as a character string and store it in the array `S[first..last]`. If the string is of length 1, then the string is a prefix expression if and only if `S[first]` is a single uppercase letter. Strings of length 1 can be the degenerate case. If the length of the string is greater than 1, then for it to be a legal prefix expression, the string must be of the form

>   <operator> <pre-exp> <pre-exp>

Thus, the algorithm must check to see that

- The first character `S[first]` is an operator

and

- `S[first + 1..last]` consists of two consecutive prefix expressions

The first task is trivial, but the second is a bit tricky. How can you determine whether you are looking at two consecutive prefix expressions? A key observation is that if you add *any* string of characters to the end of a prefix expression, you will no longer have a prefix expression. That is, if E is a prefix expression and Y is any nonempty string, then $E\ Y$ cannot be a prefix expression. This is a subtle point; Exercise 18 at the end of this chapter asks you to prove it.

If E is a prefix expression, $E\ Y$ cannot be

Given this observation, you can begin to determine whether the string `S[first + 1..last]` consists of two consecutive prefix expressions by identifying a first prefix expression. If you cannot find one, then the original string itself is not a prefix expression. If you do find one, you need to know where it ends. Notice that the previous observation implies that there is only one possible endpoint for this first expression: Given that `S[first + 1..end1]` is a prefix expression, there can be no other prefix expression that begins at `S[first + 1]`. That is, it is not possible that `S[first + 1..end2]` is a prefix expression for any *end2 ≠ end1*.

If you find that the first prefix expression ends at position *end1*, you then attempt to find a second prefix expression beginning at position *end1 + 1* and ending at or before position *last*. If you find the second expression, you must check that you are at the end of the string in question. That is, you must make sure that there are no nonblank characters in *S* between the end of the second expression and position *last*.

You can construct a function *EndPre(S, first, last)* that returns either the position of the end of the prefix expression that begins at `S[first]` or the value 0, which signals that there is no prefix expression that begins at `S[first]`. The function appears in pseudocode as follows:

```
function EndPre(S, first, last) : returns an index into
                                   array S
{ Returns the index of the end of the prefix expression that
begins at S[first], if there is one. Otherwise, returns 0. }

    if (first < 1) or (first > last) then
```

If there is a prefix expression beginning at `S[first]`, `EndPre` determines its end

```
        EndPre := 0

    else if S[first] is an identifier then
        EndPre := first

    else if S[first] is an operator then
        begin
            { find the end of the first prefix expression }
            firstend := EndPre(S, first + 1, last)

            { find the end of the second prefix expression
                if the end of the first one was found }
            if (firstend > 0)
                then EndPre := EndPre(S, firstend + 1, last)
                else EndPre := 0
        end

    else EndPre := 0
```

Now you can use the function *EndPre* to determine whether *S[1..size]* is a prefix expression as follows:

A recognition algorithm for
prefix expressions

```
function IsPre(S, size) : returns a boolean value
{ Determines if S[1..size] is a legal prefix expression. }
    lastchar := EndPre(S, 1, size)
    if (lastchar ≠ 0) and there are no nonblank characters
            in S[lastchar+1..size]
        then IsPre := true
        else IsPre := false
```

The following Pascal program demonstrates how you can use the previous functions to determine whether or not an expression is in prefix form. The recursive function *EndPre* is nested within the function *IsPre* so that *EndPre* can access *S* and *last* globally.

```
program RecPre(input, output);
{ ********************************************************
  RECOGNIZES A PREFIX EXPRESSION.
  Input: An expression (string of characters). An operand is
  a single uppercase letter; an operator is one of +, −, *,
  and /.
  Output: Prints a message that indicates whether or not the
  string is a prefix expression.
  Subprograms: IsBlank, IsPre, and ReadWriteExpr.
  ******************************************************** }
const  size = 20;        { global string size }
type   string = array[1..size] of char;
var    PRE : string;

function IsBlank(STR : string; index : integer) : boolean;
{ ----------------------------------------------------------
  Determines if a string is all blank.
```

Precondition: STR[index..size] is a string, index <= size.
Postcondition: Returns true if the string is all blanks;
else returns false.
Assumption: Substring is small, so it is searched in its
entirety.
-- }

```
var i : integer;
begin
    IsBlank := true;
     for i := index to size do
         if STR[i] <> ' '
            then IsBlank := false
end;  { IsBlank }


function IsPre(PRE : string) : boolean;
{ ---------------------------------------------------------
  Determines if a string is a valid prefix expression.
  Precondition: PRE contains a string.
  Postcondition: Returns true if PRE is in prefix form; else
  returns false. PRE is unchanged.
  Calls: IsBlank and the local recursive function EndPre.
  -------------------------------------------------------- }
var lastchar : integer;


    function EndPre(first : integer) : integer;
    { ---------------------------------------------------
      Finds the end of the legal prefix expression that
      begins at a given character. Uses the grammar <pre> =
      <letter> | <operator><pre><pre> where <letter> is a
      single uppercase letter.
      Precondition: PRE[first..size] contains a string; PRE
      and size are global to this function.
      Postcondition: Returns the index of the last character
      in the prefix expression that begins at first, or
      returns 0 if there is no such prefix expression.
      --------------------------------------------------- }
    var firstend : integer;
    begin
       { test the bounds }
       if (first < 1) or (first > size) then
           EndPre := 0        { assume empty string }

       { degenerate case — a single letter }
       else if PRE[first] in ['A'..'Z'] then
           EndPre := first

       { general case — apply the recursive definition }
       else if PRE[first] in ['+','—','*','/'] then
```

```pascal
          begin
              { find the end of the first prefix expression }
              firstend := EndPre(first+1);

              { find the end of the second prefix expression }
              if firstend > 0
                  then EndPre := EndPre(firstend+1)
                  else EndPre := 0
          end

      else EndPre := 0
  end;   { EndPre }

begin   { body of IsPre }
    { the end of the legal expression that begins at index 1
      must be the last nonblank character of the input string }
    lastchar := EndPre(1);
    IsPre := IsBlank(PRE, lastchar+1) and (lastchar > 0)
end; { IsPre }

procedure ReadWriteExpr(var PRE : string);
{ ------------------------------------------------------------
  Reads and echo prints an expression.
  Precondition: size is a global constant.
  Postcondition: PRE contains input expression. PRE is
  printed, but is not followed by a carriage return.
  ------------------------------------------------------------ }
var i : integer;
begin
    for i := 1 to size do          { initialize PRE }
        PRE[i] := ' ';

    writeln('Enter expression: ');
    for i := 1 to size do          { read expression into PRE }
        if not eoln
            then read(PRE[i]);
     readln;

    writeln;
    for i := 1 to size do { write the input expression }
        write(PRE[i])
end;   { ReadWriteExpr }

begin   { Main Program — demonstrate function IsPre }
    ReadWriteExpr(PRE);    { read and echo print expression }
    if IsPre(PRE)           { test expression for prefix form }
       then writeln(' is a legal prefix expression.')
       else writeln(' is NOT a legal prefix expression.')
end.   { Program }
```

The following provides samples of the program's output:

```
A                is a legal prefix expression.
+AB              is a legal prefix expression.
+/AB-CD          is a legal prefix expression.
A+B              is NOT a legal prefix expression.
                 is NOT a legal prefix expression.
+A               is NOT a legal prefix expression.
+ABC             is NOT a legal prefix expression.
AB               is NOT a legal prefix expression.
A B              is NOT a legal prefix expression.
```

Postfix expressions. A grammar that defines the language of all postfix expressions is

> *<post-exp>* = *<letter>* | *<post-exp>* *<post-exp>* *<operator>*
> *<operator>* = + | − | * | /
> *<letter>* = A | B | ⋯ | Z

Chapter 8 presents a nonrecursive algorithm for *evaluating* postfix expressions. Here we shall develop an algorithm for converting a prefix expression to a postfix expression. These two algorithms, combined with the prefix recognition algorithm, give you a method for evaluating a prefix expression *E*, as Figure 6-10 illustrates. To simplify the conversion algorithm, assume that by using the prefix recognition algorithm, you have a syntactically correct prefix expression.

If you think recursively, the conversion from prefix form to postfix form is straightforward. If the prefix expression *E* is a single letter, then

> *Convert(E)* = *E*

Otherwise *E* must be of the form

> *<operator>* *<pre-exp1>* *<pre-exp2>*

The corresponding postfix expression is then

> *<post-exp1>* *<post-exp2>* *<operator>*

where *<pre-exp1>* converts to *<post-exp1>* and *<pre-exp2>* converts to *<post-exp2>*. Therefore,

> *Convert(E)* = *Convert(pre-exp1)* · *Convert(pre-exp2)* · *<operator>*

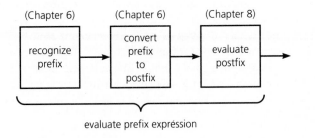

(Chapter 6) (Chapter 6) (Chapter 8)

recognize prefix → convert prefix to postfix → evaluate postfix →

evaluate prefix expression

Figure 6-10

Combining algorithms to evaluate a prefix expression

The conversion algorithm is

An algorithm that converts a prefix expression to postfix form

```
if E is a single letter
    then Convert(E) := E
    else Convert(E) := Convert(pre-exp1) · Convert(pre-exp2)
                                            · <operator>
```

The following Pascal procedure `Convert` accomplishes this conversion process. The array `PRE` contains the prefix expression, and the array `POST` will contain the postfix expression that the procedure constructs. The recursive procedure `doconvert` is nested within the nonrecursive `Convert` procedure so that `doconvert` can access the arrays `PRE` and `POST` globally. Notice that each recursive call to `doconvert` returns the index `preptr`; `preptr` points to the location within the array `PRE` that follows the end of the prefix expression that `doconvert` just converted. This index is the starting point of the prefix expression that the next recursive call to `doconvert` will convert. (Note that although pointers are mentioned, they are array indexes and not pointer variables.)

```
const  size = 20;          { global string size }
type   string = array[1..size] of char;

procedure Convert(PRE : string; var POST : string);
{ ---------------------------------------------------------
  Converts a prefix expression to postfix form.
  Precondition: PRE is an algebraic expression in
  syntactically correct prefix form. An operand is a single
  uppercase letter; an operator is one of +, —, *, and /.
  Postcondition: POST is the equivalent postfix expression;
  PRE is unchanged.
  Calls: The local recursive procedure doconvert.
  --------------------------------------------------------- }

var preptr, postptr : integer;

    procedure doconvert(var preptr, postptr : integer);
    { ---------------------------------------------------------
      Recursively converts a prefix expression to postfix
      form.
      Precondition: The prefix expression in PRE begins at
      the index preptr. PRE and POST are global to this
      procedure.
      Postcondition: Converts the prefix expression into
      postfix form and places the result in POST beginning
      at the index postptr. Sets preptr and postptr to 1
      past the ends of the respective substrings.
      --------------------------------------------------------- }
    var ch : char;
```

```
    begin
        { check the first character of the prefix string }
        ch := PRE[preptr];          { get first character }
        preptr := preptr + 1;       { advance pointer }

        if ch in ['A'..'Z']         { check character }
            then
            begin   { degenerate case — single identifier }
                POST[postptr] := ch;
                postptr := postptr+1
            end

            else
            begin   { do the conversion recursively }
                doconvert(preptr, postptr);   { first operand }
                doconvert(preptr, postptr);   { second operand }
                POST[postptr] := ch;          { operator }
                postptr := postptr+1
            end
    end;   { doconvert }
begin   { body of Convert }
    { initialize pointers to the beginning of the strings }
    preptr := 1;
    postptr := 1;

    { do the conversion }
    doconvert(preptr, postptr)
end;   { Convert }
```

Fully parenthesized expressions. Most programmers would object to using prefix or postfix notation for their algebraic expressions, so most programming languages use infix notation. However, infix notation requires parenthesization, precedence rules, and rules for association to avoid ambiguity within the expressions.

The simplest scheme for recognizing and evaluating infix expressions requires all expressions to be *fully parenthesized*. A grammar for the language of all fully parenthesized expressions is

$$<expression> = <letter> \mid (<expression> <operator> <expression>)$$
$$<operator> = + \mid - \mid * \mid /$$
$$<letter> = A \mid B \mid \cdots \mid Z$$

A grammar for the language of fully parenthesized algebraic expressions

This definition requires that you place parentheses around each pair of operands together with their operator so that there is no possibility for ambiguity. Thus, precedence and association rules are unnecessary. However, the scheme is rather inconvenient for programmers.

Therefore, most programming languages support a definition of algebraic expressions that includes both precedence rules for the operators and rules of association so that fully parenthesized expressions are not required. However, the grammars for defining such languages are more involved and the algorithms for recognizing and evaluating their expressions are more difficult than those you have seen in this section. Project 20 at the end of this chapter involves algebraic expressions with precedence rules. Chapter 8 presents a nonrecursive algorithm for evaluating algebraic expressions that allow both precedence and left-to-right association rules.

THE RELATIONSHIP BETWEEN RECURSION AND MATHEMATICAL INDUCTION

A very strong relationship exists between recursion and mathematical induction. Recursion solves a problem by specifying a solution to one or more degenerate cases and then demonstrating how to derive the solution to a problem of an arbitrary size from the solutions to smaller problems of the same type. Similarly, mathematical induction proves a property about the natural numbers by proving the property about a base case—usually 0 or 1—and then proving that the property must be true for an arbitrary natural number N if it is true for the natural numbers smaller than N.

You can use induction to prove that a recursive algorithm is either correct or performs a certain amount of work

Given the similarities between recursion and mathematical induction, it should not be surprising that induction is often employed to prove properties about recursive algorithms. What types of properties? You can, for example, prove that an algorithm actually performs the task that you intended. As an illustration, we will prove that the recursive *Factorial* algorithm of Chapter 5 does indeed compute the factorial of its argument. Another use of mathematical induction is to prove that a recursive algorithm performs a certain amount of work. For example, we will prove that the solution to the Towers of Hanoi problem makes exactly $2^N - 1$ moves when it starts with N disks.

Correctness of the Recursive Factorial Function

The following pseudocode describes a recursive function that computes the factorial of a nonnegative integer n:

```
Factorial(n)

    if n = 0
        then Factorial := 1
        else Factorial := n * Factorial(n - 1)
```

You can prove that the function `Factorial` returns the values

$$Factorial(0) = 0! = 1$$
$$Factorial(n) = n! = n * (n-1) * (n-2) * \cdots * 1 \text{ if } n > 0$$

The proof is by induction on n.

Basis. *Show that the property is true for n = 0.* That is, you must show that `Factorial(0)` returns 1. But this result is simply the degenerate case of the function: `Factorial(0)` returns 1 by its definition.

You now must establish that

property is true for an arbitrary k ⇒ property is true for k + 1

Inductive hypothesis. *Assume that the property is true for n = k.* That is, assume that

$$Factorial(k) = k * (k-1) * (k-2) * \cdots * 2 * 1$$

Inductive conclusion. *Show that the property is true for n = k + 1.* That is, you must show that `Factorial(k + 1)` returns the value

$$(k+1) * k * (k-1) * (k-2) * \cdots * 2 * 1$$

By definition of the function `Factorial`, `Factorial(k + 1)` returns the value

$$(k+1) * Factorial(k)$$

But by the inductive hypothesis, `Factorial(k)` returns the value

$$k * (k-1) * (k-2) * \cdots * 2 * 1$$

Thus, `Factorial(k + 1)` returns the value

$$(k+1) * k * (k-1) * (k-2) * \cdots * 2 * 1$$

which is what you needed to show to establish that

property is true for an arbitrary k ⇒ property is true for k + 1

The inductive proof is thus complete.

Cost of Towers of Hanoi

At the beginning of this chapter, we presented the following solution to the Towers of Hanoi problem:

```
Towers(count, source, dest, spare)

    if count = 1
        then move the disk directly from source to dest

        else
        begin
            Solve Towers(count-1, source, spare, dest)
            Solve Towers(1, source, dest, spare)
            Solve Towers(count-1, spare, dest, source)
        end
```

We now pose the following question: If you begin with *N* disks, how many moves does `Towers` make to solve the problem?

Let *Moves(N)* be the number of moves made starting with *N* disks. When $N = 1$, the answer is easy:

$$Moves(1) = 1$$

When $N > 1$, the value of *Moves(N)* is not so apparent. An inspection of the `Towers` procedure, however, reveals three recursive calls. Therefore, if you knew how many moves the procedure made starting with $N - 1$ disks, you could figure out how many moves it made starting with *N* disks; that is,

$$Moves(N) = Moves(N - 1) + Moves(1) + Moves(N - 1)$$

Thus, you have a recurrence relation for the number of moves required for *N* disks:

A recurrence relation for the number of moves that `Towers` *requires for N disks*

$$Moves(1) = 1$$
$$Moves(N) = 2 * Moves(N - 1) + 1 \text{ if } N > 1$$

For example, you can determine *Moves(3)* as follows:

$$
\begin{aligned}
Moves(3) &= 2 * Moves(2) + 1 \\
&= 2 * (2 * Moves(1) + 1) + 1 \\
&= 2 * (2 * 1 + 1) + 1 \\
&= 7
\end{aligned}
$$

Although the recurrence relation gives you a way to compute *Moves(N)*, a **closed-form formula**—such as an algebraic expression—would be more satisfactory because you could substitute any given value for *N* and obtain the number of moves made. However, the recurrence relation is useful because there are techniques for obtaining a closed-form formula from it. Unfortunately, these techniques are beyond the scope of this book. Therefore, we simply pull the formula out of the blue and use mathematical induction to prove that it is correct.

The solution to the previous recurrence relation is

A closed-form formula for the number of moves that `Towers` *requires for N disks*

$$Moves(N) = 2^N - 1, \text{ for all } N \geqslant 1$$

Notice that $2^3 - 1$ agrees with the value 7 that was just computed for *Moves(3)*.

The proof that $Moves(N) = 2^N - 1$ is by induction on *N*.

Basis.   *Show that the property is true for N = 1.* Here, $2^1 - 1 = 1$, which is consistent with the recurrence relation's specification that *Moves(1) = 1*.
You now must establish that

property is true for an arbitrary k $\Rightarrow$ property is true for k + 1

Inductive hypothesis.   *Assume that the property is true for N = k.* That is, assume

$$Moves(k) = 2^k - 1$$

Inductive conclusion. *Show that the property is true for N = k + 1.* That is, you must show that $Moves(k + 1) = 2^{k+1} - 1$. Now

$$
\begin{aligned}
Moves(k + 1) &= 2 * Moves(k) + 1 && \text{from the recurrence relation} \\
&= 2 * (2^k - 1) + 1 && \text{by the inductive hypothesis} \\
&= 2^{k+1} - 1
\end{aligned}
$$

which is what you needed to show to establish that

property is true for an arbitrary k $\Rightarrow$ property is true for k + 1

The inductive proof is thus complete.

We do not wish to leave you with the false impression that proving properties of programs is an easy matter. These two proofs are about as easy as any will be. We do, however, wish to reiterate that well-structured programs are far more amenable to these techniques than are poorly structured programs.

Appendix A provides more information about mathematical induction.

SUMMARY

1. Recursion allows you to solve problems whose iterative solutions are difficult to conceptualize. The Towers of Hanoi is such a problem.

2. You can use recursion to perform operations on linked lists. Such use will eliminate special cases and the need for a trailing pointer.

3. Backtracking is a solution strategy that involves both recursion and a sequence of guesses that ultimately lead to a solution. If a particular guess leads to an impasse, you back up, replace that guess, and try to complete the solution again.

4. A grammar is a device for defining a language, which is a set of strings of symbols. A benefit of using a grammar to define a language is that you often can construct a recognition algorithm that is directly based on the grammar. Grammars are frequently recursive, which allows you to describe vast languages concisely.

5. We illustrated the use of grammars by defining several different languages of algebraic expressions. These different languages have their relative advantages and disadvantages. Prefix and postfix expressions, while difficult for the programmer to use, eliminate problems of ambiguity. Infix expressions, on the other hand, require parentheses, precedence rules, and rules of association to eliminate ambiguity.

6. There is a very close relationship between mathematical induction and recursion. Induction is often used to establish the correctness of a recursive algorithm and to prove properties about it. For exam-

ple, you can prove that an algorithm is correct and derive the amount of work an algorithm requires.

COMMON PITFALLS / DEBUGGING

1. When developing a recursive solution, you must be sure that the solutions to the smaller problems really do give you a solution to the original problem. For example, the recursive insertion algorithm for a sorted linked list works because each smaller linked list is also sorted. When the algorithm makes an insertion at the beginning of one of these lists, the inserted node will be in the proper position in the original list.

2. You must be sure that the subproblems that a recursive solution generates eventually reach a degenerate case. Failure to do so could result in an algorithm that does not terminate. For example, the recursive insertion algorithm for a sorted linked list is guaranteed to terminate because each smaller list contains one fewer node than the preceding list and because the empty list is a degenerate case.

3. Grammars, like recursive algorithms, must have carefully chosen degenerate cases. You must ensure that when a string is decomposed far enough, it will always reach the form of one of the grammar's degenerate cases.

4. The subtleties of some of the algorithms you encountered in this chapter indicate the need for mathematical techniques to prove their correctness. The application of these techniques during the design of the various components of a solution can help to eliminate errors in logic before they appear in the program. One such technique is mathematical induction; another is the use of loop invariants, which we discussed in Chapter 1 and will discuss again in the next chapter.

SELF-TEST EXERCISES

1. Trace the execution of the procedure *Towers* to solve the Towers of Hanoi problem for two disks.

2. Write a recursive Pascal procedure that retrieves the contents of the ith integer in a linked list of integers. Assume that $i \geq 1$ and that the linked list contains at least i nodes. (*Hint:* If $i = 1$, return the first integer in the list; otherwise retrieve the $(i-1)^{st}$ integer from the rest of the list.)

3. Consider a Four Queens problem, which has the same rules as the

Eight Queens problem but uses a 4 by 4 board. Find all solutions to this new problem by applying backtracking by hand.

4. Write the prefix expression that represents the following infix expression:

$(A / B) * C - (D + E) * F$

5. Write the postfix expression that represents the following infix expression:

$(A * B - C) / D + (E - F)$

6. Write the infix expression that represents the following prefix expression:

$--A/B+C*DEF$

7. Consider the language of these strings: $, cc\$d, cccc\$dd, cccccc\$ddd, and so on. Write a recursive grammar for this language.

EXERCISES

1. Consider the following recursive function:

```
function p(x : integer) : integer;
begin
    if x < 3
        then p := x
        else p := p(x−1) * p(x−3)
end
```

Let $A(n)$ be the number of multiplication operations that the execution of p(n) performs. Write a recursive definition of $A(n)$.

2. Consider palindromes that consist only of lowercase letters such as "level" and "deed," but not "RadaR," "ADA," or "101." Let $C(n)$ be the number of palindromes of length n. Give a recursive definition of $C(n)$.

3. Let L be the language

$L = \{S : S \text{ is of the form } A^n B^{2n}, \text{ for some } n >= 0\}$

Thus, a string is in L if and only if it starts with a sequence of A's and is followed by a sequence of twice as many B's. For example, AABBBB is in L, but ABBB and ABBABB are not in L.

a. Give a grammar for the language L.
b. Write a recursive function that determines whether the character string in A[first..last] is in L.

4. Consider the language that the following grammar defines:

$<S> = \$ \mid <W> \mid \$<S>$

<W> = abb | a<W>bb

Write all strings that are in this language and that contain seven or fewer characters.

5. Is +*A–B/C++DE–FG a prefix expression? Explain in terms of the grammar for prefix expressions.

6. Is AB/C*EFG*H/+D–+ a postfix expression? Explain in terms of the grammar for postfix expressions.

7. Consider the language that the following grammar defines:

    <S> = <L> | <D> <S> <S>
    <L> = A | B
    <D> = 1 | 2

    a. Write all three-character strings that are in this language.
    b. Write one string in this language that contains more than three characters.

8. Consider a language of the following character strings: The letter A; the letter B; the letter C followed by a string that is in the language; the letter D followed by a string in the language. For example, these strings are in this language: A, CA, CCA, DCA, B, CB, CCB, DB, and DCCB.

    a. Write the grammar for this language.
    b. Is CAB in this language? Explain.

9. Trace the following recursive subprograms:

    a. *EndPre* with the expression –*/ABCD
    b. *Pal* with the string abcdeba
    c. *Towers* with three disks

10. Consider the language that the following grammar defines:

    <word> = $ | a<word>a | b<word>b | ⋯ | y<word>y | z<word>z

    Equivalently,

    L = {w$reverse(w) : w is a string of letters of length ≥ 0}

    Note that this language is very similar to the language of palindromes, but there is a special middle character here.

    The algorithm that we gave for recognizing palindromes can be adapted easily to this language. The algorithm, which is recursive and processes the string from both ends toward the middle, is based on the following facts:

    • A string with no characters (*last* < *first*) is not in the language.

    • A string with exactly one character (*first* = *last*) is in the language if the character is a $.

    • A longer string (*first* < *last*) is in the language if the ends are identical letters and the inner string (*first*+1 to *last*−1) is in the language.

Describe a recursive recognition algorithm that processes the string from left to right, reading one character at a time and not explicitly saving the string for future reference. Write a Pascal function that implements your algorithm.

11. Write recursive procedures that will perform insertion and deletion operations on a sorted linked list.

12. Write a recursive procedure that will reverse a linked list. (See Exercise 10 in Chapter 3.)

13. Write a recursive procedure that will merge two sorted linked lists into a single sorted linked list. You need not preserve the original lists. (See Exercise 18 in Chapter 3.)

14. Write a nonrecursive solution to the Towers of Hanoi problem. By studying the recursive solution that was presented in this chapter, you can gain some insight into how to proceed.

15. Complete the program that solves the Eight Queens problem.

16. Revise the program that you just wrote for the Eight Queens problem so that it answers the following questions:

    a. How many backtracks occur? That is, how many times does the program remove a queen from the board?

    b. How many calls to *Attack* are there?

    c. How many recursive calls to *PlaceNextQueen* are there?

    d. Can you make *Attack* more efficient? For example, as soon as you detect that a queen can attack a given square, do you still look for another queen?

*17. You can begin the Eight Queens problem by placing a queen in the second square of the first column instead of the first square. You can then call *PlaceNextQueen* to begin with the second column. This revision should lead you to a new solution. Write a program that finds all solutions to the Eight Queens problem.

*18. Prove the following for single-letter operands: If *E* is a prefix expression and *Y* is a nonempty string of characters, then *E Y* cannot be a legal prefix expression. (*Hint*: Use a proof by induction on the length of *E*.)

19. Chapter 5 gave the following definition for $C(n, k)$, where n and k are assumed to be nonnegative integers:

$$C(n, k) = \begin{cases} 1 & \text{if } k = 0 \\ 1 & \text{if } k = n \\ C(n-1, k-1) + C(n-1, k) & \text{if } 0 < k < n \\ 0 & \text{if } k > n \end{cases}$$

Prove by induction on n that the following is a closed form for $C(n, k)$:

$$C(n, k) = \frac{n!}{(n - k)!k!}$$

PROJECTS

20. The following is a grammar that allows you to omit parentheses in infix algebraic expressions when the precedence rules remove ambiguity. For example, $a + b * c$ means $a + (b * c)$. However, the grammar requires parentheses when ambiguity would otherwise result. That is, the grammar does not permit left-to-right association when several operators have the same precedence. For example, $a / b * c$ is illegal. Notice that the definitions introduce **factors** and **terms**.

<expression> = <term> | <term> + <term> | <term> – <term>
<term> = <factor> | <factor> * <factor> | <factor> / <factor>
<factor> = <letter> | (<expression>)
<letter> = A | B | ⋯ | Z

With this grammar, you can apply the operators * and / only to a factor—that is, to an operand that is either a single letter or enclosed in parentheses. You can apply the operators + and – to any term—that is, to an operand that is either a factor or the (possibly unparenthesized) product or quotient of a pair of factors.

The recognition algorithm is based on a recursive chain of subtasks: *find an expression → find a term → find a factor*. What makes this a recursive chain is that *find an expression* uses *find a term*, which in turn uses *find a factor*. *Find a factor* either detects a degenerate case or uses *find an expression*, thus forming the recursive chain.

The pseudocode for the recognition algorithm follows:

```
FIND AN EXPRESSION
{ The grammar specifies that an expression is either a
  single term or a term followed by a + or a —, which
  then must be followed by a second term. }

      Find a term
      if the next symbol is a + or a —
          then find a term

FIND A TERM
{ The grammar specifies that a term is either a single
  factor or a factor followed by a * or a /, which must
  then be followed by a second factor. }

      Find a factor
      if the next symbol is a * or a /
          then find a factor
```

FIND A FACTOR

```
{ The grammar specifies that a factor is either a
  single letter (the degenerate case) or an expression
  enclosed in parentheses. }

        if the next symbol is a letter then
            done
        else if the next symbol is a '(' then
            begin
                Find an expression
                Check for ')'
            end
        else there is no factor
```

Implement this recognition algorithm. Use conventions similar to those in this chapter. The following sample output indicates the results that your program should produce:

```
A+(B—C) is a legal expression.
((A)(B) is NOT a legal expression.
A+B—C   is NOT a legal expression.
   A    is NOT a legal expression.
```

(The last expression is not legal because it contains leading blanks.)

21. Instead of using an 8 by 8 array to represent the board in the Eight Queens program, you can use a one-dimensional array to represent only the squares that contain a queen. Let $Col[1..8]$ be an array of integers such that

$Col[k]$ = row number of the queen in column k

For example, if $Col[2]$ = 4, then there is a queen in the fourth row (square) of the second column; that is, in $Board[4, 2]$. Thus, you use $Col[k]$ to represent a queen instead of $Board[Col[k], k]$.

This scheme requires that you also store information about whether each queen is subject to attack. Because only one queen per column is permitted, you do not have to check columns. To check for a row attack, define a boolean array $RowAttack$ such that

$RowAttack[k]$ is true if the queen in column k can be attacked by a queen in its row

To check for diagonal attacks, observe that diagonals have either a positive slope or a negative slope. Those with a positive slope are parallel to the diagonal that runs from the lower left corner of the board to the upper right corner. Diagonals with a negative slope are parallel to the diagonal that runs from the upper left corner to the lower right corner. Convince yourself that if $Board[i, j]$ represents a square, then $i + j$ is constant for squares that are in a diagonal with a positive slope, and $i - j$ is constant for squares that are in a diagonal with a negative slope. You will find that $i + j$ ranges from 2 to 16 and that $i - j$ ranges from –7 to +7. Thus, define boolean arrays *PosDiagonal* and *NegDiagonal* such that

PosDiagonal[k] is true if the queen in column k can be attacked by a queen in its positive-sloped diagonal, and

NegDiagonal is true if the queen in column k can be attacked by a queen in its negative-sloped diagonal

Use these ideas to write a program that solves the Eight Queens problem.

22. You can use backtracking to find your way through a maze. Consider a rectangular maze that you divide into squares. Imagine that you color certain squares to indicate the walls of the maze. By representing the maze with a two-dimensional array and by using backtracking, write a program that finds a path through your maze.

CHAPTER *7*

Algorithm Efficiency and Sorting

PREVIEW   This chapter will show you how to analyze the efficiency of algorithms. The basic mathematical techniques for analyzing algorithms are central to more advanced topics in computer science and give you a way to formalize the notion that one algorithm is significantly more efficient than another. As examples, you will see analyses of some algorithms that you have studied before, including those that search data. In addition, this chapter examines the important topic of sorting data. You will study some simple algorithms, which you may have seen before, and some more sophisticated recursive algorithms. Sorting algorithms provide varied and relatively easy examples of the analysis of efficiency.

MEASURING EFFICIENCY OF ALGORITHMS

The comparison or **analysis of algorithms** is a topic that is central to computer science. Measuring an algorithm's efficiency is quite important because your choice of algorithm for a given application often makes a great deal of difference. Previous chapters have informally compared different methods for performing a task. For example, we compared a sequential search of an array with a binary search and concluded that the binary search is significantly faster. Before formalizing this comparison, we need to give a more rigorous meaning to the term "significantly faster." This section introduces **order-of-magnitude analysis** and illustrates how you can use it to formalize the intuitive notion that one algorithm is significantly faster than another.

Suppose you have two algorithms that perform the same task, such as searching. What does it mean to compare the algorithms and conclude that one is better than the other? Chapter 1 discussed the cost of a computer program and the several components that constitute this cost. Some of these components involve the cost of human time—the time of the people who develop, maintain, and use the program. The other components involve the cost of program execution—that is, the program's efficiency—measured by the amount of computer time and space that the program requires to execute.

We have, up to this point, emphasized the human cost components. The early chapters of this book stressed style and readability. They pointed out that well-structured algorithms reduce the human costs of implementing the algorithm with a program, of maintaining the program, and of modifying the program. Our primary concern has been that you develop good problem-solving skills and programming style. We have and shall continue to concentrate our efforts in that direction; we have not changed our minds about what is important. However, we are also interested in the *Consider efficiency when select-* efficiency of algorithms. Efficiency is a criterion that you should use when *ing an algorithm* selecting an algorithm and its implementation. The solutions in this book, in addition to illustrating what we feel to be a good programming style, are frequently based on algorithms that are relatively efficient.

The analysis of algorithms is the area of computer science that provides tools for contrasting the differing efficiency of methods of solution. Notice that we said methods of solution rather than programs because we want to emphasize that the analysis concerns itself primarily with *significant* differences in efficiency—differences that you usually can obtain only through superior methods of solution and rarely through clever tricks in coding. Reductions in computing costs due to clever coding tricks are often more than offset by reduced program readability, which increases human costs. An analysis should focus on gross differences in the efficiency of algorithms that are likely to dominate the overall cost of a solution. To do otherwise could very well result in the selection of an algorithm that runs a small fraction of a second faster than another algorithm yet requires many more hours of human time to implement and maintain.

A comparison of algorithms should focus on significant differences in efficiency

How do you compare the time efficiency of two algorithms that solve the same problem? One possible approach is to implement the two algorithms in Pascal and run the programs. There are at least three fundamental difficulties with this approach:

1. **How are the algorithms coded?** If algorithm A_1 runs faster than A_2, it could be the result of better programming. Thus, if you compare the running times of the programs, you are really comparing implementations of the algorithms rather than the algorithms themselves. You should not compare implementations, because they are sensitive to factors such as programming style that tend to cloud the issue of which algorithm is inherently more efficient.

Three difficulties with comparing programs instead of algorithms

2. **What computer should you use?** The particular computer on which the programs are run also obscures the issue of which algorithm is inherently more efficient. It may be that because of the particular operations that the algorithms require, A_1 runs faster than A_2 on one computer, while the opposite is true on another computer. You should compare the efficiency of the algorithms independently of a particular computer.

3. **What data should the programs use?** Perhaps the most important difficulty in this list is the selection of the data for the programs to use. There is always the danger that you will select instances of the problem for which one of the algorithms runs uncharacteristically fast. For example, when comparing a sequential and a binary search, you might happen to search for the smallest item in a sorted array. In such a case, the sequential search will find the item more quickly than the binary search because the item is first in the array and so is the first item that the sequential search will examine. Any analysis of efficiency must be independent of specific data.

Order-of-Magnitude Analysis

To overcome the previous problems, computer scientists employ mathematical techniques that analyze algorithms independently of specific implementations, computers, or data. The mathematical approach consid-

Algorithm analysis should be independent of specific implementations, computers, and data ers an algorithm's time requirement as a function of the problem size. The way to measure a problem's size depends on the application—typical examples are the size of an array, the number of nodes on a linked list, the number of records in a file, or the number of items on an ordered list.

What specifically do you want to know about the time requirement of an algorithm? The most important thing to learn is how quickly the algorithm's time requirement grows as a function of the problem size. Typically, this growth rate is stated as a proportion of the problem size. For example, if N is the size of the problem, you might conclude that an algorithm requires time proportional to N, N^2, 2^N, or log N. (When speaking of proportional growth rates, you need not specify the base of the log. Exercise 10 at the end of this chapter asks you to show why you can omit the base.)

Measure an algorithm's time requirement as a function of the problem size

Consider the statement

Algorithm A requires time proportional to N^2

What can you conclude from this statement? One thing that you cannot conclude is the exact amount of time that A will require to solve a problem of size N: The statement is equally valid if A required N^2 seconds, $5 * N^2$ seconds, or $N^2/10$ seconds to solve a problem of size N.

Such characterizations of an algorithm's efficiency might thus appear to be of little use. However, what would it mean if you said that

A requires $5 * N^2$ seconds to solve a problem of size N

The previous discussion indicated the difficulties with such a statement: On what computer does the algorithm require $5 * N^2$ seconds? What implementation of the algorithm requires $5 * N^2$ seconds? Is there another implementation of the algorithm that requires only $3 * N^2$ seconds, but is perhaps less readable? On the other hand, an assertion like "A requires time proportional to N^2" is exactly the kind of statement that characterizes the inherent efficiency of an algorithm independently of such factors as particular computers and implementations.

The significance of an algorithm's proportional time requirement will become apparent if you compare two algorithms for which the requirement differs. For example, suppose that you have a second algorithm B such that

B requires time proportional to N

Compare algorithm efficiencies for large problems

Although you cannot determine the exact amount of time that either algorithm A or algorithm B requires, you can determine that for large problems, B will require significantly less time than A. That is, the amount of time—as a function of the problem size N—that B requires increases at a slower rate than the amount of time that A requires, because N increases at a slower rate than N^2. Even if B actually requires $5 * N$ seconds and A actually requires $N^2/10$ seconds, as N increases, the amount of time that B requires will become significantly less than the time that A requires.

(a)

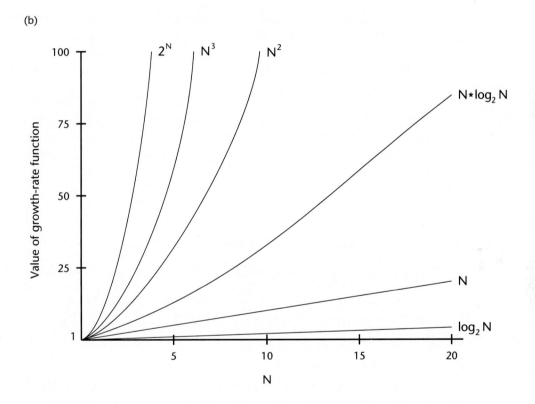

Function	10	100	1,000	10,000	100,000	1,000,000
$\log_2 N$	3	6	9	13	16	19
N	10	100	1,000	10,000	100,000	1,000,000
$N * \log_2 N$	30	664	9,965	10^5	10^6	10^7
N^2	10^2	10^4	10^6	10^8	10^{10}	10^{12}
N^3	10^3	10^6	10^9	10^{12}	10^{15}	10^{18}
2^N	10^3	10^{30}	10^{301}	$10^{3,010}$	$10^{30,103}$	$10^{301,030}$

(using the fact that $2^{10} \cong 10^{3.0103}$)

Figure 7-1

A comparison of growth-rate functions: (a) in tabular form; (b) in graphical form

(b)

To further dramatize the significance of an algorithm's proportional growth rate, consider the table and graph in Figure 7-1. The table (Figure 7-1a) gives for various values of N the approximate values of six common growth-rate functions, which are listed in order of growth. The table demonstrates how much more quickly the value of a function grows than does that of the functions that precede it in the table. (Figure 7-1b represents the growth-rate functions graphically.) If algorithm A requires time that is proportional to function f and algorithm B requires time that is proportional to a slower-growing function g, then it is apparent that B will always be significantly more efficient than A for large enough problems. For large problems, the proportional growth rate dominates all other factors in determining an algorithm's efficiency.

Big O Notation

We now formalize the concept of an algorithm's proportional growth rate. The statement

Algorithm A requires time proportional to f(N)

means that given any (reasonable) implementation of the algorithm and any (reasonable) computer, there is some **constant of proportionality** c such that A requires no more than

c * f(N) time units (such as seconds)

to solve a problem of size N. Algorithm A is said to be **order** $f(N)$, which is denoted as $O(f(N))$; $f(N)$ is called the algorithm's **growth-rate function**. Because the notation uses the capital letter O to denote *order*, it is called the **Big O notation**.

KEY CONCEPTS　　*Definition of the Order of an Algorithm*

Algorithm A is order $f(N)$ (denoted $O(f(N))$) if for any (reasonable) implementation of the algorithm and any (reasonable) computer, there is some constant c such that for all but a finite number of values of N, A requires no more than $c * f(N)$ time units to solve a problem of size N.

If a problem requires a constant time that is independent of the problem's size N, the problem is $O(1)$. If a problem of size N requires time that is directly proportional to N, then the problem is $O(N)$. If the time requirement is directly proportional to N^2, then the problem is $O(N^2)$, and so on.

Notice that the definition of $O(f(N))$ does allow A to require more than $c * f(N)$ time units for a finite number of problem sizes. This characteristic simply allows you to discount finitely many values of N, that is, to consider only sufficiently large values of N. For example, the function $\log N$ takes on the value 0 when $N = 1$. Thus, the fact $c * \log 1 = 0$ for all constants c implies an unrealistic time requirement; presumably, all algorithms require more than 0 time units even to solve a problem of size 1. Thus, you can discount problems of size $N = 1$ in this case.

There are many important mathematical properties of Big O notation that you will see in later courses. However, some of these properties are simple enough to cover now:

1. **You can ignore low-order terms in an algorithm's growth-rate function.** For example, if an algorithm is $O(N^3 + 4 * N^2 + 3 * N)$, then it is also $O(N^3)$. By examining the table in Figure 7-1a, you can see that the N^3 term is significantly larger than either $(4 * N^2)$ or $(3 * N)$, particularly for large values of N. For large N, the growth rate of $N^3 + 4 * N^2 + 3 * N$ is the same as the growth rate of N^3. Realize that the growth rate of $f(N)$, not the value of $f(N)$, is what is important here. Thus, even if an algorithm is $O(N^3 + 4 * N^2 + 3 * N)$, we say that it is simply $O(N^3)$. In general, you are usually able to conclude that an algorithm is $O(f(N))$, where f is a function similar to the ones listed in Figure 7-1.

2. **You can ignore a multiplicative constant in the high-order term of an algorithm's growth-rate function.** For example, if an algorithm is $O(5 * N^3)$, then it is also $O(N^3)$. This observation follows from the definition of $O(f(N))$, if you let $c = 5$.

3. **$O(f(N)) + O(g(N)) = O(f(N) + g(N))$.** You can combine growth-rate functions. For example, if an algorithm is $O(N) + O(N)$, then it is also $O(2 * N)$, which you write simply as $O(N)$ by applying property 2.

Some properties of growth-rate functions

There is one final point to make about the definition of the order of an algorithm: Algorithm A might require different times to solve different problems of the same size. For example, the time that an algorithm requires to search N items might depend on the nature of the items. Usually you consider the maximum amount of time that an algorithm can require to solve a problem of size N—that is, the worst case. **Worst-case analysis** concludes that A is $O(f(N))$ if, in the worst case, A requires no more than $c * f(N)$ time units to solve a problem of size N for all but a finite number of values of N.

An algorithm can require different times to solve different problems of the same size

An **average-case analysis** attempts to determine the average amount of time that an algorithm requires to solve problems of size N. In an average-case analysis, A is $O(f(N))$ if the average amount of time that A requires to solve a problem of size N is no more than $c * f(N)$ time units for all but a finite number of values of N. Average-case analysis is, in general, far more difficult to perform than worst-case analysis. One difficulty is determining the relative probabilities of encountering various problems of a given size; another is determining the distributions of various data values. Worst-case analysis is more practical to calculate and is thus more common.

An Example: The Efficiency of List Traversal

As an example of how to analyze the efficiency of a particular algorithm, consider a traversal of a linked list. Recall from Chapter 3 that you can print the contents of a linked list by using the `PrintList` procedure, which appears in pseudocode as

An example of list traversal

```
PrintList(head)
{ Prints the data in a linked list. }
    cur := head
    while cur <> nil do
    begin
        writeln(cur^.data)
        cur := cur^.next
    end
```

If there are N nodes in the list, then the number of operations that the procedure requires is proportional to N. For example, there are $N + 1$ assignments and N print operations, which together are $2 * N + 1$ operations. According to the previous discussion, you ignore both the coefficient 2 and the constant 1. Therefore, `PrintList` is $O(N)$; that is, the time that

PrintList is O(N)

`PrintList` requires to print N nodes is proportional to N. This conclusion makes sense intuitively: It takes longer to print, or traverse, a list of 100 items than it does a list of 10 items.

The Effect of Different ADT Implementations on Efficiency

You can use order-of-magnitude analysis to help you choose an implementation for an abstract data type. Recall that Chapter 4 introduced the ADT ordered list and presented two implementations. One implementation stored the list's items in an array, whereas a pointer-based implementation stored the items in a linked list. There is a potentially significant difference in the efficiency with which the two implementations support the ADT operations.

For example, one ordered list operation is `Retrieve(L, N)`, which retrieves the value of the item at the Nth position in the list. The array-based implementation can access the Nth item directly because it is stored in `L.Items[N]`. This access is independent of N; `Retrieve` takes the same time to access either the 100th item or the first item on the list. Thus, the

An array-based Retrieve is O(1)

array-based implementation of `Retrieve` is $O(1)$. However, the pointer-based implementation must traverse the list from its beginning until the Nth node is reached. Like the previous `PrintList` algorithm, the pointer-

A pointer-based Retrieve is O(N)

based implementation of `Retrieve` is $O(N)$.

Throughout the course of an analysis, you should always keep in mind that you are interested only in *significant* differences in efficiency. Is the difference in efficiency for the two implementations of `Retrieve` significant? Notice that as the size of the list grows, the pointer-based implementation might require more time to retrieve the desired node, because the node can be farther away from the beginning of the list. In contrast, regardless of how large the list is, the array-based implementation always requires the same constant amount of time to retrieve any particular item. Thus, no matter what your notion of a significant difference in time is, you will reach this time difference if the list is large enough.

In this example, observe that the difference in efficiency for the two implementations is worth considering only when the problem is large enough. If the ordered list never has more than 10 elements, for example, the difference in the implementation is not significant at all.

Keeping Your Perspective

Before continuing with additional order-of-magnitude analyses of specific algorithms, it is appropriate to present a few words about perspective. Frequently when evaluating an algorithm's efficiency, you have to weigh carefully the trade-offs between a solution's execution time requirements and its memory requirements. You rarely are able to make a statement as strong as "Method *A* is the best method of performing the task." A solution that requires a relatively small amount of computer time often also requires a relatively large amount of memory. It may not even be possible to say that one solution requires less time than another. Solution *A* may perform some components of the task faster than solution *B*, while solution *B* performs other components of the task faster than solution *A*. Often you must analyze the solutions in the light of a particular application. For example, the most appropriate implementation of an ADT for a given application strongly depends on the frequency with which the application is to perform the operations.

When choosing an ADT's implementation, consider the frequency at which particular ADT operations occur in a given application

Soon we will compare a searching algorithm that is O(*N*) with one that is O($\log_2 N$). While it is true that an O($\log_2 N$) searching algorithm requires significantly less time on large arrays than an O(*N*) algorithm, on small arrays—say $N < 25$—the time requirements might not be significantly different at all. In fact, it is entirely possible that, because of factors such as the size of the constant of proportionality—that is, the *c* in the definition of Big O—the O(*N*) algorithm will run faster on small problems. It is only on large problems that the slower growth rate of an algorithm necessarily gives it a significant advantage. Thus, in general, if the maximum size of a given problem is small, the time requirements of any two solutions for that problem likely will not differ significantly. If you know that your problem size will always be small, do not overanalyze: Simply choose the algorithm that is easiest to code and understand.

If the problem size is always small, you can probably ignore an algorithm's efficiency

In summary, it is important to examine an algorithm for both style and efficiency. The analysis should focus only on gross differences in efficiency and not reward coding tricks that save milliseconds. Any finer differences in efficiency are likely to interact with coding issues, which we feel should not interfere with the development of your programming style. If you find a method of solution that is significantly more efficient than others, you should select it, unless you know that the maximum problem size is quite small. If you will solve only small problems, it is possible that a less efficient algorithm is more appropriate. That is, other factors, such as the simplicity of the algorithm, would become more significant than minor differences in efficiency. In fact, performing an order-of-magnitude analysis implicitly assumes that an algorithm will be used to solve large problems. This assumption allows you to focus on growth rates because, regardless of

Compare algorithms for both style and efficiency

Order-of-magnitude analysis focuses on large problems

other factors, an algorithm with a slow growth rate will require less time than an algorithm with a fast growth rate, provided that the problems to be solved are sufficiently large.

The Efficiency of Searching Algorithms

As another example of order-of-magnitude analysis, consider the efficiency of two search algorithms: the sequential search and the binary search of an array.

Sequential search. Worst-case: O(N); average case: O(N); best case: O(1)

Sequential search.   In a sequential search of N array elements, you look at each element in turn, beginning with the first one, until either you find the desired element or you reach the end of the data collection. In the best case, the desired element is the first one that you examine, so only one comparison is necessary. Thus, in the best case, a sequential search is O(1). In the worst case, the desired element is the last one you examine, so N comparisons are necessary. Thus, in the worst case, the algorithm is O(N). In the average case, you would find the desired element in the middle of the collection, making $N/2$ comparisons; thus, the algorithm is O(N) in the average case.

What is the algorithm's order when you do not find the desired element? Does the algorithm's order depend on whether or not the initial data is sorted? We leave these questions for you in Self-Test Exercise 10 at the end of this chapter.

Binary search.   Is a binary search of an array more efficient than a sequential search? The binary search algorithm, which was presented in Chapter 5, searches a sorted array for a particular item by repeatedly dividing the array in half. The algorithm determines which half the item must be in—if it is indeed present—and discards the other half. Thus, the binary search algorithm searches arrays of successively smaller sizes: The size of an array is approximately one-half the size of the array previously searched.

At each division, the algorithm makes a comparison. How many comparisons does the algorithm make when it searches an array of N elements? The exact answer depends, of course, on where the sought-for item resides in the array. However, you can compute the maximum number of comparisons that a binary search requires—that is, the worst case. The number of comparisons is equal to the number of times that the algorithm divides the array in half. Suppose that $N = 2^k$ for some k. The search requires the following steps:

1. Inspect the middle item of an array of size N.
2. Inspect the middle item of an array of size $N/2$.
3. Inspect the middle item of an array of size $N/2^2$, and so on.

To inspect the middle item of an array, you first must divide the array in half. If you divide an array of N elements in half, then divide one of those halves in half, and continue dividing halves until only one element remains, you will have performed k divisions. This fact is true because $N/2^k$ = 1. (Remember, we assumed that $N = 2^k$.) In the worst case, the algorithm performs k divisions and, therefore, k comparisons. Because $N = 2^k$,

$$k = \log_2 N$$

Thus, the algorithm is $O(\log_2 N)$ in the worst case when $N = 2^k$.

What if N is not a power of 2? You can easily find the smallest k such that

$$2^{k-1} < N < 2^k$$

(For example, if N is 30, then $k = 5$, because $2^4 = 16 < 30 < 32 = 2^5$.) The algorithm still requires at most k divisions to obtain a subarray with one element. Now it follows that

$$k - 1 < \log_2 N < k$$
$$k < 1 + \log_2 N < k + 1$$
$$k = 1 + \log_2 N \text{ rounded down}$$

Thus, the algorithm is still $O(\log_2 N)$ in the worst case when $N \neq 2^k$. In general, the algorithm is $O(\log_2 N)$ in the worst case for any N.

Binary search is $O(\log_2 N)$ in the worst case

Is a binary search better than a sequential search? Much better! For example $\log_2 1,000,000 = 19$, so a sequential search of one million sorted items can require one million comparisons, but a binary search of the same items will require at most 20 comparisons. For large arrays, the binary search has an enormous advantage over a sequential search.

Realize, however, that maintaining the array in sorted order requires an overhead cost. The next section examines the cost of sorting an array.

SORTING ALGORITHMS AND THEIR EFFICIENCY

Sorting is a process that organizes a collection of data into either ascending or descending order. The need for sorting arises in many situations. You may simply want to sort a collection of data before displaying it for human consumption. Often, however, you must perform a sort as an initialization step for certain algorithms. For example, searching for data is one of the most common tasks performed by computers. When the collection of data to be searched is large, an efficient method for searching—such as the binary search algorithm—is desirable. However, the binary search algorithm requires that the data be sorted. Thus, sorting the data is a step that must precede a binary search on a collection of data that is not already sorted. Good sorting algorithms, therefore, are quite valuable.

There are two categories of sorting algorithms. An **internal sort** requires that the collection of data fit entirely in the computer's main memory. The algorithms that are presented in this chapter are internal

The sorts in this chapter are internal sorts

sorting algorithms. An **external sort** is used when the collection of data will not fit in the computer's main memory all at once, but must reside in secondary storage, such as on a disk. Chapter 14 examines external sorts.

The data elements to be sorted might be integers, character strings, or even records. It is easy to imagine the results of sorting a collection of integers or character strings, but consider a collection of records. If there is one field in each record, sorting the records is really no different than sorting a collection of integers. However, when each record contains several fields, you must know which field determines the order of the entire record within the collection of data. This field is called the **sort key**. For example, if the records contain information about people, then you might want to sort on their names, their ages, or their zip codes. Regardless of your choice of sort key, the sorting algorithm orders entire records based on only one field, the sort key.

For simplicity, this chapter assumes that the data elements are quantities such as numbers or character strings. Data elements that are records with several fields are considered in the exercises. All algorithms in this chapter sort the data into ascending order. Modifying these algorithms to sort data into descending order is simple. Finally, each example assumes that the data resides in an array and that the indexes to that array are integers.

Selection Sort

Select the largest element

Imagine some data that you can examine all at once. To sort it, you could select the largest item and put it in its place, select the next largest and put it in its place, and so on. For a card player, this process is analogous to looking at an entire hand of cards and ordering it by selecting cards one at a time in their proper order. The **selection sort** formalizes these intuitive notions. To sort an array into ascending order, you first search it for the largest element. Because you want the largest element to be in the last position of the array, you swap the last element with the largest element, even if these elements happen to be identical. Now, ignoring the last—and largest—element of the array, you search the rest of the array for its largest element and swap it with its last element, which is the next-to-last element in the original array. You continue until you have selected and swapped $N - 1$ of the N elements in the array. The remaining element, which is now in the first position of the array, is in its proper order, so it is not considered further.

Figure 7-2 provides an example of a selection sort. Beginning with five integers, you select the largest—37—and swap it with the last integer—13. (As the elements in this figure are ordered, they appear in boldface. We will use this convention throughout this chapter.) Next you select the largest integer—29—from among the first four integers in the array and swap it with the next-to-last integer in the array—13. Notice that the next selection—14—is already in its proper position, but the algorithm ignores this fact and performs a swap of 14 with itself. It is more efficient in general to occasionally perform an unnecessary swap than to continually ask

Figure 7-2

A selection sort of an array of five integers

Underlined elements are selected;
boldface elements are in order.

Initial array:	29	10	14	<u>37</u>	13
After 1st swap:	<u>29</u>	10	14	13	**37**
After 2nd swap:	13	10	<u>14</u>	**29**	**37**
After 3rd swap:	<u>13</u>	10	**14**	**29**	**37**
After 4th swap:	**10**	**13**	**14**	**29**	**37**

whether the swap is necessary. Finally, you select the 13 and swap it with the element in the second position of the array—10. The array is now sorted into ascending order.

A Pascal procedure that performs a selection sort on an array A of *N* elements follows:

```
const  maxsize = <maximum number of elements in array>;
type   datatype = <type of array element>;
       arraytype = array[1..maxsize] of datatype;

procedure SelectionSort(var A : arraytype; N : integer);
{ ------------------------------------------------------
  Sorts the elements of an array into ascending order.
  Precondition:  A[1..N] is an array of N elements.
  Postcondition: The array A is sorted into ascending order,
  N is unchanged.
  Calls: IndexOfLargest, Swap.
  ------------------------------------------------------ }
var    L : integer;      { index of largest element found }
       last : integer;   { index of last element in subarray }
begin
    for last := N downto 2 do
    { Invariant: A[last+1..N] is sorted and > A[1..last] }
    begin

        { select largest element in A[1..last] }
        L := IndexOfLargest(A, last);

        { swap largest element A[L] with A[last] }
        Swap(A[L], A[last])
    end  { for }
end  { SelectionSort }
```

The procedure uses two simple subprograms as follows:

```
function IndexOfLargest(var A : arraytype;
                        size : integer) : integer;
{ ------------------------------------------------------
  Finds the largest element in an array.
  Precondition: A[1..size] is an array, size >= 1.
```

```
            Postcondition: Returns the index of the largest element in
            the array. The parameters are unchanged.
            ----------------------------------------------------------- }
        var L, j : integer;
        begin
            L := 1;
            for j := 2 to size do
            { Invariant: A[L] >= A[1..j—1] }
                if A[j] > A[L]
                    then L := j;

            IndexOfLargest := L
        end;   { IndexOfLargest }

        procedure Swap(var x, y : datatype);
        { -----------------------------------------------------------
            Swaps x and y.
            Precondition: None.
            Postcondition: Contents of actual locations that x and y
            represent are swapped.
            ----------------------------------------------------------- }
        var Temp : datatype;
        begin
            Temp := x;
            x := y;
            y := Temp
        end   { Swap }
```

Analysis.   As you can see from the previous sorting algorithm, sorting in general requires both comparisons and exchanges of elements. As a first step in analyzing algorithms, you should count the number of comparisons and exchanges that sorting N elements requires. It is easy to see that the *for* loop in the procedure *SelectionSort* executes $N - 1$ times. Thus, there are $N - 1$ calls to each of the subprograms *IndexOfLargest* and *Swap*. Each call to *IndexOfLargest* causes its loop to execute *last* $- 1$ times for values of *last* that range from N down to 2. Thus, the $N - 1$ calls to *IndexOfLargest* cause its loop to execute in total the following number of times:

$$(N - 1) + (N - 2) + \cdots + 1 = \frac{N * (N - 1)}{2}$$

Each execution of *IndexOfLargest*'s loop performs one comparison. Therefore, a selection sort of N elements requires

$$\frac{N * (N - 1)}{2}$$

comparisons.

The $N - 1$ calls to $Swap$ result in $N - 1$ exchanges. Each exchange requires three assignments, or data moves. Thus, a selection sort of N elements requires

$$3 * (N - 1)$$

moves.

Together, there are

$$N * (N - 1)/2 + 3 * (N - 1)$$
$$= N^2/2 + 5 * N/2 - 3$$

major operations.

Thus, selection sort is $O(N^2)$. Note that the computation does not depend on the initial arrangement of the data, which is an advantage of a selection sort. However, $O(N^2)$ grows rapidly.

Selection sort is $O(N^2)$

Also, notice that while there are $O(N^2)$ comparisons, there are only $O(N)$ data moves. A selection sort could be a good choice over other methods when data moves are costly but comparisons are not. Such might be the case if each data item is lengthy but the sort key is short. Of course, storing the data in a linked list allows inexpensive data moves for any algorithm.

Bubble (Exchange) Sort

The next sorting algorithm is one that you may have seen already. That is precisely why we want to include it for analysis later, because it is not a particularly good algorithm. The **bubble sort**, or **exchange sort**, compares adjacent elements and exchanges them if they are out of order. This sort requires several passes over the data. During the first pass, you compare the first two elements in the array. If they are out of order, you exchange them. You then compare the elements in the next pair—that is, in positions 2 and 3 of the array. If they are out of order, you exchange them. You proceed, comparing and exchanging elements two at a time until you reach the end of the array.

Figure 7-3a illustrates the first pass of a bubble sort of an array of five integers. You compare the elements in the first pair—29 and 10—and exchange them because they are out of order. Next you consider the second pair—29 and 14—and exchange these elements because they are out of order. The elements in the third pair—29 and 37—are in order, and so you do not exchange them. Finally, you exchange the elements in the last pair—37 and 13.

Although the array is not sorted after the first pass, the largest element has "bubbled" to its proper position at the end of the array. During the second pass of the bubble sort, you return to the beginning of the array and consider pairs of elements in exactly the same manner as the first pass. You do not, however, include the last—and largest—element of the array. That is, the second pass considers the first $N - 1$ elements of the array. After the second pass, the second largest element in the array will be in its proper place in the next-to-last position of the array, as Figure 7-3b illustrates.

When you order successive pairs of elements, the largest element bubbles to the top (end) of the array

Bubble sort requires several passes through the array

Figure 7-3

The first two passes of a bubble sort of an array of five integers: (a) pass 1; (b) pass 2

(a) Pass 1

Initial array:

```
29  10  14  37  13
10  29  14  37  13
10  14  29  37  13
10  14  29  37  13
10  14  29  13  37
```

(b) Pass 2

```
10  14  29  13  37
10  14  29  13  37
10  14  29  13  37
10  14  13  29  37
```

Now, ignoring the last two elements, which are in order, you continue with subsequent passes until the array is sorted.

Notice that although a bubble sort requires at most $N - 1$ passes to sort the array, it is possible that fewer passes will be necessary to sort a particular array. Thus, you could terminate the process if no exchanges occur during any pass. The following Pascal procedure *BubbleSort* uses a boolean variable to signal when an exchange occurs during a particular pass. The procedure uses the previous *Swap* procedure.

```pascal
procedure BubbleSort(var A : arraytype; N : integer);
{ -------------------------------------------------------
  Sorts the elements of an array into ascending order.
  Precondition:  A[1..N] is an array of N elements.
  Postcondition: The array A is sorted into ascending order,
  N is unchanged.
  Calls: Swap.
  ------------------------------------------------------- }
var    j, Pass : integer;
       Exchanges : boolean;  { true when exchanges occur }
begin
   Pass := 1;
   Exchanges := true;

   while (Pass < N) and Exchanges do
   { Invariant: A[N+2-Pass..N] is sorted
                  and > A[1..N+1-Pass] }
   begin
      Exchanges := false;
      for j := 1 to N-Pass do
```

```
      { Invariant: A[1..j—1] <= A[j] }
         if A[j] > A[j+1]
            then
            begin
               Swap(A[j], A[j+1]); { exchange elements }
               Exchanges := true    { signal exchange }
            end;  { if, for }
      { Assertion: A[1..N—Pass] < A[N—Pass+1] }
      Pass := Pass + 1
   end  { while }
end  { BubbleSort }
```

Analysis. As was noted earlier, the bubble sort requires at most $N - 1$ passes through the array. During pass 1, there are $N - 1$ comparisons and at most $N - 1$ exchanges; during pass 2, there are $N - 2$ comparisons and at most $N - 2$ exchanges. In general, during pass i, there are $N - i$ comparisons and at most $N - i$ exchanges. Therefore, in the worst case, there will be a total of

$$(N - 1) + (N - 2) + \cdots + 1 = \frac{N * (N - 1)}{2}$$

comparisons and the same number of exchanges. Recall that each exchange requires three data moves. Thus, altogether there are

$$2 * N * (N - 1) = 2 * N^2 - 2 * N$$

major operations in the worst case. Therefore, the bubble sort algorithm is $O(N^2)$ in the worst case.

Bubble sort. Worst case: $O(N^2)$; best case: $O(N)$

The best case occurs when the original data is already sorted: `BubbleSort` uses one pass, during which there are $N - 1$ comparisons and no exchanges. Thus, the bubble sort is $O(N)$ in the best case.

Insertion Sort

Imagine once again arranging a hand of cards, but now you pick up one card at a time and insert it into its proper position; in this case you are performing an **insertion sort**. Chapter 3 introduced the insertion sort algorithm in the context of a linked list; the procedure `BuildSortedList` created a sorted linked list from a file of unsorted integers. You can use the insertion sort strategy to sort items that reside in an array. This version of the insertion sort partitions the array into two regions: sorted and unsorted, as Figure 7-4 depicts. Initially, the entire array is the unsorted region. At each step, the insertion sort takes the first item of the unsorted region and places it into its correct position in the sorted region. However, the first step is trivial: Moving $A[1]$ from the unsorted region to the sorted region really does not require moving data. Therefore, you can omit this first step by considering the initial sorted region to be $A[1]$ and the initial

Take each element from the unsorted region and insert it into its correct order in the sorted region

Figure 7-4

An insertion sort partitions the array into two regions

after i iterations

unsorted region to be $A[2..N]$. Note that an invariant of the algorithm is that the items in the sorted region are sorted among themselves. Because at each step the size of the sorted region grows by 1 and the size of the unsorted region shrinks by 1, the entire array will be sorted when the algorithm terminates.

Figure 7-5 illustrates an insertion sort of an array of five integers. Initially, the sorted region is $A[1]$, which is 29, and the unsorted region is the rest of the array. You take the first element in the unsorted region—the 10—and insert it into its proper position in the sorted region. Notice that insertion into the sorted region requires that you shift array elements to make room for the insertion. You then take the first element in the new unsorted region—the 14—and insert it into its proper position in the sorted region, and so on.

A Pascal procedure that performs an insertion sort on an array of *N* elements follows:

```
procedure InsertionSort(var A : arraytype; N : integer);
{ -----------------------------------------------------------
  Sorts the elements of an array into ascending order.
  Precondition:  A[1..N] is an array of N elements.
  Postcondition: The array A is sorted into ascending order,
  N is unchanged.
  ----------------------------------------------------------- }
var    unsorted : integer;  { first index of unsorted region }
       loc : integer;       { index of insertion in sorted
                              region }
       NextItem : datatype; { next item in unsorted region }
       Done : boolean;

{ Initially, sorted region = A[1] and unsorted region =
  A[2..N]. In general, sorted region = A[1..unsorted-1] and
  unsorted region = A[unsorted..N] }
begin
    for unsorted := 2 to N do
    { Invariant: A[1..unsorted-1] is sorted }
    begin
       { find the proper position (loc) in A[1..unsorted]
         for A[unsorted], which is the first element in the
         unsorted region--shift, if necessary, to make room }
       NextItem := A[unsorted];
```

```
        loc := unsorted;
        Done := false;
        while (loc > 1) and (not Done) do
        begin
            if A[loc-1] > NextItem
                then
                begin { shift A[loc-1] to the right }
                    A[loc] := A[loc-1];
                    loc := loc - 1
                end   { then }

                else Done := true
        end;  { while }
        { Assertion: A[loc] is where NextItem belongs }

        { insert NextItem into sorted region }
        A[loc] := NextItem
    end   { for }
end   { InsertionSort }
```

Analysis. The *for* loop in the procedure *InsertionSort* executes $N-1$ times. Within this loop there is a *while* loop that executes at most *unsorted* -1 times for values of *unsorted* that range from 2 to N. Thus, in the worst case, the algorithm's comparison occurs the following number of times:

$$1 + 2 + \cdots + (N-1) = \frac{N*(N-1)}{2}$$

In addition, the algorithm moves data items at most the same number of times. Together, there are

$$N*(N-1) = N^2 - N$$

major operations in the worst case.

Therefore, the insertion sort algorithm is $O(N^2)$ in the worst case. For small arrays—say, fewer than 50 items—the simplicity of the insertion sort makes it an appropriate choice. For large arrays, however, an insertion sort can be prohibitively inefficient.

Insertion sort is $O(N^2)$ in the worst case

Initial array:	**29** 10 14 37 13	copy 10
	29 29 14 37 13	shift 29
	10 **29** 14 37 13	insert 10; copy 14
	10 29 29 37 13	shift 29
	10 14 **29** 37 13	insert 14; copy 37, insert 37 on top of itself
	10 14 29 37 13	copy 13
	10 14 14 29 37	shift 14, 29, 37
Sorted array:	**10 13 14 29 37**	insert 13

Figure 7-5

An insertion sort of an array of five elements

Figure 7-6

A mergesort with an auxiliary temporary array

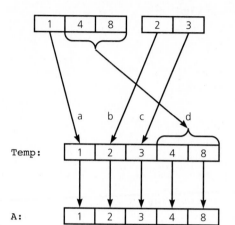

A: 8   1   4   3   2   Divide the array in half

     1   4   8   2   3   Sort the halves

Merge the halves:
     a. 1 < 2, so move 1 from left half to Temp
     b. 4 > 2, so move 2 from right half to Temp
     c. 4 > 3, so move 3 from right half to Temp
     d. Right half is finished, so move rest of left half to Temp

Temp: 1   2   3   4   8

Copy temporary array back into original array

A: 1   2   3   4   8

Mergesort

Divide and conquer

Two important divide-and-conquer sorting algorithms, mergesort and quicksort, have elegant recursive formulations and are highly efficient. The presentations here are in the context of sorting arrays, but—as you shall see in Chapter 14—mergesort generalizes to external files. It will be convenient to express the algorithms in terms of the array `A[F..L]`.

Halve the array, recursively sort its halves, and then merge the halves

Mergesort is a recursive sorting algorithm that always gives the same performance, regardless of the initial order of the array elements. Suppose that you divide the array into halves, sort each half, and then merge the sorted halves into one sorted array, as Figure 7-6 illustrates. The merge step proceeds in a manner similar to the way two sorted files are merged into one sorted file, as Figure 2-20 in Chapter 2 illustrated. You may want to review that figure and compare it with Figure 7-6. This merge step compares an element in one half of the array with an element in the other half and moves the smaller element to a temporary array. This process continues until there are no more elements to consider in one half. At that time, you simply move the remaining elements to the temporary array. Finally, you copy the temporary array back into the original array.

Although the merge step of mergesort produces a sorted array, how do you sort the array halves prior to the merge step? Mergesort sorts the array halves by using mergesort—that is, by calling itself recursively. Thus, the pseudocode for mergesort is

```
Mergesort(A, F, L)
{ Sorts A[F..L]. }

    if F < L
        then
        begin
```

```
mid := (F + L) div 2      { get midpoint }
Mergesort(A, F, mid)      { sort A[F..mid] }
Mergesort(A, mid+1, L)    { sort A[mid+1..L] }

{ merge sorted halves A[F..mid] and
  A[mid+1..L] }
Merge(A, F, mid, L)
```

end

else quit

Clearly, most of the effort in the mergesort algorithm is in the merge step, but does this algorithm actually sort? The recursive calls continue dividing the array into pieces until each piece contains only one element; obviously an array of one element is sorted. The algorithm then merges these small pieces into larger sorted pieces until one sorted array results. Figure 7-7 illustrates both the recursive calls and the merge steps in a mergesort of an array of six integers.

The following Pascal procedures implement the *Mergesort* algorithm. Note that to sort an array *A[1..N]* of integers, you would invoke *Mergesort* by writing *Mergesort(A, 1, N)*.

```
const   maxsize = 10;
type    datatype = integer;
        arraytype = array[1..maxsize] of datatype;

procedure Merge(var A : arraytype; F, mid, L : integer);
{ -----------------------------------------------------------
  Merges two sorted array segments A[F..mid] and A[mid+1..L]
  into one sorted array.
  Precondition: F <= mid <= L; The subarrays A[F..mid] and
  A[mid+1..L] are each sorted in increasing order.
  Postcondition: A[F..L] is sorted.
```

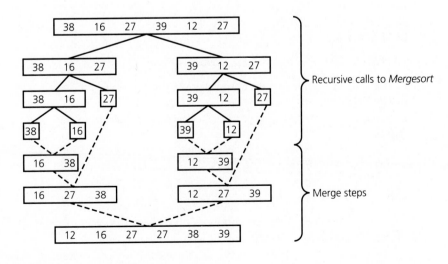

Figure 7-7

A mergesort of an array of six integers

Implementation note: This procedure merges the two subarrays into a temporary array, and copies the result into the original array A.

```
--------------------------------------------------------- }
var     TempArray : arraytype;   { temporary array }
        first1, last1, first2, last2, index : integer;
begin
    { initialize the local indexes to the subarrays }
    first1 := F;                    { beginning of first subarray }
    last1 := mid;                   { end of first subarray }
    first2 := mid + 1;              { beginning of second subarray }
    last2 := L;                     { end of second subarray }

    { next available location in TempArray }
    index := first1;

    { while both subarrays are not empty, copy the smaller
      element into the temporary array. }
    while ( (first1 <= last1) and (first2 <= last2) ) do
    { Invariant: TempArray[first1..index-1] is in order }
    begin
        if A[first1] < A[first2]
        then
        begin
            TempArray[index] := A[first1];
            first1 := first1 + 1;
            index := index + 1
        end

        else
        begin
            TempArray[index] := A[first2];
            first2 := first2 + 1;
            index := index + 1
        end
    end;  { while }

    { finish off the nonempty subarray }

    { finish off the first subarray if necessary }
    while (first1 <= last1) do
    { Invariant: TempArray[first1..index-1] is in order }
    begin
        TempArray[index] := A[first1];
        first1 := first1 + 1;
        index := index + 1
    end;  { while }

    { finish off the second subarray if necessary }
    while (first2 <= last2) do
    { Invariant: TempArray[first1..index-1] is in order }
```

```
    begin
        TempArray[index] := A[first2];
        first2 := first2 + 1;
        index := index + 1
    end;  { while }

    { copy the result back into the original array }
    for index := F to L do
        A[index] := TempArray[index]

end;  { Merge }

procedure Mergesort(var A : arraytype; F, L : integer);

{ --------------------------------------------------------

    Sorts an array  by using mergesort.
    Mergesort is a recursive algorithm that sorts by:
        1. sorting the first half of the array
        2. sorting the second half of the array
        3. merging the two sorted halves

    Precondition: A[F..L] is an array.
    Postcondition: A[F..L] is sorted in ascending order.
    Calls: Merge.
    --------------------------------------------------- }

var mid : integer;
begin
    if F < L
        then
        begin
            { sort each half }
            mid := (F + L) div 2;
            Mergesort(A, F, mid);   { sort left half A[F..mid]}
            Mergesort(A, mid+1, L); { sort right half A[mid+1..L]}

            { merge the two halves }
            Merge(A, F, mid, L)
        end
end  { Mergesort }
```

Notice that because each call to the procedure *Mergesort* must alter the array *A*, *A* is passed as a variable parameter. Recall from Chapter 5 that when you use the box method to trace the execution of a recursive procedure, you must represent variable parameters differently than value parameters. You view a variable parameter as external to the boxes instead of as part of the local environment of each recursive call. Within each box that corresponds to a call's local environment, you associate the name of the formal parameter with the actual parameter, as Figure 5-17 of Chapter 5 illustrates. References to the formal parameter from within different recursive calls to the subprogram lead to the same actual parameter.

Pass the array **A** *as a variable parameter*

Analysis. Because the merge step of the algorithm requires the most effort, we begin the analysis there. Each merge step merges `A[F..mid]` and `A[mid+1..L]`. Figure 7-8 provides an example of a merge step that requires the maximum number of comparisons. If the total number of elements in the two array segments to be merged is m, then merging the segments requires at most $m - 1$ comparisons. (For example, in Figure 7-8 there are six elements in the segments and five comparisons.) In addition, there are m moves from the original array to the temporary array, and m moves from the temporary array back to the original array. Thus, there are $3 * m - 1$ major operations in each merge step.

Each call to `Mergesort` recursively calls itself twice. As Figure 7-9 illustrates, if the original call to `Mergesort` is at level 0, then there are two calls to `Mergesort` at level 1 of the recursion. Each of these calls then calls `Mergesort` twice, so there are four calls to `Mergesort` at level 2 of the recursion, and so on. How many levels of recursion are there?

Each call to `Mergesort` halves the array. After halving the array the first time, there are two pieces. The next recursive calls to `Mergesort` halve each of these two pieces to produce four pieces of the original array; the next recursive calls halve each of these four pieces to produce eight pieces, and so on. The recursive calls continue until the array pieces each contain one element—that is, until there are N pieces, where N is the number of elements in the original array. If N is a power of 2 ($N = 2^k$), then the recursion goes $k = \log_2 N$ levels deep. For example, in Figure 7-9 there are eight elements in the original array. Because $8 = 2^3$, there are three levels of recursive calls to `Mergesort`. If N is not a power of 2, then there are $1 + \log_2 N$ (rounded down) calls to `Mergesort`.

The original call to `Mergesort` (at level 0) calls `Merge` once. `Merge` merges all N elements and requires $3 * N - 1$ operations, as was shown earlier. At level 1 of the recursion, there are two calls to `Mergesort`, and hence to `Merge`. Each of these two calls to `Merge` merges $N/2$ elements and requires $3 * (N/2) - 1$ operations. Together these two calls to `Merge` require $2 * (3 * (N/2) - 1)$, or $3 * N - 2$ operations. At level m of the recursion there are 2^m calls to `Merge`; each of these calls merges $N/2^m$ elements and so requires $3 * (N/2^m) - 1$ operations. Together the 2^m calls to `Merge` require $3 * N - 2^m$ operations. Thus, there are $O(N)$ operations at each level of the recursion. Because there are either $\log_2 N$ or $1 + \log_2 N$ levels, `Mergesort` is $O(N * \log_2 N)$ in both the worst and average cases. You should look at Figure

*Mergesort is O(N * log₂N)*

Figure 7-8

A worst-case instance of the merge step in `Mergesort`

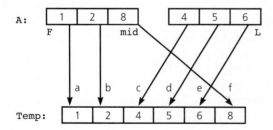

Merge the halves:
 a. 1 < 4, so move 1 from `A[F..mid]` to `Temp`
 b. 2 < 4, so move 2 from `A[F..mid]` to `Temp`
 c. 8 > 4, so move 4 from `A[mid+1..L]` to `Temp`
 d. 8 > 5, so move 5 from `A[mid+1..L]` to `Temp`
 e. 8 > 6, so move 6 from `A[mid+1..L]` to `Temp`
 f. `A[mid+1..L]` is finished, so move 8 to `Temp`

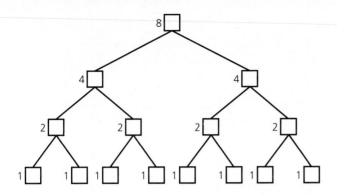

Level 0: *Mergesort* 8 elements

Level 1: 2 calls to *Mergesort* with 4 elements each

Level 2: 4 calls to *Mergesort* with 2 elements each

Level 3: 8 calls to *Mergesort* with 1 element each

Figure 7-9

Levels of recursive calls to `Mergesort`, **given an array of eight elements**

7-1 again to convince yourself that $O(N * \log_2 N)$ is significantly faster than $O(N^2)$.

Although `Mergesort` is an extremely efficient algorithm with respect to time, it does have one drawback: To perform the step

```
Merge sorted halves A[F..mid] and A[mid+1..L]
```

the algorithm requires an auxiliary array whose size equals the size of the original array. In situations where storage is limited, this requirement might not be acceptable.

Quicksort

Consider the first two steps of the solution to the problem of finding the kth smallest element of the array `A[F..L]` that was discussed in Chapter 5:

Another divide-and-conquer algorithm

```
Choose a pivot element p from A[F..L]
Partition the elements of A[F..L] about p
```

Recall that this partition, which is pictured again in Figure 7-10, has the property that all elements in $S_1 = A[F..pivotindex-1]$ are less than the pivot p, and all elements in $S_2 = A[pivotindex+1..L]$ are greater than or equal to p. Though this property does not imply that the array is sorted, it does imply an extremely useful fact: The elements in positions F through `pivotindex` $-$ `1` remain in positions F through `pivotindex` $-$ `1` when the array is properly sorted, although their positions relative to one another may change. Similarly, the elements in positions `pivotindex` + `1` through L will remain in positions `pivotindex` + `1` through L when the array is sorted, although their relative positions may change. Finally, the pivot element remains in its position in the final, sorted array.

Quicksort partitions an array into elements that are < the pivot and those that are ≥ the pivot

Partitioning places the pivot in its correct position within the array

The partition induces relationships between the array elements that are the ingredients of a recursive solution. Arranging the array elements around the pivot p generates two smaller sorting problems—sort the left section of the array (S_1), and sort the right section of the array (S_2). The relationships between the array elements imply that once you solve the

Figure 7-10

A partition about a pivot

left and right sorting problems, you will have solved the original sorting problem. That is, partitioning the array before the recursive calls places the pivot in its correct position and ensures that when the smaller array segments are sorted, their elements will be in the proper relation to the rest of the array. Notice that you are assured that the left and right sorting problems are indeed smaller problems and are each closer than the original sorting problem to the degenerate case—which is an array containing one element—because the pivot is not part of either S_1 or S_2. Thus, the quicksort algorithm will eventually terminate.

The pseudocode for quicksort follows:

```
Quicksort(A, F, L)
{ Sorts A[F..L]. }

    if F < L
        then
        begin
            Choose a pivot element p from A[F..L]
            Partition the elements of A[F..L] about p
            { the partition is A[F..pivotindex..L] }

            Quicksort(A, F, pivotindex-1)      { sort S₁ }
            Quicksort(A, pivotindex+1, L)      { sort S₂ }
        end
    { if F >= L, there is nothing to do }
```

It is worth contrasting *Quicksort* with the pseudocode function given for the *k*th smallest integer problem in Chapter 5:

```
function Select(k, A, F, L) : returns a value from the array

    Choose a pivot element p from A[F..L]
    Partition the elements of A[F..L] about p

    if k < pivotindex - F + 1 then
        Select := Select(k, A, F, pivotindex-1)
    else if k = pivotindex - F + 1 then
        Select := p
    else Select := Select(k-(pivotindex-F+1),A, pivotindex+1,L)
```

There are two fundamental differences between *Select* and *Quicksort*:

Differences between *Select* *and* *Quicksort*

- *Select* is called recursively only on the section of the array that contains the desired element, and it is not called at all if the desired element is the pivot. On the other hand, *Quicksort* is called recursively on both unsorted sections of the array. Figure 7-11 illustrates this difference.

- *Select* is a function that does not alter the array it is passed—it simply returns a value—whereas *Quicksort* is a procedure that does alter the array it is passed.

Using an invariant to develop a partition procedure. Now consider the partition procedure that both *Select* and *Quicksort* require. Partitioning an array section about a pivot element is actually the most difficult part of these two problems.

The partition procedure will receive an array segment *A[F..L]* as a parameter. The procedure must arrange the elements of the array segment into two regions: S_1, the set of elements less than the pivot, and S_2, the set of elements greater than or equal to the pivot. The procedure arranges the array so that S_1 is *A[F..pivotindex−1]* and S_2 is *A[pivotindex+1..L]*, as you saw in Figure 7-10.

What pivot should you use? If the elements in the array are arranged randomly, you can choose a pivot randomly. For example, you can choose *A[F]* as the pivot. (We will say more about the choice of pivot later.) While you are developing the partition, it is convenient to retain the pivot in the *A[F]* position.

It is also useful to impose another region, called the unknown region, on the array. Thus, you should view the array as shown in Figure 7-12. The array indices *F*, *lastS1*, *firstunknown*, and *L* divide the array as was just described. Throughout the entire partitioning process, the following is true:

> *The elements in the region S_1 are all less than the pivot, and those in S_2 are all greater than or equal to the pivot.*

Invariant

This statement is the invariant for the partitioning algorithm. The relationship between the elements in the unknown region—which is *A[firstunknown..L]*—and the pivot is, simply, unknown!

Figure 7-11

Select versus *Quicksort*

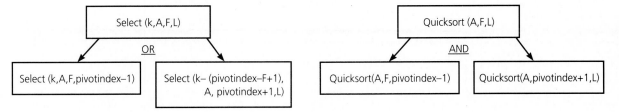

Figure 7-12

Invariant for the partition algorithm

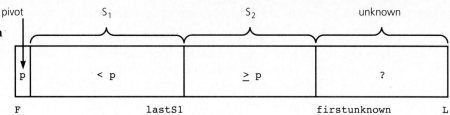

For the invariant to be true at the start of the procedure, the array's indexes must be initialized as follows so that the unknown region spans all of the array segment to be partitioned except the pivot:

Initially, all elements except the pivot A[F] constitute the unknown region

```
lastS1 := F
firstunknown := F + 1
```

Figure 7-13 shows the initial status of the array.

At each step of the partition procedure, you examine one element of the unknown region, determine in which of the two regions S_1 or S_2 it belongs, and place it there. Thus, the size of the unknown region decreases by 1 at each step. The procedure terminates when the size of the unknown region reaches 0—that is, when *firstunknown = L*.

The following pseudocode describes the partitioning algorithm:

The partitioning algorithm
```
Partition(A, F, L, pivotindex)
{ Partition A[F..L] }

   { choose the pivot, p, initialize S₁ and S₂
     to empty and unknown to A[F+1..L] }
   p := A[F]
   lastS1 := F
   firstunknown := F + 1

   while (firstunknown <= L) do
   begin
      { consider the placement of the "leftmost"
          element in the unknown region }
      if A[firstunknown] < p then
          Move A[firstunknown] into S₁
```

Figure 7-13

Initial state of the array

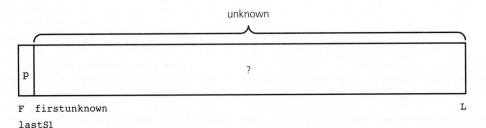

```
        else Move A[firstunknown] into S₂
end

{ place pivot in proper position between S₁ and S₂ and
    mark its new location }
Swap A[F] with A[lastS1]
pivotindex := lastS1
```

The algorithm is straightforward enough, but its move operations need clarification. Consider the two possible actions that you need to take at each iteration of the *while* loop:

Move A[firstunknown] into S₁. S_1 and the unknown region are, in general, not adjacent: S_2 is between the two regions. However, if you swap A[firstunknown] with the first element of S_2—which is A[lastS1 + 1], as Figure 7-14 illustrates—and then increment *lastS1* by 1, the element that was in A[firstunknown] will be at the rightmost position of S_1. Now, what about the element of S_2 that was moved to A[firstunknown]? If you increment *firstunknown* by 1, then that element becomes the rightmost member of S_2. Thus, you should execute the following statements to move A[firstunknown] into S_1:

```
Swap A[firstunknown] with A[lastS1+1]
lastS1 := lastS1 + 1
firstunknown := firstunknown + 1
```

This strategy works even when S_2 is empty. In this case, after *lastS1* is incremented, it will equal *firstunknown*, and thus the swap simply exchanges an element with itself. *Note that this move preserves the invariant.*

Move A[firstunknown] into S₂. This move is simple. Recall that the rightmost boundary of the region S_2 is at position *firstunknown − 1*; that is, regions S_2 and the unknown region are adjacent, as Figure 7-15 illustrates. Thus, to move A[firstunknown] into S_2, simply increment *firstunknown* by 1: S_2 expands to the right. *Note that this move preserves the invariant.*

Figure 7-14

Moving A[firstunknown] into S_1 by swapping it with A[lastS1+1] and by incrementing both *lastS1* and *firstunknown*

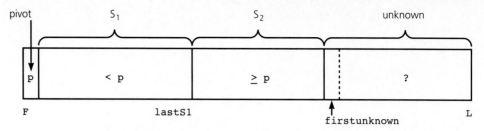

Figure 7-15

Moving `A[firstunknown]` into S_2 by incrementing `firstunknown`

After all elements have been moved from the unknown region into S_1 and S_2, there is one final task to perform. You must place the pivot between the segments S_1 and S_2. Observe that `A[lastS1]` is the rightmost element in S_1. If you interchange this element with the pivot, which is in `A[F]`, you will place the pivot in its correct location. Then the statement

        `pivotindex := lastS1`

allows the procedure to return the location of the pivot. Note that you can use this index to determine the boundaries of S_1 and S_2. Figure 7-16 shows a partition of an array of six integers when the pivot is the first element.

Before continuing the implementation of `Quicksort`, note that you can establish the correctness of the partition algorithm by using invariants. Again, the loop invariant for the partition procedure is

> *All elements in S_1 (`A[F+1..lastS1]`) are less than the pivot, and all elements in S_2 (`A[lastS1+1..L]`) are greater than or equal to the pivot.*

Recall that when you use invariants to establish the correctness of an iterative algorithm, a four-step process is required:

The proof that the partitioning algorithm is correct uses an invariant and requires four steps

1. **The invariant must be true initially,** before the loop begins execution. In the partition algorithm, before the loop that swaps array elements is entered, the pivot is `A[F]`, the unknown region is `A[F+1..L]`, and S_1 and S_2 are empty. The invariant is clearly true initially.

2. **An execution of the loop must preserve the invariant.** That is, if the invariant is true before any given iteration of the loop, then you must show that it is true after the iteration. In the partition algorithm, at each iteration of the loop a single element moves from the unknown region into either S_1 or S_2, depending on whether or not the element is less than the pivot. Thus, if the invariant was true before the move, it will remain true after the move.

3. **The invariant must capture the correctness of the algorithm.** That is, you must show that if the invariant is true when the loop terminates, the algorithm is correct. In the partition algorithm, the termination condition is that the unknown region is empty. But if the unknown region is empty, each element of `A[F+1..L]` must be in

Figure 7-16

The first partition of an array when the pivot is the first element

either S_1 or S_2—in which case the invariant implies that the partition algorithm has done what it was supposed to do.

4. **The loop must terminate.** That is, you must show that the loop will terminate after a finite number of iterations. In the partition algorithm, the size of the unknown region decreases by 1 at each iteration. Therefore, the unknown region becomes empty after a finite number of iterations, and thus the termination condition for the loop will be met.

The following Pascal procedures implement the quicksort algorithm. Note that the required procedure *Swap* is the same one that *Selection-Sort* uses. To sort an array *A[1..N]* of integers, you invoke *Quicksort* by writing *Quicksort(A, 1, N)*.

```
const  maxsize = 10;
type   datatype = integer;
       arraytype = array[1..maxsize] of datatype;

procedure Partition(var A : arraytype ; F, L : integer;
                    var PivotIndex : integer);
{ ------------------------------------------------------------
  Partitions A[F..L] for quicksort.
  Precondition: F <= L; assumes pivot is in A[F].
  Postcondition: Partitions A[F..L] such that:
     S1 =  A[F..PivotIndex-1] <  Pivot
           A[PivotIndex]      =  Pivot
     S2 =  A[PivotIndex+1..L] >= Pivot
  Calls: Swap
  ------------------------------------------------------------ }
```

```
var     firstunknown : integer;
        lastS1 : integer;
        Pivot : datatype;
begin
    { initially, everything but pivot is in unknown }
    Pivot := A[F];
    lastS1 := F;
    firstunknown := F + 1;

    { move one element at a time until unknown region is empty }
    while (firstunknown <= L) do
    { Invariant: A[F+1..lastS1] <  Pivot
                 A[lastS1+1..firstunknown—1] >= Pivot }
    begin
        { move element from unknown to proper region }
        if A[firstunknown] < Pivot
           then
           begin    { element from unknown belongs in S1 }
               Swap(A[firstunknown], A[lastS1+1]);
               lastS1 := lastS1 + 1;
               firstunknown := firstunknown + 1
           end

           { else element from unknown belongs in S2 }
           else firstunknown := firstunknown + 1
    end; { while }

    { place pivot in proper position and mark its location }
    Swap(A[F], A[lastS1]);
    PivotIndex := lastS1
end;  { Partition }

procedure Quicksort(var A : arraytype; F, L : integer);
{ ------------------------------------------------------------
  Sorts an array by using quicksort.
  Precondition: A[F..L] is an array.
  Postcondition: A[F..L] is sorted.
  Calls: Partition.

  ------------------------------------------------------------ }
var PivotIndex : integer;
begin
   if F < L
     then
     begin
        { create the partition: S1, pivot, S2 }
        Partition(A, F, L, PivotIndex);

        { sort regions S1 and S2 }
```

```
        Quicksort(A, F, PivotIndex—1);
        Quicksort(A, PivotIndex+1, L)
     end
end  { Quicksort }
```

As was true with *Mergesort*, each call to the procedure *Quicksort* must alter the array *A*, so *A* is passed as a variable parameter.

Pass the array A as a variable parameter

You can use an element other than *A[F]* as the pivot: Simply interchange your pivot with *A[F]* and then use the previously described partition algorithm. In the analysis to follow, you will learn that it is desirable to avoid a pivot that makes either S_1 or S_2 empty. A good choice of pivot is one that is near the median of the array elements. Exercise 12 at the end of this chapter considers this choice of pivot.

Place your choice of pivot in A[F] before partitioning

Quicksort and *Mergesort* are similar in spirit, but whereas *Quicksort* does work before its recursive calls, *Mergesort* does work after its recursive calls. That is, while *Quicksort* has the form

```
Quicksort(A, F, L)

   if F < L
      then
      begin
        Prepare array for recursive calls
        Quicksort(S₁ region of A)
        Quicksort(S₂ region of A)
      end

      else quit
```

Mergesort has the general form

```
Mergesort(A, F, L)

   if F < L
      then
      begin
        Mergesort( Left half of A )
        Mergesort( Right half of A )
        Tidy up array after the recursive calls
      end

      else quit
```

The preparation in *Quicksort* is to partition the array into regions S_1 and S_2. The algorithm then sorts S_1 and S_2 independently, because every element in S_1 belongs to the left of every element in S_2. In *Mergesort*, on the other hand, no work is done before the recursive calls: The algorithm sorts each half of the array with respect to itself. However, the algorithm still must deal with the interaction between the elements of the two halves. That is, the algorithm merges the two halves of the array after the recursive calls.

Analysis. The major effort in the `Quicksort` procedure occurs during the partitioning step. As you consider each element in the unknown region, you compare `A[firstunknown]` with the pivot and move `A[firstunknown]` into either S_1 or S_2. It is possible for one of S_1 or S_2 to remain empty. For example, if the pivot is the smallest element in the array segment, then S_1 will remain empty. This occurrence is the worst case because S_2 decreases in size by only 1 at each recursive call to `Quicksort`. Thus, the maximum number of recursive calls to `Quicksort` will occur.

Quicksort is slow when the array is already sorted

Notice what happens when the array is already sorted into ascending order. Figure 7-17 shows the results of the first call to `Partition` for a sorted array. The pivot is the smallest element in the array, and S_1 remains empty. `Partition` requires $N - 1$ comparisons to partition the N elements in this array. On the next recursive call to `Quicksort`, `Partition` is passed $N - 1$ elements, so it will require $N - 2$ comparisons to partition them. Again S_1 will remain empty. Because the array segment that `Quicksort` considers at each level of recursion decreases in size by only 1, $N - 1$ levels of recursion are required. Therefore, `Quicksort` requires

$$1 + 2 + \cdots + (N - 1) = \frac{N * (N - 1)}{2}$$

comparisons. However, recall that a move into S_2 does not require an exchange of array elements; it requires only a change in the index `firstunknown`.

Similarly if S_2 remains empty at each recursive call, $N * (N - 1) / 2$ comparisons are required. In addition, however, an exchange is necessary to move each unknown element to S_1. Thus, $N * (N - 1) / 2$ exchanges are necessary. (Again each exchange requires three data moves.) Thus, you can conclude that `Quicksort` is $O(N^2)$ in the worst case.

In contrast, Figure 7-18 shows an example in which S_1 and S_2 contain the same—or in general, nearly the same—number of elements. In this average case, assuming random arrangements of array items, fewer recursive calls to `Quicksort` occur. As you did in the previous analysis of `Mergesort`, you can conclude that there are either $\log_2 N$ or $1 + \log_2 N$ calls

Figure 7-17

A worst-case partitioning with `Quicksort`

Original array:	5	6	7	8	9	
	5	6	7	8	9	
	5 ‖ 6	7	8	9		S_1 is empty
	5 ‖ 6	7	8	9		S_1 is empty
	5 ‖ 6	7	8	9		S_1 is empty
First partition:	5	6	7	8	9	4 comparisons, 0 exchanges

(S_1 is empty)   pivot S_2

Original array: 5   3   6   7   4

        5 | 3   6   7   4

        5 | 3 | 6   7   4

        5 | 3 | 6 | 7   4

        5 | 3 | 6   7 | 4

        5 | 3   4 | 7   6 S_1 and S_2 are created

First partition: 4   3 | 5 | 7   6   Place pivot between S_1 and S_2

         S_1 pivot S_2

Figure 7-18

An average-case partitioning with Quicksort

to `Quicksort`. Each call to `Quicksort` involves *m* comparisons and at most *m* exchanges, where *m* is the number of elements in the subarray to be sorted. Clearly $m \leq N - 1$.

A formal analysis of `Quicksort`'s average-case behavior would show that it is $O(N * \log_2 N)$. Thus, on large arrays you can expect `Quicksort` to run significantly faster than `InsertionSort`, although in its worst case `Quicksort` will require roughly the same amount of time as an insertion sort.

It might then seem surprising that `Quicksort` is often used to sort large arrays. The reason for `Quicksort`'s popularity is that it is usually extremely fast in practice, despite its unimpressive theoretical worst-case behavior. Although a worst-case situation is not typical, even if the worst case occurs, `Quicksort`'s performance is acceptable for moderately large arrays.

The fact that `Quicksort`'s average-case behavior is far better than its worst-case behavior distinguishes it from the other sorting algorithms considered in this chapter. If the original arrangement of data in the array is "random," `Quicksort` performs at least as well as any known sorting algorithm that involves comparisons. Unless the array is already ordered, `Quicksort` is best.

`Mergesort`'s efficiency is somewhere between the possibilities for `Quicksort`: Sometimes `Quicksort` is faster, and sometimes `Mergesort` is faster. While the worst-case behavior of `Mergesort` is of the same order of magnitude as `Quicksort`'s average-case behavior, in most situations `Quicksort` will run somewhat faster than `Mergesort`. However, in its worst case `Quicksort` will be significantly slower than `Mergesort`.

Quicksort. Worst case: $O(N^2)$; average case: $O(N * log_2 N)$

Radix Sort

The final sorting algorithm in this chapter is quite different from the others. It is for this reason that we include it here.

Imagine one last time you are sorting a hand of cards. This time you pick up the cards one at a time and arrange them by rank into 13 possible groups in this order: 2, 3, ⋯ , 10, J, Q, K, A. Combine these groups and place the cards face down on the table so that the 2's are on top and the aces are on the bottom. Now pick up the cards one at a time and arrange them by suit into four possible groups in this order: clubs, diamonds, hearts, and spades. When taken together, the groups result in a sorted hand of cards.

A **radix sort** uses this idea of forming groups and then combining them to sort a collection of data. The sort treats each data element as a character string. As a first simple example of a radix sort, consider this collection of three-letter strings:

        ABC, XYZ, BWZ, AAC, RLT, JBX, RDT, KLT, AEO, TLJ

The sort begins by organizing the data according to their rightmost (least significant) letters. Although none of the strings end in A or B, two strings end in C. Place those two strings into a group. Continuing through the alphabet, you will form the following groups:

Group strings by rightmost letter

        (ABC, AAC) (TLJ) (AEO) (RLT, RDT, KLT) (JBX) (XYZ, BWZ)

The strings in each group end with the same letter, and the groups are ordered by that letter. The strings within each group retain their relative order from the original list of strings.

Now combine the groups into one as follows. Take the elements in the first group in their present order, follow them with the elements in the second group in their present order, and so on. The following group results:

Combine groups

        ABC, AAC, TLJ, AEO, RLT, RDT, KLT, JBX, XYZ, BWZ

Next, form new groups as you did before, but this time use the middle letter of each string instead of the last letter:

Group strings by middle letter

        (AAC) (ABC, JBX) (RDT) (AEO) (TLJ, RLT, KLT) (BWZ) (XYZ)

Now the strings in each group have the same middle letter, and the groups are ordered by that letter. As before, the strings within each group retain their relative order from the previous group of all strings.

Combine these groups into one group, again preserving the relative order of the elements within each group:

Combine groups

        AAC, ABC, JBX, RDT, AEO, TLJ, RLT, KLT, BWZ, XYZ

Now form new groups according to the first letter of each string:

Group strings by first letter

        (AAC, ABC, AEO) (BWZ) (JBX) (KLT) (RDT, RLT) (TLJ) (XYZ)

Finally, combine the groups into the final sorted collection of data, again maintaining the relative order within each group:

Sorted strings

        AAC, ABC, AEO, BWZ, JBX, KLT, RDT, RLT, TLJ, XYZ

The strings are now in sorted order.

In the previous example, all character strings had the same length. If the character strings have varying lengths, you can treat them as if they were the same length by padding them on the right with blanks as necessary.

To sort numeric data, the radix sort treats a number as a character string. You can treat numbers as if they were padded on the left with zeros, making them all appear to be the same length. You then form groups according to the rightmost digits, combine the groups, form groups according to the next-to-last digits, combine them, and so on, just as you did in the previous example. Figure 7-19 shows a radix sort of eight integers.

The following pseudocode describes the algorithm for a radix sort of N decimal integers of d digits each:

```
RadixSort(A, N, d)
{ Sorts N d-digit integers in the array A. }

    for j := d downto 1 do
    begin
        Initialize 10 groups to empty
        Initialize a counter for each group to 0

        for i := 1 to N do
        begin
            k := jᵗʰ digit of A[i]
            Place A[i] at the end of group k
            Increase kᵗʰ counter by 1
        end   { end for i }

        Replace the elements in A with all the elements in
            group 1, followed by all the elements in group 2,
            and so on.
    end { for j }
```

Analysis. From the pseudocode for the radix sort, you can see that this algorithm requires N moves each time it forms groups and N moves to combine them again into one group. The algorithm performs these $2 * N$

0123, 2154, 0222, 0004, 0283, 1560, 1061, 2150	Original array
(1560, 2150) (1061) (0222) (0123, 0283) (2154, 0004)	Grouped by fourth digit
1560, 2150, 1061, 0222, 0123, 0283, 2154, 0004	Combined
(0004) (0222, 0123) (2150, 2154) (1560, 1061) (0283)	Grouped by third digit
0004, 0222, 0123, 2150, 2154, 1560, 1061, 0283	Combined
(0004, 1061) (0123, 2150, 2154) (0222, 0283) (1560)	Grouped by second digit
0004, 1061, 0123, 2150, 2154, 0222, 0283, 1560	Combined
(0004, 0123, 0222, 0283) (1061, 1560) (2150, 2154)	Grouped by first digit
0004, 0123, 0222, 0283, 1061, 1560, 2150, 2154	Combined (sorted)

Figure 7-19

A radix sort of eight integers

Figure 7-20

Approximate growth rates with respect to time of seven sorting algorithms

	Worst Case	Average Case
Selection sort	N^2	N^2
Bubble sort	N^2	N^2
Insertion sort	N^2	N^2
Mergesort	N * log N	N * log N
Quicksort	N^2	N * log N
Radix sort	N	N
Heapsort	N * log N	N * log N

Even though radix sort is O(N), it is not appropriate as a general-purpose sorting algorithm

moves *d* times. Therefore, the radix sort requires $2 * N * d$ moves to sort *N* strings of *d* characters each. However, notice that no comparisons are necessary. Thus, radix sort is $O(N)$.

Despite its efficiency, radix sort has some difficulties that make it inappropriate as a general-purpose sorting algorithm. For example, to perform a radix sort of strings of uppercase letters, you need to accommodate 27 groups—one group for blanks and one for each letter. If there are *N* strings in the original data collection, each group must be able to contain *N* strings. For large *N* this requirement demands substantial memory, if you use arrays for both the original data and the resulting groups. However, you can save memory by using a linked list for each of the 27 groups. Thus, a radix sort is more appropriate for a linked list than for an array.

A Comparison of Sorting Algorithms

Figure 7-20 summarizes the worst-case and average-case orders of magnitude for the sorting algorithms that appear in this chapter. For reference purposes, we have included another algorithm—**heapsort**—here, even though you will not see it until Chapter 12.

SUMMARY

1. Order-of-magnitude analysis and Big O notation enable you to analyze the efficiency of an algorithm without regard for such factors as computer speed and programming skill that are beyond your control. When you compare the inherent efficiencies of algorithms, you typically concentrate only on significant differences in their growth-rate functions.

2. Worst-case analysis considers the maximum amount of work an algorithm will require on a problem of a given size, while average-case analysis considers the expected amount of work that it will require.

3. Quicksort and mergesort are two very efficient recursive sorting algorithms. In the "average" case, quicksort is among the fastest known sorting algorithms. However, for certain cases quicksort

can be significantly slower than other sorting algorithms. For example, quicksort's worst-case behavior is not nearly as good as mergesort. Fortunately, these cases rarely occur in practice. Mergesort is not quite as fast as quicksort in the average case, but its performance is consistently good in all cases. Mergesort has the disadvantage of requiring extra storage equal to the size of the array to be sorted.

COMMON PITFALLS / DEBUGGING

1. In general, you should avoid analyzing an algorithm solely by studying the running times of a specific implementation. Running times are influenced by such factors as programming style, the particular computer, and the data on which the program is run.

2. When comparing the efficiencies of various solutions, look only at significant differences. This rule is consistent with the multidimensional view of the cost of a computer program.

3. If a problem is small, do not overanalyze it. In such a situation, the primary concern should be simplicity. For example, if you are sorting an array that contains only a small number of elements—say, fewer than 50—a simple $O(N^2)$ algorithm such as an insertion sort is appropriate.

4. If you are sorting a very large array, an $O(N^2)$ algorithm could well be too inefficient. Although quicksort's worst-case behavior is $O(N^2)$, the worst case rarely occurs in practice. Quicksort is appropriate when you are confident that the data in the array to be sorted is arranged randomly.

SELF-TEST EXERCISES

1. Trace the selection sort as it sorts the following array into ascending order:

   20 80 40 25 60 30

2. Repeat Self-Test Exercise 1, but instead sort the array into descending order.

3. Trace the bubble sort as it sorts the following array into ascending order:

   25 30 20 80 40 60

4. Trace the insertion sort as it sorts the array in Self-Test Exercise 3 into ascending order.

5. Show that the mergesort algorithm satisfies the four criteria of recursion that Chapter 5 describes.

6. Trace `Quicksort`'s partitioning algorithm as it partitions the following array. Use the first element as the pivot.

    38 16 40 39 12 27

7. How many comparisons of array elements do the following loops contain?

    ```
    for j := 1 to N-1 do
    begin
        i := j+1;
        repeat
            if A[i] < A[j]
                then Swap(A[i], A[j]);
            i := i + 1
        until i > N
    end   {for}
    ```

8. Repeat Self-Test Exercise 7, but first replace the statement $i := j+1$ with $i := j$.

9. What order is an algorithm that has as a growth-rate function
    a. $8 * N^3 - 9 * N$ b. $7 * \log_2 N + 20$ c. $7 * \log_2 N + N$

10. Consider a sequential search of N data elements.
    a. If the data is sorted into ascending order, how can you determine that your desired element is not in the data collection without always making N comparisons?
    b. What is the order of the sequential search algorithm when the desired element is not in the data collection? Do this for both sorted and unsorted data, and consider the best, average, and worst cases.
    c. Show that if the sequential search algorithm finds the desired element in the data collection, then the algorithm's order does not depend upon whether or not the data is sorted.

EXERCISES

1. Trace the insertion sort as it sorts the following array into ascending order:

    20 80 40 25 60

2. Apply selection sort, bubble sort, and insertion sort to
    a. an inverted array: 8 6 4 2
    b. an ordered array: 2 4 6 8

3. Find an array that makes `BubbleSort` exhibit its worst behavior.

4. Revise the procedure `SelectionSort` so that it sorts records according to one field, which is the search key.

5. Write the procedure `SelectionSort` so that it uses recursion.

6. Trace mergesort as it sorts the following array into ascending order:

   20 80 40 25 60 30

7. Trace quicksort as it sorts the following array into ascending order:

   20 80 40 25 60 10 15

8. Suppose you remove the call to `Merge` from the `Mergesort` algorithm to obtain

```
Mystery(A, N)
{ Mystery algorithm for A[1.. N]. }

    if N > 1
        then
        begin
            Mergesort( Lefthalf(A) )
            Mergesort( Righthalf(A) )
        end

        else quit
```

What does this new algorithm do?

9. Show that any polynomial $f(x) = c_k x^k + c_{k-1} x^{k-1} + \cdots + c_1 x + c_0$ is $O(x^k)$.

10. Show that for all constants $a, b > 1$, $f(N)$ is $O(\log_a N)$ if and only if $f(N)$ is $O(\log_b N)$. Thus, you can omit the base when you write $O(\log N)$. (*Hint*: Use the identity $\log_a N = \log_b N / \log_b a$ for all constants $a, b > 1$.)

11. Recall that the partition procedure that `Quicksort` uses moves one item at a time from the unknown region into the appropriate region S_1 or S_2. Note that if the item to be moved belongs in region S_1, and if S_2 is empty, then the procedure will swap an array element with itself. Modify the partition procedure to eliminate this unnecessary swapping.

12. You can choose any element of the array as pivot in `Quicksort`. Simply interchange elements so that your pivot is in `A[F]`. One way to choose a pivot is to take the middle value of the three values `A[1]`, `A[L]`, and `A[(F + L) div 2]`. How many recursive calls are necessary to sort an array of size N if you always choose the pivot in this way?

13. Use invariants to show that the procedure `SelectionSort` is correct.

14. Add a counter to the procedures `InsertionSort` and `Mergesort` that counts the number of comparisons that are made. Run the two procedures on problems of various sizes. On what size does the difference in the number of comparisons become significant? How does

this size compare with the size that the Big O's for these algorithms predict?

*15. Describe an iterative version of *Mergesort*. Define an appropriate invariant and show the correctness of your algorithm.

16. One criterion used to evaluate sorting algorithms is stability. A sorting algorithm is **stable** if it does not exchange records with the same sort key. That is, records with the same sort key (possibly differing in other fields) will maintain their positions relative to one another. For example, you might want to take an array of student records that is sorted by name and produce an array that is sorted by class. Sorting the array (by class) with a stable sorting algorithm will ensure that within each class the students will remain sorted by name. Some applications mandate a stable sorting algorithm. Others do not. Which of the sorting algorithms described in this chapter are stable?

17. When we introduced the radix sort, we sorted a hand of cards by first ordering the cards by rank and then by suit. To implement a radix sort for this example, you could use two characters to represent a card, if you used T to represent a 10. For example, S2 is the 2 of spades and HT is the 10 of hearts.

   a. Trace the radix sort for this example.

   b. Suppose that you did not use T to represent a 10—that is, suppose that H10 is the 10 of hearts—and that you padded the two-character strings on the right with a blank to form three-character strings. How would a radix sort order the entire deck of cards in this case?

18. You can sort a large array of integers that are in the range 1..100 by using an array `count[1..100]` to count the number of occurrences of each integer in the range 1..100. Fill in the details of this sorting algorithm, which is called a **bucket sort**, and write a Pascal procedure that implements it. What is the order of the bucket sort? Why is the bucket sort not useful as a general sorting algorithm?

19. Implement the radix sort for both a linked list and an array.

20. Besides the radix sort, are there other sorting algorithms that are appropriate for linked lists? Discuss sorting a linked list and implement several procedures that do so.

PROJECT

21. a. Modify the partition procedure for *Quicksort* so that S_1 and S_2 will never be empty.

   b. Another partitioning strategy for *Quicksort* is possible. Let an index *low* traverse the array segment *A[F..L]* from *F* to *L* and stop when it encounters the first element that is greater than the pivot element. Similarly, let a second index *high* traverse the array segment from L to F and stop when it encounters the first element that is smaller than the pivot element. Then swap these two elements, increment *low*, decrement *high*, and continue until *high* and *low* meet somewhere in the middle. Implement this version of *Quicksort* in Pascal. How can you ensure that the regions S_1 and S_2 are not empty?

c. There are several variations of this partitioning strategy. What other strategies can you think of? How do they compare to the two that have been given?

III

Problem Solving with Abstract Data Types

CHAPTER *8*

Stacks

PREVIEW   This chapter introduces a well-known ADT called a stack and presents both array-based and pointer-based implementations. You will see how the operations on a stack give it a last-in, first-out behavior. Two of the several important applications of a stack that the chapter considers are evaluating algebraic expressions and searching for a path between two points. Finally, the chapter discusses the important relationship between stacks and recursion.

INTRODUCTION

Parts I and II of this book reviewed aspects of problem solving that are closely related to programming issues; developed the linked list, which is an important data structure that you will see throughout this book; introduced recursion, a problem-solving tool useful in the construction of algorithms; studied the efficiency of algorithms; and compared sorting algorithms. The primary concerns of Parts III and IV are the aspects of problem solving that involve the *management of data*—that is, the identification and implementation of some of the more common data-management operations.

Part III deals both with data organized by *position* and with data organized by *value*. In general, these organizations are appropriate for applications of rather different natures. For example, if an application needs to ask a question about the first person in a line, the data should be organized by position. On the other hand, if an application needs to ask a question about the employee named Smith, the data should be organized by value. Part IV considers a few advanced techniques for organizing data by value, including techniques for organizing data stored in an external file.

Our study of data management has three aspects. The first is the identification of useful sets of operations—that is, the identification of abstract data types. The second aspect is the presentation of applications that use these abstract data types. The third aspect is the development of implementations for the abstract data types—that is, the development of data structures. As you will discover, the nature of the operations of an abstract data type, along with the application in which you will use it, greatly influence the choice of its implementation.

The next section defines an important ADT known as a stack and, in doing so, illustrates how to use an ADT approach in program development.

THE STACK AS AN EXAMPLE OF AN ADT IN PROGRAM DEVELOPMENT

Suppose that you want to read a single line of text and then print it in reversed order. Assume that your terminal has no backspace key; thus, if you make a data-entry error, you must use the # character to correct your mistake as follows: Each # erases the previous character entered, but consecutive # characters do not cancel out; instead they are applied in sequence and so erase several characters. For instance, if the input line is

```
abc defgh#2klmnopqr##wxyz
```

the corrected input would be

```
abc defg2klmnopwxyz
```

Given that this line is the corrected input, the reversed output is

```
zyxwponmlk2gfed cba
```

Consider now the process of constructing a solution to this problem. One design decision that you must make eventually is how to store the input line. In accordance with the ADT approach, you should postpone this decision until you have a better idea of what operations you will need to perform on the data. You can begin by breaking the problem into two tasks:

Two tasks solve the problem

```
Read the line, correcting "errors" along the way
Print the line in reversed order
```

You can refine the first of these tasks as

Initial refinement of the first task

```
{ Read the line, correcting "errors" along the way }
while (not end of line) do
begin
    Read a new character Ch
    if Ch is not a '#'
        then add Ch to the data structure
        else remove from the data structure the
            item that was added most recently
end
```

This refinement calls to attention two of the operations that the ADT will have to include:

Two ADT operations that are required

- Insert a new item into the data structure.
- Remove from the data structure the item that was added most recently.

Notice that there is a potential for trouble if you type a # when the data structure is empty, that is, when there are no characters in the data structure. If this situation should occur, you have two options: (1) have the program terminate and print an error message, or (2) have the program ignore the # and continue. Either option is reasonable: Suppose that you decide to ignore the # and continue. Therefore, the algorithm becomes

The "read and correct" algorithm

```
{ Read the line, correcting "errors" along the way }
while (not end of line) do
```

```
begin
    Read a new character Ch
    if Ch is not a '#' then
        Add Ch to the data structure
    else if the data structure is not empty then
        Remove from the data structure the
            item that was added most recently
    else ignore the #
end
```

From this pseudocode you can identify a third operation required by the ADT:

- *Determine whether the data structure is empty.*

Another ADT operation that is required

By reading the line, you have performed the first task, so now move on to the second task, printing the line in reversed order. At first, it appears that you can accomplish this task by using the three ADT operations already identified, as follows:

```
{ Print the line in reversed order }
while the data structure is not empty do
begin
    Remove from the data structure the item
        that was added most recently
    Print .....Uh, Oh!
end
```

A false start at printing the line in reverse order

Because the *Remove* operation deletes the item from the data structure, the item is gone, so you cannot print it. What you should have done was to *retrieve* from the data structure the item that was added most recently. Recall that the *Retrieve* operation in Chapter 4 meant to *look at, but leave unchanged*. Only after retrieving and printing the item should you remove it from the data structure. The print-backward algorithm therefore becomes

```
{ Print the line in reversed order }
while the data structure is not empty do
begin
    Retrieve from the data structure the item
        that was added most recently and put it in Ch
    Print Ch
    Remove from the data structure the item
        that was added most recently
end
```

The "print-backward" algorithm

Thus, a fourth operation is required by the ADT:

- *Retrieve from the data structure the item that was added most recently.*

Another ADT operation that is required

You now have a high-level solution to the problem. Although you have yet to think about what the data structure is, you know that you must be able to perform the following four operations:

*Four operations that the solu-
tion requires*

- `Determine whether the data structure is empty.`
- `Insert a new item into the data structure.`
- `Remove from the data structure the item that was added most recently.`
- `Retrieve from the data structure the item that was added most recently.`

These operations define the ADT you need. It turns out that this is a very well-known ADT, which is usually called a **stack**.

There is a fifth operation, which seems so obvious that there might be a tendency to neglect it. This operation creates a new stack. In terms of a Pascal implementation, `Create` corresponds roughly to declaring a variable of the appropriate type and initializing the variable so that it represents an empty stack. The `Create` operation is also important from a more theoretical point of view, as it allows you to state precisely the results of performing a sequence of one or more operations beginning with an empty stack.

Thus, the following operations define the ADT stack. The operation names given here conform to convention:

KEY CONCEPTS   **ADT Stack Operations**

`Create(S)`
`{ Creates an empty stack S. }`

`IsEmpty(S)`
`{ Determines if stack S is empty. }`

`Push(S, newitem)`
`{ Adds newitem to stack S. }`

`Pop(S)`
`{ Removes from stack S the item that was added most`
`  recently. }`

`StackTop(S)`
`{ Retrieves from stack S the item that was added`
`  most recently, leaving S unchanged. }`

As was mentioned in Chapter 4, intuitive definitions such as these are not really sufficient to define an ADT formally. For example, to capture formally the intuitive notion that the last item inserted into the stack is the first item to be removed, you could write an axiom such as

```
Pop(Push(S, newitem)) = S
```

An example of an axiom

In addition, before you implement any ADT operations, you should specify both their preconditions and their postconditions. Realize, however, that during program design, the first attempt at specification is often informal and is only later made precise by the writing of preconditions and postconditions. The preconditions and postconditions for the ADT stack operations appear later in this chapter as comments in their Pascal implementations.

You can now put together the solution to the line-reversal problem. You can write a nearly complete pseudocode solution by using the previous stack operations. Notice that not only are these operations as yet unwritten, but also that you do not know what a stack looks like. Because the ADT approach builds a wall around the implementation of the stack, you can write the rest of the program independently of the stack's implementation. So long as the rest of the program correctly uses the ADT operations—that is, so long as it honors the contract—it will work regardless of how you implement the ADT.

The pseudocode solution follows:

```
program LineReverse

{ The following subprograms are the specified stack
operations. }

Create(S)          { Creates an empty stack }

IsEmpty(S)         { Determines if stack is empty }

Push(S, newitem)   { Adds newitem to stack }

Pop(S)             { Removes most recently added item from
                     stack }

StackTop(S)        { Retrieves most recently added item from
                     stack}

ReadAndCorrect(S)
{ Reads the input line. For each character read, either
  enters it into stack S or, if it is #, corrects the
  contents of S. }

begin
    while (not end of line) do
    begin
        read(newchar)

        if newchar <> '#' then
            Push(S, newchar)
        else if not IsEmpty(S) then
            Pop(S)
```

```
    end   { while }
end   { ReadAndCorrect }

PrintBackward(S)
{ Prints the reversed line by printing contents of stack S. }
begin
    while ( not IsEmpty(S) ) do
    begin
        newchar := StackTop(S)
        write(newchar)
        Pop(S)
    end
end   { PrintBackward }

begin   { Main Program }
    Create(S)
    ReadAndCorrect(S)
    PrintBackward(S)
end   { Program }
```

MORE ON THE NATURE OF THE ABSTRACT DATA TYPE STACK

The term "stack" is intended to conjure up visions of objects encountered in daily life, such as a stack of dishes in the school cafeteria, a stack of books on your desk, or a stack of assignments waiting for you to work on. In common English usage, "stack of" and "pile of" are synonymous. To computer scientists, however, a stack is not just any old pile. A stack of objects has the property that the last object placed on the stack will be the

Last in, first out first object removed. This property is commonly referred to as **last in, first out**, or simply LIFO.

A stack of dishes in a cafeteria makes a very good analogy of the abstract data type stack, as Figure 8-1 illustrates. As new dishes are added, the old dishes drop farther into the well beneath the surface. At any particular time, only the dish last placed on the stack is above the surface and visible. This dish is the one that must be removed next. In general, the dishes are removed in exactly the opposite order from that in which they were added.

The LIFO property of stacks seems inherently unfair. Think of the poor person who finally gets the last dish on the cafeteria's stack, a dish that may have been placed there six years ago. Or how would you like to be the first person to arrive on the stack for a movie—as opposed to the line for a movie. You would be the last person allowed in! These examples demonstrate the reason that stacks are not especially prevalent in everyday life. The property that we usually desire in our daily lives is **first in, first out**, or FIFO. A **queue**, which we present in the next chapter, is the abstract data type with the FIFO property. Most people would much prefer to wait in a movie *queue*—as a line is commonly called in Britain—than in a movie *stack*. However, while the LIFO property of stacks is not appropriate for very many day-to-day situations, it is precisely what is needed for a large number of problems that arise in computer science.

Notice how well the analogy holds between the abstract data type stack and the stack of cafeteria dishes. The five operations that define the ADT stack are the *only* operations of the ADT stack, and they correspond to the only things that you can do to a stack of dishes. You can determine whether the stack of dishes is empty but not how many dishes are on the stack; you can inspect the top dish but no other dish; you can place a dish on top of the stack but at no other position; and you can remove a dish from the top of the stack but from no other position. If you were permitted to perform any other operations, or if you were not permitted to perform all five of the operations, the data type would not be a stack.

We should point out, however, that there are some common variations of our definition of a stack. For example, you could define *Pop(S, item)*, which removes the top item and returns its value in *item*, and omit the operation *StackTop(S)*. If you were to adopt this definition of a stack, how could you inspect the top item of a stack without removing it? If this inspection were necessary, you could write an auxiliary function *AuxStackTop* that utilizes both *Pop* and *Push* as follows:

An alternate definition of Pop

```
function AuxStackTop(S)

    Pop(S, item)
    Push(S, item)
    AuxStackTop := item
```

This function is a bit awkward, but on the other hand it is very common to have to inspect and remove the top item of a stack simultaneously. Whereas the original definition of a stack requires the sequence

```
item := StackTop(S)
Pop(S)
```

to make a copy of the top item and then remove it, this task is accomplished by the single operation

```
Pop(S, item)
```

under the alternative definition. Both definitions of a stack are reasonable, each having its relative advantage. For the remainder of this book, we shall use the original definition presented.

Figure 8-1

Stack of cafeteria dishes

IMPLEMENTATIONS OF THE ADT STACK

This section develops two Pascal implementations of the ADT stack: array based and pointer based. The array-based implementation uses an array to represent the stack, while the pointer-based implementation uses a linked list. Figure 8-2 illustrates these two implementations. Once again the issue

Fixed size versus dynamic size

of fixed versus dynamic size is the primary consideration for making the choice between implementations. If you were to choose an array-based implementation, you would have to place a restriction on the *Push* operation so that it would not attempt to add an item to the stack if the stack's size limit, which is the size of the array, has been reached. If this restriction is not acceptable, you must use a pointer-based implementation. For the line-reversal problem, for example, it is conceivable that the fixed-size restriction does not present a problem: If the terminal allows a line length of only 80 characters, you could use the array-based implementation, which is described in the next section.

An Array-Based Implementation of the ADT Stack

Consider the array-based implementation of the ADT stack in Figure 8-3. This figure suggests that you represent a stack with a record that contains both the array *Items* and an index *Top* to a position in *Items*. In Pascal, the stack *S* could be declared as follows:

```
const   maxstack = <maximum size of stack>;

type    itemtype = <desired type of stack item>;

        stack  = record
             Top   : 0..maxstack;
             Items : array[1..maxstack] of itemtype
        end;

var     S : stack
```

Assuming the previous type definitions, the following Pascal subprograms provide an array-based implementation of the ADT stack:

```
{ ************************************************************
  BASIC STACK OPERATIONS — Array-Based Implementation

     Create, IsEmpty, Push, Pop, and StackTop

  ************************************************************ }
procedure Create(var S : stack);
{ ----------------------------------------------------------
  Creates an empty stack.
  Precondition: None.
  Postcondition: The stack S is empty.
  ---------------------------------------------------------- }
```

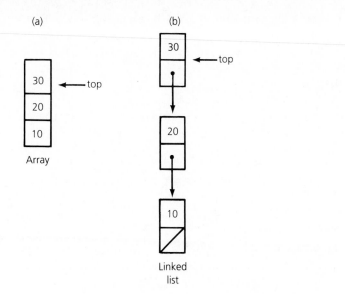

Figure 8-2

Implementations of the ADT stack: (a) array based; (b) pointer based

Figure 8-3

An array-based implementation

```
begin
    S.Top := 0
end;  { Create }

function IsEmpty(S : stack) : boolean;
{ -----------------------------------------------------------
  Determines if a stack is empty.
  Precondition: Stack S has been created.
  Postcondition: Returns true if S is empty, else returns
  false.
  ----------------------------------------------------------- }
begin
    IsEmpty := (S.Top = 0)
end;  { IsEmpty }

procedure Push(var S : stack; newitem : itemtype;
               var success : boolean);
{ -----------------------------------------------------------
  Adds an item to the top of a stack.
  Precondition: Stack S has been created.
  Postcondition: If S is not full, newitem is placed on the
```

```
    top of the stack S and success is set to true; otherwise
    success is set to false.
    Note: S is full if it has maxstack items.
    ------------------------------------------------------ }
begin
    if S.Top = maxstack
       then success := false           { stack is full }
       else
       begin
           S.Top := S.Top + 1;
           S.Items[S.Top] := newitem;
           success := true
       end
end;  { Push }

procedure Pop(var S : stack; var success : boolean);
{ ------------------------------------------------------
  Removes the top of a stack.
  Precondition: Stack S has been created.
  Postcondition: If S is not empty, the item that was added
  most recently to S is removed and success is set to true.
  However, if S is empty, deletion is impossible and success
  is set to false.
  ------------------------------------------------------ }
begin
    if IsEmpty(S)
       then success := false           { stack is empty }
       else
       begin
           S.Top := S.Top - 1;
           success := true
       end
end;  { Pop }

procedure StackTop(S : stack; var getitem : itemtype;
                   var success : boolean);
{ ------------------------------------------------------
  Retrieves the top of a stack.
  Precondition: Stack S has been created.
  Postcondition: If S is not empty, getitem contains the
  item that was added most recently to S and success is set
  to true. However, if S is empty, the operation fails and
  success is set to false. S is unchanged.
  ------------------------------------------------------ }
begin
    if IsEmpty(S)
    then success := false           { stack is empty }
    else
```

```
      begin
          getitem := S.Items[S.Top];
          success := true
      end
end;  { StackTop }
```

There are several points to make about this implementation. Consider the point when the programmer and the program designer draw a contract for the implementation of the ADT stack in Pascal. Suppose that you are the programmer. The program designer tells you that the following five operations are needed:

```
Create(S)            { Creates an empty stack. }

IsEmpty(S)           { Determines whether stack is empty. }

Push(S, newitem)     { Adds newitem to stack. }

Pop(S)               { Removes most recently added item from
                       stack }

StackTop(S)          { Retrieves most recently added item from
                       stack, leaving stack unchanged. }
```

In the course of developing these Pascal routines, you and the program designer would have to work out a few details of the contract. For example, consider the implementation of the *Push* operation. Presumably, you and the designer determined at the outset that the fixed-size restriction of the array-based implementation was acceptable. Even so, both of you still must agree on the details of how the *Push* operation should handle an attempt to add an item to a full stack. The decision made in the previous implementation is that the procedure *Push* will return a flag—that is, a boolean-valued variable parameter—with the value *false* if *Push* attempts to add an item to a full stack. This flag allows the calling routine to take appropriate action.

The designer and the programmer must agree on some details in their contract

Furthermore, you and the designer would have to decide how to handle two other eventualities: What to do if either *StackTop* or *Pop* is called when the stack is empty. The previous implementation handles these situations in a manner analogous to the way it handles the stack-full situation. If either *StackTop* or *Pop* is called with an empty stack, it will return a flag with the value *false*, thereby allowing the calling routine to take appropriate action.

Finally, you and the designer need to decide whether *StackTop* is a procedure or a function. In the previous implementation, *StackTop* is a procedure. The primary reason for this choice is to allow full generality of what *itemtype* can be—that is, what type of items the stack can contain. Because Pascal allows functions to return only simple values, you could not use a function *StackTop* if *itemtype* were, for instance, a record or an array. The limitations of Pascal have forced you to bend slightly the definition of a stack for the sake of generality.

These decisions regarding the boolean *success* parameters and the proper calling sequences for the operations all should be summarized in the final version of the contract between the designer and the programmer.

A Pointer-Based Implementation of the ADT Stack

Many applications require a pointer-based implementation of a stack so that it can grow and shrink dynamically. Figure 8-4 illustrates a pointer-based implementation of a stack where *S* is a pointer to the head of a linked list of items.

In Pascal, this implementation is realized as follows:

```
type    itemtype = <desired type of stack item>;
        nodeptr  = ^node;
        node = record
            item : itemtype;
            next : nodeptr
        end;

        stack = nodeptr;

var     S : stack
```

Assuming the previous type definitions, the following Pascal routines provide a pointer-based implementation of the ADT stack:

```
{ ***********************************************************
  BASIC STACK OPERATIONS - Pointer-Based Implementation

      Create, IsEmpty, Push, Pop, and StackTop

  *********************************************************** }
procedure Create(var S : stack);
{ ---------------------------------------------------------
  Creates an empty stack.
  Precondition: None.
  Postcondition: The stack S is empty.
  --------------------------------------------------------- }
begin
   S := nil
end;   { Create }

function IsEmpty(S : stack) : boolean;
{ ---------------------------------------------------------
  Determines if a stack is empty.
  Precondition: Stack S has been created.
  Postcondition: Returns true if S is empty, else returns
  false.
  --------------------------------------------------------- }
```

S

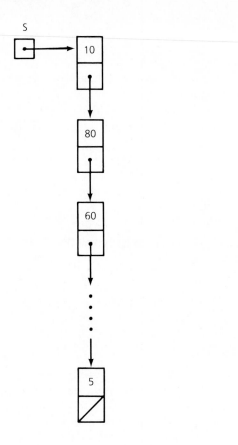

Figure 8-4

**A pointer-based
implementation**

```
begin
    IsEmpty := (S = nil)
end;  { IsEmpty }

procedure Push(var S : stack; newitem : itemtype );
{ ---------------------------------------------------------
  Adds an item to the top of a stack.
  Precondition: Stack S has been created.
  Postcondition: newitem is placed on the top of the stack S.
  --------------------------------------------------------- }
var p : nodeptr;
begin
    { create a new node }
    new(p);
    p^.item := newitem;

    { insert the new node }
    p^.next := S;
    S := p
end;  { Push }
```

```
procedure Pop(var S : stack; var success : boolean);
{ ----------------------------------------------------------
  Removes the top of a stack.
  Precondition: Stack S has been created.
  Postcondition: If S is not empty, the item that was added
  most recently to S is removed and success is set to true.
  However, if S is empty, deletion is impossible and success
  is set to false.
  ---------------------------------------------------------- }
var delptr : nodeptr;
begin
    if IsEmpty(S)
        then success := false
        else
        begin
            delptr := S;
            S := S^.next;
            dispose(delptr);
            success := true
        end
end;   { Pop }

procedure StackTop(S : stack; var getitem : itemtype;
                   var success : boolean);
{ ----------------------------------------------------------
  Retrieves the top of a stack.
  Precondition: Stack S has been created.
  Postcondition: If S is not empty, getitem contains the
  item that was added most recently to S and success is set
  to true. However, if S is empty, the operation fails and
  success is set to false. S is unchanged.
  ---------------------------------------------------------- }
begin
    if IsEmpty(S)
        then success := false
        else
        begin
            getitem := S^.item;
            success := true
        end
end;   { StackTop }
```

As they did with the array-based implementation, here the program
designer and the programmer must work out some points in the contract.
There is no concern about the stack-full condition for the *Push* operation,
as there was in the array-based implementation, but the comments made
about boolean flags with respect to the array-based implementation's *Pop*
and *StackTop* operations apply here as well. As it did for the array-based

implementation, the final version of the contract for the pointer-based implementation should include all this information.

TWO SIMPLE APPLICATIONS OF THE ADT STACK

This section and the next present several applications for which the LIFO property of stacks is appropriate. The first two examples are rather simple; the others are more substantial. Keep in mind throughout that you are using the ADT stack to solve the problems. You can use the five stack operations, but you may not assume any particular implementation. You choose a specific implementation only as a last step.

Checking for Balanced Parentheses

One application of a stack is to verify that a given input string contains balanced parentheses. For example, the parentheses in the string

        abc(defg(ijk)(l(mn))op)qr

are balanced, while the parentheses in the string

        abc(def))(ghij(kl)m

are not balanced. You can check whether a string contains balanced parentheses by traversing it from left to right. As you move from left to right, you match each successive close parenthesis ")" with the most recently encountered unmatched open parenthesis "("; that is, the "(" must be to the left of the current ")". The parentheses are balanced if

1. Each time you encounter a ")", it matches an already encountered "("
2. When you reach the end of the string, you have matched each "("

Requirements for balanced parentheses

The solution requires that you keep track of each unmatched "(" and discard one each time you encounter a ")". One way to perform this task is to push each "(" encountered onto a stack and pop one off each time you encounter a ")". Thus, a first-draft pseudocode solution is

Initial draft of a solution

```
while not at the end of the string do
begin
    if the next character is a '(' then
        Push(S, '(')
    else if the character is a ')' then
        Pop(S)
end
```

Although this solution correctly keeps track of parentheses, missing from it are the checks that conditions 1 and 2 are met—that is, that the parentheses are indeed balanced. To verify condition 1 when a ")" is encountered, you must check to see whether the stack is empty before popping from it. If it is empty, you terminate the loop and report that the string is not balanced. To verify condition 2, you check that the stack is empty when the end of the string is reached.

The pseudocode solution thus becomes

A detailed pseudocode solution

```
Create(S)
continue := true
while (not eoln) and continue do
begin
    { ignore all characters other than parentheses }
    if (input^ <> ')') and (input^ <> '(') then
        get(input)

    { push an open parenthesis }
    else if input^ = '(' then
    begin
        Push(S, '(')
        get(input)
    end

    { close parenthesis: pop a matching open parenthesis }
    else if not IsEmpty(S) then
    begin
        Pop(S)
        get(input)
    end

    { close parenthesis, but no matching open parenthesis }
    else continue := false
end   { while }

{ note that eoln cannot be true if continue
  is false, so no test of continue is necessary }
if eoln and IsEmpty(S)
    then is balanced
    else not balanced
```

Figure 8-5 shows the stacks that result when this algorithm is applied to several simple examples.

It may have occurred to you that a simpler solution to this problem is possible. You need only keep a count of the current number of unmatched left parentheses. Each time you encounter a left parenthesis, you increment the count; each time you encounter a right parenthesis, you decrement the count. If this count ever falls below zero or if it is greater than zero when the end of the string is reached, then the string is unbalanced. You need not actually store the left parentheses on a stack. However, the stack-based solution is conceptually useful as it previews more legitimate uses of stacks, such as those in the next example.

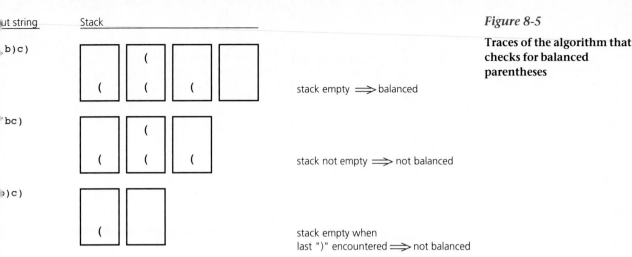

ut string   Stack

b)c)

stack empty ⟹ balanced

bc)

stack not empty ⟹ not balanced

)c)

stack empty when
last ")" encountered ⟹ not balanced

Figure 8-5

Traces of the algorithm that checks for balanced parentheses

Exercise 2 at the end of this chapter asks you to extend the algorithm given here to check for balanced square brackets and braces in addition to parentheses.

Recognizing Strings in a Language

Consider the problem of recognizing whether or not a particular string is in the language

$L = \{w\$w' : w$ is string of characters other than \$, w' = reverse(w) $\}$

For example, the string *ABC\$CBA* is in the language. (Exercise 10 in Chapter 6 introduced a similar language.) A stack is very useful in determining whether a given string is in L. If you traverse the first half of the string and push each character onto a stack, when you reach the \$ you can undo the process: For each character in the second half of the string, you pop a character off the stack. However, you must match the popped character with the current character in the string to ensure that the second half of the string is the reverse of the first half. The stack must be empty when—and only when—you reach the end of the string; otherwise, one "half" of the string is longer than the other, and so the string is not in L.

The following algorithm implements this strategy. To avoid unnecessary complications, assume that the input string contains exactly one \$.

```
Create(S)

{ push the characters in string w onto stack }
while (input^ <> '$') do
begin
    Push(S,input^)
    get(input)
end
```

A pseudocode recognition algorithm for the language **L**

```
{ skip the $ }
get(input)

{ match the reverse of w }
continue := true
while (not eoln) and continue do
begin
    { first half is shorter than second half }
    if IsEmpty(S) then
      continue := false

    { characters do not match }
    else if (StackTop(S) <> input^) then
      continue := false

    { characters match }
    else
    begin
      Pop(S)
      get(input)
    end
end   { while }

{ note that eoln cannot be true if continue
  is false, so no test of continue is needed }
if eoln and IsEmpty(S)
    then in language
    else not in language
```

Notice that the two algorithms presented in this section depend only on the fact that the stack operations are supported and not on how the stack is implemented. The primary consideration in choosing between an array-based and a pointer-based implementation for the stack in the previous examples is whether there is a reasonable limit on the size of the string to be analyzed. For example, if the string is stored in an array, an array-based stack implementation can use a maximum stack size that corresponds to the size of the array that holds the string. On the other hand, if the string is stored in a linked list or in a file, a pointer-based stack implementation might be required.

MORE COMPLEX APPLICATIONS OF STACKS

This section contains several problems that you can solve neatly by using the ADT stack. The first problems involve algebraic expressions, which were discussed in Chapter 6.

Algebraic Expressions

Chapter 6 presented recursive grammars that specified the syntax of algebraic expressions. Recall that prefix and postfix expressions avoid the ambiguity inherent in the evaluation of infix expressions. We now present stack-based solutions to the problems of evaluating infix and postfix expressions. To avoid distracting programming issues, we will allow only the binary operators *, /, +, and –, and disallow unary operators and exponentiation.

The strategy we shall adopt here is first to develop an algorithm for evaluating postfix expressions and then to develop an algorithm for transforming an infix expression into an equivalent postfix expression. This strategy eliminates the need for an algorithm that directly evaluates infix expressions, a more difficult problem.

To evaluate an infix expression, first convert it to postfix form and then evaluate the postfix expression

Evaluating postfix expressions.   Consider an example that illustrates how you can evaluate a postfix expression. Some hand-held calculators use a postfix convention. For example, to compute the value of

$$2 * (3 + 4)$$

you would enter the sequence 2, 3, 4, +, *, which corresponds to the postfix expression

$$2\ 3\ 4 + *$$

Each time you enter an operand, the calculator pushes it onto a stack. When you enter an operator, the calculator applies it to the top two operands on the stack, pops the operands from the stack, and pushes the result of the operation onto the stack. Thus, the action of the calculator for the previous sequence is as shown in Figure 8-6. The final result, 14, is on the

Key entered	Calculator action	Stack S
2	Push(S, 2)	2
3	Push(S, 3)	2 3
4	Push(S, 4)	2 3 4
+	oprnd2 ← StackTop(S)	2 3 4
	Pop(S)	2 3
	oprnd1 ← StackTop(S)	2 3
	Pop(S)	2
	result ← oprnd1 + oprnd2	2
	Push(S, result)	2 7
*	oprnd2 ← StackTop(S)	2 7
	Pop(S)	2
	oprnd1 ← StackTop(S)	2
	Pop(S)	
	result ← oprnd1 * oprnd2	
	Push(S, result)	14

Figure 8-6

The action of a postfix calculator when evaluting the expression 2 * (3 + 4)

top of the stack. Thus, the ADT stack provides the required operations for this problem.

You can formalize the action of the calculator to obtain an algorithm that evaluates a postfix expression, which is entered as a string of characters. To avoid issues that cloud the algorithm with programming details, assume that

Simplifying assumptions

- The string is a syntactically correct postfix expression.
- There are no unary operators.
- There is no exponentiation operator.
- Operands are single uppercase letters that represent integer values.

A pseudocode algorithm that evaluates postfix expressions

```
for each character Ch in the string do
begin
    if Ch is an operator named op
        then
        begin
            { evaluate and push the result }
            oprnd2 := StackTop(S)
            Pop(S)
            oprnd1 := StackTop(S)
            Pop(S)
            result := oprnd1 op oprnd2
            Push(S, result)
        end   { then }

        else Push(S, Ch) { Ch is an operand }
end
```

Upon termination of the algorithm, the value of the expression will be on the top of the stack. Exercise 11 at the end of this chapter asks you to implement this algorithm.

Converting infix expressions to postfix form.   The next problem is to convert an infix expression into a postfix expression. Taken together, the solution to the previous problem of evaluating a postfix expression and the solution to this new problem provide a way to evaluate infix expressions.

The infix expressions here are the familiar ones. They allow parentheses, operator precedence, and left-to-right association. If you manually convert a few infix expressions to postfix form, you will discover three important facts:

Facts about converting from infix to postfix

- The operands always stay in the same order with respect to one another.
- An operator will move only "to the right" with respect to the operands; that is, if, in the infix expression, the operand X pre-

cedes the operator *op,* it is also true that in the postfix expression the operand *X* precedes the operator *op.*

- All parentheses are removed.

As a consequence of these three facts, the primary task of the conversion algorithm is determining where to place each operator.

The following high-level pseudocode solution converts an infix expression to a postfix expression, which is the string *PE*:

```
Initialize PE to the null string
for each character Ch in the infix expression do
   case Ch of
      Ch is an operand    : Append Ch to the end of PE
      Ch is an operator   : Store Ch until it can be
                            determined where to place it
      Ch is '(' or ')'    : Discard Ch
   end  { case }
```

A high-level algorithm that converts an infix expression to postfix form

You may have guessed that you really do not want simply to discard the parentheses, as they play an important role in determining the placement of the operators. Because in any infix expression a set of matching parentheses defines an isolated unit that consists of an operator and its two operands, the algorithm must evaluate the unit independently of the rest of the expression. Regardless of what the rest of the expression looks like, the operator within the unit belongs with the operands in that unit. The parentheses tell the rest of the expression

> *You can have the value of this unit after it is evaluated; simply ignore the operators and operands inside.*

Parentheses are thus one of the factors that determine the placement of the operators in the postfix expression. The other factors are precedence and left-to-right association.

Parentheses, operator precedence, and left-to-right association determine where to place operators in the postfix expression

If the infix expression were always fully parenthesized, the conversion to postfix form would be conceptually straightforward. Because each operator would correspond to a pair of parentheses, you would simply move the operator to the position marked by the ")"—this position follows the operands of the operator. All parentheses would then be removed. For example, consider the infix expression

$$((A + B) \star C)$$

First, you move each operator to the position marked by its corresponding ")":

$$((A\ B)\ C\ )$$
$$+\quad \star$$

Converting a fully parenthesized infix expression to postfix form is simple

Next, you remove the parentheses:

$$A\ B + C \star$$

The actual problem is more difficult, however, because the infix expression is not always fully parenthesized. Instead, the problem allows precedence and left-to-right association, which requires a more complex algorithm. The following is a high-level description of what you must do when you encounter each character as you read the infix string from left to right.

Five steps in the conversion process

1. When an operand is encountered, append it to the output string *PE*. *Justification*: The order of the operands in the postfix expression agrees with the order in the infix expression, and the operands that appear to the left of an operator in the infix expression also appear to its left in the postfix expression.

2. Push each "(" onto the stack.

3. When you encounter a ")", you pop operators off the stack, appending them to the end of *PE* until you encounter the matching "(". *Justification*: Within a "( )" grouping, precedence and left-to-right association determine the order of the operators, and Step 4, which follows, has already ordered the operators in accordance with these rules.

4. When you encounter an operator, if the stack is empty, push the operator onto the stack. However, if the stack is not empty, pop operators of greater or equal precedence from the stack, appending them to *PE*. You stop when you encounter either a "(" or an operator of lower precedence or when the stack becomes empty. You then push the new operator onto the stack. Thus, this step orders the operators by precedence and in accordance with left-to-right association. Notice that you continue popping from the stack until you encounter an operator of strictly lower precedence than the current operator in the infix expression. You do not stop on equality, because the left-to-right association rule says that in case of a tie in precedence, the leftmost operator is applied first—and this operator is the one that is already on the stack.

5. When you reach the end of the string, you append the remaining contents of the stack to *PE*.

For example, Figure 8-7 traces the action of the algorithm on the infix expression $A-(B+C*D)/E$, assuming that the stack S and the string *PE* are initially empty. *PE* contains the resulting postfix expression $ABCD*+E/-$.

You can use the previous five-step description of the algorithm to develop a fairly concise pseudocode solution. Both the stack S and the postfix expression *PE* are empty initially. In the pseudocode that follows, the symbol · means concatenate (append), so *PE* · *x* means concatenate the string currently in *PE* and the character *x*—that is, follow the string in *PE* with the character *x*.

A pseudocode algorithm that converts an infix expression to postfix form

```
for each character Ch in the infix expression do
   case Ch of
      operand :  PE := PE · Ch
      '(' :  Push(S, Ch)
```

```
')' :    begin { pop down to the matching open
                   parenthesis}
              while StackTop(S) <> '(' do
              begin
                  PE := PE · StackTop(S)
                  Pop(S)
              end  { while }

              Pop(S)  { remove the open parenthesis }
         end  { ')' }

  operator :

       begin
           while not IsEmpty(S) Cand ((StackTop(S) <> '(')
               and (precedence(StackTop(S)) >=
                                    precedence(Ch))) do
           begin
               PE := PE · StackTop(S)
               Pop(S)
           end  { while }

           Push(S, Ch)
        end  { operator }
   end  { case }

{ append to PE the operators remaining on the stack }
while not IsEmpty(S) do
begin
    PE := PE · StackTop(S)
    Pop(S)
end  { while }
```

Ch	S	PE
A		A
–	–	A
(	–(	A
B	–(	AB
+	–(+	AB
C	–(+	ABC
*	–(+*	ABC
D	–(+*	ABCD
)	–(+	ABCD* { move operators }
	–(	ABCD*+ { from stack }
	–	ABCD*+ { to PE until "(" }
/	–/	ABCD*+
E	–/	ABCD*+E
		ABCD*+E/– { copy operators from stack to PE}

Figure 8-7

A trace of the algorithm that converts the infix expression $A - (B + C * D)/E$ to postfix form

A complete Pascal program follows. Notice that auxiliary subprograms, including the stack operations, are hidden within the procedure *ConvToPost*.

```pascal
program InfixToPostfix(input, output);
{ **********************************************************
  INFIX TO POSTFIX CONVERSION

  Input: A legal infix expression.
  Output: The equivalent postfix expression.
  Assumptions:

  1. The input string is a legal infix expression, which can
     contain parentheses.
  2. The operators are the binary operators +, −, *, and /.
  3. Every character that is not an operator or a
     parenthesis is a legal operand.
  4. The stack operations are available.
  ********************************************************** }

const   maxsize = 20;

type    expression = array[1..maxsize] of char;

var     IEin  : expression; { infix expression − input }
        PEout : expression; { prefix expression − output }
        lastin, : integer;  { index of last character in IEin}
        lastout : integer;  { index of last character in PEout }

procedure ConvToPost(IEin : expression; lastin : integer;
            var PEout : expression; var lastout : integer);
{ --------------------------------------------------------
  Converts an infix expression to postfix form.
  Precondition: The input expression IEin[1..lastin] is an
  array of characters that represents a legal infix
  expression as follows: operators are +, −, *, or /
                        open and close parentheses
                        operands, which are any other
                        character.
  Postcondition: PEout[1..lastout] is the equivalent postfix
  expression.
  Calls: Local subprograms Prec, CharType, ProcessOperand,
  ProcessCloseParen, ProcessOperator, stack operations.
  -------------------------------------------------------- }
const   maxstack = maxsize;
type    charclass = (operand, operator, open, close);
                                        { classes of character }
        itemtype = char;               { define the stack }
        stack = record
```

```
            Top   : 0..maxstack;
            Items : array[1..maxstack] of itemtype
      end;

var   done, success : boolean;
      Ch, checktop : char;
      i : integer;
      S : stack;

   #include StackOps;        { include the stack operations }

   function Prec(op : char) : integer;
   { -------------------------------------------------------
     Computes the precedence of an operator op.
     Precondition: None.
     Postcondition: Returns 1 for + and —, 2 for * and /,
     and 0 for any other character.
     ------------------------------------------------------- }
   begin
       if op in ['+', '—', '*', '/']
           then
           case op of
               '+', '—' : Prec := 1;
               '*', '/' : Prec := 2
           end   { case }

           else Prec := 0
   end;   { Prec }

   function CharType(Ch : char) : charclass;
   { -------------------------------------------------------
     Computes the type of a character Ch.
     Precondition: Ch is a legal character.
     Postcondition: Returns a data type -- operand,
     operator, open, close -- according to the class of the
     character Ch.
     ------------------------------------------------------- }
   begin
       if Ch in ['+', '—', '*', '/'] then
           CharType := operator
       else if Ch = '(' then
           CharType := open
       else if Ch = ')' then
           CharType := close
       else CharType := operand
   end;   { CharType }

   procedure ProcessOperand(Ch : char; var PEout : expression;
                               var lastout : integer);
```

```
{ -----------------------------------------------------
  Processes operands.
  Precondition: Ch is an operand; lastout points to last
  character in PEout; lastout is 0 when PEout is empty.
  Postcondition: Operand Ch is appended to the postfix
  expression PEout; lastout points to position of added
  character Ch.
  ----------------------------------------------------- }
begin
    lastout := lastout + 1;
    PEout[lastout] := Ch
end;  { ProcessOperand }

procedure ProcessCloseParen(var PEout : expression;
                              var lastout : integer);
{ -----------------------------------------------------
  Processes right parentheses.
  Precondition: lastout points to last character in
  PEout; lastout is 0 when PEout is empty; stack S is
  not empty.
  Postcondition: Pops operators from stack S and appends
  them to postfix expression PEout until a matching open
  paren is found; lastout points to last character in
  PEout.
  Calls: Stack operations.
  ----------------------------------------------------- }
var checktop : char;
    success : boolean;

begin
    StackTop(S, checktop, success);
    while checktop <> '(' do
    begin
        lastout := lastout + 1;
        PEout[lastout] := checktop;
        Pop(S, success);
        StackTop(S, checktop, success)
    end;  { while }

    Pop(S, success)
end;  { ProcessCloseParen }

procedure ProcessOperator(Ch : char;
            var PEout : expression; var lastout : integer);
{ -----------------------------------------------------
  Processes operators.
  Precondition: Ch is an operator; lastout points to
  last character in PEout; lastout is 0 when PEout is
  empty; stack S is not empty.
```

```
        Postcondition: Pops operators from stack S whose
        precedence is >= present operator Ch and appends them
        to postfix expression PEout, lastout points to last
        character in PEout.
        Calls: Stack operations.
        ------------------------------------------------- }
    var checktop : char;
        done, success : boolean;

    begin
        done := false;
        while (not IsEmpty(S)) and (not done) do
        begin
            StackTop(S, checktop, success);
            if (checktop <> '(') and (Prec(checktop) >= Prec(Ch))
                then
                begin
                    lastout := lastout + 1;
                    PEout[lastout] := checktop;
                    Pop(S, success)
                end   { then }

                else done := true
        end;   { while }

        Push(S, Ch, success)
    end;   { ProcessOperator }

begin   { ConvToPost }
    Create(S);        { create a stack }
    lastout := 0;    { initialize the output string index}
    { process each character in the expression }
    for i := 1 to lastin do
    begin
        Ch := IEin[i];
        case CharType(Ch) of
            { operand — concatenate to the output string }
            operand: ProcessOperand(Ch, PEout, lastout);

            { open paren — push onto the stack }
            open: Push(S, Ch, success);

            { close paren — pop operators until a matching
              open paren is found }
            close: ProcessCloseParen(PEout, lastout);

            { operator — pop operators of >= precedence }
            operator: ProcessOperator(Ch, PEout, lastout);
        end   { case }
```

```
            end;   { for }

            { move the rest of the stack to the output string }
            while not IsEmpty(S) do
            begin
               StackTop(S, checktop, success);
               Pop(S, success);
               lastout := lastout + 1;
               PEout[lastout] := checktop
            end   { while }

      end;   { ConvToPost }

      procedure ReadExpr(var IEin : expression; var lastin : integer);
      { -------------------------------------------------------
        Reads an expression from standard input.
        Precondition: None.
        Postcondition: IEin[1..lastin] contains the expression.
        -------------------------------------------------- }
      begin
            { read an infix expression }
            lastin := 0;
            while (input^ <> ' ') and (lastin < maxsize) do
            begin
               lastin := lastin + 1;
               read(IEin[lastin])
            end;   { while }
            readln
      end;   { ReadExpr }

      procedure WriteExpr(E : expression; last : integer);
      { -------------------------------------------------------
        Writes an expression to standard output.
        Precondition: E[1..last] is the expression.
        Postcondition: Writes an expression, moves to the next line.
        -------------------------------------------------- }
      var i : integer;
      begin
            for i := 1 to last do
               write(E[i]);
            writeln
      end;   { WriteExpr }

      begin   { Main Program — demonstrate procedure ConvToPost }
            ReadExpr(IEin, lastin);   { read infix expression }

            { convert the infix expression to postfix form }
            ConvToPost(IEin, lastin, PEout, lastout);

            { write out the infix and postfix expressions }
```

```
    write('Infix expression: ');
    WriteExpr(IEin, lastin);
    write('Postfix expression: ');
    WriteExpr(PEout, lastout)
end.   { Program }
```

The following are samples of the program's output:

```
Infix expression: A
Postfix expression: A

Infix expression: (A)
Postfix expression: A

Infix expression: A+B
Postfix expression: AB+

Infix expression: (A+B)
Postfix expression: AB+

Infix expression: A+B*C
Postfix expression: ABC*+

Infix expression: A*B+C
Postfix expression: AB*C+

Infix expression: A*(B+C)
Postfix expression: ABC+*

Infix expression: (A+B)*C
Postfix expression: AB+C*

Infix expression: A—B+C
Postfix expression: AB—C+

Infix expression: A—(B+C)
Postfix expression: ABC+—
```

A Search Problem

Our final application of stacks is designed to give you the flavor of a general type of problem for which stacks are very useful. This type of problem, known as a **search problem**, requires that you find a way to perform a given task such as getting from some point of origin to some destination point. We shall solve this problem first by using stacks and then by using recursion. The recursive solution will bring to light the close relationship between stacks and recursion.

The particular search problem here is to write a program that will act as a simple travel agent for the High Planes Airline Company (HPAir). Given all of the flight information for HPAir, the program will process customer requests to fly from some origin city to some destination city. So that you

Determine whether HPAir flies from one city to another

can focus on the issue at hand—the use of stacks as a problem-solving tool—the program will produce only a yes or no answer for each customer request. That is, the program will indicate whether or not there exists a sequence of HPAir flights from the origin city to the destination city. The more realistic problem of actually producing an itinerary—that is, the sequence of flights—is considered in Project 19 at the end of this chapter.

INPUT   There are three input textfiles as follows. All the numbers in the files are integers, and all the names are character strings.

`Cityfile`	Each line is the name of a city that HPAir services. The names are in alphabetical order.
`Flightfile`	Each line is a pair of city names that represents the origin and destination of one of HPAir's flights.
`Requestfile`	Each line is a pair of city names that represents a request to fly from some origin to some destination

OUTPUT   For each customer request, a message indicates whether or not a sequence of HPAir flights can satisfy the request.

ASSUMPTIONS

1. Each city name contains at most 12 characters.
2. HPAir services at most 20 cities.
3. The input data is correct.

EXAMPLE

Input Files

```
Cityfile:       Albuquerque
                Chicago
                San Diego

Flightfile:     Chicago      San Diego
                Chicago      Albuquerque
                Albuquerque  Chicago

Requestfile:    Albuquerque  San Diego
                Albuquerque  Paris
                San Diego    Chicago
```

Corresponding Output

```
Request is to fly from Albuquerque to San Diego.
HPAir has service from Albuquerque to San Diego.

Request is to fly from Albuquerque to Paris.
Sorry. HPAir does not service Paris.
```

```
Request is to fly from San Diego to Chicago.
Sorry. HPAir does not have service from San Diego to
Chicago.
```

Representing the flight data. The flight map in Figure 8-8 represents the routes that HPAir flies. There is an arrow from city C_1 to city C_2 if there is a flight from C_1 to C_2. In this case C_2 is **adjacent** to C_1 and the path from C_1 to C_2 is called a **directed path**. Notice that if C_2 is adjacent to C_1, it does not follow that C_1 is adjacent to C_2. For example, in Figure 8-8, there is a flight from city R to city X, but not from city X to city R. As you will see in Chapter 11, the map in Figure 8-8 is called a **graph**.

C_2 is adjacent to C_1 if there is a directed path from C_1 to C_2

Searching a flight map by using a stack. When processing a customer's request to fly from some origin city to some destination city, you must determine from the flight map whether there is a route from the origin to the destination. For example, by examining the flight map in Figure 8-8, you can see that a customer could fly from city P to city Z by flying first to city W, then to city Y, and finally to city Z; that is, there is a directed path from P to Z: $P \rightarrow W, W \rightarrow Y, Y \rightarrow Z$. Thus, you must develop an algorithm that searches the flight map for a directed path from the origin city to the destination city. Such a path might involve either a single flight or a sequence of flights. The solution developed here performs an **exhaustive search**. That is, beginning at the origin city, the solution will try every possible sequence of flights until either it finds a sequence that gets to the destination city or it determines that no such sequence exists. You will see that the ADT stack is useful in organizing this search.

Use a stack to organize an exhaustive search

First consider how you might perform the search by hand. One approach is to start at the origin city C_0 and select an arbitrary path to travel—that is, select an arbitrary flight departing from the origin city. This flight will lead you to a new city, C_1. If city C_1 happens to be the destination city, you are done; otherwise, you must attempt to get from C_1 to the destination city. To do this, you select a path to travel out of C_1. This path will lead you to a city C_2. If C_2 is the destination, you are done; otherwise, you must attempt to get from C_2 to the destination city, and so on.

Figure 8-8

Flight map for HPAir

Consider the possible outcomes of applying the previous strategy:

Possible outcomes of the
exhaustive search strategy

1.   You eventually reach the destination city and can conclude that it is possible to fly from the origin to the destination.

2.   You reach a city C from which there are no departing flights.

3.   You go around in circles. For example, from C_1 you go to C_2, from C_2 you go to C_3, and from C_3 you go back to C_1. You might continue this tour of the three cities forever; that is, the algorithm is in an infinite loop.

If you always obtained the first outcome, everyone would be happy. However, because HPAir does not fly between all pairs of cities, you certainly cannot expect that the algorithm will always find a path from the origin city to the destination. For example, if city P in Figure 8-8 is the origin city and city Q is the destination city, the algorithm could not possibly find a path from city P to city Q.

Even if there were a sequence of flights from the origin city to the destination, it would take a bit of luck for the previous strategy to discover it—the algorithm would have to select a "correct" flight at each step. For example, even though there is a way to get from city P to city Z in Figure 8-8, the algorithm might not find it and instead would reach outcome 2 or 3. That is, suppose that from city P the algorithm chose to go to city R. From city R the algorithm would have to go to city X, from which there are no flights out (outcome 2). On the other hand, suppose that the algorithm chose to go to city W from city P. From city W the algorithm might choose to go to city S. It would then have to go to city T and then back to W. From W it might once again choose to go to city S and continue to go around in circles (outcome 3).

You thus need to make the algorithm more sophisticated, so that it always finds a path from the origin to the destination, if such a path exists, and otherwise terminates with the conclusion that there is no such path. Suppose that the earlier strategy results in outcome 2: You reach a city C from which there are no departing flights. This certainly does not imply that there is no way to get from the origin to the destination; it implies only that there is no way to get from city C to the destination. In other words, it was a mistake to go to city C. After discovering such a mistake, the algorithm can retrace its steps, or *backtrack*, to the city C' that was visited just before city C was visited. Once back at city C', the algorithm can select a flight to some city other than C. Notice that it is possible that there are no other flights out of city C'. If this were the case, it would mean that it was a mistake to visit city C', and thus you would want to backtrack again, this time to the city that was visited just before city C'.

Use backtracking to recover
from a wrong choice

For example, you saw that, in trying to get from city P to city Z in Figure 8-8, the algorithm might first choose to go from city P to city R and then on to city X. As there are no departing flights from city X, the algorithm must backtrack to city R, the city visited before city X. Once back at city R, the algorithm would attempt to go to some city other than city X, but would discover that this is not possible. The algorithm would thus back-track once more, this time to city *P*, which was visited just before city *R*. From city *P* the algorithm would choose to go to city *W*, which is a step in the right direction!

For the algorithm to implement this new strategy, it must maintain information about the order in which it visits the cities. First notice that when the algorithm backtracks from a city *C*, it must retreat to the city that it visited most recently before *C*. This observation suggests that you main-tain the sequence of visited cities in a stack. That is, each time you decide to visit a city, you push its name onto the stack. You select the next city to visit from those adjacent to the city on the top of the stack. When you need to backtrack from the city *C* at the top of the stack (for example, because there are no flights out of the city), you simply pop a city from the stack. After the pop, the city on the top of the stack is the city on the current path that you visited most recently before *C*.

The algorithm as developed so far is as follows:

```
{ push the origin city onto the stack }
Push(S, Origin)

while it is unknown whether there is a sequence of
      flights from the origin to the destination do
begin
    if you need to backtrack from the city on the stack's top
        then Pop(S)

        else
        begin
            Select a city C to fly to from the city
                on the top of the stack
            Push(S, C)
        end  { if }
end  { while }
```

The search algorithm with backtracking

Notice that at any point in the algorithm, the contents of the stack corre-spond to the sequence of flights currently under consideration. The city on the top of the stack is the city you are visiting currently, directly "below" it is the city visited previously, and so forth down to the bottom city, which is the first city visited in the sequence, or the origin city. In other words, an *invariant* of the while loop is that *the stack contains a directed path from the origin city at the bottom of the stack to the city at the top of the stack*. You can, therefore, always retrace your steps as far back through the sequence as needed.

Now consider the question of when to

```
Backtrack from the city on the top of the stack
```

You have already seen one case when backtracking is necessary. You must backtrack from the city on the top of the stack when there are no flights out of that city. Another time when you need to backtrack is related to the problem of going around in circles, described previously as the third possible outcome of the original strategy.

A key observation that will tell you when to backtrack is, *You never want to visit a city that the search has already visited.* As a consequence, you must backtrack from a city whenever there are no more unvisited cities to fly to. To see why you never want to visit a city a second time, consider two cases:

Two reasons for not visiting a city more than once

- If you have visited city C and it is still somewhere in the stack—that is, it is part of the sequence of cities that you are exploring currently—you do not want to visit C again. Any sequence that goes from C through C_1, C_2, $\cdots$, C_k, back to C, and then to C' might just as well skip the intermediate cities and go from C directly to C'.

  For example, suppose that the algorithm starts at P in Figure 8-8 and, in trying to find a path to Y, visits W, S, and T. There is now no reason for the algorithm to consider the flight from T to W because W is already on the stack. Anywhere you could fly to by going from W to S, from S to T, and then back to W, such as city Y, you could fly to directly from W without first going through S and T. Because you do not allow the algorithm to visit W a second time, it will backtrack from S and T to W and then go from W directly to Y. Figure 8-9 shows how the stack would appear if revisits were allowed and how it looks after backtracking when revisits are not allowed. Notice that backtracking to W is very different from visiting W for a second time.

- If you have visited city C, but it is no longer in the stack—because you backtracked from it and popped it from the stack—you do not want to visit C again. This situation is subtle; consider two cases that depend on why you backtracked from the city.

  If you backtracked from C because there were no flights out of it, then you certainly do not ever want to try going through C again. For example, if, starting at P in Figure 8-8, the algorithm goes to R and then to X, it will backtrack from X to R. At this point, although X is no longer on the stack, you certainly do not want to visit it again, because you know there are no flights out of X.

  Now suppose that you backtracked from C because all cities adjacent to it had been visited. This implies that you have already tried all possible flights from C and have failed to find a way to get to the destination city. There is thus no reason to go to C again. For example, suppose that starting from P in Figure 8-8, the algorithm executes the following sequence: Visit R, visit X, backtrack to R (because there are no flights out of X), backtrack to P (because there are no more unvisited cities adjacent to R), visit W, visit Y. At this point the stack contains P-W-Y, with Y on top, and you need to choose a flight out of Y. You do not

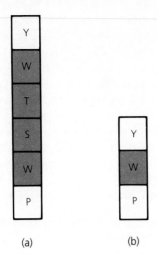

Figure 8-9

**The stack of cities (a) allow-
ing revisits and (b) after
backtracking when revisits
are not allowed**

(a)   (b)

want to fly from *Y* to *R,* because you have visited *R* already and
tried all possible flights out of *R.*

In both cases, visiting a city a second time does not gain you
anything, and in fact it may cause you to go around in circles.

To implement the rule of not visiting a city more than once, you simply   *Mark the visited cities*
mark a city when it has been visited. When choosing the next city to visit,
you restrict consideration to unmarked cities adjacent to the city on the
top of the stack. The algorithm thus becomes

```
{ push the origin city onto the stack }
Push(S, Origin)
Mark the origin as visited

while it is unknown whether there is a sequence of
      flights from the origin to the destination do
{ loop invariant: stack S contains a directed path from the
  origin city at the bottom of S to the city at the top of S }
begin
    if there are no flights to unvisited cities
      from the city on the top of the stack

      then Pop(S) { backtrack }

      else
      begin
          Select an unvisited city C to fly to from
            the city on the top of the stack
          Push(S, C)
          Mark C as visited
      end  { if }
end  { while }
```

Finally, you need to refine the condition in the *while* statement. That is, you need to refine the algorithm's final determination of whether there exists a path from the origin to the destination. The loop invariant, which states that the stack contains a directed path from the origin city to the city on the top of the stack, implies that the algorithm can reach an affirmative conclusion if the city at the top of the stack is the destination city. On the other hand, the algorithm can reach a negative conclusion only after it has exhausted all possibilities—that is, after the algorithm has backtracked to the origin and there remain no unvisited cities to fly to from the origin. At this point, the algorithm will pop the origin city from the stack and the stack will become empty.

With this refinement, the final version of the algorithm appears as follows:

The final version of the search algorithm

```
SearchS(Origin, Destination)

    { push the origin city onto the stack }
    Push(S, Origin)
    Mark the origin as visited

    while (not IsEmpty(S)) Cand (StackTop(S) <> Destination) do
    { loop invariant: stack S contains a directed path from
      the origin city at the bottom of S to the city at the
      top of S}
    begin
        if there are no flights to unvisited cities
            from the city on the top of the stack

            then Pop(S) { backtrack }

            else
            begin
                Select an unvisited city C to fly to from
                    the city on the top of the stack
                Push(S, C)
                Mark C as visited
            end   { if }
    end   { while }
```

Notice that the algorithm does not specify the order of selection for the unvisited cities. It really does not matter what selection criteria the algorithm uses, because the choice will not affect the final outcome: There is either a sequence of flights or there is not. The choice, however, will affect your trace of the algorithm's action by affecting the specific sequence of flights. For the sake of the example, suppose that the algorithm always flies to the alphabetically earliest unvisited city from the city on the top of the stack.

Figure 8-10 contains a trace of the algorithm's action, given the map in Figure 8-8 and assuming that *P* is the origin city and *Z* is the destination city. The algorithm terminates with success.

Action	Reason	Contents of stack
Push P	Initialize	P
Push R	Next unvisited adjacent city	PR
Push X	Next unvisited adjacent city	PRX
Pop X	No unvisited adjacent city	PR
Pop R	No unvisited adjacent city	P
Push W	Next unvisited adjacent city	PW
Push S	Next unvisited adjacent city	PWS
Push T	Next unvisited adjacent city	PWST
Pop T	No unvisited adjacent city	PWS
Pop S	No unvisited adjacent city	PW
Push Y	Next unvisited adjacent city	PWY
Push Z	Next unvisited adjacent city	PWYZ

Figure 8-10

A trace of the search algorithm, given the flight map in Figure 8-8

When you turn to the Pascal implementation of the algorithm, you must decide how to represent the flight map. The primary operation that the algorithm must perform on the map is to determine which cities are adjacent to a given city. If there are N cities numbered $1, 2, \cdots, N$, you can use N linked lists to represent the flight map. There is a node on list i for city j if and only if there is a directed path from city i to city j. Such a data structure is called an **adjacency list**; Figure 8-11 illustrates an adjacency list for the flight map in Figure 8-8. Chapter 11 discusses adjacency lists further when it presents ways to represent graphs. At that time, you will learn why an adjacency list is a good choice for the present program.

Represent the flight map by using an adjacency list

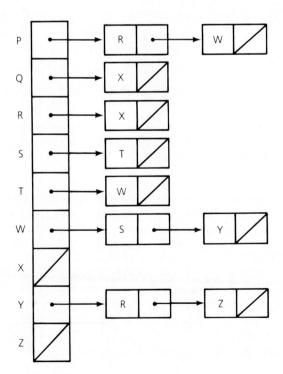

Figure 8-11

Adjacency list for the flight map in Figure 8-8

The program associates each city name with an integer as follows. As the program reads in the names of the cities that HPAir services, it places them in the array *CityNames* such that the *i*th city read is in *City-Names[i]*. The program refers to *CityNames[i]* as city *i*. If you require that the cities in the input file be in alphabetical order, the array *City-Names* must be sorted. This requirement allows you to perform a binary search on the array for a given name and then to associate the name with the correct city number. This scheme allows you to place integers rather than strings on the stack.

The following is a Pascal program that implements the solution to the HPAir problem:

```
program HPAir(Cityfile, Flightfile, Requestfile, output);
{ ************************************************************
  HPAIR — TRAVEL AGENT

  Given data describing all of the flights operated by
  HPAir, this program determines whether or not there is a
  sequence of flights from city A to city B.

  Input: There are three input textfiles:

        Cityfile    -   Each line is the name of a city
                        serviced by HPAir. The names must be in
                        alphabetical order.

        Flightfile  -   Each line is a pair of city names
                        representing the origin and destination
                        of one of HPAir's flights.

        Requestfile -   Each line is a pair of city names
                        representing a request to fly from some
                        origin to some destination.

  Output: For each customer request, a message indicating
          whether or not a sequence of HPAir flights can
          satisfy the request.

  Assumptions:
    1. City names are up to 12 characters in length.
    2. There are at most 20 cities that HPAir services.
    3. The input data is correct.

  Data Structures:
    1.  CityNames - array of city names in alphabetical
        order and indexed by city number.
    2.  Flights  - adjacency list representation of HPAir's
        flights. Flights[i] is a pointer to the list of
        city numbers adjacent to city i (i.e., there is an
        HPAir flight from i to each city on its list).
```

```
  Major Variables:
    NumCities - actual number of cities serviced by HPAir
    CityNames - list of city names
    Flights   - adjacency lists for the flight information

  The actual search for a path between two cities is done by
  the boolean-valued function IsPath.
  ********************************************************* }
const  maxcities = 20;
       namesize  = 12;

type   name     = packed array[1..namesize] of char;
       namelist = array[1..maxcities] of name;

       { nodes for the adjacency list }
       adjptr   = ^adjnode;
       adjnode  = record
            data : integer;
            next : adjptr
       end;

       adjlist  = array[1..maxcities] of adjptr;

var    Cityfile, Flightfile, Requestfile : text; { input files }
       CityNames : namelist;      { cities serviced by HPAir }

       { adjacency list for the flight information }
       Flights  : adjlist;

       NumCities : integer;       { number of cities }

procedure Getname(var Infile : text ; var City : name);
{ ---------------------------------------------------------
  Reads a city name from Infile.
  Precondition: Infile represents a textfile of city names.
  Postcondition: City contains the name read from the file.
  --------------------------------------------------------- }
var i : integer;
begin
    { skip over leading blanks on a line }
    while (Infile^ = ' ') do
       get(Infile);

    { read the name }
    for i := 1 to namesize do
    begin
        if not eoln(Infile)
            then read(Infile, City[i])
            else City[i] := ' '
    end  { for }
end;  { Getname }
```

```
procedure Putname(City : name);
{ ----------------------------------------------------------
  Writes a city name up to the last nonblank character.
  ---------------------------------------------------------- }
var i, last : integer;
begin
    { find the last nonblank character in the name }
    for i := 1 to namesize do
      if City[i] <> ' '
          then last := i;

    { write the name }
    for i :=1 to last do
      write(City[i])
end;   { Putname }

function FindIndex(CityNames : namelist; NumCities : integer;
                                ACity : name) : integer;
{ ----------------------------------------------------------
  Searches a list of city names for a particular city.
  Precondition: The NumCities names in CityNames must be
  sorted alphabetically. ACity is the desired city.
  Postcondition: Returns the index of ACity in CityNames, or
  returns 0 if the city is not found.
  Implementation note: An iterative binary search is used.
  ---------------------------------------------------------- }
var first, last, mid : integer;
begin  { binary search }
    first := 1;
    last := NumCities;
    while first < last do
    begin
        mid := (first + last) div 2;
        if CityNames[mid] < ACity
            then first := mid + 1
            else last := mid
    end;   { while }

    { test termination conditions }
    if CityNames[first] = ACity
       then FindIndex := first
       else FindIndex := 0
end;   { FindIndex }

function IsPath(FromCity, ToCity : integer;
               Flights : adjlist) : boolean;
{ ----------------------------------------------------------
  Determines if there is a sequence of flights from city
  FromCity to city ToCity.
```

Precondition: The adjacency list Flights is defined.
Postcondition: Returns true if there is a sequence of
flights from FromCity to ToCity, otherwise returns false.
Parameters are unchanged.
Calls: Stack operations, which are local to this function.
Note: Uses a local stack S for the city numbers of a
potential path and a local boolean array Visited to keep
track of cities that have been visited by the search.
--- }

```
const    maxstack  = maxcities;

type     { array-based implementation of a stack }
         itemtype  = integer;
         stack = record
              Items : array[1..maxstack] of itemtype;
              Top   : 0..maxstack
         end;

var      S : stack;
         Visited : array[1..maxcities] of boolean;
         checktop, topcity, nextcity, i : integer;
         done, success, solved : boolean;
         cityptr : adjptr;

#include StackOps;     { include the stack operations }

begin
    { initialize for the search }
    Create(S);
    solved := false;
    for i := 1 to maxcities do
       Visited[i] := false;

    { search - stack version }
    { push origin city onto stack, mark it visited }
    Push(S, FromCity, success);
    Visited[FromCity] := true;

    while (not IsEmpty(S)) and (not solved) do
    { loop invariant: stack S contains a directed path from
      the origin city at the bottom of S to the city at the
      top of S}
    begin
        { find an unvisited city adjacent to the city on the
          top of the stack - note that the search starts at
          the beginning of the adjacency list each time
          (see Exercise 16) }
        StackTop(S, topcity, success);
        cityptr := Flights[topcity];
        done := false;
```

```
              while not done do
              begin
                  if cityptr = nil then
                      done := true
                  else if not Visited[cityptr^.data] then
                      done := true
                  else cityptr := cityptr^.next
              end;  { while }

              { pop the stack at a dead end, or push
                the next city and continue the search }
              if cityptr = nil
                 then Pop(S, success) { backtrack }

                 else                    { continue search }
                 begin
                     nextcity := cityptr^.data;
                     Push(S, nextcity, success);
                     Visited[nextcity] := true;

                     { test for a solution }
                     StackTop(S, checktop, success);
                     if checktop = ToCity
                         then solved := true
                 end
          end;  { while }

      IsPath := not IsEmpty(S)
  end;  { IsPath }

  procedure ReadCountAndWriteCities(var Cityfile : text;
              var CityNames : namelist; var NumCities : integer);
  { ------------------------------------------------------------
    Reads and counts city names serviced by HPAir.
    Precondition: Cityfile is a textfile of city names.
    Postcondition: There are NumCities names in the array
    CityNames.
    Calls: Getname.
    File: Cityfile.
    ------------------------------------------------------------ }
  var i : integer;
  begin
      { read in and count the city names }
      reset(Cityfile);
      NumCities := 0;
      while not eof(Cityfile) do
      begin
        NumCities := NumCities + 1;
        Getname(Cityfile, CityNames[NumCities]);
        readln(Cityfile)
```

```
      end;   { while }

      { write out the city names }
      writeln('******************************************');
      writeln('********  HPAir FLIGHT INFORMATION  ********');
      writeln('******************************************');
      writeln;
      writeln('Cities serviced by HPAir:');
      writeln;
      for i := 1 to NumCities do
          writeln('  ', CityNames[i])
end;   { ReadCountAndWriteCities }

procedure ReadAndWriteFlightInfo(var Flightfile : text;
                CityNames : namelist; NumCities : integer;
                var Flights : adjlist);
{ ---------------------------------------------------------
  Reads and writes flight information and creates the
  adjacency list.
  Precondition: Flightfile is a textfile of city pairs,
  CityNames is a list of NumCities cities that HPAir
  services.
  Postcondition: Flights is the adjacency list; displays
  flights operated by HPAir.
  File: Flightfile.
  --------------------------------------------------------- }
var FromName, ToName : name;
    FromNum, ToNum, i : integer;
    cityptr : adjptr;
begin
    { initialize the adjacency lists }
    for i := 1 to maxcities do
      Flights[i] := nil;

    { read in all of the flight information }
    reset(Flightfile);
    while not eof(Flightfile) do
    begin
      Getname(Flightfile, FromName);
      Getname(Flightfile, ToName);
      readln(Flightfile);
      FromNum := FindIndex(CityNames, NumCities, FromName);
      ToNum := FindIndex(CityNames, NumCities, ToName);

      { add ToNum to FromNum's adjacency list }
      if (ToNum = 0) or (FromNum = 0)
          then writeln('Warning.  Bad input data.')

          else
```

```
                    begin
                        new(cityptr);
                        cityptr^.data := ToNum;
                        cityptr^.next := Flights[FromNum];
                        Flights[FromNum] := cityptr
                    end
            end;  { while }

            { write out all of the flight information }
            writeln;
            writeln('Flights operated by HPAir:');
            writeln;
            for i := 1 to NumCities do
            begin
                cityptr := Flights[i];
                while cityptr <> nil do
                begin
                    writeln('  From ', CityNames[i],
                            ' to ', CityNames[cityptr^.data]);
                    cityptr := cityptr^.next
                end  { while }
            end  { for }
    end;  { ReadAndWriteFlightInfo }

    procedure TestSolution(CityNames : namelist;
                Flights : adjlist; FromNum, ToNum : integer);
    { ------------------------------------------------------------
      Tests for a solution.
      Precondition: CityNames is a list of cities that HPAir
      services, Flights is the adjacency list, FromNum and ToNum
      are the city numbers of the origin and destination cities.
      FromNum and ToNum cannot exceed the number of cities in
      CityNames.
      Postcondition: Indicates whether a flight between the 2
      cities exists by printing a message.
      ------------------------------------------------------------ }
    begin
        { test for a solution }
        if IsPath(FromNum, ToNum, Flights)
            then write('HPAir has service from ')
            else write('Sorry. HPAir does not have service from ');

        Putname(CityNames[FromNum]);
        write(' to ');
        Putname(CityNames[ToNum]);
        writeln('.')
    end;  { TestSolution }

    procedure WriteErrorMessage(FromName, ToName : name;
                                   FromNum, ToNum : integer);
```

```
{ --------------------------------------------------------
  Writes appropriate messages for an illegal request.
  Precondition: FromName and ToName are the names of the
  origin and destination cities. FromNum and ToNum are the
  corresponding city numbers.
  Postcondition: Prints a message that indicates an illegal
  request.
  -------------------------------------------------------- }
begin
   { unknown city of origin }
   if FromNum = 0
      then
      begin
         write('HPAir does not service ');
         Putname(FromName);
         writeln('.')
      end;

   { unknown destination city }
   if ToNum = 0
      then
      begin
         write('HPAir does not service ');
         Putname(ToName);
         writeln('.')
      end;

   { origin equals destination }
   if FromNum = ToNum
      then writeln('Walk!!!')
end;   { WriteErrorMessage }

procedure ProcessRequests(var Requestfile : text;
                CityNames : namelist; NumCities : integer;
                Flights : adjlist);

{ --------------------------------------------------------
  Processes flight requests in the textfile Requestfile.
  Precondition: CityNames is a list of NumCities cities that
  HPAir services, Flights is the adjacency list, Requestfile
  is a textfile of flight requests.
  Postcondition: Prints messages about the feasibility of
  flight requests. Parameters are unchanged.
  File: Requestfile.
  -------------------------------------------------------- }
var FromName, ToName : name;
    FromNum, ToNum : integer;

begin  { ProcessRequests }
   reset(Requestfile);
```

```
            { write heading }
            writeln;
            writeln('****************************************');
            writeln('*********   ITINERARY REQUESTS   ********');
            writeln('****************************************');
            writeln;

            { process each request until end of file }
            while not eof(Requestfile) do
            begin
                { read a request }
                Getname(Requestfile, FromName);
                Getname(Requestfile, ToName);
                readln(Requestfile);

                { write the request }
                write('Request is to fly from ');
                Putname(FromName);
                write(' to ');
                Putname(ToName);
                writeln('.');

                { process the request }
                FromNum := FindIndex(CityNames, NumCities, FromName);
                ToNum := FindIndex(CityNames, NumCities, ToName);

                { test for legal to and from cities }
                if (FromNum <> 0) and (ToNum <> 0) and (FromNum <> ToNum)
                    then TestSolution(CityNames, Flights, FromNum, ToNum)
                    else WriteErrorMessage(FromName, ToName, FromNum,
                                                               ToNum);

                writeln
            end  { while }
        end;  { ProcessRequests }


    begin  { Main Program }
        { read in, count, and write city names }
        ReadCountAndWriteCities(Cityfile, CityNames, NumCities);

        { read in and write out all of the flight information
          and create the adjacency list }
        ReadAndWriteFlightInfo(Flightfile, CityNames, NumCities,
                                                             Flights);

        { Look for solution for each request }
        ProcessRequests(Requestfile, CityNames, NumCities,
    Flights)
    end.  { Program }
```

Searching a flight map by using recursion.   Recall the initial attempt at a solution to the HPAir problem of searching for a sequence of flights from some origin city to some destination city. Consider how you might perform the search "by hand." One approach is to start at the origin city and select an arbitrary flight that departs from the origin city. This flight will lead you to a new city, C_1. If city C_1 happens to be the destination city, you are done; otherwise, you must attempt to get from C_1 to the destination city by selecting a flight out of C_1. This flight will lead you to city C_2. If C_2 is the destination, you are done; otherwise, you must attempt to get from C_2 to the destination city, and so on. There is a distinct recursive flavor to this search strategy, which can be restated as follows:

```
To fly from the origin to the destination:

    Select a city C adjacent to the origin
    Fly from the origin to city C
    if C is the destination city
        then terminate--the destination is reached
        else fly from city C to the destination
```

A recursive search strategy

This statement of the search strategy makes its recursive nature very apparent. The first step in flying from the origin city to the destination city is to fly from the origin city to city C. Once at city C, you are confronted with another problem of the same type—you now must fly from city C to the destination.

This recursive formulation is nothing more than a restatement of the initial (incomplete) strategy developed previously. As such it has the same three possible outcomes:

1. You eventually reach the destination city and can conclude that it is possible to fly from the origin to the destination.

2. You reach a city C from which there are no departing flights.

3. You go around in circles.

Possible outcomes of the recursive search strategy

The first of these outcomes corresponds to a degenerate case of the recursive algorithm. If you ever reach the destination city, no additional problems of the form "fly from city C to the destination" are generated, and the algorithm terminates. However, as was observed previously, there is no guarantee that the algorithm will produce this outcome, that is, that it will reach this degenerate case. The algorithm might reach a city C from which there are no departing flights (notice that the algorithm does not specify what to do if you reach a city C from which there are no departing flights— in this sense the algorithm is incomplete), or it might repeatedly cycle through the same sequence of cities and thus never terminate.

You can resolve these problems by mirroring what you did in the previous solution. Consider the following refinement, in which you mark visited cities and never fly to a city that has been visited already:

```
SearchR(FromCity, Destination)
{ Search for a sequence of flights from
  FromCity to Destination. }

    Mark FromCity as visited
```

A refinement of the recursive search algorithm

```
if FromCity is the destination city
    then terminate--the destination is reached

    else
        for each unvisited city C adjacent to FromCity do
            SearchR(C, Destination)
```

Now consider what happens when the algorithm reaches a city that has no unvisited city adjacent to it. For example, consider the piece of a flight map in Figure 8-12. When *SearchR* reaches city X—that is, when the parameter *FromCity* has the value X—the *for* loop will not be entered, because there are no unvisited cities adjacent to X. Hence, the procedure *SearchR* returns. This return has the effect of backtracking to city W, from which the flight to X originated. In terms of the previous pseudocode, the return is made to the point from which the call *SearchR(X, Destination)* occurred. This point is within the *for* loop, which iterates through the unvisited cities adjacent to W; that is, the parameter *FromCity* has the value W.

Figure 8-12

A piece of a flight map

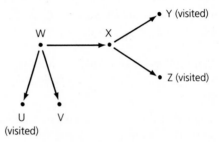

After backtracking from X to W, the *for* loop will again execute; this time the loop chooses city V, resulting in the recursive call *SearchR(V, Destination)*. From this point, the algorithm will eventually either reach the destination city and terminate, or it will backtrack once again to city W. If it backtracks to W, the *for* loop will terminate because there are no more unvisited cities adjacent to W, and a return from *SearchR* will occur. The effect is to backtrack to the city where the flight to W originated. If the algorithm ever backtracks to the origin city and there remain no unvisited cities adjacent to it, the algorithm will terminate, and you can conclude that there is no sequence of flights from the origin to the destination. Notice that the algorithm will always terminate in one way or another, because it will either reach the destination city or run out of unvisited cities to try.

You can transform the previous program, which implements the stack-based search, to one that implements this recursive search simply by replacing the function *IsPath* with the following version. The new function is a nonrecursive shell around the local recursive function *Try*. As you learned in Chapter 5, the nonrecursive shell avoids multiple copies of the array *Visited*.

```
function IsPath(FromCity, ToCity : integer;
               Flights : adjlist) : boolean;
{ ------------------------------------------------------
  Determines if there is a sequence of flights from city
  FromCity to city ToCity.
  Precondition: The adjacency list Flights is defined.
  Postcondition: Returns true if there is a sequence of
  flights from FromCity to ToCity, otherwise returns false.
  Parameters are unchanged.
  Implementation note: The local recursive function Try
  performs the search. The array Visited is used to prevent
  the search from looping--that is, from having the same
  cities searched repeatedly.
  ------------------------------------------------------- }
var   Visited : array[1..maxcities] of boolean;
      i : integer;
function Try(FromCity : integer) : boolean;
{ ----------------------------------------------------
  Performs the recursive search.  For each city that has a
  flight from FromCity, tries to find a sequence of flights
  to ToCity.
  Precondition: ToCity and Visited are global.
  Postcondition: Returns true if there is a sequence of
  flights from FromCity to ToCity, otherwise returns false.
  Parameters are unchanged.
  ----------------------------------------------------- }
var NextCity : integer;
    cityptr : adjptr;
    solved : boolean;
begin
    { mark the current city visited }
    Visited[FromCity] := true;

    { degenerate case - the destination is reached }
    if FromCity = ToCity
       then Try := true

       else
       begin
           cityptr := Flights[FromCity];
           solved := false;
           { try a flight to each unvisited city }
           while (cityptr <> nil) and (not solved) do
           begin
               {find an unvisited city adjacent to
                  FromCity and visit it }
               if Visited[cityptr^.data]
```

You can replace the `IsPath` function in the previous program with this recursive function

```
                    then        {check next one}
                        cityptr := cityptr^.next
                    else        { visit the next city }
                    begin
                        NextCity := cityptr^.data;
                        solved := Try(NextCity)
                    end   { else }
            end;   { while }

            Try := solved
        end   { else }
    end;   { Try }

begin   { IsPath }
    { initialize for search }
    for i := 1 to maxcities do
        Visited[i] := false;

    IsPath := Try(FromCity)
end;   { IsPath }
```

You have probably noticed a close parallel between this recursive algorithm and the earlier stack-based algorithm $SearchS(Origin, Destination)$. (Compare the function Try with the stack-based function $IsPath$.) In fact, the two algorithms simply employ different mechanisms to implement the identical search strategy. The next section will elaborate on the relationship between the two algorithms.

THE RELATIONSHIP BETWEEN STACKS AND RECURSION

The previous section solved the HPAir problem once by using the ADT stack and again by using recursion. The goal of this section is to relate the way that the stack organizes the search for a sequence of flights to the way a recursive algorithm organizes the search. You will see that the ADT stack has a hidden presence in the concept of recursion and, in fact, that stacks have an active role in most computer implementations of recursion.

Consider how the two search algorithms implement three key aspects of their common strategy.

A comparison of key aspects of two search algorithms

- **Visiting a new city.** The recursive algorithm $SearchR$ visits a new city C by making the call $SearchR(C, Destination)$. The algorithm $SearchS$ visits city C by pushing C onto a stack. Notice that if you were to use the box method to trace the execution of $SearchR$, the call $SearchR(C, Destination)$

would generate a box in which the city *C* is associated with the formal parameter *FromCity* of *SearchR*.

   For example, Figure 8-13 shows both the state of the box trace for *SearchR* and the stack for *SearchS* at corresponding points of their search for a path from city *P* to city *Z* in Figure 8-8.

- **Backtracking.** Both search algorithms attempt to visit an unvisited city that is adjacent to the current city. Notice that this current city is the value associated with the formal parameter *FromCity* in the deepest (rightmost) box of *SearchR*'s box trace. Similarly, the current city is on the top of *SearchS*'s stack. In Figure 8-13, this current city is *X*. If there are no unvisited cities adjacent to the current city, the algorithms must backtrack to the previous city. The algorithm *SearchR* backtracks by returning from the current recursive call. You represent this action in the box method by crossing off the deepest box. The algorithm *SearchS* backtracks by explicitly popping from its stack. For example, from the state depicted in Figure 8-13, both algorithms backtrack to city *R* and then to city *P*, as Figure 8-14 illustrates.

- **Termination.** The search algorithms terminate either when they reach the destination city or when they exhaust all possibilities. All possibilities are exhausted when, after backtracking to the origin city, there remain no unvisited adjacent cities. This situation occurs for *SearchR* when all boxes have been crossed off in the box trace and a return occurs to the point of the original call, which, for example, occurred in the main program. For *SearchS* there remain no unvisited cities adjacent to the origin when the stack becomes empty.

Thus, the two search algorithms really do perform the identical action. In fact, provided that they use the same rule to select an unvisited city—for example, traverse the current city's list of adjacent cities alphabetically—they will always visit the identical cities in the identical order. The similarities between the algorithms are far more than coincidence. In fact, it is always possible to capture the actions of a recursive subprogram by using a stack.

Figure 8-13

Visiting a new city: (a) box trace versus (b) stack

Search has visited city P then R then X.

(a) Boxes:

(b) Stack: PRX (X is top)

Search backtracks from X then R back to P.

(a)   Boxes:

    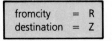

(b)   Stack: originally PRX, then PR, then P

Figure 8-14

Backtracking: (a) box trace versus (b) stack

Typically, stacks are used to implement recursive subprograms

An important context in which the close tie between stacks and recursion is explicitly utilized is a compiler's implementation of a recursive subprogram. It is common for a compiler to use a stack to implement a recursive subprogram in a manner that greatly resembles the box method. When a recursive call to a subprogram occurs, the implementation must remember certain information. This information consists essentially of the same local environment that you place in the boxes—values of both parameters and local variables, and a reference to the point from which the recursive call was made.

During execution, the compiled program must manage these boxes of information, or **activation records**, just as you must manage them on paper. As the HPAir example has indicated, the operations needed to manage the activation records are those that a stack provides. When a recursive call occurs, a new activation record is created and pushed onto a stack. This action corresponds to the creation of a new box at the deepest point in the sequence. When a return is made from a recursive call, the stack is popped, bringing the activation record that contains the appropriate local environment to the top of the stack. This action corresponds to crossing off the deepest box and following the arrow back to the preceding box. Although we have greatly simplified the process, most implementations of recursion are based on stacks of activation records.

Each recursive call generates an activation record that is pushed into a stack

You can use stacks when implementing a nonrecursive version of a recursive algorithm

Programmers use a similar strategy when coding a nonrecursive version of a recursive algorithm. There are several reasons why you might need to recast a recursive algorithm into a nonrecursive form; the most obvious of these is that there are languages such as BASIC that do not support recursion. The previous discussion should give you a taste of the techniques for removing recursion from a program. You will encounter recursion removal as a formal topic in more advanced courses, such as compiler construction.

SUMMARY

1.   The ADT stack operations have a last-in, first-out (LIFO) behavior.

2.   Algorithms that operate on algebraic expressions are an important application of stacks. The LIFO nature of stacks is exactly what the algorithm that evaluates postfix expressions needs to organize the operands. Similarly, the algorithm that transforms infix expres-

sions to postfix form uses a stack to organize the operators in accordance with precedence rules and left-to-right association.

3. You can use a stack to determine whether a sequence of flights exists between two cities. The stack keeps track of the sequence of visited cities and enables the search algorithm to backtrack easily. Because the origin city is at the bottom of the stack and the destination is at the top, it is awkward to print the sequence of cities in their normal order from origin to destination.

4. There is a strong relationship between recursion and stacks. Most implementations of recursion maintain a stack of activation records in a manner that resembles the box method.

COMMON PITFALLS / DEBUGGING

1. Operations such as *StackTop* and *Pop* must take reasonable action when the data structure is empty. One possibility is to return a boolean flag whose value is *false* in this event.

2. Algorithms that evaluate an infix expression or transform one to postfix form must determine to which operands a given operator applies. Doing so allows for precedence and left-to-right association so that you can omit parentheses.

3. When searching for a sequence of flights between cities, you must take into account the possibility that the algorithm will make wrong choices. For example, the algorithm must be able to backtrack when it hits a dead end, and you must eliminate the possibility that the algorithm will cycle.

SELF-TEST EXERCISES

1. If you push the letters A, B, C, and D in order onto a stack of characters and then pop them, in what order will they be deleted from the stack?

2. What do the stacks *S* and *T* "look like" after the following sequence of operations:

```
Create(S)
Push(S, 1)
Push(S, 2)
Create(T)
Push(T, 3)
Push(T, 4)
Pop(S)
Push(S, StackTop(T))
```

(continues)

Figure 8-15

Flight map for Self-Test Exercise 8 and Exercise 12

```
Push(S, 5)
Pop(T)
Push(T, 6)
```

3. Under what conditions in the line-reversal problem would you choose an array-based implementation for the stack? Under what conditions would you choose a pointer-based implementation?

4. For each of the following strings, trace the execution of the balanced-parentheses algorithm and show the contents of the stack at each step.

    a. `x((yz)))`
    b. `(x(y((z)))`
    c. `(((x)))`

5. Use the stack algorithms in this chapter to evaluate the postfix expression $AB-C+$. Assume the following values for the identifiers: $A = 7$; $B = 3$; $C = -2$. Show the status of the stack after each step.

6. Use the stack algorithms in this chapter to convert the infix expression $A/B*C$ to postfix form. Be sure to account for left-to-right association. Show the status of the stack after each step.

7. Explain the significance of the precedence tests in the infix-to-postfix conversion algorithm. Why is a $\geq$ test used rather than a $>$ test?

8. Execute the HPAir algorithm with the map in Figure 8-15 for the following requests. Show the state of the stack after each step.

    a. Fly from A to D
    b. Fly from A to B
    c. Fly from C to G

EXERCISES

1. For the following input line, trace the execution of the *LineReverse* pseudocode and show the contents of the stack at each step:

    `abc#de##fg#h`

Figure 8-16

Railroad switching system

2. Revise the solution to the balanced-parentheses problem so that the expression can contain three types of parentheses: ( ), [ ], and { }. Thus, {ab(c[d])e} is valid, but {ab(c)) is not.

3. The diagram of a railroad switching system in Figure 8-16 is commonly used to illustrate the notion of a stack. Identify the three stacks and show how they relate to one another. How can you use this system to construct any possible permutation of railroad cars?

4. List the changes that you must make to change a program that uses an array-based implementation of a stack to one that uses a pointer-based implementation of a stack.

5. Suppose that you have a stack S and an empty auxiliary stack T. Show how you can do each of the following tasks by using the ADT stack operations:

   a. Print the contents of S in reverse order.
   b. Count the number of items in S, leaving S unchanged.
   c. Delete every occurrence of a specified item from S, leaving the order of the remaining items unchanged.

6. For each of the following strings, trace the execution of the language-recognition algorithm described in the section "Recognizing Strings in a Language," and show the contents of the stack at each step.

   a. xy$xy   c. y$yx
   b. xy$x   d. xx$xx

7. Implement in Pascal the line-reversal problem described in the section "The Stack As an Example of an ADT in Program Development."

8. Evaluate the following postfix expressions. Assume the following values for the identifiers: $A = 7$; $B = 3$; $C = -2$; $D = -5$; $E = 1$.

   a. $ABC+-$
   b. $ABC-D*+$
   c. $AB+C-DE*+$

9. Convert the following infix expressions to postfix form. Do not forget to account for the precedence rules and left-to-right association.

    a. *A–B+C*   e. *A–(B/C∗D)*
    b. *A/(B∗C)*   f. *A/B/C–(D+E)∗F*
    c. *(A+B)∗C*   g. *A∗(B/C/D)+E*
    d. *A–(B+C)*   h. *A–(B+C∗D)/E*

10. Repeat Exercises 8 and 9, but this time use the algorithms given in this chapter. Show the status of the stack after each step.

11. Implement the algorithm that evaluates postfix expressions in Pascal. For illustrative purposes, recognize only the operands *A, B, C, D,* and *E*, and write a procedure that assigns values to the operands as follows: $A = 5, B = 7, C = -1, D = 11,$ and $E = 25.$ Assign the value zero to any other operand. Although the pseudocode treats *StackTop* as a function, you may want to implement it as a procedure.

12. Execute the HPAir algorithm with the map in Figure 8-15 (see Self-Test Exercise 8) for the following requests. Show the state of the stack after each step.

    a. Fly from *A* to *G*
    b. Fly from *F* to *H*
    c. Fly from *E* to *I*
    d. Fly from *I* to *G*

13. Consider a popular variation of the ADT stack. Instead of the *Pop* and *StackTop* operations, define *Pop* to both retrieve and remove the top element from a stack. Modify the pointer-based and array-based implementations of the original ADT stack accordingly.

    How does this new definition of the ADT stack affect the infix-to-postfix conversion program and the HPAir program? How does it affect the postfix evaluation program that you wrote in Exercise 11?

14. You can implement two stacks in one array by having them grow toward each other from the opposite ends of the array, as shown in Figure 8-17. What are the advantages of one array rather than two separate arrays of half the size? Work out the details of an implementation. How are the limiting conditions (empty and full) recognized? Note that it is important that the two stacks do not run into each other.

15. Suppose that you redefine the *Pop* operation for a stack as follows:

    Pop(S, n)
    { Removes from stack S the n items that were most
    * recently added. It is an error if there are fewer*
    * than n items on S. }*

    Modify the pointer-based and array-based implementations of the original *Pop* operation to reflect this change. Could you define the new operation in terms of the old operations? Which implementation of the new operation would be more efficient?

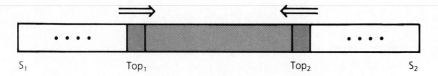

Figure 8-17

Two stacks implemented in a single array

S_1 Top_1 Top_2 S_2

16. In the implementation of the HPAir program, the search for the next unvisited city adjacent to a city *i* always starts at the beginning of the ith linked list in the adjacency list. This approach is actually a bit inefficient, because a city can never become unvisited after it has already been visited by the search. Modify the program so that the search for the next city begins where the last search left off. That is, maintain an array of *trynext* pointers into the adjacency list.

17. Write a nonrecursive procedure that solves the Towers of Hanoi problem, discussed in Chapter 6, by using stacks.

*18. As Chapter 4 pointed out, you can define ADT operations in a mathematically formal way by using axioms. For example, you can formally define the ADT stack by using the following axioms, where *S* is an arbitrary stack and *item* an arbitrary stack item. Note that *Create* is treated as a constant that represents a "newly created empty stack."

IsEmpty(Create) = true (A newly created stack is empty.)

IsEmpty(Push(S, item)) = false

Pop(Create) = Create (You could define this to be an error.)

Pop(Push(S, item)) = S

StackTop(Create) = error

StackTop(Push(S, item)) = item

You can use the axioms, for example, to prove that the stack defined by the sequence of operations

```
Create an empty stack
Push a 5
Push a 7
Push a 3
Pop (the 3)
Push a 9
Push a 4
Pop (the 4)
```

which you can write as

Pop(Push(Push(Pop(Push(Push(Push(Create,5),7),3)),9),4))

is exactly the same as the stack defined by the sequence

```
Create an empty stack
Push a 5
```

Push a 7

Push a 9

which you can write as

Push(Push(Push(Create,5),7),9)

Similarly, you can use the axioms to show

IsEmpty(Pop(Pop(Push(Pop(Push(Push(Create,1),2)),3))))
= true

a. The representation of a stack as a sequence *Push(Push(· · · Push(Create, · · ·)* without any *Pop* operations is called a **canonical form**. Prove that any stack is equal to a stack that is in canonical form.

b. Prove that the canonical form is unique. That is, a stack is equal to exactly one stack that is in canonical form.

c. Use the axioms to formally show the following:

StackTop(Pop(Push(Push(Pop(Push(Push(Pop(Pop(Push
(Create,6))),9),2)),3),1))) = 3

PROJECT

19. Consider an expanded statement of the HPAir problem. In addition to the "from" and "to" cities, each line of input contains a flight number (an integer) and the cost of the flight (an integer). Modify the HPAir program so that it will produce a complete itinerary for each request, including the flight number of each flight, the cost of each flight, and the total cost of the trip.

EXAMPLE

Input Files

Cityfile:	Albuquerque		
	Chicago		
	San Diego		

Flightfile:	703 Chicago	San Diego	125
	111 Chicago	Albuquerque	450
	178 Albuquerque	Chicago	450

Requestfile:	Albuquerque	San Diego
	Albuquerque	Paris
	San Diego	Chicago

Corresponding Output

```
Request is to fly from Albuquerque to San Diego.
Flight #178 from Albuquerque  to Chicago    Cost: $450
Flight #703 from Chicago      to San Diego Cost: $125
Total Cost ............  $575
```

```
Request is to fly from Albuquerque to Paris.
Sorry. HPAir does not service Paris.

Request is to fly from San Diego to Chicago
Sorry. HPAir does not have service from San Diego to
Chicago.
```

When the HPAir program in this chapter finds a sequence of flights from the origin city to the destination city, its stack contains the corresponding path of cities. The stumbling block to reporting this path is that the cities appear on the stack in reverse order; that is, the destination city is at the top of the stack and the origin city is at the bottom. For example, if you use the program to find a path from city *P* to city *Z* in Figure 8-8, the final contents of the stack will be *P-W-Y-Z*, with *Z* on top. You want to print the origin city *P* first, but it is at the bottom of the stack. If you restrict yourself to the stack operations, the only way that you can print the path in its correct order is first to reverse the stack by popping it onto a temporary stack and then to print the cities as you pop them off the temporary stack. Note that this approach requires that you process each city on the path twice.

Evidently a stack is not the appropriate ADT for the problem of printing the path of cities in the correct order; the appropriate ADT is a **traversable stack**. In addition to the five standard stack operations, *Create*, *IsEmpty*, *Push*, *Pop*, and *StackTop*, a traversable stack includes the operation *Traverse*. *Traverse* begins at one end of the stack and *visits* each item in the stack until it reaches the other end of the stack. For this project, you want *Traverse* to begin at the bottom of the stack and move toward the top.

What modifications are required to find a least-cost trip for each request? How can you incorporate time considerations into the problem?

CHAPTER 9

Queues

PREVIEW   The operations that define a queue give this ADT a behavior opposite from that of a stack. While a stack's behavior is characterized as last in, first
out, a queue's behavior is characterized as first in, first out. This chapter defines
the queue's operations and discusses strategies for implementing them.
Queues are important in simulation, a technique for analyzing the behavior of
complex systems. As an example of this application of queues, this chapter
presents a simulation of people waiting in line at a bank. The first-in, first-out
behavior of a queue makes this ADT an appropriate model for the behavior of
people in a line.

THE ABSTRACT DATA TYPE QUEUE

You can think of a stack as having only one end, because all operations are
performed at the top of the stack. This characteristic of the operations gives
a stack its last-in, first-out behavior. A **queue**, on the other hand, has two
ends: a **rear**, where new items are inserted, and a **front**, from which items
are deleted. This characteristic gives a queue its **first-in, first-out** (FIFO)
behavior, which makes it appropriate for modeling real-world structures
such as a line of customers.

FIFO: *The first item inserted into
a queue is the first item out*

The abstract data type queue is defined by five operations:

*ADT **Queue Operations***

KEY CONCEPTS

```
Create(Q)
{ Creates an empty queue Q. }

IsEmpty(Q)
{ Determines if queue Q is empty. }

Add(Q, newitem)
{ Adds newitem to queue Q. }

Remove(Q)
{ Removes from queue Q the item that was added earliest. }

QueueFront(Q)
{ Retrieves from queue Q the item that was added earliest,
  leaving Q unchanged. }
```

Figure 9-1 illustrates these operations with a queue of integers. Notice
that *Add* inserts an item at the rear of the queue and that *QueueFront*
looks at the item at the front of the queue, while *Remove* deletes the item
at the front of the queue.

Figure 9-1

Some queue operations

Operation	Queue after operation
	Front
	↓
`Create(Q)`	
`Add(Q, 5)`	5
`Add(Q, 2)`	5 2
`Add(Q, 7)`	5 2 7
`QueueFront(Q)`	5 2 7 (returns 5)
`Remove(Q)`	2 7

Consider how you might formalize the FIFO property of a queue by using axioms. For example, you need an axiom that indicates that after a series of *Add* operations, *QueueFront* returns the item I_1 added earliest. Intuitively, you want the axiom to say

`QueueFront(Add(···Add(Add(empty queue, I₁), I₂),···,Iₙ)) = I₁`

This attempt at an axiom is not completely rigorous, however, because the meaning of the dots, ··· , is not well defined. Exercise 8 at the end of this chapter discusses further the formal axioms that define the ADT queue.

A SIMPLE APPLICATION OF THE ADT QUEUE

Recall from Chapter 6 that a palindrome is a string of characters that reads the same from left to right as it does from right to left. In the previous chapter, you learned that you can use a stack to reverse the order of occurrences. You should realize now that you can use a queue to preserve the order of occurrences. Thus, you can use both a queue and a stack to determine whether a string is a palindrome.

You can use a queue in conjunction with a stack to recognize palindromes

As you read the character string from left to right, you can insert each character into both a queue and a stack. Figure 9-2 illustrates the result of this action for the string "abcbd." You can see that the first character in the string is at the front of the queue and at the bottom of the stack. Likewise, the last character in the string is at the rear of the queue but at the top of the stack.

Thus, you can compare the characters at the top of the stack and the front of the queue. If the characters are the same, you can delete them. You can repeat this process until either the ADT's become empty, in which case the original string is a palindrome, or the two characters are not the same, in which case the string is not a palindrome.

The following is a pseudocode version of a nonrecursive recognition algorithm for the language of palindromes:

```
function Pal(w) : returns a boolean value
{ Determines if w is a palindrome. }
```

```
    Create(Q)        { create a queue }
    Create(S)        { create a stack }

    { insert each character into both the queue and the stack }
    while (not end of line) do
    begin
        read(newchar)
        Add(Q, newchar)
        Push(S, newchar)
    end   { while }

    { compare the queue characters with the stack characters }
    Pal := true
    while (not IsEmpty(Q)) and Pal do
    begin
        if (QueueFront(Q) = StackTop(S))
            then
            begin
                Remove(Q)
                Pop(S)
            end   { if }

            else Pal := false
    end   { while }
```

String: a b c b d

Queue:

Front   Rear

Stack:

Figure 9-2

The results of inserting a string into both a queue and a stack

IMPLEMENTATIONS OF THE ADT QUEUE

As with stacks, there are array-based and pointer-based implementations of queues. The choice between the two implementations once again depends on whether or not your problem can use the fixed-size queue that an array-based implementation provides.

For queues, the pointer-based implementation is a bit more straightforward than the array-based one, so we start with it.

A Pointer-Based Implementation of the ADT Queue

You might expect a pointer-based implementation to use two external pointers, one to the front and one to the rear, as Figure 9-3a illustrates. However, as Figure 9-3b shows, you can actually get by with a single external pointer—to the rear—if you make the queue circular.

When a circular linked list represents a queue, the node at the rear of the queue points to the node at the front. Thus,

A circular linked list can represent a queue

Q points to the node at the rear of the queue, and

$Q^\wedge.next$ points to the node at the front

Insertion at the rear and deletion from the front are straightforward. Figure 9-4 illustrates the addition of an item to a nonempty queue. Inserting the new node, which p points to, at the rear of the queue requires three pointer changes: the next pointer in the new node, the next pointer in the rear node, and the external pointer Q. Figure 9-4 depicts these changes and

Figure 9-3

A pointer-based implementation of a queue: (a) with two external pointers; (b) circular

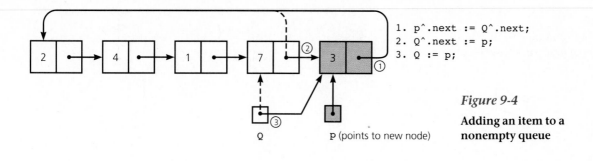

1. p^.next := Q^.next;
2. Q^.next := p;
3. Q := p;

Figure 9-4

Adding an item to a nonempty queue

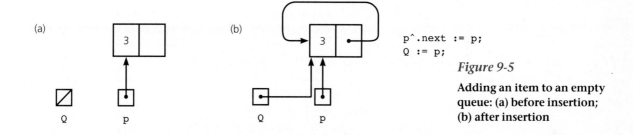

p^.next := p;
Q := p;

Figure 9-5

Adding an item to an empty queue: (a) before insertion; (b) after insertion

indicates the order in which they must occur. (The dashed lines indicate pointer values before the changes.) The addition of an item to an empty queue is a special case, as Figure 9-5 illustrates.

Deletion from the front of the queue is simpler than insertion at the rear. Figure 9-6 illustrates the removal of the front of a queue that contains more than one item. Notice that you need to change only one pointer. Deletion from a queue of one item is a special case that sets the external pointer *Q* to *nil*.

A pointer-based implementation in Pascal of the ADT queue operations follows.

```
{ ***********************************************************

BASIC QUEUE OPERATIONS - Pointer-Based Implementation

Create, IsEmpty, Add, Remove, and QueueFront

The following definitions are assumed:

type    itemtype = <desired type of queue item>;
        nodeptr  = ^node;
        node     = record
             item : itemtype;
             next : nodeptr
        end;
        queue = nodeptr
```

Figure 9-6

Removing an item from a queue of more than one item

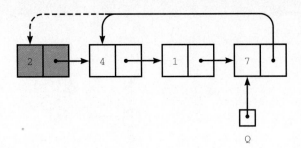

```
The queue is implemented as a circular linked list. The
single external pointer Q points to the rear of the queue.
*********************************************************** }
procedure Create(var Q : queue);
{ --------------------------------------------------------
  Creates an empty queue.
  Precondition: None.
  Postcondition: The queue Q is empty.
  -------------------------------------------------------- }
begin
    Q := nil
end;  { Create }

function IsEmpty(Q : queue) : boolean;
{ --------------------------------------------------------
  Determines if a queue is empty.
  Precondition: Queue Q has been created.
  Postcondition: Returns true if Q is empty, else returns
  false.
  -------------------------------------------------------- }
begin
    IsEmpty := (Q = nil)
end;  { IsEmpty }

procedure Add(var Q : queue; newitem : itemtype);
{ --------------------------------------------------------
  Adds an item to the rear of a queue.
  Precondition: Queue Q has been created.
  Postcondition: newitem is placed at the rear of Q.
  -------------------------------------------------------- }
var p : nodeptr;
begin
    { get a new node }
    new(p);
    p^.item := newitem;

    { insert the new node }
```

```
        if IsEmpty(Q)
            then p^.next := p { insertion into empty queue }

            else                { insertion into nonempty queue }
            begin
                p^.next := Q^.next;
                Q^.next := p
            end;
        Q := p
end;  { Add }

procedure Remove(var Q : queue; var success : boolean);
{ --------------------------------------------------------
  Removes the item at the front of a queue.
  Precondition: Queue Q has been created.
  Postcondition: If Q is not empty, the item that was added
  to Q earliest is removed and success is set to true.
  However, if Q is empty, removal is impossible and success
  is set to false.
  -------------------------------------------------------- }
var front : nodeptr;
begin
    if IsEmpty(Q)
        then success := false { empty queue - insertion fails }

        else
        begin
            front := Q^.next;
            if front = Q     { special case - one node in queue }
                then Q := nil
                else Q^.next := front^.next;
            dispose(front);
            success := true
        end  { if }
end;  { Remove }

procedure QueueFront(Q : queue; var getitem : itemtype;
                    var success : boolean);
{ --------------------------------------------------------
  Retrieves the item at the front of the queue.
  Precondition: Queue Q has been created.
  Postcondition: If Q is not empty, getitem contains the
  item that was added to Q earliest and success is set to
  true. However, if Q is empty, the operation fails and
  success is set to false. Q is unchanged.
  -------------------------------------------------------- }
begin
    if IsEmpty(Q)
        then success := false { empty queue - retrieval fails }
```

```
            else
            begin
                getitem := Q^.next^.item;
                success := true
            end { if }
    end   { QueueFront }
```

An Array-Based Implementation of the ADT Queue

An array-based implementation is appropriate for applications in which a fixed-sized queue does not present a problem. As Figure 9-7a illustrates, a naive array-based implementation might define a queue as follows:

A naive array-based implementation of a queue suffers from rightward drift

```
    const   maxqueue = <maximum size of queue>;
    type    itemtype = <desired type of queue item>;
            queue = record
                Front : 1..maxqueue;
                Rear  : 0..maxqueue;
                Items : array[1..maxqueue] of itemtype
            end;

    var     Q : queue
```

The queue is initialized with *Front* = 1 and *Rear* = 0. When a new item is added to the queue, *Rear* is incremented and the item is placed in the position that the new value of *Rear* references. When an item is removed, *Front* is incremented. The queue is empty whenever *Rear* < *Front*. The queue is full when *Rear* = *maxqueue*.

Rightward drift can cause a queue-full condition even though the queue contains few entries

The problem with this strategy is **rightward drift**—that is, after a sequence of additions and removals, the items in the queue will drift down to the high end of the array, and *Rear* could equal *maxqueue* even when there are only a few items currently in the queue. Figure 9-7b illustrates this situation.

Figure 9-7

(a) A naive array-based implementation of a queue; (b) rightward drift

(a)

(b)

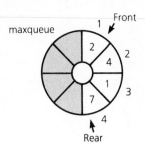

Figure 9-8

A circular implementation of a queue

One possible solution to this problem is to shift array elements to the left, either after each deletion or whenever *Rear* = maxqueue. This solution guarantees that the queue can always contain up to *maxqueue* items. Shifting is not really satisfactory, however, as it would dominate the cost of the implementation.

Shifting elements to compensate for rightward drift is expensive

A much more elegant solution is possible by viewing the array as circular, as Figure 9-8 illustrates. You advance the queue indexes *Front*—to remove an item—and *Rear*—to add an item—by moving them clockwise around the array. Figure 9-9 illustrates the effect of a sequence of three queue operations on *Front*, *Rear*, and the array. When either *Front* or *Rear* advances past location *maxqueue*, it wraps around to location 1. This wraparound eliminates the problem of rightward drift, which occurred in the previous implementation, because here the circular array has no end.

A circular array eliminates right-ward drift

The only difficulty with this scheme is the detection of the queue-empty and queue-full conditions. It seems reasonable to select as the queue-empty condition

Front and Rear cannot be used to distinguish between queue-full and queue-empty conditions

> *Front is one slot ahead of Rear*

since this appears to indicate that *Front* "passes" *Rear* when the queue becomes empty, as Figure 9-10a depicts. However, it is also possible that this condition signals a full queue: Because the queue is circular, *Rear* might in fact "catch up" with *Front* as the queue becomes full; Figure 9-10b illustrates this situation.

Figure 9-9

No drifting

Figure 9-10

(a) **Front** passes **Rear** when
the queue becomes empty;
(b) **Rear** catches up to
Front when the queue
becomes full

(a)

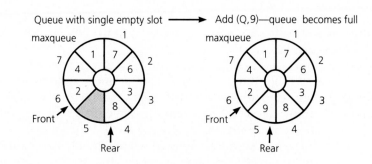

(b)

Obviously, you need a way to distinguish between the two situations.
One such way is to keep a count of the number of items in the queue.
Before adding to the queue, you check to see if the count is equal to *max-queue*; if it is, the queue is full. Before removing an item from the queue,
you check to see if the count is equal to zero; if it is, the queue is empty.

*By counting queue items, you
can detect queue-full and queue-
empty conditions*

The implementation of this scheme in Pascal uses the following
definitions:

An array-based queue

```
const   maxqueue = <maximum size of queue>;

type    itemtype = <desired type of queue item>;
        queue = record
              Items : array[1..maxqueue] of itemtype;
              Front, Rear : 1..maxqueue;
              Count : 0..maxqueue
        end;

var     Q : queue
```

Initialize **Front**, **Rear**, *and*
Count

The queue is initialized with *Front* = 1, *Rear* = *maxqueue*, and *Count*
= 0. You obtain the wraparound effect of a circular queue by using modulo
arithmetic (that is, Pascal's *mod* operator) when incrementing *Front* and
Rear. For example, you can add *newitem* to the queue by using the
statements

```
      Q.Rear := (Q.Rear mod maxqueue) + 1;
      Q.Items[Q.Rear] := newitem;
      Q.Count := Q.Count + 1
```

Adding to the rear of a queue

Notice that if *Rear* equaled *maxqueue* before the addition of *newitem*, the first statement, $Q.Rear := (Q.Rear \ mod \ maxqueue) + 1$, would have the effect of wrapping *Rear* around to location 1.

Similarly, you can remove an item from the front of the queue by using the statements

```
      Q.Front := (Q.Front mod maxqueue) + 1;
      Q.Count := Q.Count − 1
```

Removing from the front of a queue

The following Pascal subprograms represent an array-based implementation of the ADT queue that uses a circular array as just described.

```
{ **********************************************************
  BASIC QUEUE OPERATIONS - Array-Based Implementation

      Create, IsEmpty, Add, Remove, and QueueFront

  The following definitions are assumed:

      const maxqueue = <maximum size of queue>;
      type  itemtype = <desired type of queue item>;
            queue = record
                Items : array[1..maxqueue] of itemtype;
                Front, Rear : 1..maxqueue;
                Count : 0..maxqueue
            end

  The array is circular. Front and Rear point respectively
  to the front and rear of the queue. Count indicates the
  number of items currently in the queue.
  ********************************************************** }
procedure Create(var Q : queue);
{ ---------------------------------------------------------
  Creates an empty queue.
  Precondition: None.
  Postcondition: The queue Q is empty.
  --------------------------------------------------------- }
begin
   Q.Front := 1;
   Q.Rear := maxqueue;
   Q.Count := 0
end; { Create }

function IsEmpty(Q : queue) : boolean;
{ ---------------------------------------------------------
  Determines if a queue is empty.
  Precondition: Queue Q has been created.
```

Postcondition: Returns true if Q is empty, else returns
false.
-- }
begin
    IsEmpty := (Q.Count = 0)
end; { IsEmpty }

procedure Add(**var** Q : queue; newitem : itemtype;
              var success : boolean);
{ --
  Adds an item to the rear of a queue.
  Precondition: Queue Q has been created.
  Postcondition: If Q is not full, newitem is placed at the
  rear of Q and success is set to true; otherwise success is
  set to false.
  Note: The queue is full if it has maxqueue items.
-- }
begin
    if Q.Count = maxqueue
        then success := false { full queue - insertion fails }

        else
        begin
            Q.Rear := (Q.Rear **mod** maxqueue) + 1;
            Q.Items[Q.Rear] := newitem;
            Q.Count := Q.Count + 1;
            success := true
        end { if }
end; { Add }

procedure Remove(**var** Q : queue; **var** success : boolean);
{ --
  Removes the item at the front of a queue.
  Precondition: Queue Q has been created.
  Postcondition: If Q is not empty, the item that was added
  to Q earliest is removed and success is set to true.
  However, if Q is empty, removal is impossible and success
  is set to false.
-- }
begin
    if IsEmpty(Q)
        then success := false   { empty queue — deletion fails }

        else
        begin
            Q.Front := (Q.Front **mod** maxqueue) + 1;
            Q.Count := Q.Count — 1;
            success := true
        end { if }
end; { Remove }

```
procedure QueueFront(Q : queue; var getitem : itemtype;
                     var success : boolean);
{ --------------------------------------------------------
  Retrieves the item at the front of the queue.
  Precondition: Queue Q has been created.
  Postcondition: If Q is not empty, getitem contains the
  item that was added to Q earliest and success is set to
  true. However, if Q is empty, the operation fails and
  success is set to false. Q is unchanged.
  -------------------------------------------------------- }
begin
   if IsEmpty(Q)
      then success := false { empty queue - retrieval fails }

      else
      begin
         getitem := Q.Items[Q.Front];
         success := true
      end { if }
end { QueueFront }
```

There are several variations of this scheme in common use that do not require a count of the number of items in the queue. In our opinion, however, these implementations are not quite as clean as the one just presented. Exercises 3 and 4 at the end of this chapter consider two of the alternate schemes.

SIMULATION AS AN APPLICATION OF THE ADT QUEUE

Simulation is a major application area for computers. It is a technique for modeling the behavior of both natural and human-made systems. Generally, the goal of a simulation is to generate statistics that summarize the performance of an existing system or to predict the performance of a proposed system. In this section we present a simple example that illustrates one important type of simulation.

Simulation models the behavior of systems

Consider the following problem. Ms. Drysdale, president of the First City Bank of Shiprock, has heard her customers complain about how long they have to wait for service. Because she fears that they may move their accounts to another bank, she is considering whether to hire a second teller.

Before Ms. Drysdale hires another teller, she would like an approximation of the average time that a customer has to wait for service from First

City's only teller. How can Ms. Drysdale obtain this information? She could stand with a stopwatch in the bank's lobby all day, but she does not find this prospect particularly exciting. Besides, she would like to use a method that also allows her to predict how much improvement she could expect if the bank hired a given number of additional tellers. She certainly does not want to hire the tellers on a trial basis and monitor the bank's performance before making a final decision.

Ms. Drysdale concludes that the best way to obtain the information she wants is to simulate the behavior of her bank. The first step in simulating a system such as a bank is to construct a mathematical model that captures the relevant information about the system. For example, how many tellers does the bank employ? How often do customers arrive? If the model accurately describes the real-world system, you can use a simulation to derive accurate predictions about the system's overall performance. For example, a simulation could predict the average time a customer has to wait before receiving service. You can also use a simulation to evaluate proposed changes to the real-world system. For example, to evaluate an increase in the number of tellers in the bank, you could make the appropriate changes in the model and use the simulation to predict the behavior of this hypothetical system. A large decrease in the time predicted for the average wait of a customer might justify the cost of hiring additional tellers.

Simulated time   Central to a simulation is the concept of simulated time. Envision a stopwatch that measures elapsed time as the simulation mimics the behavior of the system under study. For example, suppose that the model of the bank specifies that there is one teller. At *Time* = 0, which is the start of the banking day, the simulated system would be in its initial state with no customers. As the simulation runs, the stopwatch ticks away units of time—perhaps minutes—and certain events occur. At *Time* = 12 the bank's first customer arrives. Since there is no line, the customer goes directly to the teller and begins her transaction. At *Time* = 20, a second customer arrives. Because the first customer has not yet completed her transaction, the second customer must wait in line. At *Time* = 38, the first customer completes her transaction and the second customer can begin his. Figure 9-11 illustrates these four times in the simulation.

To gather the information you need, you run this simulation for a specified period of simulated time. During the course of the run, you need to keep track of certain statistics, such as the average time a customer has to wait for service. Notice that in the small example of Figure 9-11, the first customer had to wait 0 minutes to begin a transaction and the second customer had to wait 18 minutes to begin a transaction—an average wait of 9 minutes.

One point not addressed in the previous discussion is how to determine when certain events occur. For example, why did we say that the first customer arrived at *Time* = 12 and the second at *Time* = 20? After studying real-world systems like our bank, mathematicians learned to model events such as the arrival of people by using techniques from probability theory. This statistical information is incorporated into the mathematical model

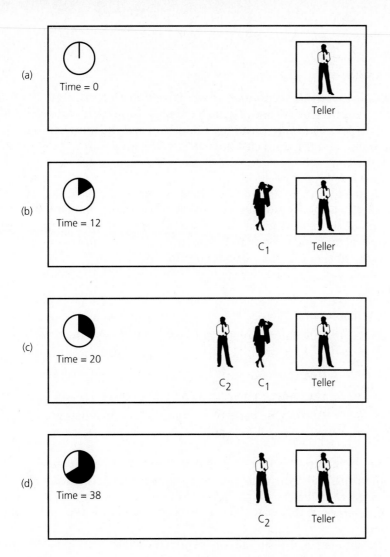

Figure 9-11

(a) *Time* = 0; (b) *Time* = 12;
(c) *Time* = 20; (d) *Time* = 38

of the system and is used to generate events in a way that reflects the real world. The simulation uses these events and is thus called an **event-driven simulation**. Note that the goal is to reflect long-term average behavior of the system rather than to predict occurrences of specific events. This goal is sufficient for the needs of the simulation.

Although the techniques for generating events to reflect the real world are interesting and important, they require a good deal of mathematical sophistication. Therefore, simply assume that you already have a list of events available for your use. In particular, for the bank problem, assume that a file contains the time of each customer's arrival—an **arrival event**—and the duration of that customer's transaction once the customer reaches the teller. For example, the data

*Sample arrival and transaction
times*

20   3

22   9

30   6

indicates that the first customer arrives 20 minutes into the simulation and that the transaction—once begun—requires 3 minutes; the second customer arrives 22 minutes into the simulation and the transaction requires 9 minutes; and the third customer arrives 30 minutes into the simulation and the transaction requires 6 minutes. Assume that the input file is ordered by arrival time.

Notice that there are no **departure events** in the data; the data does not specify when a customer will complete the transaction and leave. It is the job of the simulation to determine when departures occur. By using the arrival time and the transaction length, the simulation easily can determine the time at which a customer departs. To see how to make this determination, you can conduct a simulation by hand with the previous data as follows:

The results of a simulation

Time	Event
20	Customer 1 enters bank and begins transaction
22	Customer 2 enters bank and stands at end of line
23	Customer 1 departs; customer 2 begins transaction
30	Customer 3 enters bank and stands at end of line
32	Customer 2 departs; customer 3 begins transaction
38	Customer 3 departs

Notice that the amount of time that elapses between a customer's arrival in the bank and the time that the customer reaches the front of the line and begins a transaction is the amount of time the customer has to wait. It is the average of this wait time over all the customers that you want to obtain.

To summarize, this simulation is concerned with two types of events:

- **Arrival events (A).** These events indicate the arrival at the bank of a new customer. The input file specifies the times at which the arrival events occur. As such, they are **external events**. When a customer arrives at the bank, one of two things happens. If the teller is idle when the customer arrives, the customer begins the transaction immediately. If the teller is busy, the new customer must stand at the end of the line and wait for service.

- **Departure events (D).** These events indicate the departure from the bank of a customer who has completed a transaction. The simulation determines the times at which the departure events occur. As such, they are **internal events**. When a customer completes the transaction, he or she departs and the next person in line—if there is one—begins a transaction.

You now must develop an algorithm to perform the simulation. The main task of the algorithm is to determine the times at which the events occur and to process the events when they do occur. The algorithm is stated at a high level as follows:

```
{ initialize }
Time := 0
Initialize the line to "no customers"

while Time ≤ time of the final event do
begin
    if an arrival event occurs at time Time
        then process the arrival event

    if a departure event occurs at time Time
        then process the departure event

    { when an arrival event and departure event occur at the
      same time, arbitrarily process the arrival event first }

    Time := Time + 1
end
```

A first attempt at a simulation algorithm

Do you really want to increment `Time` by 1? You would for a **time-driven simulation**, where you would determine arrival and departure times randomly and compare those times to `Time`. In such a case, you would increment `Time` by 1 to simulate the ticking of a clock. Recall, however, that this simulation is **event driven**, so you have a file of arrival times and transaction times. Because you are interested only in those times at which arrival and departure events occur, and as no action is required at the time steps between the occurrences of events, you can advance `Time` from the time of one event directly to the time of the next.

A time-driven simulation simulates the ticking of a clock

An event-driven simulation considers only times of certain events, in this case, arrivals and departures

Thus, you can revise the pseudocode solution as follows:

```
{ initialize }
Initialize the line to "no customers"

while there remain events to be processed do
begin
    Time := time of next event

    if an arrival event occurs
        then process the arrival event
        else process the departure event { the other possibility}

    { when an arrival event and departure event occur at the
      same time, arbitrarily process the arrival event first }
end
```

First revision of the simulation algorithm

You must determine the time of the next arrival or departure event so that you can implement the statement

```
        Time := time of next event
```

An event list contains all future events

This determination entails the maintenance of an **event list.** An event list contains all arrival and departure events that will occur but have not occurred yet. The times of the events in the event list are in ascending order, and thus the next event to be processed is always at the head of the list. The algorithm simply gets the event from the head of the list, advances to the time specified, and processes the event. The difficulty lies in successfully managing such an event list.

The particular event list here contains at most one arrival event and one departure event

For this particular problem you can manage the event list so that it always contains at most one event of each kind. Recall that the arrival events are specified in the input file and that they appear in ascending time order. You thus never need to worry about an arrival event until you have processed all the arrival events that precede it in the file. You simply keep the earliest unprocessed arrival event on the event list. When you eventually process this event—that is, when it is time for this customer to arrive—you replace it on the event list with the next unprocessed arrival event, which is the next item in the input file.

Similarly, you need to place only the next departure event to occur on the event list. But how can you determine the times for the departure events? Observe that the next departure event always corresponds to the customer that the teller is currently serving. As soon as a customer begins service, you can determine the time of his or her departure. This time is simply

time of next departure = time service begins + length of customer's transaction

Recall that the length of the customer's transaction is in the input file along with the arrival time. Thus, as soon as a customer begins service, you place a departure event corresponding to this customer on the event list. Figure 9-12 illustrates a typical instance of the event list for this particular simulation.

Now consider how you can process an event when it is time for the event to occur. You must perform two general types of actions:

Two tasks are required to process each event

- **Update the line:** Add or remove customers.
- **Update the event list:** Add or remove new events.

Figure 9-12

A typical instance of the event list

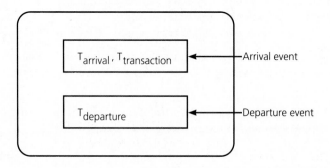

Notice that as customers arrive, they are added to the rear of the line. The current customer, who is at the front of the line, is receiving service, and it is this customer that you remove from the system next. It is thus natural to use a queue to manage the customers in the system. For this problem, the only information that you store in the queue about each customer is the time of arrival and the length of the transaction.

A queue represents the customers in line

To summarize, you process an event as follows:

```
TO PROCESS AN ARRIVAL EVENT FOR CUSTOMER C
```

The event-processing algorithm

```
Update the line:

    Add the new customer C to the queue

Update the event list:

    Remove the arrival event for Customer C from the event list
    if not at the end of the input file
        then add a new arrival event to the event list
          (time of event = time specified in file)

    if the new customer C began service immediately
    { i.e., the queue was empty so customer C went directly
      to the teller }
        then add a departure event for customer C to the event list
          (time of event = current time + transaction length)

TO PROCESS A DEPARTURE EVENT

Update the line:

    Remove the first customer from the queue
    { if the queue does not become empty, then the new first
      customer begins service }

Update the event list:

    Remove the departure event from the event list
    if the queue has not become empty
        then add to the event list the departure event for
            the person now at the front of the queue (time of
            event = current time + transaction length)
```

Examining the event list more closely will help explain the workings of the algorithm. Although the event list has no general form among various simulations, for this particular simulation, it has four possible configurations as follows. Initially, the event list contains an arrival event A after you read the first arrival event from the input file but before you process it:

> Event List: A

Generally, the event list for this simulation contains exactly two events: one arrival event A and one departure event D. Either the departure event is first or the arrival event is first as follows:

Event List: *D A*   (general case—next event is a departure),

or

Event List: *A D*   (general case—next event is an arrival)

If the departure event is first and that event leaves the teller's line empty, a new departure event does not replace the just-processed event. Thus, in this case, the event list appears as

Event List: *A*   (a departure leaves the teller's line empty)

Notice that this instance of the event list is the same as its initial state.

If the arrival event is first and if, after it is processed, there are no more arrival events in the input file, the event list contains only a departure event:

Event List: *D*   (the input has been exhausted)

Also notice that new events may be inserted either at the beginning of the event list or at the end, depending on the relative times of the new event and the event currently on the list. For example, suppose that the event list contains only an arrival event *A* and that you generate a departure event *D* for the customer who is now at the front of the line and beginning a transaction. If the customer's departure time is before the time of the arrival event *A*, then you must insert the departure event *D* before the event *A* in the event list. However, if the departure time is after the time of the arrival event, you must insert the departure event *D* after the arrival event *A*. In the case of a tie, you need a rule to determine which event should take precedence. In this solution we have arbitrarily chosen to place the departure event after the arrival event.

You can now combine and refine the pieces of the solution into an algorithm that performs the simulation. The following algorithm uses the ADT queue operations to manage the bank line. Notice that the procedure *ProcessA* updates the event list before it updates the line. This ordering allows the use of the function *IsEmpty* to determine whether the new arrival begins service immediately; if so, then you must add a departure event for the new arrival to the event list. Also, before calling procedures *ProcessA* and *ProcessD*, the main program removes from the event list the event that is about to be processed. This removal is thus not performed by procedures *ProcessA* and *ProcessD*. The other refinements to the algorithm should be self-explanatory.

The final pseudocode for the
event-driven simulation

```
ProcessA(event)
{ Procedure to process an arrival event. }

    { update the event list }
    if IsEmpty(Q)
        then { the line is empty, so the customer
               goes directly to the teller }
```

```
        Add to the event list a departure event that corresponds
        to the new customer and has Time = Time + transaction
        length

    if not at the end of the input file
        then
        begin
            Get the next arrival event from the input file
            Add the event--with time as specified in the input
                file--to the event list

    { update the line by adding the new customer to the queue }
    item := information about new customer
    Add(Q, item)

ProcessD(event)
{ Procedure to process a departure event. }

    { update the line by removing the first customer }
    Remove(Q, success)

    { update the event list }
    if not IsEmpty(Q)
        then add to the event list a departure event that
            corresponds to the customer now at the front of the
            line and has Time = Time + transaction length

{ MAIN PROGRAM }

    { initialize the event list }
    Get the first arrival event from the input file
    Place event on the event list

    { initialize the bank line }
    Create(Q)
    while the event list is not empty do
    begin
        { get next event from the beginning of the event list }
        Let newevent be the first event on the event list
        Remove the first event from the event list

        Time := time specified by newevent

        if newevent is an arrival event
            then ProcessA(newevent)
            else ProcessD(newevent)
    end   { while }
```

A Pascal implementation of the simulation follows. Note that this demonstration program uses a global record to count customers and to keep track of their cumulative waiting time. These statistics are sufficient to compute the average waiting time after the last event has been processed.

```
program SimulationDemo(input, Inputfile, output);
{ *********************************************************
  SAMPLE EVENT-DRIVEN SIMULATION

  Simulation of a single waiting line of people.

  There are two kinds of events:

      A : arrival - enter the line
      D : departure - complete transaction and leave the line

  Input:  The textfile Inputfile. Each line contains the
          arrival time and required transaction time for a
          person.

  Assumption: The arrival times are ordered by increasing time.

  Output: A trace of the events executed.
          Summary statistics (total number of arrivals,
          average time spent waiting in line).

  Data Structures:
      Line of people--a queue
      Event list--a linked list of 2 kinds of event nodes:
        arrival event - an arrival time and a transaction time
        departure event - a departure time

  Subprograms:
      Einsert    - inserts event node into event list
      getA       - reads arrival event from input file,
                     inserts it into event list
      ProcessA   - executes an arrival event
      ProcessD   - executes a departure event
      ADT Queue operations

  Major Global Variables:
      Q           - queue (line of people)
      E           - event list
      Stats       - a record with two fields as follows:
        totnum    - total number of arrivals (customers)
        totwait   - cumulative time spent waiting in line
  ********************************************************* }

      { queue }
type  itemtype = record
          trans,                              { transaction time }
          arrive : integer;                   { arrival time }
      end;  { record }
      nodeptr = ^node;
      node  = record
          item : itemtype;
          next : nodeptr
      end;  { record }
```

```
          queue = nodeptr;

          { event list }
          events = (A, D);                    { arrival/departure }
          enodeptr = ^enode;
          enode = record
                next : enodeptr;              { next event }
                time : integer;               { time of event }
                case etype : events of        { type of event }
                     A : (trans : integer);   { transaction time }
                     D : ()
                end;  { record }

          statistics = record
                totnum  : integer;  { total no. of customers }
                totwait : integer   { cumulative waiting time }
          end;  { record }
var   Q : queue;               { the waiting line }
      E : enodeptr;            { the event list }
      Stats : statistics;      { global statistics }
      Inputfile : text;        { arrival and transaction times }
      NewEvent : enode;        { the current event node }

#include QueueOps;             { include the queue operations }

procedure Einsert(var E : enodeptr; newnode : enodeptr);
{ --------------------------------------------------------
  Inserts an event node into the event list ordered by time.
  Precondition: Event list E is empty or has 1 node.
  Postcondition: newnode is added to E such that times are
  ordered. (In case of nodes with the same times, arrival
  events come before departure events.)
  -------------------------------------------------------- }
begin
   { if the event list is empty }
   if E = nil then
      E := newnode

   { if the event list is not empty, then insert new node at
     front or end of list according to time }

   { new node has earliest time or has same time, but is
     arrival event - insert at front of list }
   else if (newnode^.time < E^.time) or
        ((newnode^.time = E^.time) and (newnode^.etype = A))
   then
   begin
       newnode^.next := E;
       E := newnode
   end
```

```
                    { new node has later time or has same time, but is
                      departure event - insert at end of the list }
                    else
                    begin
                       newnode^.next := nil;
                       E^.next := newnode
                    end
                end;   { Einsert }

                procedure getA(var E : enodeptr);
                { ------------------------------------------------------------
                  Reads data for the next arrival event, and inserts the new
                  arrival node into the event list E.
                  Precondition: Inputfile is a textfile of arrival and
                  transaction times, E is the current event list.
                  Postcondition: Event read from Inputfile and inserted into
                  E. At end-of-file, does nothing to E.
                  Calls: Einsert.
                  File: Inputfile.
                  ------------------------------------------------------------ }
                var p : enodeptr;
                begin
                    if not eof(Inputfile)
                       then
                       begin
                           { create a new event node }
                           new(p);                { get pointer to new node }
                           p^.etype := A;         { tag field = arrival event }
                           p^.next := nil;
                           readln(Inputfile, p^.time, p^.trans);

                           { insert the node into the event list }
                           Einsert(E, p)
                       end
                end;   { getA }

                procedure ProcessA(doevent: enode; var E : enodeptr);
                { ------------------------------------------------------------
                  Executes an arrival event.
                  Precondition: Event node doevent contains the arrival
                  event, E is the event list, the queue Q has been created,
                  an input file of arrival events is available, global
                  Stats.totnum is the total number of arrivals.
                  Postcondition: If waiting line (queue) is empty, departure
                  event is inserted into event list. A new arrival event
                  read from the input file is inserted into event list,
                  doevent is added to waiting line (queue). Stats.totnum
                  (total no. of arrivals) is updated.
```

```
  Calls: Einsert, getA, IsEmpty, Add.
  ----------------------------------------------------------- }
var current : integer;          { arrival time of current person }
    PersonInLine : itemtype; { data about person in queue }
    event : enodeptr;           { event in event list }
begin
  { update the global statistics }
  Stats.totnum := Stats.totnum + 1;

  { get current time }
  current := doevent.time;
  writeln('Processing an arrival event at time: ', current:4);

  { update the event list }

  { if the line is empty, then the person starts transaction }
  if IsEmpty(Q)
     then
     begin
         { create a departure event }
         new(event);            { get pointer to new node }
         event^.etype := D;  { tag field = departure event }
         event^.next := nil;
         event^.time := current + doevent.trans;

         { insert the node into the event list }
         Einsert(E, event)
     end;

  { get the next arrival event from input file }
  getA(E);

  { person arrives: update the waiting line (queue) }
  PersonInLine.trans := doevent.trans;
  PersonInLine.arrive := current;
  Add(Q, PersonInLine )
end;   { ProcessA }

procedure ProcessD(doevent : enode; var E : enodeptr);
{ -----------------------------------------------------------
  Executes a departure event.
  Precondition: Event node doevent contains the departure
  event, E is the event list, the queue Q has been created,
  global Stats.totwait is the total waiting time.
  Postcondition: A person is removed from the queue; the
  event list is updated by adding a departure event for the
  next customer, if any; Stats.totwait (total waiting time)
  is updated.
  Calls: Einsert, IsEmpty, Remove, QueueFront.
  ----------------------------------------------------------- }
```

```pascal
var current : integer;          { arrival time of current person }
    PersonInLine : itemtype; { data about person in queue }
    event : enodeptr;          { event in event list }
    success : boolean;          { flag for queue ops - ignored }
begin
   current := doevent.time;
   writeln('Processing a departure event at time: ',
                                              current:3);

   { person departs - update the line (queue) }
   Remove(Q, success);      { remove person from queue }

   { update the event list }

   { if the line is not empty, then the
     next person starts a transaction }
   if not IsEmpty(Q)
      then
      begin
         { create a departure node }
         QueueFront(Q, PersonInLine, success);
         new(event);          { get pointer to new node }
         event^.etype := D; { tag field = departure event }
         event^.next := nil;
         event^.time := current + PersonInLine.trans;

         { insert the node into the event list }
         Einsert(E, event);

         { update the global statistics }
         Stats.totwait := Stats.totwait + (current -
                                     PersonInLine.arrive)

      end
end;   { ProcessD }

begin   { Main Program }

   { initialize }
   Create(Q);
   E := nil;
   reset(Inputfile);
   Stats.totnum := 0;
   Stats.totwait := 0;

   writeln('Simulation Begins');

   { get the first arrival event }
   getA(E);

   { process events until the event list is empty }
   while E <> nil do
   begin
      NewEvent := E^; { next event at beginning of event list }
```

```
        E := E^.next;   { delete event from event list }
      if NewEvent.etype = A
          then ProcessA(NewEvent, E)   { process arrival }
          else ProcessD(NewEvent, E)   { process departure }
    end;   { while }

    writeln('Simulation Ends');

    { write out the final statistics }
    writeln;
    writeln('Final Statistics:');
    writeln(' Total number of people processed: ',
                                    Stats.totnum:3);
    write(' Average amount of time spent on line: ');
    if Stats.totnum = 0
      then writeln(' 0.0')
      else writeln((Stats.totwait)/(Stats.totnum):5:1)
end.  { program }
```

If this program were run with the input file shown in the left columns of the following table, it would produce the output shown in the right column:

Input file		Output
1	5	Simulation Begins
2	5	Processing an arrival event at time: 1
4	5	Processing an arrival event at time: 2
20	5	Processing an arrival event at time: 4
22	5	Processing a departure event at time: 6
24	5	Processing a departure event at time: 11
26	5	Processing a departure event at time: 16
28	5	Processing an arrival event at time: 20
30	5	Processing an arrival event at time: 22
88	3	Processing an arrival event at time: 24
		Processing a departure event at time: 25
		Processing an arrival event at time: 26
		Processing an arrival event at time: 28
		Processing an arrival event at time: 30
		Processing a departure event at time: 30
		Processing a departure event at time: 35
		Processing a departure event at time: 40
		Processing a departure event at time: 45
		Processing a departure event at time: 50
		Processing an arrival event at time: 88
		Processing a departure event at time: 91
		Simulation Ends
		Final Statistics:
		Total number of people processed: 10
		Average amount of time spent on line: 5.6

A SUMMARY OF POSITION-ORIENTED ADT'S

Operations for the ADT's ordered list, stack, and queue reference the position of items

So far, we have introduced three abstract data types—the ordered list, the stack, and the queue—that have a common theme: All of their operations are defined in terms of the positions of their data items. Stacks and queues greatly restrict the positions that their operations can affect; their operations apply only to the end positions of their structures. The ordered list removes this restriction.

There is really a great deal of similarity between stacks and queues. This similarity becomes apparent if you pair off their operations. In the following list of pairs, we have changed the names of the operations where necessary to avoid ambiguity.

A comparison of stack and queue operations

- *CreateStack(S)* and *CreateQueue(Q)*. These operations create an empty structure of the appropriate type.

- *StackEmpty(S)* and *QueueEmpty(Q)*. These operations tell whether there are any items in the structure. Notice that in both cases the operations do not look beyond the ends of their structures to see how many items are present. Rather, the operations tell only if there is an item present at one of the ends.

- *Push(S, newitem)* and *Add(Q, newitem)*. These operations insert a new item into one end (the top and rear) of their structures.

- *Pop(S)* and *Remove(Q)*. *Pop* deletes the last item, which is at the top of the stack, and *Remove* deletes the first item, which is at the front of the queue.

- *StackTop(S)* and *QueueFront(Q)*. *StackTop* retrieves the last item, which is at the top of the stack, and *QueueFront* retrieves the first item, which is at the front of the queue.

The ADT ordered list, introduced in Chapter 4, allows you to insert into, delete from, and inspect the item at any position of the structure. Thus, it has the most flexible operations of the three position-oriented ADT's. You can view the ordered list operations *Length*, *Insert*, *Delete*, and *Retrieve* as generalizing the stack and queue operations to the logical extreme as follows:

Ordered list operations generalize stack and queue operations

- *Length(L)*. If you remove the restriction that *StackEmpty* and *QueueEmpty* can tell only when an item is present at the ends of their structures, you obtain an operation that can count the number of items that are present.

- *Insert(L, i, newitem)*. If you remove the restriction that *Push* and *Add* can insert new items only into one position, you obtain a general *Insert* operation that can insert a new item into any position *i* of the list.

- *Delete(L, i)*. If you remove the restriction that *Pop* and *Remove* can delete items only from one position, you obtain a general *Delete* operation that can delete an item from any position i of the list.

- **Retrieve(L, i)**. If you remove the restriction that *StackTop* and *QueueFront* can retrieve items only from one position, you obtain a general *Retrieve* operation that can retrieve the item from any position i of the list.

Because each of these three ADT's defines its operations in terms of an item's position in the structure, we have presented implementations for them that can provide easy access to specified positions. For example, both of the stack implementations allow the first position (top) to be accessed quickly, while both of the queue implementations allow the first position (front) and the last position (rear) to be accessed quickly.

In the remainder of this book, you will study ADT's that organize their data by value. That is, rather than asking for the ith item on a list, the operations of these ADT's will ask, for example, for the item with name John Smith. To support these types of operations efficiently, you will need new and more complex data structures.

SUMMARY

1. The definition of the queue operations gives this ADT first-in, first-out (FIFO) behavior.

2. As is the case for the other ADT's that you have studied, the primary criterion for choosing between an array-based and a pointer-based implementation of a queue is the issue of fixed versus dynamic size.

3. Models of real-world systems often use queues. The event-driven simulation in this chapter used a queue to model a line of customers.

4. Central to a simulation is the notion of simulated time. In a time-driven simulation, simulated time is advanced by a single time unit, whereas in an event-driven simulation, simulated time is advanced to the time of the next event. To implement an event-driven simulation, you maintain an event list that contains events that have not yet occurred. The list is ordered by the time of the events so that the next event to occur is always at the head of the list.

COMMON PITFALLS / DEBUGGING

1. The pointer-based queue implementation is straightforward, but a linear array-based implementation has to overcome the problem

of rightward drift of the elements in the array. This problem can lead to a queue-full condition even though only a few items are present.

2. You can solve the problem of rightward drift by viewing the array as circular. However, you must be able to distinguish between the queue-full and queue-empty conditions. One way to make this distinction is to maintain a count of the number of items in the queue.

3. The management of an event list in an event-driven simulation typically is more difficult than it was in the example presented in this chapter. For instance, if there were more than one line in the bank, the structure of the event list would be much more complex.

SELF-TEST EXERCISES

1. If you add the letters A, B, C, and D in order to a queue of characters and then remove them, in what order will they be deleted from the queue?

2. What do the queues *Q* and *T* "look like" after the following sequence of operations?

   Create(Q)
   Add(Q, 1)
   Add(Q, 2)
   Create(T)
   Add(T, 3)
   Add(T, 4)
   Remove(Q)
   Add(Q, QueueFront(T))
   Add(Q, 5)
   Remove(T)
   Add(T, 6)

   Compare these results with Self-Test Exercise 2 in Chapter 8.

3. Trace the palindrome-recognition algorithm described in the section "A Simple Application of the ADT Queue" for each of the following strings:
   a. abcda
   b. radar

4. For each of the following situations, which of these ADT's
   (1) a queue; (2) a stack; (3) an ordered list; (4) none of these
   would be most appropriate?
   a. The customers at the deli counter who take numbers to mark their turn

b. An alphabetic list of names
c. Integers that need to be sorted
d. The boxes in a box trace of a recursive function
e. A grocery list ordered by the occurrence of the items in the store
f. The items on a cash register tape
g. A word processor that allows you to correct typing errors by using the Backspace key
h. A program that uses backtracking
i. A list of ideas in chronological order
j. Airplanes that stack above a busy airport, waiting to land
k. People who are put on hold when they call an airline to make reservations
l. An employer who fires the most recently hired person

EXERCISES

1. Consider the language

   $L = \{w\$w' : w$ is string of characters other than $\$, w' = \text{reverse}(w)\}$

   as defined in Chapter 8. Write a recognition algorithm for this language that uses both a queue and a stack. Thus, as you read the input string, you insert each character of w into a queue and each character of w' into a stack. Assume that each input string contains exactly one $.

2. Revise the infix-to-postfix conversion algorithm of Chapter 8 so that it uses a queue instead of an array to represent the postfix expression.

3. Consider the array-based implementation of a queue described in the text. Instead of counting the number of items in the queue, you could maintain a boolean flag `IsFull` to distinguish between the full and empty conditions. Revise the array-based implementation by using the `IsFull` flag.

4. Another popular array-based implementation of a queue uses no special data field—such as `Count` or `IsFull` (see Exercise 3)—to distinguish between the full and empty conditions. In this implementation, you declare the array `Items` to be `[0..maxqueue]` instead of `[1..maxqueue]` and sacrifice one of the array locations as follows. By convention, `Front` will always point to the array location that precedes the location holding the item that is at the front of the queue. That is, the front item of the queue is always at the location one past the location that `Front` points to. (Note that location 0 follows location `maxqueue`.) Before adding to the queue, you check to see if `Rear + 1` is equal to `Front`. If this is the case, you disallow the insertion because it would violate the rule that at least one array location be empty. How does this allow you to distinguish between

the full and empty conditions? Revise the array-based implementation by using this convention.

5. Consider a slight variation of the ADT queue. In this variation, new items can be added to and deleted from either end. This ADT is commonly called a **doubly ended queue**, or **deque**. Construct array-based and pointer-based implementations of the deque.

6. With the following data, hand-trace the execution of the bank-line simulation that this chapter describes. Show the state of the queue and the event list at each step.

5	9
7	5
14	5
30	5
32	5
34	5

Note that at *Time* = 14 there is a tie between the execution of an arrival event and a departure event.

7. Consider the stack-based search of the flight map in the HPAir problem of Chapter 8. You can replace the stack that the search uses with a queue. That is, you can replace every call to *Push* with a call to *Add*, every call to *Pop* with a call to *Remove*, and every call to *StackTop* with a call to *QueueFront*. Trace the resulting algorithm when applied to the flight map in Figure 8-8. Indicate the contents of the queue after every operation on it.

*8. As Chapter 4 pointed out, you can define ADT operations in a mathematically formal way by using axioms. Consider the following axioms for the ADT queue, where Q is an arbitrary queue and x is an arbitrary queue item.

IsEmpty(Create) = true   (a newly created queue is empty)

IsEmpty(Add(Q, x)) = false

Remove(Create) = error

Remove(Add(Create, x)) = Create

IsEmpty(Q) = false ⇒
                          Remove(Add(Q, x)) = Add(Remove(Q), x)

QueueFront(Create) = error

QueueFront(Add(Create, x)) = x

IsEmpty(Q) = false ⇒
                          QueueFront(Add(Q, x)) = QueueFront(Q)

  a. Note the recursive nature of the definition of the operation *QueueFront*. What is the degenerate case? What is the recursive step? What is the significance of the *IsEmpty* test? Why is *QueueFront* recursive in nature while the operation *StackTop* for the ADT stack is not?

b. The representation of a stack as a sequence

    Push(Push(···Push(Create, ···)

without any *Pop* operations was called a canonical form. (See Exercise 18 in Chapter 8.) Is there a canonical form for the ADT queue that uses only *Add* operations? That is, is every queue equal to a queue that can be written with only *Add*s? Prove your answer.

PROJECTS

9. Modify and expand the event-driven simulation program that this chapter describes. Here are a few suggestions:

a. Add some statistics to the simulation. For example, compute the maximum wait in line, the average length of the line, and the maximum length of the line.

b. Modify the simulation so that it accounts for three tellers, each with a distinct line. You should keep in mind that there should be

- Three queues, one for each teller
- A rule that chooses a line when processing an arrival event (for example, enter the shortest line)
- Three distinct departure events, one for each line
- Rules for breaking ties in the event list

Run both this simulation and the original simulation on several sets of input data. How do the statistics compare?

c. The bank is considering the following change: Instead of having three distinct lines (one for each teller), there will be a single line for the three tellers. The person at the front of the line will go to the first available teller. Modify the simulation of part *b* to account for this variation. Run both simulations on several sets of input data. How do the various statistics compare (averages and maximums)? What can you conclude about having a single line as opposed to having distinct lines?

10. The people that run the Motor Vehicle Department (MVD) have a problem. They are concerned that people do not spend enough time waiting in lines to appreciate the privilege of owning and driving an automobile. The current arrangement is as follows:

- When people walk in the door, they must wait in a line to sign in.
- Once they have signed in, they are told either to stand in line for registration renewal or to wait until they are called for license renewal.
- Once they have completed their desired transaction, they must go and wait in line for the cashier.
- When they finally get to the front of the cashier's line, if they expect to pay by check, they are told that all checks must get approved. To do this, it is necessary to go to the check-approver's table and then reenter the cashier's line at the end.

The object of this problem is to write an event-driven simulation to help the Motor Vehicle Department gather statistics.

INPUT

Each line of input will contain

- An arrival time (integer).
- A name. To simplify reading in the data, you can assume that every name will contain exactly eight characters, possibly ending in blanks.
- A desired transaction code (L for license renewal, R for registration renewal).
- A method-of-payment code ($ for cash, C for check).

OUTPUT

Write out the details of each event (when, who, what, and so on).

FINAL STATISTICS

Licenses—total number and average time spent in MVD (arrival until completion of payment)

Registrations—total number and average time spent in MVD (arrival until completion of payment)

DETAILS OF THE SIMULATION

a. Define the following events: arrive, sign in, renew license, renew registration, and cope with the cashier (make a payment or find out about check approval).

b. In case of ties, let the order be determined by the order of the events just given—that is, arrivals have the highest priority.

c. Assume that the various transactions take the following amounts of time:

Sign in	10 seconds
Renew license	90 seconds
Register automobile	60 seconds
See cashier (payment)	30 seconds
See cashier (check not approved)	10 seconds

d. As ridiculous as it may seem, the people waiting for license renewal are called in alphabetical order. Note, however, that people are not pushed back once their transactions have started.

e. For the sake of this simulation, you can assume that checks are approved instantly. Therefore, the rule for arriving at the front of the cashier's line with a check that has not been approved is to go to the rear of the cashier's line with a check that has been approved.

PREVIEW   The ADT's presented in earlier chapters are appropriate for problems that must manage data by position. This chapter considers the ADT table, which is appropriate for problems that must manage data by value.

Several implementations of a table will be presented, along with their advantages and disadvantages. These implementations range from familiar data structures based on arrays and linked lists to new and important data structures based on trees. Thus, this chapter also discusses general trees, binary trees, and binary search trees.

To make an intelligent choice among the various possible table implementations, you must analyze the efficiency with which each of the implementations supports the table operations. For example, this chapter analyzes the efficiency of array-based and pointer-based table implementations and concludes that, in many applications, the implementations do not support the table operations as efficiently as possible. This conclusion motivates the use of a more sophisticated table implementation based on the binary search tree.

INTRODUCTION

In a broad sense, the following operations are what the management of data is all about:

- Operations that insert data into a data structure
- Operations that delete data from a data structure
- Operations that ask questions about the data in a data structure

General categories of data-management operations

The operations of the ADT's presented in the previous chapters each fit into at least one of these categories. The ADT's ordered list, stack, and queue are all **position oriented.** The operations of these ADT's have the form

- Insert a data item into the ith position of a data structure
- Delete a data item from the ith position of a data structure
- Ask a question about the data item in the ith position of a data structure

The form of operations on position-oriented ADT's

As you have seen, the ADT ordered list places no restriction on the value of *i*, while the other ADT's do impose some restrictions. For example, the operations of the ADT stack are restricted to inserting into, deleting from, and asking a question about one end of the data structure (the top of the stack). Thus, although they differ with respect to the flexibility of their operations, all the previous ADT's manage an association between data items and *positions.*

This chapter introduces **value-oriented** ADT's whose operations are of the form

- Insert a data item containing the *value x* into a data structure

The form of operations on value-oriented ADT's

- Delete a data item containing the *value x* from a data structure
- Ask a question about a data item containing the *value x*

Although these operations, like position-oriented operations, fit into the three general categories of operations listed at the beginning of this section—they insert data, delete data, and ask questions about data—the operations are based upon *values* of data items instead of *positions*. Applications that require such value-oriented operations are extremely prevalent, as you might imagine. For example, the tasks

- `Find the phone number of John Smith.`
- `Delete all the information about the employee with ID number 12908.`

involve values instead of positions. The next section presents an example of a value-oriented ADT.

THE ADT TABLE

The name of an ADT often suggests images of familiar objects that possess properties resembling those of the ADT. For example, the name "stack" might remind you of a stack of dishes. What does the name "table" bring to mind? If you had heard the question before you began reading this chapter, you might have answered, "My favorite mahogany coffee table." However, your answer now should be something more like, "A table of the major cities of the world," such as the following one:

An ordinary table

City	Country	Population
Athens	Greece	2,500,000
Barcelona	Spain	1,800,000
Cairo	Egypt	9,500,000
London	England	9,400,000
New York	U.S.A.	7,300,000
Paris	France	2,200,000
Rome	Italy	2,800,000
Toronto	Canada	3,200,000
Venice	Italy	300,000

This table of cities contains several pieces of information about each city. Its design allows you to look up this information. For example, suppose that you want to know the population of London. You could scan the column of city names, starting at the top, until you came to London. However, because the cities are listed in alphabetical order, you could also mimic a binary search. You could begin the search near the middle of the table, determine in which half London lies, and recursively apply the binary search to the appropriate half. As you know, a binary search is far more efficient than scanning the entire table from the beginning.

Now suppose that you want to find which of the major cities are in Italy. To answer this question, you have no choice but to scan the entire table. The fact that the city names are in alphabetical order does not help you for this problem at all. The table's arrangement facilitates the search for a given city, but other types of questions require a complete scan of the table.

The ADT **table** also allows you to look up information easily and has a special operation for this purpose. Frequently, the ADT table also contains several pieces of information—that is, the items of a table are often records. Other ADT's that you saw earlier also allowed the items to be records. In the implementations of ordered lists, stacks, and queues, you could define *itemtype* to be a record, and the operations would still make sense without modification. Because the ADT table is value oriented, however, there is greater significance to the fact that its items are records.

ADT table

By designating one of the record's fields as the **search key**, you can facilitate the retrieval of items based on a specified value for this field. In the table of cities, for example, you could designate *City* as the search key if you often needed to retrieve the information about a city. You can devise implementations of a table that allow the rapid retrieval of the item(s) whose search key matches some specified value. However, if you need to retrieve the item(s) whose non-search-key field matches some specified value, you will have to inspect the entire table. Therefore, by designating a given field to be a search key, the problem solver sends the ADT implementer the following message:

Search-key field

> *Arrange the data in a way that facilitates the search for an item that has a specified value in its search key.*

The basic operations that define the ADT table are as follows:

ADT *Table Operations*

KEY CONCEPTS

```
Create(T)
{ Creates an empty table T. }

Insert(T, newitem, success)
{ Inserts newitem into table T, if T is not already full,
  and sets success to true. Otherwise sets success to false.
  It is assumed that there is no item in the table with the
  same search key as newitem and that no two table items
  have the same search key. (Note that if the table items
  are records, newitem must specify a value for each
  field.) }
```

```
Delete(T, X, success)
{ Deletes from table T the item with search key X. The
  operation fails if there is no such item. The flag success
  indicates whether the operation succeeded. }

Retrieve(T, X, getitem, success)
{ Retrieves into getitem from table T the item with search
  key X. The operation fails if there is no such item. The
  flag success indicates whether the operation succeeded. }

Traverse(T, Visit)
{ Traverses the table T and calls the procedure Visit for
  each item. }
```

*Various sets of table operations
are possible*

You should realize that these operations are only one possible set of table operations. The problem solver may require either a subset of these operations or other operations not listed here to fit the application at hand. It also may be convenient to modify the definitions of some of the operations. For example, these operations assume that no two table items have the same values in their search keys. In addition, `Insert` assumes that no table item has the same search key as the item to be inserted. However, in many applications it is quite reasonable to expect duplicate search-key values. If this is the case, you must redefine several of the operations to eliminate the ambiguity that would arise from duplicate search-key values. For example, which item should `Retrieve` return if several items have the specified value in their search keys? The point is that you should tailor your definition of the ADT table to the problem at hand. (The problem of duplicate search-key values is the subject of Exercises 8 through 10 at the end of this chapter.)

Although the first four operations—*Create, Insert, Delete,* and *Retrieve*—in the previous set of operations are sufficient for some applications, you cannot do several significant things without additional operations. For instance, you cannot perform an important task such as

```
Print out all the items that are in the table
```

because you cannot `Retrieve` a data item unless you know the value of its search key. Thus, you cannot print out all the items that are in the table unless you can *traverse* the table.

*Traverse visits all table items
in a specified order*

The definition of the `Traverse` operation is intuitively simple: The operation *visits* each item in the table. In defining the `Traverse` operation, you must specify the order in which `Traverse` should visit the items. One common specification is to visit the items sorted by search key. It is also possible that you do not care in what order `Traverse` visits the items. As you will see, the way you define `Traverse`—if you request it at all— may affect the way that you implement the table.

The notion of traversing an ADT is quite important and is actually more difficult than you might imagine. Although traversal means to visit each item in the ADT, it can be difficult because you do something with each item when you visit it. You might simply print each item or you might assign its value to a variable or even place a copy of it into another data structure.

The details of *Traverse* are thus very application dependent, which makes it difficult to define the operation within the ADT framework. You could have a different *Traverse* operation for each task that you wanted to do as you visited items. Or the *Traverse* operation could call a user-defined procedure, whose name you passed as a parameter. *Traverse* would call this procedure for each item in the table. Thus, the header of a *Traverse* operation that visits the items in a table is

```
procedure Traverse(T: table; procedure Visit(Item: itemtype));
{ Traverses table T and calls procedure Visit for each item. }
```

Note that not all versions of Pascal allow you to pass a procedure name as a parameter. In such cases, you will have to define a different traversal procedure for each necessary operation.

Because you can define the *Visit* procedure to do any number of things—including access the table via the ADT operations—*Traverse* is a versatile operation. This versatility is illustrated with three brief examples, which represent the previous table of major cities as an ADT table.

Suppose that the items in the table are records of the form

```
type    itemtype = record
            City ··· ;          { city's name }
            Country ··· ;       { city's country }
            Pop ···             { city's population }
        end;
```

Three tasks that you could perform on this table are

- *Print, in alphabetical order, the name of each city and its population.*
- *Increase the population of each city by 10 percent*
- *Delete all cities with a population of less than 1,000,000.*

Tasks that use City as the search key

Each task suggests that you designate the *City* field as the search key.

The first task requires you to print the city names in alphabetical order. Thus, *Traverse* must visit items alphabetically by search key.

To perform the first task, you pass to *Traverse* the name of the procedure *PrintInfo*, which appears in pseudocode as follows:

```
PrintInfo(T, Item)

    Print(Item.City, Item.Pop)
```

First task

Traverse's visitation order is immaterial for the other two tasks. To perform the second task, you pass to *Traverse* the name of the procedure *UpdatePop*:

Second task

```
UpdatePop(T, Item)

    Item.Pop := Item.Pop + Round(0.1 * Item.Pop)
    Delete(T, Item.City, success)
    Insert(T, Item, success)
```

Note that to update the population of a city, you must delete the old item and insert a new one that contains the updated field. Because *UpdatePop* is on the user's side of the wall, you must use the ADT operations; that is, you cannot update the record directly. If an application frequently requires a replace operation such as this, it would be wise to include *Replace* as one of the ADT table operations. (See Exercise 2 at the end of this chapter.)

To perform the third task, you pass to *Traverse* the name of the procedure *DelSmall*:

Third task

```
DelSmall(T, Item)

    if Item.Pop < 1,000,000
        then Delete(T, Item.City, success)
```

However, this task is not as simple as it may seem. By deleting an item, you alter the table during *Traverse*'s traversal. Which item will *Traverse* visit next? Clearly it should visit the one after the deleted item, but will *Traverse* skip that item? Notice that during the second task (update), the deletion is followed by an insertion, so that the number and order of the items are unchanged in the table. Thus, for the update task, *Traverse* visits the correct next item. However, when deletion is the only task, you must ensure that *Traverse* does not skip a node. The traversal of a table while deleting parts of it is left as a difficult exercise.

Despite the fact that the ADT operation *Traverse* calls a user-supplied procedure, the sanctity of the wall between the program and the implementation of the ADT has not been violated. Because *Visit* is on the user's side of the wall, the procedure can access the data only through the ADT operations.

Selecting an Implementation

A major goal of this chapter is to indicate how the requirements of a particular application influence the selection of an implementation. The five operations given earlier make table a powerful ADT. Some applications will require all the operations; others only a subset of them. It is important that, before requesting the implementation of a set of table operations, the problem solver carefully analyze which operations are really needed for the application at hand. It is tempting always to request that all the operations be supported. This strategy, however, is a poor one. The sections that follow discuss the trade-offs between various implementations of a table. You will see that frequently one implementation supports some of the

What operations are needed?

operations more efficiently than another implementation. Therefore, if you request an operation that you never use, the implementer of the ADT might select an implementation that is not best suited for what you are really doing.

In addition to knowing what operations you need for a given application, it is often important that the ADT implementer know approximately how frequently the application will perform each of the operations. Although some applications may require many occurrences of every operation, other applications may not. For example, if you maintained a table of major cities such as the one given earlier in this chapter, you would expect to perform far more retrieve operations than insertions or deletions. Other applications may require many more insertions and deletions than retrieves. Thus, if you seldom retrieve items, you can tolerate a table implementation that results in an inefficient *Retrieve* operation, as long as the operations that you will use frequently are efficient. The mix of operations is therefore one of the factors that influences which implementation of table you should select for a particular application.

How often is each operation required?

The next section presents several different application scenarios. Each of these scenarios involves an application that requires a particular mix of the table operations. The scenarios will present successively more challenging problems. For the first scenarios, adequate table implementations are possible through the use of arrays and linked lists. The later scenarios require a new type of data structure. The analysis of various implementations of the ADT table will illustrate some of the basic concerns of the analysis of algorithms. Given an application, you will see how to select an implementation that supports in a reasonably efficient manner the required mix of table operations. You should, however, remain conscious of factors other than efficiency, as was discussed in Chapter 7 in the section "Keeping Your Perspective."

LINEAR IMPLEMENTATIONS OF THE ADT TABLE

Linear implementation is a generic term that covers both array-based and pointer-based implementations. A linear implementation represents items one after another in the data structure and thus mirrors the flat, listlike appearance of the table of cities that was presented earlier in this chapter. Linear implementations are less sophisticated and less efficient than other implementations that you will see later in this chapter, but they are nevertheless appropriate for many applications. Because linear implementations are easy to understand conceptually, they are appropriate for tables that will contain only a small number of items. In such cases efficiency is not as great a concern as simplicity and clarity.

Even when a table is large, a linear implementation may still be appropriate. Whether or not it is appropriate depends upon the mix of operations that the given application requires. As a first step in examining this issue, observe that the linear implementations fall into four categories:

Four categories of linear implementations

- Unsorted, array-based
- Unsorted, pointer-based
- Sorted (by search key), array-based
- Sorted (by search key), pointer-based

Whether sorted or unsorted, the array-based and pointer-based implementations have the basic structures shown in Figure 10-1.

Under the array-based implementation, the table T is a record with two fields:

```
Size : 0..maxitems; { number of items currently in the table }
Items : array[1..maxitems] of itemtype; { table items }
```

Under the pointer-based implementation, T is a pointer to the first node of a linked list. Each node contains both an item of data type *itemtype* and a pointer to the next node. Note that the items in either implementation can be records with several fields.

The unsorted implementations store the items in no particular order; they can insert a new item into any convenient location. The sorted implementations must insert a new item into its proper position as determined by the value of its search key. You should review the techniques for inserting into and deleting from a sorted linked list that were first presented in Chapter 3. As you will see, the unsorted and sorted implementations have their relative advantages and disadvantages.

Next, we analyze the effectiveness of the linear table implementations for four application scenarios. The analysis of the last two scenarios leads to the development of a nonlinear implementation, the binary search tree.

Scenario A: Insert and Traverse in No Particular Order

Figure 10-1

Implementations of the ADT table: (a) array based; (b) pointer based

Consider an application where the predominant tasks are to insert a new item into a table and print out a report of the items currently present. Suppose that the organization of the report is irrelevant: The items can be sorted or unsorted. If the application needs to perform any of the operations *Retrieve*, *Delete*, or *Traverse* in sorted order, it does so infrequently enough in this scenario that these operations should not influence your choice of an implementation.

For this application there is no advantage to maintaining the items in a sorted order. In fact, by not maintaining a sorted order, the *Insert* operation can be quite efficient: Under either unsorted implementation, you can insert a new item into any convenient location. Under the unsorted array-based implementation, it is convenient to insert a new item at the end of the used portion of the array—that is, at location *Items[Size + 1]* in Figure 10-1a. Figure 10-2a shows the result of this insertion after *Size* has been updated. Under the pointer-based implementation, it is convenient to insert a new item at the beginning of the linked list—that is, *T* points to the new item and the new item points to the item previously first in the list. (See Figure 10-2b.) Thus, not only can you insert a new item quickly into either unsorted implementation of a table, but also the *Insert* operation requires a constant time for either implementation regardless of the table size.

An unsorted order is efficient

As for whether you should choose the array-based or pointer-based implementation, there is really only one significant issue, given this particular mix of operations. As you have seen with other ADT's, the dynamic nature of a pointer-based implementation makes it appropriate if you do not have a good estimate of the maximum possible size of the table. In other situations, the choice is mostly a matter of style. The space requirements of the array-based implementation are slightly less than for the pointer-based implementation—because no explicit pointer is stored—but in most situations the difference is not likely to be significant.

Array based versus pointer based

Scenario B: Traverse in Sorted Order

It is perhaps most common for an application to traverse a table's items in sorted order according to their search keys. Consider an application where

Figure 10-2

Insertion for unsorted implementations: (a) array based; (b) pointer based

(a)

(b)

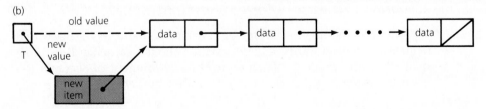

such a traversal is the predominant operation, and the `Insert` and `Delete` operations occur only infrequently. Suppose that your local library has computerized its catalog of the books currently in its collection. Furthermore, suppose that the library's computer prints this catalog for each person who enters the library. This task will thus occur much more frequently than updates to the catalog. In addition, the catalog will be of greatest use to the patron if the books' titles appear in alphabetical order. Therefore, the most frequently required task is a sorted `Traverse` operation.

Order the table items by their search keys

This application obviously requires that you choose the book title as the search key and order the table items by their search keys. Now the question becomes, should you use a sorted implementation that is array based or pointer based? In general, there are three issues to consider:

Issues that affect the implementation choice

1. Do you require the dynamic nature of a pointer-based implementation?

2. How quickly can you locate an item with a given value in its search key?

3. How quickly can you insert and delete a given item?

For the present library problem, the second and third issues are not of great importance, because insertions and deletions are infrequent and there is no mention of a `Retrieve` operation. Thus, if you do not have a good idea of the maximum number of books that the library can contain, the pointer-based implementation is necessary.

What if you do know the maximum capacity of the library? For this mix of operations (many sorted traversals, few insertions and deletions), the two implementations do not differ significantly in their efficiency, because the time required to traverse the table under the two implementations is roughly the same.

Array-based and pointer-based implementations are comparable here

To summarize, the array-based and pointer-based implementations have approximately the same efficiency when the predominant operation is `Traverse` in sorted order. The choice is thus mostly one of personal taste, unless the lack of a good estimate of the maximum size of the table mandates that you choose a pointer-based implementation because of its dynamic nature.

In fact, it is possible to do quite a bit better than either of these implementations. If the table is large, neither the array-based nor the pointer-based implementation would be satisfactory. For a large table you should use a different implementation—one that you will see later in this chapter.

Scenario C: Traverse in Sorted Order and Retrieve

Suppose that the librarian from the previous scenario has realized that frequently a patron wants only information about a particular title rather than the entire catalog. Therefore, to the environment of Scenario *B*— frequent sorted `Traverse` operations, infrequent `Insert` and `Delete` operations—add frequent *Retrieve* operations. The addition of the *Retrieve* operation requires a table implementation that allows you to efficiently search for an item that has a specified value in its search key.

Under an array-based implementation, you can use a binary search to retrieve a particular title. On the other hand, under a pointer-based implementation, you must traverse the list from its beginning until you encounter the title on the list. The binary search performs this retrieval in significantly less time than the time required to traverse a linked list. Two questions come to mind at this point:

1. Is a binary search possible under a linear pointer-based implementation?

2. How much more efficient is a binary search under an array-based implementation than the linear pointer-based implementation's traversal from the beginning of a linked list?

Questions

Can you perform a binary search under a pointer-based implementation? Yes, but too inefficiently to be practical. Consider the very first step of the binary search algorithm:

A binary search is impractical with a pointer-based implementation

```
Look at the "middle" item in the table
```

If the items are in a linked list, how can you possibly get to the middle item on the list? The only way that comes to mind (for now) is to traverse the list from the beginning until you have visited *N div 2* items. But, as you will see in the answer to the second question, the time required to do just this first step often will be more than the time required to perform the entire binary search algorithm on an array. Further, you would have the same problem of finding the "middle" element at each recursive step. It is thus not practical to perform a binary search under the pointer-based implementation. This observation is extremely significant.

On the other hand, if the items are in an array *Items[1..N]*, then the middle item is at location *N div 2* and can be accessed directly. Thus, a binary search of an array requires considerably less time than an algorithm that must inspect every item in the table. What does "considerably less time" mean? As you know, without the ability to perform a binary search, you may have to inspect every item in the table, either to locate an item with a particular value in its search key or to determine that such an item is not present. In other words, if a table has size N, then you will have to inspect as many as N items; thus, such a search is $O(N)$. How much better can you do with a binary search? Recall from Chapter 7 that a binary search is $O(\log_2 N)$ in its worst case and that an $O(\log_2 N)$ algorithm is substantially more efficient than an $O(N)$ algorithm. For example, $\log_2 1024 = 10$ and $\log_2 1,048,576 = 20$. For a large table, the binary search has an enormous advantage.

What impact will this discussion have on the implementation decisions for Scenario C? Because *Retrieve* is one of the predominant operations, unless you know that the library's catalog is quite small, you must choose an implementation under which a binary search is practical. As you have just seen, this decision eliminates both the sorted and unsorted linear pointer-based implementations and leaves only the sorted array-based implementation. This choice is fine if you have a good estimate of the maximum size of the table. Unfortunately, a good estimate is not always possible, and you will thus require the dynamic nature offered by a pointer-based implementation.

Linear implementations are not suitable here

This situation seems to be irreconcilable. The requirement that a binary search be used mandates an array-based implementation, yet most applications will require the dynamic storage allocation available only to a pointer-based implementation. Thus, for this problem, the linear implementations are not suitable. A satisfactory solution requires a new type of implementation. The sections that follow introduce a nonlinear pointer-based implementation on which you can perform a binary search-like algorithm. First, however, there is one more scenario to discuss. This scenario also finds the linear implementations unsatisfactory.

Scenario D: Traverse in Sorted Order, Insert, and Delete

Scenario *B* introduced the library catalog problem. In that scenario the predominant operation was `Traverse` in sorted order, with occasional `Insert` and `Delete` operations. The linear implementations were satisfactory for this mix of operations. Scenario *C* required, in addition, frequent `Retrieve` operations, which made the linear implementations inadequate. If, instead of adding the `Retrieve` operation to Scenario *B,* you add frequent insertions and deletions, the same inadequacy will result, as you will now see.

To insert into the table an item that has the value X in its search key, you must first determine where the item belongs in the table's sorted order. Similarly, to delete from the table an item that has the value X in its search key, you must first locate the item. Thus, both the `Insert` and `Delete` operations perform the following steps:

Both `Insert` and `Delete` perform these two steps

1.   Find the appropriate position in the table.
2.   Insert into (or delete from) this position.

Use an array-based implementation for Step 1

Step 1 is accomplished far more efficiently under an array-based implementation than it is under a pointer-based implementation. Under an array-based implementation, you can—in the case of insertion—use a binary search to determine where the new item X belongs and—in the case of deletion—where the item is located. On the other hand, under a pointer-based implementation, you know from the discussion in Scenario *C* that a binary search is impractical, and so you must traverse the list from its beginning until you encounter the appropriate location on the list. You also saw in Scenario *C* that an array-based implementation's binary search performs this step in significantly less time than the time required to traverse a linked list.

Thus, because it facilitates a binary search, the array-based implementation is superior with respect to Step 1 of *Insert* and *Delete*. However, as you may have guessed, the pointer-based implementation is better for Step 2, which is the actual insertion or deletion of the item at the located position in the table. Under the array-based implementation, *Insert* must shift array items to make room for the new item, while *Delete* must shift array items to fill in the gap created when the item is removed. (See Figure 10-3a.) The worst case would require that every array item be shifted. On the other hand, under the pointer-based implementation, you can accomplish this second step simply by changing at most two pointers, as Figure 10-3b illustrates.

Use a pointer-based implementation for Step 2

When you take Steps 1 and 2 together, you will find that both the sorted array-based and sorted pointer-based implementations of *Insert* or *Delete* require roughly the same amount of time. However, neither implementation supports these operations particularly well. Once again you find yourself in what seems to be an irreconcilable position. If the table is large, the speed of a binary search in performing Step 1 is desirable and thus an array-based implementation is required. On the other hand, a pointer-based implementation avoids shifting array elements in Step 2. Once again, what is really needed is a pointer-based structure on which you can perform a binary search.

You have seen scenarios in which the linear table implementations are adequate and other scenarios in which they are not. Those latter scenarios provide the motivation to develop a different type of implementation for a table, one that combines the best features of the linear implementations. Such an implementation is the topic of much of the remainder of this chapter. However, we first conclude this section by presenting the sorted array-based implementation of the ADT table.

Figure 10-3

Insertion for sorted implementations: (a) array based; (b) pointer based

The Sorted Array-Based Implementation of the ADT *Table*

A Pascal version of the sorted array-based implementation follows. Exercise 1 at the end of this chapter asks you to write the other linear implementations.

Recall that the given ADT table operations assume that no two table items contain the same search key. Furthermore, *Insert* assumes that no item already in the table has a search key equal to that of the new item to be inserted. Exercises 8, 9, and 10 at the end of this chapter ask you to remove these assumptions.

```
{ *************************************************************
  BASIC TABLE OPERATIONS (Sorted Array-Based Implementation):

    Create, Insert, Delete, Retrieve, and Traverse (sorted)

  The following definitions are assumed:

    const   maxitems = <maximum size of table>;
    type    keytype = <desired type of search key>;

            itemtype = record
                key : keytype;
                 <... and possibly other fields>
            end;

            table = record
                Size : 0..maxitems;
                Items : array[1..maxitems] of itemtype
            end;

  Assumption: A table contains at most one item with a given
  search key at any time. (See Exercise 8.)

  Notes:
    If T is of type table, then
      1. 0 <= T.Size <= maxitems
      2. T.Items[1..T.Size] contains the current table items
      3. if 0 <= i < j <= T.Size, then T.Items[i] < T.Items[j]

    The auxiliary function Locate determines where a search
    key belongs in the sorted list by using a binary search.
    ********************************************************* }

function Locate(T : table ; keyval : keytype) : integer;
{ -------------------------------------------------------
  Finds the position of a table item or its insertion point.
  Precondition: Table T has been created and no two items of
  T have the same search key. T's items are sorted by search
  key; keyval is the value of the search key sought in the
  table.
```

Postcondition: Returns the index (between 1 and T.Size) of the item in T whose search key equals keyval. If there is no such item, returns the position (between 1 and T.Size + 1) that the item would occupy if inserted. Locate does not alter T.

Calls: Local recursive function dosearch.

--- }

```
   { local function for the recursive binary search }
   function dosearch(first, last : integer) : integer;
   var mid : integer;
   begin
      if first > last
         then dosearch := first

         else
         begin
            mid := (first + last) div 2;
            if T.Items[mid].key = keyval then
               dosearch := mid
            else if T.Items[mid].key > keyval then
               dosearch := dosearch(first, mid-1)
            else dosearch := dosearch(mid+1, last)
         end  { if }
end;  { dosearch }

begin  { Locate }
   Locate := dosearch(1, T.Size)
end;  { Locate }

procedure Create(var T : table);
{ -------------------------------------------------------
   Creates an empty table.
   Precondition: None.
   Postcondition: The empty table T is created.
   ------------------------------------------------------- }
begin
   T.Size := 0 { set count field to 0 }
end;  { Create }

procedure Insert(var T : table; newitem : itemtype;
                 var success : boolean);
{ -------------------------------------------------------
   Inserts an item into a table in its proper sorted order
   according to the item's search key.
   Precondition: Table T has been created and no two items of
   T have the same search key. T's items are sorted by search
   key. The item to be inserted into T is newitem, whose
```

search key differs from all search keys presently in T.
Postcondition: If T was not already full, newitem is
inserted into its proper order in T and success is set to
true. Otherwise, T is unchanged and success is set to
false.
Calls: Locate.
-- }

```
var i,loc : integer;
begin
    if T.Size = maxitems
        then success := false    { table is full }

        else                     { insert in proper order }
        begin
            { locate the position where keyval belongs }
            loc := Locate(T, newitem.key);

            { shift up to make room for the new item }
            for i := T.Size downto loc do
                T.Items[i + 1] := T.Items[i];

            T.Items[loc] := newitem;
            T.Size := T.Size + 1;
            success := true
        end   { if }
end;   { Insert }

procedure Delete(var T : table; keyval : keytype;
                 var success : boolean);
```
{ --
  Deletes an item with a given search key from a table.
  Precondition: Table T has been created and no two items of
  T have the same search key. T's items are sorted by search
  key; keyval is the search key of the item to be deleted.
  Postcondition: If the item whose search key equals keyval
  exists in T, the item is deleted and success is set to
  true. Otherwise, T is unchanged and success is set to false.
  Calls: Locate.
  -- }

```
var i, loc : integer;
begin
    { locate the position where keyval exists or belongs }
    loc := Locate(T, keyval);

     { delete if present }
    if loc > T.Size then
        success := false
    else if T.Items[loc].key <> keyval then
        success := false
```

```
      else
      begin   { delete the item }
         { shift down to fill the gap }
         for i := loc to T.Size − 1 do
            T.Items[i] := T.Items[i + 1];

         T.Size := T.Size − 1;
         success := true
      end   { if }
end;   { Delete }

procedure Retrieve(T : table; keyval : keytype;
                   var getitem : itemtype; var success : boolean);
{ ------------------------------------------------------------
  Retrieves an item with a given search key from a table.
  Precondition: Table T has been created and no two items of
  T have the same search key. T's items are sorted by search
  key; keyval is the search key of the item to be retrieved.
  Postcondition: If retrieval is successful, getitem
  contains the retrieved item and success is true. If there
  is no such item, getitem is unchanged and success is
  false. T and keyval remain unchanged.
  Calls: Locate.
  ------------------------------------------------------------ }
var loc : integer;
begin
   { locate the item }
   loc := Locate(T, keyval);

   { retrieve if present }
   if loc > T.Size then
      success :=false
   else if T.Items[loc].key <> keyval then
      success := false
   else
   begin
      getitem := T.Items[loc];
      success := true
   end   { if }
end;   { Retrieve }

procedure Traverse(var T:table; procedure Visit(var T:table;
                                              item : itemtype));
{ ------------------------------------------------------------
  Traverses a table in sorted order, calling procedure Visit
  for each item.
  Precondition: Table T has been created and no two items of
  T have the same search key. T's items are sorted by search
```

key. The procedure represented by Visit exists outside of
the ADT implementation.
Postcondition: Visit's action occurs for each item in T.
-- }

```
var i : integer;
begin
   for i := 1 to T.Size do
      Visit(T, T.Items[i])
end   { Traverse }
```

BINARY TREES

The desired nonlinear implementation of the ADT table requires a new data
structure, which this section presents. You will learn about general trees,
binary trees, and binary search trees. Although they are treated here as data
structures, some people think of trees as ADT's, just as you can think of a
linked list either as a data structure or as an ADT. Exercise 24 at the end of
this chapter considers this issue.

Tree Terminology

Computer scientists use **general trees** to represent relationships between
objects. Previous chapters informally used tree diagrams to represent the
relationships between the calls of a recursive algorithm. Recall, for example, Figure 5-12 of Chapter 5 for the *Rabbit* algorithm. The diagram is actually a tree. Each call to *Rabbit* is represented by a box, or a **node** in the tree.
The lines between the nodes (boxes) are called **directed edges.** For this
tree, the directed edges indicate recursive calls. For example, the directed
edges from *Rabbit(7)* to *Rabbit(6)* and *Rabbit(5)* indicate that subproblem
Rabbit(7) makes calls to *Rabbit(6)* and *Rabbit(5)*.

Trees are hierarchical   All trees are **hierarchical** in nature. Intuitively, hierarchical means that
there is a "parent-child" relationship between the nodes in the tree. If
there is a directed edge from node *n* to node *m*, then *n* is the **parent** of *m*,
and *m* is a **child** of *n*. In the tree in Figure 10-4, nodes *B* and *C* are children
of node *A*. Children of the same parent—for example, *B* and *C*—are called
siblings. Each node in a tree has at most one parent, and there is exactly
one node, called the **root** of the tree, which has no parent. Node *A* is the
root of the tree in Figure 10-4. A node that has no children is called a **leaf**
of the tree. The leaves of the tree in Figure 10-4 are *C, D, E,* and *F*.

The parent-child relationship between the nodes is generalized to the
relationships **ancestor** and **descendant.** In Figure 10-4, *A* is an ancestor of
D, and thus *D* is a descendant of *A*. Notice that not all nodes are related by
the ancestor or descendant relationship: *B* and *C*, for instance, are not so

Figure 10-4

A general tree

related. However, the root of any tree is an ancestor of every node in that tree. A **subtree** of a tree is any node in the tree together with all of its descendants. A **subtree of a node** *n* is a subtree rooted at a child of *n*. For example, Figure 10-5 shows a subtree of the tree in Figure 10-4. This subtree has *B* as its root and is a subtree of the node *A*.

A subtree is any node and its descendants

Because trees are hierarchical in nature, you can use them to represent information that itself is hierarchical in nature—for example, organization charts and family trees, as Figure 10-6 depicts. It may be disconcerting to discover, however that the nodes in the family tree in Figure 10-6b that represent Caroline's parents are the children of the node that represents Caroline! That is, the nodes in the family tree that represent Caroline's ancestors are the descendants of Caroline's node. It's no wonder that computer scientists often seem to be confused by reality.

A **binary tree** is a tree in which each node has no more than two children. Thus, the trees in Figures 5-12 and 10-6b are binary, but the trees in Figures 10-4 and 10-6a are not; they are general trees. The remainder of this chapter will focus on binary trees.

A formal, recursive definition of a binary tree follows:

A set *T* of elements—called nodes—is a binary tree if either

Formal definition of a binary tree

1. *T* is empty, or
2. *T* is partitioned into three disjoint sets:

   - A single element *r*, its root
   - Two sets that are binary trees, called **left and right subtrees** of *r*

Figure 10-5

A subtree of the tree in Figure 10-4

Figure 10-6

(a) An organization chart;
(b) a family tree

(a)

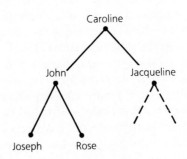

(b)

It is useful to have the following intuitive restatement of the definition of a binary tree:

Intuitive definition of a binary
tree

T is a binary tree if either

1. T has no nodes, or
2. T is of the form

$$r$$
$$T_L \qquad T_R$$

where r is a node and T_L and T_R are both binary trees.

Notice that the formal definition agrees with this intuitive one: If r is the root of T, then the binary tree T_L is the left subtree of T and the binary tree T_R is the right subtree of T. (Alternatively, T_L is the left subtree of node r and T_R is the right subtree of node r.) If T_L is not empty, its root is the **left child** of r, and if T_R is not empty, its root is the **right child** of r. Notice that if both subtrees of a node are empty, that node is a leaf.

As an example of how you can use a binary tree to represent data in a hierarchical form, consider Figure 10-7. The binary trees in this figure represent algebraic expressions that involve the binary operators +, −, *, and

/. To represent an expression such as *a* – *b*, you place the operator in the root node and the operands *a* and *b* into left and right children, respectively, of the root. (See Figure 10-7a.) Figure 10-7b represents the expression *a* – *b*/*c*. Notice that a subtree represents the subexpression *b*/*c*. A similar situation exists in Figure 10-7c, which represents (*a* – *b*) * *c*. Notice that parentheses do not appear in the tree. Also notice that the leaves of the tree contain the expression's operands, while other tree nodes contain the operators. The binary tree provides a hierarchy for the operations— that is, the tree specifies an unambiguous order for evaluating an expression.

The nodes of a tree typically contain values. A **binary search tree** is a binary tree that is in a sense sorted according to the values in its nodes. For each node *n*, a binary search tree satisfies the following three properties:

- *n*'s value is greater than all values in its left subtree T_L.
- *n*'s value is less than all values in its right subtree T_R.
- Both T_L and T_R are binary search trees.

Properties of a binary search tree

Figure 10-8 is an example of a binary search tree. As its name suggests, a binary search tree organizes data in a way that facilitates searching it for a particular data item. As you will see later, the binary search tree will solve the difficulties with the linear implementations of the ADT table.

The height of trees.   Trees come in many shapes. For example, although the binary trees in Figure 10-9 all contain the same nodes, their structures are quite different. Although each of these trees has seven nodes, some are "taller" than others. Intuitively, the **height** of any general tree is the dis-

Figure 10-7

Binary trees that represent algebraic expressions

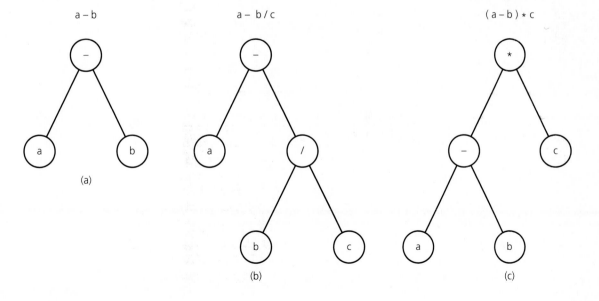

a – b

(a)

a – b / c

(b)

(a – b) * c

(c)

Figure 10-8

A binary search tree of names

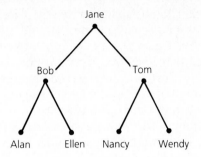

tance from its root to its farthest leaf. More precisely, the height is the number of nodes on the longest path from the root to a leaf. For example, the trees in Figure 10-9 have respective heights of 3, 5, and 7. Many people's intuitive notion of height of would lead them to say that these trees have heights of 2, 4, and 6. Indeed, many authors define height to agree with this intuition. However, the definition of height given here leads to a cleaner statement of many algorithms and properties of trees.

There are other equivalent ways to define the height of a general tree *T*. One way uses the following definition of the **level** of a node *n*:

Level of a node
- If *n* is the root of *T*, then it is at level 1.
- If *n* is not the root of *T*, then its level is 1 greater than the level of its parent.

For example, in Figure 10-9a, node *A* is at level 1, node *B* is at level 2, and node *D* is at level 3.

Now the **height** of a general tree *T* in terms of the levels of its nodes is defined as follows:

Height of a tree in terms of levels
- If *T* is empty, then its height is 0.

Figure 10-9

Binary trees with the same nodes but different heights
- If *T* is not empty, then its height is equal to the maximum level of its nodes.

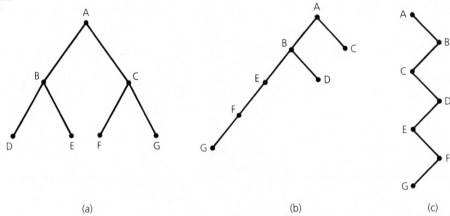

(a)   (b)   (c)

Apply this definition to the trees in Figure 10-9 and show that their heights are respectively 3, 5, and 7, as was stated earlier.

For binary trees, it is often convenient to use an equivalent recursive definition of height:

- If T is empty, its height is 0.   *Recursive definition of height*

- If T is a nonempty binary tree, then because T is of the form

$$r$$
$$T_L \qquad T_R$$

    the height of T can be defined as 1 greater than the height of its root's taller subtree; that is,

$$height(T) = 1 + max\{\ height(T_L),\ height(T_R)\ \}$$

Later, when we discuss the efficiency of searching a binary search tree, it will be necessary to determine the maximum and minimum heights of a binary tree of N nodes.

Full, complete, and balanced binary trees.   A **full binary tree** of height h has all its leaves at level h, and all nodes that are at a level less than h each have two children. Figure 10-10 pictures a full binary tree of height 3.

When proving properties about full binary trees—such as how many nodes they have—it is convenient to use the following recursive definition of a full binary tree:

- If T is empty, then T is a full binary tree of height 0.   *A full binary tree*

- If T is not empty and has height $h > 0$, then T is a full binary tree if its root's subtrees are both full binary trees of height $h - 1$.

Notice that this definition closely reflects the recursive nature of a binary tree.

A **complete binary tree** of height h is a binary tree that is full down to level $h - 1$, with level h filled in from left to right, as Figure 10-11 illustrates. More formally, a binary tree T of height h is complete

1. If all nodes at level $h - 2$ and above have two children   *A complete binary tree*

2. If, when a node has a right descendant at level h (that is, a

Figure 10-10

A full binary tree of height 3

Figure 10-11

A complete tree

descendant at level *h* in its right subtree) all leaves in its left subtree are at level *h*

Full binary trees are complete

Notice that part 2 of this definition formalizes the requirement that level *h* be filled in from left to right. Also notice that *if a binary tree is full, it is necessarily complete.*

Finally, a binary tree is **height balanced**, or simply **balanced**, if the height of any node's right subtree differs from the height of the node's left subtree by no more than 1. A binary tree is **completely balanced** if the left and right subtrees of every node have the same height. The binary tree in Figure 10-11 is balanced, and the binary tree in Figure 10-9a is completely balanced, but the other trees in Figure 10-9 are not balanced. Notice that a complete binary tree is balanced, whereas a full binary tree is completely balanced.

The following is a summary of the major tree terminology presented so far.

KEY CONCEPTS *Summary of Tree Terminology*

Parent of *n*	The node directly above node *n* in the tree
Child of *n*	A node directly below node *n* in the tree
Root	The only node in the tree with no parent
Leaf	A node with no children
Siblings	Nodes with a common parent
Ancestor of *n*	A node on the path from the root to *n*
Descendent of *n*	A node on a path from *n* to a leaf
Empty tree	A tree with no nodes

Subtree of *n*	A tree that consists of a child of *n* and the child's descendents
Height	The number of nodes on the longest path from the root to a leaf
General tree	A set of nodes that is either empty or has a root node and zero or more subtrees of the root
Binary tree	A tree in which each node has at most two children, the **left child** and the **right child**
Left (right) subtree of *n*	In a binary tree, the left (right) child of node *n* plus its descendents
Binary search tree	A binary tree where the value in any node *n* is greater than the value in every node in *n*'s left subtree, but less than the value of every node in *n*'s right subtree
Full binary tree	A binary tree of height *h* whose leaves are all at level *h* and whose nonleaves each have two children
Complete binary tree	A binary tree of height *h* that is full to level *h* − 1 and has level *h* filled from left to right
Balanced binary tree	A binary tree in which the left and right subtrees of any node have heights that differ by at most 1
Completely balanced binary tree	A binary tree in which the left and right subtrees of any node have the same height

Implementations of a Binary Tree

There are two common ways in which you can implement a binary tree by using the constructs of Pascal. One way uses pointers and the other uses arrays. Suppose that you want to implement the binary tree of names in Figure 10-8. Each node in this tree contains a name and, because the tree is a binary tree, each node is followed by at most two descendant nodes.

Pointer-based implementation. You can use Pascal pointers to link the nodes in the tree. Thus, you can represent a tree by using the following Pascal statements:

```
const  maxlen = 20;        { maximum length of name }
type   string = packed array[1..maxlen] of char;
       bintree = ^node;
```

Figure 10-12

**A pointer-based implemen-
tation of a binary tree**

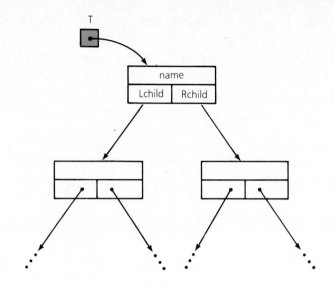

```
node = record
    name : string;
    Lchild : bintree;{ pointer to the left child }
    Rchild : bintree { pointer to the right child }
end;

var    T : bintree;           { pointer to the tree's root }
```

The external pointer *T* points to the tree's root. If the tree is empty, *T* is *nil*. Figure 10-12 illustrates this implementation.

Recall from the recursive definition of a binary tree that every nonempty binary tree consists of a left subtree and a right subtree, each of which is a binary tree. Under the pointer-based implementation, if *T* points to the root *r* of a binary tree, then $T^\wedge.Lchild$ points to the root of the left subtree of *r* and $T^\wedge.Rchild$ points to the root of the right subtree of *r*.

Array-based implementation. Another way to represent the nodes in a tree is by using an array of records. Array indexes can indicate a node's children, as the following Pascal statements indicate:

```
const  maxnodes = 100;     { maximum number of nodes }
       maxlen = 20;        { maximum length of name }
type   string = packed array[1..maxlen] of char;
       index = 0..maxnodes;

       node = record
           name : string;
           Lchild : index;  { index to the left child }
           Rchild : index   { index to the right child }
       end;
```

```
          bintree = array[1..maxnodes] of node;

  var     Tree : bintree;
          T : index;          { index of root }
          Free : index;       { index of free list }
```

The variable T is an index to the tree's root within the array $Tree$. If the tree is empty, T is 0. Both $Lchild$ and $Rchild$ within a node are indexes to the children of that node. A zero value for either index indicates that there is no child.

As the tree changes due to insertions and deletions, its nodes may not be in consecutive elements of the array. Therefore, this implementation requires you to establish a list of available nodes, which is called a **free list**. To insert a new node into the tree, you first obtain an available node from the free list. If you delete a node from the tree, you place it into the free list so that you can reuse the node at a later time. The variable $Free$ is the index to the first node in the free list and, arbitrarily, the field $Rchild$ of each node is the index of the next node in the free list. Figure 10-13 illus-

A free list keeps track of available nodes

Tree

	name	Lchild	Rchild
1	Jane	2	3
2	Bob	4	5
3	Tom	6	7
4	Alan	0	0
5	Ellen	0	0
6	Nancy	0	0
7	Wendy	0	0
8		0	9
9		0	10

T: 1   Free: 8

free list

Figure 10-13

An array-based implementation of the binary tree in Figure 10-8

trates this array-based implementation for the binary tree in Figure 10-8. Note that *Free* points to the next available node in the array—the first node in the free list—and that the *Rchild* field of that node points to next node in the free list.

Under this array-based implementation, if *T* points to the root *R* of a binary tree, then *Tree[T].Lchild* points to the root of the left subtree of *R* and *Tree[T].Rchild* points to the root of the right subtree of *R*.

Traversals of Binary Trees

The definitions of a binary tree make apparent its recursive nature, which is reflected in many algorithms. As an illustration, consider algorithms for traversing a binary tree *T*—that is, for visiting each node in *T*. These algorithms will be useful later. For illustrative purposes, assume that visiting a node simply means printing the data portion of the node.

With the recursive definition of a binary tree in mind, you can construct a recursive traversal algorithm as follows. According to the definition, the binary tree *T* is either empty or is of the form

$$r$$
$$T_L \qquad T_R$$

If *T* is empty, then the traversal algorithm takes no action—an empty tree is the degenerate case. If *T* is not empty, then the traversal algorithm must perform three tasks: It must print the data in the root *r*, and it must traverse the two subtrees T_L and T_R, each of which is a binary tree smaller than *T*.

Thus, the general form of the recursive traversal algorithm is

A recursive traversal algorithm

```
Traverse(T)
{ Traverses the binary tree T. }

    if T is not empty
        then
        begin
            Traverse(Left subtree of T)
            Traverse(Right subtree of T)
        end
```

This algorithm is not quite complete, however. What is missing is the instruction to print out the data in the root. When traversing any binary tree, the algorithm has three choices of when to process the root *r*. It can process *r* before it traverses both of *T*'s subtrees, it can process *r* after it has traversed *T*'s left subtree T_L, but before it traverses its right subtree T_R, or it can process *r* after it has traversed both of *T*'s subtrees. These traversals are called **preorder**, **inorder**, and **postorder**, respectively.

The preorder traversal algorithm is as follows:

Preorder traversal

```
Preorder(T)
{ Traverses the binary tree T in preorder.
  Visit a node means print out its data. }
```

```
if T is not empty
    then
    begin
        Print the data in the root of T
        Preorder(Left subtree of T)
        Preorder(Right subtree of T)
    end
```

The preorder traversal of the tree in Figure 10-14a visits the nodes in this order: 60, 20, 10, 40, 30, 50, 70. If you apply preorder traversal to a binary tree that represents an algebraic expression, such as any tree in Figure 10-7, you will obtain the prefix form of the expression.

The inorder traversal algorithm is as follows:

```
Inorder(T)
{ Traverses the binary tree T in inorder.
  Visit a node means print out its data. }

    if T is not empty
        then
        begin
            Inorder(Left subtree of T)
            Print the data in the root of T
            Inorder(Right subtree of T)
        end
```

Inorder traversal

The result of the inorder traversal of the tree in Figure 10-14b is 10, 20, 30, 40, 50, 60, 70. If you apply inorder traversal to a binary search tree, you will visit the nodes in order according to their data values. Such is the case for the tree in Figure 10-14b.

Figure 10-14

Traversals of a binary tree: (a) preorder; (b) inorder; (c) postorder

  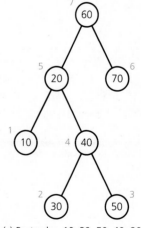

(a) Preorder: 60, 20, 10, 40, 30, 50, 70   (b) Inorder: 10, 20, 30, 40, 50, 60, 70   (c) Postorder: 10, 30, 50, 40, 20, 70, 60

Finally, the postorder traversal algorithm is as follows:

Postorder traversal

```
Postorder(T)
{ Traverses the binary tree T in postorder.
  Visit a node means print out its data. }

    if T is not empty
       then
          begin
             Postorder(Left subtree of T)
             Postorder(Right subtree of T)
             Print the data in the root of T
          end
```

The result of the postorder traversal of the tree in Figure 10-14c is 10, 30, 50, 40, 20, 70, 60. If you apply postorder traversal to a binary tree that represents an algebraic expression, such as any tree in Figure 10-7, you will obtain the postfix form of the expression.

You can easily implement each of these traversals as a recursive Pascal procedure. For example, if you have a pointer-based implementation of a binary tree, as was described previously, the inorder traversal appears in Pascal as follows. (The two points from which a recursive call is made are marked for future reference.)

Inorder traversal in Pascal for a pointer-based implementation

```
procedure Inorder(T : ptr);
{ Traverses the binary tree T in inorder.
  Visit a node means print out its data. }

begin
   if T <> nil
      then
      begin
         Inorder(T^.Lchild); { Point 1 }
         writeln(T^.name);
         Inorder(T^.Rchild)  { Point 2 }
      end  { if }
end  { Inorder }
```

Nonrecursive traversal.   Before leaving the topic of traversals, it will be useful to develop a *nonrecursive* traversal algorithm. Remember that some popular programming languages do not support recursion. Thus, it will be desirable to see a traversal of a binary tree in a nonrecursive environment. However, there is a less obvious reason for developing a nonrecursive traversal algorithm: The process will illustrate further the relationship between stacks and recursion that was first discussed in Chapter 8.

As an example of nonrecursive traversal techniques, consider a nonrecursive *inorder* traversal for the pointer-based implementation of a binary tree. The conceptually difficult part of the nonrecursive traversal is determining where to go next after a particular node has been visited. To gain some insight into this problem, consider how the recursive inorder traversal works. Notice that the preceding *Inorder* procedure has its recursive calls marked as points 1 and 2.

In the course of the traversal's execution, the current value of the pointer *T* actually marks the position in the tree. Each time *Inorder* makes a recursive call (from either point 1 or point 2), the effect is to descend the tree. In terms of the stack that is implicit to recursive subprograms, a call to *Inorder* pushes a pointer to the new current node—that is, the new value of *T*—onto the stack. At any given time, the stack contains pointers to the nodes along the path from the tree's root to the current node *n*, with the pointer to *n* at the top of the stack and the pointer to the root at the bottom, as Figure 10-15 illustrates.

Now consider what happens when *Inorder* returns from a recursive call. The effect of the return is to backtrack up the tree from a node *n* to its parent *p*, from which the recursive call to *n* was made. (Note that *n* is possibly "empty"—that is, is indicated by a *nil* value for *T* at the top of the stack.) A pointer to *p* comes to the top of the stack when, as the return is made from the recursive call, the pointer to *n* is popped from the stack.

What happens next depends on which subtree of *p* has just been traversed. If, as Figure 10-16a illustrates, the process has just finished traversing *p*'s left subtree (that is, *n* is the left child of *p* and thus the return is made to point 1 in the *Inorder* procedure), then control is returned to the statement that prints out the data in node *p*. After the data in *p* has been printed, a recursive call is made from point 2 and the right subtree of *p* is traversed. However, if, as Figure 10-16b illustrates, you have just traversed *p*'s right subtree (that is, if *n* is the right child of *p* and thus the return is made to point 2), then control is returned to the end of the procedure. As a consequence another return is made, the pointer to *p* is popped off the stack, and you backtrack up the tree to *p*'s parent, from where the recursive call to *p* was made. Notice that in this latter case, the

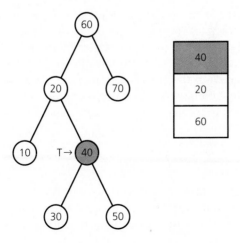

Figure 10-15

Inorder traversal using a stack

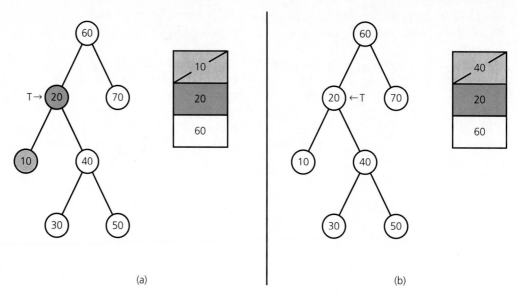

(a)   (b)

Figure 10-16

Traversing (a) the left and
(b) the right subtrees of 20

data in *p* is not printed—it was printed before the recursive call to *n* was made from point 2.

Thus, two facts emerge from the recursive version of the *Inorder* procedure when a return is made from a recursive call:

Actions at a return from a recursive call to ***Inorder***

1. The implicit recursive stack of pointers is used to find the node *p* to which the traversal must backtrack.

2. Once the traversal backtracks to node *p*, it either visits *p* (for example, prints out its data) or backtracks further up the tree. It visits *p* if *p*'s left subtree has just been traversed or backtracks if its right subtree has just been traversed. The appropriate action is taken simply as a consequence of the point—1 or 2—to which control is returned.

You could directly mimic this action by using an iterative procedure and an explicit stack, as long as some bookkeeping device kept track of which subtree of a node had just been traversed. However, you can use the following observation both to eliminate the need for the bookkeeping device and to speed up the traversal somewhat. Consider the subtree in Figure 10-17. After you have finished traversing the subtree rooted at node *R*, there is no need to return to nodes *B* and *C*, because the right subtrees of these nodes have already been traversed. You can instead return directly to node *A*, *which is the nearest ancestor of R, whose right subtree has not yet been traversed.*

It is a simple matter to implement this strategy of not returning to a node after its right subtree has been traversed. All that is required is that you place a pointer to a node on the stack only before the node's left subtree is traversed, and not before its right subtree is traversed. Thus, in

Figure 10-17

A subtree with a stack

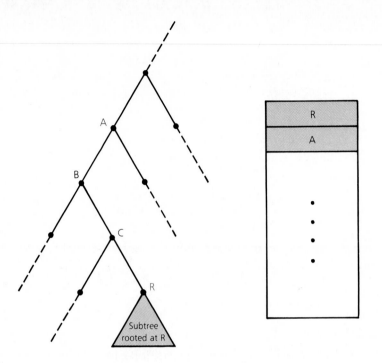

Figure 10-17, when you are at node *R* the contents of the stack is *A-R* (with *R* on top). Nodes *B* and *C* are not on the stack because you are currently traversing their right subtrees; on the other hand, *A* is on the stack because you are currently traversing its left subtree. When you return from node *R*, nodes *B* and *C* are thus bypassed because you have finished with their right subtrees and do not need to return to these nodes. Thus, you go directly to node *A*, whose left subtree has just been traversed. You then visit *A*, pop its pointer from the stack, and traverse *A*'s right subtree.

This nonrecursive traversal strategy is captured by the following pseudocode:

Nonrecursive inorder traversal

```
{ initialize }
p := root
Push(S, p)
done := false

while not done do
begin
    if p <> nil
        then   { traverse the left subtree }
        begin
            p := p^.Lchild
            Push(S, p)
        end
```

```
            else  { backtrack from the empty subtree }
        begin
            Pop(S)  { pop the nil pointer }
            { visit the node at the top of the stack.
              However, if the stack is empty, you are done. }
            if not IsEmpty(S)
                then
                begin
                    p := StackTop(S)
                    Visit(p)

                    { traverse the right subtree
                      of the node just visited }
                    Pop(S)
                    p := p^.Rchild
                    Push(S, p)
                end  { then }

                else done := true
        end  { else backtrack }
end  { while }
```

You should note that eliminating recursion can be more complicated than the example given here. However, the general case is beyond the scope of this book.

A NONLINEAR IMPLEMENTATION OF THE ADT TABLE

A nonlinear implementation of the ADT table that uses a binary search tree provides the best features of the linear implementations of the ADT table that were presented earlier in this chapter. You can insert and delete data items by changing either pointers or indexes, without shifting data. You can locate data items by using a binary search-like algorithm, a technique you previously could apply only to an array-based implementation. Finally, in its pointer-based form, the binary search tree allows you to take advantage of dynamic storage allocation.

Despite certain difficulties, linear implementations of a table can be appropriate

If all of these claims are indeed true, you might wonder why you studied the linear implementations of the ADT table at all. There are three main reasons why it is appropriate to discuss the linear table implementations before introducing the nonlinear implementation. The first and foremost reason is perspective. Chapter 7 spoke of the dangers of overanalyzing a problem. If the size of the problem is small, it is unlikely that there will be a significant difference in efficiency among the possible solutions. In particular, if the size of the table is small, you should select a linear implementation because it is simple to code and read.

The second reason is that there actually are scenarios for which a linear implementation is quite efficient. Recall that a linear implementation was adequate for Scenario *A*, where the predominant operations are `Insert` and `Traverse` in no particular order; Scenario *B*, where the predominant operation is `Traverse` in sorted order; and, if the maximum number of items is known, Scenario *C*, where the predominant operations are `Traverse` in sorted order and `Retrieve`. For these situations, a concern for simplicity suggests that you use a linear implementation and not a binary search tree, even for large tables.

The third reason is motivation. By seeing scenarios for which the linear implementations are not adequate, you can appreciate binary search trees more fully. Recall that in these scenarios there seemed to be conflicting needs that could not be reconciled. For the task of locating a table item for both the `Retrieve` operation and the first steps of the `Insert` and `Delete` operations, a binary search is desirable. Thus, an array-based implementation is preferable. On the other hand, the need for dynamic storage allocation and the desire not to shift items during the `Insert` and `Delete` operations make a pointer-based implementation equally desirable. The binary search tree reconciles this conflict.

The recursive definition of a binary search tree, whose nodes each contain one field designated as the search key, can be restated as follows:

> For each node *n*, a **binary search tree** satisfies the following three properties:
>
> - *n*'s search key is greater than all search keys in its left subtree T_L.
> - *n*'s search key is less than all search keys in its right subtree T_R.
> - Both T_L and T_R are binary search trees.

A recursive definition of a binary search tree

The sorted nature of a binary search tree allows efficient `Retrieve`, `Insert`, `Delete`, and `Traverse` operations.

For example, suppose that you want to locate the name Ellen in the binary search tree of Figure 10-18. Beginning with Jane, which is in the root node of the tree, you know that if the name Ellen is present in the

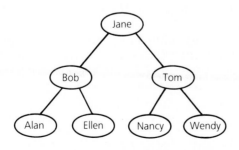

Figure 10-18

A binary search tree

tree, it must be in Jane's left subtree because Ellen is before Jane alphabetically. From the recursive definition, you know that Jane's left subtree is also a binary search tree, so you use exactly the same strategy to search this subtree for Ellen. The name Bob is in the root of this binary search tree, and because Ellen is greater than Bob it must be in Bob's right subtree. Bob's right subtree is also a binary search tree, and it happens that Ellen is in the root node of this tree. Thus, the search has located the name.

This search strategy for the pointer-based implementation of the binary search tree is formalized as follows:

A search algorithm for a pointer-based binary search tree

```
Find(T, X)
{ Searches the binary search tree T for the name X. }

   if T = nil then
      Print 'X is not present'  { empty tree }

   else if T^.name = X then
      Print 'X is present'       { name is found }

   else if X < T^.name then
      Find(T^.Lchild, X)         { search the left subtree }

   else Find(T^.Rchild, X)       { search the right subtree }
```

As you will see, this *Find* algorithm is the basis of the operations *Insert*, *Delete*, and *Retrieve*.

Several different binary search trees are possible for the same data

Many different binary search trees can contain the names Alan, Bob, Ellen, Jane, Nancy, Tom, and Wendy. For example, in addition to the tree in Figure 10-18, each tree in Figure 10-19 is a valid binary search tree for these names. Although these trees have different shapes, the shape of the tree in no way affects the validity of the *Find* algorithm. The only property that *Find* needs is that a tree be a binary search tree.

Find works more efficiently on some trees than on others, however. For example, with the tree in Figure 10-19c, the *Find* algorithm inspects every node before locating Wendy. In fact, this binary tree really has the same structure as a sorted linear list. In contrast, with the full tree in Figure 10-18, the *Find* algorithm inspects only the nodes that contain the names Jane, Tom, and Wendy. Notice that these are exactly the same names that a binary search of the sorted array in Figure 10-20 would inspect. Later in this chapter, you will learn more about how the shape of a binary search tree affects efficiency and how the *Insert* and *Delete* operations affect this shape.

Now consider the operation *Traverse* in sorted order. The inorder traversal that you saw earlier in this chapter will visit the nodes of a binary search tree in sorted order. Recall that the inorder traversal algorithm appears as follows:

```
Inorder(T)
{ Traverses the binary tree T in inorder. }
```

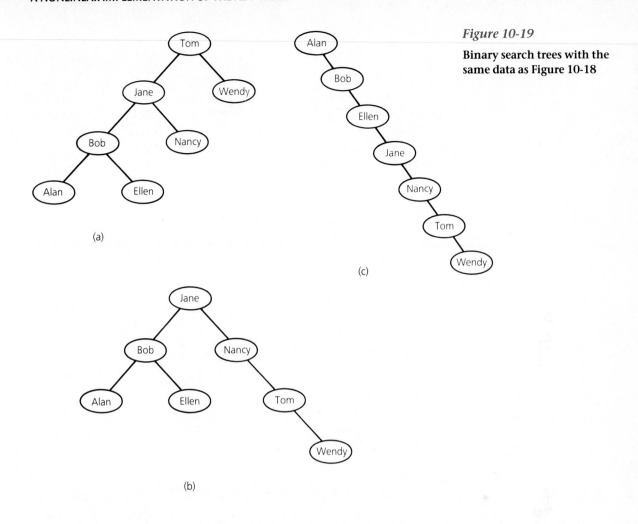

Figure 10-19

Binary search trees with the same data as Figure 10-18

(a)

(b)

(c)

Figure 10-20

An array of names in sorted order

Alan	Bob	Ellen	Jane	Nancy	Tom	Wendy
1	2	3	4	5	6	7

```
if T is not empty
   then
   begin
      Inorder(Left subtree of T)
      Visit the root of T
      Inorder(Right subtree of T)
   end
```

THEOREM 10-1. The inorder traversal of a binary search tree *T* will visit its nodes in sorted search-key order.

PROOF.   The proof is by induction on h, the height of T.

Basis: $h = 0$. When T is empty, the algorithm does not visit any nodes. This is the proper sorted order for the zero names that are in the tree!

Inductive hypothesis: Assume the theorem is true for all k, $0 \leqslant k < h$. That is, assume for all k ($0 \leqslant k < h$) that the inorder traversal visits the nodes in sorted order.

Inductive conclusion: You must show that the theorem is true for $k = h > 0$. Recall that T has this form:

$$r$$
$$T_L \qquad T_R$$

Because T is a binary search tree, all the search keys in the left subtree T_L are less than the search key in the root r, and all the search keys in the right subtree T_R are greater than the search key in r. The `Inorder` algorithm will visit all the nodes in T_L, then visit r, and then visit all the nodes in T_R. Thus, the only concern is that `Inorder` visit the nodes within each of the subtrees T_L and T_R in the correct sorted order. But because T is a binary search tree of height h, each subtree is a binary search tree of height less than h. Therefore, by the inductive hypothesis, `Inorder` visits the nodes in each subtree T_L and T_R in the correct sorted order. **(End of proof.)**

Use inorder traversal to visit nodes of a binary search tree in search-key order

As a result of this theorem, you can use inorder traversal to visit the nodes of a binary search tree in search-key order.

To summarize, the structure of a binary search tree allows you to traverse it in sorted order by using inorder traversal and to search it by using a binary search-like algorithm, `Find`.

Details of the Nonlinear Implementation of the ADT Table

This section examines the details of a pointer-based nonlinear implementation of the ADT table that uses a binary search tree. A binary search tree is recursive by nature, and it is thus natural to formulate the algorithms recursively. Chapter 6 examined a recursive implementation of the linked list operations, which this section will now use.

Insert.   Suppose that you want to insert the name Frank into the binary search tree of Figure 10-18. As a first step, imagine that you instead want to *find* the item with a search key of Frank. The `Find` algorithm first searches the tree rooted at Jane, then the tree rooted at Bob, and then the tree rooted at Ellen. It then searches the tree rooted at the right child of Ellen. Because this tree is empty, as Figure 10-21 illustrates, the `Find` algorithm has reached a degenerate case and will terminate with the report that Frank is not present. What does it mean that `Find` looked for Frank in the right subtree of Ellen? For one thing, it means that if Frank were the right child of Ellen, `Find` would have found Frank there.

Figure 10-21

Empty subtree where *Find* terminates

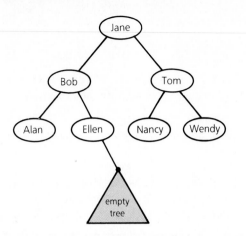

This observation indicates that a good place to insert Frank is as the right child of Ellen. Because Ellen has no right child, the insertion is simple, requiring only that Ellen's *Rchild* pointer field be set to point to Frank. More importantly, Frank belongs in this location—*Find* will look for Frank here. Specifically, inserting Frank as the right child of Ellen will preserve the tree's binary search tree property. Because *Find*, when searching for Frank, would follow a path that leads to the right child of Ellen, you are assured that Frank is in the proper relation to the names above it in the tree.

Notice that the use of *Find* to determine the insertion point in the tree for the new name always leads to an easy insertion. No matter what new name you insert into the tree, *Find* will always terminate at an empty subtree, and thus it will always indicate that you should insert the name as a new leaf. Because adding a leaf requires only that you set the appropriate pointer field in the parent, the work required for an insertion is virtually the same as that for the corresponding find.

*Use **Find** to determine the insertion point*

The following high-level pseudocode describes this insertion process:

```
Insert(T, newitem)
{ Inserts newitem into table T, where no item
  in T has the same search key as newitem. }

    { X is the search key of newitem }
    Let N be the parent of the empty subtree
      at which Find(T, X) terminates

    if the empty subtree is the left subtree of N
        then set Lchild of N to point to newitem
        else set Rchild of N to point to newitem
```

Insertion algorithm at a high level

Observe that the appropriate pointer of node *N* must be set to point to the new node. The recursive nature of the algorithm provides an elegant means of setting the pointer, provided that you pass *T* as a variable parameter. Thus, *Insert* is refined as follows:

```
Insert(T, newitem)
{ Inserts newitem into table T, where no item
  in T has the same search key as newitem. }

   if T = nil then
      { create a new record with T pointing to it }
      begin
         new(T)
         Set the data fields of the new record
            to the values in newitem
         Set the pointer fields of the new record to nil
      end

   else if newitem.key < T^.key then
         Insert(T^.Lchild, newitem)

   else Insert(T^.Rchild, newitem)
```

Does this procedure really set the appropriate pointer variable to point to the new node? The situation is quite similar to the recursive *Insert* procedure for the sorted linked list that you saw in Chapter 6. If the tree was empty before the insertion, the external pointer to the root of the tree would be *nil* and the procedure would not make a recursive call. In this case the actual parameter is therefore the external pointer to the root of the tree. Because *T* is a variable parameter, when it is set to point to the new record, the effect is to set the external pointer to point to the new record. Figure 10-22a illustrates insertion into an empty tree.

The general case of *Insert* is similar to the special case when the tree is empty. When the formal parameter *T* becomes *nil*, the corresponding actual parameter is the *Lchild* or *Rchild* pointer field of the parent of the empty subtree; that is, this pointer field has the value *nil*. This pointer field was passed to the *Insert* procedure by one of the recursive calls

```
Insert(T^.Lchild, newitem)
```

or

```
Insert(T^.Rchild, newitem)
```

Thus, when *T* is set to point to the new record, the effect is to set the actual parameter, which is the appropriate pointer field of the parent, to point to the new record. Parts *b* and *c* of Figure 10-22 illustrate the general case of insertion.

You can create a binary search tree by using *Insert*. For example, beginning with an empty tree, if you insert the names Jane, Bob, Alan, Ellen, Tom, Nancy, and Wendy in order, you will get the binary search tree in Figure 10-18. It is interesting to note that the inserted names Jane, Bob,

(a)

(b)

(c)

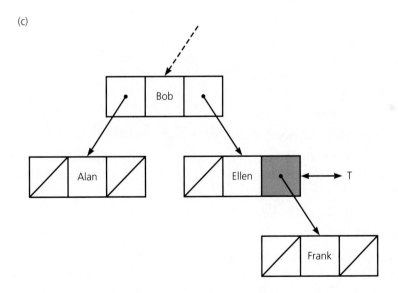

Alan, Ellen, Tom, Nancy, and Wendy constitute the preorder traversal of the tree in Figure 10-18. Thus, if you take the output of a preorder traversal of a binary search tree and use it with *Insert* to create a binary search tree, you will obtain a duplicate tree.

By inserting the previous names in a different order, you will get a different binary search tree. For example, by inserting the previous names in alphabetic order, you will get the binary search tree in Figure 10-19c.

Delete.   The `Delete` operation is a bit more involved than `Insert`. First, you use the `Find` algorithm to locate the node with the specified search key and then, if it is found, you must remove the node from the tree. A first draft of the algorithm follows:

First draft of the deletion algorithm

```
Delete(T, X, success)
{ Deletes from table T the item with search key X. The
  operation fails if there is no such item. The flag success
  indicates whether the operation succeeded. }

    Find(T, X)      { locate node N with value X }

  if X is found
     then
     begin
        Remove node N from the tree
        success := true
     end

     else success := false
```

The essential task here is

```
    Remove node N from the tree
```

There are three cases to consider:

Three cases for the node, N, to be deleted

1. *N* is a leaf.
2. *N* has only one child.
3. *N* has two children.

Case 1: Set the pointer in a leaf's parent to `nil`

The first case is the easiest. To remove a leaf, you need only set the pointer field of its parent to `nil`. The second case is a bit more difficult. If *N* has only one child, there are really two possibilities:

Case 2: Two possibilities for N

- *N* has only a left child.
- *N* has only a right child.

Let N's parent adopt N's child

The two possibilities are symmetric, so it is sufficient to illustrate the solution for a left child. In Figure 10-23a *L* is the left child of *N*, and *P* is the parent of *N*. Notice that *N* can be either the left or right child of *P*. If you deleted *N* from the tree, *L* would be without a parent, and *P* would be without one of its children. Suppose you let *L* take the place of *N* as one of *P*'s children, as in Figure 10-23b. Does this adoption preserve the binary search tree property?

If *N* is the left child of *P*, for example, then all the search keys in the subtree rooted at *N* are less than the search key in *P*. Thus, all the search

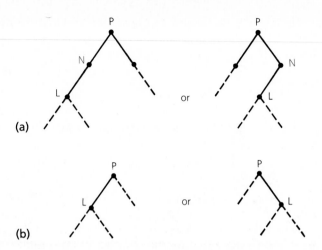

Figure 10-23

(a) *N* with only a left child—*N* can be either the left or right child of *P*; (b) after deleting node *N*

keys in the subtree rooted at *L* are less than the search key in *P*. Therefore, after *N* is removed and *L* is adopted by *P*, all the search keys in *P*'s left subtree are still less than the search key in *P*. This deletion strategy thus preserves the binary search tree property. A parallel argument holds if *N* is a right child of *P*, and therefore the binary search tree property is preserved in either case.

The most difficult of the three cases occurs when the node *N* to be deleted has two children, as in Figure 10-24. Recall that when *N* has one child, the child replaces *N*; that is, *N*'s parent adopts the child. However, when *N* has two children, these children cannot both replace *N*: *N*'s parent has room for only one of *N*'s children as a replacement for *N*. A different strategy is necessary.

Case 3: N *has two children*

In fact, you will not delete *N* at all. You can find another node that is easier to delete and delete it instead of *N*. That may sound like cheating. After all, the programmer who requests

```
Delete(T, X, success)
```

expects that the item whose search key contains the value *X* will be deleted from the tree. However, the programmer expects the *item* will be deleted and has no right, because of the wall between the program and the ADT

Figure 10-24

N with two children

implementation, to expect a particular *node* in the tree to be deleted. In fact, because of the wall, the programmer has no right to even expect that there is a tree at all!

Consider then an alternate strategy. To delete from a binary search tree an item that resides in a node *N* that has two children, take the following steps:

Deleting an item whose node has two children

1. Locate another node *M* that is easier to remove from the tree than is the node *N*.

2. Copy the item that is in *M* to *N*, thus effectively deleting from the table the item originally in *N*.

3. Remove the node *M* from the tree.

What kind of node *M* is easier to remove than the node *N*? Because you know how to delete a node that has no children or one child, *M* could be such a node. You have to be careful, though. Can you choose any node and copy its value into *N*? No, because you must preserve the tree's status as a binary search tree. For example, if in the tree of Figure 10-25, you copied the value from *M* to *N*, the result would no longer be a binary search tree.

What value, when copied into the node *N*, will preserve the tree's status as a binary search tree? All search keys in the left subtree of *N* are less than the search key in *N*, and all the search keys in the right subtree of *N* are greater than the search key in *N*. You must retain this property when you replace the search key *X* in node *N* with the search key *Y*. There are two suitable possibilities for the value *Y*: It can come immediately after or immediately before *X* in the sorted order of search keys. If *Y* comes immediately after *X*, then clearly all search keys in the left subtree of *N* are smaller than *Y*, because they are all smaller than *X*, as Figure 10-26 illustrates. Further, all search keys in the right subtree of *N* are greater than or equal to *Y*, because they are greater than *X* and, by assumption, there are no search keys in the tree between *X* and *Y*. A similar argument illustrates

Figure 10-25

Not any node will do

Figure 10-26

Search key *X* can be replaced by *Y*

that if *Y* comes immediately before *X* in the sorted order, then it is greater than or equal to all search keys in the left subtree of *N* and smaller than all search keys in the right subtree of *N*.

You can thus copy into *N* either of the two items whose search keys are the two values of *Y*, as just described. How can you locate one of these items? Suppose that arbitrarily, you decide to locate the search key *Y* that comes immediately after *X*. Recall that the inorder traversal will visit the search keys of a binary search tree in proper sorted order. Therefore, search key *Y* is contained in the node that the inorder traversal visits immediately after node *N*. This node is called *N*'s **inorder successor**. Given that *N* has two children, its inorder successor is the leftmost node of *N*'s right subtree. That is, to find the node that contains *Y*, you follow *N*'s `Rchild` pointer to its right child *R*, which must be present because *N* has two children. You then descend the tree rooted at *R* by taking left branches at each node until you encounter a node *M* with no left child. You copy the value of the item in this node *M* into node *N* and, because *M* has no left child, you can remove *M* from the tree as one of the two easy cases (see Figure 10-27).

Inorder successor of N: *the left-most node in* N*'s right subtree*

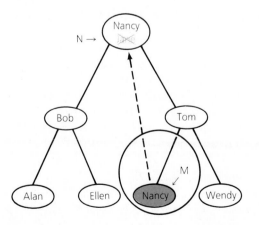

Figure 10-27

Copying *N*'s inorder successor to *N*

A more detailed high-level description of the `Delete` algorithm follows:

Second draft of the deletion
algorithm

```
Delete(T, X, success)
{ Deletes from table T the item with search key X. The
  operation fails if there is no such item. The flag success
  indicates whether the operation succeeded. }

    Find(T, X)  { locate node N with value X }

    if X is found
       then
       begin
          Delitem(N) { Delitem is defined next }
          success := true
       end

       else success := false

Delitem(N)
{ Deletes the item in the node N of a binary search tree. }

    if N is a leaf then
       Remove N from the tree

    else if N has only one child C then
       begin
          if N was a left child of its parent P
             then make C the left child of P
             else make C the right child of P
       end

    else  { N has two children }
    begin
       Find N's inorder successor M
       Copy the item from M into N
       Remove M from the tree by using the previous
          technique for a leaf or a node with one child
    end
```

In the following refinement, `Find`'s algorithm is adapted and inserted directly into `Delete`. Also, the procedure `Delitem` uses the procedure `Leftmost` to find the node that contains the inorder successor of the item in N. `Leftmost` deletes this node from the tree and returns the inorder successor. This item then replaces in node N the item to be deleted from the binary search tree.

Final draft of the deletion
algorithm

```
Delete(T, X, success)
{ Deletes from table T the item with search key X. The
  operation fails if there is no such item. The flag success
  indicates whether the operation succeeded. }
```

```
    if T = nil then
        success := false

    else if T^.key = X then
        begin     { remove the item in the node pointed to by T }
            Delitem(T)
            success := true
        end

    else if X < T^.key then
        Delete(T^.Lchild, X, success) { search left subtree }

    else
        Delete(T^.Rchild, X, success) { search right subtree }

Delitem(delptr)
{ Removes the item in the node N pointed to by delptr. }

    if N is a leaf then
        { remove from the tree }
        begin
            dispose(delptr)
            delptr := nil
        end

    else if N has only one child C then
        { C replaces N as the child of N's parent }
        begin
            p := delptr
            if C is the left child of N
                then delptr := delptr^.Lchild
                else delptr := delptr^.Rchild
            dispose(p)
        end

    else { N has two children }
    begin
        { find the inorder successor of the value in N: It is
          in the leftmost node of the subtree rooted at N's
          right child }
        Leftmost(delptr^.Rchild, ReplacementItem)
        Put ReplacementItem in N
    end

Leftmost(p, getitem)
{ Retrieves into getitem the item in the leftmost descendent
  of the node pointed to by p. Deletes the node that
  contains this item. }

    if p^.Lchild = nil
        then
        { this is the node you want - it has no left
          child but it might have a right subtree }
```

Figure 10-28

Recursive deletion of node *N*

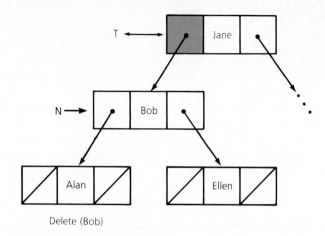

Delete (Bob)

Any change to T while deleting node N (Bob) changes Lchild of Jane

```
begin
    getitem := p^.item
    temp := p

    { notice that the actual parameter corresponding
      to p is a child-pointer field of p's parent -
      the following thus correctly "moves up" p's
      right subtree }
    p := p^.Rchild

    dispose(temp)
end

else Leftmost(p^.Lchild, getitem)
```

Observe that, as in the case of the *Insert* procedure, the actual parameter that corresponds to *T* is either one of the pointer fields of the parent of *N* or is the external pointer to the root in the case where *N* is the root of the original tree, as Figure 10-28 depicts. Thus, any change you make to *T*, which points to node *N*, by calling the procedure *Delitem* with actual parameter *T* changes the pointer field of the parent of *N*. The recursive procedure *Leftmost*, which is called by *Delitem* if *N* has two children, also uses this strategy to remove the node that contains the inorder successor of the item to be deleted.

Exercise 22 at the end of this chapter discusses an easier deletion algorithm. However, that algorithm tends to increase the height of the tree and, as you will see later, an increase in height can decrease the efficiency of searching the tree.

Retrieve. By refining the *Find* algorithm, you can implement the *Retrieve* operation. Recall that the *Find* algorithm is

```
Find(T, X)
{ Searches the binary search tree T for the name X. }

    if T = nil then
        Print 'X is not present'  { empty tree }

    else if T^.name = X then
        Print 'X is present'       { name is found }

    else if X < T^.name then
        Find(T^.Lchild, X)         { search the left subtree }

    else Find(T^.Rchild, X)        { search the right subtree }
```

There are only two minor issues to consider. First, recall that the items of a table are, in general, records with one of the fields designated as the search key. Therefore, the nodes of the tree may contain, in addition to the two pointer fields, several data fields, one of which is named *key*. The implementation of the `Retrieve` operation must reflect this fact. The second issue is that `Retrieve` must return the item with the desired search key if it exists, and otherwise it must return the boolean flag *success* with the value *false*. These actions replace the `Print` statements in the `Find` algorithm.

The `Retrieve` procedure, therefore, appears as follows:

```
Retrieve(T, X, getitem, success)          Retrieve is a refinement of
{ Retrieves into getitem from the binary search tree T the    Find
  item with search key X. The operation fails if there is no
  such item. The flag success indicates whether the
  operation succeeded. }

    if T = nil then
        success := false          { T is empty }

    else if T^.key = X then        { item is found }
        begin
            getitem := data fields of record pointed to by T
            success := true
        end

    else if X < T^.key then
        Retrieve(T^.Lchild, X)     { search the left subtree }

    else Retrieve(T^.Rchild, X)    { search the right subtree }
```

Pascal implementation. The Pascal nonlinear implementation of the ADT table follows.

```
{ **************************************************************
  BASIC TABLE OPERATIONS (Pointer-Based Binary Search Tree
  Implementation):

    Create, Insert, Delete, Retrieve, and Traverse (sorted)
```

The following definitions are assumed:

```
type    keytype = <desired type of search key>;

        itemtype = record
            key : keytype;
            <... and possibly other fields>
        end;

        bintree = ^node;
        node = record
            item : itemtype;
            Lchild, Rchild : bintree
        end;

var    T : bintree;
```

Assumption: At any time a binary search tree contains at most one item with a given search key. (See Exercises 8 through 10 at the end of this chapter.)
** }
```
procedure Create(var T : bintree);
{ ------------------------------------------------------
  Creates an empty table.
  Precondition: None.
  Postcondition: The empty table T is created.
  ------------------------------------------------------ }
begin
   T := nil
end;  { Create }

procedure Insert(var T : bintree; newitem : itemtype);
{ ------------------------------------------------------
  Inserts an item into a table in its proper sorted order
  according to the item's search key.
  Precondition: Table T has been created and no two items of
  T have the same search key. T's items are sorted by search
  key. The item to be inserted into T is newitem, whose
  search key differs from all search keys presently in T.
  Postcondition: newitem is inserted into its proper
  position in T.
  ------------------------------------------------------ }
begin
   { the position has been found - insert after leaf }
   if T = nil then
      begin
         new(T);
         T^.item := newitem;
         T^.Lchild := nil;
         T^.Rchild := nil
      end
```

```
      { search for the position }
      else if newitem.key < T^.item.key then
          Insert(T^.Lchild, newitem)
      else Insert(T^.Rchild, newitem)
end; { Insert }

procedure Delete(var T : bintree; keyval : keytype;
                    var success : boolean);
{ ----------------------------------------------------------
  Deletes an item with a given search key from a table.
  Precondition: Table T has been created and no two items of
  T have the same search key. T's items are sorted by search
  key; keyval is the search key of the item to be deleted.
  Postcondition: If the item whose search key equals keyval
  exists in T, the item is deleted and success is set to
  true. Otherwise, T is unchanged and success is set to
  false.
  Calls: Local procedure Delitem, which calls Leftmost.
  ---------------------------------------------------------- }

    procedure Leftmost(var p : bintree;
                          var getitem : itemtype);
      { --------------------------------------------------------
        Retrieves and deletes the leftmost descendent of a
        given node.
        Precondition: p is a node in a binary search tree,
        which contains at most one item with a given search
        key.
        Postcondition: getitem contains the item in the
        leftmost descendent of the node pointed to by p. The
        leftmost descendent of p is deleted.
        -------------------------------------------------------- }
    var delnode : bintree;
    begin
    if p <> nil
      then
      begin
        if p^.Lchild = nil
            then
            begin
              getitem := p^.item;
              delnode := p;
              p := p^.Rchild;
              dispose(delnode)
            end

            else Leftmost(p^.Lchild, getitem)
      end  { if }
  end;  { Leftmost }
```

```pascal
procedure Delitem(var delptr : bintree);
{ ------------------------------------------------------
  Deletes the item in the root of a given tree.
  Precondition: Binary search tree delptr has been
  created and contains at most one item with a given
  search key.
  Postcondition: The item in the root of the given tree
  is deleted.
  Algorithm note: There are four cases to consider:
     1. The root is a leaf.
     2. The root has no left child.
     3. The root has no right child.
     4. The root has two children.
  Calls: Leftmost.
  ------------------------------------------------------ }
var p : bintree;
    replitem : itemtype;
begin
  if delptr <> nil
      then
      begin
         { test for a leaf }
         if (delptr^.Lchild = nil) and
               (delptr^.Rchild = nil) then
            begin
               dispose(delptr);
               delptr := nil
            end

         { test for no left child }
         else if delptr^.Lchild = nil then
            begin
               p := delptr;
               delptr := delptr^.Rchild;
               dispose(p)
            end

         { test for no right child }
         else if delptr^.Rchild = nil then
            begin
               p := delptr;
               delptr := delptr^.Lchild;
               dispose(p)
            end

         { there are two children - delete and
           retrieve the inorder successor }
         else
```

```
                    begin
                        Leftmost(delptr^.Rchild, replitem);
                        delptr^.item := replitem
                    end
            end  { if delptr <> nil }
    end; { Delitem }

begin  { Delete }
    if T = nil then
        success := false

    { the item is found - the node is the root of some subtree }
    else if keyval = T^.item.key then
        begin
            Delitem(T);
            success := true
        end

    { search for the item }
    else if keyval < T^.item.key then
        Delete(T^.Lchild, keyval, success)

    else Delete(T^.Rchild, keyval, success)
end;  { Delete }

procedure Retrieve(T : bintree; keyval : keytype;
                var getitem : itemtype; var success : boolean);
{ -------------------------------------------------------
  Retrieves an item with a given search key from a table.
  Precondition: Table T has been created and no two items of
  T have the same search key. T's items are sorted by search
  key; keyval is the search key of the item to be retrieved.
  Postcondition: If retrieval is successful, getitem
  contains the retrieved item and success is true. If there
  is no such item, getitem is unchanged and success is
  false. T and keyval remain unchanged.
  ------------------------------------------------------- }
begin
    if T = nil then
        success := false

    else if keyval = T^.item.key then
        { the item has been found }
        begin
            getitem := T^.item;
            success := true
        end

    { search for the item }
    else if keyval < T^.item.key then
        Retrieve(T^.Lchild, keyval, getitem, success)
```

```
        else Retrieve(T^.Rchild, keyval, getitem, success)
end;   { Retrieve }

procedure Traverse(T : bintree;
                              procedure Visit(item : itemtype));
{ --------------------------------------------------------
  Traverses a table in sorted order, calling procedure Visit
  for each item.
  Precondition: Table T has been created and no two items of
  T have the same search key. T's items are sorted by search
  key. The procedure represented by Visit exists outside of
  the ADT implementation.
  Postcondition: Visit's action occurs for each item in T.
  -------------------------------------------------------- }
begin
  { inorder traversal }
  if T <> nil
    then
    begin
      Traverse(T^.Lchild, Visit);
      Visit(T^.item);
      Traverse(T^.Rchild, Visit)
    end
end   { Traverse }
```

The Efficiency of the Nonlinear Implementation of the ADT Table

An analysis of this nonlinear implementation of the ADT table will show whether it succeeds where the linear implementations failed. You saw binary search trees in many shapes. For example, even though the binary search trees in Figures 10-18 and 10-19c have seven nodes each, they have radically different shapes and heights. You saw that to locate Wendy in Figure 10-19c, you would have to inspect all seven nodes, but to locate Wendy in Figure 10-18 would require you to inspect only three nodes (Jane, Tom, and Wendy). Consider now the relationship between the height of a binary search tree and the efficiency of the operations *Retrieve*, *Insert*, and *Delete*.

Each of these operations compares the specified value *keyval* to the search keys in the nodes along a **path** through the tree. This path always starts at the root of the tree and, at each node *n*, follows the left or right branch, depending on the comparison of *keyval* to the search key in *n*. The path terminates at the node that contains *keyval* or, in the case that *keyval* is not present, at an empty subtree. The number of comparisons that each operation requires is thus equal to the number of nodes along this path.

The number of comparisons that *Retrieve*, *Insert*, and *Delete* require therefore depends on the location in the tree of the node (or empty subtree) at which the path terminates. This location in turn depends on both the value `keyval` and the values in the tree. Thus, the maximum number of comparisons that the operations can require is the number of nodes on the longest path through the tree. In other words, the *maximum number of comparisons that these operations can require is equal to the height of the binary search tree.* What then are the maximum and minimum heights of a binary search tree of *N* nodes?

The maximum number of comparisons for `Retrieve`, `Insert`, *or* `Delete` *is the height of the tree*

The maximum and minimum heights of a binary search tree. You can maximize the height of a binary tree with *N* nodes simply by giving each internal node (nonleaf) exactly one child, as shown in Figure 10-29. This process will result in a tree of height *N*. Notice that an *N*-node tree with height *N* strikingly resembles a linear list.

N *is the maximum height of a binary tree with* N *nodes*

A minimum-height binary tree with *N* nodes is a bit more difficult to obtain. It is useful first to consider the number of nodes that binary trees with a given height *h* can have. For example, if *h* = 3, the possible binary trees include those in Figure 10-30. Thus, binary trees of height 3 can have between 3 and 7 nodes. In addition, Figure 10-30 shows that 3 is the minimum height for a binary tree with 4, 5, 6, or 7 nodes. Similarly, binary trees with more than 7 nodes require a height greater than 3.

Intuitively, to minimize the height of a binary tree given *N* nodes, you must fill each level of the tree as completely as possible. That is, you want a complete tree. Notice that the trees b, c, d, and e of Figure 10-30 are complete trees. If a complete binary tree of a given height *h* is to have the maximum possible number of nodes, it should be full (as in Figure 10-30e). Figure 10-31 counts these nodes by level and shows the following:

THEOREM 10-2. A full binary tree of height *h* ($h \geq 0$) has $2^h - 1$ nodes.

A formal proof by induction of this theorem appears in Appendix B.
    It follows then that

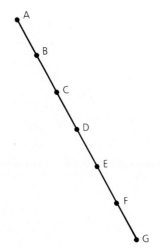

Figure 10-29

A maximum-height binary tree with seven nodes

Figure 10-30

Binary trees of height 3

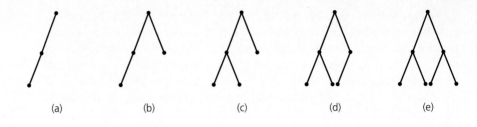

(a)   (b)   (c)   (d)   (e)

THEOREM 10-3. The maximum number of nodes that a binary tree of height h can have is $2^h - 1$.

The formal proof of this theorem, which closely parallels that of Theorem 10-2, is left as an exercise.

The following theorem uses Theorems 10-2 and 10-3 to determine the minimum height of a binary tree that contains some given number of nodes.

THEOREM 10-4. The minimum height of a binary tree with N nodes is $\lceil \log_2(N + 1) \rceil$.

PROOF. Let h be the smallest integer such that $N \leq 2^h - 1$. To find the minimum height of a binary tree with N nodes, first establish the following facts:

1. *A binary tree whose height is $\leq h - 1$ has $< N$ nodes.*
    By Theorem 10-3, a binary tree of height $h - 1$ has at most $2^{h-1} - 1$

Figure 10-31

Counting the nodes in a full binary tree of height h

Level	Number of nodes at this level	Number of nodes at this and previous levels
1	$1 = 2^0$	$1 = 2^1 - 1$
2	$2 = 2^1$	$3 = 2^2 - 1$
3	$4 = 2^2$	$7 = 2^3 - 1$
4	$8 = 2^3$	$15 = 2^4 - 1$
h	2^{h-1}	$2^h - 1$

nodes. If it is possible that $N \leq 2^{h-1} - 1 < 2^h - 1$, then h is not the smallest integer such that $N \leq 2^h - 1$. Therefore, N must be greater than $2^{h-1} - 1$ or, equivalently, $2^{h-1} - 1 < N$. Because a binary tree of height $h - 1$ has at most $2^{h-1} - 1$ nodes, it must have fewer than N nodes.

2. *There exists a complete binary tree of height h that has exactly N nodes.*
   Consider the full binary tree of height $h - 1$. By Theorem 10-2, it has $2^{h-1} - 1$ nodes. As you just saw, $N > 2^{h-1} - 1$ because h was selected so that $N \leq 2^h - 1$. You can thus add nodes to the full tree from left to right until you have N nodes, as Figure 10-32 illustrates. Because $N \leq 2^h - 1$ and a binary tree of height h cannot have more than $2^h - 1$ nodes, you will reach N nodes by the time level h is filled up.

3. *The minimum height of a binary tree with N nodes is the smallest integer h such that $N \leq 2^h - 1$.*
   If h is the smallest integer such that $N \leq 2^h - 1$, and if a binary tree has height $\leq h - 1$, then by fact 1 it has fewer than N nodes. Because by fact 2 there is a binary tree of height h that has exactly N nodes, h must be as small as possible.

The previous discussion implies that

$$2^{h-1} - 1 < N \leq 2^h - 1$$
$$2^{h-1} < N + 1 \leq 2^h$$
$$h - 1 < \log_2(N + 1) \leq h$$

If $\log_2(N + 1) = h$, the theorem is proven. Otherwise, $h - 1 < \log_2(N + 1) < h$ implies that $\log_2(N + 1)$ cannot be an integer. Therefore, *round $\log_2(N + 1)$ up* to get h. The standard way of writing X rounded up is $\lceil X \rceil$, which is read the **ceiling of X**. (For example, $\lceil 6 \rceil = 6$, $\lceil 6.1 \rceil = 7$, and $\lceil 6.8 \rceil = 7$.)

Thus, $h = \lceil \log_2(N + 1) \rceil$ is the minimum height of a binary tree with N nodes. (**End of proof.**)

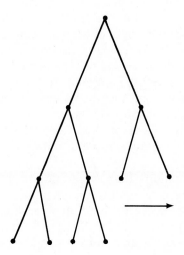

Figure 10-32

Filling in the last level of a tree

Complete trees and full trees
have minimum height

Complete trees and full trees with N nodes thus have heights of $\lceil \log_2(N + 1) \rceil$, which, as you just saw, is the theoretical minimum. Notice that this minimum height agrees with the maximum number of comparisons a binary search must make to search an array with N elements. Therefore, if a binary search tree is complete and therefore balanced, the time it takes to search it for a value is about the same as is required by a binary search of an array. On the other hand, as you go from balanced trees toward trees with a linear structure, the height approaches the number of nodes N. This number agrees with the maximum number of comparisons that you must make when searching a linked list of N nodes.

The height of an N-node binary
search tree ranges from
$\lceil log_2(N + 1) \rceil$ *to N*

Given that the height of an N-node binary search tree can vary from a maximum of N to a minimum of approximately $\log_2 N$, what height should you use when comparing the linear and nonlinear implementations of the ADT table? Suppose that the height of the binary search tree is close to the theoretical minimum of $\lceil \log_2(N + 1) \rceil$. Although this height may seem overly optimistic, you will soon see that the optimism is quite justified.

If the height of the binary search tree is $\lceil \log_2(N + 1) \rceil$, the nonlinear implementation of the ADT table certainly succeeds where the linear implementations failed. By using a binary search tree, you can, with efficiency comparable to that of a binary search, locate an item in both the `Retrieve` operation and the first steps of the `Insert` and `Delete` operations. In addition, the pointer-based implementation of the binary search tree permits dynamic allocation of its nodes, so that it can handle a table whose maximum size is unknown. This implementation also efficiently performs the second step of the `Insert` and `Delete` operations: The actual insertion and removal of a node is accomplished via a few pointer changes (plus a short traversal to the inorder successor if the node to be removed has two children) rather than via the possible shifting of all the table items, as the array-based implementations require. The nonlinear implementation of the ADT table therefore combines the best aspects of the two linear implementations.

However, the outstanding efficiency of the nonlinear implementation hinges on the assumption that the height of the binary search tree is $\lceil \log_2(N + 1) \rceil$. What will the height of a binary search tree actually be? The factor that determines the height of a binary search tree is the order in which you perform the `Insert` and `Delete` operations on the tree. Recall that, starting with an empty tree, if you insert names in the order Alan, Bob, Ellen, Jane, Nancy, Tom, Wendy, you would obtain a binary search tree of maximum height, as shown in Figure 10-19c. On the other hand, if you insert names in the order Jane, Bob, Tom, Alan, Ellen, Nancy, Wendy, you would obtain a binary search tree of minimum height, as shown in Figure 10-18.

Insertion in search-key order
produces a maximum-height
binary search tree

Insertion in random order pro-
duces a near-minimum-height
binary search tree

Which of these situations should you expect to encounter in the course of a real application? It can be proven mathematically that if the `Insert` and `Delete` operations occur in a random order, the height of the binary search tree will be quite close to $\log_2 N$. Thus, in this sense, the previous analysis is not unduly optimistic. However, in a real-world application, is

	Sorted array based	Sorted pointer based	Nonlinear
Retrieve	O(log N) comparisons	O(N) comparisons	O(log N) comparisons
Insert	O(log N) comparisons O(N) item shifts	O(N) comparisons O(1) pointer changes	O(log N) comparisons O(1) pointer changes
Delete	O(log N) ccomparisons O(N) item shifts	O(N) comparisons O(1) pointer changes	O(log N) comparisons O(1) pointer changes

Figure 10-33

The order of the *Retrieve*, *Insert*, and *Delete* operations for three implementations of the ADT table

it realistic to expect the *Insert* and *Delete* operations to occur in random order? In many applications, the answer is yes. There are, however, applications in which this assumption would be dubious. For example, the person preparing the previous sequence of names for the *Insert* operations might well decide to "help you out" by arranging the names to be inserted into sorted order. This arrangement, as has been mentioned, would lead to a tree of maximum height. Thus, while in many applications you can expect the behavior of a binary search tree to be excellent, you should be wary of the possibility of poor performance due to some characteristic of a given application.

Is there anything you can do if you suspect that the operations might not occur in a random order? Similarly, is there anything you can do if you have an enormous number of items and need to ensure that the height of the tree is close to $\log_2 N$? Chapter 13 presents a variation of the basic binary search tree, called a **2-3 tree**, which is guaranteed always to remain balanced. The fact that you can, if need be, always keep the height of a binary search tree near $\log_2 N$ justifies the claim that it provides the best aspects of the two linear implementations of the ADT table.

Figure 10-33 summarizes the order of the operations *Retrieve*, *Insert*, and *Delete* for the three implementations discussed in this chapter.

SUMMARY

1. The ADT table supports value-oriented operations such as *Retrieve all the information about John Smith*.

2. The linear implementations (array based and pointer based) of a table are adequate only in limited situations, such as when the table is small or for certain operations. The fundamental problem with the linear implementation is this paradox: A binary search, which you use to locate either a specified value or the point of insertion, requires an array-based implementation; however, insertions and deletions can avoid the shifting of items only under a pointer-based implementation.

3. A nonlinear (pointer-based binary search tree) implementation of the ADT table provides the best aspects of the two linear implementations. The pointer-based implementation allows the table to grow dynamically and allows insertions and deletions of data to occur through pointer changes instead of data movement. In addition, the binary search tree allows you to use a binary search-like algorithm when searching for an item with a specified value. These characteristics make a nonlinear table implementation far superior to the linear implementations in many applications.

4. Traversing an ADT is an important concept. Intuitively, traversing an ADT means to visit every item in the ADT. If you need to traverse an ADT, you should include a *Traverse* operation in the ADT's definition. Because the meaning of "visit" is application dependent, you can pass a user-defined *Visit* procedure to the *Traverse* operation.

5. Binary search trees come in many shapes. The height of a binary search tree with N nodes can range from a minimum of $\lceil \log_2(N + 1) \rceil$ to a maximum of N. The shape of a binary search tree determines how efficiently it is able to support the table operations. The closer a binary search tree is to a balanced tree (and the further it is from a linear structure), the closer will be the behavior of the *Find* algorithm to a binary search (and the further will it be from the behavior of a linear search).

COMMON PITFALLS/DEBUGGING

1. When defining an ADT to solve a particular problem, do not request unnecessary operations. The proper choice of an implementation depends on the mix of requested operations, and if you request an operation that you do not need, you might get an implementation that does not best support what you are really doing.

2. Although a linear pointer-based implementation of the ADT table eliminates the need to shift data, it does not support the *Insert* and *Delete* operations any more efficiently than does an array-based implementation, because you cannot perform a binary search in a reasonable fashion.

3. Usually a binary search tree can support the ADT table operations quite efficiently. However, in the worst case, when the tree approaches a linear shape, the performance of the table operations is comparable to that of a linear pointer-based implementation. If you must avoid such a situation for a given application, you should use the balancing methods presented in Chapter 13.

SELF-TEST EXERCISES

1. Consider the tree in Figure 10-34. What node or nodes are
   a. The tree's root
   b. Parents
   c. Children of the parents in Part *b*
   d. Siblings
   e. Ancestors of 50
   f. Descendants of 20
   g. Leaves

2. What are the levels of all nodes in the tree in
   a. Figure 10-9b
   b. Figure 10-9c

3. What is the height of the tree in Figure 10-34?

4. Consider the binary trees in Figure 10-30. Which are complete? Which are full? Which are balanced?

5. What are the preorder, inorder, and postorder traversals of the binary tree in Figure 10-9a?

6. Is the tree in Figure 10-35 a binary search tree?

7. Beginning with an empty binary tree, what binary search tree is formed when you insert the following values in the order given: J, N, B, A, W, E, T?

8. By using the ADT table operations, write pseudocode for a *Replace* operation that replaces the table item whose search key is X with another item whose search key is also X.

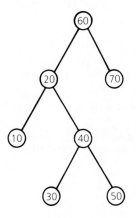

Figure 10-34

A tree for Self-Test Exercises 1, 3, and 9, and Exercise 6

Figure 10-35

A tree for Self-Test Exercise 6 and Exercise 3a

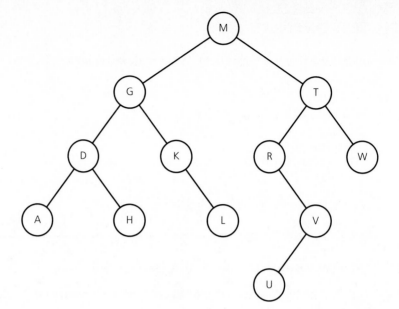

9. Trace the algorithm that searches a binary search tree when the tree is the one in Figure 10-34 and the search key is

    a. 30
    b. 15

    In each case, list the nodes in the order in which the search visits them.

EXERCISES

1. Complete the sorted pointer-based, unsorted array-based, and unsorted pointer-based implementations of the ADT table described in this chapter.

2. Many applications require a `Replace` operation in the definition of the ADT table. Although you can simulate this operation by using other ADT operations, it is more efficient to implement the operation directly. Write implementations of `Replace` for the five implementations (four linear and the binary search tree) of the ADT table described in this chapter.

3. What are the preorder, inorder, and postorder traversals of the binary trees in

    a. Figure 10-35
    b. Figure 10-9b
    c. Figure 10-9c

4. Beginning with an empty binary tree, what binary search tree is formed when you insert the following values in the order given?

    a. W, T, N, J, E, B, A
    b. W, T, N, A, B, E, J
    c. A, B, W, J, N, T, E

5. Arrange nodes that contain the letters A, C, E, F, L, V, and Z into two binary search trees: one that has maximum height and one that has minimum height.

6. Consider the binary search tree in Figure 10-34.

    a. What tree results after you insert the nodes 80, 65, 75, 45, 35, and 25?
    b. After inserting the nodes mentioned in Part *a,* what tree results when you delete the nodes 50 and 20?

7. Does the sequence of operations `Delete(T, X)` followed by `Insert(T, X)` ever change the shape of the binary search tree `T`?

Exercises 8 through 10 discuss the problem of duplicates in an ADT or data structure. Duplicates could mean either items that are identical in all fields or, more subtly, items that have identical search keys but differ in other fields.

8. The implementations of the ADT table given in this chapter make the following assumption: At any time, a table contains at most one item with a given search key. Although the ADT definition required for a specific application may not allow duplicates, it is probably wise to test for them rather than simply to assume that they will not occur. Why? What are the implications of a user inserting duplicate items? What are the implications of a user inserting items that have the same search key but that have other data fields that differ? Specifically, what would the implementations of `Insert`, `Delete`, and `Retrieve` do?

    Modify the table implementations so that they test for—and disallow—any duplicates. What table operations are affected? What are the implications for the unsorted linear implementations?

9. Although disallowing duplicates (see Exercise 8) is reasonable for some applications, it is just as reasonable to have an application that will allow duplicates. What are the implications of allowing duplicates for the definitions of the ADT table operations? In particular, how can the `Retrieve` and `Delete` operations be defined?

*10. If duplicates are allowed in a binary search tree, it is important to have a convention that determines the relationship between the duplicates in the data structure. Items that duplicate the root of a tree should either all be in the left subtree or all be in the right subtree, and, of course, this property must hold for every subtree. Why is this convention critical to the effective use of the binary search tree?

This chapter stated that you can delete an item from a binary search tree by replacing it with either its inorder successor or its inorder predecessor. If duplicates are allowed, however, the choice between inorder predecessor and inorder successor is no longer arbitrary. How does the convention of putting duplicates in either the left or right subtree affect this choice?

11. The following procedure constructs a binary tree from two binary trees and a data item for its root:

```
type    bintree = ^node;
        node = record
            data : integer;
            Lchild, Rchild : bintree
        end;
var     p, q, r, s, t : bintree;

procedure MakeTree(var Tree:bintree; RootValue:datatype;
                    LeftTree, RightTree : bintree);
begin
    new(Tree);
    with Tree^ do
    begin
        data := RootValue;
        Lchild := LeftTree;
        Rchild := RightTree
    end
end;  { MakeTree }
```

What tree(s) would the following sequence of statements produce?

```
MakeTree(t, 1, nil, nil);
MakeTree(t^.Lchild, 2, nil, nil);
MakeTree(t^.Rchild, 3, nil, nil);
MakeTree(t^.Lchild^.Rchild, 4, nil, nil);
MakeTree(t^.Lchild, 5, nil, nil); { subtree is "lost" }
MakeTree(p, 6, nil, nil);
MakeTree(q, 7, nil, nil);
MakeTree(r, 8, p, q);
MakeTree(r, 9, nil, r);
new(r^.Lchild);
s := r^.Lchild;
s^.data := 10;
s^.Lchild := t;
s^.Rchild := nil;
```

12. Consider an array-based implementation of a binary search tree. Figure 10-13 illustrates such a representation for the binary search tree in Figure 10-8.

    a. Depict the arrays in an array-based implementation for the binary search tree in Figure 10-19a.

b. Show the effect of each of the following sequential operations on the arrays in Part *a* of this exercise.

```
Insert(T, Doug)
Delete(T, Nancy)
Delete(T, Bob)
Insert(T, Sarah)
```

c. Repeat Parts *a* and *b* of this exercise for the tree in Figure 10-19b.

13. Given the recursive nature of the tree, a good strategy for writing a Pascal subprogram that operates on a binary tree is often first to write a recursive definition of the task. For example, suppose that the task is to count the number of nodes in a binary tree. An appropriate recursive definition for the number of nodes $C(T)$ of binary tree T is

$$C(T) = \begin{cases} 0 & \text{if } T \text{ is the empty tree} \\ C(\text{left subtree of } T) + C(\text{right subtree of } T) + 1 & \text{otherwise} \end{cases}$$

Given such a recursive definition, a Pascal implementation is often straightforward.

Write recursive definitions that perform the following tasks on arbitrary binary trees. Implement the definitions in Pascal. For simplicity, assume that a tree data item is a single integer and that there are no duplicates.

a. Compute the height of a tree.
b. Find the maximum element.
c. Find the sum of the elements.
*d. Find the average of the elements.
e. Find a specific item.
f. Determine whether one item is an ancestor of another (that is, whether one item is in the subtree rooted at the other item).
g. Determine the highest level that is full (that is, has the maximum number of nodes for that level [see Exercise 18]).
*h. Dispose of all of the nodes.

14. Consider a nonempty binary tree with two types of nodes: **min** nodes and **max** nodes. Each node has an integer value initially associated with it. You can define the **value** of such a tree as follows:

- If the root is a min node, then the value of the tree is equal to the *minimum* of

  The integer stored in the root

  The value of the left subtree, but only if it is nonempty

  The value of the right subtree, but only if it is nonempty

- If the root is a max node, then the value of the tree is equal to the *maximum* of the above three values.

a. Compute the value of the tree in Figure 10-36. Each node is labeled with its initial value.

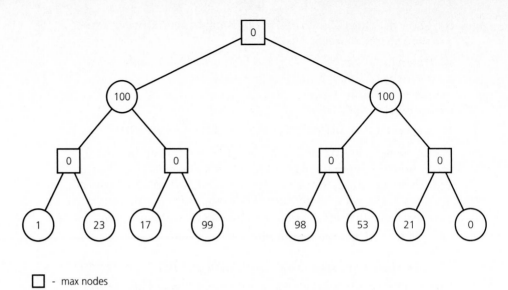

□ - max nodes
○ - min nodes

Figure 10-36

Minimax tree

   b. Write a general solution for representing and evaluating these trees in Pascal.

*15. Recall that a binary search tree with a given set of data items can have several different structures that conform to the definition of a binary search tree. Suppose that you are given a list of data items. Is there always at least one binary search tree whose preorder traversal matches the order of the items on your list? Is there ever more than one binary search tree that has the given preorder traversal?

*16. How many different (in shape) binary trees are there with N nodes? How many different binary search trees are there with N nodes? (Write recursive definitions.)

17. Prove Theorem 10-3 by induction.

18. What is the maximum number of nodes that can exist at level N of a binary tree? Prove your answer by induction. Use this fact to do the following:

   a. Rewrite the formal definition of a complete tree of height h.
   b. Derive a closed form for the formula

$$\sum_{i=1}^{h} 2^{i-1}$$

   What is the significance of this sum?

19. Prove by induction that a binary tree with N nodes has exactly $N + 1$ empty subtrees (or, in Pascal terms, $N + 1$ *nil* pointers).

20. A binary tree is **strictly binary** if every nonleaf node has exactly two children. Prove by induction on the number of leaves that a strictly binary tree with N leaves has exactly $2 * N - 1$ nodes.

21. Consider two algorithms for traversing a binary tree. Both are non-recursive algorithms that use an extra list for bookkeeping. Both algorithms have the following basic form:

```
Put the root of the tree on the list
while the list is not empty do
begin
    Remove a node from the list and call it N
    Visit N
    Put the left child of N on the list (if it exists)
    Put the right child of N on the list (if it exists)
end
```

The difference between the two algorithms is the method for choosing a node N to remove from the list.

Algorithm X: Remove the newest (most recently added) node from the list.

Algorithm Y: Remove the oldest (earliest added) node from the list.

a. In what order would each algorithm visit the nodes of the tree in Figure 10-18?

b. For each algorithm, describe an ADT that is appropriate for maintaining the bookkeeping list. What should the list item be? Do not use extra memory unnecessarily for the bookkeeping list. Also, note that the traversal of a tree should not alter the tree in any way.

22. Consider another algorithm to delete nodes from a binary search tree. This algorithm differs from the one described in this chapter when the node N has two children. First let N's right child take the place of the deleted node N in the same manner in which you delete a node with one child. Next reconnect N's left child (along with its subtree, if any) to the left side of N's inorder successor. *Hint:* If N is the left child of P, let `Delete(P^.Lchild)` be the call to the `Delete` procedure.

23. Write an iterative `Insert` procedure to insert a node into a binary search tree.

24. Some people define a binary search tree as an ADT instead of a data structure. List the operations that are suitable for such an ADT.

25. Recall that the motivation for a doubly linked list is the need to locate and delete a node on a list without traversing the list. The analogy for a binary search tree is to maintain parent pointers. That is, every node except the root will have a pointer to its parent in the tree. Write `Insert` and `Delete` operations for this structure.

*26. A node in a general tree, such as the one in Figure 10-4, can have an arbitrary number of children.

    a. Describe a Pascal implementation of a general tree in which every node contains an array of child pointers. What are the advantages and disadvantages of this implementation?

    b. What happens if you replace the array of children with a linked list of children? Observe that every node will have two pointers: a pointer to its oldest child—that is, to the first node on its linked list of children—and a pointer to its next sibling, which follows this node on its parent's list of children. Consider a tree T in which every node has at most two children. Compare the oldest-child/next-sibling representation of T to the left-child/right-child representation described in this chapter. Are the two representations ever the same?

*27. Implement a `Traverse` operation that permits `Visit` to delete the node visited.

CHAPTER **11**

Graphs

PREVIEW   Graphs are an important mathematical concept that have significant applications in computer science. You can view a graph as a mathematical construct, a data structure, or an abstract data type. This chapter provides an introduction to graphs that allows you to view a graph in any of these three ways. It also presents the major operations and applications of graphs that are relevant to the computer scientist.

TERMINOLOGY

You are undoubtedly familiar with graphs: Line graphs, bar graphs, and pie charts are in common use. The simple line graph in Figure 11-1 is illustrative of the type of graph that this chapter considers: a set of points that are joined by lines. Clearly, graphs provide a way to illustrate data. However, graphs also represent the relationships between data, and it is this feature of graphs that is important here.

$G = \{V, E\}$

Formally, a **graph** G consists of two sets: a set V of **vertices**, or **nodes**, and a set E of **edges** that connect the vertices. For example, the portion of the campus map in Figure 11-2 is a graph whose vertices represent buildings and whose edges represent the sidewalks between the buildings. This definition of a graph is more general than the definition of a line graph. In fact, a line graph, with its points and lines, is a special case of the general definition of a graph.

A **subgraph** consists of a subset of a graph's vertices and a subset of its edges. Figure 11-3 shows a subgraph of the graph in Figure 11-2. Two vertices of a graph are **adjacent** if they are joined by an edge. In Figure 11-3, the Library and the Student Union are adjacent. A **path** between two vertices is a sequence of edges that begins at one vertex and ends at another

Adjacent vertices

Figure 11-1

An ordinary line graph

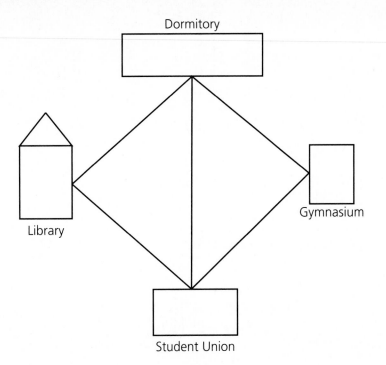

Figure 11-2

A portion of a campus map

vertex. For example, there is a path that begins at the Dormitory, leads first to the Library, then to the Student Union, and finally back to the Library. Although a path may pass through the same vertex more than once, a **simple path** may not. The path Dormitory-Library-Student Union is a simple path. A **cycle** is a path that begins and ends at the same vertex but does not pass through other vertices more than once. The path Library-Student Union-Gymnasium-Dormitory-Library is a cycle in the graph in Figure 11-2. A graph is **connected** if there is a path between every pair of vertices. Figure 11-4a shows a connected graph, while Figure 11-4b shows a **disconnected** graph. A graph is **complete** if there is an edge between every pair of vertices. The graph in Figure 11-4c is complete. Clearly, a complete graph is also connected, but the converse is not true; notice that the graph in Figure 11-4a is connected but is not complete.

Path, cycle

Connected, disconnected

A complete graph is connected

You can label the edges of a graph. When these labels represent numeric values, the graph is called a **weighted graph**. The graph in Figure 11-5 is a weighted graph whose edges are labeled with the distances between cities.

Weighted

All of the previous graphs are examples of **undirected** graphs because there is at most one edge between any two vertices and the edges do not indicate a direction. That is, you can travel in either direction along the edges between the vertices of an undirected graph. In contrast, each edge in a **directed graph**, or **digraph**, has a direction and is called a **directed**

Undirected, directed

Figure 11-3

A subgraph of the graph in Figure 11-2

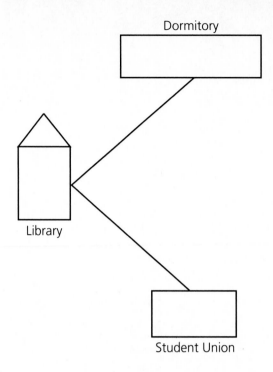

edge. Although there can be only one edge between two vertices of an undirected graph, a directed graph can have two edges between a pair of vertices. For example, the airline flight map in Figure 11-6 is a directed graph. There are flights in both directions between Providence and New York but, although there is a flight from San Francisco to Albuquerque, there is no flight from Albuquerque to San Francisco. Notice that you can convert an undirected graph to a directed graph by replacing each edge with two edges that point in opposite directions.

The definitions just given for undirected graphs apply also to directed graphs, with changes that account for direction. For example, a **directed path** is a sequence of **directed edges** between two vertices, such as the

Figure 11-4

Graphs that are (a) connected; (b) disconnected; and (c) complete

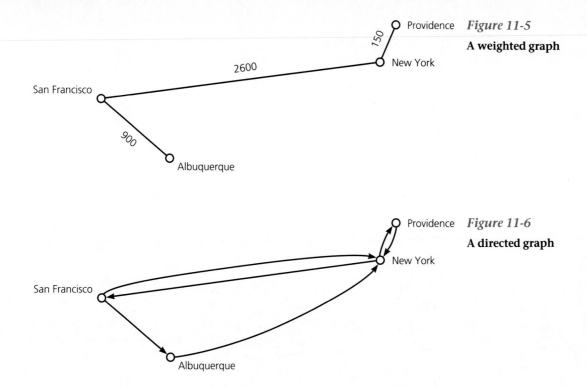

Figure 11-5

A weighted graph

Figure 11-6

A directed graph

directed path in Figure 11-6 that begins in Providence, goes to New York, and ends in San Francisco. However, the definition of adjacent vertices is not quite as obvious for a digraph. If there is a directed edge from vertex *x* to vertex *y*, then *y* is **adjacent** to *x*. (Alternatively, *y* is a **successor** of *x*.) It does not necessarily follow, however, that *x* is adjacent to *y*. Thus, in Figure 11-6, Albuquerque is adjacent to San Francisco, but San Francisco is not adjacent to Albuquerque.

GRAPHS AS ADT'S

You can treat graphs as abstract data types. Insertion and deletion operations are somewhat different for graphs than for other ADT's that you have studied in that they apply to either vertices or edges. You can define the ADT graph so that its vertices either do or do not contain values. A graph whose vertices do not contain values represents the relationships only between vertex positions. It is not unusual for a graph problem to involve only the relationships between vertex positions and to have no need for vertex values. However, the following ADT graph operations assume that the graph's vertices contain values.

KEY CONCEPTS   *ADT **Graph Operations***

Create(G)
{ Creates an empty graph G. }

IsEmpty(G)
{ Returns true if the graph G is empty, otherwise returns
  false. }

InsertVertex(G, v, success)
{ Inserts a vertex v into the graph G and returns success =
  true. If there already is a vertex with the same search
  key, no insertion takes place and returns success = false. }

InsertEdge(G, v1, v2, success)
{ Inserts an edge between vertices v1 and v2 in the graph G
  and returns success = true. If there already is an edge
  between the specified vertices, returns success = false. }

DeleteVertex(G, v, success)
{ Deletes the vertex v from the graph G and returns success
  = true. If there is no vertex at the specified position,
  returns success = false. }

DeleteEdge(G, v1, v2, success)
{ Deletes the edge between vertices v1 and v2 in the graph G
  and returns success = true. If there is no edge between
  the specified vertices, returns success = false. }

Retrieve(G, searchkey, v, success)
{ Retrieves the vertex v that contains searchkey. Returns
  success = true if vertex is found, otherwise returns
  false. }

Replace(G, searchkey, v, success)
{ Replaces the vertex that contains searchkey with v.
  Returns success = true if vertex is found, otherwise
  returns false. }

IsEdge(G, v1, v2)
{ Returns true if there is an edge between the vertices v1
  and v2. }

Several variations of this ADT are possible. For example, if the graph is directed, you can replace references to edges in the previous specifications with directed edges. You can also add traversal operations to the ADT. This chapter discusses graph-traversal algorithms shortly.

Implementing Graphs

The two most common implementations of a graph are the adjacency matrix and the adjacency list. In both implementations, it is convenient to imagine that the vertices are numbered 1, 2, and so on to N. An **adjacency matrix** for a graph with N vertices is an N by N boolean array A such that A[i, j] is *true* if and only if there is an edge from vertex i to vertex j. Figure 11-7 shows a directed graph and its adjacency matrix. Notice that A[i, i] is *false*. However, there may be times when it is preferable to set the diagonal entries of the adjacency matrix to *true*. You should choose the value that is most convenient for your application. Finally, note that the adjacency matrix for an undirected graph is symmetric, that is, A[i, j] = A[j, i].

When the graph is weighted, it is convenient to let A[i, j] be the weight that labels the edge from vertex i to vertex j, instead of the boolean value *true*, and to let A[i, j] equal ∞ instead of *false* when there is no edge from vertex i to vertex j. In addition, the diagonal entries A[i, i] are zero, which implies that there is no distance between a vertex and itself. For example, Figure 11-8 contains a weighted undirected graph and its adjacency matrix.

Notice that with an adjacency matrix, there is no mention of the value in a vertex. However, if you do need to associate values with vertices, you can use a one-dimensional array *Values* of N items that represent vertex values; that is, *Values[i]* is the value in vertex i.

Adjacency matrix

Vertices can have values

Figure 11-7

(a) A directed graph and (b) its adjacency matrix

(a)

(b)

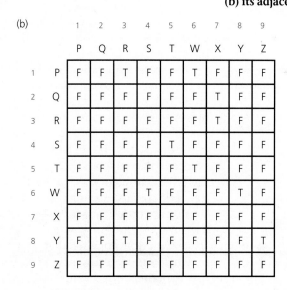

		1 P	2 Q	3 R	4 S	5 T	6 W	7 X	8 Y	9 Z
1	P	F	F	T	F	F	T	F	F	F
2	Q	F	F	F	F	F	F	T	F	F
3	R	F	F	F	F	F	F	T	F	F
4	S	F	F	F	F	T	F	F	F	F
5	T	F	F	F	F	F	T	F	F	F
6	W	F	F	F	T	F	F	F	T	F
7	X	F	F	F	F	F	F	F	F	F
8	Y	F	F	T	F	F	F	F	F	T
9	Z	F	F	F	F	F	F	F	F	F

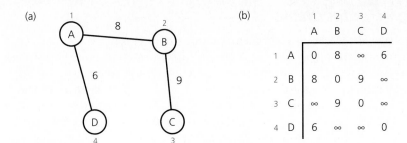

Figure 11-8

(a) A weighted undirected graph and (b) its adjacency matrix

Adjacency list

An **adjacency list** for a graph with N vertices numbered 1, 2, $\cdots$, N consists of N linked lists. There is a node in the ith linked list for vertex j if and only if there is an edge from vertex i to vertex j. Figure 11-9 shows the adjacency list for the graph in Figure 11-7a.

Which of these two implementations of a graph—the adjacency matrix or the adjacency list—is better? The answer depends on how your particular application uses the graph. For example, the two most commonly performed graph operations are

Two common operations on graphs

1. Given two vertices i and j, determine whether there is an edge from i to j.

2. Find all vertices adjacent to a given vertex i.

An adjacency matrix supports operation 1 more efficiently

The adjacency matrix supports the first operation somewhat more efficiently than does the adjacency list. To determine whether there is an edge from i to j by using an adjacency matrix, you need only examine the value of $A[i, j]$. If you use an adjacency list, however, you must traverse the ith linked list to determine whether a vertex corresponding to vertex j is present.

An adjacency list supports operation 2 more efficiently

The second operation, on the other hand, is supported more efficiently by the adjacency list. To determine all vertices adjacent to a given vertex i given the adjacency matrix, you must traverse the ith row of the array; however, given the adjacency list, you must traverse the ith linked list. For a graph with N vertices, the ith row of the adjacency matrix always has N entries, whereas the ith linked list has only as many nodes as there are vertices adjacent to vertex i, a number typically far less than N. Notice that the HPAir problem of Chapter 8 used an adjacency list because its most frequent operation was to find all vertices adjacent to a given vertex.

Consider now the space requirements of the two implementations. On the surface it might appear that the matrix implementation requires less space than does the linked list implementation, because each entry in the matrix is simply a single boolean value, whereas each entry in the linked lists contains both a value and a pointer. Notice, however, that the adjacency matrix always has N^2 entries, whereas the number of entries in an adjacency list is equal to the number of edges in the graph. Because the number of edges is often much smaller than N^2, an adjacency list often requires less space than an adjacency matrix.

An adjacency list usually requires less space than an adjacency matrix

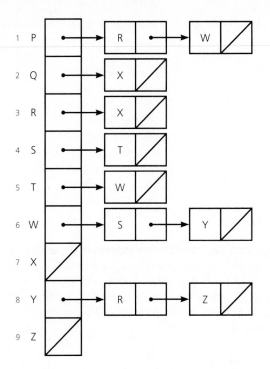

Figure 11-9

Adjacency list for the graph in Figure 11-7a

Thus, when choosing a graph implementation for a particular application, you must consider such factors as what operations you will perform most frequently on the graph and the number of edges that the graph is likely to contain.

GRAPH TRAVERSALS

Chapter 8 presented the HPAir problem, which was to determine whether an airline provided a sequence of flights from an origin city to a destination city. The flight map for that problem is in fact a directed graph and appeared earlier in this chapter in Figure 11-7a. The solution to the HPAir problem involved an exhaustive search of an adjacency list to determine a directed path from the origin vertex (city) to the destination vertex (city). The algorithm *SearchS* started at a given vertex and traversed edges to other vertices until it either found the desired vertex or determined that no directed path existed between the two vertices.

What distinguishes *SearchS* from a standard graph traversal is that *SearchS* stops when it first encounters the designated destination vertex. A **graph-traversal algorithm**, on the other hand, will not stop until it has visited *all the vertices that it can reach*. That is, a graph traversal that starts at

A graph traversal visits only the vertices that it can reach

vertex *v* will visit all vertices *w* for which there is a path between *v* and *w*. Notice that unlike a tree traversal, which always visits *all* the nodes in a tree, a graph traversal does not necessarily visit all the vertices in the graph unless the graph is connected. In fact, a graph traversal visits every vertex in the graph if and only if the graph is connected, regardless of where the traversal starts. (See Exercise 12.). If a graph is not connected, then a graph traversal that begins at vertex *v* will visit only a subset of the graph's verti-ces. This subset is called the **connected component** containing *v*.

Two basic graph-traversal algorithms are presented next. These algo-rithms visit the vertices in different orders, but if they both start at the same vertex, they will visit the same set of vertices.

Depth-First Search

DFS traverses as far as possible from a vertex before backtracking

From a given vertex *v*, the **depth-first search** (DFS) strategy of graph tra-versal goes as deep into the graph as it can before backtracking. That is, after visiting vertex *v*, DFS visits, if possible, an unvisited vertex *u* adjacent to *v*. The algorithm continues from *u* as far as possible before returning to *v* to visit the next unvisited vertex adjacent to *v*. An iterative version of this algorithm follows.

Iterative DFS traversal algorithm

```
DFS(v)
{ Traverses a graph beginning at vertex v by using depth-
  first search — Iterative version. }

    { push v onto the stack and mark it }
    Push(S, v)
    Mark v as visited

    { loop invariant: there is a path from vertex v at the
      bottom of the stack S to the vertex at the top of S}
    while (not IsEmpty(S)) do
    begin
        if there are no unvisited vertices adjacent to the
            vertex on the top of the stack

            then Pop(S) { backtrack }

            else
            begin
                Select an unvisited vertex u adjacent to
                    the vertex on the top of the stack
                Push(S, u)
                Mark u as visited
            end  { if }
    end  { while }
```

Notice that *DFS* is similar to *SearchS* of Chapter 8, but *SearchS* contains the termination condition *StackTop(S) = destination* in its *while* statement.

The depth-first search algorithm does not completely specify the order in which it should visit the vertices adjacent to *v*. One possibility is to visit the vertices adjacent to *v* in sorted (that is, alphabetic or numerically increasing) order. This possibility is natural either when an adjacency matrix represents the graph or when the nodes in each linked list of an adjacency list are linked in sorted order.

Order in which adjacent vertices are visited

As an example of DFS traversal, consider the graph in Figure 11-10. Figure 11-11 shows the contents of the stack as the procedure *DFS* visits vertices in this graph beginning at vertex *a*. Because the graph is connected, *DFS* will visit every vertex. In fact, the traversal visits the vertices in this order: *a, b, c, d, g, e, f, h, i*.

A recursive version of *DFS* is also possible:

```
DFS(v)
{ Traverses a graph beginning at vertex v by using depth-
    first search — Recursive version. }

    Mark v as visited

    for each unvisited vertex u adjacent to v do
        DFS(u)
```

Recursive DFS traversal algorithm

Notice that the vertex from which *DFS* embarks is the vertex that it visited most recently. This *last visited, first explored* strategy is reflected both in the explicit stack of vertices that the iterative *DFS* uses and in the implicit stack of vertices that the recursive *DFS* generates with its recursive calls.

Breadth-First Search

After visiting a given vertex *v*, the **breadth-first search** (BFS) strategy of graph traversal visits every vertex adjacent to *v* that it can. Thus, the traversal will not embark from any of the vertices adjacent to *v* until it has visited all possible vertices adjacent to *v*. Whereas DFS is a *last visited, first explored* strategy, BFS is a *first visited, first explored* strategy. It is not surpris-

BFS visits all vertices adjacent to a vertex before going forward

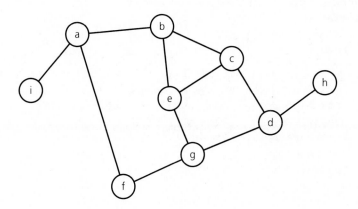

Figure 11-10

A connected graph with cycles

Figure 11-11

The results of a depth-first traversal, beginning at vertex *a*, of the graph in Figure 11-10

Node visited	Stack (bottom → top)
a	a
b	a b
c	a b c
d	a b c d
g	a b c d g
e	a b c d g e
(backtrack)	a b c d g
f	a b c d g f
(backtrack)	a b c d g
(backtrack)	a b c d
h	a b c d h
(backtrack)	a b c d
(backtrack)	a b c
(backtrack)	a b
(backtrack)	a
i	a i
(backtrack)	a
(backtrack)	(empty)

ing, then, that a breadth-first search uses a queue. An iterative version of this algorithm follows.

Iterative BFS traversal algorithm

```
BFS(v)
{ Traverses a graph beginning at vertex v by using breadth-
   first search — Iterative version. }

   { add v to queue and mark it }
   Add(Q, v)
   Mark v as visited

   while (not IsEmpty(Q)) do
   begin
      w := QueueFront(Q)
      Remove(Q)

      { loop invariant: there is a path from vertex w to
         every vertex in the queue Q }
      for each unvisited vertex u adjacent to w do
      begin
         Mark u as visited
         Add(Q, u)
      end   { for }
   end   { while }
```

Node visited	Queue (front → rear)
a	a
	(empty)
b	b
f	b f
i	b f i
	f i
c	f i c
e	f i c e
	i c e
g	i c e g
	c e g
	e g
d	e g d
	g d
	d
	(empty)
h	h
	(empty)

Figure 11-12

The results of a breadth-first traversal, beginning at vertex *a*, of the graph in Figure 11-10

Figure 11-12 shows the contents of the queue as the procedure BFS visits vertices in the graph in Figure 11-10 beginning at vertex *a*. BFS will visit the same vertices as DFS: In this example, all of them. The traversal visits the vertices in this order: *a, b, f, i, c, e, g, d, h.*

BFS does not have a recursive counterpart. Exercise 13 at the end of this chapter asks you to think about why this is so.

BFS is not recursive

Recall that a connected component of a vertex *v* contains all vertices that a traversal algorithm visits when it begins at *v*. You can generate all the connected components of a graph by repeatedly starting a traversal at an unvisited vertex.

Generating connected components

APPLICATIONS OF GRAPHS

There are many useful applications of graphs. This section surveys some of these common applications.

Topological Sorting

There is a natural order in a directed graph without cycles, such as the one in Figure 11-13. For example, vertex *a* precedes *b*, which precedes *c*. Such a graph has significance in ordinary life. Suppose that the vertices represent

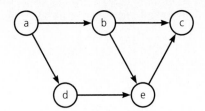

Figure 11-13

A directed graph without cycles

academic courses and that the graph represents the prerequisite structure for the courses. For example, course *a* is a prerequisite to course *b*, which is a prerequisite to course *c*. In what order should you take all five courses so that you will satisfy all prerequisites? There is a linear order, called the **topological order**, of the vertices in a directed graph without cycles that answers this question. In a list of vertices in topological order, vertex *x* precedes vertex *y* if there is a directed edge from *x* to *y* in the graph. There may be several topological orders for a given graph; Figure 11-14 shows two possible topological orders for the vertices in the graph in Figure 11-13. Note that arranging the vertices into a topological order is called **topological sorting.**

A simple topological sorting algorithm

There are several simple algorithms for finding a topological order. First, you could find a vertex that has no successor, remove it from the graph, and add it to the beginning of an ordered list of vertices. You add each subsequent vertex that has no successor to the beginning of the ordered list. When the graph is empty, the ordered list of vertices will be in topological order. By applying this algorithm to the graph in Figure 11-13, you get one of the topological orders in Figure 11-14.

The DFS topological sorting algorithm

Another algorithm is a simple modification of the iterative depth-first search algorithm *DFS*. Each time you pop a vertex from the stack, you add it to the beginning of the ordered list of vertices. When the traversal ends, the ordered list of vertices will be in topological order. Figure 11-15 traces this algorithm for the graph in Figure 11-13. The resulting topological order is shown in Figure 11-14a.

Spanning Trees

A tree is an undirected, connected graph without cycles

A **tree** is a special kind of undirected graph, one that is connected but has no cycles. The graph in Figure 11-4a is a tree. Although all trees are graphs,

Figure 11-14

Two topological orders for the graph in Figure 11-13

(a)

(b)

Action	Stack (bottom → top)	Ordered List
Push a	a	
Push b	a b	
Push c	a b c	
Pop c	a b	c
Push e	a b e	c
Pop e	a b	e c
Pop b	a	b e c
Push d	a d	b e c
Pop d	a	d b e c
Pop a	(empty)	a d b e c

Figure 11-15

A trace of the DFS topological-sorting algorithm for the graph in Figure 11-13

not all graphs are trees. The nodes (vertices) of a tree are arranged in a hierarchy that is not required of all graphs.

A **spanning tree** of a connected undirected graph G is a subgraph of G that contains all of G's vertices and enough of its edges to form a tree. For example, Figure 11-16 shows a spanning tree for the graph in Figure 11-10. The dashed lines in Figure 11-16 indicate edges that were omitted from the graph to form the tree. There may be several spanning trees for a given graph.

If you have a connected undirected graph with cycles and you remove edges until there are no cycles, you will obtain a spanning tree for the graph. It is relatively simple to determine whether a graph contains a cycle. One way to make this determination is based on the following observations about undirected graphs:

1. **A connected undirected graph that has N vertices must have at least $N – 1$ edges.** To establish this fact, recall that a connected graph has a path between every pair of vertices. Suppose that you choose one vertex and draw an edge between it and any other vertex. Next, draw an edge between this second vertex and any other unattached vertex.

Observations about undirected graphs

Figure 11-16

A spanning tree for the graph in Figure 11-10

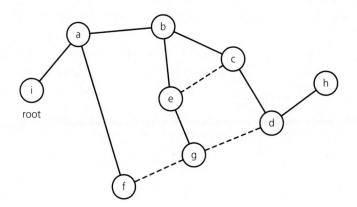

If you continue this process, you will get a connected graph like the one in Figure 11-1. Notice that if there are N vertices, there are $N - 1$ edges. In addition, if you remove an edge, the graph will not be connected.

2. **A connected undirected graph with N vertices and $N - 1$ edges cannot contain a cycle.** To see this, begin with the previous observation: A graph with N vertices must have at least $N - 1$ edges to be connected. If a connected graph did have a cycle, you could remove any edge along that cycle and still have a connected graph. Thus, if a connected graph with N vertices and $N - 1$ edges did contain a cycle, removing an edge along the cycle would leave you with a connected graph with only $N - 2$ edges, which is impossible.

3. **A connected undirected graph with N vertices and more than $N - 1$ edges must contain at least one cycle.** This fact is harder to establish and is left as an exercise. (See Exercise 11 at the end of this chapter.)

Thus, you can determine whether a connected graph contains a cycle simply by counting its vertices and edges.

It follows, then, that a tree, which is a connected undirected graph without cycles, must connect its N nodes with $N - 1$ edges. Thus, to obtain the spanning tree of a connected graph of N vertices, you must remove edges along cycles until there are $N - 1$ edges left.

Two algorithms for determining a spanning tree of a graph are based on the previous traversal algorithms and are presented next. In general, these algorithms will produce different spanning trees for any particular graph.

The DFS spanning tree.   One way to determine a spanning tree for a connected undirected graph is to traverse the graph's vertices by using a depth-first search. As you traverse the graph, mark the edges that you follow. After the traversal is complete, the graph's vertices and the marked edges form a spanning tree, which is called the **depth-first search (DFS) spanning tree.** (Alternatively, you can remove the unmarked edges from the graph to form the spanning tree.) Simple modifications to the previous iterative and recursive versions of the procedure *DFS* result in algorithms to create a DFS spanning tree. For example, the recursive algorithm follows:

DFS spanning tree algorithm

```
DFSTree(v)
{ Forms a spanning tree for an undirected graph beginning at
  vertex v by using depth-first search — Recursive version. }

   Mark v as visited

   for each unvisited vertex u adjacent to v do
   begin
      Mark the edge from u to v
      DFS(u)
   end
```

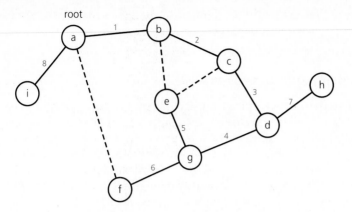

Visitation order of vertices: a, b, c, d, g, e, f, h, i

Figure 11-17

The DFS **spanning tree rooted at vertex *a* for the graph in Figure 11-10**

Figure 11-17 shows the DFS spanning tree rooted at vertex *a* for the graph in Figure 11-10. The figure indicates the order in which the procedure visits vertices and marks edges.

The BFS spanning tree.   Another way to determine a spanning tree for a connected undirected graph is to traverse the graph's vertices by using a breadth-first search. As you traverse the graph, mark the edges that you follow. After the traversal is complete, the graph's vertices and the marked edges form a spanning tree, which is called the **breadth-first search (BFS) spanning tree.** (Alternatively, you can remove the unmarked edges from the graph to form the spanning tree.) You can modify the previous iterative procedure *BFS* by marking the edge between *w* and *u* before you add *u* to the queue. The result will be an algorithm to create a BFS spanning tree.

Figure 11-18 shows the BFS spanning tree rooted at vertex *a* for the

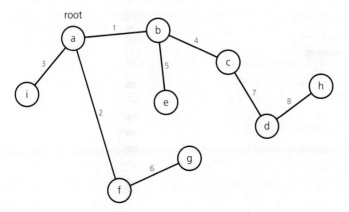

Visitation order of vertices: a, b, f, i, c, e, g, d, h

Figure 11-18

The BFS **spanning tree rooted at vertex *a* for the graph in Figure 11-10**

graph in Figure 11-10. The figure indicates the order in which the procedure visits vertices and marks edges.

Minimum Spanning Trees

Suppose that a developing country has hired you to design its telephone
system to allow all the cities in the country to call one another. Obviously,
one solution is to place telephone lines between every pair of cities. However, your engineering team has determined that due to the country's
mountainous terrain, it is impossible to put lines between certain pairs of
cities. The team's report contains the weighted undirected graph in Figure
11-19. The vertices in the graph represent N cities. An edge between two
vertices indicates that it is feasible to place a telephone line between the
cities that the vertices represent, and each edge's weight represents the
installation cost of the telephone line. Note that if this graph is not connected, you will be unable to link all of the cities with a network of telephone lines. The graph in Figure 11-19 is connected, however, making the
problem feasible.

If you install a telephone line between each pair of cities that is connected by an edge in the graph, you will certainly solve the problem. However, this solution may be too costly. From observation 1 in the previous
section, you know that $N - 1$ is the minimum number of edges necessary
for a graph of N vertices to be connected. Thus, $N - 1$ is the minimum
number of lines that can connect N cities.

If the cost of installing each line is the same, the problem is reduced to
one of finding any spanning tree of the graph. The total installation cost,
that is, the **cost of the spanning tree**, is the sum of the costs of the edges
in the spanning tree. However, suppose that the cost of installing each line
varies. Because there may be more than one spanning tree, and because
the cost of different trees may vary, you can solve the problem by selecting
a spanning tree with the least cost, that is, you select a spanning tree for
which the sum of the edge costs is minimal. Such a tree is called the **minimum spanning tree**, and it need not be unique. Although there may be
several minimum spanning trees for a particular graph, their costs are
equal.

*Minimum spanning tree of a
connected undirected graph*

One simple algorithm that finds a minimum spanning tree begins at
any vertex and moves to an unvisited vertex along a least-cost edge. At
each stage, the algorithm selects a least-cost edge from among those that
begin with a visited node and end with an unvisited node. The following
pseudocode describes this algorithm:

*Minimum spanning tree
algorithm*

```
MST(v)
{ Determines a minimum spanning tree for a weighted
   connected undirected graph beginning with any vertex v. }

   Mark vertex v as visited and include it in the minimum
      spanning tree
```

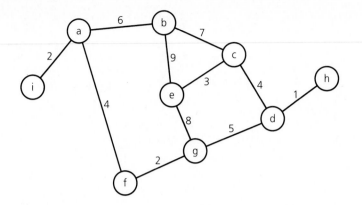

Figure 11-19

A weighted, connected, undirected graph

```
while there are unvisited vertices do
begin
    Find the least-cost edge (v, u) from a visited vertex
      v to some unvisited vertex u
    Mark u as visited
    Add the vertex u and the edge (v, u) to the minimum
      spanning tree
end
```

Figure 11-20 traces *MST* for the graph in Figure 11-19 beginning at vertex *a*. Edges added to the tree appear as solid lines, while edges under consideration appear as dashed lines.

The fact that *MST* selects a least-cost edge from among those that begin with a visited node and end with an unvisited node does not necessarily imply that the spanning tree will be minimal. However, the proof that *MST* is correct is beyond the scope of this book.

Shortest Paths

Suppose that a weighted directed graph represents a map of airline routes: The vertices are cities, and the edges indicate existing flights between cities. The edge weights represent the mileage between cities (vertices); as such, the weights are not negative. For example, you could combine the graphs in Figures 11-5 and 11-6 to get such a weighted directed graph.

Often for weighted directed graphs you need to know the shortest path between two particular vertices. The **shortest path** between two given vertices in a weighted graph is the path that has the smallest sum of its edge weights. Although we use the term "shortest," realize that the weights could be a measure other than distance, such as the cost of each flight in dollars or the duration of each flight in hours. The sum of the weights of the edges of a path is called the path's **length**, or **weight**, or **cost**.

It turns out that the algorithm to determine the shortest path between two given vertices actually determines the shortest paths between a given

(a) Mark a, consider edges from a

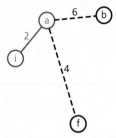

(b) Mark i, include edge (a, i)

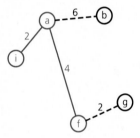

(c) Mark f, include edge (a, f)

(d) Mark g, include edge (f, g)

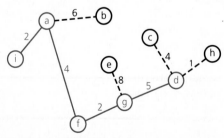

(e) Mark d, include edge (g, d)

(f) Mark h, include edge (d, h)

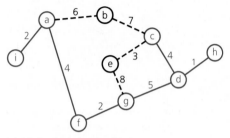

(g) Mark c, include edge (d, c)

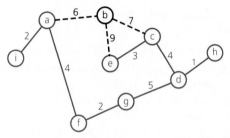

(h) Mark e, include edge (c, e)

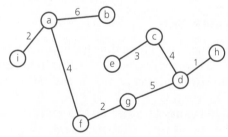

(i) Mark b, include edge (a, b)

Figure 11-20

A trace of the *MST* algorithm for the graph in Figure 11-19 beginning at vertex *a*

vertex—the origin—and *all* other vertices. The algorithm is attributed to E. Dijkstra. For convenience, let the given vertex be vertex 1 and number the other vertices in the graph from 2 to *N*, as in the graph in Figure 11-21a. Notice the graph's adjacency matrix *A* in Figure 11-21b.

Finding the shortest paths between vertex 1 and all other vertices

The algorithm uses a set *S* of selected vertices and an array *W*, where *W*[*v*] is the weight of the shortest (cheapest) path from vertex 1 to vertex *v* that passes through vertices in *S*. If *v* is in *S*, then the shortest path involves only vertices in *S*. However, if *v* is not in *S*, then *v* is the only vertex along the path that is not in *S*. That is, the path ends with an edge from a vertex in *S* to *v*. Initially, *S* contains only vertex 1 and *W* contains the weights of the single-edge paths from vertex 1 to *v* for all *v*. That is, *W*[*v*] equals *A*[1, *v*] for all *v*. Thus, initially *W* is simply the first row of the adjacency matrix *A*.

After this initialization step, you select vertices from those that you have not selected, add them to *S*, and adjust W as follows. You select a vertex *v* from among those not in *S* such that *W*[*v*] is a minimum. After adding *v* to *S*, you check the values *W*[*u*] for all unselected vertices *u*, that is, for those vertices not in *S*, to ensure that these values are indeed minimums. In other words, you must determine whether it is possible to reduce *W*[*u*]—the weight of a path from vertex 1 to vertex *u*—by passing through the newly selected vertex *v*.

To make this determination, break the path from 1 to *u* into two pieces and find their weights as follows:

$W[v]$ = weight of the shortest path from 1 to v

$A[v, u]$ = weight of the edge from v to u

Then compare $W[u]$ with $W[v] + A[v, u]$ and let

$W[u]$ = the smaller of the values $W[u]$ and $W[v] + A[v, u]$

The pseudocode for **Dijkstra's shortest-path algorithm** is as follows:

```
ShortestPath(G, W)
{ Finds the minimum-cost path between vertex 1 and all other
  vertices in a weighted directed graph G of N vertices. }

   { Step 1: initialization }
```

The shortest-path algorithm

(a)   origin

(b)

Figure 11-21

(a) A weighted directed graph and (b) its adjacency matrix *A*

```
S := [1]
for v := 1 to N do
   W[v] := A[1, v]

{ Steps 2 through N }
```

Loop invariant

```
{ Invariant : For v not in S, W[v] is the smallest
   weight of all paths from 1 to v that pass through only
   vertices in S before reaching v. For v in S, W[v] is
   the smallest weight of all paths from 1 to v
   (including paths outside S) and the shortest path from
   1 to v lies entirely in S. }
for Step := 2 to N do
begin
   Find the smallest W[v] such that v is not in S
   S := S + [v]    { Add v to S }

   { Check W[u] for all u not in S }
   for all vertices u not in S do
       if W[u] > W[v] + A[v, u]
             then W[u] := W[v] + A[v, u]
end   { for }
```

The loop invariant states that once a vertex v is placed in S, $W[v]$ is the weight of the absolutely shortest path from 1 to v and will not change.

Figure 11-22 traces the algorithm for the graph in Figure 11-21a. The algorithm takes the following steps:

A trace of the shortest-path algorithm

Step 1. S is initialized to 1 and W is initialized to the first row of the graph's adjacency matrix, shown in Figure 11-21b.

Step 2. $W[5] = 4$ is the smallest value in W, ignoring $W[1]$ because 1 is in S. Thus, $v = 5$, so add 5 to S. For vertices not in S, that is, for $u = 2$, 3, and 4, check whether it is shorter to go from 1 to 5 and then along an edge to u instead of directly from 1 to u along an edge. For vertices 2 and 4, it is not shorter to include vertex 5 in the path. However, for vertex 3 notice that $W[3] = \infty > W[5] + A[5, 3] = 4 + 1 = 5$. Therefore, replace $W[3]$ with 5. You can also verify this conclusion by examining the graph directly, as Figure 11-23a shows.

Figure 11-22

A trace of the shortest-path algorithm applied to the graph in Figure 11-21

Step	v	S	W[1]	W[2]	W[3]	W[4]	W[5]
1	–	[1]	0	8	∞	9	4
2	5	[1, 5]	0	8	5	9	4
3	3	[1, 5, 3]	0	7	5	8	4
4	2	[1, 5, 3, 2]	0	7	5	8	4
5	4	[1, 5, 3, 2, 4]	0	7	5	8	4

Step 3. $W[3] = 5$ is the smallest value in W, ignoring $W[1]$ and $W[5]$ because 1 and 5 are in S. Thus, $v = 3$, so add 3 to S. For vertices not in S, that is, for $u = 2$ and 4, check whether it is shorter to go from 1 to 3 and then along an edge to u instead of directly from 1 to u along an edge. (See parts b and c of Figure 11-23.) Notice that

$W[2] = 8 > W[3] + A[3, 2] = 5 + 2 = 7$. Therefore, replace $W[2]$ with 7.

$W[4] = 9 > W[3] + A[3, 4] = 5 + 3 = 8$. Therefore, replace $W[4]$ with 8.

Step 4. $W[2] = 7$ is the smallest value in W, ignoring $W[1]$, $W[3]$, and $W[5]$ because 1, 3, and 5 are in S. Thus, $v = 2$, so add 2 to S. For vertex 4, which is the only vertex not in S, notice that

$W[4] = 8 < W[2] + A[2, 4] = 7 + \infty$

as Figure 11-23d shows. Therefore, leave $W[4]$ as it is.

Step 5. The only remaining vertex not in S is 4, so add it to S and stop.

Does this algorithm work? That is, are the weights in W the smallest possible? The answer to both questions is yes as long as the loop invariant is true. The proof that the loop invariant is true is by induction on *step*, and is left as a difficult exercise. (See Exercise 15.)

Some Difficult Problems

The next three applications of graphs have solutions that are beyond the scope of this book.

The traveling salesperson problem. A **circuit** is a path that begins at a *Circuit* vertex v, passes through every vertex in the graph exactly once, and terminates at v. Obviously, a graph that is not connected cannot contain a circuit. However, determining whether or not an arbitrary graph contains a circuit can be difficult. A well-known variation of this problem—the traveling salesperson problem—involves a weighted graph that represents a road map. Each edge has an associated cost, such as the mileage between cities or the time required to drive from one city to the next. The salesperson must begin at an origin city, visit every other city exactly once, and return to the origin city. However, the circuit traveled must be the least expensive. Unfortunately for this traveler, solving the problem is no easier than determining whether a circuit exists.

The three utilities problem. Suppose that there are three houses A, B, and C and three utilities X, Y, and Z (such as telephone, water, and electricity). If the houses and the utilities are vertices in a graph, is it possible to connect each house to each utility with edges that do not cross one another? The answer to this question is no.

A graph is **planar** if you can draw it in a plane in at least one way so *Planar graph* that no two edges cross. The generalization of the three utilities problem

Figure 11-23

Checking $W[u]$ by examining the graph: (a) $W[3]$ in Step 2; (b) $W[2]$ in Step 3; (c) $W[4]$ in Step 3; (d) $W[4]$ in Step 4

(a)

Step 2. The path (1, 5, 3) is
        shorter than (1, 3)

(b)

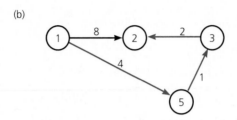

Step 3. The path (1, 5, 3, 2) is
        shorter than (1, 2)

(c)

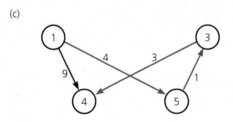

Step 3 continued. The path (1, 5, 3, 4) is
                  shorter than (1, 4)

(d)

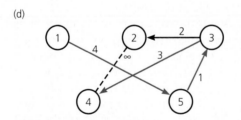

Step 4. The path (1, 5, 3, 4) is
        shorter than
        (1, 5, 3, 2, 4)

determines whether or not a given graph is planar. Making this determination has many important applications. For example, a graph can represent an electronic circuit where the vertices represent components and the edges represent the connections between components. Is it possible to design the circuit so that the connections do not cross? The solutions to these problems are also beyond the scope of this book.

The four-color problem.   Given a planar graph, can you color the vertices so that no adjacent vertices have the same color, if you use at most four colors? For example, the graph in Figure 11-10 is planar because none of its edges cross. You can solve the coloring problem for this graph by using only three colors. Color vertices *a, c, g,* and *h* red, color vertices *b, d, f,* and *i* blue, and color vertex *e* green.

The answer to our question is yes, but it is difficult to prove. In fact, this problem was posed more than a century before it was proven in the 1970s with the use of a computer.

SUMMARY

1. Graph searching is an important application of stacks. Depth-first search is a graph-traversal algorithm that uses a stack to keep track of the sequence of visited vertices. It goes as deep into the graph as it can before backtracking. Breadth-first search uses a queue to keep track of the sequence of visited vertices. It visits all possible adjacent vertices before traversing further into the graph.

2. The two most common implementations of a graph are the adjacency matrix and the adjacency list. Each has its relative advantages and disadvantages. The choice should depend on the needs of the given application.

3. Topological sorting produces a linear order of the vertices in a directed graph without cycles. Vertex *x* precedes vertex *y* if there is a directed edge from *x* to *y* in the graph.

4. Trees are connected undirected graphs without cycles. A spanning tree of a connected undirected graph is a subgraph that contains all the graph's vertices and enough of its edges to form a tree. DFS and BFS traversals produce DFS and BFS spanning trees.

5. A minimum spanning tree is a spanning tree for a weighted undirected graph whose edge-cost sum is minimal. There may be several minimum spanning trees for a particular graph. However, their edge-cost sums will be equal.

6. The shortest path between two vertices in a weighted directed graph is the path that has the smallest sum of its edge weights.

COMMON PITFALLS/DEBUGGING

1. When searching a graph, realize that the algorithm might take wrong turns. For example, you must eliminate the possibility of cycling within the algorithm; the algorithm must be able to backtrack when it hits a dead end.

SELF-TEST EXERCISES

1. Describe the graphs in Figure 11-24. For example, are they directed?
    Connected? Complete? Weighted?

2. Use the depth-first strategy and the breadth-first strategy to traverse
    the graph in Figure 11-24a, beginning with vertex 1. List the vertices
    in the order in which each traversal visits them.

3. Write the adjacency matrix for the graph in Figure 11-24a.

4. Add an edge to the directed graph in Figure 11-13 that runs from ver-
    tex *d* to vertex *b*. Write all possible topological orders for the vertices
    in this new graph.

5. Is it possible for a connected undirected graph with 5 vertices and 4
    edges to contain a cycle? Explain.

6. Draw the DFS spanning tree whose root is 1 for the graph in Figure 11-
    25.

7. Draw the minimum spanning tree whose root is 1 for the graph in
    Figure 11-25.

8. What are the shortest paths from vertex 1 to each vertex of the graph
    in Figure 11-21a? (Note the weights of these paths in Figure 11-22.)

Figure 11-24

Graphs for Self-Test Exercises 1, 2, and 3

(a)

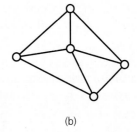

(b)

Figure 11-25

A graph for Self-Test Exercises 6 and 7 and Exercises 1 and 3

EXERCISES

1. Write the adjacency matrix for the weighted graph in Figure 11-25.

2. Consider the directed graph in Figure 11-26. Give the adjacency matrix and adjacency list representations of the graph.

3. Use both the depth-first strategy and the breadth-first strategy to traverse the graph in Figure 11-25, beginning with the vertex 1, and the graph in Figure 11-27, beginning with the vertex a. List the vertices in the order in which each traversal visits them.

4. Trace the DFS topological sorting algorithm and indicate the resulting topological order of the vertices for each graph in Figure 11-28.

5. Trace the DFS and BFS spanning tree algorithms, beginning with vertex a of the graph in Figure 11-10, and show that the spanning trees are the trees in Figures 11-17 and 11-18, respectively.

6. Draw the DFS and BFS spanning trees rooted at a for the graph in Figure

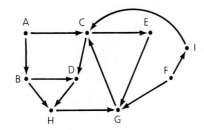

Figure 11-26

A graph for Exercise 2

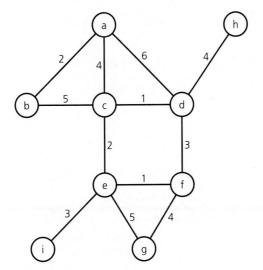

Figure 11-27

A graph for Exercises 3 and 6

11-27. Then draw the minimum spanning tree rooted at *a* for this graph.

7. Draw the minimum spanning tree for the graph in Figure 11-19 when you start with (a) vertex *g* and (b) vertex *c*.

8. Trace the shortest-path algorithm for the graph in Figure 11-29.

9. Write Pascal procedures that determine the DFS and BFS spanning trees for a connected graph.

10. Implement the shortest-path procedure in Pascal. How can you modify this procedure so that any vertex can be the origin?

11. Prove that a connected undirected graph with *N* vertices and more than *N* − 1 edges must contain at least one cycle. *Hint:* Take an arbitrary connected undirected graph with *N* vertices and *N* − 1 edges,

Figure 11-28

Graphs for Exercise 4

(a)

(b)

(c)

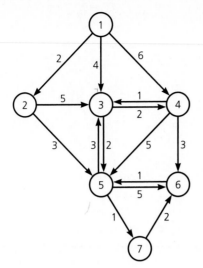

Figure 11-29
A graph for Exercise 8

which, because of observation 2 in the section "Spanning Trees," you know cannot contain a cycle, and add any edge.

*12. Prove that a graph-traversal algorithm visits every vertex in the graph if and only if the graph is connected, regardless of where the traversal starts.

*13. Although the DFS traversal algorithm has both iterative and recursive forms, the BFS traversal algorithm is iterative. Explain why the BFS traversal algorithm does not have a recursive form.

14. Implement the ADT graph operations first by using an adjacency matrix to represent the graph and then by using an adjacency list to represent the graph.

*15. Prove that the loop invariant of Dijkstra's shortest-path algorithm is true by using a proof by induction on *Step*.

CHAPTER *12*

Priority Queues and Heaps

PREVIEW   This chapter introduces an important variation of the ADT table, the priority queue. This ADT supports operations that allow the item with the largest value to be retrieved and deleted easily. Although you can implement a priority queue by using a binary search tree, a simpler tree structure, known as a heap, is often more appropriate for this purpose. The case study in this chapter is an enhancement of the case study in Chapter 3.

The table is one of the most useful abstract data types that you have studied. In addition to the basic table presented in Chapter 10, there are several classical variations of the ADT table. This chapter presents one of these variants, the ADT priority queue.

The chapter contains two main sections. The first defines a priority queue and develops implementations for it. The second section presents a case study that illustrates modifications to the videocassette inventory system originally developed in Chapter 3. One of the modifications to the system serves to illustrate an application of the ADT priority queue.

A VARIATION OF THE ADT TABLE: THE ADT PRIORITY QUEUE

The **priority queue** is an abstract data type whose operations make it useful in the solution to many problems. For example, it is desirable to enhance the videocassette inventory system developed in Chapter 3 so that it manages the repair of cassettes. If a cassette in the inventory is in need of repair, it is placed on a *repair queue*. When a worker becomes available to fix a cassette, a cassette is selected from the repair queue, as Figure 12-1 illustrates. The videocassette dealer wants the tapes that are most important to the inventory to be repaired as quickly as possible. That is, the dealer does not necessarily want the *first in, first out* rule of a standard queue to govern the behavior of the repair queue. Rather, the dealer would like to assign some measure of importance, or **priority**, to the cassettes awaiting repair and to select for repair the tape with the highest priority.

When a cassette first enters the repair queue, the videocassette dealer assigns a **priority value** *P*, which reflects the urgency with which the tape

A priority queue is not FIFO

A priority queue orders by priority values

Figure 12-1

A repair queue

should be repaired. What quantity should the dealer use for this priority value? There are many reasonable possibilities, including those that take into account the title's popularity, its selling price, and the number of copies of the title currently in the inventory. Recall from the case study in Chapter 3 that the inventory system maintains a *have value* and a *want value* for each title. The have value of a title is the number of copies of the title currently in stock. The want value is the number of copies that should be in stock. The want value, which presumably reflects the popularity of a title, is used to determine how many new copies should be ordered— enough are ordered so that the have value is brought up to the want value. Thus, you could use, for example, the following ratio for a cassette's priority value:

$$P = \frac{\text{want value of title}}{\text{have value of title}}$$

To summarize, when a defective cassette is found, the dealer assigns it a priority value and places it on the repair queue. The next available worker selects the cassette with the highest priority value from the repair queue. This management of the repair queue describes an ADT known as a priority queue. More formally, a priority queue is an abstract data type that supports the following operations:

KEY CONCEPTS   **ADT *Priority Queue Operations***

```
Create(PQ)
{ Creates an empty priority queue PQ. }

IsEmpty(PQ)
{ Determines whether priority queue PQ is empty. }

Insert(PQ, newitem)
{ Adds newitem to priority queue PQ. }

Remove(PQ, getitem)
{ Removes and retrieves from priority queue PQ the item with
  the highest priority value. }
```

Remove is the difference between a priority queue and a table

These operations resemble a subset of the ADT table operations. The significant difference is the *Remove* operation. While the sequence *Retrieve-Delete* of table operations allows you to retrieve and delete an item that has a specified value in its search key, *Remove* allows you to retrieve and delete the item with the highest priority value. Notice that *Remove*, unlike *Retrieve* and *Delete*, is not told the value in question. Since in general you will not know what the highest priority value is, *Retrieve* and *Delete* could not easily perform this task. On the other hand, you could not use *Remove* to retrieve and delete an item with some specified value.

The ADT priority queue and the ADT table are thus both similar and dissimilar, a fact that is reflected in their implementations. A binary search tree implementation is good for both a table and a priority queue. On the other hand, this chapter develops an implementation that, for many applications, is the most appropriate one for a priority queue but that is not at all appropriate as an implementation of a table.

To begin, consider some of the table implementations as implementations for a priority queue. The sorted linear implementations are appropriate if the number of items in the priority queue is small. The array-based implementation would maintain the items sorted in ascending order of priority value, so that the item with the highest priority value would be at the end of the array, as Figure 12-2a illustrates. Thus, *Remove* simply returns the item in *PQ[Last]* and decrements *Last*. However, the *Insert* operation, after using a binary search to find the correct position for the insertion, must shift the array elements to make room for the new item.

Possible implementations

The pointer-based implementation (Figure 12-2b) maintains the items sorted in descending order of priority value, so that the item with the highest priority value is at the beginning of the list. Thus, *Remove* simply returns the item pointed to by *PQ* and changes *PQ* to point to the next item. The *Insert* operation, however, must traverse the list to find the correct position for the insertion. Thus, the linear implementations of priority queues suffer from the same problems as the linear implementations of tables.

Instead, consider a binary search tree as an implementation for a priority queue, as Figure 12-2c illustrates. Although you can perform the *Insert* operation exactly as you can in the case of a table, the *Remove* operation has no direct analogue among the table operations. *Remove* must locate the item with the highest priority value, without knowing what this value is. The task is not difficult, however, because this item is always in the rightmost node of the tree. (Why?) You thus need only follow *Rchild* links until you encounter a node with a *nil Rchild* link. (A procedure analogous to the binary search tree's *Leftmost* can accomplish this task). The removal of this node from the tree is particularly easy because it has at most one child.

The binary search tree is thus a very good implementation of a priority queue. For some applications, however, you can do even better. A **heap** is an important array-based implementation of a priority queue. Because it is array-based, a heap is appropriate only for applications in which a fixed-size data structure is not a problem.

An Array-Based Representation of Complete Trees

Chapter 10 discussed both array-based and pointer-based representations of a binary tree. There is another array-based representation of a binary tree that is useful, provided that the tree is complete. As you will see, a heap is a binary tree that happens to be complete.

(a)

(b)

(c)

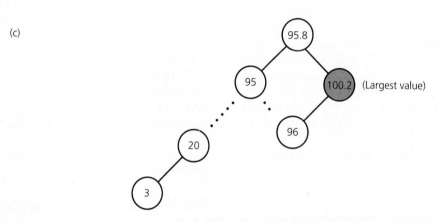

Figure 12-2

Implementations of the ADT priority queue: (a) array based; (b) pointer based; (c) binary search tree

Reminder: a complete binary tree

Recall the definition of a complete binary tree from Chapter 10:

A binary tree T of height h is **complete**

1. If all nodes at level $h - 2$ and above have two children
2. If, when a node has a right descendant at level h, all leaves in its left subtree are at level h

Recall that criterion 2 of this definition formalizes the requirement that level h be filled in from left to right.

Figure 12-3 shows a complete tree with nine nodes. The nodes are numbered according to a standard level-by-level numbering scheme. The root is numbered 1, and the children of the root (the next level of the tree) are numbered left to right 2 and 3. The nodes at the next level are numbered left to right 4, 5, 6, and 7, and so forth. This level-by-level numbering scheme for a complete tree allows you to conveniently develop a simple array-based implementation.

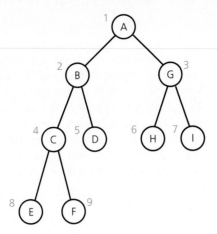

Figure 12-3

Level-by-level numbering of a complete binary tree

The array-based representation of a complete binary tree is rather elegant. If *Tree* is an array that represents the tree, then *Tree[1]* contains node 1 (the root), *Tree[2]* contains node 2, and so forth, as Figure 12-4 illustrates. The key observation is that, given any node, you can easily locate both of its children and its parent. If you study the tree in Figure 12-3, you will observe that for any node *i*, its left child (if it exists) is node *2 * i*, and its right child (if it exists) is node *2 * i + 1*. Further, the parent of node *i* (assuming the node is not the root) is node *i div 2*. Because the array representation stores node *i* in *Tree[i]*, it is quite simple to go from any node to either of its children or to its parent.

For this array-based representation to be appropriate for a binary tree, two conditions must occur. First, the tree must be complete. If nodes were missing from the middle of the tree, the numbering scheme would be thrown off, and there would be ambiguity as to who was the child of whom. In addition, because the representation is array based, you must know the maximum number of nodes.

An array can represent a complete binary tree, if you know the maximum number of nodes in the tree

Figure 12-4

An array representation of the complete binary tree in Figure 12-3

1	A
2	B
3	G
4	C
5	D
6	H
7	I
8	E
9	F

Heaps

A heap differs from a binary
search tree in two ways

A **heap** is a data structure similar to a binary search tree, although it differs from a binary search tree in two significant ways. First, while you can view a binary search tree as sorted, a heap is ordered in a much weaker sense. However, the manner in which a heap is ordered is sufficient for the efficient performance of the priority queue operations (`Create`, `IsEmpty`, `Insert`, and `Remove`). The second significant difference is that while binary search trees come in many different shapes, heaps are always complete binary trees. As a consequence, if you know the maximum size of a heap, you can use the array-based implementation that was just described.

Heap

A **heap** is a complete binary tree

1. That is empty

or

2a. In which the (priority) value in the root is greater than or equal to the priority value in each of its children, and

2b. In which both subtrees of the root are themselves heaps

For example, Figure 12-5 shows a heap along with its array representation. Notice that, unlike the node values in a binary search tree, the value of each node in a heap is greater than or equal to the value in each of its children. Further, in a heap there is no relationship between the values of the children; that is, you do not know which child contains the larger value.

A Heap As an Implementation of a Priority Queue

Consider how you can use a heap to implement the priority-queue operations `Remove` and `Insert`. Let the priority queue `PQ` be a record with two fields:

Priority queue as a record with
two fields

*   `Items`: an array of priority-queue items
*   `Last`: an integer that indicates the number of items in the priority queue

Figure 12-5

A heap with its array representation

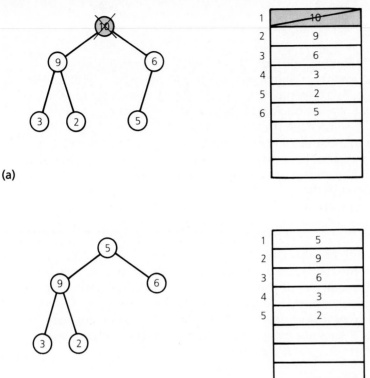

Figure 12-6

(a) Disjoint heaps; (b) a semiheap

(a)

(b)

The array *Items* corresponds to the array-based representation of a tree, as was described earlier. (To simplify the following examples, assume that the priority-queue items are integers.)

First consider the *Remove* operation. Where is the largest value in the heap? Because the value of every node is greater than or equal to that of either of its children, the largest value must be in the root of the tree. Thus, the first step of the *Remove* operation is

```
{ return the item in the root }
Return the item in PQ.Items[1]
```

Remove's first step

That was easy, but you must do more. Once you have removed the largest value, you are left with two disjoint heaps, as Figure 12-6a indicates.

Therefore, you need to transform the nodes that remain after the root is removed back into a heap. To begin this transformation, you take the item in the last node of the tree and place it in the root as follows:

```
{ copy the item from the last node into the root }
PQ.Items[1] := PQ.Items[Last]
```

Remove's second step produces a semiheap

```
                            { remove the last node }
                            Last := Last — 1
```

As Figure 12-6b suggests, the result of this step is *not* necessarily a heap. It is, however, a complete binary tree whose left and right subtrees are both heaps. The only problem is that the item in the root may be (and usually is) out of place. Such a structure is called a **semiheap**. You thus need a way to transform a semiheap into a heap. One strategy allows the value in the root to *trickle down* the tree until it reaches a node in which it will not be out of place; that is, the value will come to rest in the first node where it would be greater than (or equal to) the value of each of its children. To accomplish this, you first compare the value in the root of the semiheap to the values in its children. If the root's value is smaller than the values of both of its children, you swap the item in the root with that of the larger child. (By larger child, we mean the child whose value is greater than the value of the other child.)

Figure 12-7 illustrates the `Remove` operation. Although the value 5 trickles down to its correct position after only one swap, in general, more swaps may be necessary. In fact, once the values in the root and the larger child *C* have been swapped, *C* becomes the root of a semiheap. (Notice that node *C* does not move; only its value changes.) This strategy suggests the following recursive algorithm:

Remove's final step transforms the semiheap into a heap

```
Adjust(H, root)
{ Converts the semiheap H rooted at position root into a
  heap. }

  { Recursively trickle the item at position root down to
    its proper position by swapping it with its larger
    child, if the child is larger than the item. If (2 *
    root) > H.Last, then the item is at a leaf and nothing
    needs to be done. }

  if (root is not a leaf, i.e. 2 * root <= H.Last) and
     ((the value in node root, stored in H.Items[root]) <
     (the value of its children, stored in H.Items[2*root]
     and H.Items[2*root + 1]))
```

Figure 12-7

Removal from a heap

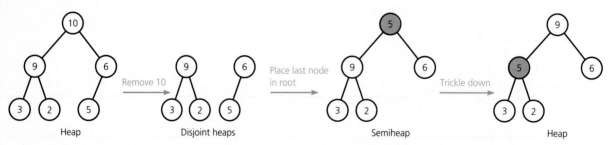

Heap → Remove 10 → Disjoint heaps → Place last node in root → Semiheap → Trickle down → Heap

```
    then
    begin
       Let child indicate the larger of the two children nodes

       { swap value in node child with value in node root }
       Swap(H.Items[root], H.Items[child])

       { recursively call Adjust on the semiheap
           rooted at node child }
       Adjust(H, child)

    else the value is in the correct place and you are done
    end
```

Figure 12-8 illustrates the recursive calls to the procedure *Adjust*. The entire *Remove* operation uses *Adjust* as follows:

```
Remove(PQ)

  { return the item in the root }
  Return the item in PQ.Items[1]

  { copy the item from the last node into the root }
  PQ.Items[1] := PQ.Items[PQ.Last]

  { remove the last node }
  PQ.Last := PQ.Last − 1

  { transform the semiheap back into a heap }
  Adjust(PQ, 1)
```

Before developing the *Insert* algorithm, consider briefly the efficiency of *Remove*. Because the tree is stored in an array, the removal of a node requires that you swap array elements rather than simply change a few pointers. These swaps may concern you, but they do not necessarily indicate that the algorithm is inefficient. You must ask, what is the largest number of array elements that you might have to swap? *Remove* first cop-

Remove's efficiency

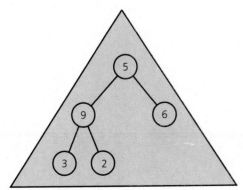

First semiheap passed to Adjust

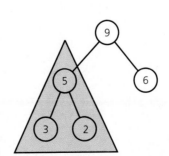

Second semiheap passed to Adjust

Figure 12-8

Recursive calls to the procedure Adjust

ies the item in the last node of the tree into the root. *Adjust* then trickles this item down the tree until its appropriate place is found. The key observation is that this item travels down a single path from the root to, at worst, a leaf. Therefore, the number of array items that *Adjust* must swap is no greater than the height of the tree. Because the height of a complete binary tree with N nodes is always approximately $\log_2 N$, *Remove* is in fact quite efficient.

Remove swaps at most $\lceil \log_2(N + 1) \rceil$ items

The strategy for the *Insert* algorithm is the opposite of that for *Remove*. A new item is inserted at the bottom of the tree and it trickles up to its proper place, as Figure 12-9 illustrates. It is easy to trickle up a node, because the parent of node *i*—other than a root—is always stored in *PQ.Items[i div 2]*. The pseudocode for *Insert* follows.

Insertion strategy

```
Insert(PQ, newitem)

    { insert the new item into the last position of the tree }
    PQ.Last := PQ.Last + 1
    PQ.Items[PQ.Last] := newitem

    { trickle the item up to the appropriate spot in the tree }
    place := PQ.Last
    parent := place div 2
    while (parent > 0) Cand
                            (PQ.Items[place] > PQ.Items[parent]) do
    begin
        Swap(PQ.Items[place], PQ.Items[parent])
        place := parent
        parent := place div 2
    end
```

The efficiency of *Insert* is like that of *Remove*. *Insert*, at worst, has to swap array elements on a path from a leaf to the root. The number of swaps, therefore, cannot exceed the height of the tree. Because the height of the tree, which is complete, is always approximately $\log_2 N$, *Insert* is also very efficient.

Insert swaps at most $\lceil \log_2(N + 1) \rceil$ items

A heap is thus an efficient implementation of a priority queue. How does a heap compare to a binary search tree as an implementation of a

Figure 12-9

Insertion into a heap

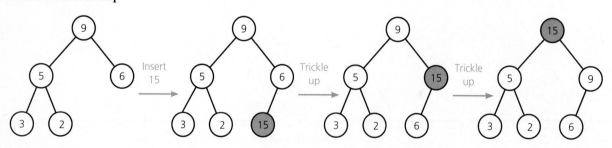

priority queue? As was stated earlier, because a heap has an array-based implementation, it is appropriate only if you know the maximum number of items that the priority queue can contain. If you know this number, a heap has several advantages over a binary search tree. For one thing, because a heap does not store explicit pointers, it requires slightly less space than a binary search tree. In most settings, however, this is not a major issue.

The real advantage of a heap is that it is always balanced. (Recall that complete is a stronger condition than balanced.) As you know, the height of a binary search tree can greatly exceed $\log_2 N$. The operations that keep a binary search tree balanced are far more complex than the heap operations. Do not think, however, that a heap can replace a binary search tree as a table implementation; as was stated earlier, a heap is not appropriate in this role. If this fact is not apparent to you, try to perform the table operation `Retrieve(T, X)` on a heap, or try to traverse a heap in sorted order.

A heap is always balanced

The Pascal code for the heap implementation of the ADT priority queue follows:

```
{ *********************************************************
   BASIC PRIORITY QUEUE OPERATIONS (Heap Implementation):

      Create, IsEmpty, Insert, and Remove

   The following definitions are assumed:

      const maxqueue = <maximum size of priority queue>;

      type  keytype = <desired type of search key>;

            itemtype = record
                key : keytype;
                <... and possibly other fields>
            end;

            pqueue = record
                Items : array[1..maxqueue] of itemtype;
                Last : 0..maxqueue
            end;

      Procedure Adjust is defined to help maintain a heap.
   ********************************************************* }

procedure Adjust(var H : pqueue; root : integer);
{ --------------------------------------------------------
   Converts a semiheap into a heap.
   Precondition: H is a semiheap rooted at position root.
   Postcondition: H is a heap rooted at position root.
   Method: Recursively trickles the item at position root
   down to its proper position by swapping it with its larger
   child, if the child is larger than the item. If (2 * root)
```

```
         > H.Last, then the item is at a leaf and nothing needs to
         be done.
         ------------------------------------------------------------ }
     var child : integer;
         temp : itemtype;
     begin
        if (2 * root) <= H.Last
             then              { root is not a leaf }
             begin
                { find index of larger child of root }
                child := 2 * root;  { index of left child of root }
                if (child + 1) <= H.Last then
                     { there is a right child; find larger child }
                     if H.Items[child + 1].key > H.Items[child].key
                         then child := child + 1;
                { child is the index of the larger child of root }

                { swap if the value at position root is smaller
                  than the value in the larger child }
                if H.Items[root].key < H.Items[child].key
                   then
                   begin  { swap }
                      temp := H.Items[root];
                      H.Items[root] := H.Items[child];
                      H.Items[child] := temp;

                      { adjust the new subtree }
                      Adjust(H, child)
                   end  { if }
          end  { if }
       { if root is a leaf, do nothing }
     end;  { Adjust }

     procedure Create(var PQ : pqueue);
     { ----------------------------------------------------------
       Creates an empty priority queue.
       Precondition: None.
       Postcondition: The priority queue PQ is empty.
       Implementation note: The Last field of PQ is 0.
       ---------------------------------------------------------- }
     begin
        PQ.Last := 0
     end;  { Create }

     function IsEmpty(PQ : pqueue) : boolean;
     { ----------------------------------------------------------
       Determines if a priority queue is empty.
       Precondition: The priority queue PQ has been created.
```

```
  Postcondition: Returns true if PQ is empty, else returns
  false.
  ------------------------------------------------------- }
begin
   IsEmpty := (PQ.Last = 0)
end;  { IsEmpty }

procedure Insert(var PQ : pqueue; newitem : itemtype;
                 var success : boolean);
{ ------------------------------------------------------
  Inserts an item into a priority queue.
  Precondition: The priority queue PQ has been created.
  Postcondition: If PQ is not full, newitem is inserted into
  PQ and success is set to true; otherwise success is set to
  false.
  Method: Inserts the new item after the last item in the
  heap and trickles it up to its proper position. The
  priority queue is full when it contains maxqueue items.
  ------------------------------------------------------- }
 var parent, place : integer;
     done : boolean;
     temp : itemtype;
begin
   if PQ.Last = maxqueue
      then success := false        { PQ is full }

      else
      begin
         { place the new item at the end of the heap }
         PQ.Last := PQ.Last + 1;
         PQ.Items[PQ.Last] := newitem;

         { trickle it up to its proper position }
         place := PQ.Last;
         parent := place div 2;
         done := false;
         while (parent > 0) and (not done) do
         begin
            if PQ.Items[place].key > PQ.Items[parent].key
               then
               begin
                  temp := PQ.Items[parent];
                  PQ.Items[parent] := PQ.Items[place];
                  PQ.Items[place] := temp;
                  place := parent;
                  parent := place div 2
               end  { if }

               else done := true
```

```
            end;   { while }

          success := true
      end   { if }
end;   { Insert }

procedure Remove(var PQ : pqueue; var getitem : itemtype;
                  var success : boolean);
{ ------------------------------------------------------------
  Deletes and retrieves the item with the largest priority
  value from a priority queue.
  Precondition: The priority queue PQ has been created.
  Postcondition: If PQ is not empty, getitem is the
  retrieved item, the item is deleted from PQ, and success =
  true. However, if PQ is empty, removal is impossible and
  success = false.
  Method: Swaps the last item in the heap with the root and
  trickles it down to its proper position.
  Calls: Adjust.
  ------------------------------------------------------------ }
begin
   if PQ.Last = 0
      then success := false

      else
      begin
         getitem := PQ.Items[1];
         PQ.Items[1] := PQ.Items[PQ.Last];
         PQ.Last := PQ.Last — 1;
         Adjust(PQ, 1);
         success := true
      end   { if }
end;   { Remove }
```

A heap of queues

Finite distinct priority values. Suppose that you have a finite number of distinct priority values, such as the integers 1 through 10. In such cases, it is likely that many items will have the same priority value, and therefore you probably will need to order these items.

A heap of queues accommodates this situation. Each priority value appears in the heap only once. To insert an item into the priority queue, you add its priority value to the heap, if it is not already there, and then add the item to the corresponding queue. To delete an item, you remove the item at the front of the queue that corresponds to the highest priority value in the heap. If this deletion leaves the queue empty, you remove the corresponding priority value from the heap.

Exercise 8 at the end of this chapter treats distinct priority values further.

Heapsort

As its name implies, the *Heapsort* algorithm uses a heap to sort an array *A* of items that are in no particular order. The first step of the algorithm transforms the array into a heap. One way to accomplish this transformation is to use the priority queue's *Insert* procedure to insert the items into the heap one by one.

Building a heap from an array of items

There is, however, a more efficient method of building a heap out of the items of *A*. Suppose, for example, that the initial contents of *A* are as shown in Figure 12-10a. You can imagine the array as a binary tree by assigning the items of *A* to the tree's nodes, beginning with the root and proceeding left to right down the tree. Figure 12-10b shows the resulting tree. You can transform this tree into a heap by calling *Adjust* repeatedly. Recall that *Adjust* transforms a semiheap—a tree whose subtrees are both heaps but whose root may be out of place—into a heap. But are there any semiheaps in the tree for *Adjust* to work on? Although *A* itself is not a semiheap, if you look at the leaves you will find semiheaps—that is, each leaf is a semiheap. (In fact, each leaf is a heap, but for the sake of simplicity ignore this fact.) You first call *Adjust* on the leaves from right to left. You then move up the tree, knowing that by the time you reach a node *i*, its subtrees are heaps, and thus *Adjust* will transform the semiheap rooted at *i* into a heap.

The following procedure transforms the array *A* into a heap and is the first step of the *Heapsort* algorithm. Notice that you need to modify the earlier version of *Adjust* slightly: In addition to the root of the semiheap, you must also pass *N*, the number of items in the array.

Figure 12-10

(a) The initial contents of **A**;
(b) **A**'s corresponding tree;
(c) the contents of **A** after
BuildHeap

```
BuildHeap(A, N)

    for i := N downto 1 do
        { the tree rooted at i is a semiheap —
          call Adjust to transform it into a heap }

        Adjust(A, i, N)
```

Now that the array of items is structured as a heap (Figure 12-10c), `Heapsort` partitions the array into two regions: the Heap region and the Sorted region. The Heap region is in `A[1..last]` and the Sorted region is in `A[last+1..N]`, as Figure 12-11 illustrates. The invariant of the `Heapsort` algorithm is that after step `i`

- The Sorted region contains the `i` largest values in `A`, and they are in sorted order—that is, `A[N]` is the largest, `A[N–1]` is the second largest, and so on.

- The items in the Heap region form a heap.

After converting `A` to a heap, `Heapsort` initializes the Heap region to be all of `A` and the Sorted region to be empty—that is, `last` is equal to `N`. Each step of the algorithm moves an item `I` from the Heap region to the Sorted region. So that the invariant holds, `I` must be the item that has the largest value in the Heap region, and therefore `I` must be in the root of the heap. To accomplish the move, you exchange the item in the root of the heap with the last item in the heap—that is, you exchange `A[1]` with `A[last]`—and then decrement the value of `last`. The result is that the item that was just swapped from the root into `A[last]` becomes the smallest item in the Sorted region (and is in the first position of the Sorted region). After the move, you must transform the Heap region back into a heap because the new root may be out of place. You can accomplish this transformation by using `Adjust`—modified as was noted earlier—to trickle down the item now in the root so that the Heap region is once again a heap.

The following algorithm summarizes the steps:

```
Heapsort(A, N)
{ Sorts A[1..N]. }

    BuildHeap(A, N)

    { initialize the regions }
    last := N
```

Figure 12-11

The invariant for *Heapsort*

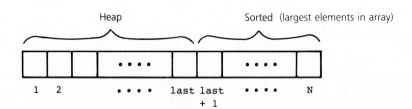

```
{ loop invariant: A[1..last] is a heap, A[last+1..N] is
  sorted and contains the largest elements of A }

for i := N downto 2 do
begin
{ Remove the largest item from the Heap region and place
  it at the beginning of the Sorted region. Since the
  Heap region is a heap, the largest item is at the
  root. To move the largest item into the first position
  of the Sorted region, swap A[1] and A[last] and
  decrement last }

    Swap(A[1], A[last])

    { expand the Sorted region, shrink the Heap region }
    last := last — 1

    { make the Heap region a heap again }
    Adjust(A, 1, last)
end
```

Heapsort, like `Mergesort`, is $O(N * \log N)$ in both the worst and average cases. It has an advantage over `Mergesort` in that it does not require a second array.

Heapsort is O(N ∗ log N)

The following Pascal procedures implement `Heapsort`. Note that to sort an array `A[1..N]` of integers, you would write `Heapsort(A, N)`.

```
const  maxsize = 10;
type   datatype = integer;
       heap = array[1..maxsize] of datatype;

procedure Adjust(var H : heap; root, last : integer);
{ ------------------------------------------------------
  Converts a semiheap into a heap.
  Precondition: H is a semiheap rooted at position root;
  last marks the end of the semiheap.
  Postcondition: H is a heap rooted at position root; last
  marks the end of the heap.
  Method: Recursively trickles the item at position root
  down to its proper position by swapping it with its larger
  child, if the child is larger than the item. If (2 * root) >
  last, then the item is at a leaf and nothing needs to be
  done.
  ------------------------------------------------------ }
var child : integer;
    temp  : datatype;
begin
    if (2 * root) <= last
      then                { root is not a leaf }
```

```
            begin
                { find index of larger child of root }
                child := 2 * root;  { index of left child of root }
                if (child + 1) <= last then
                    { there is a right child; find larger child }
                    if H[child + 1] > H[child]
                        then child := child + 1;
                    { child is the index of the larger child of root }

                    { swap if the value at position root is smaller
                      than the value in the larger child }
                    if H[root] < H[child]
                        then
                        begin  { swap }
                            temp := H[root];
                            H[root] := H[child];
                            H[child] := temp;

                            { adjust the new subtree }
                            Adjust(H, child, last)
                        end  { if }
            end  { if }
        { if root is a leaf, do nothing }
end;  { Adjust }

procedure BuildHeap(var H : heap; N : integer);
{ ------------------------------------------------------------
  Builds the initial heap.
  Precondition: H is an array of N items.
  Postcondition: H is a heap of N items.
  ------------------------------------------------------------ }
var i : integer;
begin
    for i := N downto 1 do
        { tree rooted at i is a semiheap —
          transform it into a heap }
        Adjust(H, i, N)
end;  { BuildHeap }

procedure Heapsort(var A: heap; N : integer);
{ ------------------------------------------------------------
  Sorts an array by using heapsort.
  Precondition: A is an array of N items.
  Postcondition: A is sorted into ascending order.
  ------------------------------------------------------------ }
var last : integer;
    temp : datatype;
begin
    BuildHeap(A, N);                    { build the initial heap }
    for last := N downto 2 do    { heapsort }
```

```
begin
    { swap A[[1] and A[last] }
    temp := A[1];
    A[1] := A[last];
    A[last] := temp;
    { change semiheap into a heap }
    Adjust(A, 1, last-1)
end   { for }
end   { Heapsort }
```

A CASE STUDY: ENHANCEMENTS TO THE VIDEOCASSETTE INVENTORY SYSTEM

The case study in this section helps to illustrate, once again, the use of ADT's in the problem-solving process. It modifies and enhances the inventory program that was presented in Chapter 3.

Although a program might meet the needs of its users at the time of the original design, those needs can change as the environment of the users changes (for example, as a company grows). Ideally, the program should evolve along with its users' needs. At least two types of changes to a program can occur:

- The program specifications might change. For example, the program could be required to do more (perform more functions) than was previously needed or desired.

Program changes that can occur

- The requirements for performance might change. When the program was originally written, the demands on computer resources may have been minimal. As the usage of the program or the size of the problem increases (for instance, as the size of an inventory grows), a simple implementation that was satisfactory before may become unsatisfactory.

One of the things that this book has stressed throughout is that a program that is properly organized into modules, with respect to both its processes and the management of its data, will be amenable to modification. Imagine that the videocassette dealership discussed in Chapter 3 has grown considerably since the design of the inventory program and that the program is no longer completely addressing its current needs. The object of this case study is to bring the implementation up to date with these needs (and with the material that you have been studying!).

Suppose that the new requirements are classified as follows:

- **Performance**. At the time of the original program design, the dealership was quite small, and efficient management of data was not a major concern. (Also, of course, you had not yet studied the issue of efficiency.) This case study will begin by reviewing the original implementation in the context of the material

New requirements of the program

you have covered since Chapter 3. As a consequence of this review, we will consider more efficient implementations of the data-management parts of the program.

- **Features.** The dealer would like the program to help keep track of the cassettes that need repair. Because the store repairperson can fix only one cassette at a time, it is important that at any time the most-needed cassette be repaired first. In particular, the program should be able to execute the following three new commands associated with the repair of cassettes:

Three new commands

B *<title>*	(broken cassette)	Move the specified cassette from the stock shelves to the repair area. (This decreases the corresponding value in the inventory by 1.) If the number of cassettes waiting to be repaired is at some prespecified maximum (that is, if the backlog is too great), send the new cassette out to be repaired somewhere else.
F	(start repairing the most-needed cassette)	The most-needed cassette in the repair area is identified (the one with the highest priority value), and the repairperson starts working on it.
P *<title>*	(put a cassette back into the inventory)	Add one copy of the specified title to the inventory. This command is executed when a repair is completed.

- Note that the B command assigns to the cassette a priority value, which determines how soon the cassette should be repaired. This value is defined to be the cassette's want value divided by its have value. That is, the more popular the cassette is (based on the want value), the sooner it should be repaired; the more copies that are on hand (based on the have value), the less urgent the repair becomes.

Make a few changes at a time   As is the case when you are designing a solution from scratch, the best approach to making changes to an existing program is to make a few related modifications at a time. The program should be fully tested and debugged with each new set of modifications before you proceed to the next set. Ideally, this strategy will ensure that you will make changes to only a few isolated modules at a time. In this spirit, the modification of the inventory program will occur in two stages that correspond to the two classes of requirements (performance and features) just described.

Improving the Performance of the Program

If you review the original implementation of the inventory program with the discussions of ADT's in mind, you can identify the key data-management operations that are performed on the inventory items. Because the operations are essentially value oriented rather than position oriented, the ADT resembles a variation of the ADT table.

For the following operations, assume that the inventory list is alphabetical by title.

BASIC TABLE OPERATIONS FOR THE INVENTORY

Operations associated with the inventory

```
Insert(invlist, title)
{ Inserts a title into an inventory list, if it is not
  already present.
  Precondition: The inventory list invlist has been created.
  Postcondition: If title is not in invlist, insert it in
  alphabetical order; otherwise do nothing.
  Called by: procAM and procD. }

Retrieve(invlist, title, getitem, success)
{ Retrieves an item from the inventory list.
  Precondition: The inventory list invlist has been created.
  Postcondition: Retrieves into getitem the inventory item
  with the specified title. The operation fails if the item
  is not present. The flag success indicates whether the
  operation succeeded.
  Calls: Find.
  Called by: procI, procAM, procD and procS. }

Replace(invlist, replitem, success)
{ Replaces an item in the inventory list.
  Precondition: The inventory list invlist has been created.
  Postcondition: If found, the item in the inventory list
  whose title matches that of replitem is replaced by
  replitem and success = true. If the item is not found, the
  operation fails and success = false.
  Calls: Find.
  Called by: procAM, procD, procR and procS. }

Traverse(invlist, Visit)
{ Traverses an inventory list in sorted order, calling
  procedure Visit for each item.
  Precondition: The inventory list invlist has been created,
  Visit is a user-defined procedure.
  Postcondition: Visit's action occurs for each item in the
  inventory list.
  Calls: Visit.
  Called by: procL, procO and procR. }
```

OPERATIONS THAT ARE PARTICULAR TO THE WAIT LIST ASSOCIATED WITH EACH INVENTORY ITEM

Waitnames(invlist, title)
{ Writes out the names on the wait list for a particular
* title.*
* **Precondition:** The inventory list invlist has been created.*
* **Postcondition:** The wait list for title is printed.*
* **Calls:** Find.*
* **Called by:** procL and procI. }*

Addwait(invlist, title, who, success)
{ Adds a name to the wait list associated with a given title.
* **Precondition:** The inventory list invlist has been created.*
* **Postcondition:** If title appears in the inventory list,*
* then title is added to the waitlist and success = true;*
* otherwise, success = false.*
* **Calls:** Find.*
* **Called by:** procS. }*

Delwait(invlist, title, getname)
{(This specification changes during the subsequent
* discussion.)}*
{ Deletes and retrieves the first name from the wait list
* associated with a particular inventory item.*
* **Precondition:** The inventory list invlist has been created.*
* **Postcondition:** getname is the first name on title's wait*
* list; deletes this name from the wait list. If wait list*
* is empty, does nothing.*
* **Calls:** Find.*
* **Called by:** procD. }*

OPERATIONS PARTICULAR TO SAVING AND RESTORING THE INVENTORY EACH DAY

Putinv(invlist, invfile, sizefile, waitfile)
{ Saves the current inventory in specified files for use by
* the restore operation.*
* **Precondition:** The inventory list invlist has been created.*
* **Postcondition:** Files associated with file parameters are*
* either created, if they do not exist already, or are*
* rewritten so that their prior contents are lost. The*
* inventory list is written to invfile. The size of the*
* structure and the associated wait lists are saved in the*
* separate files sizefile and waitfile. Items that have zero*
* have and want values and empty wait lists are eliminated.*
* Files remain open for output.*
* **Calls:** Putwait.*
* **Called by:** The main program. }*

```
Getinv(invlist, invfile, sizefile, waitfile)
{ Restores the inventory from a sorted file into a binary
  search tree of minimum height. Restores the corresponding
  wait lists.
  Precondition: The following files, created by the save
  operation, are available but need not be open:
                    invfile — the main inventory structure
                    sizefile — the size of the inventory
                    waitfile — the associated wait lists
  Postcondition: The inventory list is read into invlist.
  Files remain open for input.
  Calls: Getwait.
  Called by: The main program. }
```

Note that there are no *Create* or *Delete* operations. There is no *Create* operation because the inventory is restored from the files—that is, the table already exists. The issue of the initial execution of the program will be discussed in Exercise 17 at the end of this chapter. There is no *Delete* operation because the only time an item is deleted is when the inventory is written to the file. The deletion of an unwanted item is therefore handled by the *Putinv* operation.

Create and Delete are unnecessary

You can rewrite the original program, which was described in Chapter 3, in terms of these ADT operations. The result is a program with a much clearer wall between the implementation of the data-management operations and the rest of the program.

The conversion to this ADT version of the program is straightforward. The ADT operations were already implemented in the original program, and all that is needed is to isolate them into separate subprograms. Here, for example, is the new version of one of the procedures (*ProcAM*) that uses the ADT operations. The rest of the transformation is left as an exercise.

An example of the ADT operations in use

```
procedure procAM(var invlist : stockptr);
{ ----------------------------------------------------------
  Adds a new title to the inventory or modifies the want
  value for a title that already exists in the inventory.
  Precondition: The inventory list invlist has been created.
  Postcondition: Modifies invlist as described above.
  Calls: Prompt, Getstring, Insert, Retrieve, Replace.
  ---------------------------------------------------------- }
var oneitem : stockinfo;
    wantval : integer;
    newtitle : string;
    success : boolean;
begin
  { get the title argument }
  Prompt(titleprompt);
  Getstring(newtitle, input);
```

```
{ insert a new stock item if necessary }
Insert(invlist, newtitle);
Retrieve(invlist, newtitle, oneitem, success);

{ update the want value for the stock item }
writeln('Title: ', newtitle);

writeln;
writeln('The current want value is ', oneitem.want:1,
        '. Enter correct value:');
readln(wantval);
if wantval < 0
    then
    begin
        writeln(' Negative want value is not allowed.');
        writeln(' The want value will be set to 0.');
        oneitem.want := 0
    end

    else oneitem.want := wantval;
    Replace(invlist, oneitem, success)
end;   { procAM }
```

Notice that in the original program, the data structure is very much integrated with the rest of the program. For example, the *Insert* routine returned a pointer to the inserted item; you could then use the pointer to make direct changes—without using ADT operations—to that item in the data structure. Note how this approach violates the spirit of the wall between the data structure and the routines that use it.

Comparing the revised program with the original one

What is the consequence of rewriting the program in terms of the previous ADT operations? Consider, for example, the old and new versions of procedure *procAM* (which adds or modifies an inventory item). In the original version, a call to *Insert* locates or inserts an item, and *procAM* directly modifies the have value of the item by referencing the pointer that *Insert* returns. In the new version, a call to *Insert* is followed by a call to *Retrieve*, which is followed by a call to *Replace*. However, unless you use a clever implementation or redefine the ADT operations (see Exercise 14), you will have to search the data structure three times instead of the one time required by the original insert-modify sequence.

On the surface it seems that there is a large price to pay for the sake of clarity and the wall. Recall, however, the comments in Chapter 7 about keeping your perspective. In this spirit, a good argument can be made that this extra cost is of no real consequence.

In contrast to procedure *procAM*, consider the old and new versions of procedure *procD* (which processes a delivery). In particular, focus on the modification of the wait list associated with a newly delivered cassette. In the original version, a call to *Insert* inserts (or locates) an item. You modify the wait list directly by referencing the pointer that *Insert* returns. In the new version, however, *Insert* does not return a pointer, because if it did, the wall around the ADT implementation would be violated. Instead, you must make a call to the ADT operation *Delwait* for each name that you want to remove from the wait list. Note that *Delwait* must search for the item each time it is called. As a consequence, if there are several copies of a single title, you might search for the same inventory item repeatedly.

It is important to appreciate how significant the difference between the old and new versions of *procD* is. One search (for each delivered title) is replaced by a number of searches that depends on the size of the shipment (the quantity of each title delivered). This number can easily be large enough to make the cost of the extra searches of the inventory prohibitive. On the other hand, in *procAM*, the original one search of the inventory is replaced by exactly three searches (calls to *Insert*, *Retrieve*, and *Replace*.)

You can eliminate the redundant searching in *procD* by modifying the definition of the operation *Delwait*. Instead of deleting and retrieving one name at a time from a specified wait list, you can pass an extra argument that allows you to delete several items at once. A consequence of this modification is that the message that must be written out for each name removed from the wait list will now be defined as part of the ADT operation.

```
Delwait(invlist, title, count)
{ Deletes count names from the wait list associated with the
  specified inventory item. Writes a message for each name. }
```

A more efficient `Delwait`

With this digression out of the way, we can examine the implementation of the ADT operations more closely. It is assumed that the inventory has grown quite large and that there is now a concern for the efficiency of the data-management operations. It should not be difficult to see that the original implementation of the inventory corresponds to the sorted linear implementation of the ADT table discussed in Chapter 10. Given that the inventory has grown quite large and that it may continue to grow, the binary search tree implementation should immediately come to mind.

The conversion to the binary search tree implementation of the ADT operations is straightforward and is left as an exercise. Most of the routines do not require special comment; we will discuss the only *Getinv* and *Putinv* operations for saving and restoring the inventory structure.

How can you save a binary search tree's data in a file so that you can restore the tree later? Two different algorithms for saving and restoring a tree will be considered here. The first algorithm will restore a tree to its original shape. The second will restore a tree to a shape that is balanced.

Saving a tree and then restoring it to its original shape. The first algorithm restores a tree to exactly the same shape that it had before it was saved. For example, consider the tree in Figure 12-12a. If you save the tree in preorder, you get the sequence 60, 20, 10, 40, 30, 50, 70. If you then use *Insert* to insert these values into a tree that is initially empty, you will get the original tree. Figure 12-12b shows this sequence of *Insert* operations. Thus, the first algorithm appears in pseudocode as follows:

Figure 12-12

(a) A binary search tree;
(b) the sequence of *Insert*'s
that result in this tree

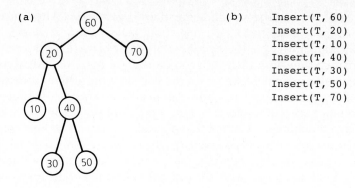

(a)

(b)
```
Insert(T, 60)
Insert(T, 20)
Insert(T, 10)
Insert(T, 40)
Insert(T, 30)
Insert(T, 50)
Insert(T, 70)
```

```
{ ALGORITHM 1 }

SAVE
{ Saves the tree in a file. }

    Write the data items to a file in the order of the
        tree's preorder traversal

RESTORE
{ Restores a tree in its original shape from a file. }

        Insert each item as it is read from the file into the
            tree by using the binary search tree Insert operation
```

Saving a tree and then restoring it to a balanced shape. Can you do
better than Algorithm 1? That is, do you necessarily want the restored tree
to have its original shape? Recall that you can organize a given set of data
items into binary search trees with many different shapes. All that is
required for the inventory program to work correctly is that the restored
tree have the binary search tree property. That is, the search key in any
node must be greater than all the search keys in its left subtree and less
than all of the search keys in its right subtree.

    Although the shape of a binary search tree has no effect whatsoever on
the correctness of the program, it will affect the efficiency of the tree operations, and efficiency is a concern. After all, that is why we are considering
a binary search tree implementation in the first place! What is needed is
an algorithm that will restore a tree to a shape that is balanced. It turns out
that this algorithm is surprisingly simple. In fact, you can even guarantee
that the restored tree will be of minimum height—a condition stronger
than balanced.

    To see how you can design an algorithm that will restore a tree to a
balanced shape, first recall that the whole purpose of a balanced binary
search tree is to facilitate a binary search of a structure that can have a
pointer-based implementation. That is, each node of the tree represents

*A balanced tree will increase the
program's efficiency*

the middle item of a subproblem that the binary search algorithm could encounter. This observation tells you exactly how to build a balanced binary search tree from a fixed set of data: Let the middle item be the root of the tree, and make the left and right subtrees into balanced binary search trees.

Consider, for example, a full tree with exactly $N = 2^h - 1$ nodes for some height h, as Figure 12-13 illustrates. Note that, as a consequence of the definition of a full tree, the root contains the item that is the exact middle of the data items, and the left and right subtrees are full trees of $2^{h-1} - 1$ nodes each (that is, half of $N - 1$ or, equivalently, N div 2, since N is odd). Thus, you can use the following recursive algorithm to restore a full tree T with N nodes, provided that you saved it in sorted order (by using an inorder traversal) and you either know or can determine N beforehand. It may be surprising that you can construct the tree directly by reading the sorted data from left to right from the file.

Building a full tree

```
Readfull(T, N)
{ Builds a full tree T from N sorted values in a file. }

  if N > 0
    then
    begin
      { construct the left subtree }
      Readfull(left subtree of T, N div 2)

      { get the root }
      read(item for root of T)

      { construct the right subtree }
      Readfull(right subtree of T, N div 2)
    end
```

This algorithm for restoring a full tree is simple, but what can you do if the tree to be restored is not full (that is, if it does not have $N = 2^h - 1$ nodes for some h)? The first thing that comes to mind is that the restored tree should be complete—full up to the last level, with the last level filled in from left to right. Actually, because you care only about minimizing the height of the restored tree, it does not matter where the nodes on the last level go, as Figure 12-14 shows.

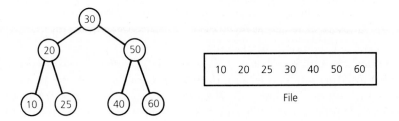

File

Figure 12-13

Building a full tree from a file

Figure 12-14

**A tree of minimum height
that is not complete**

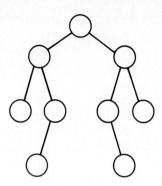

Procedure *Readfull* is essentially correct even if the tree is not full. However, you do have to be a bit careful when computing the sizes of the left and right subtrees. If *N* is odd, then both subtrees are of size *N* div 2, as before. (The root is automatically accounted for.) If *N* is even, however, you have to account for the root and the fact that one subtree will have one more node than the other. In this case, you can arbitrarily choose to put the extra node in the left subtree. The following algorithm makes these compensations:

Building a minimum-height tree

```
Readtree(T, N)
{ Builds a minimum-height tree T from N sorted values in a
  file. }

   if N > 0
      then
      begin
         { construct the left subtree }
         Readtree(left subtree of T, N div 2)

         { get the root }
         read(item for root of T)

         { construct the right subtree }
         Readtree(right subtree of T, (N-1) div 2)
      end
```

You should trace this algorithm and convince yourself that it is correct for both even and odd values of *N*.

   To summarize, you can easily restore a tree as a balanced binary search tree if the data is sorted—that is, produced from the inorder traversal—and you know the number *N* of nodes in the tree. You need *N* so that you can determine the middle item and, in turn, the number of nodes in the left and right subtrees. Knowing these numbers is a simple matter of counting nodes as you traverse the tree and then saving the number in a file that the restore operation can read. Thus, the second algorithm appears in pseudo-code as follows:

```
{ ALGORITHM 2}

SAVE
{ Saves the tree in a file. }

    Write the data items to a file in the order of the
        tree's inorder traversal, counting the number of
        nodes in the tree

    Save the size of the tree

RESTORE
{ Restores a tree from a file and balances it. }

    Read the size of the tree
    Execute the recursive Readtree procedure
```

So far, the primary differences between the revised program and the original program are as follows:

- The revised program uses identified ADT operations. This use further modularizes the program by separating the implementation of the data-management operations from that of the rest of the program. The implication is that if the underlying data structure changes, you need modify only the implementations of the ADT operations—behind the wall.

The program revisions so far

- The data structure that supports the inventory is a binary search tree instead of a sorted linked list. The intended outcome is to support the data-management operations more efficiently.

Adding New Features to the Program

The second major task in bringing the program up to date with the users' current needs is to add new features to the new ADT version of the program that was just described. The videocassette dealer has requested that the program help keep track of cassettes that need to be repaired. In particular, the new commands B, F, and P, which were described earlier, are desired. The addition of these new features requires the following seven subtasks:

I. Process command B (*procB*).
II. Process command F (*procF*).
III. Process command P (*procP*).
IV. Identify the ADT operations needed to support the repair queue.
V. Choose an implementation for the defined ADT.
VI. Modify the main program to accommodate the B, F, and P commands and the repair queue.
VII. Modify the H command (*procH*) to list the B, F, and P commands.

Seven tasks that the new features require

Subproblem I: Process command B.   Move a specified cassette from the inventory to the repair queue.

FIRST PASS

```
procB(invlist, repair)

  Read in a title argument
  Retrieve the inventory item

  { add the title to the repair queue }
  Compute the priority value for the cassette
  Add the title to the repair queue

  { update the inventory item }
  Decrement the have value by 1
  Replace the inventory item
```

Because you are modifying an existing program, many of the implementation details have already been worked out. Therefore, the second refinement can be fairly complete.

SECOND PASS

```
procB(invlist, repair)

  Prompt(titleprompt)
  Getstring(title, input)
  Retrieve(invlist, title, oneitem, success)
  if (not success) Cor (oneitem.have < 1)
     then write a message

     else
     begin
       { add the title to the repair queue }
       priority := oneitem.want/oneitem.have
       Add the title to the repair queue
       if the add is not successful (repair area is full)
          then write a message (send cassette out for repair)

       { update the inventory item }
       oneitem.have := oneitem.have − 1
       Replace(invlist, oneitem, success)
     end
```

Subproblem II: Process command F.   Identify the most-needed cassette and start repairing it.

```
procF(invlist, repair)

  if the repair queue is empty
     then write a message
```

```
    else remove from the repair queue the cassette with
         highest priority value
```

Subproblem III: Process command P.   Put a cassette into the inventory.

FIRST PASS

procP(invlist)

```
  Read a title argument
  Insert a new item if necessary
  Retrieve the item
  Add 1 to the have value (call Delwait if necessary)
  Replace the modified item
```

SECOND PASS

procP(invlist)

```
  Prompt(titleprompt)
  Getstring(title, input)
  Insert(invlist, title)
  Retrieve(invlist, title, oneitem, success)
  if oneitem.have < 0
     then Delwait(invlist, title, 1)
  oneitem.have := oneitem.have + 1
  Replace(invlist, oneitem, success)
```

Subproblem IV: Identify the ADT operations needed to support the repair queue.   So far, the following operations are necessary to support the previous subproblems:

```
Insert
{ Adds a title to the repair queue. }
```

```
Remove
{ Removes the title with highest priority value. }
```

```
IsEmpty
{ Determines whether the repair queue is empty. }
```

In addition to these operations, *Save* and *Restore* operations are necessary to save the repair queue along with the rest of the inventory at the end of the day. As was true for the table for the inventory structure, here a *Create* operation is unnecessary because the queue will be restored from a file. Notice that these operations define a variation of the classic priority queue.

Subproblem V: Choose an implementation for the repair queue.   The fixed maximum size of the repair queue suggests a heap implementation of the priority queue, which was presented earlier in this chapter. The following Pascal definitions describe the repair queue:

```
const   maxqueue = <desired size of repair queue>;

type    keytype = real;
        itemtype = record
            key : keytype;
            title : string
        end;

        pqueue = record
            Items : array[1..maxqueue] of itemtype;
            Last : 0..maxqueue
        end;

var     repair : pqueue;      { repair queue }
```

This implementation, in turn, suggests an extremely simple implementation for the *Save* and *Restore* operations. By defining a file of type *pqueue* as follows:

```
type   pqfile = file of pqueue;
var    repairfile : pqfile
```

you can save or restore a heap by using simple Pascal *write* or *read* statements. Thus, the pseudocode for the *Save* and *Restore* operations appears as follows:

```
Save(repair, repairfile)

    rewrite(repairfile)
    write(repairfile, repair)

Restore(repair, repairfile)

    reset(repairfile)
    read(repairfile, repair)
```

Subproblem VI: Modify the main program to accommodate the B, F, and P commands and the repair queue.   You simply make the following additions to the program:

- Add B, F, and P to the list of recognized command characters.
- Add calls to *procB*, *procF*, and *procP* in the *case* statement.
- Add calls to *Save* and *Restore*, along with *Putinv* and *Getinv*.

Subproblem VII: Modify the H command (*procH*) to list the B, F, and P commands.   The modification to *procH* is simply a matter of listing the three new commands in the help listing.

The implementation of the previous modifications is left as an exercise. The following guidelines summarize the approach to program modification used here.

Modifying or Enhancing a Program

1. When making changes to a program, it is best to make a few at a time. By maintaining a modular design, you can reduce a fairly large modification to a set of small and relatively simple modifications to isolated parts of the program.

2. You can add new features to a program by applying the same techniques that you use in an original design. These techniques include the use of top-down design and data abstraction.

3. If a program is properly modularized, it is a simple matter to replace implementations of specific algorithms or data structures with new implementations.

SUMMARY

1. A priority queue is a variation of the ADT table. Its operations allow you to retrieve and remove the item in the queue with the largest priority value.

2. A heap that uses an array-based representation of a complete binary tree is a good implementation of a priority queue when you know the maximum number of items that will be stored at any one time.

3. *Heapsort* like *Mergesort*, has very good worst-case and average-case behaviors, but neither algorithm is as good in the average case as *Quicksort*. *Heapsort* has an advantage over *Mergesort* in that it does not require a second array.

4. The case study illustrated that a modular program is easy to modify and expand. It is a simple matter to replace implementations of algorithms and data structures with new ones. You should add new features to a program in accordance with the principles of top-down design and data abstraction.

5. The case study developed a simple algorithm for saving an arbitrary binary search tree in a file and restoring it to a binary search tree of the minimum possible height.

COMMON PITFALLS / DEBUGGING

1. Although a heap is a good implementation of a priority queue, it is not appropriate for a table. Specifically, a heap does not support the sorted *Retrieve* and *Traverse* operations efficiently.

2. The array-based representation of a binary tree is appropriate only when the tree is complete and the maximum number of nodes is known.

SELF-TEST EXERCISES

1. Represent the full binary tree in Figure 12-13 with an array.

2. What complete binary tree does the array in Figure 12-15 represent? Is the tree a heap?

3. Is the full binary tree in Figure 12-13 a semiheap? Is it a heap?

4. Consider the heap in Figure 12-5. Draw the heap after you insert 12 and then remove 12.

5. What does the array that represents the priority queue *PQ* contain after the following sequence of operations?

   ```
   Create(PQ)
   Insert(PQ, 5)
   Insert(PQ, 9)
   Insert(PQ, 6)
   Insert(PQ, 7)
   Insert(PQ, 3)
   Insert(PQ, 4)
   Remove(PQ)
   Insert(PQ, 9)
   Insert(PQ, 2)
   Remove(PQ)
   ```

6. Execute *Buildheap* on the array in Figure 12-15.

7. a. What binary tree results when you execute *Readtree*, which the case study describes, with a file of the six integers 2, 4, 6, 8, 10, 12?
   b. Is the resulting tree's height a minimum? Is the tree complete? Is it full?

Figure 12-15

**Array for Self-Test Exercises
2 and 6, and Exercise 6**

5	1	2	8	6	10	3	9	4	7
1	2	3	4	5	6	7	8	9	10

EXERCISES

1. How does the order in which you insert into a heap two items that have the same priority value affect the order in which they will be deleted? What can you do if you need elements with equal priority value to be served on a first-come, first-served basis?

2. Prove that the root of a heap is the largest element in the tree.

3. The heap that this chapter described is called a **maxheap** because the largest element is at the root. (See Exercise 2.) This organization is appropriate because the *Remove* operation for the heap implementation of the priority queue deletes the element with the highest priority value. Imagine that the *Remove* operation deletes the element with the lowest priority value instead. You would then use a **minheap**. Convert the maxheap implementation to a minheap implementation.

4. Suppose that you want to maintain the index of the item with smallest priority value in a maxheap. That is, in addition to a *Removemax* operation, you might want to support a *Retrievemin* operation. How difficult will it be to maintain this index under *Insert* and *Removemax* operations?

5. Show that in the *BuildHeap* procedure of *Heapsort*, you can replace the *for* loop

   for i := N **downto** 1 **do**

   with

   for i := (N **div** 2) **downto** 1 **do**

6. Trace the action of *Heapsort* on the array in Figure 12-15.

7. As Figure 12-2 illustrates, you can use data structures other than a heap to implement the ADT priority queue.

   a. Write the Pascal declarations for a pointer-based implementation.
   b. Write the Pascal declarations for a binary search tree implementation.
   c. Implement the ADT's four operations first by using pointers and then by using a binary search tree.

8. Suppose that you want to implement a priority queue under the assumption that there are only 10 distinct priority values.

   a. Implement the priority queue as a heap of queues, as described in this chapter.
   b. Another solution uses an array of 10 queues, one for each priority value. Use this approach to implement the priority queue.

9. Implement the ADT operations *Insert*, *Retrieve*, *Replace*, *Traverse*, *Waitnames*, *Addwait*, *Delwait*, *Putinv*, and *Getinv* as described in the case study. Note that the restore operation is part of the procedure *Getinv* and that the save operation is part of the procedure *Putinv*. The following auxiliary procedures will be helpful:

    function *Find(invlist, title)*
    { *Finds title in the inventory list.*
      Precondition: *The inventory list invlist has been created.*
      Postcondition: *Returns a pointer to the title. However, if title is not found, returns nil.*
      Called by: *Retrieve, Replace, Waitnames, Addwait, Delwait.* }

    Putwait(stockitem, waitfile)
    { *Writes the wait list for an inventory item into a file.*
      Precondition: *The file associated with waitfile is open for output.*
      Postcondition: *The wait list for stockitem is written to waitfile, which remains open for further output.*
      Note: *The size of the wait list is the negative of the have value of the inventory item.*
      Called by: *Putinv.* }

    Getwait(stockitem, waitfile)
    { *Reads the wait list for an inventory item from waitfile.*
      Precondition: *The file associated with waitfile is open for output.*
      Postcondition: *The wait list is created from the data in waitfile, which remains open for output.*
      Note: *The wait list is a singly linked list. The size of the list is the negative of the have value of the inventory item.*
      Called by: *Getinv.* }

10. Implement the procedures *procB*, *procF*, and *procP*, as described in the case study.

11. Rewrite the original inventory program from Chapter 3 in terms of the ADT operations described in this chapter.

12. Suppose that you want to count the total number of copies sold of each title in the inventory. Which routines in the inventory program have to be modified? How might you use this sales information to determine a priority value for the repair queue?

13. If you modify the inventory structure for an existing inventory (for example, if you add a new data field to a stock item), the restore operation that executes at the very beginning of the program will not be valid. (Why?) Write a program that will convert all the files asso-

ciated with a saved inventory to a new format. Keep your conversion program as general as possible to account for future modifications to the inventory program.

14. Suppose that you know in advance that you tend to access a given item several times in a row before accessing a different item. You would like to take advantage of this knowledge to avoid searching for the same item repeatedly.

   In the case study, you were faced with this problem to some extent when you had to perform *Insert-Retrieve-Replace* sequences for a given title. More significantly, you faced the problem with the *Delwait* operation when you had to delete several names at a time from a wait list associated with an inventory item. Recall that we resolved this problem by redefining the *Delwait* operation to include an integer argument that specified the number of names to delete. Unfortunately, it will not always be easy to address this problem by redefining a simple ADT operation.

   Another way to address this problem is to add an extra bookkeeping component to your implementation. That is, you can maintain a last-accessed indicator that will always reference the last item that was accessed in the table (by any operation). Whenever you perform an operation that references the location of a specific table item, you can check the last-accessed item before starting the search.

   For example, if you use this scheme with a binary search tree implementation of a table, *T* becomes a record of the following type:

```
type   table = record
           root, lastaccessed : nodeptr
       end
```

Complete the implementation of the basic ADT table operations under this scheme. Note that the operations that are currently implemented recursively cause a problem: The initial call is passed a record (of type *table*) as an argument, but the recursive calls are passed a pointer (of type *nodeptr*). You can resolve this problem by adding a nonrecursive shell around the recursive procedures (as you did for the binary search in Chapter 5).

15. Suppose that you want to support deletion operations for two different search keys—for example, *DeleteN* (delete by name) and *DeleteS* (delete by Social Security number). Describe an efficient implementation.

16. Repeat Exercise 15, but instead organize one of the search keys with a binary search tree and the other with a sorted linked list.

17. Note that the inventory program assumes the existence of a previously saved inventory. How must you modify the program to start a new inventory from scratch?

*18. Recall the use of the repair queue in the inventory program. Imagine that you would like to adjust the priority of an item in the queue after each sale. For example, if a title that is on the repair queue sells out, then it becomes important to repair it more quickly.

   a.   How can you adjust a heap if a single priority value changes?
   b.   How can you link the two main structures (the inventory and the repair queue) together to make updates easy?

PROJECT

19.   Write an interactive program that will monitor the flow of patients in a large hospital. The program should account for patients checking in and out of the hospital and should allow access to information about a given patient. In addition, the program should manage the scheduling of three operating rooms. Doctors make a request that includes a patient's name and a priority value between 1 and 10 that reflects the urgency of the operation. Patients are chosen for the operating room by priority value, and patients with the same priority are served on a first-come, first-served basis. The basic control of the program should be with external commands (as in the inventory case studies). Although this problem is very similar in spirit to the inventory case studies that were developed previously, the object of this exercise is to design a program from scratch by incorporating the techniques of data abstraction into your problem-solving process. That is, as you design your solution, try to identify the essential operations (excuse the pun) that will be performed on the data, and only then choose an appropriate data structure for implementation. This approach will allow you to maintain the wall between the main part of the program and the implementations. An interesting exercise would be to recast this problem as an event-driven simulation.

IV

Advanced Techniques for the Management of Data

CHAPTER 13

Advanced Implementations of the ADT Table

PREVIEW   This chapter introduces several advanced implementations of the ADT table. The first topic discussed is balanced search trees. In Chapter 10 you saw that the efficiency of the binary search tree implementation of a table depends on the balance of the tree. This chapter discusses modifications to the basic binary search tree algorithms that ensure efficiency by dealing with the balance of the search tree.

This chapter then considers a completely different implementation of the ADT table that attempts to provide direct access to the data item with a given key value. In principle the algorithm, which is called hashing, calculates where to look for the data, given the search key value, rather than searching for it.

Finally, the problem of organizing data to support diverse kinds of operations simultaneously is considered. One such implementation uses doubly linked lists.

INTRODUCTION

This final part of the book looks at several fundamentally important techniques for managing data. These techniques can all be characterized as advanced methods for implementing the ADT table and its variants. Some of the techniques provide improvements to the table implementations that you have already studied, while others adopt approaches to implementing a table that are completely different from anything you have seen so far. In addition, the next chapter considers methods for implementing a table that, because of its great size, must reside on an external storage device such as a disk.

The following thumbnail description previews the major topics that you will encounter in the last two chapters.

- **Balanced search trees.** The high degree of efficiency with which a binary search tree can implement a table depends on the balance of the tree. This chapter examines a slightly different type of search tree, which remains balanced in all situations and thus can always be searched with efficiency comparable to a binary search.

- **Hashing.** Hashing is a technique that, for many applications, can provide a table implementation that is even more efficient than a search tree. Hashing locates a data item by calculating the location where it should be stored rather than by searching for it.

- **Data with multiple organizations.** Some problems require that you maintain data in different organizations simultaneously. For example, you may want to organize data according to a first in, first out order, but you may also require the data to be in sorted order. The problem is how to avoid storing the data more than once.

- **External methods.** All of the table implementations discussed so far assume that the table will reside in the computer's internal memory when the operations are performed. In many real-world applications, however, the size of a table greatly exceeds the amount of available internal memory. In such situations you must be able to operate on the table while it resides on an external device. Chapter 14 briefly examines the nature of external storage and describes methods for implementing a table that must be stored externally.

Most computer scientists would agree that these are fairly advanced topics. Indeed, aspects of this material are often encountered in graduate courses and even in research articles. Interestingly enough, however, while the details and mathematical analyses of these techniques are quite difficult, their underlying concepts are at a level compatible with this book. Therefore, by focusing on only the basic concepts, this last part of the book will present a useful introduction to material that is central to the efficient management of data.

BALANCED SEARCH TREES

Recall from the presentation of binary search trees in Chapter 10 that a tree's performance is related to its height. To perform the table operations *Retrieve*, *Insert*, and *Delete*, you must follow a path from the root of the tree down to the node that contains the desired item (or, in the case of the *Insert* operation, to the node that is to become the parent of the new item). At each node along the path, you compare the search value to the value in the node and determine which branch to follow next. Because the maximum number of nodes that can be on such a path is equal to the height of the tree, the maximum number of comparisons that the table operations can require is equal to this height.

You learned in Chapter 10 that a binary search tree of N items has a height that ranges from a maximum of N to a minimum of $\lceil \log_2(N + 1) \rceil$. As a consequence, the number of comparisons that could be required to locate a particular item in a binary search tree can be anywhere between that required by a sequential search of a linked list and that required by a binary search of an array. Because the motivation for developing the binary search tree implementation was to obtain a linked structure that could be searched with speed comparable to that of a binary search, it is

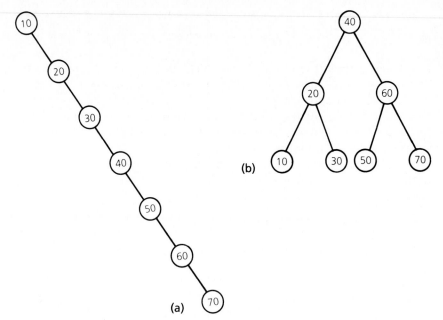

Figure 13-1

(a) A search tree of maximum height; (b) a search tree of minimum height

certainly critical that the most optimistic behavior of a binary search tree be realized.

Consider the factors that determine the height of a binary search tree. The algorithms developed in Chapter 10 that maintain a binary search tree make the height of the tree very sensitive to the order in which items are inserted and deleted. For example, consider a binary search tree that contains the items 10, 20, 30, 40, 50, 60, and 70. (For simplicity, assume that each item consists solely of an integer search key.) If you inserted the items into the tree in ascending order, as was just given, you would obtain a binary search tree of maximum height, as shown in Figure 13-1a. If, on the other hand, you inserted the items in the order 40, 20, 60, 10, 30, 50, 70, you would obtain a binary search tree of minimum height, as shown in Figure 13-1b.

The height of a binary search tree is sensitive to the order of insertions and deletions

Thus, if you use the algorithms in Chapter 10 to maintain a binary search tree, it is always possible that the tree will approach a linear shape and, as a consequence, that its behavior will be no better than that of a linked list. For this reason, it is desirable in many applications to use one of several variations of the basic binary search tree together with algorithms that can prevent the shape of the tree from degenerating. Two of the better-known variations are the **2-3 tree** and the AVL **tree**.

This chapter will consider 2-3 trees in greater detail than AVL trees. One reason for concentrating on the 2-3 tree is that a generalization of the 2-3 tree, the **B-tree**, is a data structure that you can use to implement a table that resides in external memory, such as on a disk. The B-tree is discussed in the next chapter.

2-3 TREES

A 2-3 tree retains its shape despite insertions and deletions

A 2-3 tree permits the number of children of an internal node to vary between two and three. As you will see, this feature allows a 2-3 tree to absorb insertions and deletions without a deterioration of the tree's shape. You can therefore search a 2-3 tree almost as efficiently as you can search a minimum-height binary search tree. However, it is far easier to maintain a 2-3 tree than a minimum-height binary search tree.

A **2-3 tree** is a tree in which each internal node (nonleaf) has either two or three children, and all leaves are at the same level. A recursive definition is as follows:

Recursive definition of a 2-3 tree

T is a 2-3 tree of height h if

1. T is empty (a 2-3 tree of height 0).

or

2. T is of the form

$$r$$
$$T_L \qquad T_R$$

where r is a node and T_L and T_R are both 2-3 trees, each of height $h - 1$. In this case T_L is called the **left subtree** and T_R is called the **right subtree**.

or

3. T is of the form

$$r$$
$$T_L \quad T_M \quad T_R$$

where r is a node and T_L, T_M, and T_R are 2-3 trees, each of height $h - 1$. In this case T_L is called the **left subtree**, T_M is called the **middle subtree**, and T_R is called the **right subtree**.

For example, Figure 13-2 shows a 2-3 tree of height 3.

A 2-3 tree is not necessarily binary

The most striking feature of a 2-3 tree is that it is not necessarily a binary tree, since a node can have three children. A 2-3 tree does, nevertheless, resemble a full binary tree. If a 2-3 tree contains no node that has three children—a situation that the definition permits—then it is in fact a full binary tree, because all its internal nodes would have two children and all its leaves would be at the same level. If, on the other hand, some of the internal nodes of a 2-3 tree do have three children, then the tree will contain more nodes than a full binary tree of the same height. Therefore, a 2-3 tree of height h always has at least as many nodes as a full binary tree of height h; that is, it always has at least $2^h - 1$ nodes. To put this another way,

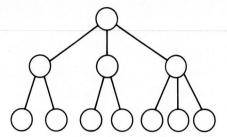

Figure 13-2
A 2-3 tree of height 3

a 2-3 tree with N nodes never has height greater than $\lceil \log_2(N + 1) \rceil$, the minimum height of a binary tree with N nodes.

A 2-3 tree with N nodes is never taller than a minimum-height binary search tree with N nodes

Given these observations, you should suspect that a 2-3 tree is a type of balanced tree that might be useful in implementing the ADT table, and this is indeed the case. You can use a **2-3 search tree**, defined as follows, to implement the ADT table.

A 2-3 search tree T is a 2-3 tree such that

A 2-3 search tree

1. T is empty.

or

2. T is of the form

$$r$$
$$T_L \qquad T_R$$

and node r contains one data item. In this case, the value of the search key in r must be greater than the value of each search key in the left subtree T_L and smaller than the value of each search key in the right subtree T_R. Also, T_L and T_R must each be a 2-3 search tree.

or

3. T is of the form

$$r$$
$$T_L \quad T_M \quad T_R$$

and node r contains two data items. In this case, the value of the smaller search key in r must be greater than the value of each search key in the left subtree T_L and smaller than the value of each search key in the middle subtree T_M. The value of the larger search key in r must be greater than the value of each search key in the middle subtree T_M and smaller than the value of each search key in the right subtree T_R. In addition, T_L, T_M, and T_R must each be a 2-3 search tree.

This definition sets the following rules for how you may place data items in the nodes of a 2-3 search tree:

***Rules for Placing Data Items in the Nodes
of a 2-3 Search Tree***

1. If a node has two children, it must contain a single data item.
2. If a node has three children, it must contain two data items.
3. If a node is a leaf, it may contain either one or two data items.

Items in a 2-3 search tree are ordered

In addition to these three structural rules, the definition of a 2-3 search tree implies that its values are ordered. For example, the tree in Figure 13-3 is a 2-3 search tree whose data items are each a single integer value. Notice that if the data items were records, nodes with three children would each have to accommodate two records.

Notice that the ordering of items in a 2-3 search tree is analogous to the ordering of values in a binary search tree. As you will see, this ordering allows you to search a 2-3 search tree efficiently for the item with a given

Searching a 2-3 search tree is efficient

search key. In fact, the `Retrieve` operation of a 2-3 search tree is quite similar to that of a binary search tree, as you can see from the following pseudocode:

```
Retrieve(T, X, getitem, success)
{ Retrieves into getitem from a nonempty table T the item
  with search key X. The operation fails if there is no such
  item. The flag success indicates whether the operation
  succeeded. }

   Let R be the root node of T

   { the item has been found }
   if X is in R then
       begin
           getitem := the appropriate item from R
           success := true
       end
```

Figure 13-3

A 2-3 search tree

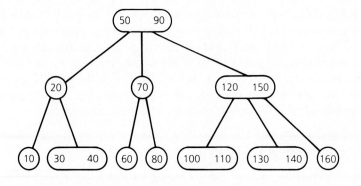

```
    { failure }
    else if R is a leaf then
        success := false

    { search the appropriate subtree }

    { R has two data items }
    else if R has two data items then
        begin
            if X < the smaller search key of R then
                Retrieve(left subtree, X, getitem, success)
            else if X < the larger search key of R then
                Retrieve(middle subtree, X, getitem, success)
            else Retrieve(right subtree, X, getitem, success)
        end

    { R has one data item }
    else
        begin
            if X < search key
                then Retrieve(left subtree, X, getitem, success)
                else Retrieve(right subtree, X, getitem, success)
        end
```

For the 2-3 search tree algorithms, it is convenient to define the degenerate case to be a leaf rather than an empty subtree. As a result, the algorithms must assume that they are not passed an empty tree as an argument. This change will allow you to avoid distracting implementation details. For example, you can traverse a 2-3 search tree in sorted order by performing the analogue of an inorder traversal:

```
Inorder(T)                                          Traversal in sorted order

    Let R be the root node of T

    if R is a leaf then
        Print the data item(s)

    { R has two data items }
    else if R has two data items then
        begin
            Inorder(left subtree)
            Print the first data item
            Inorder(middle subtree)
            Print the second data item
            Inorder(right subtree)
        end

    { R has one data item }
    else
```

```
begin
    Inorder(left subtree)
    Print the data item
    Inorder(right subtree)
end
```

Consider now what you have gained by using a 2-3 tree rather than a binary search tree. (Most people use the term "2-3 tree" to mean "2-3 search tree"; we will also.) Earlier you saw that a 2-3 tree with N nodes can have a height no greater than $\lceil \log_2(N + 1) \rceil$. Thus, a 2-3 tree that represents a given table of items always has a height less than or equal to that of the *best possible* binary search tree for that same table. This fact, plus the fact that no node in a 2-3 tree has more than two items, can be shown to imply that you can search a table represented by a 2-3 tree with approximately the same efficiency as that obtained if the table is represented by a binary search tree that is *as balanced as possible*.

From now on, the term "2-3 tree" will mean "2-3 search tree"

It may have surprised you that the efficiency of searching a 2-3 tree is not greater than the efficiency of searching a binary search tree. After all, by allowing the nodes of a 2-3 tree to have three children, it seems possible that the 2-3 tree could be shorter than the balanced binary search tree. Although the height of a 2-3 tree might indeed be less than that of a balanced binary search tree, this advantage is canceled out by the fact that, when searching a 2-3 tree for a given value X, at some nodes you must compare X with two search-key values instead of just one. In other words, although you might visit fewer nodes when searching a 2-3 tree, you might have to make more comparisons at each node. As a consequence, the number of comparisons required to search a 2-3 tree for a given value is *approximately equal* to the number of comparisons required to search a binary search tree that is as balanced as possible. This number is approximately $\log_2 N$, where N is the number of items in the table.

Searching a 2-3 tree is O(log₂N)

If you can search a 2-3 tree and a balanced binary search tree with approximately the same efficiency, why then should you use a 2-3 tree? The answer is that, although it is difficult to maintain the balance of a

Figure 13-4

(a) A balanced binary search tree; (b) a 2-3 tree with the same elements

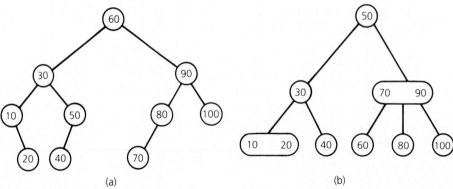

(a)   (b)

binary search tree in the face of *Insert* and *Delete* operations, it is relatively simple to maintain the shape of a 2-3 tree. For example, consider the two trees in Figure 13-4. The first tree is a binary search tree and the second is a 2-3 tree. Both trees contain the same data items. The binary search tree is as balanced as possible, and you can thus search both it and the 2-3 tree for a value with approximately the same efficiency. If, however, you perform a sequence of insertions on the binary search tree—by using the *Insert* algorithm of Chapter 10—the tree can quickly lose its balance, as Figure 13-5a indicates. As you will soon see, you can perform the same sequence of insertions on the 2-3 tree without a degradation in the tree's shape—it will retain its structure, as Figure 13-5b shows.

Notice that the new values (32 through 39) that were inserted into the binary search tree of Figure 13-4a appear along a single path in Figure 13-5a. The insertions increased the height of the binary search tree from 4 to 12—an increase of 8. On the other hand, the new values have been

Maintaining the shape of a 2-3 tree is relatively easy

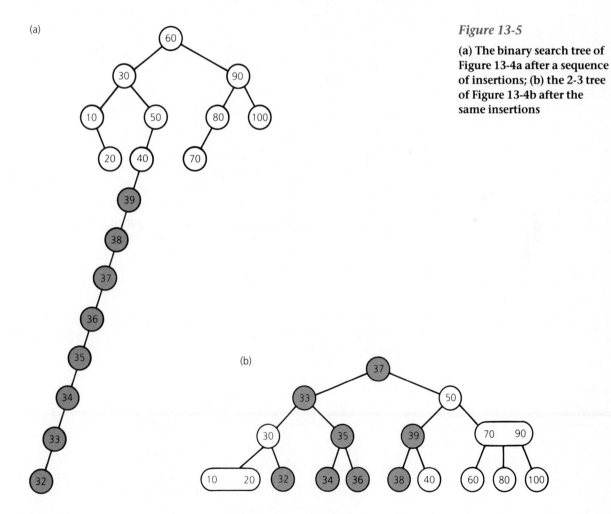

Figure 13-5

(a) The binary search tree of Figure 13-4a after a sequence of insertions; (b) the 2-3 tree of Figure 13-4b after the same insertions

spread throughout the 2-3 tree in Figure 13-5b. As a consequence, the height of the resulting tree is only 1 greater than the height of the original 2-3 tree in Figure 13-4b. The next section demonstrates these insertions into the original 2-3 tree.

Insertion into a 2-3 Tree

The fact that the nodes of a 2-3 tree can have either two or three children and can contain one or two values allows you to insert items into the tree while maintaining its shape. Suppose you were to make the same sequence of insertions that Figure 13-5a indicates into the 2-3 tree in Figure 13-4b. Consider an informal description of these insertions.

Insert 39. As is true with a binary search tree, the first step in inserting a node into a 2-3 tree is to locate the node at which the search for 39 would terminate. To do this, you can use the search strategy of the *Retrieve* algorithm given previously; an unsuccessful search will then always terminate at a leaf. With the tree in Figure 13-4b, the search for 39 terminates at the leaf <40>. Since this node contains only one item, you can simply insert the new item into this node. The result is the 2-3 tree in Figure 13-6.

Insert 38. In a manner similar to that just described, you would search the tree in Figure 13-6 for 38 and find that the search terminates at the node containing <39 40>. As a conceptual first step, you should place 38 in this node, as Figure 13-7a illustrates.

    The problem with this placement is that a node cannot contain three values. Suppose that you divide these three values into the smallest (38), middle (39), and largest (40) values. You can move the middle value (39) up to the node's parent *P* and separate the remaining values, 38 and 40, into two nodes that you attach to *P* as children, as Figure 13-7b indicates. Notice that since you chose to move up the middle value of <38 39 40>, the parent correctly separates the values of its children; that is, 38 is less than 39, which is less than 40. The result of the insertion is the 2-3 tree in Figure 13-7c.

Insert 37. The insertion of 37 into the tree in Figure 13-7c is easy because 37 belongs in a leaf that currently contains only one value, 38. The result of this insertion is the 2-3 tree in Figure 13-8.

Figure 13-6

Insert 39

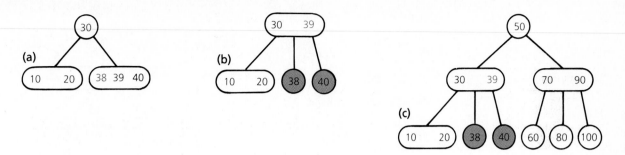

Figure 13-7

Insert 38

Insert 36. The search strategy determines that 36 belongs in the node <37 38>. Again, as a conceptual first step, place it there, as Figure 13-9a indicates.

Because the node <36 37 38> now contains three values, you divide it—as you did previously—into the smallest (36), middle (37), and largest (38) values. You then move the middle value (37) up to the node's parent *P*, and attach to *P*—as children—nodes that contain the smallest (36) and largest (38) values, as Figure 13-9b illustrates.

This time, however, you are not finished: You have a node <30 37 39> that contains three values and has four children. What should you do next? (*Hint*: Think recursively.) This situation is familiar, with the slight difference that the overcrowded node is not a leaf but rather has four children. As you did before, you divide the node into the smallest (30), middle (37), and largest (39) values, and then move the middle value up to the node's parent. Because you are splitting an internal node, you now must account for its four children; that is, what happens to nodes <10 20>, <36>, <38>, and <40>, which were the children of node <30 37 39>? The solution is to attach the left pair of children (nodes <10 20> and <36>) to the smallest value (30) and attach the right pair of children (nodes <38> and <40>) to the largest value (39), as shown in Figure 13-9c. The final result of this insertion is the 2-3 tree in Figure 13-9d.

Insert 35, 34, and 33. Each of these insertions is similar to those done previously. Figure 13-10 shows the tree after the three insertions.

Before performing the final insertion of the value 32, consider the 2-3 tree's insertion strategy.

Figure 13-8

Insert 37

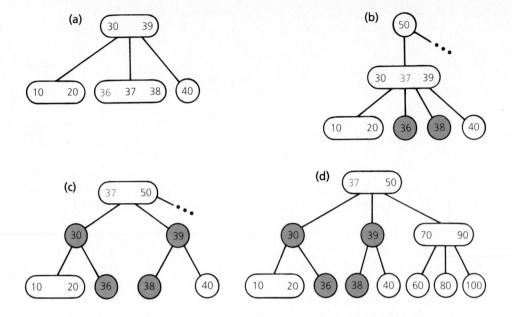

Figure 13-9

Insert 36

The insertion algorithm.   To insert the value X into a 2-3 tree, you first locate the leaf L at which the search for X would terminate. You insert the new value X into L, and if L now contains only two values, you are done. *Splitting a leaf*   However, if L contains three values, you must split it into two nodes, L_1 and L_2. L_1 gets the smallest of the three values in L, L_2 gets the largest of the values, and the middle value is moved up to L's parent P. Nodes L_1 and L_2 then become children of P, as Figure 13-11a illustrates.

If P now has only three children (and contains two values), you are finished. If, on the other hand, P now has four children (and contains three *Splitting an internal node*   values), you must split P. You split the internal node P as you just split the leaf L, except that you must also take care of P's four children. As Figure 13-11b illustrates, you split P into P_1 and P_2, give P_1 the smallest value in P, attach P's two leftmost children to P_1, move the middle value of P up to its

Figure 13-10

The tree after the insertion of 35, 34, and 33

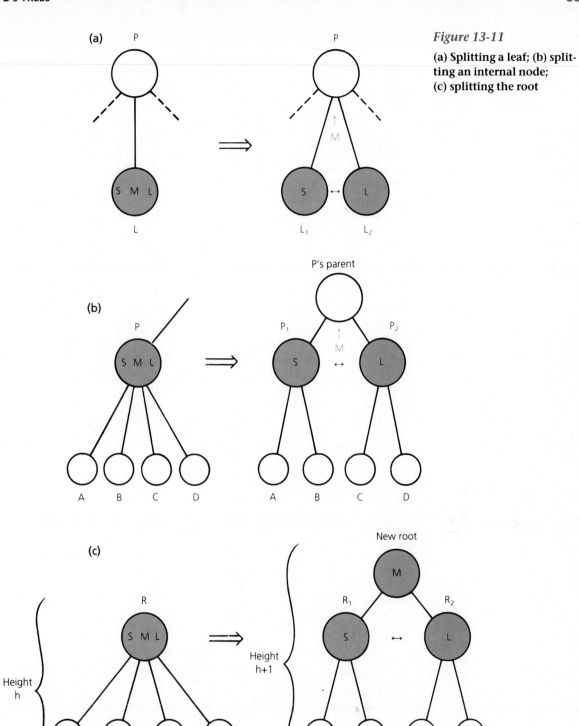

parent, give P_2 the largest value in P, and attach P's two rightmost children to P_2.

After this, the process of splitting a node and moving a value up to the parent continues recursively until a node is reached that had only one value before the insertion and thus has only two values after it takes on a new value. Notice in the previous sequence of insertions that the tree's height never increased from its original value of 3. In general, *an insertion will not result in an increase in the height of the tree* as long as there is at least one node on the path from the root to the leaf into which the new value is inserted that contains only one value. The insertion strategy of a 2-3 tree has thus postponed the growth of the tree's height much more effectively than did the strategy of a basic binary search tree.

When the height of a 2-3 tree does grow, it does so from the top. An increase in the height of a 2-3 tree will occur if every node on the path from the root of the tree to the leaf into which the new value is inserted contains two values. In this case, the recursive process of splitting a node and moving a value up to the node's parent will eventually reach the root

Splitting the root R, so you must now split R into R_1 and R_2 exactly as you would any other internal node. However, you must create a new node that contains the middle value of R and becomes the parent of R_1 and R_2. Thus, the new node is the new root of the tree, as Figure 13-11c illustrates.

The following algorithm summarizes the entire insertion strategy:

2-3 tree insertion algorithm

```
Insert(T, newitem)
{ Inserts newitem into table T implemented as a 2-3 tree. }

    Let X be the search key of newitem
    Locate the leaf L in which X belongs
    Add newitem to L

    if L now has three items
        then Split(L)

Split(N)
{ Splits node N which contains 3 items. Note that if N is
  internal, it has 4 children. }

    Let P be the parent of N
      (if N is the root, then create a new node P)

    Replace node N with two nodes, N₁ and N₂
    Give N₁ the item in N with the smallest search-key value
    Give N₂ the item in N with the largest search-key value

    if N is an internal node
        then
        begin
            N₁ becomes the parent of N's two leftmost children
            N₂ becomes the parent of N's two rightmost children
        end
```

```
Move up to P the item in N with the middle search key value

if P now has three items
    then Split(P)
```

Insert 32.   To be sure that you fully understand the insertion algorithm, go through the steps of inserting the value 32 into the 2-3 tree in Figure 13-10. The result should be the tree shown in Figure 13-5b.

Once again, compare this tree with the binary search tree in Figure 13-5a and notice the dramatic advantage of the 2-3 tree's insertion strategy.

Deletion from a 2-3 Tree

The deletion strategy for a 2-3 tree is the mirror image of its insertion strategy. Just as a 2-3 tree spreads insertions throughout the tree by splitting nodes when they become too full, it spreads deletions throughout the tree by merging nodes when they become empty. As an illustration of the 2-3 tree's delete strategy, consider the deletion of 70, 100, and 80 from the tree in Figure 13-4b.

Delete 70.   By searching the tree, you will discover that the value 70 is in the node <70 90>. Because you always want to begin the deletion process at a leaf, the first step is to swap the value 70 with its inorder successor— the value that follows it in the sorted order. Because 70 is the smaller of the two values in the node, its inorder successor (80) is the smallest value in the node's middle subtree. (The inorder successor of an item in an internal node will always be in a leaf.) After the swap, the tree appears as shown in Figure 13-12a. The value 80 is in a legal position of the search tree, because it is larger than all the values in its node's left subtree and smaller than all the values in its node's right subtree. The value 70, however, is not in a legal position, but this is of no concern, because the next step is to delete this value from the leaf.

Swap the value to be deleted with its inorder successor

In general, after you delete a value from a leaf, another value may remain in the leaf (because the leaf contained two values before the deletion). If this is the case, you are done, because a leaf of a 2-3 tree may contain a single value. In this example, however, once you delete 70 from the leaf, the node is left without a value, as Figure 13-12b indicates. You then delete the node by merging it with one of its siblings, as Figure 13-12c illustrates.

Empty node

At this point you see that the parent of the deleted node contains two values (80 and 90) but has two children (60 and 100). This situation is not allowed in a 2-3 tree (see rule 1). You can remedy the problem by moving the smaller value (80) down from the parent into the left child, as Figure 13-12d illustrates. The 2-3 tree that results from this deletion is shown in Figure 13-12e.

Moving a value down

Figure 13-12

Delete 70

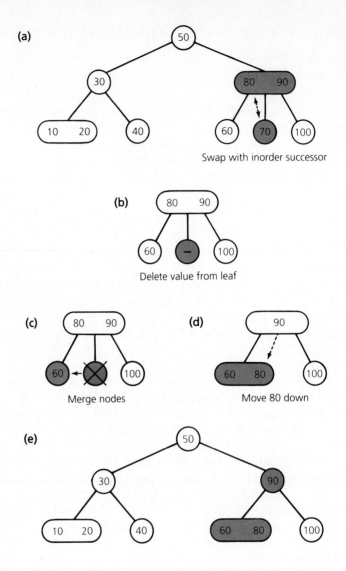

(a)

Swap with inorder successor

(b)

Delete value from leaf

(c)

Merge nodes

(d)

Move 80 down

(e)

Delete 100. The search strategy discovers that 100 is in the leaf <100> of the tree in Figure 13-12e. When you delete the value from this leaf, the node becomes empty, as Figure 13-13a indicates. In this case, however, no merging of nodes is required, because the sibling <60 80> can spare a value. That is, the sibling has two values, whereas a 2-3 tree requires only that it have at least one value. However, if you simply move the value 80 into the empty node—as Figure 13-13b illustrates—you find that the search-tree order is destroyed: The value in 90's right child is 80, whereas it should be *Redistribution of values*   greater than 90. The solution to this problem is to redistribute the values among the empty node, its sibling, and its parent. Here you can move the larger value (80) from the sibling into the parent and move the value 90

Figure 13-13

Delete 100

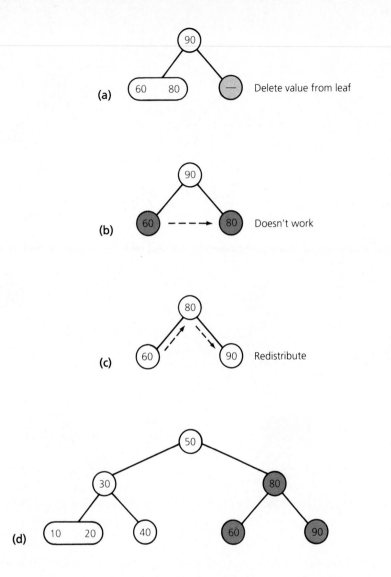

down from the parent into the node that had been empty, as Figure 13-13c shows. Notice that this distribution preserves the search-tree order, and you have thus completed the deletion. The resulting 2-3 tree is shown in Figure 13-13d.

Delete 80. The search strategy finds that 80 is in an internal node of the tree in Figure 13-13d. You must thus swap 80 with its inorder successor, 90, as Figure 13-14a illustrates. When you delete 80 from the leaf, the node becomes empty (see Figure 13-14b). Because the sibling of the empty node has only one value, you cannot redistribute as you did in the deletion of

Figure 13-14

Delete 80

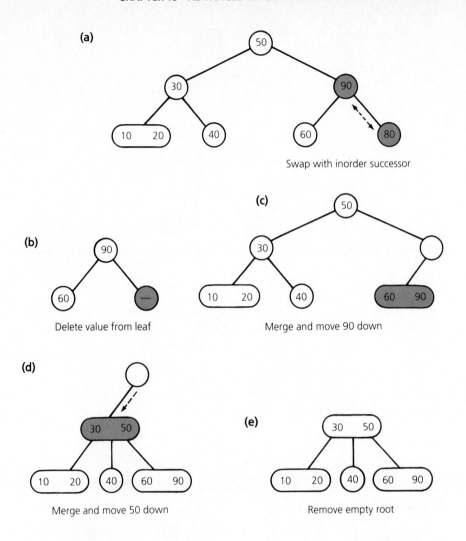

(a) Swap with inorder successor

(b) Delete value from leaf

(c) Merge and move 90 down

(d) Merge and move 50 down

(e) Remove empty root

100. Instead you must merge the nodes, bringing the value 90 down from the parent, as Figure 13-14c indicates.

You are not yet finished, however, because the parent now contains no values and has only one child. You must recursively apply the deletion strategy to this internal node without a value. First, you should check to see if the node's sibling can spare a value. Because the sibling <30> contains only the single value 30, you cannot redistribute—you must merge the nodes. The merging of two internal nodes is identical to the merging of leaves, except that the child <60 90> of the empty node must be adopted. Because the sibling of the empty node contains only one value (and hence can have only two children, as stated in rule 1), it can become the parent of <60 90> if you bring the value 50 down from the sibling's parent. The tree now appears as shown in Figure 13-14d. Note that this operation preserves the search property of the tree.

Now the parent of the merged nodes is left with no values and only a single child. You would usually simply apply the recursive deletion strategy to this node, but this is a special case because the node is the root. Because the root is empty and has only one child, you can simply delete it, allowing <30 50> to become the root of the tree, as Figure 13-14e illustrates. This deletion has thus caused the height of the tree to shrink by 1.

In contrast, consider the same deletions from the balanced binary search tree in Figure 13-4a. After deleting 70, 100, and 80 from the binary search tree, you are left with the tree in Figure 13-15. Notice that the deletions affected only one part of the tree, causing it to lose its balance. The left subtree has not been affected at all, and thus the overall height of the tree has not been diminished.

The deletion algorithm.   The deletion procedure is summarized as follows: To delete X from a 2-3 tree, you first locate the node N that contains it. If N is an internal node, you find X's inorder successor and swap it with X. As a result of the swap, the deletion always begins at a leaf L. If L contains a value in addition to X, you simply delete X from L and you are done. On the other hand, if L contains only X, then deleting it would leave L without a value. In this case you must perform some additional work to complete the deletion.

You first check the siblings of the now-empty leaf L. If a sibling has two values, you redistribute the values among L, L's sibling, and L's parent, as Figure 13-16a illustrates. If no sibling of L has two values, you merge L with an adjacent sibling and bring down a value from L's parent. (The sibling had only one value before, so it has room for another.) This case is shown in Figure 13-16b.

The merging of L may have caused its parent P to be left without a value and with only one child. If so, you recursively apply the deletion procedure to P. If P has a sibling with two values (and three children), you redistribute the values among P, the sibling, and P's parent. You also give P one of its sibling's children, as Figure 13-16c indicates.

If P has no sibling with two values, you merge P with a sibling (Figure 13-16d). You move a value down from the parent and let the sibling adopt P's one child. (At this point you know that the sibling previously had only

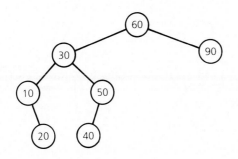

Figure 13-15

The binary search tree of Figure 13-4a after the deletion of 70, 100, and 80

Figure 13-16

**(a) Redistributing values;
(b) merging a leaf; (c) redistributing values and children; (d) merging internal nodes; (e) deleting the root**

(a)

(b)

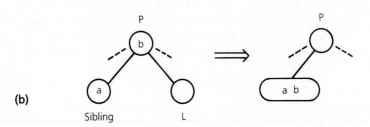

Merge and bring down value

(c)

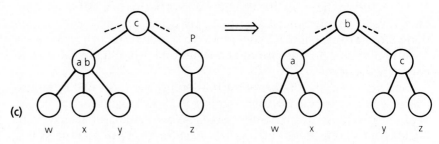

Redistribute between P, its parent, and its sibling

(d)

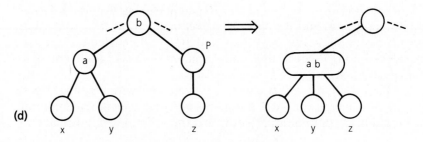

Merge and bring value down

(e)

Remove empty root

one value and two children.) If the merge causes *P*'s parent to be without a value, you recursively apply the deletion process to it.

If the merging continues so that the root of the tree is without a value (and has only one child), you simply delete the root. When this step occurs, the height of the tree is reduced by 1, as Figure 13-16e illustrates.

The following is a high-level statement of the algorithm for deleting from a 2-3 tree:

```
Delete(T, X, success)
{ Deletes from table T the item with search key X. The
  operation fails if there is no such item. The flag success
  indicates whether the operation succeeded. (The table is
  implemented as a 2-3 tree.) }

    Attempt to locate item I with search key X

    if I is present
       then
       begin
           Swap item I with its inorder successor, which will
              be in a leaf L

           { the deletion always begins at a leaf }
           Delete item I from leaf L

           if L now has no items
                then Fix(L)
           success := true
       end

       else success := false
```

2-3 tree deletion algorithm

```
Fix(N)
{ Completes the deletion when node N is empty. Note that if
  N is internal, then it has one child. }

    Let P be the parent of N--if N is the root, delete it and
       return
    if some sibling of N has two items
       then
       begin
           Distribute items appropriately among N, the
              sibling, and P

           if N is internal
                then move the appropriate child from sibling
                         to N
       end

       else    { must merge the node }
       begin
           Choose an adjacent sibling S of N
```

> *Bring the appropriate item down from P into S*
>
> **if** *N is internal*
>   **then** *move N's child to S*
>
> *Delete node N*
>
> **if** *P is now empty*
>   **then** *Fix(P)*
>
> **end**

The details of the Pascal implementation of the insertion and deletion algorithms for 2-3 trees, which were just developed, are rather involved. The implementation is left as a challenging programming project.

Concluding Remarks About 2-3 Trees

A 2-3 tree is always balanced

The algorithms for inserting into and deleting from a 2-3 tree have just been described. Given that a 2-3 tree is always balanced, you can search it in all situations with the logarithmic efficiency of a binary search.

You might be concerned that the insertion and deletion algorithms incur some overhead in the course of maintaining the 2-3 structure of the tree. That is, after the search strategy locates either the item or the position for the new item, the `Insert` and `Delete` algorithms sometimes have to perform extra work, such as splitting and merging nodes. However, this extra work is not a real concern. A rigorous mathematical analysis would show that the extra work required to maintain the structure of a 2-3 tree after an insertion or a deletion is not significant. In other words, when analyzing the efficiency of the `Insert` and `Delete` algorithms, it is suffi-

A 2-3 implementation of a table is $O(\log_2 N)$ for all table operations

cient to consider only the time required to locate the item (or the position for the insertion). As you have seen, this step is highly efficient in all situations. Thus, the 2-3 tree implementation of the ADT table is guaranteed to support all the table operations in logarithmic time.

Before leaving the topic of 2-3 trees, consider one final question: If a 2-3 tree is so good, are trees whose nodes can have more than three children even better? Recall that the advantage of a 2-3 tree is that it is a balanced structure that is easy to maintain, not that it might be shorter than a balanced binary search tree. The reduction in height of a 2-3 tree is offset by the fact that at each node the search algorithm may require more comparisons to determine which branch to take than those necessary if you use a balanced binary search tree. Similarly, although a tree whose nodes can

Allowing nodes with more than three children is counter-productive

have 100 children would be shorter than a 2-3 tree, its search algorithm would require more comparisons at each node in order to determine the appropriate subtree to search. It can be shown, in fact, that a binary search tree that is as balanced as possible minimizes the amount of work required to support the ADT table operations. The problem with a binary search tree is, of course, that its balance is difficult to maintain. A 2-3 tree is a compromise—although searching it may not be quite as efficient as searching a binary search tree of minimum height, it is relatively simple to maintain.

Allowing the nodes of a tree to have more than three children would be counterproductive because searches would require more comparisons.

Although searching a tree whose nodes have more than three children requires more comparisons than does searching a 2-3 tree, there are contexts in which you should use them. In the next chapter, for example, you will see that when a search tree is implemented in external storage, it is desirable to reduce its height, even at the expense of additional comparisons. The justification is that when a search tree is implemented externally, it is far more expensive to go from node to node than it is to perform comparisons with the data values in a node. As a consequence, you will want a search tree with the minimum possible height, even if it means that you will have to perform several comparisons at each node. Chapter 14 will discuss this point further and introduce an external search tree known as a **B-tree**.

AVL TREES

An **AVL tree**—named for its inventors, Adel'son-Vel'skii and Landis—is a balanced binary search tree. Recall that the heights of the left and right subtrees of any node in a balanced binary tree differ by no more than 1. Like a 2-3 tree, an AVL tree can be searched almost as efficiently as a minimum-height binary search tree. This section will simply introduce you to the notion of an AVL tree and leave the details for another course.

An AVL tree is a balanced binary search tree

It is, in fact, possible to rearrange any binary search tree to obtain a binary search tree with the minimum possible height, that is, $\lceil \log_2(N + 1) \rceil$ for a tree with N nodes. Recall, for example, the algorithm developed in the case study of Chapter 12. The algorithm starts with an arbitrary binary search tree, saves its values in a file, and then constructs a new binary search tree of minimum height that contains these same values. Although this approach was appropriate in the context of the inventory system (since the rebuilding was performed only once a day), it requires too much work to be performed every time an insertion or deletion leaves the tree unbalanced. The cost of repeatedly rebuilding the tree could very well outweigh the benefit of searching a tree of minimum height.

The AVL method is a compromise. It maintains a binary search tree with a height close to the minimum, but it is able to do so with far less work than would be necessary to keep the height of the tree exactly equal to the minimum. The basic strategy of the AVL method is to monitor the shape of the binary search tree. You insert or delete nodes just as you would for any binary search tree, but after each insertion or deletion, you check that the tree is still an AVL tree. That is, you determine whether any node in the tree has left and right subtrees that differ in height by more than 1. For example, suppose that the binary search tree in Figure 13-17a is the result of a sequence of insertions and deletions. The heights of the left and right

An AVL tree maintains a height close to the minimum

Figure 13-17

(a) An unbalanced binary search tree; (b) a balanced tree after rotation; (c) a balanced tree after insertion

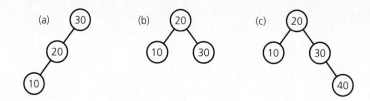

Rotations restore the balance

subtrees of the root 30 differ by 2. You can restore this tree's AVL property, that is, its balance, by rearranging its nodes. For instance, you can **rotate** the tree so that the node 20 becomes the root with left child 10 and right child 30, as in Figure 13-17b. Notice that you cannot arbitrarily rearrange the tree's nodes, because you must take care not to destroy the search tree's ordering property in the course of the rebalancing.

Rotations are not necessary after every insertion or deletion. For example, you can insert 40 into the AVL tree in Figure 13-17b and still have an AVL tree. (See Figure 13-17c.) However, when a rotation is necessary to restore a tree's AVL property, the rotation will be one of two possible types. We will demonstrate these rotations by example.

Suppose that you have the tree in Figure 13-18a after the insertion or deletion of a node. (Perhaps you obtained this tree by inserting 60 into an AVL tree.) An imbalance occurs at the node 20; that is, 20's left and right subtrees differ in height by more than 1. A **single rotation** to the left is necessary to obtain the balanced tree in Figure 13-18b: 40 becomes the parent of 20, which adopts 30 as its right child. Figure 13-19 shows this rotation in a more general form. It shows, for example, that before the rotation the left and right subtrees of the node 40 have heights h and $h + 1$, respectively. After the rotation the tree is balanced and, in this particular case, has decreased in height from $h + 3$ to $h + 2$. Figures 13-20 and 13-21 show examples of a single left rotation that restores a tree's balance but does not affect its height. Mirror images of the examples shown here will demonstrate single right rotations.

A more complex rotation may be necessary. For example, consider the tree in Figure 13-22a, which is the result of nodes being added to or deleted from an AVL tree. The left and right subtrees of 20 differ in height by more

Figure 13-18

(a) An unbalanced binary search tree; (b) a balanced tree after a single left rotation

(a)   (b)

Figure 13-19

Before and after a single left rotation that decreases the tree's height

Before rotation   After rotation

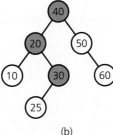

(a)   (b)

Figure 13-20

(a) An unbalanced binary search tree; (b) a balanced tree after a single left rotation

Figure 13-21

Before and after a single left rotation that does not affect the tree's height

Before rotation   After rotation

Figure 13-22

(a) Before; (b) during; and (c) after a double rotation

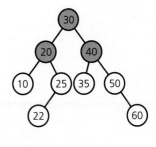

(a)   (b)   (c)

Figure 13-23

Before and after a double rotation that decreases the tree's height

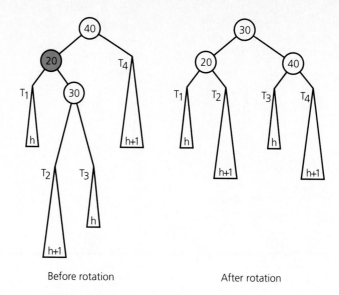

Before rotation   After rotation

than 1. A **double rotation** is necessary to restore this tree's balance. Figure 13-22b shows the result of a left rotation about 20, and Figure 13-22c shows the result of a right rotation about 40. Figure 13-23 illustrates this double rotation in a more general form. Mirror images of these figures provide examples of other possible double rotations.

It can be proven that the height of an AVL tree with N nodes will always be very close to the theoretical minimum of $\lceil \log_2(N + 1) \rceil$. The AVL tree is, therefore, one method for guaranteeing binary search-like efficiency in the search-tree implementation of a table.

HASHING

The binary search tree and its balanced variants, such as 2-3 and AVL trees, provide excellent implementations of the ADT table. They allow you to perform all the table operations quite efficiently. If, for example, a table contains 10,000 items, the operations *Retrieve*, *Insert*, and *Delete* each require approximately $\log_2 10{,}000 \approx 13$ steps. Though it may be difficult for you—given the applications that you have studied—to imagine situations in which the search-tree implementations are not adequate, nevertheless consider the question, is there an even better implementation of a table? One reason for asking this question is that, in the context of searching external storage, which will be discussed in the next chapter, even a small number of steps can actually require a good deal of time.

A radically different strategy is necessary to locate an item with fewer than the $\log_2 N$ comparisons that a search tree requires. Try to imagine a method that would allow you to locate (and insert or delete) an item virtually instantaneously.

Suppose that you have an array *T[0..N−1]*, with each array slot capable of holding a single table item. You also have a seemingly magical box called an "address calculator." Whenever you have a new item that you want to insert into the table, the address calculator will tell you where you should place it in the array. Figure 13-24 illustrates this scenario.

You thus can easily perform an insertion into the table as follows:

```
Insert(T, newitem)

    Tell the address calculator the search key of newitem

    Let i be the location where the address calculator
        tells you to put the new item

    T[i] := newitem
```

An insertion is performed virtually instantaneously.

You also use the address calculator for the *Retrieve* and *Delete* operations. If you want to retrieve the item whose search key is *X*, you simply ask the address calculator where it would tell you to insert such an item. Because you would have inserted the item earlier by using the *Insert* algorithm just given, if the desired item is present in the table, it would be in the array location that the address calculator specifies. Thus, the *Retrieve* operation appears as follows:

```
Retrieve(T, X, getitem, success)

    Let i be the location where the address calculator
        would put an item with search key X

    if T[i].key = X
        then
        begin
            getitem := T[i]
            success := true
```

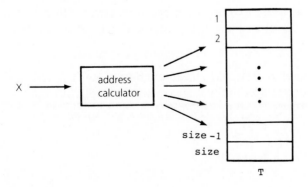

Figure 13-24

Address calculator

```
    end

    { the item is not in the table }
    else success := false
```

Similarly, the pseudocode for the `Delete` operation is

```
Delete(T, X, success)

    Let i be the location where the address calculator
        would put an item with search key X

    if T[i].key = X
        then
        begin
            Delete the item from T[i]
            success := true
        end

        { the item is not in the table }
        else success := false
```

It thus appears that you can perform the operations `Retrieve`, `Insert`, and `Delete` virtually instantaneously. You never have to search for an item; instead, you simply let the address calculator determine where the item should be. The amount of time required to carry out the operations depends only on how quickly the address calculator can perform this computation.

If you are to implement such a scheme, you must, of course, be able to construct an address calculator that can, with very little work, tell you where a given item should be. Address calculators are actually not as mysterious as they seem and, in fact, there are many well-known address calculators that can approximate the idealized behavior just described. Such an address calculator is usually referred to as a **hash function**. The scheme just described is an idealized description of a method known as **hashing**, and the array `T` is called the **hash table**.

To illustrate how a hash function works, suppose that the array `T` has locations `0..100`. Suppose also that the search keys of the table items are positive integers, such as employee ID numbers. Then a hash function h must take an arbitrary positive integer x and map it into an integer in the range `0..100`; that is, h is a function such that for any positive integer x,

A hash function $h(x) = n$, where n is an integer in the range `0..100`

Once you have selected a hash function h, the table operations are easy to write. For example in the `Retrieve` procedure, the step

```
    Let i be the location where the address calculator
        would put an item with search key X
```

is implemented simply as

```
    i := h(X)
```

The table operations appear to be virtually instantaneous. But is hashing really as good as it sounds? If it really were this good, there would have been little reason for developing all those other table implementations. Hashing would beat them hands down!

Why is hashing not quite as simple as it seems? You might first notice that since the hashing scheme stores the items in an array, it would appear to suffer from the familiar problems associated with a fixed-size implementation. Obviously, the hash table must be large enough to contain all items that you want to store. This requirement, however, is not the crux of the implementation's difficulty, for—as you will see later—there are ways to allow the table to grow dynamically. There is, however, a major pitfall in the implementation, even given the assumption that the number of items in the table will never exceed the size of the hash table.

Ideally, you want the hash function to map each *x* into a unique integer *n*. The hash function in the ideal situation is called a **perfect hash function.** In fact, it is possible to construct perfect hash functions, if you know all possible search keys. Although as you will see, this requirement is not impossible, you usually will not know the values of the search keys in advance.

A perfect hash function is possible if you know all the search keys

Typically, a hash function will map two or more search keys *x* and *y* into the *same* integer *n*. That is, the hash function tells you to store two or more items in the same array location $T[i]$. This occurrence is called a **collision.** Thus, even if fewer than 101 items are present in the hash table $T[0..100]$, *h* could very well tell you to place more than one item into the same array location. For example, if two items have search keys 123445678 and 123445779, and if

Typically, collisions occur

$$h(123445678) = h(123445779) = 44$$

then *h* will tell you to place the two items into the same array location, $T[44]$. That is, the search keys 123445678 and 123445779 have collided.

Even if the number of items that can be in the array at any one time is small, the only way to avoid collisions completely is for the hash table to be large enough so that each possible search-key value can have its own location. If, for example, Social Security numbers were the search keys, you would need an array location for each integer in the range 000000000 through 999999999. This situation would certainly require a good deal of storage! Because reserving vast amounts of storage is usually not practical, collision-resolution schemes are necessary to make hashing a viable method. Such resolution schemes usually require that the hash function place items evenly throughout the hash table.

To summarize, a typical hash function must

- Be easy and fast to compute
- Place items evenly throughout the hash table

Requirements for a hash function

In addition, the hash table must be large enough to allow the hash function to distribute the items evenly throughout the table.

Consider now several hash functions and collision-resolution schemes.

Hash Functions

It is sufficient to consider hash functions that operate on search keys that are arbitrary integers. Why? If a search key is not an integer, there are simple ways to map the search key into an integer, which you then hash. If, for example, the search key is a character string—such as a name—you could convert it into an integer in one of several ways. The simplest way is first to assign each character in the string an integer value. For example, you could use the character's ASCII value—by using Pascal's *ord* function—or simply assign arbitrary values such as A = 1, B = 2, and so on. You could then add the values of the characters in the string. For example, you could convert the word "THE" either into the integer 2,085 by adding the ASCII values of the letters T, H, and E or into the integer 33 because T = 20, H = 8, and E = 5, and 20 + 8 + 5 = 33.

There are many ways to convert an arbitrary integer x into an integer within a certain range, such as 0 through 100. Here are several simple hash functions that assume that the search keys are positive integers.

Selecting digits.   Suppose that your search key is the nine-digit employee ID number 001364825. You could select the fourth digit and the last digit to obtain 35 as the index to the hash table. That is,

$$h(001364825) = 35 \quad \{ \text{select the fourth and last digits} \}$$

Therefore, you would store the item whose search key is 001364825 in *T[35]*.

You do need to be careful about which digits you choose in a particular situation. For example, the first three digits of a Social Security number are based on geography. If you select only these digits, you will map all people from the same state into the same location of the hash table.

Digit-selection hash functions are simple and fast, but generally they do not evenly distribute the items in the hash table.

Folding.   One way to improve upon the previous method of selecting digits is to add the digits. For example, you can add all the digits in 001364825 to obtain

$$0 + 0 + 1 + 3 + 6 + 4 + 8 + 2 + 5 = 29 \qquad \{ \text{add the digits} \}$$

Therefore, you would store the item whose search key is 001364825 in *T[29]*. Notice that if you add all digits from a nine-digit search key,

$$0 \leq h(\text{search key}) \leq 81$$

That is, you would use only *T[0]* through *T[81]* of the hash table. To change this situation or to increase the size of the hash table, you can group the digits in the search key and add the groups. For example, you could form three groups of three digits from the search key 001364825 and add them as follows:

$$001 + 364 + 825 = 1,190$$

For this hash function,

$$0 \leqslant h(\text{search key}) \leqslant 3 * 999 = 2{,}997$$

Clearly, if 2,997 is larger than the size of the hash table that you want, you can alter the groups that you choose. Perhaps not as obvious is that you can apply more than one hash function to a search key. For example, you could select some of the digits from the search key before adding them, or you could either select digits from the previous result 2,997 or apply folding to it once again by adding 29 and 97.

Applying more than one hash function to a single search key

Dividing (modular arithmetic). Modular arithmetic provides a simple and effective hash function. For example, consider the function

$$h(x) = x \bmod \textit{TableSize}$$

where the hash table T has *TableSize* elements. In particular, $h(x) = x \bmod 101$ maps any integer x into the range 0 through 100. This hash function maps 001364825, for example, into array location 12 (001364825 mod 101).

There are many x's that map into $T[0]$, because $x \bmod \textit{TableSize} = 0$, many x's that map into $T[1]$ because $x \bmod \textit{TableSize} = 1$, and so on. However, you can distribute the table items evenly over all of T—thus reducing collisions—by choosing a prime number as *TableSize*. For instance, 101 in the previous example is prime.

The table size should be prime

Resolving Collisions

Consider the problems caused by a collision. Suppose that you want to insert an item whose search key is 123445678 into the hash table T, as was described previously. If you apply the hash function $h(x) = x \bmod 101$ to 123445678, you will find that you should place the new item in $T[44]$. Suppose, however, that $T[44]$ already contains an item whose search key is 123445779, as Figure 13-25 illustrates. That is, earlier you had placed 123445779 into $T[44]$ because 123445779 mod 101 equals 44. The question is, what do you do with the new item? You certainly do not want to disallow the insertion on the grounds that the table is full: You could have a collision even when inserting into a table containing only a single item!

There are two general approaches to collision resolution. One approach allocates another location *within* the hash table to the new item. A second approach changes the structure of the hash table so that each location $T[i]$ can accommodate more than one item. The four collision-resolution schemes that appear next exemplify these two approaches.

Two approaches to collision resolution

Linear probing. Some commonly used methods for resolving collisions are based on the notion of **open addressing.** That is, during an attempt to insert a new item into a table, if the hash function indicates a location in the hash table that is already occupied, you **probe** for some other empty, or *open*, location in which to place the item. The concern, of course, is that you must be able to find a table item efficiently after you have inserted it. That is, the insertion-probe sequence must be reproducible by the `Delete` and `Retrieve` operations.

The difference between the various open addressing schemes is the method used to probe for an empty location. One common scheme is called **linear probing.** In this scheme, you search the hash table sequentially, starting from the original hash location. More specifically, if `T[h(key)]` is occupied, you check `T[h(key) + 1]`, `T[h(key) + 2]`, and so on until you find an available location. Typically you *wrap around* from the last table location to the first table location if necessary.

Begin at the hash location and search the table sequentially

In the absence of deletions, it is straightforward to implement the `Retrieve` operation under this scheme. You need only follow the same probe sequence that the `Insert` operation used until you find the item you are searching for; reach an empty location, which indicates that the item is not present; or visit every table location.

The presence of deletions, however, adds a slight complication. The `Delete` operation itself is no problem. You merely find the desired item, as in the `Retrieve` operation, and delete it, making the location empty. But what happens to the `Retrieve` operation after deletions? The new empty locations that `Delete` created along a probe sequence could cause the `Retrieve` operation to stop prematurely, incorrectly indicating a failure. You can resolve this problem by allowing a table location to be in one of three states: *occupied* (currently in use), *empty* (has not been used), or *deleted* (was once occupied, but is now available). You then modify the `Retrieve` operation to continue probing when it encounters a location in the deleted state. Similarly, you modify the `Insert` operation to insert into either empty or deleted locations.

Three states: occupied, empty, deleted

Efficiency

How efficient is linear probing? As the hash table fills, the chance of collision increases. As collisions increase, the probe sequences increase in

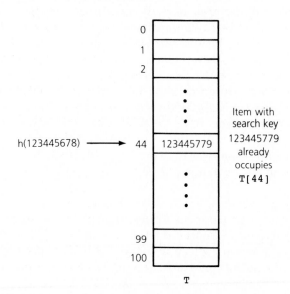

Figure 13-25

A collision

length, causing increased search times. An unsuccessful search requires more time in general than a successful search. For example, for a table that is two-thirds full, an average unsuccessful search might require at most five comparisons, or probes, while an average successful search might require at most two comparisons. To maintain efficiency, it is important to prevent the hash table from filling up.

One of the problems with the linear-probing scheme is that table items tend to **cluster** together in the hash table. That is, one part of the table might be quite dense, even though another part has relatively few items. It can be shown that this form of clustering is detrimental to the overall efficiency of hashing because it causes long probe searches.

Clustering

Double hashing. Double hashing, which is a second open-addressing scheme, drastically reduces clustering. Notice that the **probe sequence** that linear probing uses is *key independent*. That is, linear probing inspects the table locations sequentially no matter what the hash key is. Double hashing defines *key-dependent* probe sequences. In this scheme the probe sequence still searches the table in a linear order, but a second hash function determines the size of the steps taken. For example, let h_1 and h_2 be the primary and secondary hash functions defined as follows:

$$h_1(key) = key \bmod 11$$
$$h_2(key) = key \bmod 7$$

A hash address and a step size determine the probe sequence

If $key = 25$, then h_1 indicates that *key* hashes to table location 3 (25 mod 11), and h_2 indicates that the probe sequence should take steps of size 4 (25 mod 7). In other words, the probe sequence will be 3, 7, 0 (wraps around), 4, 8, 1 (wraps around), 5, 9, 2, 6, 10, 3. On the other hand, if $key = 9$, then h_1 indicates that *key* hashes to table location 9 (9 mod 11), and h_2 indicates that the probe sequence should take steps of size 2 (9 mod 7), and so the probe sequence would be 9, 0, 2, 4, 6, 8, 10, 1, 3, 5, 7, 9.

Note that each of these probe sequences visits *all* the table locations. This phenomenon always occurs if the size of the table and the size of the probe step are relatively prime, that is, if their greatest common divisor is 1. Because the size of a hash table is commonly a prime number, it will be relatively prime to all step sizes.

On the average, double hashing requires fewer comparisons than linear probing. As a result, you can use a smaller hash table for double hashing than you can for linear probing. However, because they are open-addressing schemes, both linear probing and double hashing suffer when you are unable to predict the number of insertions and deletions that will occur. If your hash table is too small, it will fill up, and search efficiency will decrease.

Buckets. Another method commonly used to resolve a collision is to change the structure of the array T—the hash table—so that it can accommodate more than one item in the same location. You could, for example, change T so that each location T[i] is itself an array—called a **bucket**—capable of holding B items. The problem with this approach, of course, is

Accommodate more than one item per hash-table location

Figure 13-26

Separate chaining

Each Table location is a linked list

choosing B. If B is too small, you will only have postponed the problem of collisions until $B + 1$ items map into some array location. If you attempt to make B large enough so that each array location can accommodate the largest number of items that might map into it, you are likely to waste a good deal of storage.

Each hash-table location is a linked list

Separate chaining.   An approach that is better than using buckets is to design the hash table as an array of linked lists. In this collision-resolution method, known as **separate chaining**, each entry $T[i]$ is a pointer to a linked list—the **chain**—of items that the hash function has mapped into location i, as Figure 13-26 illustrates. The following Pascal statements describe such a hash table:

```
const   size = 100;
type    keytype = <desired type of search key>;
        itemtype = record
            key : keytype;
            <... and possibly other fields>
        end;

        ptr = ^node;
        node = record
            item : itemtype;
            next : ptr
        end;

        hashtable = array[0..size] of ptr;
var     T : hashtable;
```

When you insert a new item into the table, you simply place it at the beginning of the linked list that the hash function indicates. The following pseudocode describes the insertion algorithm for a linked hash table:

```
Insert(T, newitem)

    Let X be the search key of newitem
    i := h(X)
    new(p)
    p^.item := newitem
    p^.next := T[i]
    T[i] := p
```

When you want to retrieve an item, you search the linked list that the hash function indicates. The following pseudocode describes the retrieval algorithm:

```
Retrieve(T, X, getitem, success)

    i := h(X)
    p:= T[i]

    while (p <> nil) Cand (p^.key <> X) do
       p := p^.next

    if p <> nil
        then
        begin
            getitem := p^.item
            success := true
        end

    else success := false
```

The Delete algorithm is very similar to Retrieve and is left as an exercise.

Separate chaining is thus a successful method of resolving collisions. Notice also that the total size of the table is now dynamic, since each linked list can be as long as necessary. This observation leads to the next question: How efficient are the table operations under this scheme? While the Insert operation is still instantaneous, the Retrieve and Delete operations are not. They require a search of the linked list of items.

Separate chaining successfully resolves collisions

To analyze the efficiency of the Retrieve and Delete operations under the separate-chaining approach, you must estimate the length of the linked lists that you need to search. If your array T has TableSize entries—that is, if it is an array T[0..TableSize-1]—and there are N items in the table, then the average length of a linked list is N/TableSize. In choosing the size of the array T, you should estimate the largest possible N and select an array size TableSize so that N/TableSize is small. For

Efficiency

example, you could select *TableSize* to be near *N*, the expected maximum number of items in the table. If you are successful at this selection, it is likely that the linked lists that *Retrieve* and *Delete* must search will be quite short.

Even if it is likely that the linked lists are short, you still should ask, in the worst case, how long can a list be? If you seriously underestimate the maximum size of the table or if you are extremely unlucky and most of the table items happen to hash into the same location, then the number of items on a linked list could be quite large. (Shortly you will see circumstances that might make you appear to be unlucky.) In fact, in the worst case, all *N* items in the table could be on the same linked list!

As you can see, the time that a *Retrieve* or *Delete* operation requires can range between almost nothing—if the linked list to be searched has only one or two items on it—to the time required to search a linked list that contains all the items in the table, if all the items hashed into the same location. Therefore, although the hashing implementation might often be faster than a search-tree implementation, in the worst case it can be much slower. If so, you should either change your hashing function or increase the size of the hash table; you should not use complex collison-resolution schemes.

Table Traversal: An Operation That Hashing Does Not Support Well

For many applications, hashing provides the most efficient implementation of the ADT table. There is, however, one important table operation not yet considered that the hashing schemes do not support well at all: the operation of traversing the table in *sorted order*. A hash function scatters

Items hashed into T[i] and T[i+1] have no ordering relationship

the items randomly throughout the array, so that there is no ordering relationship between the search keys that hash into *T[i]* and those that hash into *T[i+1]*. (In fact, as you will see, a good hash function necessarily scatters the search keys as randomly as possible.) As a consequence, if you must traverse the table in sorted order—for example, to print it out—you would first have to perform a sort on the items. If this operation were required frequently, hashing would be a far less attractive implementation than a search tree.

Traversing a table in sorted order is really just one example of a whole class of operations that hashing does not support well. Many similar operations that you often wish to perform on a table require the items to be ordered. For example, consider an operation that must find the table item with the smallest or largest value in its search key. If you use a search-tree implementation, then these items are in the leftmost and rightmost nodes of the tree, respectively. If you use a hashing implementation, however, there is no way of knowing where these items are—you would have to search the entire table. A similar type of operation is a **range query**, which requires that you retrieve all items that have a search key that falls into a given range of values. For example, you might want to retrieve all of the items whose search keys are in the range 129 to 755. This task is relatively easy to perform by using a binary search tree (see Exercise 1), but if you use hashing, there is no efficient way to answer the range query.

In general, if an application requires any of these ordered operations, you should probably use a search tree. Although hashing does support the `Retrieve`, `Insert`, and `Delete` operations somewhat more efficiently than does a balanced search tree, the balanced search tree supports these operations so efficiently itself that, in most contexts, the difference in speed for these operations is negligible (whereas the advantage of the search tree over hashing for the ordered operations is significant). In the context of external storage, however, the story is different. For data that is stored externally, the difference in speed between hashing's implementation of `Retrieve` and a search tree's implementation may well be significant. As you will see in Chapter 14, in an external setting it is not uncommon to see a hashing implementation used to support the `Retrieve` operation and a search-tree implementation used simultaneously to support the ordered operations.

Hashing versus balanced search trees

What Constitutes a Good Hash Function?

Before concluding this introduction to hashing, consider in more detail the issue of choosing a hash function to perform the address calculations for a given application. A great deal has been written on this subject, most of which is beyond the mathematical level of this book. However, this section will present a brief summary of the major concerns.

- **A hash function should be easy and fast to compute.** If a hashing scheme is to perform table operations almost instantaneously, you certainly must be able to calculate the hash function rapidly. Most of the common hash functions require only a single division (like the modulo function), a single multiplication, or some kind of "bit-level" operation on the internal representation of the search key. In all these cases, the requirement that the hash function be easy and fast to compute is satisfied.

- **A hash function should evenly scatter the data throughout the hash table.** No matter what hash function you use, there is in general no way to avoid collisions entirely. (Of course, a perfect hashing function avoids collisions.) For example, to achieve the best performance from a separate chaining scheme, each entry `T[i]` should contain approximately the same number of items on its chain; that is, each chain should contain approximately `N/TableSize` items (and thus no chain should contain significantly more than `N/TableSize` items). To accomplish this goal, your hash function should scatter the search keys evenly throughout the hash table.

You cannot avoid collisions entirely

There are two issues to consider with regard to how evenly a hash function scatters the search keys.

- **How well does the hash function scatter random data?** If every search-key value is equally likely, will the hash function scatter the search keys evenly? For example, consider the following scheme for hashing nine-digit ID numbers:

  $T[0..39]$ is the hash table, and
  the hash function is $h(x) = $ (first two digits of x) mod 40

  The question is, given the assumption that all employee ID numbers are equally likely, does a given ID number x have equal probability of hashing into any one of the 40 array locations? For this hash function, the answer is no. Notice that there are three different ID *prefixes*—that is, the first two digits of an ID number—that map into each array location $0..19$, while there are only two different prefixes that map into each array location $20..39$. For example, ID numbers that start with 19, 59, and 99 map into $T[19]$, while only ID numbers that start with 20 and 60 map into $T[20]$. Given that all ID numbers are equally likely—and thus that all prefixes 00 through 99 are equally likely—a given ID number is 50 percent more likely to hash into one of the locations $0..19$ than it is to hash into one of the locations $20..39$. As a result, each array location $0..19$ would contain, on average, 50 percent more items than each location $20..39$.

  Thus, the hash function

A function that does not scatter random data evenly

  $h(x) = $ (first two digits of x) mod 40

  does not scatter random data evenly throughout the array $T[0..39]$. On the other hand, it can be shown that the hash function

A function that does scatter random data evenly

  $h(x) = x \bmod 101$

  does, in fact, scatter random data evenly throughout the array $T[0..100]$.

- **How well does the hash function scatter nonrandom data?** Even if a hash function scatters random data evenly, it may have trouble with nonrandom data. In general, no matter what hash function you select, it is always possible that the data will have some unlucky pattern that will result in uneven scattering. Although there is no way to guarantee that a hash function will scatter all data evenly, there are hashing techniques that can greatly increase the likelihood of uniformity.

  As an example, consider the following scheme:

  $T[0..99]$ is the hash table, and
  the hash function is $h(x) = $ first two digits of x

If every ID number is equally likely, then it is apparent that *h* will scatter the search keys evenly throughout the array. But what if every ID number is not equally likely? A company might assign employee ID's according to department. For instance, suppose that ID numbers are assigned according to the following convention:

10xxxxx   Sales

20xxxxx   Customer Relations

. . .

90xxxxx   Data Processing

Under this assignment, only 9 out of the 100 array locations would contain any items at all. Further, those locations corresponding to the largest departments (Sales, for example, which corresponds to $T[10]$) would contain more items than those locations corresponding to the smallest departments. This scheme certainly does not scatter the data evenly. There is a large body of theoretical results describing types of hash functions that you should use to guard against various types of patterns in the data. These results are really in the province of more advanced courses, but two general principles can be noted here:

1. The calculation of the hash function should *involve the entire search key*. Thus, for example, computing a modulo of the entire ID number is much safer than using only its first two digits.

2. If a hash function uses modulo arithmetic, *the base should be prime;* that is, if *h* is of the form

    $h(x) = x \bmod TableSize$

    then *TableSize* should be a prime number. This selection of *TableSize* is a safeguard against many subtle kinds of patterns in the data (for example, search keys whose digits are likely to be multiples of one another). Although each application can have its own particular kind of patterns and thus should be analyzed on an individual basis, choosing *TableSize* to be prime is an easy way to safeguard against some common types of patterns in the data.

General requirements of a hash function

To summarize, hashing is a table implementation that in many cases can support the operations `Retrieve`, `Insert`, and `Delete` even faster than a balanced search tree. Although hashing does not efficiently support operations that require the table items to be ordered—for example, traversing the table in sorted order—it is nevertheless the most efficient table implementation for many types of applications. The next chapter uses hashing in a discussion of external searching techniques.

DATA WITH MULTIPLE ORGANIZATIONS

Many applications require a data organization that simultaneously supports several different data-management tasks. As a simple example, suppose that you must maintain a waiting list of customers, that is, a queue of customer records. Suppose that in addition to requiring the standard queue operations *Isempty*, *Add*, *Remove*, and *QueueFront*, the application frequently requires a listing of the records of the customers in the queue. This listing is more useful if the records appear sorted by customer name. You thus need a *Traverse* operation that visits the customer records in sorted order.

This scenario presents an interesting problem. If you simply store the customer records in a queue, they will not, in general, be sorted by name. If, on the other hand, you simply store the records in sorted order, you will not be able to perform the queue operations; that is, you will be unable to process the customers on a first-come, first-served basis. Apparently, this problem requires you to organize the data in two different ways.

One solution is to maintain two independent data structures, one organized to support the sorted traversal and the other organized to support the queue operations. Figure 13-27 depicts a sorted linked list of customer records and a pointer-based implementation of the queue. The pointer-based data structures are a good choice because there is no good estimate of the maximum number of customer records that must be stored.

Several independent data structures waste space

One obvious disadvantage of this scheme is the space that it requires to store two copies of each customer record. In addition, not all of the required operations are supported as efficiently as possible. How well does this scheme support the required operations?

Figure 13-27

Independent data structures: (a) a sorted linked list; (b) a pointer-based queue

The operations that require you only to *retrieve* data—sorted *Traverse* and *QueueFront*—are easy to perform. You can obtain a sorted listing of customer records by traversing the sorted linked list, and you can perform the *QueueFront* operation by inspecting the record at the front of the

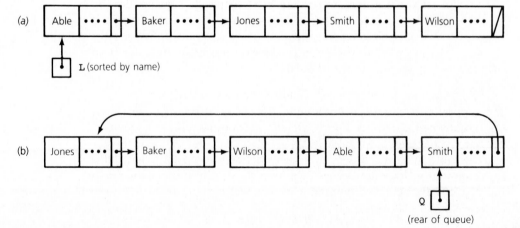

queue. The operations *Add* and *Remove* are, however, more difficult to perform because they must *modify* the data.

The *Add* operation has two steps:

1. Insert a copy of the new customer record at the rear of the queue. This step requires only a few pointer changes.

2. Insert a copy of the new customer record into its proper position in the sorted linked list. This step requires a traversal of the sorted linked list.

Similarly, the *Remove* operation has two steps:

1. Delete the customer at the front of the queue, but retain a copy of the name. This step requires only a few pointer changes.

2. Scan the sorted linked list for the name just removed from the queue, and delete from the list the customer record containing this name. This step requires a traversal of the sorted linked list.

Thus, although the scheme efficiently supports the *Traverse* and *QueueFront* operations, *Add* and *Remove* require a traversal of the sorted linked list (whereas in a basic queue *Add* and *Remove* require only a small, constant number of steps). Is there any way to improve this scheme? One possibility is to store the customer records in a binary search tree rather than a sorted linked list. This approach would allow you to perform the second steps of the *Add* and *Remove* operations much more efficiently. While the binary search tree strategy is certainly an improvement over the original scheme, the *Add* and *Remove* operations would still require significantly more work than they would for a normal queue.

Several independent data structures do not support all operations efficiently

In fact, a different kind of scheme, one that supports the *Remove* operation almost as efficiently as if you were maintaining only a basic queue, is possible by allowing the data structures to communicate with each other. This concept is demonstrated here first with a sorted linked list and a queue, and then with more complex structures, such as a binary search tree.

In the data structure shown in Figure 13-28, the sorted linked list still contains customer records, but the queue now contains only pointers to customer records. That is, each entry of the queue points to the record in the sorted linked list of the customer at the given queue position. An obvious advantage of storing only pointers in the queue is that the storage requirements are reduced, since a pointer is likely to be much smaller than a customer record (which could contain a large number of fields). As you will soon see, this scheme also significantly improves the efficiency of the *Remove* operation.

A better way

The efficiency of the *Traverse*, *QueueFront*, and *Add* operations does not differ significantly from the original scheme that Figure 13-27 depicts. You still perform the *Traverse* operation by traversing the sorted linked list. However, you perform *QueueFront* and *Add* as follows:

```
QueueFront(Q)

    Let p be the pointer stored at the front of the queue
```

```
                     { p points to the record in the sorted linked list
                       corresponding to the customer at the front of the
                       queue }

                     Return the record pointed to by p

            Add(Q, newitem)

                     Find the proper position for newitem in the sorted
                       linked list
                     Insert a record containing newitem into this position
                     Add to the rear of the queue a pointer to the new record
```

The real benefit of the new scheme is in the implementation of the *Remove* operation.

```
            Remove(Q)

              Remove the item from the front of the queue and retain its
                value p

              { p points to the customer record to be deleted }
              Delete from the sorted linked list the customer record
                pointed to by p
```

Because the front of the queue contains a pointer to the customer record that you want to delete, there is no need to search the sorted linked list. You have a pointer to the appropriate record, and all you need to do is delete it.

There is one big problem, however. Because you are able to go directly to the record *R* that you want to delete, without traversing the list from its beginning, you have no trailing pointer to the record that precedes *R* on

Figure 13-28

A queue pointing into a sorted linked list

the linked list! Recall that you must have a trailing pointer to delete the record. As the scheme now stands, the only way to obtain the trailing pointer is to traverse the linked list from its beginning, but this requirement negates the advantage gained by having the queue point into the linked list. However, as you saw in Chapter 3, you can solve this problem by replacing the singly linked list in Figure 13-28 with a doubly linked list.

A doubly linked list is required

To summarize, you have seen a fairly good scheme for supporting the queue operations plus a sorted traversal. The only operation whose efficiency you might improve significantly is *Add*. Recall that to perform the *Add* operation, you still must traverse the linked list to find the proper place to insert a new customer record.

The choice to store the customer records in a linear linked list was made to simplify the discussion. However, figure 13-29 illustrates a more effi-

Figure 13-29

A queue pointing into a binary search tree

cient scheme in which the queue points into a binary search tree rather than a linked list. This data structure allows you to perform the *Add* operation in logarithmic time, assuming that the tree remains balanced. Notice, however, that you need the analogue of a doubly linked tree to support the *Remove* operation efficiently. That is, each node in the tree must point to its parent so that you can easily delete the node to which the front of the queue points. This implementation is further discussed in Exercise 11.

In general, it is possible to impose several different organizations simultaneously on a set of data items. This concept is discussed further in Chapter 14 in the context of indexing external storage.

SUMMARY

1. A 2-3 tree is a variant of a binary search tree. The internal nodes of a 2-3 tree can have either two or three children. By allowing the number of children to vary, the insertion and deletion algorithms can easily maintain the balance of the tree.

2. An AVL tree is a binary search tree that is guaranteed to remain balanced. The insertion and deletion algorithms perform rotations in the event that the tree starts to stray from a balanced shape.

3. Hashing is a table implementation that allows for very efficient retrievals, insertions, and deletions. Rather than searching for a data item, hashing calculates where it should be.

4. The hash function should be extremely easy to compute—it should require only a few operations—and it should scatter the search keys evenly throughout the hash table.

5. A collision occurs when two different search keys hash into the same array location. Two ways to resolve collisions are through probing and chaining.

6. Hashing does not efficiently support operations such as traversing a table in sorted order.

7. It is possible to impose several independent organizations on a given set of data. For example, you can store records in a sorted doubly linked list and impose a FIFO order by using a queue of pointers into the list.

COMMON PITFALLS / DEBUGGING

1. Even though search trees that allow their nodes to have more than two children are shorter than binary search trees, they are not nec-

essarily easier to search: More comparisons are necessary at each node to determine which subtree should be searched next.

2. A hashing scheme in general must provide a means of resolving collisions. Choose a hash function that keeps the number of collisions to a minimum. You should be careful to avoid a hash function that will map more items into one part of the hash table than another.

3. Hashing is not a good table implementation if, for example, you need to either traverse the table in sorted order or find the item with the largest search-key value.

SELF-TEST EXERCISES

1. What is the result of inserting 5, 40, 10, 20, 15, and 30—in the order given—into an initially empty 2-3 tree? Note that insertion of an item into an empty 2-3 tree will create a single node that contains the inserted item.

2. What is the result of deleting the 10 from the 2-3 tree that you created in Self-Test Exercise 1?

3. Write the pseudocode for the *Delete* operation when linear probing is used to implement the hash table.

4. What is the probe sequence that double hashing uses when $h_1(key) = key \bmod 11$, $h_2(key) = key \bmod 7$, and $key = 19$.

5. If $h(x) = x \bmod 7$ and separate chaining resolves collisions, what does the hash table look like after the following insertions occur: 8, 10, 24, 15, 32, 17? Assume that each table item contains only a search key.

EXERCISES

1. Write a procedure to implement a **range query** for a binary search tree. That is, write a procedure that will visit all items that have a search key in a given range of values (such as all values between 100 and 1,000).

2. Write the pseudocode for a range-query procedure for a 2-3 tree. (See Exercise 1.)

3. What are the advantages of implementing the ADT table with a 2-3 tree instead of a binary search tree? Why do you not, in general, maintain a completely balanced binary search tree?

4. Execute the following sequence of operations on
   a. An empty binary search tree
   b. An empty 2-3 tree
   c. An empty AVL tree

   ```
   Insert(10)
   Insert(100)
   Insert(30)
   Insert(80)
   Insert(50)
   Delete(10)
   Insert(60)
   Insert(70)
   Insert(40)
   Delete(80)
   Insert(90)
   Insert(20)
   Delete(30)
   Delete(70)
   ```

5. Write the pseudocode for the `Delete` operation when separate chaining resolves collisions.

6. Consider search keys that are English words instead of integers.
   a. Write a program that will implement a hash table for English words by using the following scheme: Let A = 1, B = 2, and so on, and let *h(key)* be the value of the first character of the search key. Thus, "THE" maps to 20. Resolve collisions by separate chaining with unsorted linked lists.
   b. How appropriate is the hash function in part *a* if you are entering random strings into a table? What if the words come from English text?
   c. Experiment with other hashing schemes. Experiment with other implementations of chaining (for example, binary search trees, 2-3 trees, and other hash functions).

7. Modify the hash implementation of the ADT table described in Exercise 6a to check for duplicates on insertion. That is, you should add an item to a table only if it is not already present. Does this change affect the amount of time required to perform an insertion?

8. Repeat Exercise 6, but this time use linear probing as the collision-resolution scheme.

9. Repeat Exercise 6, but this time use double hashing as the collision-resolution scheme.

10. The success of a hash-table implementation of the ADT table is related to the choice of a good hash function. A good hash function is one that is easy to compute and will evenly distribute the possible data.

Comment on the appropriateness of the following hash functions. What patterns would hash to the same location?

a. The hash table has size 2,048. The search keys are identifier names in Pascal. The hash function is

$h(key) = $ (position of first letter of *key* in alphabet) mod 2048

b. The hash table is 10,000 entries long. The search keys are integers in the range *0..9999*. The hash function is

$h(key) = (key * random)$ truncated to an integer

where *random* represents a sophisticated random-number generator that returns a real value between 0 and 1.

c. The search keys are integers in the range *0..9999*. The hash function is given by the following Pascal function:

```
function hash(x : integer) : 0..TableSize;
var i : integer;
begin
    for i := 1 to 1000000 do
        x := (x * x) mod TableSize;
    hash := x
end;
```

d. The keys are English words. The hash function is

$h(key) = $ (sum of positions in alphabet of *key*'s letters) mod
    TableSize

11. Recall that you can delete a node from a doubly linked list without traversing the list to locate the previous node. The analogy for binary search trees is to maintain parent pointers. That is, every node—except the root—will have a pointer to its parent in the tree. Write *Add* and *Remove* operations for the structure pictured in Figure 13-29.

PROJECT

*12. Implement the ADT table with a 2-3 tree. Include the operations *Insert*, *Delete*, and *Retrieve*.

External Methods

PREVIEW This chapter considers a table that is so large you must store it in an external file. By using a direct access file as a model of external storage, the chapter shows how you can modify *Mergesort* to sort data that resides in a file. Finally, you will see how to search an external file by using generalizations of the hashing and search-tree schemes developed previously.

A LOOK AT EXTERNAL STORAGE

This chapter considers the problem of data management in a different type of environment. Whereas previous tables of data items were stored in the internal memory of the computer, assume now that the table resides on an external storage device such as a disk.

Until now, your only contact with external storage involved reading data from and writing data to Pascal files. For example, recall the videocassette inventory program developed in the case studies of Chapters 3 and 12. At the end of each business day, the program saves the current inventory in a Pascal file so that at the beginning of the next day, it can restore the inventory by reading the file. This scenario illustrates one of the advantages of external storage: It exists beyond the execution period of a program.

External storage exists after program execution

Another advantage of external storage is that, in general, it is available in a far greater quantity than is internal memory. If you have a table of 1,000,000 data items, each of which is a record of moderate size, it is not likely that you will be able to store the entire table in internal memory at one time. On the other hand, this much data can easily reside on an external disk. As a consequence, when dealing with tables of this magnitude, you cannot simply read the entire table into memory when you want to operate on it, and write it out when you are finished. Instead, you must devise ways to operate on data—for example, sort it and search it—while it resides externally.

Generally, there is more external storage than internal memory

The files that you have considered up to now have been Pascal files. Compared to the file interaction that many programming languages and operating systems provide, Pascal's file interaction is rather clumsy. The fundamental problem is that Standard Pascal can interact only with **sequential access files**. That is, to access the data stored at a given position in a Pascal (sequential access) file, you must advance the file window beyond all the intervening data. In this sense, a sequential access file resembles a linked list. To access a particular node on the list, you must traverse the list from its beginning until you reach the desired node. In contrast, many types of files allow you to access the data at a given position directly. These **direct access files** resemble arrays in that you can access the element at $A[i]$ without first accessing $A[1]$, $A[2]$, $\cdots$, $A[i-1]$.

Standard Pascal files are sequential access

Direct access files are essential for external tables

Without direct access files, it would be impossible to efficiently support the table operations in an external environment. Because Standard Pascal does not support direct access files, you must construct a model of an environment that does. This model will be a simplification of reality, but will include the features necessary for this discussion. (Note, however, that several dialects of Pascal do support direct access files.)

Imagine that a computer's memory is divided into two parts: internal memory and external memory, as Figure 14-1 illustrates. Assume that an executing program, along with its nonfile data, resides in the computer's internal memory; the permanent files of a computer system reside in the external memory. Further assume that the external storage devices have the characteristics of a disk (though some systems use other devices, such as tapes).

A file consists of **data records.** A data record can be anything from a simple value, such as an integer, to a multifield Pascal-like record, such as an employee record. For simplicity, assume that the data records in any one file are all of the same type.

A file contains records that are partitioned into blocks

The records of a file are partitioned into one or more **blocks,** each of which typically contains many data records, as Figure 14-2 shows. The size of a block, that is, the number of bits of data it can contain, is determined by both the hardware configuration and the system software of the computer. In general, an individual program has no control over this size. Therefore, the number of records that can fit per block is a function of the size of the records in the file. For example, a file of integer records will have more records per block than a file of employee records.

Much as you number the elements of an array, you can number the blocks of a file linearly. With a direct access file, a program can read a given block from the file by specifying its block number, and similarly, it can write data out to a particular block. In this regard a direct access file resembles an array of arrays, with each block of the file analogous to a single array entry, which is itself an array that contains several records.

Direct access I/O involves blocks instead of records

Notice that in this direct access model, *all input and output is at the block level rather than at the record level.* That is, you can read and write a block of records, but you cannot read or write an individual record. It is interesting to note that several programming languages have commands that make it *appear* that you can access records one at a time. In general, however, the system actually performs I/O (input and output) at the block level and perhaps hides this fact from the program. For example, if a programming language includes the command

Figure 14-1

Internal and external memory

External memory

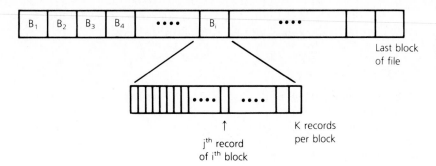

Figure 14-2

A file partitioned into blocks of records.

```
ReadRecord(F, i, R)
{ Reads the iᵗʰ record of file F into variable R. }
```

the system probably accesses the entire block that contains the ith record. The previous model of I/O therefore approximates reality reasonably well.

In the algorithms that this chapter presents, you should assume that your programming language has two commands for performing block I/O. The statement

```
ReadBlock(F, i, B)
```

will read the ith block of file F and place it in program variable B. Notice that variable B must accommodate the many records that each block of file F contains. For example, if each block contains 100 employee records, program variable B must be an array, such as $B[1..100]$, of employee records.

Once the system has read a block into B, the program can process—for example, inspect or modify—the records in the block. It is important to note that you can process data only after you have copied (read) it from the file into the internal memory of the computer. Also, because the records in the program variable B are only copies of the records in the file F, if a program does modify the records in B, the program must write B back out to F, so that the file also reflects the modifications. You can use the statement

```
WriteBlock(F, i, B)
```

to write the contents of B to the ith block of the file F. If F contains n blocks, you can use the statement

```
WriteBlock(F, n+1, B)
```

to append a new block to F, and thus the file can grow dynamically, just like a Pascal file.

Again, realize that these I/O commands allow you to read and write only entire blocks. As a consequence, even if you need to operate on only a single record of the file, you must access an entire block. For example, suppose that you want to give employee Smith a $1,000 raise. If Smith's record is in block i (how to determine the correct block is discussed later in the chapter), you would perform the following steps:

Updating a field within a record
within a block

```
{ read block i from file F into array B }
ReadBlock(F, i, B)

Find the entry B[j] that contains the record with Name =
   "Smith"

{ increment the Salary field of Smith's record }
B[j].Salary := B[j].Salary + 1000

{ write block back to file F so that the change is reflected }
WriteBlock(F, i, B)
```

There is one final issue to consider in this introduction to external storage: the time required to read or write a block of data. The amount of time that a **block access** (a read or write) requires is typically much larger than the time required to operate on the block's data once it is in the computer's internal memory. For example, it is reasonable to assume that the time necessary to inspect every record in a block is less than the time required to read or write that block. Thus, in most external data-management applications, the time required for block accesses typically dominates all other factors. As a consequence, in the next two sections, which devise schemes to sort and search data that is stored externally, *the goal will be to reduce the number of required block accesses*. You should pay little attention to the time required to operate on a block of data once it has been read into internal memory.

File access time is the dominant
factor when considering an
algorithm's efficiency

SORTING DATA IN AN EXTERNAL FILE

This section considers the following problem of sorting data that resides in an external file:

A sorting problem

> An external file contains 1,600 employee records. You want to sort these records by the Social Security number field. Each block contains 100 records, and thus the file contains 16 blocks of records B_1, B_2, and so on to B_{16}. Suppose that the program can only access enough internal memory to manipulate about 300 records (three blocks' worth) at one time.

Sorting the file might not sound like a difficult problem, because you have already seen several sorting algorithms in earlier chapters. There is, however, a fundamental difference here in that the file is far too large to fit into internal memory all at once. This restriction creates somewhat of a difficulty because the sorting algorithms presented earlier assume that all the data to be sorted is available at one time in internal memory (for example, that it is all in an array). Fortunately, however, `Mergesort` can be modified so that this assumption is not necessary.

The basis of the `Mergesort` algorithm is that you can easily merge two sorted segments—such as arrays—of data records into a third sorted segment that is the combination of the two. What makes `Mergesort` appropriate for the problem of sorting external files is that the merge step needs to look only at the *leading edge* of each of the segments. For example, if S_1 and S_2 are sorted segments of records, the first step of the merge is to compare the first record of each segment and select the record with the smaller search key. If the record from S_1 is selected, the next step is to compare the second record of S_1 to the first record of S_2. This process is continued until all the records are exhausted. The key observation is that at any step, the merge never needs to look beyond the leading edge of either segment.

Now consider the details of modifying `Mergesort` so that you can use it for external files. Suppose that the 1,600 records to be sorted are in the file F_1 and that you are not permitted to alter this file. You have two work files, F_2 and F_3. One of the work files will contain the sorted records when the algorithm terminates. The algorithm has two phases: Phase 1 sorts each block of records, and Phase 2 performs a series of merges.

> **Phase 1.** Read a block from F_1 into internal memory, sort its records by using an internal sort, and write the sorted block out to F_2 before you read the next block from F_1. After you process all 16 blocks of F_1, F_2 contains 16 **sorted runs** R_1, R_2, and so on to R_{16}; that is, it contains 16 groups of records, with the records within each group sorted among themselves, as Figure 14-3a illustrates.
>
> **Phase 2.** Phase 2 is a sequence of merge steps. Each merge step merges pairs of sorted runs to form larger sorted runs. Each merge step doubles the number of blocks in each sorted run and thus halves the total number of sorted runs. For example, as Figure 14-3b shows, the first merge step merges eight pairs of sorted runs from F_2 (R_1 with R_2, R_3 with R_4, $\cdots$, R_{15} with R_{16}) to form eight sorted runs, each two blocks long, which are written to F_3. The next merge step merges four pairs of sorted runs from F_3 (R_1 with R_2, R_3 with R_4, $\cdots$, R_7 with R_8) to form four sorted runs, each four blocks long, which are written to F_2, as Figure 14-3c illustrates. The next step merges the two pairs of sorted runs from F_2 to form two sorted runs, which are written to F_3 (see Figure 14-3d). The final step merges the two sorted runs into one, which is written to F_2. At this point, F_2 will contain all of the records of the original file in sorted order.

External Mergesort

Given this overall strategy, how can you merge the sorted runs at each step of Phase 2? The statement of the problem specifies that there is only sufficient internal memory to manipulate at most 300 records at once. However, the later steps of Phase 2 require that you merge runs that contain more than 300 records, so you must merge the runs a piece at a time.

Merging sorted runs in Phase 2

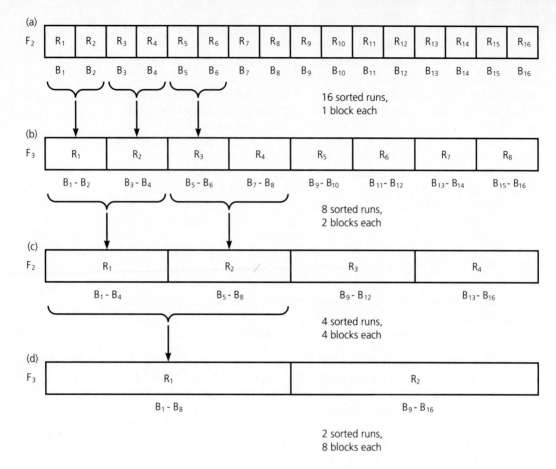

Figure 14-3

(a) 16 sorted runs, 1 block each, in file F_2; (b) 8 runs, 2 blocks each, in file F_3; (c) 4 runs, 4 blocks each, in file F_2; (d) 2 runs, 8 blocks each, in file F_3

To accomplish this merge, you must divide the program's internal memory into three arrays, `In1`, `In2`, and `Out`, each capable of holding 100 records (the block size). You read block-sized pieces of the runs into the two `In` arrays and merge them into the `Out` array. Whenever an `In` array is exhausted—that is, when all its elements have been copied to `Out`—you read the next piece of the run into the `In` array; whenever the `Out` array becomes full, you write this completed piece of the new sorted run to one of the files.

Consider how you can perform the first merge step. You start this step with the pair of runs R_1 and R_2, which are in the first and second blocks, respectively, of the file F_2. (See Figure 14-3a.) Because at this first merge step each run contains only one block, an entire run can fit into one of the `In` arrays. You can thus read R_1 and R_2 into the arrays `In1` and `In2`, and then merge `In1` and `In2` into `Out`. However, although the result of merging `In1` and `In2` is a sorted run two blocks long (200 records), `Out` can hold only one block (100 records). Thus, when in the course of the merge `Out` becomes full, you write its contents to the first block of F_3, as Figure

14-4a illustrates. The merging of $In1$ and $In2$ into Out then resumes. The array Out will become full for a second time only after all the records in $In1$ and $In2$ are exhausted. At that time, write the contents of Out to the second block of F_3. You merge the remaining seven pairs from F_1 in the same manner and append the resulting runs to F_3.

This first merge step is conceptually a bit easier than the others because the initial runs are only one block in size, and thus each can fit in its entirety into one of the In arrays. What do you do in the later steps when the runs to be merged are larger than a single block? Consider, for example, the merge step in which you must merge runs of size four blocks each to form runs of size eight blocks each. (See Figure 14-3c.) The first pair of these runs to be merged is in blocks 1 through 4 and 5 through 8 of F_2.

The algorithm will read the first block of R_1—which is the first block B_1 of the file—into $In1$ and the first block of R_2—which is B_5—into $In2$, as Figure 14-4b illustrates. Then, as it did earlier, the algorithm merges $In1$ and $In2$ into Out. The complication here is that as soon as you finish moving all of the records from either $In1$ or $In2$, you must read the next block from the corresponding run. For example, if you finish $In2$ first, you must read the next block of R_2—which is B_6—into $In2$ before the merge can continue. The algorithm thus must detect when the In arrays become exhausted as well as when the Out array becomes full.

(a)

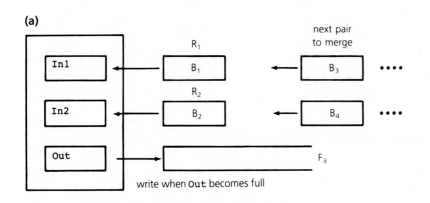

Figure 14-4

(a) **Merging single blocks;**
(b) **merging long runs**

(b)

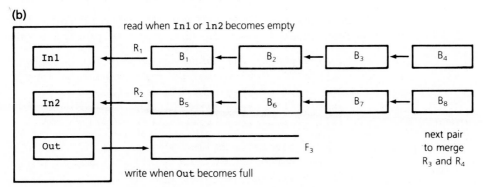

A high-level description of the algorithm for merging arbitrary-sized sorted runs R_i and R_j from F_2 into F_3 is as follows:

Pseudocode to merge sorted runs

```
Read the first block of R_i into In1
Read the first block of R_j into In2

while (either In1 or In2 is not exhausted) do
begin
    Select the smaller "leading" record of In1 and In2 and
        place it into the next position of Out (if one of the
        arrays is exhausted, select the leading record from
        the other)

    if Out is full
        then write its contents to the next block of F_3

    if In1 is exhausted
        then if more blocks remain in R_i
                then read the next block into In1

    if In2 is exhausted
        then if more blocks remain in R_j
                then read the next block into In2
end
```

A pseudocode version of the external sorting program follows. Notice that it uses the procedures *ReadBlock* and *WriteBlock*, introduced in the previous section, and assumes a procedure *CopyFile* that copies a file. To avoid further complications, the solution assumes that the number of blocks in the file is a power of 2. This assumption allows the program always to pair off the sorted runs at each step of the merge phase. Also note that the program uses two scratch files and copies the final sorted scratch file to the designated output file.

A pseudocode mergesort program

```
program ExtMerge(infile, outfile)
{ ****************************************************************

  EXTERNAL MERGESORT

  Sorts file infile and places the result in outfile.

  Calls: Procedures ReadBlock and WriteBlock to perform
  direct access input and output, and CopyFile to copy a file.

  Simplifying Assumption: The number of blocks in the file is
  an exact power of 2. The removal of this assumption involves
  special end-of-file testing that would obscure the
  algorithm that this program illustrates.
  **************************************************************** }

Blocksort(infile, outfile, numblocks)
{ ------------------------------------------------------------
  Sorts each block of records in a file.
```

```
    Precondition: infile is available.
    Postcondition: outfile contains the blocks of infile.
    Each block is sorted; numblocks is the number of blocks
    processed.
    -------------------------------------------------------- }
begin
    reset(infile)
    rewrite(outfile)

    numblocks := 0
    while not eof(infile) do
    begin
        numblocks := numblocks + 1
        ReadBlock(infile, numblocks, buffer)

        { sort with some internal sort }
        Sort(buffer)

        WriteBlock(outfile, numblocks, buffer)
    end   { while }
end   { Blocksort }

Merge(fromfile, tofile, start, size)
{ -------------------------------------------------------
  Merges two consecutive sorted runs in a file.
  Precondition: fromfile is an external file of sorted runs
  open for input; tofile is an external file of sorted runs
  open for output; start is the block number of the first
  run on fromfile to be merged; this run contains size
  blocks.
      Run 1: block start to block start + size — 1
      Run 2: block start + size to start + (2 * size) — 1
  Postcondition: The merged runs from fromfile are appended
  to tofile.
  -------------------------------------------------------- }
begin
    { initialize the input buffer for Run 1 with the first
      block of the run }
    ReadBlock(fromfile, first block of Run 1, In1)

    { initialize the input buffer for Run 2 with the first
      block of the run }
    ReadBlock(fromfile, first block of Run 2, In2)

{ merge until one of the runs is finished. Whenever an
  input buffer is exhausted, the next block is read in.
  Whenever the output buffer is full, it is written out. }

while neither run is finished do
```

```
begin
    { Invariant: Out is ordered. Each block in tofile is
      ordered. }
    Select the smaller "leading edge" of In1 and In2, and
      place it in the next position of Out

    if Out is full
        then WriteBlock(tofile, next block of tofile, Out)

    if In1 is exhausted
        then if more blocks remain in Run 1
            then ReadBlock(fromfile, next block of Run 1, In1)

    if In2 is exhausted
        then if more blocks remain in Run 2
            then ReadBlock(fromfile, next block of Run 2, In2)
end   { while }

{ At this point, exactly one of the runs is complete.
  The remainder of the incomplete run must be appended
  to the output file. The program must

  1. Append the remainder of the unfinished input buffer
     to the output buffer and write it out.

  2. Append the remaining complete blocks. }

{ finish off the remaining input buffer and write out
  the output buffer — only one of these loops will
  execute }

while In1 is not exhausted do
    { Invariant: Out is ordered }
    Place next item of In1 into the next position of Out

while In2 is not exhausted do
    { Invariant: Out is ordered }
    Place next item of In2 into the next position of Out

WriteBlock(tofile, next block of tofile, Out)

{ finish off the remaining complete blocks — only one of
  these loops will execute }

while there remain blocks in Run 1 do
{ Invariant: Each block in tofile is ordered }
begin
    ReadBlock(fromfile, next block of Run 1, In1)
    WriteBlock(tofile, next block of tofile, In1)
end   { while }

while there remain blocks in Run 2 do
{ Invariant: Each block in tofile is ordered }
```

```
      begin
         ReadBlock(fromfile, next block of Run 2, In2)
         WriteBlock(tofile, next block of tofile, In2)
      end   { while }
   end   { Merge }

   MergeFile(infile, outfile, runsize, numblocks)
   { -----------------------------------------------------------
     Merges blocks from one file to another.
     Precondition: infile is an external file that contains
     numblocks sorted blocks organized into runs of runsize
     blocks each.
     Postcondition: outfile contains the merged runs of infile.
     ----------------------------------------------------------- }
   begin
      reset(infile)
      rewrite(outfile)

      next := 1
      while next <= numblocks do
      { Invariant: runs in outfile are ordered }
      begin
         Merge(infile, outfile, next, runsize)
         next := next + (2 * runsize)
      end   { while }
   end   { MergeFile }

   begin   { Main Program }

      { Phase 1: sort the file block by block and count how
        many blocks there are }
      Blocksort(infile, tempfile1, numblocks)

      { Phase 2: merge runs of size 1, 2, 4,... , numblocks/2.
        Uses two temporary files; a toggle keeps track of the
        from file and the to file for each merge step }

      size := 1
      toggle := 1
      while size < numblocks do
      begin
         if toggle = 1
            then MergeFile(tempfile1, tempfile2, size, numblocks)
            else MergeFile(tempfile2, tempfile1, size, numblocks)
         size := 2 * size
         toggle := — toggle
      end   { while }

      { copy the current temporary file to outfile }
      if toggle = 1
```

```
    then CopyFile(tempfile1, outfile)
    else CopyFile(tempfile2, outfile)
end   { Program }
```

SEARCHING EXTERNAL TABLES

This section discusses techniques for organizing records in external storage so that you can perform ADT table operations such as *Retrieve*, *Insert*, *Delete*, and *Traverse* efficiently. Although this discussion will only scratch the surface of this topic, you do have a head start: Two of the most important external table implementations are variations of the 2-3 tree and hashing, methods you studied in Chapter 13.

Suppose you have a direct access file of records that are to be table items. The file is partitioned into blocks, as was described earlier in this chapter. One of the simplest table implementations stores the records in order by their search key, perhaps sorting the file by using the external sorting algorithm developed in the previous section. Once it is sorted, you can easily traverse the file in sorted order by using the following algorithm:

A simple external table implementation: records stored in search-key order

Sorted-order traversal

```
Traverse(F, Visit)
{ Traverses in sorted order the sorted file F, calling
  procedure Visit for each item. }

    { read each block of file F into an internal array B }
    for i := 1 to NumberOfBlocks do
    begin
        ReadBlock(F, i, B)

        { visit each record in the block }
        for j := 1 to RecordsPerBlock do
            Visit(B[j])
    end
```

To perform the *Retrieve* operation on the sorted file, you can use a binary search algorithm as follows:

Retrieval by using a binary search

```
Retrieve(F, first, last, X, getitem, success)
{ Searches blocks first through last of file F and retrieves
  into getitem the record whose search key is X. The
  operation fails if there is no such item. The flag success
  indicates whether the operation succeeded. }

    { read the middle block of file F into internal array B }
    mid := (first + last) div 2 { number of middle block of F }
    ReadBlock(F, mid, B)

    { the desired block has been found }
```

```
if (X >= B[1].key) and (X <= B[RecordsPerBlock].key) then
   begin
        Search array B for record B[j] whose search key is X
        if record is found
           then
           begin
                getitem := B[j]
                success := true
           end

           else success := false
   end

{ there are no more blocks in the file to search }
else if F is one block in size then
   success := false

{ the desired block is in the first half of the file }
else if X < B[1].key then
   Retrieve(F, first, mid-1, X, getitem, success)

{ the desired block is in the second half of the file }
else Retrieve(F, mid+1, last, X, getitem, success)
```

The previous `Retrieve` algorithm recursively splits the file in half and reads the middle block into the internal array B. Note that splitting a file segment requires that you know the numbers of the first and last blocks of the segment. You would pass these values as parameters, along with the file name, to the `Retrieve` procedure.

Once you have read the middle block of the file segment into B, you determine if a record with search key X could be in this block. You can make this determination by comparing X to the smallest search key in B—which is in B[1]—and to the largest search key in B—which is in B[RecordsPerBlock]. If X does not lie between the values of the smallest and largest search keys in B, you must recursively search one of the halves of the file (which half to search depends on whether X is less than or greater than the search keys in the block you just examined). If, on the other hand, X does lie between the values of the smallest and largest search keys of the block in B, you must search B for the record. Notice that because the records within the block B are sorted, you could use a binary search on the records within this block. However, the number of records in the block B is typically small, and thus the time required to scan the block sequentially is insignificant compared to the time required to read the block from the file. It is therefore common simply to scan the block sequentially.

This external implementation of the ADT table is not very different from the internal sorted array-based implementation. As such, it has many of the same advantages and disadvantages. Its main advantage is that because the records are sorted sequentially, you can use a binary search to locate the block that contains a given search key. The main disadvantage

Insert and Delete for an external implementation of the ADT table can require many costly file accesses due to shifting records

of the implementation is that, as is the case with an array-based implementation, the `Insert` and `Delete` operations must shift table items. Shifting records in an external file is, in general, far more costly than shifting array items. A file may contain an enormous number of large records, which are organized as several thousand blocks. As a consequence, the shifting could require a prohibitively large number of block accesses.

Consider, for example, Figure 14-5. If you insert a new record into block *K*, you must shift the records not only in block *K*, but also in every block after it. Note that you must shift some records across block boundaries. Thus, for each of these blocks, you must read the block into internal memory, shift its records by using an assignment such as

```
B[i+1] := B[i]
```

and write the block to the file so that the file reflects the change. This large number of block accesses makes the external sorted array-based implementation practical only for tables where insertions and deletions are rare. (See Exercise 1 at the end of this chapter.)

Indexing an External File

Two of the best external table implementations are variations of the internal hashing and search-tree schemes. The biggest difference between the internal and external versions of these implementations is that in the external versions, it is often advantageous to organize an **index** to the data file rather than to organize the data file itself. An index to a data file is conceptually similar to other indexes with which you are familiar. For example, consider a card catalog in a library. Rather than looking all over the library for a particular title, you can simply search the card catalog. The catalog is typically organized alphabetically by title (or by author), so it is a simple matter to locate the appropriate entry. The entry for each book contains a *pointer* (for example, a Dewey decimal number), which indicates where on the shelves you can find the book.

There are at least three benefits to using a card catalog to index the books in a library:

Advantages of a library card catalog

- The library can organize the books on the shelves in any way, without regard to how easy it will be for a patron to scan the shelves for a particular book. To locate a particular book, the patron searches the card catalog for the appropriate entry.

Figure 14-5

Shifting across block boundaries

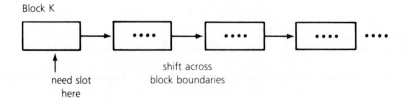

Block K

need slot here

shift across block boundaries

- Because each catalog entry is small (for example, a 3-inch by 5-inch index card), the entire catalog for a large library can fit into a small area. A patron can thus locate a particular book without running all over the library.

- The library can have different types of catalogs to facilitate different types of searches. For example, it can have one catalog organized by title and another organized by author.

Now consider how you can use an index to a data file to much the same advantage as the card catalog. As Figure 14-6 illustrates, you can leave the data file in a disorganized state and maintain an index to it. When you need to locate a particular record in the data file, you search the index for the corresponding entry, which will tell you where to find the desired record in the data file.

An index to the data file is simply a file, called the **index file**, that contains an **index record** for each record in the data file, just as a card catalog contains an entry for each book in the library. An index record has two fields: a **key field**, which contains the same value as the search key of its corresponding record in the data file, and a **pointer field**, which shows the number of the block in the data file that contains this data record. (Despite its name, the pointer field contains an integer, not a Pascal pointer.) You can thus determine which block of the data file contains the record whose search key field is X by searching the index file for the index record whose key field is X. (This type of index is often called a **dense index** to distinguish it from other types of indexes.)

An index to a data file

Maintaining an index to a data file has benefits analogous to those provided by the library's card catalog:

- Because you do not need to maintain the data file in any particular order, you can insert new records in any convenient location, such as at the end of the file. As you will see, this flexibility eliminates the need for shifting the data records during insertions and deletions.

Advantages of an index file

- In general, an index record will be much smaller than a data record. While the data record may contain many fields, an index

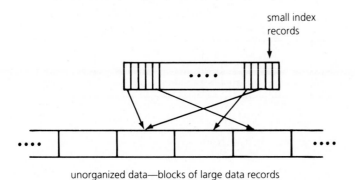

small index records

unorganized data—blocks of large data records

Figure 14-6

A data file with an index

record contains only two fields: the search key, which is also one of the fields of the data record, and a single integer pointer, which is the block number. Thus, just as the library's card catalog occupies only a small fraction of the space occupied by the books it indexes, an index file is only a fraction of the size of the data file. As you will see, the small size of the index file often allows you to manipulate it with fewer block accesses than would be required to manipulate the data file.

- You can maintain several indexes simultaneously. Just as a library can have one card catalog organized by title and another organized by author, you can have one index file that indexes the data file by one search key (for example, an index file that consists of `<Name, Pointer>` records), and a second index file that indexes the data file by another search key (for example, an index file that consists of `<SocSec, Pointer>` records). Such **multiple indexing** is discussed briefly at the end of this chapter.

Organize the index file but not the data file

Although you do not organize the data file, you must organize the index file so that you can search and update it rapidly. Before considering how to organize an index file by using either hashing or search-tree schemes, first consider a less complex organization that illustrates the concepts of indexing. Suppose that the index file simply stores the index records sequentially, sorted by their key fields, as shown in Figure 14-7. Because the index records are far smaller than the data records, the index file contains far fewer blocks than the data file. For example, if the index records are one-tenth the size of the data records and the data file contains 1,000 blocks, the index file will require only about 100 blocks. As a result, you can perform the operations `Retrieve`, `Insert`, and `Delete` with fewer block accesses.

For example, to perform the `Retrieve` operation, you can use a binary search on the index file as follows:

Figure 14-7

A data file with a sorted index file

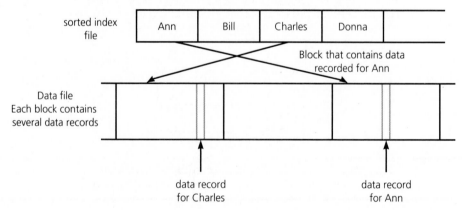

```
Retrieve(Tindex, Tdata, X, getitem, success)
{ Retrieves into getitem the record whose search key is X,
  where Tindex is the index file and Tdata is the data file.
  The operation fails if there is no such record. The flag
  success indicates whether the operation succeeded. }

    { read middle block of index file into internal array B }
    mid := middle block of index file Tindex
    ReadBlock(Tindex, mid, B)

    { the desired block of the index file has been found }
    if (X >= B[1].key) and (X <= B[IndexRecordsPerBlock].key)
        then
        begin
            { determine desired block number of the data file }
            Search array B for index record B[j] with key
              value X

            if record is found
                then
                begin
                    blocknum := block number of the data file
                                   pointed to by B[j]

                    { read the block from the data file into
                      internal array D }

                    ReadBlock(Tdata, blocknum, D)

                    { search for the table item }
                    Find data record D[k] whose search key is X
                    getitem := D[k]

                    success := true
                end

                else success := false

        end   { then }
    { there are no more blocks in the file to search }
    else if Tindex is one block in size then
        success := false

    { desired block is in the first half of the index file }
    else if X < B[1].key then
        Retrieve(first half of Tindex, Tdata, X, getitem, success)

    { desired block is in the second half of the index file }
    else Retrieve(second half of Tindex, Tdata, X, getitem,
                                                      success)
```

Retrieval by searching an index file

An index file reduces the number of required block accesses for table operations

For the previous example, the use of an index cuts the number of block accesses down from about $\log_2 1000 = 10$ to about $1 + \log_2 100 = 8$. (The one additional block access is into the data file once you have located the appropriate index record.)

The reduction in block accesses is far more dramatic for the *Insert* and *Delete* operations. In the implementation of an external table that was discussed earlier in this section, if you insert a record into or delete a record from the first block of data, for example, you have to shift records in every block, requiring that you access all 1,000 blocks of the data file. (See Figure 14-5.)

Shift index records instead of data records

However, when you perform an insertion or a deletion by using the index scheme, you have to shift only index records. When you use an index file, you do not keep the data file in any particular order, so you can insert a new data record into any convenient location in the data file. This flexibility means that you can simply insert a new data record at the end of the file or at a position left vacant by a previous deletion (as you will see). As a result, you never need to shift records in the data file. However, you do need to shift records in the index file to create an opening so that you can insert the corresponding index entry into its proper sorted position. Because there are only 100 blocks in the index file, the maximum number of block accesses that are necessary is greatly reduced. A secondary benefit of shifting index records rather than data records is that, because the records themselves are smaller, the amount of time required for a single shift is diminished; that is, the time required for the assignment *B[i + 1] := B[i]* is decreased.

Deletions under the index scheme reap similar benefits. Once you have searched the index file and located the data record to be deleted, you can simply leave its location vacant in the data file, and thus you need not shift any data records. You can keep track of the vacant locations in the data file (see Exercise 2), so that you can insert new data records into the vacancies, as was mentioned earlier. The only shifting required is in the index file to fill the gap created when the index record that corresponds to the deleted data record is removed.

An unsorted data file with a sorted index is more efficient than a sorted data file, but other schemes are even better

Even though this scheme is an improvement over maintaining a sorted data file, in many applications it is far from satisfactory. The 100 block accesses that could be required to insert or delete an index record would often be prohibitive. Far better implementations are possible when you use either hashing or search trees to organize the index file.

External Hashing

The external hashing scheme is quite similar to the internal scheme described in Chapter 13. Recall that in the internal hashing scheme each entry of the array *T[0..TableSize-1]* contains a pointer to the beginning of the list of items that hash into that location. In the external hashing scheme, each entry of *T* still contains a pointer to the beginning of a list, but here each list consists of *blocks of index records*. In other words, you hash an index file rather than the data file, as Figure 14-8 illustrates. (In many applications the array T is itself so large that you must keep it in external storage—for example, in the first K blocks of the index file. To avoid this extra detail, you can assume that the array T is an internal array.)

Hashed index file

In Figure 14-8, you see that associated with each entry $T[i]$ is a linked list of blocks of the index file. Each block of $T[i]$'s linked list contains index records whose keys (and thus whose corresponding data-records' search keys) hash into location i. To form the linked lists, you must reserve space in each block for a block pointer—the integer block number of the next block in the chain—as Figure 14-9 illustrates. That is, in this linked list the pointers are integers, not Pascal pointers. By convention, the value zero is placed in the last block on the chain (which is analogous to setting a Pascal pointer to nil).

The following is a high-level description of the $Retrieve$ algorithm that uses external hashing:

```
Retrieve(Tindex, Tdata, X, getitem, success)
{ Retrieves into getitem the item whose search key is X,
  where Tindex is the index file which is hashed, and Tdata
  is the data file. The operation fails if there is no such
  record. The flag success indicates whether the operation
  succeeded. }

{ apply the hash function to the search key X }
i := h(X)
```

Retrieval under external hashing of an index file

Table hashes index file

Blocks of index file—each block contains several index records

Each index record points to a block of the data file

Data file—each block contains several data records

Figure 14-8

A hashed index file

Figure 14-9

A single block with a pointer

pointer to next
block on chain

```
{ find the first block on the chain of index blocks —
  these blocks contain index records that hash into
  location i }
p := T[i]

{ if p = 0 then no values have hashed into location i }
if p <> 0
    then ReadBlock(Tindex, p, B)

{ search for the block with the desired index record }
while (p <> 0) Cand
    (B does not contain an index record with key value X) do
begin
    p := block number of next block on chain

    { if p = 0, you are at the last block in the chain }
    if p <> 0
        then ReadBlock(Tindex, p, B)
end   { while }

{ retrieve the data item if present }
if p <> 0
    then
    begin { B[j] is the index record whose key value = X }
        blocknum := block number of data file pointed
                         to by B[j]
        { read the block from the data file into
          internal array D }
        ReadBlock(Tdata, blocknum, D)

        { search for the table item }
        Find data record D[k] whose search key is X
        getitem := D[k]

        success := true
    end   { then }

    else success := false
```

The *Insert* and *Delete* algorithms are also similar to those for internal hashing. The major difference is that, in the external environment, you must insert or delete both a data record and the corresponding index record. First consider the steps of the insertion algorithm.

INSERT A NEW DATA RECORD WHOSE SEARCH KEY IS *X*

1. **Insert the data record into the data file.** Because the data file is not ordered, the new record can go anywhere you want. If a previous deletion has left a free slot in the middle of the data file, you can insert it there. (See Exercise 2.)

    If there are no free slots, you insert the new data record at the end of the last block or, if necessary, you append a new block to the end of the data file and store the record there. In either case, let *p* denote the number of the block that contains this new data record.

2. **Insert a corresponding index record into the index file.** You need to insert into the index file an index record that has key value *X* and pointer value *p*. (Recall that *p* is the number of the block in the data file into which you inserted the new data record.) Because the index file is hashed, you first apply the hash function to the search key *X*, letting

    `i := h(X)`

    You then insert the index record `<X, p>` into the chain of blocks pointed to by the entry `T[i]`. You can insert this record into any block on the chain that contains a free slot or, if necessary, you can allocate a new block and link it to the beginning of the chain.

The steps for a deletion are as follows:

DELETE A DATA RECORD WHOSE SEARCH KEY IS *X*

1. **Search the index file for the corresponding index record.** You apply the hash function to the search key *X*, letting

    `i := h(X)`

    You then search the chain of index blocks pointed to by entry `T[i]` for an index record whose key value is *X*. If you do not find such a record, you can conclude that there is no record in the data file whose search key is *X*. However, if you find an index record `<X, p>`, you delete it from the index file after noting the block number *p*, which indicates where in the data file you can find the data record to be deleted.

2. **Delete the data record from the data file.** You know that the data record is in block *p* of the data file. You simply access this block, search the block for the record, delete the record, and write the block back to the file.

Observe that for each of the operations `Retrieve`, `Insert`, and `Delete`, the number of block accesses is very low. You never have to access more than one block of the data file, and at worst you have to access all of the blocks along a single hash chain of the index file. Like internal hashing, with external hashing you can take measures to keep the length of each of the chains quite short (for example, one or two blocks long). You should

Insertion under external hashing of an index file

Deletion under external hashing of an index file

make the size of the array T large enough so that the average length of a chain is near one block, and the hash function should scatter the keys evenly. If necessary, you can even structure each chain as an external search tree—a **B-tree**—by using the techniques described next.

Choose external hashing for
Retrieve, Insert, and
Delete operations

The hashing implementation is the one to choose when you need to perform the operations `Retrieve`, `Insert`, and `Delete` on a large external table. As is the case with internal hashing, however, there are operations that this implementation does not support well. These are operations such as sorted traversal, retrieval of the smallest or largest item, and range queries that require ordered data. When these types of operations are added to the basic table operations `Retrieve`, `Insert`, and `Delete`, a search-tree implementation may be more appropriate than hashing.

B-Trees

Another way to search an external table is to organize it as a search tree. Just as you applied external hashing to the index file, you organize the index file, not the data file, as an external search tree. The implementation developed here is a generalization of the 2-3 tree of Chapter 13.

Observe that you can organize the blocks of an external file into a tree structure by using block numbers for child pointers. In Figure 14-10, for

Figure 14-10

(a) Blocks organized into a 2-3 tree; (b) a single node of the 2-3 tree

example, the blocks are organized into a 2-3 tree. Each block of the file is a node in the tree and contains three child pointers, each of which is the integer block number of the child. A child pointer value of zero plays the role of a *nil* pointer, and thus, for example, a leaf will contain three child pointers with the value zero.

If you organized the index file into a 2-3 tree, each node (block of the index file) would contain either one or two index records, each of the form *<Key, Pointer>*, along with three child pointers. It is important to remember that the pointer field of the record *<X, p>* indicates the block (of the data file) that contains the data record whose search key is *X* and has nothing to do with the tree structure of the index file. To help avoid confusion, the term **child pointers** is used here to refer to the pointers that are used to maintain the tree structure of the index file.

Organize the index file as an external 2-3 tree

You must organize the index records in the tree so that their keys obey the same search-tree ordering property as an internal 2-3 tree. This organization allows you to retrieve the data record with a given value in its search key as follows:

```
Retrieve(Tindex, Tdata, rootnum, X, getitem, success)
{ Retrieves into getitem the record whose search key is X.
  Tindex is the index file, which is organized as a 2-3
  tree. Rootnum is the block number (of the index file) that
  contains the root of the tree. Tdata is the data file. The
  operation fails if there is no such item. The flag success
  indicates whether the operation succeeded. }

    { read into internal array B the block of the index file
      that contains the root of the 2-3 tree }
    ReadBlock(Tindex, rootnum, B)

    { search for the index record whose key value is X }
    if X is in the root
      then
      begin
          blocknum := block number of the data file
                      specified by the index record

          { read the block from the data file into internal
            array D }
          ReadBlock(Tdata, blocknum, D)

          { search for the table item }
          Find data record D[k] whose search key is X
          getitem := D[k]

          success := true
      end { then }

      else
      begin
          { search the appropriate subtree }
```

Retrieval when the index file is a 2-3 tree

```
if the root is a leaf
    then success := false

else
begin
    child := block number of the root of the
                appropriate subtree
    Retrieve(Tindex, Tdata, child, X,
                getitem, success)
end
end { else }
```

You can also perform insertions and deletions in a manner similar to the internal version, with the addition that you must insert records into and delete records from both the index file and the data file (as was the case in the external hashing scheme described earlier). In the course of insertions into and deletions from the index file, you must split and merge nodes of the tree just as you do for the internal version. You perform insertions into and deletions from the data file—which, recall, is not ordered in any way—exactly as described for the external hashing implementation.

An external 2-3 tree is adequate, but an improvement is possible

You can thus support the table operations fairly well by using an external version of the 2-3 tree. However, you can generalize the 2-3 tree to a structure that is even more suitable for an external environment. Recall the discussion in Chapter 13 about search trees that allow their nodes to have more than three children. You saw that any reduction in the height of the search tree obtained by allowing its nodes to have more than three children is offset by the fact that, in the course of searching for a value, more comparisons are necessary at each node visited. In an external environment, however, the advantage of keeping a search tree short far outweighs the disadvantage of performing extra work at each node.

Keep an external search tree short

In an external environment, as you traverse the search tree you must perform a block access for each node visited. Because the time required to access a block of an external file is, in general, far greater than the time required to operate on that block once it has been read in (for example, the time required to inspect its data), the overriding concern is to reduce the number of block accesses required. This fact implies that you should attempt to reduce the height of the tree, even at the expense of requiring more comparisons at each node. In an external search tree, you should thus allow each node to have as many children as possible, with only the block size as a limiting factor.

How many children can a block of some fixed size accommodate? If a node is to have m children, then clearly you must be able to fit m child pointers in the node. In addition to child pointers, however, the node must also contain index records.

Before you can answer the question of how many children a block can accommodate, you must first consider this related question: If a node N in a search tree has m children, how many key values—and thus how many index records—must it contain?

In a binary search tree, if the node N has two children, then it must contain one key value, as Figure 14-11a indicates. You can think of the key value in node N as separating the key values in N's two subtrees—all the key values in N's left subtree are less than N's key value, and all the key values in N's right subtree are greater than N's key value. When you are searching the tree for a given key value, the key value in N tells you which branch to take.

Binary search tree: the number of records and children per node

Similarly, if a node N in a 2-3 tree has three children, then it must contain two key values. (See Figure 14-11b.) These two values separate the key values in N's three subtrees—all the key values in the left subtree are less than N's smaller key value, all the key values in N's middle subtree lie between N's two key values, and all the key values in N's right subtree are greater than N's larger key value. As is the case with a binary search tree, this requirement allows a search algorithm to know which branch to take at any given node.

2-3 tree: the number of records and children per node

In general, if a node N in a search tree is to have m children, then it must contain $m - 1$ key values to separate the values in its subtrees correctly. (See Figure 14-11c.) Suppose that you denote the subtrees of N as S_0, S_1, and so on to S_{m-1} and denote the key values in N as K_1, K_2, and so on to K_{m-1} (with $K_1 < K_2 < \cdots < K_{m-1}$). The key values in N must separate the values in its subtrees as follows:

General search tree: the number of records and children per node

- All the values in subtree S_0 must be less than the key value K_1.
- For all i, $1 \leq i \leq m - 2$, all the values in subtree S_i must lie between the key values K_i and K_{i+1}.
- All the values in subtree S_{m-1} must be greater than the key value K_{m-1}.

If every node in the tree obeys this property, you can search the tree by

(a)

left   right

(b)

left   middle   right

(c)

Figure 14-11

(a) A node with two children; (b) a node with three children; (c) a node with m children

using the following generalized version of a search tree's retrieval algorithm:

```
Retrieve(Tindex, Tdata, rootnum, X, getitem, success)
{ Retrieves into getitem the record whose search key is X.
  Tindex is the index file, which is organized as a search
  tree. Rootnum is the block number (of the index file) that
  contains the root of the tree. Tdata is the data file. The
  operation fails if there is no such item. The flag success
  indicates whether the operation succeeded. }

    { read into internal array B the block of the index file
      that contains the root of the tree }
    ReadBlock(Tindex, rootnum, B)

    { search for the index record whose key value is X }
    if X is in the root (is one of the Kᵢ)
        then
        begin
            blocknum := block number of the data file
                        specified by the index record

            { read the block from the data file into internal
              array D }
            ReadBlock(Tdata, blocknum, D)

            { search for the table item }
            Find the data record D[k] whose search key is X
            getitem := D[k]

            success := true
        end { then }

        else
        begin
            { search the appropriate subtree }
            if root is a leaf
                then success := false

                else
                begin
                    Determine which subtree Sᵢ to search
                    child := block number of the root of Sᵢ
                    Retrieve(Tindex, Tdata, child, X,
                             getitem, success)

                end
        end  { else }
```

Now return to the question of how many children the nodes of the search tree can have—that is, how big can *m* be? If you wish to organize the index file into a search tree, then the items that you store in each node will be records of the form `<Key, Pointer>`. Thus, if each node in the tree (which, recall, is a block of the index file) is to have m children, it must be large enough to accommodate m child pointers and $m - 1$ records of the form `<Key, Pointer>`. You should choose m to be the largest integer such that m child pointers (which, recall, are integers) and $m - 1$ `<Key, Pointer>` records can fit into a single block of the file. Actually, the algorithms are somewhat simplified if you always choose m to be odd. That is, you should choose m to be the largest odd integer such that m child pointers and $m - 1$ index records can fit into a single block.

Ideally then, you should structure the external search tree so that every internal node has m children, where m is chosen as just described, and all leaves are at the same level, as is the case with full trees and 2-3 trees. For example, Figure 14-12 shows a full tree whose internal nodes each have five children. Although this structure would give you the search tree with the minimum possible height, it is too difficult to maintain in the face of insertions and deletions. As a consequence, you must make a compromise. You can still insist that all the leaves of the search tree be at the same level—that is, that the tree be balanced—but you must allow each internal node to have between m and (m div 2) + 1 children. *Number of children per node*

This type of search tree is known as a **B-tree of degree** m. A B-tree of degree m is a search tree such that *B-tree of degree* m

- All leaves are at the same level.

- Each node contains between $m - 1$ and (m div 2) records, and each internal node has one more child than it has records. An exception to this rule is that the root of the tree can contain as few as one record and can have as few as two children. This exception is necessitated by the insertion and deletion algorithms described next.

Figure 14-12

(a) **A full tree of order 5;**
(b) **the format of a single node**

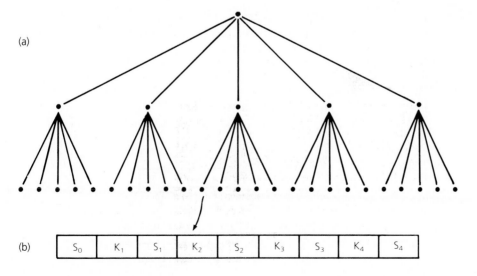

Notice that a 2-3 tree is a B-tree of degree 3. Furthermore, the manner in which the B-tree insertion and deletion algorithms maintain the structure of the tree is a direct generalization of the 2-3 tree's strategy of splitting and merging nodes.

The B-tree insertion and deletion algorithms are illustrated next by means of an example. Suppose that the index file is organized into a B-tree of degree 5—that is, 5 is the maximum and 3 is the minimum number of children that an internal node (other than the root) in the tree can have. (Typically, a B-tree will be of a higher degree, but the diagrams would get out of hand!)

Insertions into a B-tree.   The steps that insert a data record with search key 55 into the tree of Figure 14-13 are as follows:

1.   **Insert the data record into the data file.** First you find block p in the data file into which you can insert the new record. As was true with the external hashing implementation, block p is either any block with a vacant slot or is a new block.

2.   **Insert a corresponding index record into the index file.** You now must insert the index record <55, p> into the index file, which is a B-tree of degree 5. The first step is to locate the leaf of the tree in which this index record belongs by determining where the search for 55 would terminate.

     Suppose that this is the leaf L shown in Figure 14-14a. Conceptually, you insert the new index record into L, causing it to contain five records (Figure 14-14b). Since a node can contain only four records, you must split L into L_1 and L_2. With an action analogous to the splitting of a node in a 2-3 tree, L_1 gets the two records with the smallest key values, L_2 gets the two records with the largest key values, and the record with the middle key value (56) is moved up to the parent P. (See Figure 14-14c.)

     In this example, P now has six children and five records, so it must be split into P_1 and P_2. The record with the middle key value (56) is

Figure 14-13

A B-tree

Figure 14-14

Insert 55

moved up to *P*'s parent, *Q*. Then *P*'s children must be distributed appropriately, as happens with a 2-3 tree when an internal node is split. (See Figure 14-14d.)

At this point the insertion is complete, since *P*'s parent *Q* now contains only three records and has only four children. In general, though, an insertion might cause splitting to propagate all the way up to the root (Figure 14-14e). Notice that if the root must be split, the new root will contain only one record and have only two children. (Recall that the definition of a B-tree allows for this eventuality.)

Deletions from a B-tree. The steps that delete a data record with a given search key from a B-tree are as follows:

1. **Locate the index record in the index file.** You use the search procedure to locate the index record with the desired key value. If this record is not already in a leaf, you swap it with its inorder successor. (See Exercise 5.) Suppose that the leaf L shown in Figure 14-15a contains the index record with the desired key value, 73. After noting the value p of the pointer field of this index record (which indicates the block of the data file that contains the data record with search key 73), you remove the record from L (Figure 14-15b). Because L now contains only one value (recall that two is the minimum number of values that a node is permitted to contain), and since L's siblings cannot spare a value, you merge L with one of the siblings and bring down a record from the parent P (Figure 14-15c). Notice that this step is analogous to the merge step for a 2-3 tree. However, P now has only one value and two children, and since its siblings cannot spare a record and child, you must merge P with its sibling P_1 and bring a record down from P's parent, Q. Since P is an internal node, its children must be adopted by P_1. (See Figure 14-15d.)

    After this merge, P's parent Q is left with only two children and one record. In this case, however, Q's sibling Q_1 can spare a record and a child, so you redistribute children and records among Q_1, Q, and the

Figure 14-15

Delete 73

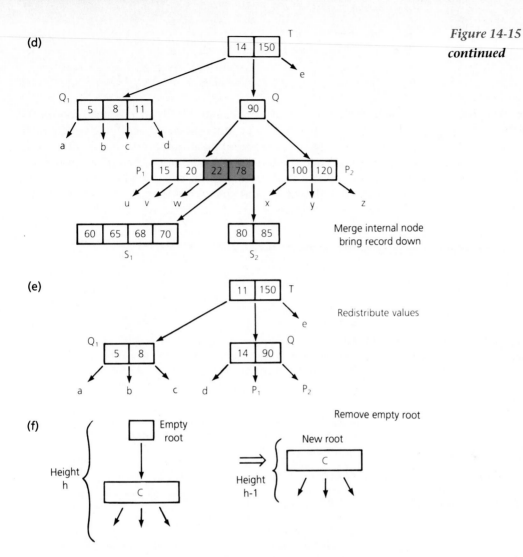

(d)

(e)

Redistribute values

Remove empty root

(f)

Figure 14-15
continued

parent T to complete the deletion. (See Figure 14-15e.) Notice that if a deletion ever propagates all the way up to the root so that it has only two children and contains only one record, you simply let this situation stand. Recall that this eventuality is accounted for in the definition of a B-tree. If a future deletion causes the root to have a single child and no records, you remove the root so that the tree's height decreases by 1, as Figure 14-15f illustrates. The deletion of the index record is complete and you now must delete the data record.

2. **Delete the data record from the data file.** Prior to deleting the index record, you noted the value p of its pointer field. Thus, you know that the data record is in block p of the data file. You simply access this block, delete the record, and write the block back to the file. The high-

level pseudocode for the insertion and deletion algorithms parallels that of the 2-3 tree and is left as an exercise.

Traversals

Accessing only the search key of each record, but not the data file

Now consider the operation `Traverse` in sorted order, which is one of the operations that hashing does not support at all efficiently. Often an application requires only that the traversal print the search keys of the records. If such is the case, then the B-tree implementation can efficiently support the operation. You can visit the search keys in sorted order by using an inorder traversal of the B-tree, and you do not have to access the data file. The algorithm is as follows:

Inorder traversal of a B-tree index file

```
Traverse(blocknum)
{ Traverses in sorted order an index file that is organized
  as a B-tree. Blocknum is the block number of the root of
  the B-tree in the index file. }

    if blocknum <> 0
        then
        begin
            { read the root into internal array B }
            ReadBlock(indexfile, blocknum, B)

            { traverse the children }

            { traverse S_0 }
            Let p be the block number of the 0th child of B
            Traverse(p)

            for i := 1 to m—1 do
            begin
                Print key K_i of B

                { traverse S_i }
                Let p be block number of the ith child of B
                Traverse(p)
            end
        end
```

This traversal accomplishes the task with the minimum possible number of block accesses because each block of the index file is read only once. Notice, however, that this algorithm assumes that there is enough internal memory to accommodate a recursive stack that contains h blocks, where h is the height of the tree. In many situations this assumption is reasonable—for example, a 255-degree B-tree that indexes a file of 16 million data records has a height of no more than 3. When internal memory cannot accommodate h blocks, you must use a different algorithm. (See Exercise 9.)

Accessing the entire data record

If the traversal must print the entire data record (and not just the search key), then the B-tree implementation is less attractive. In this case, as you traverse the B-tree, you must access the appropriate block of the data file. The traversal becomes

```
Traverse(blocknum)
{ Traverses in sorted order a data file that is indexed with
  a B-tree. Blocknum is the block number of the root of the
  B-tree. }

    if blocknum <> 0
        then
        begin
            { read the root into internal array B }
            ReadBlock(indexfile, blocknum, B)

            { traverse S₀ }
            Let p be the block number of the 0ᵗʰ child of B
            Traverse(p)

            for i := 1 to m—1 do
            begin
                Let pdata be the pointer in the iᵗʰ index
                    record of B
                ReadBlock(datafile, pdata, D)
                Extract from D the data record with search
                    key Kᵢ
                Print the data record

                { traverse Sᵢ }
                Let p be block number of the iᵗʰ child of B
                Traverse (p)
            end
        end
    end
```

Sorted-order traversal of a data file indexed with a B-tree

Notice that this traversal requires you to read a block of the data file before you print each data record; that is, the number of data-file block accesses is equal to the number of data records. In general, such a large number of block accesses would not be acceptable. If you must perform this type of traversal frequently, you probably would modify the B-tree scheme so that the data file itself is kept nearly sorted.

Generally, the previous traversal is unacceptable

Multiple Indexing

There is one final point to make before we conclude the discussion of external implementations. This point concerns the multiple indexing of a data file. Chapter 13 presented a problem where you had to support multiple organizations for data stored in internal memory. Such a problem is also common for data stored externally. For example, suppose that a data file contains a collection of employee records on which you need to perform two types of retrievals:

```
RetrieveN(name)
{ Retrieves the item whose Name field contains the value
  name. }

RetrieveS(ss)
{ Retrieves the item whose SocSec field contains the value
  ss. }
```

Multiple index files allow multiple data organizations

One solution to this problem is to maintain two independent index files to the data file. For example, you could have one index file that contains index records of the form `<Name, Pointer>` and a second index file that contains index records of the form `<SocSec, Pointer>`. These index files could both be hashed, could both be B-trees, or could be one of each, as Figure 14-16 indicates. The choice would depend on the operations you wanted to perform with each search key. (Similarly, if an application requires extremely fast retrievals on `SocSec` and also requires operations such as traverse in sorted `SocSec` order and range queries on `SocSec`, it might be reasonable to have two `SocSec` index files—one hashed, the other a B-tree.)

Notice that while you can perform each `Retrieve` operation by using only one of the indexes (that is, use the `Name` index for `RetrieveN` and the `SocSec` index for `RetrieveS`), insertion and deletion operations must update both indexes. For example, the delete-by-name operation `DeleteN(Jones)` requires that you

1. Search the `Name` index file for Jones and delete the index record.
2. Delete the appropriate data record from the data file, noting the `SocSec` value `S` of this record.
3. Search the `SocSec` index file for `S` and delete this index record.

Figure 14-16

Multiple index files

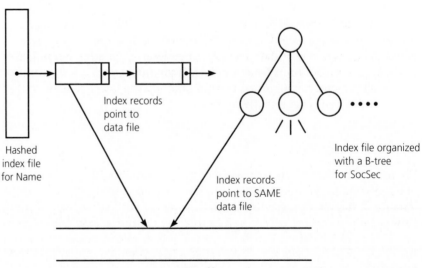

Hashed index file for Name

Index records point to data file

Index records point to SAME data file

Index file organized with a B-tree for SocSec

Data file

In general, the price paid for multiple indexing is more storage space and an additional overhead for updating each index whenever you modify the data file.

This chapter has presented at a very high level the basic principles of managing data in external storage. The details of implementing the algorithms are quite complex and depend heavily on the specific computing system. Particular situations often mandate either variations of the methods described here or completely different approaches. In future courses and work experience, you will undoubtedly learn much more about these techniques.

SUMMARY

1. An external file is partitioned into blocks. Each block typically contains many data records, and a block is generally the smallest unit of transfer between internal and external memory. That is, to access a record, you must access the block that contains it.

2. You can access the ith block of a direct access file without accessing the blocks that precede it. In this sense direct access files resemble arrays.

3. *Mergesort* can be modified so that it can sort a file of records without requiring all the records to be in internal memory at one time.

4. A dense index to a data file is a file that contains an index record for each record in the data file. An index record contains both the search key of the corresponding data record and the number of the block that contains that record.

5. You can organize the index file by using either hashing or B-trees. These schemes allow you to perform the basic table operations by using only a few block accesses.

6. It is possible to have several index files for the same data file. Such multiple indexing allows you to perform different types of operations efficiently, such as retrieve by name and retrieve by Social Security number.

COMMON PITFALLS / DEBUGGING

1. Before you can process (for example, inspect or update) a record, you must read it from an external file into internal memory. Once you modify a record, you must write it back to the file.

2. Block accesses are typically quite slow when compared to other computer operations. Therefore, you must carefully organize a file

so that you can perform tasks by using only a few block accesses. Otherwise, response time can be very poor.

3. If a record is inserted into or deleted from a data file, you must make the corresponding change to the index file. If a data file has more than one index file, you must update each index file. Thus, there is an overhead associated with multiple indexing.

4. Although external hashing generally supports retrievals, insertions, and deletions more quickly than does a B-tree, it does not support such operations as sorted traversals or range queries. This deficiency is one motivation for multiple indexing.

SELF-TEST EXERCISES

1. Consider two files of 1,600 employee records each. The records in each file are organized into sixteen 100-record blocks. One file is sequential access and the other is direct access. Describe how you would append one record to the end of each file.

2. Trace the external *Mergesort* algorithm with an external file of 16 blocks. Assume that the arrays *In1*, *In2*, and *Out* are each one block long. List the calls to the various procedures in the order in which they occur.

3. Trace the *Retrieve* algorithm for an indexed external file when the search key is less than all keys in the index. Assume that the index file is sorted by its search key, the data file contains 100 blocks, and each block contains 10 employee records. The index file contains 20 blocks of 50 records each. List the calls to the various procedures in the order in which they occur.

4. Repeat Self-Test Exercise 3, but this time assume that the search key equals the key field of record 26 in block 12 of the index. Also assume that record 26 of the index points to block 98 of the data file.

EXERCISES

1. Assuming the existence of *ReadBlock* and *WriteBlock* procedures, write a pseudocode program for shifting data to make a gap at some specified location of a sorted file. Pay particular attention to the details of shifting the last item out of one block and into the first position of the next block. You can assume that the last record of the file is in record *LastRec* of block *LastBlock* and that *LastBlock* is not full. (Note that this assumption permits shifting without allocating a new block to the file.)

2. The problem of managing the blocks of an external data file indexed by a B-tree or external hashing scheme is similar to that of managing memory for internal structures. When an external structure such as a data file needs more memory (for example, to insert a new record), it gets a new block from a **free list** that the system manages. That is, if the file contains N blocks, then the system can allocate to it an $(N + 1)^{st}$ block. When the file no longer needs a block, you can deallocate it and return it to the system.

The complication in the management of external storage is that a block allocated to a file may have available space interspersed with data. For example, after you delete a record from the middle of a data file, the block that contained that record now has space available for at least one record, even though it may not be completely empty. Therefore, you must be able to keep track of blocks that have space available for one or more records as well as recognize when blocks are completely empty (so that you can return them to the system).

Assuming the existence of *AllocateBlock* and *ReturnBlock* procedures that get empty blocks from and return empty blocks to the system, write pseudocode implementations of the following external memory-management procedures:

```
GetSlot(F, blocknum, recnum)
{ Determines the block number (blocknum) and record
  number (recnum) of an available slot in file F. A new
  block is allocated to the file from the system if
  necessary. }
```

```
FreeSlot(F, blocknum, recnum)
{ Makes record recnum in block blocknum of file F
  available. The block is returned to the system if it
  becomes empty. }
```

What data structure is appropriate to support these operations? You may assume that you can distinguish slots of a block that do not contain a record from those that do. You can make this distinction either by having a convention for *nil* values in the fields of a record or by adding an empty/full boolean field.

3. Describe pseudocode algorithms for insertion into and deletion from a table implemented externally with a hashed index file.

4. Execute the following sequence of operations on an empty B-tree of order 5. Note that insertion into an empty B-tree will create a single node that contains the inserted item.

```
Insert(10)
Insert(100)
Insert(30)
Insert(80)
Insert(50)
```

```
Delete(10)
Insert(60)
Insert(70)
Insert(40)
Delete(80)
Insert(90)
Insert(20)
Delete(30)
Delete(70)
```

5. Describe a pseudocode algorithm for finding an item's inorder successor in an external B-tree.

6. Describe pseudocode algorithms for insertion into and deletion from a table implemented with an index file organized as a B-tree.

7. Implement a *RangeQuery* procedure for a B-tree in pseudocode. (See Exercises 1 and 2 of Chapter 13.) Assume that only the key values are needed (as opposed to the entire data record).

8. Integrate calls to the appropriate memory-management procedures (see Exercise 2) into the pseudocode for *Insert* and *Delete* under both the B-tree and hashing schemes. (See Exercises 3 and 6.)

9. The B-tree traversal algorithm presented in this chapter assumes that internal memory is large enough to accommodate the recursive stack that contains up to h blocks, where h is the height of the B-tree. Suppose that you are in an environment where this assumption is not true. Modify the traversal algorithm so that the recursive stack contains block numbers rather than the actual blocks. How many block accesses does your algorithm have to perform?

10. **a.** Suppose that traversals and range queries need to access entire data records, not simply the search key. Write pseudocode implementations of such operations against a B-tree. How many block accesses do your procedures require?

  b. To reduce the number of block accesses required by these operations, various modifications of the basic B-tree structure are frequently used. The central idea behind such structures is to keep the data file itself sorted. First, assume that you can keep the data file in sequential sorted order—that is, so that the records are sorted within each block and the records in B_{i-1} are less than the records in B_i for $i = 2, 3$, and so on to the number of blocks in the file. Rewrite your implementations of the traversal and range-query operations to take advantage of this fact. How many block accesses do these operations now require?

  c. Because it is too inefficient to maintain a sequentially sorted data file in the face of frequent insertions and deletions, a compromise scheme is often employed. One such possible compromise is as follows. If a data record belongs in block B and B is full, a new block is allocated and linked to *B*, allowing the new record to be inserted into its proper sorted location. The difficulty is that you must now view each index record in the B-tree as indicating the first of possibly several blocks on a chain of blocks that might contain the corresponding data record. Rewrite the *Insert*, *Delete*, *Retrieve*, *Traverse*, and *RangeQuery* operations in terms of this implementation. What is the effect on their efficiency?

11. Write an iterative (nonrecursive) version of internal *Mergesort* that is based on the external version. That is, merge sorted runs that double in size at each pass of the array.

PROJECT

*12. **a.** Implement the external *Mergesort* in a version of Pascal that allows seek operations. Assume that the file to be sorted is a file of type *integer* and that it has 2^N blocks for some integer N.

b. Write Standard Pascal routines to simulate the procedures *ReadBlock* and *WriteBlock*. Implement the external *Mergesort* by using these procedures.

c. Extend your implementation of *Mergesort* by removing the restriction that the file contains 2^N blocks.

Mathematical Induction

Many proofs of theorems or invariants in computer science use a technique called **mathematical induction**, or simply **induction**. Induction is a principle of mathematics that is like a row of dominoes stood on end. If you push the first domino, all the dominoes will fall one after another. What is it about the dominoes that allows us to draw this conclusion? If you know that when one domino falls the next domino will fall, then pushing the first domino will cause them all to fall in succession. More formally, you can show that all the dominoes will fall if you can show the following two occurrences:

- The first domino falls.
- For any $k \geq 1$, if the kth domino falls, the $(k + 1)$st domino will fall.

The principle of mathematical induction is an axiom that is stated as follows:

AXIOM A-1. **The principle of mathematical induction.** A property $P(n)$ that involves an integer n is true for all $n \geq 0$ if the following are true:

1. $P(0)$ is true.
2. If $P(k)$ is true for any $k \geq 0$, then $P(k + 1)$ is true.

A **proof by induction on n** is one that uses the principle of mathematical induction. Such a proof consists of the two steps given in Axiom A-1. The first step is called the **basis**, or **base case**. The second step is the **induc-**

tive step. We usually break the inductive step into two parts: the **inductive hypothesis** ("if $P(k)$ is true for any $k \geqslant 0$") and the **inductive conclusion** ("then $P(k + 1)$ is true").

Example 1

Chapter 5 presented the following recursive function that computes x^n:

```
function Pow2(x, n)

    if n = 0
        then Pow2 := 1
        else Pow2 := x * Pow2(x, n−1)
```

You can prove that *Pow2* returns x^n for all $n \geqslant 0$ by using the following proof by induction on n:

Basis. *Show that the property is true when n = 0.* That is, you must show that *Pow2(x, 0)* returns x^0, which is 1. However, as you can see from the definition of *Pow2*, *Pow2(x, 0)* is 1.

Now you must establish the inductive step. By assuming that the property is true when $n = k$ (the inductive hypothesis), you must show that the property is true when $n = k + 1$ (the inductive conclusion).

Inductive hypothesis. *Assume that the property is true when n = k.* That is, assume that

   $Pow2(x, k) = x^k$

Inductive conclusion. *Show that the property is true when n = k + 1.* That is, you must show that *Pow2(x, k + 1)* returns the value x^{k+1}. By definition of the function *Pow2*,

   $Pow2(x, k + 1) = x * Pow2(x, k)$

By the inductive hypothesis, *Pow2(x, k)* returns the value x^k, so

   $Pow2(x, k + 1) = x * x^k$
   $= x^{k + 1}$

which is what you needed to show to establish the inductive step.

The inductive proof is thus complete. We demonstrated that the two steps in Axiom A-1 are true, so the principle of mathematical induction guarantees that *Pow2* returns x^n for all $n \geqslant 0$. (**End of proof.**)

Example 2

Prove that

$$1 + 2 + \cdots + n = \frac{n(n+1)}{2} \text{ when } n \geqslant 1$$

It will be helpful to let S_n represent the sum $1 + 2 + \cdots + n$.

Basis. Sometimes the property to be proven is trivial when $n = 0$, as is the case here. You can use $n = 1$ as the basis instead. (Actually, you can use any value of $n \geqslant 0$ as the basis, but a value of 0 or 1 is typical.)

You need to show that the sum S_1, which is simply 1, is equal to $1(1 + 1)/2$. This fact is obvious.

Inductive hypothesis. Assume that the formula is true when $n = k$; that is, assume that $S_k = k(k + 1)/2$.

Inductive conclusion. Show that the formula is true when $n = k + 1$. To do so, you can proceed as follows:

$$S_{k+1} = (1 + 2 + \cdots + k) + (k + 1)$$
$$= S_k + (k + 1)$$
$$= k(k + 1)/2 + (k + 1)$$
$$= (k(k + 1) + 2(k + 1))/2$$
$$= (k + 1)(k + 2)/2$$

The last expression is $n(n + 1)/2$ when n is $k + 1$. Thus, if the formula for S_k is true, the formula for S_{k+1} is true. Therefore, by the principle of mathematical induction, the formula is true when $n \geqslant 1$. (**End of proof.**)

Example 3

Prove that $2^n > n^2$ when $n \geqslant 5$.

Basis. Here is an example where the base case is not $n = 0$ or 1, but instead is $n = 5$. It is obvious that the relationship is true when $n = 5$ because

$$2^5 = 32 > 5^2 = 25$$

Inductive hypothesis. Assume that the relationship is true when $n = k \geqslant 5$; that is, assume that $2^k > k^2$ when $k \geqslant 5$.

Inductive conclusion. Show that the relationship is true when $n = k + 1$; that is, show that $2^{k+1} > (k + 1)^2$ when $k \geqslant 5$. To do so, you can proceed as follows:

$$(k + 1)^2 = k^2 + (2k + 1)$$
$$< k^2 + k^2 \text{ when } k \geqslant 5$$
$$< 2^k + 2^k \text{ when } k \geqslant 5$$
$$= 2^{k+1}$$

Therefore, by the principle of mathematical induction, $2^n > n^2$ when $n \geqslant 5$. (**End of proof.**)

Sometimes, the inductive hypothesis in Axiom A-1 is not sufficient. That is, you may need to assume more than $P(k)$. The following axiom is a stronger form of the principle of mathematical induction:

AXIOM A-2. **The principle of mathematical induction (strong form).** A property $P(n)$ that involves an integer n is true for all $n \geqslant 0$ if the following are true:

1. $P(0)$ is true.
2. If $P(0)$, $P(1)$, $\cdots$, $P(k)$ are true for any $k \geqslant 0$, then $P(k + 1)$ is true.

Notice that the inductive hypothesis of Axiom A-2 ("If $P(0)$, $P(1)$, $\cdots$, $P(k)$ are true for any $k \geqslant 0$") includes the inductive hypothesis of Axiom A-1 ("If $P(k)$ is true for any $k \geqslant 0$").

Example 4

Prove that every integer greater than 1 can be written as a product of prime integers.

Recall that a prime number is one that is divisible only by 1 and itself. The inductive proof is as follows:

Basis. The statement that you must prove involves integers greater than 1. Thus, the base case is $n = 2$. However, 2 is a prime number and, therefore, it trivially is a product of prime numbers.

Inductive hypothesis. Assume that the property is true for each of the integers 2, 3, $\cdots$, k, where $k \geqslant 2$.

Inductive conclusion. Show that the property is true when $n = k + 1$; that is, show that $k + 1$ can be written as a product of prime numbers.

If $k + 1$ is a prime number, then there is nothing more to show. However, if $k + 1$ is not a prime number, it must be divisible by an integer x such that $1 < x < k + 1$. Thus,

$$k + 1 = x * y$$

where $1 < y < k + 1$. Notice that x and y are each less than or equal to k, so the inductive hypothesis applies. That is, x and y can each be written as a product of prime numbers. Clearly $x * y$, which is equal to $k + 1$, must be a product of prime numbers. Because the formula holds for $n = k + 1$, it holds for all $n \geqslant 2$ by the principle of mathematical induction. (**End of proof.**)

Example 5

Chapter 5 discusses the following recursive definition:

$Rabbit(1) = 1$
$Rabbit(2) = 1$
$Rabbit(n) = Rabbit(n - 1) + Rabbit(n - 2)$ when $n > 2$

Prove that

$$Rabbit(n) = (a^n - b^n)/\sqrt{5}$$

where $a = (1 + \sqrt{5})/2$ and $b = (1 - \sqrt{5})/2 = 1 - a$.

Basis. *Rabbit*(0) is undefined, so begin at $n = 1$. Some algebra shows that *Rabbit*(1) = $(a^1 - b^1)/\sqrt{5} = 1$. However, notice that *Rabbit*(2) is also a special case. That is, you cannot compute *Rabbit*(2) from *Rabbit*(1) by using the recurrence relationship given here. Therefore, the basis in this inductive proof must include $n = 2$.

When $n = 2$, some more algebra will show that *Rabbit*(2) = $(a^2 - b^2)/\sqrt{5} = 1$. Thus, the formula is true when n is either 1 or 2.

Inductive hypothesis. Assume that the formula is true for all n such that $1 \leqslant n \leqslant k$, where k is at least 2.

Inductive conclusion. Show that the formula is true for $n = k + 1$. To do so, you can proceed as follows:

$$\begin{aligned}
Rabbit(k + 1) &= Rabbit(k) + Rabbit(k - 1) && \text{(recurrence relation)} \\
&= [(a^k - b^k) + (a^{k-1} - b^{k-1})]/\sqrt{5} && \text{(inductive hypothesis)} \\
&= [a^{k-1}(a + 1) - b^{k-1}(b + 1)]/\sqrt{5} && \text{(factorization)} \\
&= [a^{k-1}(a^2) - b^{k-1}(b^2)]/\sqrt{5} && (a + 1 = a^2;\ b + 1 = b^2) \\
&= (a^{k+1} - b^{k+1})/\sqrt{5}
\end{aligned}$$

Because the formula holds for $n = k + 1$, it holds for all $n > 2$ by the principle of mathematical induction. (**End of proof.**)

Note that the previous proof requires that you show that $a + 1 = a^2$ and $b + 1 = b^2$. Although simple algebra will demonstrate the validity of these equalities, exactly how did we discover them after the factorization step? Some experience with inductive proofs will give you the confidence to determine and verify the auxiliary relationships—such as $a + 1 = a^2$—that are necessary in a proof. Here, after we introduced the factors $(a + 1)$ and $(b + 1)$, we observed that if these factors were equal to a^2 and b^2, respectively, we could finish the proof. Thus, we tried to show that $a + 1 = a^2$ and $b + 1 = b^2$; indeed, we were successful. Inductive proofs often require adventurous algebraic manipulations!

SELF-TEST EXERCISES

1. Prove that $1 + 2^1 + 2^2 + \cdots + 2^m = 2^{m+1} - 1$ for all $m \geqslant 0$.

2. Prove that the sum of the first n odd positive integers is n^2.

3. Prove that $Rabbit(n) \geqslant a^{n-2}$ when $n \geqslant 2$ and $a = (1 + \sqrt{5})/2$.

EXERCISES

1. Prove that the sum of the first n even positive integers is $n(n + 1)$.

2. Prove that $1^2 + 2^2 + \cdots + n^2 = n(n + 1)(2n + 1)/6$ for all $n \geqslant 1$.

3. Prove that $n^3 - n$ is divisible by 6 for all $n \geqslant 0$.

4. Prove that $2^n > n^3$ when $n \geqslant 10$.

5. Prove that $n! > n^3$ when n is large enough.

6. Recall the following recursive definition from Chapter 5:

    $C(n, 0) = 1$
    $C(n, n) = 1$
    $C(n, k) = C(n - 1, k - 1) + C(n - 1, k)$ when $0 < k < n$

    a. Prove that $C(n, 0) + C(n, 1) + \cdots + C(n, n) = 2^n$.
        Hint: Use $C(n + 1, 0) = C(n, 0)$ and $C(n + 1, n) = C(n, n)$.

    b. Prove that $(x + y)^n = \displaystyle\sum_{k=0}^{n} C(n, k)\, x^k y^{n-k}$

7. Prove that $Rabbit(n) \leqslant a^{n-1}$ when $n \geqslant 1$ and $a = (1 + \sqrt{5})/2$.

8. Suppose that the rabbit population doubles every year. If you start with two rabbits, find and prove a formula that predicts the rabbit population after n years.

Proof of Theorem 10–2

The proofs of both Theorem 10–1 in Chapter 10 and Theorem 10–2 in this appendix use Axiom A-2, as given in Appendix A, but with a slight change in notation. The inductive step of Axiom A-2 is

If $P(0)$, $P(1)$, $\cdots$, $P(k)$ are true for any $k \geqslant 0$, then $P(k + 1)$ is true.

However, you can also write this step as

If $P(0)$, $P(1)$, $\cdots$, $P(k - 1)$ are true for any $k \geqslant 0$, then $P(k)$ is true

or as

If $P(0)$, $P(1)$, $\cdots$, $P(h - 1)$ are true for any $h \geqslant 0$, then $P(h)$ is true.

The previous form is equivalent to

If $P(k)$ is true for all k such that $0 \leqslant k < h$, then $P(h)$ is true.

The proofs of Theorem 10–1 and 10–2 use this last form of the inductive step.

THEOREM 10–2. **A full binary tree of height h ($h \geqslant 0$) has $2^h - 1$ nodes.**

PROOF. The proof is by induction on h.

Basis. When $h = 0$, the full binary tree is empty, and it contains $0 = 2^0 - 1$ nodes.

Inductive hypothesis. Assume that the theorem is true for all k, $0 \leqslant k < h$. That is, assume for all k, $0 \leqslant k < h$, that a full binary tree of height k has $2^k - 1$ nodes.

Inductive conclusion. You must show that the theorem is true for h ($h > k \geq 0$). That is, you must show that a full binary tree of height h has $2^h - 1$ nodes.

If T is a full binary tree of height $h > 0$, then from the definition of a full tree, it is of the form

$$r$$
$$T_L \qquad T_R$$

where T_L and T_R are full binary trees of height $h - 1$. The number of nodes in T is thus

1 (for the root) + (number of nodes in T_L) + (number of nodes in T_R)

By the inductive hypothesis, T_L and T_R each have $2^{h-1} - 1$ nodes because each is a full binary tree of height $h - 1$. Thus, the number of nodes in T is

$$1 + (2^{h-1} - 1) + (2^{h-1} - 1) = 1 + 2 \star (2^{h-1} - 1)$$
$$= 2^h - 1$$

which is what you needed to show. (**End of proof.**)

Pascal Reserved Words and Standard Identifiers

Reserved Words

and	end	mod	repeat
array	file	nil	set
begin	for	not	then
case	forward	of	to
const	function	or	type
div	goto	packed	until
do	if	procedure	var
downto	in	program	while
else	label	record	with

Standard Identifiers

Constants: false, true, maxint

Types: integer, real, char, boolean, text

Files: input, output

Functions: abs, arctan, chr, cos, eof, eoln, exp, ln, odd, ord, pred, round, sin, sqr, sqrt, succ, trunc

Procedures: read, readln, get, reset

write, writeln, put, rewrite, page

new, dispose

pack, unpack

APPENDIX D

Pascal Operators

Operators

Arithmetic:	+, −, *, /, div, mod
Assignment:	:=
Boolean:	and, or, not
Relational:	<, <=, =, <>, >=, >
Set:	in, =, <>, <=, >=, *, +, −

Operator Precedence

In the absence of parentheses, which override operator precedence, operators are executed in the following order:

1. not
2. *, /, div, mod, and
3. +, −, or
4. <, <=, =, <>, >=, >, in

Operators of equal precedence are executed in left-to-right order.

Standard Functions

Name	Parameter Type	Result Type	Returns
abs(x)	*integer* or *real*	same as parameter	absolute value of *x*
arctan(x)	*integer* or *real*	*real*	arctangent of *x* (*x* in radians)
chr(x)	*integer*	*char*	character whose ordinal value is *x*
cos(x)	*integer* or *real*	*real*	cosine of *x* (*x* in radians)
eof(x)	*file* or *text*	*boolean*	*true* if end of file, *false* if not end of file
eoln(x)	*text*	*boolean*	*true* if end of line, *false* if not end of line and not end of file, undefined if end of file
exp(x)	integer or *real*	*real*	e to the power *x*
ln(x)	*integer* or *real*	*real*	natural logarithm of *x*
odd(x)	*integer*	*boolean*	*true* if *x* is odd, *false* if *x* is even
ord(x)	ordinal, except *real*	*integer*	ordinal position of *x*
pred(x)	ordinal, except *real*	same as parameter	predecessor of *x*, except if *x* is first

Name	Parameter Type	Result Type	Returns
round(x)	real	integer	x rounded to an integer
sin(x)	integer or real	real	sine of x (x in radians)
sqr(x)	integer or real	same as parameter	x squared
sqrt(x)	integer or real	real	square root of x
succ(x)	ordinal, except real	same as parameter	successor of x, except if x is last
trunc(x)	real	integer	x truncated to an integer

Standard Procedures

Name	Action
dispose(p)	Frees memory to which pointer *p* points.
get(F)	Advances file window to next component and assigns new value to *F^*.
new(p)	Allocates a new memory cell and sets pointer *p* to point to it.
pack(U, i, P)	Copies elements from array *U* beginning at index *i* into packed array *P* beginning at *P*'s first element.
page(F)	Positions printer at the top of a new page before printing lines from the textfile *F*.
read(F, <variable_list>)	Reads values from file *F* and assigns them to variables in *<variable_list>*. (Assumes standard input file, if *F* is omitted.)
readln(F, <variable_list>)	Same as *read*, but then advances file window beyond the next end-of-line character. Valid only with textfiles.
reset(F)	Opens file *F* for input and positions file window at the beginning of the file.
rewrite(F)	Opens file *F* for output. If *F* exists already, it is erased; otherwise a new file is created.
unpack(P, U, i)	Copies elements from array *P* beginning with *P*'s first element into array *U* beginning at index *i*.
write(F, <variable_list>)	Writes values specified in *<variable_list>* to the file *F*. (Assumes standard output file, if *F* is omitted.)
writeln(F, <variable_list>)	Same as *write*, but then writes an end-of-line character and advances file window beyond it. Valid only with textfiles.

APPENDIX G

Character Codes

Codes are given for printable characters only.

ASCII

32	blank	44	, (comma)	65–90	A to Z
33	!	45	–	91	[
34	"	46	.	92	\
35	#	47	/	93	]
36	$	48–57	0 to 9	94	^
37	%	58	:	95	_ (underscore)
38	&	59	;	96	` (reverse quote)
39	' (apostrophe)	60	<	97–122	a to z
40	(	61	=	123	{
41	)	62	>	124		
42	*	63	?	125	}
43	+	64	@	126	~

EBCDIC

64	blank	96	–	129–137	a to i
74	¢	97	/	145–153	j to r
75	.	106	^	162–169	s to z
76	<	107	, (comma)	177	\
77	(	108	%	178	{
78	+	109	_ (underscore)	179	}
79			110	>	180	[
80	&	111	?	181	]
90	!	122	:	193–201	A to I
91	$	123	#	209–217	J to R
92	*	124	@	226–233	S to Z
93	)	125	' (apostrophe)	240–249	0 to 9
94	;	126	=		
95	¬	127	"		

abstract data type (ADT)   A collection of data values together with a set of well-specified operations on that data.

access time   The time required to access a particular item in a data structure such as an array, a linked list, or a file.

activation record   A record that contains a subprogram's local environment at the time of and as a result of the call to the subprogram.

actual parameter   A variable or expression that is passed to a subprogram. An actual parameter appears in a call to a subprogram and corresponds to a formal parameter in the heading of the subprogram's definition. See also *variable parameter* and *value parameter*.

address   A number that labels a location in a computer's memory.

adjacency list N linked lists that implement a graph of N vertices numbered $1, 2, \cdots, N$ such that there is a node in the ith linked list for vertex j if and only if there is an edge from vertex i to vertex j.

adjacency matrix   An N-by-N boolean array A that implements a graph of N vertices numbered $1, 2, \cdots, N$ such that $A[i, j]$ is $true$ if and only if there is an edge from vertex i to vertex j.

adjacent vertices   Two vertices of a graph that are joined by an edge. In a directed graph, vertex y is adjacent to vertex x if there is a directed edge from vertex x to vertex y.

ADT   See *abstract data type*.

algorithm   A concise specification of a method to solve a problem.

analysis of algorithms   A branch of computer science that measures the efficiency of algorithms.

ancestor of a node N A node on the path from the root of a tree to N.

array   A finite collection of elements of the same data type that are referenced by means of an index, or subscript.

array-based implementation   An implementation of an ADT or a data structure that uses an array to store the data values.

assertion   A statement about a particular condition at a certain point in an algorithm.

average-case analysis   A determination of the average amount of time that an algorithm requires to solve problems of size N.

AVL tree   A balanced binary search tree in which rotations restore the tree's balance after each insertion or deletion of a node.

axiom   A mathematical rule or relationship. Axioms can be used to specify the behavior of an ADT operation. The principle of mathematical induction is an axiom.

B-tree of degree m A search tree whose leaves are at the same level and whose nodes each contain between $m - 1$ and (m `div` 2) records. Each internal node has one more child than it has records. The root of the tree can contain as few as one record and can have as few as two children.

backtracking   A problem-solving strategy that backs up when it reaches an impasse.

balanced binary tree   A binary tree in which the left and right subtrees of any node have heights that differ by at most 1.

base case   See *basis*.

base type of a set   The data type of permissible elements in a set.

basis   The known case in either a recursive definition or an inductive proof. Also called the base case or degenerate case.

best-case analysis   A determination of the minimum amount of time that an algorithm requires to solve problems of size N.

BFS   See *breadth-first search*.

BFS spanning tree   A spanning tree formed by using a breadth-first search to traverse a graph's vertices.

Big O notation   Notation used to specify an algorithm's order. "O($f(N)$)" means "order $f(N)$". See also *order of an algorithm*.

binary file   See *general file*.

binary search   An algorithm that locates an item in a sorted collection by repeatedly halving the collection and determining which half can contain the item.

binary search tree   A binary tree where the search key in any node N is greater than the search key in any node in N's left subtree but less than the search key in any node in N's right subtree.

binary tree   A tree in which each node has at most two children, the left child and the right child.

block   A group of data records in a file.

block access time   The time required to read or write a block of data associated with a file.

bottom-up implementation An implementation method that starts at the submodules that make up larger modules.

box method A systematic way to trace the actions of a recursive function or procedure.

breadth-first search (BFS) A graph-traversal strategy that visits every vertex adjacent to a vertex v that it can.

bubble sort A sorting algorithm that compares adjacent elements and exchanges them if they are out of order. This sort requires several passes over the data. Also called exchange sort.

bucket A structure associated with a hash address that can accommodate more than one item. An array of buckets can be used as a hash table to resolve collisions.

Cand See *conditional and.*

chain A linked list used within separate chaining, which is a collision-resolution scheme associated with hashing.

chaining See *separate chaining.*

child of a node N A node directly below node N in a tree.

circuit A path in a graph that begins at a vertex v, passes through every vertex in the graph exactly once, and terminates at v.

circular doubly linked list A doubly linked list whose first node contains a *previous* pointer to the list's last node and whose last node contains a *next* pointer to the list's first node.

circular linked list A linked list whose last node points to the first node on the list.

closed-form formula A nonrecursive algebraic expression.

clustering A difficulty with the linear probing collision-resolution scheme in hashing whereby items tend to map into a cluster of locations in the hash table, rather than randomly scattered locations. This difficulty can cause lengthy search times.

code Statements in a programming language.

coding Implementing an algorithm in a programming language.

collision A condition that occurs when a hash function maps two or more different search keys into the same location.

collision-resolution scheme The part of hashing that assigns locations in the hash table to items with different search keys when they are involved in a collision. See also *bucket, chain, clustering, double hashing, linear probing, open addressing, probe sequence,* and *separate chaining.*

compiler A program that translates a program written in a high-level language, such as Pascal, into machine language.

compile time The time during which a compiler translates a program from source form into machine language.

complete binary tree A binary tree of height h that is full to level $h - 1$ and has level h filled from left to right.

complete graph A graph such that there is an edge between every pair of vertices.

completely balanced binary tree   A binary tree in which the left and right subtrees of any node have the same height.

conditional and   An *and* operator in pseudocode that does not evaluate its second operand if the first operand is false.

conditional or   An *or* operator in pseudocode that does not evaluate its second operand if the first operand is true.

connected component   For a graph that is not connected, a subset of the graph's vertices that a traversal visits beginning at a given vertex.

connected graph   A graph such that there is a path between every pair of vertices.

Cor   See *conditional or.*

cost of a path   The sum of the weights of the edges of a path in a weighted graph. Also called the weight or length of a path.

cost of a program   Factors such as the computer resources (computing time and memory) that the program consumes, the difficulties encountered by those who use the program, and the consequences when a program does not behave correctly.

cost of a spanning tree   The sum of the weights of the edges in a weighted graph's spanning tree.

cycle   In a graph, a path that begins and ends at the same vertex, but does not pass through other vertices more than once.

data abstraction   A design principle that separates the operations that can be performed on a collection of data from the implementation of the operations.

data flow   The flow of data between modules.

data record   An element in a file. A data record can be anything from a simple value, such as an integer, to a multifield Pascal-like record, such as an employee record. See also *block.*

data structure   A construct that is defined within a programming language to store a collection of data.

degenerate case   See *basis.*

depth-first search (DFS)   A graph-traversal strategy that goes as deep into the graph as it can before backtracking. That is, after visiting vertex *v*, DFS visits, if possible, an unvisited vertex *u* adjacent to *v*. The algorithm continues from *u* as far as possible before returning to *v* to visit the next unvisited vertex adjacent to *v*.

descendent of a node *N*   A node on a path from *N* to a leaf of a tree.

DFS   See *depth-first search.*

DFS **spanning tree**   A spanning tree formed by using a depth-first search to traverse a graph's vertices.

digraph   See *directed graph.*

direct access   A process that provides access directly by position to any element in a data structure without the need to first access other elements in the structure.

direct access file   A file whose elements you can access directly by position without first accessing previous elements.

directed edge An edge in a directed graph; that is, an edge that has a direction.

directed graph A graph whose edges indicate a direction. Also called a digraph.

directed path A sequence of directed edges between two vertices in a directed graph.

disconnected graph A graph that is not connected; that is, a graph that has at least one pair of vertices without a path between them.

divide and conquer A problem-solving strategy that divides a problem into smaller problems, each of which are solved separately.

double hashing A collision-resolution scheme that uses two hash functions. The hash table is searched for an unoccupied location, starting from the location that one hash function determines and considering every n^{th} location, where n is determined from a second hash function.

doubly linked list A linked list whose nodes each contain pointers to both the next node and the previous node.

dummy head node In a linked list, a first node that is not used for data but is always present. The item at the first position of the list is thus actually in the second node.

dynamic allocation The assignment of memory to a variable during program execution, as opposed to during compilation. See also *static allocation*.

edge The connection between two vertices of a graph.

empty string A string of length zero.

empty tree A tree with no nodes.

event An occurrence, such as an arrival or a departure, in an event-driven simulation. See also *external event* and *internal event*.

event-driven simulation A simulation that uses events generated by a mathematical model that is based on statistics and probability. The times of events are either read as input or computed from other event times. Because only those times at which the events occur are of interest, and because no action is required at times between the occurrence of events, the simulation can advance from the time of one event directly to the time of the next.

event list A data structure within an event-driven simulation that keeps track of arrival and departure events that will occur but have not occurred yet.

exchange sort See *bubble sort*.

exhaustive search A search strategy that tries every possibility until either it is successful or it determines that the item sought does not exist.

external event An event that is determined from the input data to an event-driven simulation.

external file A file that exists after program execution.

external methods Algorithms that require external files because the data will not fit entirely into the computer's main memory.

external sorting A sorting algorithm that is used when the collection of data will not fit in the computer's main memory all at once but must reside on secondary storage such as a disk.

fail-safe programming　Including checks in a program for anticipated errors.

Fibonacci sequence　A sequence of integers that is defined by a particular recurrence relationship and that models many naturally occurring phenomena.

field　A component of a record.

field identifier　An identifier of a field in a record.

FIFO　See *first in, first out.*

file　A sequence of components of the same data type.

file buffer　A special variable that is associated with each file in a program and that has the same data type as each individual component of the file. You specify it by appending a caret (^) to the file identifier and use it to read or write file components.

file variable　A Pascal identifier that names a file.

file window　A marker of the current position in the file.

first in, first out (FIFO)　A property of a queue whereby the item inserted first (earliest) is the first item removed.

fixed size　A characteristic of a data structure that contains a fixed amount of memory. See *static allocation.*

formal parameter　An identifier that appears in the heading of a subprogram definition and represents the actual parameter that the calling program will pass to the subprogram. See also *variable parameter* and *value parameter.*

free list　A list of available nodes used in an array-based implementation of a binary tree.

front of a queue　The end of a queue at which items are removed.

full binary tree　A binary tree of height h whose leaves are all at level h and whose nonleaves each have two children.

general file　A file that is not a textfile and whose elements are in the computer's internal representation. A general file does not contain end-of-line characters. Also called a binary file or a nontext file.

general tree　A set of nodes that is either empty or has a root node and zero or more subtrees of the root.

global variable　A variable declared in the outermost (main) block of a program; that is, a variable whose scope is the entire program.

grammar　The rules that define a language.

graph　A set V of vertices, or nodes, and a set E of edges that connect the vertices.

graph traversal　A process that starts at vertex v and visits all vertices w for which there is a path between v and w. A graph traversal visits every vertex in a graph if and only if the graph is connected, regardless of where the traversal starts.

growth-rate function　A function of the size of a problem, used to specify an algorithm's order.

hash function　A function that maps the search key of a table item into a location that will contain the item.

hashing A method that enables access to table items in time that is relatively constant and independent of the items by using a hash function and a scheme for resolving collisions.

hash table An array that contains the table items, as assigned by a hash function.

head pointer A pointer to the first node on a linked list. Also called head.

head record A record that contains the external pointer to the first node on a linked list, along with global information about the list, such as its length.

heap A complete binary tree whose nodes each contain a priority value that is greater than or equal to the priority values in the node's children.

heapsort A sorting algorithm that first transforms an array into a heap, then removes the heap's root (the largest element) by exchanging it with the heap's last element, and finally transforms the resulting semiheap back into a heap.

height-balanced binary tree See *balanced binary tree.*

height of a tree The number of nodes on the longest path from the root of the tree to a leaf.

hierarchical relationship The "parent-child" relationship between the nodes in a tree.

host type A single ordinal data type that includes the subrange or subranges that define a set.

implement (1) To create a program for an algorithm. (2) To use a data structure to realize an ADT.

index An ordinal value that references the elements of an array. Also called a subscript. Index can also mean index file.

index file A data structure whose entries—called index records—are used to locate items in an external file. Also called the index.

index record An entry in an index to a data file that points to a record in the data file. This entry contains a key field and a pointer field.

induction See *mathematical induction.*

inductive conclusion See *inductive step.*

inductive hypothesis See *inductive step.*

inductive proof A proof that uses the principle of mathematical induction.

inductive step The step in an inductive proof that begins with an inductive hypothesis ("if $P(k)$ is true for any $k \geq 0$") and demonstrates the inductive conclusion ("then $P(k + 1)$ is true").

infix expression An algebraic expression in which every binary operator appears between its two operands.

information hiding A process that hides certain implementation details within a module and makes these details inaccessible from outside the module.

inorder successor of a node N The node in a tree that an inorder traversal visits immediately after node N. This node is the leftmost node of N's right subtree.

inorder traversal A traversal of a binary tree that processes (visits) a node after it traverses the node's left subtree but before it traverses the node's right subtree.

insertion sort   A sorting algorithm that considers items one at a time and inserts each item into its proper sorted position.

interface   The communication mechanisms between modules.

internal event   An event that is determined by a computation within an event-driven simulation, as opposed to an external event, which is determined by the reading of data.

internal file   A file that is temporary and exists only during program execution.

internal sort   A sorting algorithm that requires the collection of data to fit entirely in the computer's main memory.

invariant   An assertion that is always true at a particular point in an algorithm.

iteration   (1) A process that is repetitive. (2) A single pass through a loop.

iterative solution   A solution that involves loops.

key field   A field in an index record that contains the same value as the search key in the record in the data file to which the index record points.

language   A set of strings of symbols that adhere to the rules of a grammar.

last in, first out (LIFO)   A property of a stack whereby the most recently inserted item is the first item removed.

leaf   A tree node with no children.

left child of a node N   A node directly below and to the left of node N in a tree.

left subtree of a node N   The left child of node N plus its descendents in a binary tree.

length of a path   The sum of the weights of the edges of a path in a weighted graph. Also called the weight or cost of a path.

level of a node   The root of a tree is at level 1. If a node is not the root, then its level is 1 greater than the level of its parent.

life cycle of software   The phases of software development: specification, design, verification, coding, testing, refining, production, and maintenance.

LIFO   See *last in, first out.*

linear implementation   An array-based implementation or a pointer-based implementation.

linear linked list   A linked list that is not circular.

linear probing   A collision-resolution scheme that searches the hash table sequentially, starting from the original location specified by the hash function, for an unoccupied location.

linked list   A list of elements, or nodes, that are linked to one another such that each element points to the next element.

local environment of a subprogram   A subprogram's formal value parameters, its local variables, a return address in the calling routine, and, in the case of functions, the value of the function itself.

local variable   A variable declared within a subprogram and available only within that subprogram. That is, a variable whose scope is the block that contains its declaration.

loop invariant   An assertion that is true before and after each execution of an algorithm's loop.

machine language   A language composed of the fundamental instructions that a computer can execute directly.

mathematical induction   A method for proving properties that involve nonnegative integers. Starting from a base case, you show that if a property is true for an arbitrary nonnegative integer k, then the property is true for the integer $k + 1$.

mergesort   A sorting algorithm that divides an array into halves, sorts each half, and then merges the sorted halves into one sorted array.

minimum spanning tree   A graph's spanning tree for which the sum of its edge weights is minimal.

modular program   A program that is divided into isolated components, or modules, that have well-specified purposes and interactions.

module   An individual component of a program, such as a procedure, function, or other block of code.

multiple indexing   A process that uses more than one index file to an external data file.

node   An element in a linked list, graph, or tree that usually contains both data and a pointer to the next element in the structure.

nonrecursive shell   A nonrecursive subprogram that contains a locally defined recursive subprogram.

nontext file   See *general file*.

O($f(N)$)   Order $f(N)$. See *order of an algorithm*.

open   A process that prepares a file for either input or output and positions the file window. A state of readiness for I/O.

open addressing   A type of collision-resolution scheme in hashing that probes for an empty, or open, location in the hash table in which to place the item. See also *linear probing* and *double hashing*.

ordered list   An ADT whose elements each have a relative ordering within the list.

order of an algorithm   An algorithm's time requirement as a function of the problem size. An algorithm A is order $f(N)$ if, for any implementation of the algorithm and any computer, there is some constant c such that for all but a finite number of values of N, A requires no more than $c * f(N)$ time units to solve a problem of size N. See also *Big O notation*.

order-of-magnitude analysis   An analysis of an algorithm's time requirement as a function of the problem size. See also *order of an algorithm*.

palindrome   A character string that reads the same from left to right as it does from right to left, for example, "deed."

parent of a node N   The node directly above node N in a tree.

partition   To divide a data structure such as an array into segments.

path   A sequence of edges in a graph that begins at one vertex and ends at another vertex. Because a tree is a special graph, you can have a path through a tree. See also *simple path*.

perfect hash function   An ideal hash function that maps each search key into a unique location in the hash table. Perfect hash functions exist when all possible search keys are known.

pivot element   A central element in an algorithm. For example, the quicksort algorithm partitions an array about a particular element called the pivot.

planar graph   A graph that can be drawn in a plane in at least one way so that no two edges cross.

pointer   A pointer variable in Pascal. Generically, a dynamic element that references a memory cell. Sometimes an indicator, such as an integer, to an element within a data structure.

pointer-based implementation   An implementation of an ADT or a data structure that uses pointers to organize its elements.

pointer field   A field in an index record that points to a data record in a data file. This field contains the number of the block that contains the data record.

pointer variable   A Pascal variable that references a memory cell. Also called a pointer.

pop   To remove an item from a stack.

position oriented   The characteristic of certain ADT's whose operations involve the ith position of a data structure.

postcondition   A statement of the conditions that exist at the end of a module.

postfix expression   An algebraic expression in which every binary operator follows its two operands.

postorder traversal   A traversal of a binary tree that processes (visits) a node after it has traversed both of the node's subtrees.

precondition   A statement of the conditions that must exist at the beginning of a module in order for the module to work correctly.

prefix expression   An algebraic expression in which every binary operator precedes its two operands.

preorder traversal   A traversal of a binary tree that processes (visits) a node before it traverses both of the node's subtrees.

primitive data types   A collection of built-in data types provided in high-level programming languages (for example, integers, reals, characters, and arrays in Pascal).

principle of locality   A principle that states that the effects of any statement should, as much as possible, be limited to other statements in its immediate vicinity.

priority queue   An ADT that orders its items by a priority value. The first item removed is the one having the highest priority value.

priority value   A value assigned to the items in a priority queue to indicate the item's priority.

private portion   The implementation of a subprogram or unit, which is hidden from the user.

probe sequence   The sequence of locations in the hash table that a collision-resolution scheme examines.

problem solving   The entire process of taking the statement of a problem and developing a computer program that solves that problem.

procedural abstraction   A design principle that separates the purpose and use of a module from its implementation.

public portion   The part of a subprogram or unit that a user can see. What you see when you want to use a subprogram or unit.

push   To add an item to a stack.

queue   An ADT whose first (earliest) inserted item is the first item removed. This property is called first in, first out, or simply FIFO. Items enter a queue at its rear and leave at its front.

quicksort   A sorting algorithm that partitions an array's elements around a pivot p to generate two smaller sorting problems: Sort the array's left section, whose elements are less than p, and sort the array's right section, whose elements are greater than or equal to p.

radix sort   A sorting algorithm that treats each data element as a character string and repeatedly organizes the data into groups.

random access   See *direct access*.

range query   An operation that retrieves all table items whose search keys fall into a given range of values.

rear of a queue   The end of a queue at which items are inserted.

recognition algorithm   An algorithm, based on a language's grammar, that determines whether a given string is a member of the language.

record   A group of related items, called fields, that are not necessarily of the same data type.

recurrence relation   A mathematical formula that generates successive terms in a sequence.

recursion   A process that solves a problem by solving smaller problems of exactly the same type as the original problem.

recursive call   A call within a subprogram to the subprogram itself.

right child of a node N   A node directly below and to the right of node N in a binary tree.

right subtree of a node N   The right child of node N plus its descendents in a binary tree.

rightward drift   In an array-based implementation of a queue, the problem of the front of the queue moving toward the end of the array. In a Pascal program, the problem of nested blocks bumping against the right-hand margin of the page.

root   The only node in a tree with no parent.

rotation   An operation used to maintain an AVL tree.

run time   The execution phase of a program. The time during which a program's instructions execute.

scope of an identifier   The blocks of a program in which an identifier has meaning.

search   A process that locates a certain item in a collection of items.

search key A field that identifies an entire record within a collection of records. A field that a search algorithm uses to locate a record within a collection of records.

selection sort A sorting algorithm that selects the largest item and puts it in its correct place, then selects the next largest item and puts it in its correct place, and so on.

semiheap A complete binary tree in which the root's left and right subtrees are both heaps.

separate chaining A collision-resolution scheme that uses an array of linked lists as a hash table. The ith linked list, or chain, contains all items that hash (map) into location i.

sequential access A process that requires elements in a data structure to be accessed one after another starting at the beginning.

sequential access file A file whose elements must be accessed sequentially. That is, to access the data stored at a given position, you must advance the file window beyond all the data that precedes it. Standard Pascal files are sequential access files.

sequential search An algorithm that locates an item in a collection by examining items in order one at a time, beginning with the first item.

set A collection of distinct elements drawn from a specific universe.

shortest path The path between two given vertices in a weighted graph that has the smallest sum of its edge weights.

siblings Tree nodes that have a common parent.

side effect A change to a variable that exists outside of the scope of a procedure or function and that is not passed as a parameter. An occurrence that is not specified by a module.

silent program A program that produces no visible output.

simple data type A data type that is not structured, such as integer, real, character, boolean, enumerated, and subrange.

simple path In a graph, a path that does not pass through a vertex more than once.

simulation A technique for modeling the behavior of both natural and artificial systems. Generally, its goal is to generate statistics that summarize the performance of an existing system or to predict the performance of a proposed system. A simulation reflects the long-term average behavior of a system rather than predicting occurrences of specific events.

software engineering A branch of computer science that provides techniques to facilitate the development of computer programs.

solution Algorithms and ways to store data that solve a problem.

sorted run Sorted data that is part of an external sort.

sorting A process that organizes a collection of data into either ascending or descending order.

sort key A field that determines the order of entire records within a collection of records. A field that a sorting algorithm uses to order records within a collection of records.

source code A program in the programming language in which it was written and that needs to be compiled. For example, a Pascal program. Also called source program.

source-inclusion facility A facility that automatically places the contents of a file at a specified point in a program before the program is compiled.

spanning tree A subgraph of a connected, undirected graph G that contains all of G's vertices and enough of its edges to form a tree. See also *BFS spanning tree* and *DFS spanning tree*.

stack An ADT whose most recently inserted item is the first item removed. This property is called last in, first out, or simply LIFO. Items enter and leave a stack at its top.

standard input file The default file, designated by *input*, from which a Pascal program reads data.

standard output file The default file, designated by *output*, to which a Pascal program writes data.

static allocation The assignment of memory to a variable during compilation, as opposed to during program execution. See also *dynamic allocation.*

structure chart An illustration of the hierarchy of modules that solve a problem.

structured data type A data type composed of multiple elements. Some examples of structured data types are arrays, records, files, and sets.

stub A dummy procedure or function that you use during the development and testing of other modules of a program.

subgraph A subset of a graph's vertices and edges.

subscript An ordinal value that references the elements of an array. Also called an index.

subtree Any node in a tree, together with all of the node's descendants.

subtree of a node N A tree that consists of a child of N and the child's descendents.

successor In a linked list, the successor of node x is the node to which x points. In a graph, vertex y is a successor of vertex x if y is adjacent to x.

symmetric matrix An N-by-N matrix A whose elements satisfy the relationship $A_{ij} = A_{ji.}$

table An ADT whose data items are stored and retrieved according to their search-key values.

tag field A field in a variant record that indicates which fields exist in a particular record.

tail recursion A type of recursion where the recursive call is the last action taken.

textfile A file of characters that are organized into lines.

time-driven simulation A simulation where the time of an event, such as an arrival or departure, is determined randomly and compared to a simulated clock.

time-sharing system An operating system that allows you to share a computer with many other users via a remote terminal.

top-down design   A process that addresses a task at successively lower levels of detail, producing independent modules.

top of a stack   The end of a stack at which items are inserted and deleted.

topological order   A list of vertices in a directed graph without cycles such that vertex x precedes vertex y if there is a directed edge from x to y in the graph. A topological order is not unique, in general.

topological sorting   The process of arranging the vertices in a directed graph without cycles into a topological order.

traversal   An operation that visits (accesses) each element in an ADT or data structure.

tree   A connected, undirected graph without cycles.

2–3 search tree   A type of search tree whose balance is readily maintained. A 2–3 tree in which, if a node has two children and contains one data item, the value of the search key in the node must be greater than the value of the search key in the left child and smaller than the value of the search key in the right child. If a node has three children and contains two data items, the value of the smaller search key in the node must be greater than the value of the search key in the left child and smaller than the value of the search key in the middle child; the value of the larger search key in the node must be greater than the value of the search key in the middle child and smaller than the value of the search key in the right child.

2–3 tree   A tree in which each internal node (nonleaf) has either two or three children, and all leaves are at the same level. A node can have a left subtree, a middle subtree, and a right subtree. People often use the term "2–3 tree" to mean "2–3 search tree."

type compatible   A characteristic of sets that have the same host type.

undirected graph   A graph that has at most one edge between any two vertices and whose edges do not indicate a direction.

unit   A collection of subprograms, constant definitions, type definitions, and variable declarations that can be compiled for later use in a program.

value oriented   The characteristic of certain ADT's whose operations involve data items with given values.

value parameter   A formal parameter whose value is initially the value of the corresponding actual parameter. Any change that the subprogram makes to a value parameter is not reflected in the corresponding actual parameter in the calling routine. The default when you do not specify the keyword *var*.

variable parameter   A formal parameter that represents an actual parameter. Any change that the subprogram makes to a variable parameter changes the corresponding actual parameter in the calling routine. A variable parameter is used when a procedure needs to return a value to the calling routine. You designate a variable parameter in the subprogram heading by writing *var* before the parameter.

variant record   A record that has both a fixed part, which contains the fields that are common to all records, and a variant part, which contains fields that differ for certain records according to the value of a tag field.

vertex   A node in a graph.

visit   The act of processing an item during a traversal of an ADT or a data structure.

weighted graph   A graph whose edges are labeled with numeric values.

weight of an edge The numeric label on an edge in a weighted graph.

weight of a path   The sum of the weights of the edges of a path in a weighted graph. Also called the length, or cost, of a path.

worst-case analysis   A determination of the maximum amount of time that an algorithm requires to solve problems of size N.

ANSWERS TO SELF-TEST EXERCISES

Chapter 1

1. $1 \leqslant j \leqslant N$ and $Sum = A[1] + \cdots + A[j]$.

2. The specifications include type definitions, parameters, and pre- and postconditions.

   ```
   const  MaxSize = 50;
   type   ElementType = integer;
          arraytype = array[1..MaxSize] of ElementType;

   procedure ComputeSum(A : arraytype; N : integer;
                            var Sum : ElementType);
   { Computes the sum of the first 5 positive elements in an array A.
   Precondition: A is an array of N elements, N >= 5,
   there are at least 5 positive elements in A.
   Postcondition: Sum = sum of first 5 positive elements, A and N are
   unchanged. }
   ```

   Another solution:

   ```
   procedure ComputeSum(A : arraytype; N : integer;
                    var Sum : ElementType; var Success : boolean);
   { Computes the sum of the first 5 positive elements in an array A.
   Precondition: A is an array of N elements.
   Postcondition: If there are at least 5 positive elements in A, then
   Sum = sum of first 5 positive elements and Success = true. Otherwise,
   Sum = 0 and Success = false. A and N are unchanged. }
   ```

Chapter 2

1. a. ```
      for d := 1 to 7 do
            write(MinTemps(d, 1):7:1)
      ```
   b. ```
      for w := 1 to 5 do
            write(MinTemps(1, w):7:1)
      ```

A30

```
c.  for w := 1 to 52 do
        begin
            for d := 1 to 7 do
                write(MinTemps(d, w):7:1);
            writeln
        end
```

2. **function** Average(X : weektype) : real;

3. **a.** Student1.Address.State; **b.** Student1.Address.Zip[1];
   c. Student1.GPA; **d.** Student1.Name[1]

4. **a.** true; **b.** [1,3,5,9]; **c.** [6,8]; **d.** A; **e.** [9]; **f.** false; **g.** [1..6,8,9];
   h. [1..5,9..15,20,22]

5.

OriginalFile	Ch	eoln	eof	CopyFile
<u>a</u> b *\<eoln\>* c d *\<eoln\>* *\<eof\>*	?	F	F	—
a <u>b</u> *\<eoln\>* c d *\<eoln\>* *\<eof\>*	a	F	F	a __
a b <u>*\<eoln\>*</u> c d *\<eoln\>* *\<eof\>*	b	T	F	a b __
				a b *\<eoln\>* __
a b *\<eoln\>* <u>c</u> d *\<eoln\>* *\<eof\>*	b	F	F	a b *\<eoln\>* __
a b *\<eoln\>* c <u>d</u> *\<eoln\>* *\<eof\>*	c	F	F	a b *\<eoln\>* c __
a b *\<eoln\>* c d <u>*\<eoln\>*</u> *\<eof\>*	d	T	F	a b *\<eoln\>* c d __
				a b *\<eoln\>* c d *\<eoln\>* __
a b *\<eoln\>* c d *\<eoln\>* <u>*\<eof\>*</u>	?	T	a b *\<eoln\>* c d *\<eoln\>* __
				a b *\<eoln\>* c d *\<eoln\>* *\<eof\>*

6.
```
i := 1;
Done := false;
while (i <= N) and (not Done) do
begin
   if A[i] = 0
       then i := i + 1
       else Done := true
end;   { while }

if i > N
    then writeln('All elements are zero.')
    else writeln('The first nonzero element is ', A[i])
```

7.
```
{ while <x> Cor <y> do }
Done := false
while <x> or (not Done) do
begin
   if <y>
       then <S>   { body of the loop }
       else Done := true
end
```

Chapter 3

1. Incorrect statements:

```
writeln(p, q);      { cannot write addresses (pointer values) }
writeln(p^, pp^); { pp^ is a pointer; use pp^^ instead }
pp^ := 20;          { cannot assign a value to a pointer }
```

Output from hand trace:

```
7     11
18    18
18    11    26
```

2. **a.** `prev^.next := cur^.next;`
`dispose(cur)`

b. `head := cur^.next;`
`dispose(cur)`

c. `new(p);`
`p^.data := 'A';`
`p^.next := head;`
`head := p`

d. The pointer *head* points to a node that contains 'A'; this node points to a node that contains 'J'. The *next* portion of the last node is *nil*.

3.
```
procedure PrintNodeN(head : ptr; N : integer);
var cur : ptr; i : integer;
begin
   cur := head;
   for i := 1 to N–1 do
       cur := cur^.next;
    write(cur^.data)
end
```

4. *N*, ignoring the assignments to *i* in the *for* statement.

5. Use *Lists[i]* instead of *head* in the procedure calls.

Chapter 4

1. A wall is a visualization of abstraction and modularity. Modules should be as independent as possible: Walls prevent other parts of the program from seeing the details of modules. A contract is a specification of what the module, which is behind the wall, is to do. The contract governs the slit in the wall; it specifies what is to be passed to the module and what will be passed out. The contract does not specify how to implement the module.

These concepts help during the problem-solving process by encouraging you to divide the problem into small parts and to focus first on what you want done rather than on how to do it.

2. `Replace(L, i, newitem)`
`{ Replaces the ith item in the ordered list L with newitem. }`

```
      Delete (L, i)
      Insert(L, i, newitem)
```

3. For example, the following specify operations for output:

   PrepareForOutput(F)
   { Readies a textfile F for output. If F exists, erases its data;
   * otherwise creates an empty textfile F. }*

   Output(F, X)
   { Places X at the end of the file F. }

   OutputLine(F, X)
   { Places X at the end of the file F and marks the end of a line. }

4. *Create(L)*
   *{ **Pre:** None.*
   * **Post:** The ordered list L is empty. }*

   Length(L)
   *{ **Pre:** The ordered list L has been created.*
   * **Post:** Returns the number of items that are in ordered list L. }*

   Insert(L, i, newitem)
   *{ **Pre:** The ordered list L has been created, 1 ≤ i ≤ Length(L) +*
   * 1.*
   * **Post:** Inserts newitem at position i of ordered list L. If i ≤*
   * Length(L), items are shifted as follows: The item at position i*
   * becomes the item at position i+1, the item at position i+1*
   * becomes the item at position i+2, ··· , the item at position*
   * Length(L) becomes the item at position Length(L)+1. }*

   Delete(L, i)
   *{ **Pre:** The ordered list L has been created, 1 ≤ i ≤ Length(L).*
   * **Post:** Deletes the item at position i of the ordered list L. If i*
   * < Length(L), items are shifted as follows: The item at position*
   * i+1 becomes the item at position i, the item at position i+2*
   * becomes the item at position i+1, ··· , the item at position*
   * Length(L) becomes the item at position Length(L)-1. }*

   Retrieve(L, i)
   *{ **Pre:** The ordered list L has been created, 1 ≤ i ≤ Length(L).*
   * **Post:** Returns the item at position i of the ordered list L. The*
   * list is left unchanged by this operation. }*

Chapter 5

1. **a.** The product of n numbers is defined in terms of the product of $n - 1$ numbers, which is a smaller problem of the same type.
   b. The recursive call computes the product of one fewer numbers.

c. The product of one number ($n = 1$) is the degenerate case.

d. If $n = 1$, you are at the degenerate case. If $n > 1$, then each recursive call reduces n by 1 so that you will eventually reach the degenerate case.

2.
```
procedure ComputeProduct(A:arraytype; n:integer;
                                    var Product:real);
begin
    if n = 1
        then Product := A[1]

        else
        begin
            ComputeProduct(A, n–1, Product);
            Product := A[n] * Product
        end
end
```

3.
```
function Product(A:arraytype; first, last : integer) : real;
{ Assumes first <= last }
begin
    if first = last
        then Product := A[first]
        else Product := A[last] * Product(A, first, last-1)
end
```

4.
```
procedure PrintIntegers(N : integer);
begin
    if N > 0
        then
        begin
            writeln(N);
            PrintIntegers(N–1)
        end
end
```

5. A nonrecursive shell provides a compromise between efficiency and style when a recursive subprogram operates on an array. The shell is a nonrecursive subprogram that contains a locally defined recursive subprogram. You define the array within the shell so that it is global to the recursive subprogram. Thus, you do not pass the array to the recursive subprogram and can avoid copies of the array.

6. *WriteBackward*, *BinSearch*, and *Select*.

Chapter 6

1. The three recursive calls result in the following moves: move a disk from *A* to *C*, from *A* to *B*, and then from *C* to *B*.

2.
```
procedure Retrieve(head:ptr; i:integer; var DataItem:integer);
begin
   if i = 1
        then DataItem:= head^.data
        else Retrieve(head^.next, i—1, DataItem)
end
```

3. The positions of the queens are given as (*row, column*) pairs.

Solution 1: (2, 1), (4, 2), (1, 3), (3, 4)

Solution 2: (3, 1), (1, 2), (4, 3), (2, 4)

4. −*/*ABC*∗+DEF*

5. *AB∗C–D/EF–+*

6. $(A - B / (C + D * E)) - F$

7. *<T>* = $ | cc*<T>*d

Chapter 7

1. 20 <u>80</u> 40 25 60 30
20 30 40 25 <u>60</u> 80
20 30 <u>40</u> 25 60 80
20 <u>30</u> 25 40 60 80
20 <u>25</u> 30 · 40 60 80
20 25 30 40 60 80

2. Find the smallest instead of the largest element at each pass.

<u>20</u> 80 40 25 60 30
30 80 40 <u>25</u> 60 20
<u>30</u> 80 40 60 25 20
60 80 <u>40</u> 30 25 20
<u>60</u> 80 40 30 25 20
80 60 40 30 25 20

3. Pass 1

<u>25 30</u> 20 80 40 60
25 <u>30 20</u> 80 40 60
25 20 <u>30 80</u> 40 60
25 20 30 <u>80 40</u> 60
25 20 30 40 <u>80 60</u>
25 20 30 40 60 80

Pass 2

<u>25 20</u> 30 40 60 80
20 <u>25 30</u> 40 60 80
20 25 <u>30 40</u> 60 80
20 25 30 <u>40 60</u> 80
20 25 30 40 60 80

There are no exchanges during pass 3, so the algorithm will terminate.

4. 25 <u>30</u> 20 80 40 60
25 30 <u>20</u> 80 40 60
20 25 30 <u>80</u> 40 60
20 25 30 80 <u>40</u> 60
20 25 30 40 80 <u>60</u>
20 25 30 40 60 80

5. a. *Mergesort* sorts an array by sorting each half of the array.
 b. Sorting half of an array is a smaller problem than sorting the entire array.
 c. An array of one element is the degenerate case.
 d. By halving an array and repeatedly halving the halves, you must reach array segments of one element each.

6. 38 | <u>16</u>   40   39   12   27   Swap 16 with itself
 38 | 16 | <u>40</u>   39   12   27
 38 | 16 | 40 | <u>39</u>   12   27
 38 | 16 | 40   39 | <u>12</u>   27   Swap 12 and 40
 38 | 16   12 | 39   40 | <u>27</u>   Swap 27 and 39
 38 | 16   12   27 | 40   39   Swap 38 and 27 to position pivot
 27   16   12 | 38 | 40   39

7. $(N-1) + (N-2) + \cdots + 1 = N * (N-1)/2$

8. $N + (N-1) + \cdots + 2 = N * (N+1)/2 - 1$

9. a. $O(N^3)$; **b.** $O(\log N)$; **c.** $O(N)$

10. a. You can stop searching as soon as *SearchValue* is less than a data element, because you will have passed the point where *SearchValue* would have occurred if it was in the data collection.
 b. Sorted data, using the scheme just described in the answer to Part *a:* best case: $O(1)$; worst case: $O(N)$; average case: $O(N)$.
   Unsorted data: $O(N)$ in all cases.
 c. Regardless of whether the data is sorted, the best case is $O(1)$ (you find the item after one comparison) and both the average and worst cases are $O(N)$ (you find the item after $N/2$ or N comparisons, respectively).

Chapter 8

1. D, C, B, A

2. *S:* 1 4 5; *T:* 3 6   (elements listed bottom to top)

3. Use an array-based implementation if you know the maximum line length in advance and you know that the average line length is not much shorter than the maximum length. Clearly, you would use a pointer-based implementation if you could not predict the maximum line length. In addition, if the maximum line length is 300, for example, but the average line length is 30, a pointer-based implementation would use less storage on average than an array-based implementation.

4. a. The stack is empty when the last close parenthesis is encountered. When the loop ends, *eoln* is false.
 b. The stack contains one open parenthesis when the end of the line is reached.
 c. The stack is empty when the end of the line is reached.

5. 2

6. *AB/C**

7. The precedence tests control association. The $\geq$ test enables left-to-right association when operators have the same precedence.

8. **a.** Stack contains A, then A B, then A B D.
   b. Stack contains A, then A B.
   c. Stack contains C, then C D, then C D H, then C D H G.

Chapter 9

1. A, B, C, D

2. Q: 2 3 5; T: 4 6   (elements listed front to rear)

3. **a.** Stack: a b c d a ← top   Queue: a b c d a ← rear
      The a at the top of the stack matches the a at the front of the queue. After deleting
      the a from both ADT's, $b \neq d$, so the string is not a palindrome.
   b. The letters that you delete from the stack and the queue are the same, so the string
      is a palindrome.

4. **a.** 1; **b.** 3; **c.** 3; **d.** 2; **e.** 3; **f.** 1; **g.** 2; **h.** 2; **i.** 1; **j.** 1; **k.** 1; **l.** 2

Chapter 10

1. **a.** 60; **b.** 60, 20, 40; **c.** 20, 70, 10, 40, 30, 50; **d.** 20 and 70, 10 and 40, 30 and 50;
   e. 60, 20, 40; **f.** 10, 40, 30, 50; **g.** 70, 10, 30, 50

2. **a.** 1: A; 2: B, C; 3: E, D; 4: F; 5: G
   b. 1: A; 2: B; 3: C; 4: D; 5: E; 6: F; 7: G

3. 4

4. Complete: b, c, d, e; Full: e; Balanced: b, c, d, e.

5. Preorder: A, B, D, E, C, F, G; Inorder: D, B, E, A, F, C, G; Postorder: D, E, B, F, G, C, A.

6. No. H should be in G's right subtree. U and V should be in T's right subtree.

7.

8. `Replace(T, X, ReplacementItem, success)`

   ```
       Delete(T, X, success)
       if success
          then Insert(T, ReplacementItem, success)
   ```

9. **a.** 60, 20, 40, 30; **b.** 60, 20, 10

Chapter 11

1. **a.** Directed, connected; **b.** Undirected, connected

2. DFS: 1 2 3 5 4; BFS: 1 2 3 4 5.

3.

	1	2	3	4	5
1	F	T	F	F	F
2	F	F	T	T	F
3	F	F	F	F	T
4	F	T	F	F	F
5	T	F	F	F	F

4. a d b e c

5. No. See Observation 2 on page 518.

6.

7.

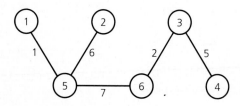

8. Path 1, 5, 3, 2 has weight 7.
Path 1, 5, 3 has weight 5.
Path 1, 5, 3, 4 has weight 8.
Path 1, 5 has weight 4.

Chapter 12

1. A: 30 20 50 10 25 40 60

2.

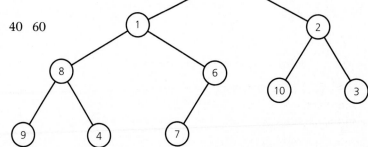

This tree is not a heap.

3. It is neither a semiheap nor a heap.

4. After inserting 12:   After removing 12:

 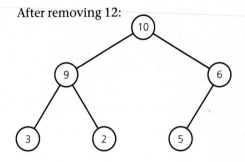

5. *PQ*: 7 5 6 4 3 2

6. The array is 10 9 5 8 7 2 3 1 4 6

7. a.

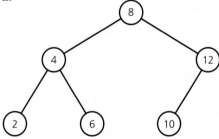

    b. The tree has minimum height and is complete but not full.

Chapter 13

1.

2.

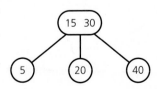

3. `Delete(T, X, success)`

```
i := h(x)
while ((T[i] is occupied) Cand (T[i] <> X))
or (T[i] is deleted) do
```

```
        i := i + 1
   if T[i] is full
      then
      begin
         Mark T[i] deleted
         success := true
      end

      else success := false
```

4. 8, 2, 7, 1, 6, 0, 5, 10, 4, 9, 3

5. $T[1] \to 15 \to 8$
$T[2]$ is nil
$T[3] \to 17 \to 24 \to 10$
$T[4] \to 32$

Chapter 14

1. Sequential access: Copy the original file *F1* into the file *F2*. Write a new block containing the desired record and 99 blank records. Copy *F2* to the original file *F1*.

Direct access: Create a new block containing the desired record and 99 blank records.
Write the new block to the file as block 17.

2.
```
Blocksort(infile, TF1, numblocks)
{ records in each block are now sorted;
  numblocks = 16}
MergeFile(TF1, TF2, 1, 16)
     Merge(TF1, TF2, 1, 1)
     Merge(TF1, TF2, 3, 1)
     Merge(TF1, TF2, 5, 1)
     Merge(TF1, TF2, 7, 1)
     Merge(TF1, TF2, 9, 1)
     Merge(TF1, TF2, 11, 1)
     Merge(TF1, TF2, 13, 1)
     Merge(TF1, TF2, 15, 1)
MergeFile(TF2, TF1, 2, 16)
     Merge(TF2, TF1, 1, 2)
     Merge(TF2, TF1, 5, 2)
     Merge(TF2, TF1, 9, 2)
     Merge(TF2, TF1, 13, 2)
MergeFile(TF1, TF2, 4, 16)
     Merge(TF1, TF2, 1, 4)
     Merge(TF1, TF2, 9, 4)
MergeFile(TF2, TF1, 8, 16)
     Merge(TF2, TF1, 1, 8)
CopyFile(TF1, outfile)
```

3. ```
Retrieve(Tindex[1..20], Tdata, X, getitem, success)
    ReadBlock(Tindex[1..20], 10, B)
    Retrieve(Tindex[1..9], Tdata, X, getitem, success)
        ReadBlock(Tindex[1..9], 5, B)
        Retrieve(Tindex[1..4], Tdata, X, getitem, success)
            ReadBlock(Tindex[1..4], 2, B)
            Retrieve(Tindex[1..1], Tdata, X, getitem, success)
                ReadBlock(Tindex[1..1], 1, B)
                success := false
```

4. ```
Retrieve(Tindex[1..20], Tdata, X, getitem, success)
    ReadBlock(Tindex[1..20], 10, B)
    Retrieve(Tindex[11..20], Tdata, X, getitem, success)
        ReadBlock(Tindex[11..20], 15, B)
        Retrieve(Tindex[11..14], Tdata, X, getitem, success)
            ReadBlock(Tindex[11..14], 12, B)
            j := 26
            blocknum := 98
            ReadBlock(Tdata, 98, D)
            Find record D[k] whose search key is X
            getitem := D[k]
            success := true
```

Appendix A

1. Proof by induction on m. When $m = 0$, $2^0 = 2^1 - 1$. Now assume that the statement is true for $m = k$; that is, assume that $1 + 2^1 + 2^2 + \cdots + 2^k = 2^{k+1} - 1$. Show that the statement is true for $m = k + 1$, as follows:

$$(1 + 2^1 + 2^2 + \cdots + 2^k) + 2^{k+1} = (2^{k+1} - 1) + 2^{k+1}$$
$$= 2^{k+2} - 1$$

2. Proof by induction on n. When $n = 1$, the first odd integer is 1 and the sum is trivially 1, which is equal to 1^2. Now assume that the statement is true for $n = k$; that is, assume that $1 + 3 + \cdots + (2k - 1) = k^2$. Show that the statement is true for $n = k + 1$, as follows:

$$[1 + 3 + \cdots + (2k - 1)] + (2k + 1) = k^2 + (2k + 1)$$
$$= (k + 1)^2$$

3. Proof by induction on n. When $n = 2$, $Rabbit(2) = 1 = a^0$. Now assume that the statement is true for all $n \leq k$; that is, assume that $Rabbit(n) \geq a^{n-2}$ for all $n \leq k$. Show that the statement is true for $n = k + 1$, as follows:

$$Rabbit(k + 1) = Rabbit(k) + Rabbit(k - 1)$$
$$\geq a^{k-2} + a^{k-3}$$
$$= a^{k-3}(a + 1)$$
$$= a^{k-3}(a^2)$$
$$= a^{k-1}$$